Communication Yearbook / 15

Communication
Yearbook / 15

edited by
STANLEY A. DEETZ

Published Annually for the
International Communication
Association

SAGE PUBLICATIONS
The International Professional Publishers
Newbury Park London New Delhi

For information address:

SAGE Publications, Inc.
2455 Teller Road
Newbury Park, California 91320

SAGE Publications Ltd.
6 Bonhill Street
London EC2A 4PU
United Kingdom

SAGE Publications India Pvt. Ltd.
M-32 Market
Greater Kailash I
New Delhi 110 048 India

Printed in the United States of America

Library of Congress: 76-45943

ISBN 0-8039-3529-3

ISSN 0147-4642

P
87
.C 5974
V15

1545.32
ma. 1992

92 93 94 95   10 9 8 7 6 5 4 3 2 1

Sage Production Editor: Judith L. Hunter

CONTENTS

THE INTERNATIONAL COMMUNICATION ASSOCIATION

The International Communication Association was formed in 1950, bringing together academicians and other professionals whose interest focused on human communication. The Association maintains an active membership of more than 2,200 individuals, of which some two-thirds are teaching and conducting research in colleges, universities, and schools around the world. Other members are in government, the media, communication technology, business law, medicine, and other professions. The wide professional and geographical distribution of the membership provides the basic strength of the ICA. The Association is a meeting ground for sharing research and useful dialogue about communication interests.

Through its Divisions and Interest Groups, publications, annual conferences, and relations with other associations around the world, ICA promotes the systematic study of communication theories, processes, and skills.

In addition to *Communication Yearbook,* the Association publishes the *Journal of Communication, Human Communication Research, Communication Theory,* the *Newsletter,* and *ICA Directory.* Several divisions also publish newsletters and occasional papers.

INTRODUCTION

Communication Yearbook 15 is the first of three volumes I will edit in the series. Custom is such that a new editor usually begins with a statement of his or her guiding philosophy. I will not, however, join in the chorus proclaiming the ultimate nature of science or research, thus justifying my own community's principles of exclusion. Nor will I erect an intellectual Statue of Liberty proclaiming to give voice to the voiceless and effectively hiding domination behind an ecstatic pluralism. Life is messier than either of these scripts envision. Yet I do have hopes and commitments that are perhaps better organized as a conversational move in a discussion than an editorial philosophy. And I should make them explicit.

I see scholarly work as a struggle, a struggle that is all too often suppressed either by exclusion at the outset or by respecting everybody without listening to anybody. It is a struggle for personal and professional respect, identity, knowledge, and meaning. It is a struggle for space and voice to ask interesting questions and propose arguable answers in a world society that thinks it already knows the right questions and often the right answers. And it is a struggle to define a past and a tradition as well as a future. A yearbook tries to reflect the critical work in a field during its period and inevitably to structure an agenda for that field. This volume enters as a player in this struggle. The question that was left to me was how to help make this a more edifying struggle.

At least on the surface, the last decade has witnessed a new ecumenical spirit in communication studies. Paradigm dialogue and ferment have been met with much self-congratulation. Our texts line up the potpourri of paradigms much as they did theoretical choices and definitions in the decades before. Despite the best of intentions, I fear that the outcome has been at best tolerance rather than productive diversity. In practice, the emphasis on the plurality of paradigms has generated more expressive monologues than dialogues. And the proclaimed presence of separate but equal paradigms has led to purification rituals within camps, since diversity is assured by the separated other. It is fairly easy to let everyone speak if listening is not required. If everyone has his or her own discourse, questions, and method, what can we talk about other than department and discipline politics? How do we get to the place where discovering a different point of view is reason to start a discussion rather than the time to end it?

THE SIGNIFICANCE OF COMMUNICATION STUDIES
WITHIN THE SOCIAL SCIENCES

The attempt to answer this begins for me with a general conception of what social science knowledge is *about* rather than with presupposing what science and research *are* in order to identify the social agenda of communication studies rather than provide a definition of the domain of communication. The production of social science knowledge is ultimately about freedom and collective decision making that at the core struggles to explore and challenge what is uncritically taken for granted. Kant would get credit for best articulating our modern form of knowledge production in proclaiming the Enlightenment as "breaking forms of self-inflicted tutelage." Knowledge replaces authority and tradition as a basis for social choice and provides the possibility of a collective determination of the future based on a self-achieved desire to choose rather than submit to authority. If social science proclaims, or establishes by its practices, itself as a new authority even if such tutelage is chosen, its very reason for existing is denied. Social science becomes the modern church, the modern master. Social science research is part of a social conversation rather than the answer to socially posed questions. The body of knowledge produced is not what is important, but rather the capacity of that body of knowledge based on its premises and methods to pose new social questions, to challenge guiding assumptions of everyday life, or to open common sense to reconsideration.

This point of view has not been used here to exclude research programs operating in a different manner, even those done with doctrine or dogma. But, following Jim Anderson's lead, I have asked authors to say more and to position their studies to engage in more general questions, to situate their own mode of knowledge production (sometimes with success). The literature reviews explicitly develop points of view as well as report and summarize the studies of the last several years. The empirical studies aim at justifying their research practices as well as their conclusions to wider reading publics. The commentaries are not just the opening up of the later stages of the review process to the public; it is hoped that they will help the reader to engage in the debate that any good work generates and will open debates that the essays themselves overlook or suppress. The goal is not to determine how good a study is with paradigmatic standards, but to ask whether being good makes any difference.

Inclusions in this volume reflect a conception of the significance of communication studies as well as a purpose of the social sciences. This to me is not a domain question—that is, Which phenomena are communication phenomena? Rather, I have asked initially what differentiates communication studies from psychological, sociological, or economic studies of similar phenomena; that is, how are *communication studies* different from *studies of communication*? First and foremost, communication is not a dependent variable, or an independent one for that matter. Communication is a constitutive process. It can be seen as the process by which psychological states are formed and transformed, social structures produced and reproduced, and economic resources and transactions assume a social life. In this sense communication is a mode of explanation as well as an academic administrative unit and a set of phenomena or questions. While this cannot be the whole story, I think it is important to highlight a view that pulls together and distinguishes communication studies from other ways of approaching the world.

Researchers in academic units called communication have often been slower than those in other fields to articulate this disciplinary mode of explanation. As many philosophers, sociologists, literary theorists, political scientists, and even psychologists have rushed to rethink their traditional phenomena of study in communicational (textual, transactional, semiotic—choose your preferred metaphor) terms, many members of communication associations continue to work primarily in psychological, sociological, or informational terms. I do not mean this to reflect negatively on the interdisciplinary character of the study of communication phenomena. The works contained within this volume contain several disciplinary modes of explanation. Clearly, all social sciences (and often their "yearbooks") are deeply interdisciplinary. Psychology, for example, has recently benefited greatly from communicational analyses of the social production of identity. But there is a loss when most significant communication theories are produced in other disciplines, and one has to wonder about the internal politics of a group of people who marginalize themselves during the periods when their contributions could prove critical.

I believe we live in a time when communication studies are of great social importance. Each mode of explanation has expanded greatly during periods of socially defined problems that are partially constructed by that mode of explanation and, more important, require that mode of explanation for studies that construct a social response. Psychological explanation has flourished with the development of the Western conception of the modern individual, an autonomous individual yet directed by hidden, unconscious, or physiological forces. Sociological explanation became widely used to articulate and respond to perceived integration and moral decay problems thought to be fostered by the decline of community and the development of modern societies.

Today, we live in a pluralistic society characterized by rapid change. And, whether we all like it or not, as a world community we are committed to respecting diversity and continued material development. Such a world cannot rely on any simple preexisting consensus of meaning, personal identity, or structures of roles and decision making. These must be constructed through a constant process of negotiation in human interaction. We live in a mediated world with an active communicational production of our personal and social experience, where different groups and valuing systems vie for definitional authority. Communication specifies in this world a social politics rather than a tool, means, or social technology. It is not, nor can it be, a neutral or transparent medium; it is a constitutive process. Neither the old Left nor the old Right, alternatively fearing or desiring a homogeneous world and seeing communication administratively as a tool of oppression or of integration, provides concepts that help us respond in this contemporary context. When communication is conceptualized as the study of influence (whether viewed positively or negatively, culturally or minimally), explanations become external to communication and the commitment to deconstructive/constructive diversity and moral/material development disappear. While higher education continues to move in the direction of training professionals rather than facilitating responsible citizenship, our research can still reclaim a self-consciousness of public responsibilities.

Clearly, communication is more usefully conceptualized and studied today in response to issues of democracy rather than those of control and social influence. If that is done, the central questions facing us concern the nature and manner of participation guided by an ideal of participatory expansion rather than the processes of influence guided by administrative ideals of effectiveness and efficiency. This of course does not deny the significance of studies of influence, but the latent presumptions of free speech, informed publics, an open marketplace of ideas, invisible hands, and autonomous decision makers provide poor alibis for value neutrality in a world with asymmetrical communication opportunities and dominant representational practices. Studies of influence look different when studied within a larger concern for advancing democracy rather than under guises of neutral yet undeniably advancing administrative control interests.

In this volume, accepting communication, community, and democracy as intrinsically intertwined does not preclude the inclusion of studies with different political orientations, but does demand that policy and value issues have a place in the discussion. Such a redirection of communication concern cuts across academic subdivisions such as interpersonal, organizational, and mass communication. As McLuskie perhaps best shows in his commentary on media effects and agenda-setting research, the concern with what the media do to or for people often fails to account for the ways the "public" as a site of informed mutual decision making itself is lost. But the "public" that is essential to a democratic pluralistic society is not lost only to mass communication but often is invisible in organizational and interpersonal contexts. The misrecognized centrality of communication in the production and reproduction of people and their experiences and the assumption that democracy has already been accomplished (once and for all) threaten to trivialize what I take to be the most important study of our times.

The centrality of communication and mutual concern with communicative processes are what pull this *Yearbook* together, rather than the similarity of sites and phenomena of study. Like any editor, I have hopes and commitments. Some of their contours should be clear by now. Despite my own scholarly commitments, I have not been a particularly heavy-handed editor. Each author must make his or her own statement and each field must define itself. While I express my scholarly commitments, I have no need to make this the forum for my own agenda. I am capable of writing my own books. Yet I fail as an editor if the *Yearbook* lacks vision, for its lack becomes its vision. I have included the essays that various reviewers found to be of high quality and expressive of contemporary issues in their areas of specialization. Several reviewers and commentators actively helped the authors to make their cases as complete and persuasive as possible. I am happier with some of the essays than with others. Even a good review process is ultimately limited by what is available at that time in each area. I hope that, collectively, the volume gives some sense of the state of the art in communication studies.

OVERVIEW OF THE ESSAYS

In putting together these essays, I have worked to provide a readable and relatively coherent volume. It is my hope that the volume as a whole will be useful for those with a general interest in communication studies and can be used in graduate and other courses to increase familiarity with the scope of communication studies. I have tried to accomplish this without losing the scholarly contribution of specific essays to specialized audiences. The essays here favor North American and, to a lesser extent, European research concerns and methods, reflecting in part the composition of the International Communication Association, but more generally the difficulty of any volume bridging large bodies of water.

Further, the topical content of this volume favors mass communication issues, though the theoretical issues raised have their readily apparent analogues in other topical areas and provide insights for scholars in those areas. The choice of mass communication reflects the seriousness of the theoretical issues being fought out there. In 1975 I would have said that the significant debates over the conception of the communication process were fought out using interpersonal topical concerns. Today, however, various national and international issues and policy debates and the intellectual response to them have situated general questions about the communication process within mass communication discussions. *Communication Yearbook 16* will focus on the emerging debates within the organizational communication area as well as contain reviews in other areas. This volume is divided into four sections, each partially reflecting and defining a significant recent issue of concern in communication studies.

Mass Entertainment, Audience Mediation, and Politics

Contemporary mass media messages are increasingly difficult to conceptualize using both everyday and scholarly separations among news, advertising, and entertainment. Perhaps even the socially produced divisions indexed in the presentation of media messages disguise central communication findings. All information today can be seen as sponsored information. The political, commercial, and private enjoyment experiences merge in mixed texts and receptions where the political is commercial and entertaining and the entertaining is political and commercial. The essays included in Section 1 take different cuts at this new context. Dennis Davis and Thomas Puckett take the issues head-on by examining the political aspects of mass entertainment. In doing so, they argue that a culture-centered paradigm is essential to investigating such phenomena. In the next essay, Sonia Livingstone passes by the question of how scholars should investigate media messages and examines how everyday viewers think through and interpret the entertainment messages they experience on a daily basis. Robert Wicks continues in a similar vein in proposing a way to examine receiver interpretive processes. It is not the media messages themselves that are at issue, but the way they are worked together with the variety of competing and complementary messages in individuals' total experience. Finally, Vladimir Shlapentokh and Dmitry Shlapentokh provide an extensive look at Soviet films, exploring how they have been produced and interpreted in a changing social and explicitly politically charged culture.

Mass Media Messages and Influence

Section 2 includes somewhat more traditionally based essays that look at the production of media messages and the influences these messages have on specific audiences. Yet the essays probe these issues more deeply than has been the custom in the various effects and minimal effects traditions. The basic concern that pulls these essays together centers on the formation of a public response and the individual decisions that members of a public must make. David Barker and Bernard Timberg provide a review of the ways in which the television image has been conceptualized. As a ground for any analysis of the politics of representational practices, questions about the nature of the media code must first be posed. As these authors show, a number of conceptions are possible, and each suggests both a conception of the nature of possible effect and the public as a recipient.

Michael Burgoon, Deborah Newton, and Thomas Birk then provide the first of three more specific essays looking at the relation of media content and representational practice to the capacity of citizens to make personal choices. As advertising is a feature of modern society, so too is deception and the production of corrective messages. But what do corrective messages do? Burgoon and his colleagues show that, at least in one case, they can have unexpectedly strong effects. Such effects raise both social policy questions and the need to reconsider models of social influence. In the next essay, Clifford Scherer and Napoleon Juanillo look at the proactive side of the media influence issue. Public health promotion programs have emerged as a central tool in preventive health care, and the use of various mediated forms of communication has increasingly become a significant part of these programs. By careful analysis of several specific cases, Scherer and Juanillo attempt to specify the concurrent factors in successful public health communication. Finally, Hans-Jürgen Weiss takes a different theoretical perspective on the issue of influence. In his essay the concern shifts to news media and the ways in which they contribute to stereotyping issue-specific conflicts. By studying the contents of media agenda-setting through what he calls "argumentation analysis," he is able to show how the conflict structure of media issue coverage mediates the agenda-setting effect.

Interaction in the Social Context

Interpersonal interaction takes place within a social-historical context. This context is composed of institutions, power relations, and symbolic traditions that both influence and contextualize interactional practices and are used as resources by specific interactants to accomplish their goals. While much of the literature regarding interpersonal interaction overlooks these contextual factors and even the historical significance of our current talk and interaction forms, it has become increasingly clear that simple interaction descriptions fail to give much guidance in response to contemporary issues.

Jo Liska takes on directly one of the most significant of these issues, the relations among gender, dominance, and language use. Through an extensive review of the literature on the "language of dominance," Liska shows that differences in language usage produce different effects based primarily on contextual differences. In the next essay, Barbara Montgomery focuses on a somewhat more basic and abstract issue, that regarding the relation of interpersonal relationships to the larger social order. Montgomery claims that a fundamental tension exists between "seeing dyadic relationships as orderly, predictable interactions that are anchored in the institutions and practices of society and seeing relationships as opportunities for spontaneous, interpersonal expressions that lead to unique relational experiences." Such a tension exists for both everyday people and interpersonal researchers. The question is, How do people use communication to manage such tension? Ultimately, the nature of the person-to-person interaction is closely tied to the couple-to-culture interface. Ian Angus, in the last essay in Section 3, presents an even more fundamental issue, the social production of personal experience represented collectively as "common sense." Angus uses the phenomenological conception of "horizon" to reconstruct "articulation theory." By doing so he is better able to describe the interplay of poetic expressions and rhetorical linkages in the constitution of common sense and the elaboration of issues raised by new social movements.

The Person in Interaction

Contemporary communication theories, particularly those grounded in some form of structuralism, have provided much insight into the social side of human interaction. Much of this work emphasizing social control and reproduction of structure has essentially replaced the earlier humanist conception of the person, which emphasized a center identity and unique personal experiences. The response to structuralism in many international circles has been to reform a conception of human agency. Individual-centered communication researchers have seemed to avoid involvement with either the structuralist move or the rekindled concern with agency. Even psychology has responded with more communicational or interactional conceptions of the personal. Clearly it is important to see how psychologically oriented communication researchers accomplish this omission as well as to see what types of claims are possible from within their perspectives.

Stanley Cunningham provides an extensive review of the literature on *intra*-personal communication. Much of his essay outlines the conceptual problems inherent within such a notion. Of particular interest is the way conceptual confusion and linguistic play across categories engender an impervious self-reflexive discourse. Pedagogical models and devices substitute for substantive ones without the recognition that there must be some substantive position that makes the pedagogical claims themselves meaningful.

ACKNOWLEDGMENTS

I would like to thank my reviewers and the divisional officers of the International Communication Association for help in identifying appropriate essays and in improving the essays here. In particular, I would like to thank Charles Conrad, John Daly, Hartmut Mokros, Robert Kubey, Malcolm Parks, David Swanson, Lawrence Grossberg, and Ellen Wartella. I have also appreciated the efforts of the commentators to provide, in addition to timely and thoughtful responses, continuous help to me as an editor and to the authors of the various major pieces.

The publication of this volume would not have been possible without the support of the International Communication Association and the Department of Communication at Rutgers University. Lea Stewart in particular has done much to secure the necessary resources. Special thanks to Celeste Hodges for compiling the index. Finally, the editorial assistance of Karen Brooks, Britten Skelton, Joseph Woelfel, Jr., and especially Lynn Bodofsky has contributed greatly to the volume.

Stanley A. Deetz
Belle Mead, New Jersey

SECTION 1

MASS ENTERTAINMENT, AUDIENCE MEDIATION, AND POLITICS

1 Mass Entertainment and Community: Toward a Culture-Centered Paradigm for Mass Communication Research

DENNIS K. DAVIS
University of North Dakota

THOMAS F. N. PUCKETT
Eastern Washington University

In this essay, we begin with a review of the arguments in the debate over media and then seek to move beyond the narrow issues raised by previous media criticism. We argue that a culture-centered paradigm for media scholarship is emerging that explicitly abandons many of the assumptions about media and audiences that were central to the old debate. This paradigm offers the possibility of integrating a broad range of current research in our field and could provide a means of stemming conflict between qualitative and quantitative scholars. After outlining this paradigm we discuss current scholarship and present an agenda for future research.

S INCE their appearance at the end of the nineteenth century, mass media have inspired dreams of Great Communities (Kreiling, 1984; Peters, 1989) and nightmares of Big Brother. With the introduction of each new medium, strikingly similar hopes and fears have been expressed by observers. During development, each new medium inspires optimism that desirable aspects of past ways of life might somehow be restored and integrated into contemporary existence. But each medium also threatens to undermine desirable features of modern life, and to aggravate social problems. Rightly or wrongly, media have been viewed both as a "leading edge" for positive social change (McLuhan, 1965; Mendelsohn, 1966) and as agents of mass society (Brantlinger, 1983). From the 1920s until the 1970s, a fundamentally sterile debate over the role of media was waged,

Correspondence and requests for reprints: Dennis K. Davis, School of Communication, University of North Dakota, Box 8118 University Station, Grand Forks, ND 58202.

Communication Yearbook 15, pp. 3-34

pitting media industry apologists and their social science allies against an array of social critics ranging from left-wing critical theorists to cultural reactionaries. During the 1970s, the very basis for this debate was challenged as its theoretical assumptions were shaken by a fundamental paradigm shift.

THE HISTORY OF MEDIA CRITICISM

Already in the nineteenth century, critics in both Europe and the United States drew parallels between the Roman circuses and new forms of mass entertainment. In a recent overview of these early theories of mass entertainment and mass culture, Brantlinger (1983) found a pervasive theme, which he labels "negative classicism." In these schools of social criticism, mass media were often identified as an important, if not a primary, corrupting influence within society. The term *mass society* came to be widely used by conservative, liberal, and radical critics to refer to modernizing social orders in which urbanization and industrialization produced widespread and deleterious social change. Critics asserted that innovative forms of media—such as pulp fiction, magazines, movies, and radio—exacerbated these changes.

In mass society, small, grass-roots social units were broken down and replaced by disorganized, sprawling urban slums. Individuals were suddenly cut off from the norms and values of folk communities and rendered vulnerable to manipulation by media. Critics such as Ortega y Gasset on the Right and the proponents of the Frankfurt school on the Left argued that the social changes unleashed by industrialization would inevitably bring a new Dark Age and a return to barbarism (Brantlinger, 1983). The rise of Stalin and Hitler provided these critics with ample evidence in support of their views. In both the Soviet Union and Nazi Germany, media were systematically used to undermine the credibility of older forms of culture and to impart legitimacy to the new regimes (Adorno, 1970/1984; Marcuse, 1964).

Two Schools of American Social Criticism

In Europe, social criticism ranged across a broad political spectrum from anarchist and communist theory to fascism and monarchism, but in the United States, Kreiling (1984) argues, it was generally limited to a much narrower ideological range. Kreiling divides American social criticism into two schools—conservative social Darwinism and reform social Darwinism. Both schools were dedicated to social evolution, or "progress," and both expressed concern about the unforeseen and sometimes tragic consequences of social changes associated with the appearance of new media. Both recognized that media had the ability to foment social unrest and disrupt local communities and the cultures on which they were based. However, the two schools offered radically different strategies for media development. Conservatives favored strong elite control and the use of media to disseminate those forms of "high" culture favored by them. Reform Darwinists were more optimistic about democratic forms of politics and the ability of media to create "Great Communities," in which new forms of mediated culture would be widely shared.

Critical Responses to Mass Society

In both Europe and the United States, social critics expressed antipathy toward new media and proposed varying strategies for limiting their detrimental effects. Cultural conservatives such as Ortega y Gasset and T. S. Eliot charged that the media were agents of barbaric mass culture, undermining high culture and pandering to the worst impulses of average persons (Brantlinger, 1983). By raising the specter of cultural decline, they hoped to mobilize reactionary movements and bring about restoration of traditional social orders. By contrast, leftist critics used dire assessments of contemporary culture as a basis for justifying efforts to transform the status quo radically and create a new social order based on egalitarian and idealistic values (i.e., communism, socialism; see, e.g., Marcuse, 1969, 1978). Rather than return to the past, left-wing thought sought to envision and implement utopian social orders in which innovative values were made dominant.

At the heart of both conservative and radical visions of media and society was distrust of average persons and a simplistic view of how a "good" social order should be created and maintained. The Right saw a need for strong and stable social institutions (i.e., church, state, schools, business) that would assume dominant, paternalistic roles, saving people from their own worst impulses and ignorance. The power of mass media had to be subordinated to and controlled by these guardian institutions if anarchy was to be avoided.

By contrast, several left-wing critics argued that people were too easily exploited because they maintained an unreasoning and unreflective faith (false consciousness) in the legitimacy of status quo institutions and elites. Consequently, it was necessary for enlightened revolutionaries to form a vanguard political party that could overthrow reactionary institutions and lead people into a better future. The party was to serve as the dominant social institution, preparing the way for a new social order, acting as an agent of the people and controlling all other institutions on their behalf. In order that progress might be assured, control of media by the party was considered necessary (Markham, 1967).

The arguments of both the Right and the Left were grounded in early social theories that shared many assumptions. These theories placed great importance upon social institutions and devalued the abilities of average persons. At the heart of these theories were simple, mechanistic, and deterministic views of both social institutions and individuals. Average persons were conceptualized as having little creative potential or skill. They were thought to be easily manipulated or coerced into doing what paternalistic or revolutionary elites judged best. Conservatives favored deterministic psychological or functionalist theories developed by behaviorists or social Darwinists (Martindale, 1960), while those on the Left preferred equally pessimistic views offered by Marxist, structuralist, or Freudian theory.

CONTEMPORARY MEDIA CRITICISM

Unbridled mass entertainment continues to provoke intense criticism inside and outside of academia from both conservative and reform critics. However, the deterministic assumptions that grounded earlier criticisms are being questioned and rejected. Audiences are now referred to as active rather than passive. It is recognized that media effects are rarely immediate and direct; rather, they tend to be subtle and long term. Nevertheless, there are echoes of arguments first raised more than a century ago. Some conservatives still maintain that mass culture distracts people from and disturbs their belief in traditional forms of culture. Traditional forms are considered essential if the social order is to be maintained. On the other hand, radicals still condemn the power of mass culture to narcotize, desensitize, and alienate. They continue to argue that mass culture erodes the will of the people to seek necessary social change and thus serves to perpetuate an increasingly untenable status quo. Recent arguments concerning the erosion of the public sphere and attendant privatization can be seen as paralleling earlier concerns over the dissolution of communities and attendant "massification":

> In all of these studies—Lasch, Sennett, Mander, DeBord, Boorstin, the Frankfurt theorists . . . —a central paradox is that the highly public mass media erode the public sphere by subjectivizing or privatizing it. But as the public sphere is hollowed out, so is the individual, the meaning of whose existence depends upon participation in a public community. The isolated, narcissistic ego becomes the hero or heroine of every mass-mediated experience, the source and aim of the grandest, most glamorous daydreams and wish fulfillments, in an infinite hall of mirrors. (Brantlinger, 1983, p. 259)

The enormous popularity of television is frequently cited by critics as evidence that average persons cannot be trusted to make wise choices for themselves—that they are easily seduced into preferring amusement to enlightenment. As Neil Postman (1985) has argued, if people are given the opportunity, they will "amuse themselves to death." It is important that such arguments be carefully formulated if they are to take into account the innovative views of media and culture that are gaining acceptance. Below, we offer a systematic description of this new paradigm and then discuss several recent studies that are grounded in it. We have indicated how notions of public sphere erosion, privatization, and narcissism can be enhanced through integration into a culture-centered paradigm.

TOWARD A NEW PERSPECTIVE ON
MASS ENTERTAINMENT AND COMMUNITY

Over the last 25 years, much has been written concerning new paradigms for social research. Not one, but several new paradigms appear to have emerged to challenge the dominant perspective. In two recent volumes a host of "paradigm dialogues" are presented in which advocates of various perspectives confront sympathetic critics (Dervin, Grossberg, O'Keefe, & Wartella, 1989a, 1989b). In this essay, we will take an alternative position on this "ferment in the field" (Gerbner, 1983) and will argue that most of these seemingly disparate perspectives can be and should be integrated into a common paradigm. The explicit development of this paradigm would have many benefits, including resolution of some of the more sterile arguments over the role of mass entertainment. We are concerned that if such theoretical integration does not occur soon, an important opportunity for unifying scholarship in our field will be lost.

As we discuss the major themes in the new paradigm, we will seek to differentiate it from the assumptions that grounded earlier forms of media criticism. Though this early work provided a starting point for contemporary analyses of media, many older theoretical assumptions require reassessment. Some should be replaced with new insights into culture, community, and social change. It is important to recognize that current neo-Marxist theory and "mainstream" effects research have undergone profound changes in a relatively short period of time. It is misleading for critics of either approach to charge that they suffer from the same limitations as earlier scholarship. Both have undergone surprisingly similar "paradigm shifts." In our view, these shifts stem from the same source and create the possibility of locating a common ground, of developing a new paradigm for communication research, which we have labeled the *culture-centered paradigm*.

Despite our view that most current changes in theory stem from the same underlying paradigm, we recognize this will not prevent our field from fragmenting into at least two opposing camps. The most likely division is one that has already emerged in the literature and pits the cultural studies perspective (Carey, 1989; Grossberg, 1989) against the communication science perspective (Berger & Chaffee, 1987; Bradac, 1989; Hawkins, Wiemann, & Pingree, 1988). Some cultural studies advocates have positioned themselves as articulators of the new paradigm and have rejected the possibility that this paradigm might also be compatible with the communication science approach (Carey, 1989). Advocates of communication science have adopted many new assumptions on a piecemeal basis. However, they are failing to address issues concerning community and the role of media implicit in the overall paradigm.

An important opportunity for integration of existing approaches will be lost if cultural studies and communication science continue to be elaborated as independent and opposing perspectives. The "territory" for media research is being carved up between these perspectives. Already there is evidence that existing Ph.D. programs are choosing to specialize in one approach or the other. Despite efforts at paradigm dialogues, adherents to each perspective remain relatively uninformed about the concepts and research methods used in the other camp. Too often, advocates of each perspective are aware only of the limitations of the opposing camp and make little effort to acknowledge strengths. While several recent volumes (e.g., Berger & Chaffee, 1987; Dervin et al., 1989a, 1989b) offer essays that provide overviews of approaches used within each of the perspectives, most of these essays are unable to articulate a common ground. Citations within individual essays tend to be limited to either the cultural studies or the communication science perspective.

Though recent theory textbooks cover both perspectives (see, e.g., DeFleur & Ball-Rokeach, 1989; Littlejohn, 1989; McQuail, 1987), these may not overcome divisiveness because the various theories that make up each perspective tend to be discussed in isolation. Shared themes and assumptions are not emphasized. Communication science is typically described as quantitative, analytical, and concerned with the application of knowledge to solve specific communication problems, while cultural studies are said to be qualitative, holistic, and more concerned with understanding the human condition (Carey, 1989).

While we recognize the validity of such categorizations, we are concerned that common themes and assumptions in both perspectives are not being recognized and highlighted. Both perspectives have made a clear break from earlier and more pessimistic theories of human nature. Both agree that great potential may exist for the constructive use of media by average persons. The communication science perspective has focused heavily on communicator activity and the ability people have to make various forms of communication accomplish planned objectives (Bryant & Street, 1988). Within cultural studies, there is growing interest in the power of average persons to resist interpreting messages as intended by media executives and to engage in "oppositional decoding" (Morley, 1980; Radway, 1986; Steiner, 1988). Thus both perspectives have come to focus on the ability of people to make media serve personal needs and desires.

Similarly, both perspectives have developed sophisticated insight into the operation of media institutions. Simplistic, functionalist notions of the role of media have been abandoned by the communication science approach and replaced by more complex notions (such as entertainment theory, as articulated by Zillman & Bryant, 1986). Cultural studies has developed several quite sophisticated analyses of the media as culture industries (Gitlin, 1983; Real, 1977, 1989).

We have taken care to avoid writing an essay that could simply widen the gulf between communication science and cultural studies. The literature of our discipline already contains several essays that provide useful summaries of recent research from the point of view of each perspective (Berger & Chaffee, 1987; Peck, 1989; Real, 1989). We chose, instead, to identify and focus on themes that are or should be common to both perspectives. After identifying these themes, we discuss specific studies that utilize them. Then, in our concluding section, we consider possibilities for future theory construction, elaboration, and clarification.

In summary, our overall purpose will be to argue for the utility of a "culture-centered" paradigm as a means of unifying scholarship in our field. If such a paradigm can be elaborated, it could guide both quantitative and qualitative work. If future media research were more explicitly and self-consciously grounded in it, findings from very different types of analyses might be integrated and common problems might be addressed. Critics of our proposal might argue that existing divisions in the field are giving rise to "heuristic dialogues." In our view, these dialogues too often consist of juxtaposed monologues (dialogues of the deaf). Within these, much effort is made to defend existing perspectives, but little is done to assess and build on common themes. Given the sterility of past debates over the nature of mass entertainment, we are skeptical that true dialogue will be possible without explicit acknowledgment of a common paradigm and a concerted effort to ground all forms of scholarship in it.

TOWARD A CULTURE-CENTERED PARADIGM

Our effort in paradigm articulation will begin with derivation of useful concepts and themes from a disparate body of work, ranging from cultural studies (Carey, 1989; Grossberg, 1989; Real, 1989) to the changing insights on media effects offered under the rubric of communication science (Berger & Chaffee, 1987; Bradac, 1989; Hawkins et al., 1988). Too often, previous work has juxtaposed these approaches and ignored their common concerns. For example, in his defense of cultural studies, Carey (1989) argues that the communication science approach should be abandoned as sterile and ill conceived (pp. 91-92). At the same time, adherents of communication science continue to ignore the rapidly growing body of work in cultural studies. For example, in a recent overview of research on media effects, Bowers (1989) cites 80 studies, but only the work of Goffman appears to have links to cultural studies.

Structuration Theory

If there is to be a culture-centered paradigm, it must have a systematically developed theoretical core. After considering several alternate theories, we chose the work of Anthony Giddens (1979, 1984) as offering the best possibility of grounding both quantitative and qualitative work in our field. We are not alone in making this assessment. Giddens (1989) himself views his work in this way. Also, he is one of the few theorists who is beginning to be cited with some regularity by persons identified with either communication science (McPhee, 1989) or cultural studies (Marvin, 1989; Murdock, 1989). His work has been influenced by such diverse approaches as structural-functionalist theory, Weberian theory, Marxism, symbolic interactionism, structuralism, and poststructuralism. His approach is especially compatible with the poststructural perspective, which attempts to account for both agents (human beings) and agencies (human institutions) without placing primacy on one or the other.

Giddens integrates a broad range of contemporary social theories to create the perspective that he labels *structuration* theory. Central to this theory is the notion that there is always a close and dynamic relation between all forms of social practice (including communication practices) and social institutions. Practices are made up of sets of actions that are structured, promulgated, and constrained by social institutions. But institutions cannot be maintained unless the practices that are essential to them are routinely carried out. Everyday, institutions must be re-created and reenacted by individuals in the course of their lives. Giddens's argument is echoed in French poststructural thought, such as in Kristeva's (1984) subject in process/on trial and Foucault's (1972) subject of discourse, among others.

Giddens argues that an intimate, dynamic interrelationship exists between the two levels of social action. Institutions operate at the macroscopic level, defining, constraining, and nurturing a broad range of social practices. Practices would quickly become disorganized or cease to be invested with meaning without the framework provided by institutions. At the microscopic level, routine enactment of social practices serves to reconfirm and legitimate the institutions that facilitate those practices. At any time, social change can arise either through gradual evolution of new practices at the microscopic level or through rapid restructuring of entire social institutions. This view parallels that of Foucault (1970). For example, Foucault (1972) argues that ruptures, understood as system failures, can completely transform a communication system (such as an institution like media) in an instant on a variety of levels.

But, although structuration theory provides a very cogent macroscopic description of how social structure is created and maintained, it is less useful in dealing with microscopic issues. What motivates individuals to learn and engage in social practices? What is their experience of these practices and how important are such experiences to the continuance of the practices and the perpetuation of institutions? What is the role of media in fostering social practices, especially if earlier notions about socialization, such as those provided by behaviorism or Freudianism, are rejected as simplistic or "overdetermined"? Giddens is less concerned about such "phenomenological" questions. To address them, it is necessary to elaborate on his perspective by adding themes taken from other recent theories of culture and community. Below, we consider several of these themes and suggest how they could extend the work of Giddens in useful ways.

The Production of Meaning

A dominant theme in recent cultural studies theory is the production of meaning within the context of a community. Several rather diverse theories share a common focus on culture as both vehicle and artifact of a complex social process involving the creation, dissemination, and consumption of meaning. Culture is conceived by these theories as a dominant force (if not *the* dominant force) in social life. Among the most important of these theories are the synthesis of American cultural studies provided by Carey (1989), British cultural studies (S. Hall, 1980), cultural anthropology (Marcus & Fischer, 1986), and symbolic interactionism (Burke, 1968; Edelman, 1988; Goffman, 1974).

Each of these theories identifies the desire to produce meaningful experience for oneself and to communicate or share such experience with others as the most fundamental motivations for human action. To produce and share meaningful experience, we use and participate in the elaboration of culture. Thus these diverse theories are "culture centered" in that they assume that the creation and dissemination of culture per se is a paramount human activity. All other forms of human action are necessarily shaped and prioritized by culture. Without culture, action would be meaningless. Similarly, following Giddens, without action, culture would be nonexistent.

All of these theories also place stress on the problematic nature of meaning production. They reject simplistic "transmission" notions inherent in earlier communication theories that assumed that after "socialization" most persons rarely change the communication practices that underlie encoding and decoding of messages. Instead, these theories assert that such practices constantly undergo changes and that as the practices change, so does the experience of meaning. The social world is thus open to constant and potentially quite radical reinterpretation and redefinition. As understanding of the external world alters, it inevitably affects self-identity and social roles. Our relationships with others and our understanding of them are subject to powerful transformations.

Social Construction of Reality

A related theme, common to cultural theories, is the social construction of reality (Berger & Luckmann, 1966). Most people are assumed to live in a social world defined and structured by shared meaning—a common culture. However, they are generally quite unaware that this culture is created and shared through complex social/communication processes. Their ability to construct and maintain this culture is based on practical knowledge, not on reflection or self-conscious action. These processes permit social worlds of endless and varied complexity to be shaped from quite mundane physical materials and ordinary social practices (Schutz, 1967, 1970). With the use of mass media, some forms of culture can even be shared across large geographic areas.

From the perspective of individuals, culture provides convenient, highly cogent definitions that permit them routinely to impose meaning on the world. It enables individuals to structure their own experiences and to anticipate and interpret the experiences of others. But culture is not simply a cookbook or dictionary that provides stock recipes or formulaic definitions. Culture consists of a broad range of artifacts and symbols that serve to direct or constrain perception. Taken as individual entities, the elements that make up culture are meaningless. They have meaning only as parts of larger patterns, just as words have meaning only within the context of a language. Culture is structural in the sense that the meanings of its symbols and artifacts are understood only in relation to other symbols and artifacts. Culture is semiotic in the sense that meaning is derived not only from language, but from "signs" that stand, ultimately, for something other than what they are (Peirce, 1985). Culture is made up of many silent (and not so silent) "languages" (E. Hall, 1959; Ruesch & Bateson, 1951/1987) that structure very different sorts of social practices and artifacts.

Thus, though culture is humanly created, it can legitimately be seen as operating independent of human control. Structuralist linguists have argued that we do not speak languages; rather, we are spoken by them. That is, the structure inherent in language/culture provides a very powerful constraint upon human thought and action—a constraint that is difficult, if not impossible, for isolated individuals to overcome. Carried to its logical extreme, this structuralist position degenerates into a cultural determinism that ignores the possibility that, under certain circumstances, culture can be creatively reshaped. For example, Lefebvre (1988) argues that "the everyday is not only programmed but is entirely mediated and mass mediated" (p. 79). Althusser (1970) has been criticized for his hard-line structural position on culture. "Subjectivity is culturally determined; it is a function of the ideological practices by which certain subject positions become historically available" (Grossberg & Nelson, 1988, p. 7). Poststructuralist theory rejects this degree of cultural determinism and argues instead that human action is motivated, that is, grounded in what a human being takes from culture to create a common boundary (i.e., a community). Thus it is when individuals form communities that they gain the ability to break the constraints of culture.

Acculturation: Beyond Behaviorism

Among the important insights emerging from the various culture-centered theories is awareness of the complexity of the social processes that socialize or acculturate individuals. These theories reject behavioristic learning notions, which asserted that culture is acquired through behavioral conditioning or rote memorization of institutional rules, mores, folkways, or values (Peck, 1989). Behavioristic theories assumed that social institutions develop and maintain their control over human action by compelling individuals to learn rules, sometimes through rewards, but frequently with the threat of punishment. The outcome of successful socialization from this viewpoint was the production of social robots—persons programmed to obey complex sets of social rules. Once programmed, people were thought to be quite fixed in their adherence to rules. In such theories, rituals were viewed as functioning merely to reinforce previously learned norms and values. Rituals reminded people of the importance of rules and provided superficial rewards for compliance or punishment for deviance. Those who persisted in their deviance were persons who "broke down," probably due to inadequate socialization or psychological instability.

By contrast, culture-centered theories emphasize the utility of conceiving of individuals as active agents who constantly engage in relatively creative efforts to produce meaning for themselves and others. Social practices are not learned out of fear or compulsion to fit into a given social order, but rather are acquired as part of the larger effort to make sense of the external environment and find one's place within it. As these practices are learned, the social world is experienced as "real," predictable, and ordered.

Socialization is also motivated by a strong desire to share meaning with others—to know what others know and to be able to empathize with what they experience. During socialization, an individual learns a broad and diverse range of social practices that permit him or her to *encode* meaning, to engage in actions that will induce specific experiences for himself, herself, or others. An individual also learns a large repertoire of social practices that guide *decoding* of the actions of others, permitting him or her to *read* those actions properly and induce appropriate, meaningful experiences. Although we must remind our readers that the code that is decoded or "read" is not necessarily a linguistic code. The edict that "the social world is structured like a language" has passed. When we decode advertising, we are not decoding a chain of nouns and pronouns. Instead, we are determining, based on our place within culture, the rules that enable that advertisement to have meaning *and* form *and* some practical (even though questionable) use. What we read are not words, but signs.

It is important to note that these experiences of meaning are not idiosyncratic; rather, they exist in some relation to a "received view" of propriety and a uniform standard of conduct. As a result, the preteenager who learns of the latest styles by watching *Dance Party USA* is being acculturated, as is the mentally handicapped person watching an orientation video for McDonald's. Acculturation results in the acquisition of a proper mode of conduct. That propriety becomes the definition for the acculturated individual.

Thus, in some culture-centered theories, the desire to experience and share meaning is seen as taking precedence over most, if not all, other motives underlying socialization. However, this desire must be satisfied within a social/cultural context (i.e., a community) in which specific norms for action are prescribed. This desire to share meaning is so strong that it can often take precedence over more biologically based survival motives, such as hunger or personal safety.

Individuals are drawn to and learn those social practices that are most useful to them in imposing order on experience. In time, they acquire great skill in accomplishing this task. An acculturated individual is one who has learned how to produce and share highly meaningful experiences by using quite complex sets of social practices to encode and decode meaning. He or she also must learn to enact complex sequences of action that the community regards as normal and proper.

Mass Media Rituals

Some culture-centered theorists argue that it is useful to regard much use of mass entertainment as serving a ritual function (Carey, 1989). They believe that the long-term consequences of such media use can be understood only if we are able to conceptualize the overarching rituals that structure it. These rituals are propagated by specific social institutions and provide important opportunities for people to produce meaning for themselves and to share this meaning with others. Given the problematic nature of meaning production and the possibility that always exists for sudden shifts in the way individuals experience the social world, themselves, and others, such rituals may be quite essential not only to the maintenance of social order, but also as a means of stabilizing personal experience. For example, Holland's (1988) and Ryan's (1988) discussions of psychoanalysis assert that film production should be and is designed to elicit commonplaces that balance the individual in society. When commonplaces (codes) are unstable, the individual loses his or her sense of place. Meyrowitz (1985) has questioned the utility of such mediated rituals and argues that they may often disrupt rather than stabilize everyday life.

Critical theorists have devoted considerable attention to the analysis of one particular media ritual—the ritual inherent in many forms of advertising. This ritual is clearly orchestrated by advertisers with the intent of marketing specific products. Conceptualized as ritual, advertising can be seen as offering a narrow and clearly quite erroneous perspective on the social world (Jhally, 1987). In advertising, the consumption of specific products is routinely portrayed as the central, if not the only, means by which meaning can be encoded and decoded. If you have problems relating to other people, consume toothpaste or mouthwash or deodorant. If you want to impress others, consume specific brands of alcohol or smoke certain cigarettes.

Media rituals impose constraint upon (provide structure for) both the decoding of media content and the encoding of experiences associated with this content. To the extent that such media rituals are structured/constrained by social institutions, these institutions may be able to retain effective control over the production of meaning by individuals. Thus the implementation of new media rituals could increase or consolidate the influence of specific social institutions, while the disappearance of specific media rituals could have serious long-term implications for the stability of other institutions. This perspective attaches considerable importance to the emergence of new industries that specialize in the orchestration of media rituals such as advertising and public relations.

While the conceptualization of media rituals has been under development for more than a decade, there is considerable disagreement concerning their prevalence and importance. Michael Real (1989, pp. 250-261) has offered some of the strongest arguments concerning the power and range of media rituals. His early work used the concept of mediated rituals to examine a broad range of media content, from Billy Graham to Walt Disney fantasies (Real, 1977). Recently, Real (1989) has argued that media provide a "near total environment . . . which serves to structure human experience at deep levels" (pp. 253-254).

While the overall argument advanced by Real is generally consistent with ours, he reaches more pessimistic conclusions. He believes that media executives wield enormous power over individuals. This position fails to recognize the constraints that culture imposes upon media entrepreneurs who attempt to manipulate it to their advantage or the countervailing influence of other social institutions. It also devalues the power of individuals to resist rituals that exploit rather than nurture meaning. Indeed, the postmodern experience of television appears to be characterized by a fullness of sense and an absence of meaning. Any meaning encountered in a postmodern text will be indexical to modes of production. In other words, instead of cleverly hiding the fact that a camera is creating a fiction, a seamless narrative, postmodern television points to the camera, to the script, to the fact that actors are acting, to the arbitrary imposition of narrative structure (Olson, 1987).

SOCIAL INSTITUTIONS AND CULTURE

Culture-centered theories recognize the importance of social institutions as stabilizing agencies within social orders. Social institutions provide an overarching structure that facilitates the teaching of specific social practices and makes available the resources necessary to engage in these practices. The establishment and sanctioning of communication rituals is only one example of the structure provided by social institutions.

Institutions establish and enforce rules that prohibit some social practices while encouraging others. By encouraging individuals to adopt certain practices, institutions assure their own survival. An "acculturated" individual is one who not only has come to rely on certain institutions as a source of social practices, but also accepts the rules these institutions set for the use of such practices. Once such rules are learned, they are routinely applied.

Symbiotic Acculturation

Some culture-centered theories imply that it is essential that the relationship between institutions and individuals be balanced. Ideally, a symbiotic relationship should be developed and maintained. In such a relationship the social practices necessary to the perpetuation of institutions are also experienced by most individuals as useful in producing and sharing meaning. If institutions are to remain stable over long periods of time, such symbiotic acculturation is crucial. Many, if not most, persons who daily engage in the practices that reenact institutions must derive meaning from their actions. If they do not, then external rewards or coercion will become increasingly necessary to force compliance. Though rewards or coercion can be quite effective in the short term for controlling small groups of people, culture-centered theories argue that they cannot be an effective means of social control if large-scale populations are to be controlled over long periods of time.

It is useful to recognize that symbiosis between institutions and individuals can be achieved in a variety of different ways within very different types of social order. It may be a temporary phenomenon, or it may endure for decades or perhaps centuries. Many culture-centered theories are "radically pluralist." That is, they assume that no specific social order or its underlying culture(s) has any claim to universal "truth" or "goodness." They also recognize that symbiosis between institutions and individuals is not a guarantee that a social order will be "just" or "good" in some ultimate sense. For example, such symbiosis might have been achieved in Nazi Germany for some persons (those not subject to coercion), but with diabolical consequences. Below, we argue that privatization of discourse may currently permit a particular kind of symbiotic acculturation that has some clear disadvantages.

Plurality of Experience

Though it is crucial that most persons use similar social practices to create/impose meaning, it may not be necessary that each person share the same physical or psychological experience of this meaning. Even persons who enact the same practices in the same situations may be likely to have widely divergent experiences. An important theme found in some culture-centered theories is that experience need not be identical for meaning to be shared. Rather, meaning experienced by individuals can be expected to range across a wide continuum and be affected by many factors—some of which are social and some of which are idiosyncratic.

Efforts to standardize the experiences associated with specific practices and to compel commonality of these experiences may be doomed to failure, especially in modern social orders, where diverse socialization agents foster a broad range of practices. Many competing or countervailing social institutions foster rituals that invest similar practices with variant meaning/ experience. One consequence of such fractured socialization is that it may allow or even force people to develop personal styles for structuring their experiences and for producing meaning. It may also allow media to play the important role of a source of information on the development of such personal styles. For example, Pfeil (1988) argues that some rock music abandons explicit signification, offering its listeners not overt meaning but implicit, idiosyncratic feeling.

Thus some culture-centered theories assume that in contemporary, liberal-pluralist social orders, great responsibility for development of decoding strategies is inevitably placed on individuals. Mass media disseminate highly ambiguous messages that can be and are decoded in highly variant ways depending upon the specific decoding strategies that audience members have learned to use. It therefore becomes more useful to categorize audiences in terms of decoding strategies, rather than their position in the social order or within specific communities. When consuming the same media content, persons with very different social statuses and geographic locations may share similar decoding strategies and produce similar experiences for themselves. For example, sports fans may be effectively categorized based on the experiences they produce for themselves using sports content.

Privatization of Discourse

Thus in contemporary social order the role of institutions in guiding/ constraining personal experience may have undergone important changes. Rather than using ritual as a mechanism for standardizing experience, modern institutions may rely on mediated rituals to give people opportunities to produce gratifying experiences for themselves. A term used to refer to this phenomenon is *privatization of discourse.* So long as institutions derive advantages from such idiosyncratic meaning production, they will foster it. For these institutions, privatization of discourse and the narcissistic focusing of experience that results may be quite useful. For example, so long as the advertising placed in mass entertainment content serves to stimulate and structure product sales, advertisers will continue to fund the production and distribution of this content. A peculiar type of symbiotic acculturation may bind together advertisers and their audiences.

Thus, in contemporary social orders, institutions may simply provide general guidelines and advice, leaving each person to be responsible for developing his or her own individualized styles of work and play, which permit him or her to derive personal meaning from the enactment of social practices. Each individual may become "atomized"—confined to the private world centered on the narcissistic production of gratifying personal experiences. Use of entertainment media content may most often be structured by consumption styles that simply serve to maximize personal satisfaction. But in learning to use media in this way, individuals may also be learning personal styles for the encoding and decoding of discourse that emphasize short-term private satisfaction over longer-term public/community good. Meyrowitz (1985) has argued that such persons lack a sense of place—they have no community to guide meaning production.

Role of Communities and
Media in Contemporary Social Orders

Though the various culture-centered theories share many assumptions, there are disagreements on specific issues that permit differentiation of these theories into differing camps. One of the most important of these issues concerns the conceptualization of community and the role assigned to it in modern social orders. Each of the culture-centered theories recognizes that prior to urbanization and industrialization most people were acculturated within geographically limited folk communities. They grew up with others who were socialized by the same social institutions. It is likely that most social practices were learned through routine observation of others within the boundaries of a physically limited community. The dominant form of communication was interpersonal. Within these highly stable, geographically isolated, hierarchically structured, and culturally homogeneous communities, the encoding and decoding of social practices should have been relatively unproblematic and static. Individuals were able to make many assumptions concerning the meaning that others imposed on the social world and their experience of it. This enabled them to share a commonality of experience that some theorists argue was especially meaningful or "deep." Persons from outside the community could never hope to share these communal experiences—even if they became expert in the practices that produced them. Such assertions have been strengthened by ethnographic research in isolated folk communities (Marcus & Fischer, 1986).

While there is growing agreement over the historic role of folk communities, there is considerable debate over the role of communities in contemporary social orders. Some theorists maintain considerable respect for the depth of meaning that they believe folk communities made possible. They argue that it may be possible and desirable to make communities the building block of modern social orders rather than rely on large-scale, bureaucratized institutions. However, these theorists are not proposing to re-create folk communities in the way that the hippie movement established communes. Rather, their intent is to create social units that can overcome obvious failings of folk communities (cultural homogeneity, hierarchical structure, social isolation, and so on) while realizing their greatest benefits—including deep sharing of meaning. Various innovative social units have been proposed, some of which would utilize new media technologies and innovative communication practices. These "new communities" might rely on media to transcend physical and social boundaries. They might also utilize mediated rituals to induce common experiences routinely.

Bureaucracy Versus Community

The interest of culture-centered theorists in establishing new forms of community stems in part from their desire to find an alternative to bureaucracy as the basic building block for society. These theorists are often quite ambivalent about the role of bureaucracy. Though some recognize that bureaucracy has proved essential in bringing about many positive social changes, they are quite skeptical about the ability of bureaucracies to sustain symbiotic acculturation and assist individuals in living meaningful lives. Instead, it is argued that bureaucracies are too inflexible and static; that they persist in fostering practices that long ago ceased to be valuable to individuals in the production or sharing of meaning. Bureaucracies are said to have inadequate mechanisms for monitoring the meanings individuals derive from social practices. Bureaucracies may be unable to cope adequately with plurality of experience. Loyal bureaucrats may be expected to play similar roles and experience these roles in similar ways. When experience cannot be closely monitored or controlled, bureaucracies may rely on material rewards or various forms of coercion to compel learning of or assure compliance with specific social practices.

In feminist and neo-Marxist cultural theories, these evils of bureaucracy are attributed instead to patriarchal culture and to capitalism, respectively. In both of these perspectives, one goal of the theory is to demonstrate that destructive social practices have been fostered and to find ways these practices might be overcome or resisted. It is assumed that individuals need to be liberated from such constraints. In the case of feminism, liberation also involves joining a feminist community in which new encoding and decoding strategies are fostered.

Community-centered theorists argue that various strategies should be explored for reducing the dominant role currently played by bureaucracies in our social institutions. A community-based social order would differ from bureaucratically based social order in two ways. First, a community-based social order would focus much more concern on assisting individuals in their efforts to impose meaning, and, second, it would integrate functions now assigned to specialized bureaucracies. Thus high priority would be given to acculturating individuals so that they could encode and decode social practices in ways they experience, on the one hand, as personally meaningful, but that also have value for a larger community. Privatization of discourse and narcissistic production of experience would be avoided.

Services currently performed by specialized bureaucracies would be replaced by services supplied from within communities. Individual communities might perform various services for members, ranging, perhaps, from religious to entertainment to social welfare functions. Media might be utilized so that relatively small communities would still be able to offer highly specialized services. For example, if such services could not be provided by community members, experts in distant communities might be contacted to provide assistance. A network of interdependent communities might be created in which expertise would be shared.

Considerable effort could be taken by such communities to assure symbiotic acculturation. Within each community, some persons might be more responsible than others for teaching social practices or for structuring institutions in which meaning is experienced. However, these persons would not be isolated from those they serve—as they now are within specialized educational, religious, or media bureaucracies. If their acculturation efforts failed, there would be immediate pressure on them to change. Their work might be routinely and easily monitored by parents, permitting families to assume a more central role in acculturation.

These arguments assume that communities would have important advantages over bureaucracies. Above all, they should be better able to achieve symbiotic acculturation while avoiding privatization of meaning. But such community-centered theories are open to serious criticism. Like folk communities, these community-centered social orders might tend to foster and maintain highly static and relatively homogeneous forms of culture. It is not clear how the limitations of folk communities will be avoided. In their search for "deep meaning," these communities might succeed only by standardizing the experience of meaning and coercing deviants to share this experience. Even relatively minor deviations from established social practices might be suppressed. Social pressure to conform might be high. Could a social order based on such communities remain committed to the values of cultural pluralism and pluralism of experience?

SPECIFIC CULTURE-CENTERED THEORIES

Though the various culture-centered theories share to a greater or lesser extent the themes described above, they all interpret these themes differently and offer quite divergent analyses of contemporary culture and the role of media. Below we discuss several of these theories. Our intent is not to provide an exhaustive summary of all or even the most important of these theories. Rather, we have chosen a subset of theories that illustrate the diverse views and conclusions offered by these theories. The theories range across the ideological spectrum from conservative to radical. They also focus on very different levels of analysis.

Coping with Everyday Life in a Pluralistic Social World

Erving Goffman (1974) provides a useful way of conceptualizing how average individuals use routine social practices to construct meaningful social worlds for themselves. His theory implies that plurality of experience need not interfere with the development of symbiotic relationships between institutions and individuals. Goffman explains how people living in complex, seemingly contradictory social orders, such as U.S. society, can nevertheless experience themselves as living within relatively well-integrated, culturally homogeneous social orders. Most do not perceive themselves to be moving among situations structured by contradictory social practices fostered by competing social institutions. Most act with the conviction that a single, "paramount" social reality underlies and provides continuity for their existence. They fail to notice even quite serious contradictions in their actions. When moving between essentially similar situations, they can perceive very different things to be important and have markedly different experiences. How can there be such apparent cultural diversity without intrusion into and disruption of everyday experience? Goffman argues that all of us seek to create and maintain for ourselves the illusion of living in an ordered and more or less rational social world—one that we experience as real. During acculturation, whatever its agent or agency, we develop very effective and highly routinized strategies (sets of social practices) for making sense of events in the situations dominated by those agencies. We rarely need to reflect consciously upon these strategies—in fact, reflection is likely to impede effective action.

Goffman uses the concept of *frame* to refer to sets of interrelated definitions that we routinely impose upon situations. We are constantly learning and then routinely utilizing frames. Frames enable us to identify quickly the most important elements in situations—to see and anticipate sequences of actions, and to screen out ambiguous or irrelevant sensory data. We quickly perceive only what is "meaningful" as defined by a socialization agency that dominates the situation. With no conscious effort, we choose from among a repertoire of social practices to create a social role suited to the situation. We experience the role as natural, rational, and right. Enactment of the role guides us through a situation. If we are successful, we produce for ourselves the experience that we anticipated at the outset and that was implicit in the frames we used to guide our actions.

If Goffman is correct, then much of our experience of the social world is quite routinized and predictable, but at the same time can be structured by diverse or even contradictory agencies. Though our experience of the social world is guided by the frames we have learned, most of us have little awareness of the extent to which our perception is structured by different agencies. Instead, many of us hold to "naive empiricist" notions that assert we are seeing "things as they are" in an external and objective "real world." We may even reject the notion that we are acting in ways that are socially sanctioned and argue instead that we are simply doing what is "right," "natural," "logical," "realistic," or "personally meaningful."

How do most of us manage to retain these notions of living in a "real world" consisting of a unified, well-integrated social order? How do we systematically reject evidence that constantly implicates us in the fabrication of this "reality"? Goffman points out that most of us have highly developed skills for coping with unusual or unexpected happenings. Our naive faith in the existence of a real world persists because of our ability to "repair" our experiences by quickly reframing situations whenever unanticipated happenings take place. Only rarely are our framing mistakes so glaring that we are forced to "flood out" and admit them to ourselves and others. In such cases, we may be unlikely to blame the social world for being overly ambiguous or for "tricking" us into making framing mistakes. It is easier and less troubling to assume personal responsibility. If we experience the world as "unreal," then it must be our own fault. We should have known better or been more logical. We need to get our act together. We need to get our heads straight.

Goffman points out that our simplistic understanding of the social world makes us exceedingly vulnerable to systematic manipulation by socialization agents or by others who take advantage of the way we frame situations. For example, we may be so convinced of the "reality" of what we think we see that we are easily "taken in" by con artists, salespersons, or anyone else who "plays along" with the way we are routinely framing a situation. We can be manipulated by persons who profess to help us, but whose intent is to exploit us.

Though Goffman's perspective is quite insightful concerning the manner in which average persons experience and manage their everyday lives, it is ultimately unsatisfying because it fails to address macroscopic issues. In Goffman's world, people seem trapped by the constraints of a subtle and ultimately quite manipulative everyday life culture. Goffman frequently resorts to theatrical metaphors in describing everyday life. Like actors, individuals are forced to accommodate themselves to roles and scripts they cannot control. At best, one succeeds by living with style, using one's creativity to play effectively the part one has "received." In his most interesting work, Goffman (1963) examined people who failed to live with "style" due to mental illness or to social stigmas that impeded their acceptance by others. Their inability to live normally doomed them to a chaotic, marginalized existence. Goffman offers little hope of transcending the constraints imposed by everyday life culture or of reshaping culture.

Michel Foucault's Cultural Perspective

Goffman's microscopic perspective contrasts sharply with the more far-reaching outlook of Michel Foucault (1970, 1972, 1978, 1979, 1980), who offers a well-developed perspective on the dynamics of culture. Foucault (1980) argues that culture emerges out of a struggle between power and desire. Power is generally tied to institutional practices. Institutional practices include both discursive practices, such as "findings" of science or medicine that express certain views about humans and treat humans in particular ways, and nondiscursive practices, which include architectural and geographical expression. In the context of entertainment media, discursive practices are the media themselves, while nondiscursive practices include the channels by which discourse is disseminated—whether it be by television, radio, or print.

Foucault maintains that institutions constitute a particular apparatus of power that is designed to control populations of people and create a uniform stereotype of particular groups or persons. Humans struggle against relations of power in order to regain their particularity and overcome "cultural" stereotypes. Entertainment media, then, become a record of the struggle between power and desire. Through a descriptive examination of particular entertainment programs, following Foucault's perspective, a particular configuration of culture can be discovered. The configuration that specifies the dialectical process of power and desire is understood by examining the points of rupture (or discontinuity) as they occur in media. Ruptures are points in a "text" where relations of power break down and the system fails. What ruptures reveal are the relations that keep the relations of power intact.

(Re)Structuring Feeling

Goffman's perspective also contrasts sharply with the cultural studies perspective as it is currently evolving in the United States (Grossberg, 1989; O'Connor, 1989). While this perspective shares with Goffman a recognition of the constraints that culture imposes on daily existence, one of its primary objectives has been to discover ways of overcoming such constraints and creating what is conceived of as revolutionary practice. Pfeil (1988) argues that "structure of feeling" constitutes an important form of revolutionary practice within postmodernity. He uses this term to describe the empirical artistic practices of musicians such as Laurie Anderson. Pfeil derives this term from Marxist literary critic Raymond Williams (1977), who defines structure of feeling as social experience in solution, as distinct from other social semantic formations which have been precipitated and are more immediately available. . . . Yet this specific solution is never mere flux. It is a structured formation which, because it is *at the very edge of semantic availability*, has many of the characteristics of a pre-formation. (pp. 133-134; quoted in Pfeil, 1988, p. 383)

Structure of feeling is exemplified by nonexpressive artistic performances. Artists valorize no position and offer warning against any value. "Post-modernism immerses us within the desire and dread it evokes without resolving their oscillation on the level of either content or form" (Williams, quoted in Pfeil, 1988, p. 386). Artistic practices present reflections of an audience's own alienation.

Pfeil argues that when viewed as a structure of feeling, postmodernity keeps the question of political and ideological value open. Such practices could be viewed as nihilistic; the "devaluation of all values" takes place at the level of the code and the utterance. The mechanism at work cuts across codes, disabling the constitution of any value. This response is an appropriate re-cognition of a modernist rationality that attempts to value *all* values. Postmodernity does not care about the hidden meaning; its practices create a surface response to felt contradictions. Pfeil is correct in conceptualizing postmodernity as an event that cuts across codes, but he overlooks the fact that as a result of the disablement of value, transformations do occur at diverse levels. We must be careful on these points. While not inherently nihilistic, postmodern theories are primarily useful as a basis for criticizing the formations of modernity. However, they have yet to offer any alternative to these formations.

Olson (1987) provides another application of the concept of structure of feeling to television. He argues that postmodern television viewers have acquired a great ability to reflect upon and decode television content in complex ways. His main argument is that "meta-television relies on the ability of the viewers to recognize artifice" (p. 284). The structure of feeling relies on its placement of audiences and concentrates primarily on artistic practices at the point of production. Meta-television explicates the express work of the audience, television's "second generation." This audience has aspired to a certain level of sophistication. With their knowledge of television's conventions and production practices, they can "interact" with its postmodern form(s). Television production caters to such audiences using three techniques of self-reflexivity. Television assumes that audiences "can reflect on the medium of television (audience awareness and intertextuality); they can reflect on particular shows or particular genres of television (metagenericism); and they can reflect on their own textuality (autodeconstruction and ilinx)" (Olson, 1987, p. 287). These techniques serve to shatter the illusion that television is portraying real life. Such practices have been exhibited in several programs, including *Moonlighting* and

Saturday Night Live. "Meta-television makes it clear that television can tell and that it usually is telling" (Olson, 1987, p. 298). Meta-television expresses the boredom and restriction of "modernist" television's claim that it is reflecting its audience.

Both Olson's and Pfeil's perspectives are exemplary of the postmodern critique of media and mass culture. These analyses result from an empirical examination of the manifestations of the contradictions brought about by the postmodern critique (of modernity). Both perspectives talk about the "structure" side of culture, that is to say, the objects and artifacts of culture.

The Cultural Economy of Television

Another cultural studies theorist, John Fiske, has developed a theory of the cultural economy of television that argues strongly for the ability of audiences to influence or even control what they are offered by the industry. His views contrast sharply with early Marxist-based theories of political economy such as those offered by Frankfurt school. These early theories assumed that audiences of popular media were cultural dupes. "The necessary implication is that they are the dupes of the industry or of ideology, and that there can be no such thing in their position as popular discrimination" (Fiske, 1989, p. 22). Cultural economy, on the other hand, conceptualizes television viewers as creators of meaning.

According to Fiske (1989), in a cultural economy, the audience produces meanings and pleasures: "The people make their own popular culture out of the offerings of the industry" (p. 25). Elsewhere, Fiske (1988) asserts that "the text is an open potential that can only be activated into a meaningful and pleasurable moment by the personified semiotic process" (p. 248). In other words, viewers interact and create the television text (i.e., the significations). Television viewers use the products of a political economy to constitute their particular culture.

Cultural economy does not assume that viewers are completely free to select meaning; "the text is no do-it-yourself meaning kit from which any meaning can be made" (Fiske, 1989, p. 28). The text is produced with a number of so-called weak points, that is, places that "present opportunities to resist or evade" (p. 29) the interpretations intended by producers. Such weak points enable alternative readings. In Marxist terminology, this is known as the "contradiction" that is assumed always to exist in culture. Popular texts are inherently ambiguous in order to broaden their appeal to diverse audiences. This ambiguity creates additional opportunities for alternative decoding.

Of those that have emerged from neo-Marxist and poststructuralist thought, Fiske's view is among the most comprehensive in its effort to integrate many of the notions about culture, media, and audiences. He seeks to go beyond other cultural studies approaches that are narrowly focused on cultural artifacts and that do not conceptualize audience members as active agents.

Schizoanalysis

Using Deleuze and Guittari's (1972/1977) notion of "schizoanalysis," Holland (1988) perceives film as operating in ways similar to Fiske's (1989) views of television. Schizoanalysis meets one of the aims of a Marxist cultural criticism, namely, the goal "to target and dismantle the processes of recoding that serve to perpetuate the power component of capitalist society and thus prevent the realization of permanent revolution" (Holland, 1988, p. 408). What schizoanalysis intends is to "produce interference between codes and so acts to undermine their authority" (p. 413). Schizoanalysis promises not to interpret a text, but instead to undermine all interpretations that constitute or "recode" values, especially those values labeled dominant. Schizoanalysis opposes interpretation and seeks to undermine any authority. "Interpretation merely reinforces semiotic despotism by translating one authorized code—that of the author or 'creator'—into another authorized code—that of the critic" (p. 413).

Recoding processes, understood here as social conventions, are located in three domains: "the sphere of production, the nuclear family, and the sphere of consumption" (Holland, 1988, p. 408). As a theory that can explicate the cultural response of postmodernity, schizoanalysis reintroduces psychoanalytic theory into the study of entertainment in a way that subverts the terms of psychoanalytic theory as utilized in film criticism. Schizoanalysis, following deconstruction's path, analyzes surfaces and sites of contradiction.

Psychoanalysis and Film: Object Relations Theory

Ryan (1988) borrows object relations theory from psychoanalysis to explicate the relationship between the phenomenological (conscious) viewer and culture. "Object relations theory holds that a person's sense of self identity is constituted through identifications with social objects, images of which are internalized" (p. 481). This perspective asserts that collective behavior can orchestrate and interpret popular film. By doing so, it is making film a site of struggle between viewers and societal (group) or cultural (institutional) points of view. "Popular film is a terrain of contesting representations that articulate a struggle between regressive and alternative models of social institutions and values" (p. 483). Object relations theory is offered as an alternative to the popular Lacanian psychoanalytic position, which views sexuality and sexual difference as key operators in film and key figures in film analysis, according to Ryan. In opposition to the structure of feeling and schizoanalysis, object relations theory argues that "it is possible to imagine a political use of popular film forms that would work to recode the prevailing social discourses" (p. 483). The idea that an encoded discourse could be recoded coincides with such perspectives as Fiske's (1988, 1989) and valorizes the role of the viewer. In addition, the notion of ideology, analysis of which is well grounded in modernity, is restructured because "ideology in this sense is an undifferentiated exercise in domination" (Ryan, 1988, p. 483). Film requires a double reading: one reading that accounts for a dominant encoding, and a second that accounts for viewer decoding. According to object relations theory, this process is constant in all viewers.

Phenomenology, Structuralism, and Semiotics

In recent work, Lanigan (1988) has argued for the development of a human science perspective that moves beyond a focus on message content and audience effects to concentrate on viewers' actual perceptions and expressions while using cultural artifacts. He argues for a methodological approach—semiotic phenomenology that integrates phenomenology, semiotics, historiography, and ethnography. The purpose of semiotic phenomenology is to explicate the role of an active audience in discerning the meaning, form, and use of cultural artifacts. Peterson (1987) used semiotic phenomenology to examine media consumption. He asked students to write brief essays about their experience of listening to Cyndi Lauper's song "Girls Just Want to Have Fun." He argues that "listening to music is a form of media consumption, a habitual practice that inscribes social meanings and organizes pleasure" (p. 37). What Peterson is attempting to discern is the structure and function of music in everyday life. "Postmodernity, the structuration of affect, and co-optation require research that can articulate their specificity" (p. 40).

In addition to the concern about how modern music structures personal experience, Peterson also argues that music can disrupt social movements or minority communities through co-optation. Co-optation occurs when marginal culture (such as radical punk or radical feminism) is transformed into mass culture through being featured in widely distributed media content. Such co-optation may devalue the group's specificity, depoliticize its epistemological claims, and make a mockery of its original intentions.

The Marketing of Meaning

One of the most insightful forms of cultural analysis to be found in current neo-Marxist theory concerns the marketing of meaning. Several recent studies have given a "new look" to critical analyses of advertising (see, e.g., Hay, 1989; Jhally, 1987). This perspective assumes that for advertising to be effective in structuring consumption, it must be part of an overall strategy in which "meaning" is packaged in the form of a mass-produced and -distributed commodity. The strategy must include an effective means of acculturating consumers so that they know what to do with (how to de-code) both material and communication commodities.

Mass media as currently structured are found to play a very central role in the marketing of meaning. Not only do media produce and distribute communication commodities designed to facilitate private production of meaning (fetishism), they also provide a constant flow of information and advice concerning the consumption of all other commodities supplied by the market. While advertising provides the most visible and explicit promotion of commodities, many other types of content provide advice concerning consumption and dramatic re-creations of the meaningful experiences facilitated by consumption. Private life-styles based on consumption of commodities are constantly promoted as practical or even ideal ways of producing meaning for oneself.

Feminism and Media Criticism

Feminist scholars have drawn upon cultural studies, poststructuralism, and neo-Marxism to formulate analyses of media that are gaining increasing recognition. Unlike most other American cultural studies scholars (O'Connor, 1989), feminists have a strong concern for community and the propagation of movement values (Long, 1989). The are committed to breaking the dominance of what they conceptualize as patriarchal culture, and replacing it with a culture grounded in feminist values. Feminist research offers the potential for being constructive as well as critical if in time feminists turn more of their attention to the development of innovative forms of community that could replace the patriarchal bureaucracies that they disdain.

An example of potentially constructive research is offered by Byars (1987), who critiques feminist conceptions grounded in psychoanalytic theory and finds useful examples of feminine discourse (i.e., communication practices appropriate to a feminist community) on prime-time television. "To move beyond the impasses met in traditional marxist and psychoanalytic theories, we must move beyond our reverence for them" (Byars, 1987, p. 293). Byars examines episodes of *Dallas, Cagney & Lacey,* and *Kate & Allie,* arguing that "we still do find alternative discourses at work, particularly of women relating to other women" (p. 296). She states that "ignoring feminine discourse already at work in mainstream texts grossly underestimates the complexity of these texts and their role in the ideological process" (p. 302).

AN AGENDA FOR MEDIA RESEARCH

The culture-centered paradigm suggests a number of potentially fruitful issues for future research. In our view, these issues are particularly timely, given the changes that are currently reshaping the media industries. We are entering a new era of mass communication, but its direction and dominant institutions are yet to be shaped. Precipitating this era are a host of new technologies that simultaneously extend the range and power of existing media (satellites, fiber-optic cables). They also offer the possibility of greater personal and local control (personal computers, camcorders, video-cassette recorders, compact discs, personal copiers). At the same time that we can begin to envision the world enmeshed in one gigantic media net-work, we are witnessing a powerful resurgence of local, ethnic cultures supported in part by new technologies. Future revolutions may be based not on pamphlets or pirate radio stations, but on computer disks, fax machines, and videotapes. The future seems quite open in that the various technolo-gies could be configured in many different ways to develop and sustain very different social and political orders.

Already, the battle lines over the exploitation of new technology are be-ginning to be drawn. A status quo position has emerged within the media industries that envisions the future as largely an extension of the present—with larger profits for media industries and more attractive commodities for audiences. From the perspective of status quo theorists, new media technol-ogies have value primarily if they enable a greater variety of attractive commodities to be produced and marketed. Technologies are appealing only if they provide an innovative means of undergirding the existing mar-ket system. They can do this by facilitating more effective promotion of all forms of commodities together with the private life-styles so essential to an economy based largely upon routinized consumption of goods and services. If the power of media to aid and constrain meaning production is thus in-creased, the overall market system, with its specialized bureaucracies, should become even more stabilized. Those forms of media that do not serve this market system either will fail to be developed or may even be ac-tively suppressed.

This position is rejected either implicitly or explicitly by most of the re-searchers we have considered in this essay. As we have seen, scholars who adopt the critical studies approach assert that the market for media com-modities may soon be exhausted or that attractive new forms of media con-tent could be developed. This would lure increasingly sophisticated audiences away from old-fashioned mass entertainment. These new forms of content could merely continue the current privatization of discourse or they could recontextualize discourse within a community. An example of such recontextualization is provided by Steiner (1988), who argues that *Ms.* magazine was able to encourage oppositional decoding of existing media content. Readers learned to decode conventional media content from the point of view of the feminist community.

Below, we discuss five topics for future research. These topics summa-rize some of the most important suggestions that have emerged out of existing work. This list is not exhaustive; rather, it suggests a range of work that might be undertaken.

Mass-Mediated Culture

Much remains to be learned about the manner in which media content serves to acculturate individuals and to perpetuate existing social institutions. Research on mass media-supported rituals appears to offer considerable promise of new insight, but we need to verify the many intriguing arguments that have been summarized by Real (1989). Research on the power of media to constrain everyday communication practices should have high priority. Is the materialistic culture so central to our market system ultimately as shallow as neo-Marxist critics assert, or does it have a power to command popular imagination and feeling that has not yet been adequately gauged? If this culture were to be displaced, what would be the consequences? Can a media system be envisioned that is not centrally linked to marketing—if not of products, then of its own communication commodities?

New Audiences for Old Content

Some of the recent culture-centered research has argued that current media content is quite polysemic (Fiske, 1989). If media audiences could be "reconstituted," then these audiences might be able to construct innovative and useful new meanings out of existing forms of content. Such reinterpretations of media might take the form of "oppositional decoding" (Steiner, 1988). The possibility of creating such audiences for media deserves exploration. Research might be conducted using either qualitative or quantitative methods. A perspective recently outlined by Fry, Alexander, and Fry (1990) might be especially useful for designing and conducting this type of audience research in that it explicitly combines concepts drawn from both cultural studies and communication science approaches.

Such research might assist existing social movements in their efforts to teach oppositional decoding when acculturating new members. Many existing movements, from fundamentalist religious groups to feminist groups, are already engaging in efforts to teach innovative strategies for decoding media. Their success or failure could be studied. Research over a period of weeks or months in which group viewing is followed by critical discussion of media content might yield important insights into the power of communities to "reframe" existing content and make it serve new purposes.

New Content for Old Audiences

Some researchers have become optimistic that new forms of media will permit the creation of content that will appeal to existing audiences, but serve innovative purposes. Such content might even have the power to transform existing social institutions gradually. While new media appear to offer many possibilities for creating attractive new forms of content, relatively little research has been done to determine the actual appeal and effectiveness of this content. Content similar enough to existing content that is able to appeal to existing audiences may also be easily misunderstood.

Creating Communities Using New Media

One of the most intriguing possibilities offered by new media technology is that of community creation. It is possible to envision and create a broad range of new forms of content that might be used within communities to acculturate members. Ideally, such content would facilitate symbiotic acculturation, in which individual desires for meaning are met at the same time institutional structures are elaborated and enhanced.

Revitalization of the Public Sphere

If the assumptions of the culture-centered paradigm prove valid, this paradigm could provide very powerful insight into the role of media in politics (Jasinski & Davis, 1990). Additional research is necessary to demonstrate that existing uses of media (i.e., to support marketing and consumption of products) do in fact encourage privatization of discourse with consequent devaluation of public politics. Such research could also provide a basis for developing strategies to revitalize politics, so that it serves the vital function of integrating diverse ethnic and racial communities. The goal of this work would be the creation of a public sphere in which a pluralistic public culture is valued and propagated. This public sphere would, in turn, permit a diversity of communities to flourish.

REFERENCES

Adorno, T. (1984). *Aesthetic theory* (C. Lenhardt, Trans.). New York: Routledge & Kegan Paul. (Original work published 1970)

Althusser, L. (1970). *For Marx* (B. Brewster, Trans.). New York: Vintage.

Berger, C. R., & Chaffee, S. H. (Eds.). (1987). *Handbook of communication science.* Newbury Park, CA: Sage.

Berger, P. L., & Luckmann, T. (1966). *The social construction of reality.* Garden City, NY: Doubleday.

Bowers, J. W. (1989). Message effects: Theory and research on mental models of messages. In J. J. Bradac (Ed.), *Message effects in communication science* (pp. 10-23). Newbury Park, CA: Sage.

Bradac, J. J. (Ed.). (1989). *Message effects in communication science.* Newbury Park, CA: Sage.

Brantlinger, P. (1983). *Bread and circuses: Theories of mass culture as social decay.* Ithaca, NY: Cornell University Press.

Bryant, J., & Street, R. L. (1988). From reactivity to activity and action: An evolving concept and *Weltanschauung* in mass and interpersonal communication. In R. P. Hawkins, J. M. Wiemann, & S. Pingree (Eds.), *Advancing communication science: Merging mass and interpersonal process.* Newbury Park, CA: Sage.

Burke, K. (1968). *Language as symbolic action: Essays on life, literature, and method.* Berkeley: University of California Press.

Byars, J. (1987). Reading feminine discourse: Prime-time television in the U.S. *Communication, 9,* 289-303.

Carey, J. W. (1989). *Communication as culture: Essays on media and society.* London: Unwin Hyman.

DeFleur, M. L., & Ball-Rokeach, S. (1989). *Theories of mass communication* (5th ed.). New York: Longman.

Deleuze, G., & Guittari, F. (1977). *Anti-Oedipus: Capitalism and schizophrenia* (R. Hurley, M. Seem, & H. Lane, Trans.). New York: Viking. (Original work published 1972)

Dervin, B., Grossberg, L., O'Keefe, B. J., & Wartella, E. (Eds.). (1989a). *Rethinking communication: Vol. 1. Paradigm issues.* Newbury Park, CA: Sage.

Dervin, B., Grossberg, L., O'Keefe, B. J., & Wartella, E. (Eds.). (1989b). *Rethinking communication: Vol. 2. Paradigm exemplars.* Newbury Park, CA: Sage.

Edelman, M. (1988). *Constructing the political spectacle.* Chicago: University of Chicago Press.

Fiske, J. (1988). Meaningful moments. *Critical Studies in Mass Communication, 5,* 246-251.

Fiske, J. (1989). Popular television and commercial culture: Beyond political economy. In G. Burns & R. J. Thompson (Eds.), *Television studies: Textual analysis* (pp. 21-37). New York: Praeger.

Foucault, M. (1970). *The order of things: An archeology of the human sciences.* New York: Random House.

Foucault, M. (1972). *The archaeology of knowledge.* New York: Random House.

Foucault, M. (1978). *The history of sexuality* (Vol. 1). New York: Random House.

Foucault, M. (1979). *Discipline and punish.* New York: Vintage.

Foucault, M. (1980). *Power/knowledge.* New York: Pantheon.

Fry, V. H., Alexander, A., & Fry, D. L. (1990). Textual status, the stigmatized self, and media consumption. In J. A. Anderson (Ed.), *Communication yearbook 13* (pp. 519-544). Newbury Park, CA: Sage.

Gerbner, G. (Ed.). (1983). Ferment in the field [Special issue]. *Journal of Communication, 33*(3).

Giddens, A. (1979). *Central problems in social theory.* London: Macmillan.

Giddens, A. (1984). *The constitution of society: Outline of the theory of structuration.* Cambridge: Polity.

Giddens, A. (1989). The orthodox consensus and the emerging synthesis. In B. Dervin, L. Grossberg, B. J. O'Keefe, & E. Wartella (Eds.), *Rethinking communication: Vol. 1: Paradigm issues* (pp. 53-65). Newbury Park, CA: Sage.

Gitlin, T. (1983). *Inside prime time.* New York: Pantheon.

Goffman, E. (1963). *Stigma: Notes on the management of spoiled identity.* Englewood Cliffs, NJ: Prentice-Hall.

Goffman, E. (1974). *Frame analysis: An essay on the organization of experience.* Cambridge, MA: Harvard University Press.

Grossberg, L. (1989). The circulation of cultural studies. *Critical Studies in Mass Communication, 6,* 413-420.

Grossberg, L., & Nelson, C. (1988). Introduction: The territory of Marxism. In C. Nelson & L. Grossberg (Eds.), *Marxism and the interpretation of culture* (pp. 1-13). Urbana: University of Illinois Press.

Hall, E. (1959). *The silent language.* Garden City, NY: Doubleday.

Hall, S. (1980). Cultural studies: Two paradigms. *Media, Culture and Society, 2*, 57-72.

Hawkins, R. P., Wiemann, J. M., & Pingree, S. (Eds.). (1988). *Advancing communication science: Merging mass and interpersonal processes.* Newbury Park, CA: Sage.

Hay, J. (1989). Advertising as a cultural text (rethinking message analysis in a recombinant culture). In B. Dervin, L. Grossberg, B. J. O'Keefe, & E. Wartella (Eds.), *Rethinking communication: Vol. 2. Paradigm exemplars* (pp. 129-152). Newbury Park, CA: Sage.

Holland, E. (1988). Schizoanalysis: The postmodern contextualization of psychoanalysis. In C. Nelson & L. Grossberg (Eds.), *Marxism and the interpretation of culture* (pp. 405-416). Urbana: University of Illinois Press.

Jasinski, J., & Davis, D. K. (1990, September). *Political communication and politics: A theory of public culture.* Paper presented to the Political Communication Division at the annual meeting of the American Political Science Association, San Francisco.

Jhally, S. (Ed.). (1987). *The codes of advertising: Fetishism and the political economy of meaning in the consumer society.* London: Frances Pinter.

Kreiling, A. (1984). Television in American ideological hopes and fears. In W. D. Rowland, Jr., & B. Watkins (Eds.), *Interpreting television: Current research perspectives* (pp. 39-57). Beverly Hills, CA: Sage.

Kristeva, J. (1984). *Revolution in poetic language.* New York: Columbia University Press.

Lanigan, R. L. (1988). *Phenomenology of communication: Merleau-Ponty's thematics in communicology and semiology.* Pittsburgh, PA: Duquesne University Press.

Lefebvre, H. (1988). Toward a leftist cultural politics: Remarks occasioned by the centenary of Marx's death. In C. Nelson & L. Grossberg (Eds.), *Marxism and the interpretation of culture* (pp. 75-88). Urbana: University of Illinois Press.

Littlejohn, S. W. (1989). *Theories of human communication* (3rd ed.). Belmont, CA: Wadsworth.

Long, E. (1989). Feminism and cultural studies. *Critical Studies in Mass Communication, 6*, 427-435.

Marcus, G. E., & Fischer, M. M. (1986). *Anthropology as cultural critique: An experimental movement in the human sciences.* Chicago: University of Chicago Press.

Marcuse, H. (1964). *One-dimensional man: Studies in the ideology of advanced industrial society.* New York: Beacon.

Marcuse, H. (1969). *The aesthetic dimension.* Boston: Beacon.

Marcuse, H. (1978). *An essay on liberation.* Boston: Beacon.

Markham, J. (1967). *Voices of the red giants.* Ames: Iowa State University Press.

Martindale, D. (1960). *The nature and types of sociological theory.* Boston: Houghton Mifflin.

Marvin, C. (1989). Experts, black boxes, and artifacts: New allegories for the history of the electric media. In B. Dervin, L. Grossberg, B. J. O'Keefe, & E. Wartella (Eds.), *Rethinking communication: Vol. 2. Paradigm exemplars* (pp. 188-198). Newbury Park, CA: Sage.

McLuhan, M. (1965). *Understanding media: The extensions of man.* New York: McGraw-Hill.

McPhee, R. D. (1989). Organizational communication: A structurational example. In B. Dervin, L. Grossberg, B. J. O'Keefe, & E. Wartella (Eds.), *Rethinking communication: Vol. 2. Paradigm exemplars* (pp. 199-212). Newbury Park, CA: Sage.

McQuail, D. (1987). *Mass communication theory: An introduction.* Newbury Park, CA: Sage.

Mendelsohn, H. (1966). *Mass entertainment.* New Haven, CT: College & University Press.

Meyrowitz, J. (1985). *No sense of place: The impact of electronic media on social behavior.* New York: Oxford University Press.

Morley, D. (1980). *The "Nationwide" audience: Structure and decoding.* London: British Film Institute.

Murdock, G. (1989). Critical activity and audience activity. In B. Dervin, L. Grossberg, B. J. O'Keefe, & E. Wartella (Eds.), *Rethinking communication: Vol. 2. Paradigm exemplars* (pp. 226-249). Newbury Park, CA: Sage.

O'Connor, A. (1989). The problem of American cultural studies. *Critical Studies in Mass Communication, 6,* 405-413.

Olson, S. R. (1987). Meta-television: Popular postmodernism. *Critical Studies in Mass Communication, 4,* 284-300.

Peck, J. (1989). The power of media and the creation of meaning: A survey of approaches to media analysis. In B. Dervin & M. J. Voigt (Eds.), *Progress in communication sciences* (Vol. 9, pp. 145-182). Norwood, NJ: Ablex.

Peirce, C. S. (1985). Logic as semiotic: The theory of signs. In R. E. Innis (Ed.), *Semiotics: An introductory anthology* (pp. 1-24). Bloomington: Indiana University Press.

Peters, J. D. (1989). Satan and savior: Mass communication in progressive thought. *Critical Studies in Mass Communication, 6,* 247-263.

Peterson, E. E. (1987). Media consumption and girls who want to have fun. *Critical Studies in Mass Communication, 4,* 37-50.

Pfeil, F. (1988). Postmodernism as a "structure of feeling." In C. Nelson & L. Grossberg (Eds.), *Marxism and the interpretation of culture* (pp. 381-404). Urbana: University of Illinois Press.

Postman, N. (1985). *Amusing ourselves to death: Public discourse in the age of show business.* New York: Penguin.

Radway, J. A. (1986). Identifying ideological seams: Mass culture, analytical method, and political practice. *Communication, 9*(1), 93-123.

Real, M. R. (1977). *Mass-mediated culture.* Englewood Cliffs, NJ: Prentice-Hall.

Real, M. R. (1989). *Super media: A cultural studies approach.* Newbury Park, CA: Sage.

Ruesch, J., & Bateson, G. (1987). *Communication and the social matrix of psychiatry.* New York: W. W. Norton. (Original work published 1951)

Ryan, M. (1988). The politics of film: Discourse, psychoanalysis, ideology. In C. Nelson & L. Grossberg (Eds.), *Marxism and the interpretation of culture* (pp. 477-486). Urbana: University of Illinois Press.

Schutz, A. (1967). *The phenomenology of the social world.* Evanston, IL: Northwestern University Press.

Schutz, A. (1970). *On phenomenology and social relations.* Chicago: University of Chicago Press.

Steiner, L. (1988). Oppositional decoding as an act of resistance. *Critical Studies in Mass Communication, 5,* 1-15.

Williams, R. (1977). *Marxism and literature.* New York: Oxford University Press.

Zillman, D., & Bryant, J. (1986). Exploring the entertainment experience. In J. Bryant & D. Zillman (Eds.), *Perspectives on message effects* (pp. 303-324). Hillsdale, NJ: Lawrence Erlbaum.

The Challenge of a Culture-Centered Paradigm: Metatheory and Reconciliation in Media Research

MICHAEL REAL
San Diego State University

S ELECTED Book of the Year in 1990 by England's *Sunday Express,*
Nice Work by David Lodge (1989) satirizes both industry and academe and offers provocative observations about the place of contemporary critical theory. During one weekend tryst, the heroine, Robyn
Penrose, muses aloud to her occasional lover:

"But doesn't it bother you at all?" Robyn said. "That the things we care so passionately about—for instance, whether Derrida's critique of metaphysics lets
idealism in by the back door, or whether Lacan's psychoanalytic theory is
phallogocentric, or whether Foucault's theory of the episteme is reconcilable
with dialectical materialism—things like that, which we argue about and read
about and write about endlessly—doesn't it worry you that ninety-nine point
nine per cent of the population couldn't give a monkey's?"

"A what?" said Charles.

"A monkey's. It means you don't care a bit."

"It means you don't give a monkey's fuck."

"Does it?" said Robyn with a snigger. "I thought it was a monkey's nut. I
should have known: 'fuck' is much more poetic in Jakobson's terms—the repe-
tition of the 'k' as well as the first vowel in 'monkey'. . . . No wonder Vic
Wilcox looked startled when I said it the other day." (p. 152)

Correspondence and requests for reprints: Michael Real, Telecommunications and Film
Department, San Diego State University, San Diego, CA 92182.

Communication Yearbook 15, pp. 35-46

Even among peers within one field, such as communication, one some-times wonders, like Robyn, whether anyone outside a small circle of like-minded souls values the research one conducts. Which leads to a more specific question: How does a culture-centered paradigm relate to its friends and enemies among paradigms and approaches? If one accepts the self-label of *cultural studies*, for instance, how does that position one in regard to communication science, reception theory, political economy, post-modernism, the social construction of reality, and additional choices among research topics, methods, and theories? If one follows the lead of Davis and Puckett in the preceding essay, there may be increasing rapprochement and accommodation between previously separated media research strategies, but there remain significant disagreements in what different researchers consider important. There is considerable tension *within* culture-centered paradigms, as well as between culture-centered and communication science paradigms, over what are important research topics and goals, in addition to more articulated tensions over research methods and theories. To put it in Lodgian terms, which kinds of studies are worth a "monkey's"?

Disputes within the culture-centered paradigms have revolved around the question, Where is the central nexus of power in the media communication process? Is it in the commercial, industrialized means of production, as Garnham, Schiller, Murdock, Golding, and other political economists have argued? Is it in the text itself, as Newcomb, Kellner, Connell, and other formalist, popular culture, and ideological critics have maintained? Or is it in the audience reading of the text, in the meaning generated among view-ers, readers, and listeners, as Fiske, Ang, and reception theory have vigor-ously posited in recent debates? These conflicts are prominent in the literature of culture-centered research and require closer examination in any effort to reconcile variant approaches to media research through the promise of a culture-centered paradigm.

Of course, media research and theory have always been conflictual. In the 1930s survey and behavioral audience research was recognized by media industries as a legitimate offspring, while the equally important criti-cal tradition associated with the Frankfurt school was scorned as a bastard child. In the 1950s the mass culture debate interposed a relatively narrow range of liberal and conservative humanists between the extremes of a Marxist Left and an empiricist Right. In the 1960s empiricists held the center in American research, often touting the "limited effects" gospel of Joseph Klapper, at the same time as a McLuhanatic fringe emerged proclaiming the centrality of media as a causal force in all human history and social change. In the past two decades a more sophisticated heir to the Frankfurt school and mass culture debates has emerged to loosen the iron grip of empiricism in mainstream communication journals, organizations, research methods, and theory. With that history, it is not surprising that the emergent "culture-centered paradigm" is combative and critical even as it contains within itself the seeds of reconciliation with the intellectually and methodologically narrower empiricist, quantitative, behavioral tradition. What today are the battle lines, and the seeds of reconciliation?

RECEPTION THEORY: MEANING, THE AUDIENCE OF THE POPULAR, AND RESISTANCE

The most active development in culture-centered paradigms in recent years has been audience reception theory. The last decade has witnessed a minor revolution in the way audiences are conceived. Following the "active audience" concept of uses and gratifications research, which challenged the passive audience of classic survey research and mass culture critiques, reception analysis shifts the audience from consumer of messages to producer of meanings (Ang, 1990a, 1990b). Janice Radway's (1984) pioneering and widely cited study of readers of romance novels found evidence that the novels provide a minor act of independence for needed time and space away from family duties and against patriarchal domination. Differential audience readings of *Dallas* identified by Tamar Liebes and Elihu Katz (1986) and by Ien Ang (1985) confirm the variety of distinct and even contradictory meanings generated by viewers of one television series. David Morley (1980, 1986) and James Lull (1988) further this clarification and describe the role of gender and context in interpreting television texts. Jesus Martin-Barbero (1987) and Michel de Certeau (1984) provide theories of mediation, the popular, and everyday life as they also confirm that the revolution in audience conceptualization is not confined to English-language works.

Among reception theorists, John Fiske has staked out perhaps the largest and most provocative position in the culture-centered debates by elaborating extensively on the resistive power of the popular audience in generating its own meaning from products of the cultural industries. Four books in the 1980s, supplemented by coauthored works, elaborate his central themes.

- On "domination": The cultural industries operate in capitalism within structures of domination. Society is a site for conflicting interests, not a scene of tranquil harmonization of interests by consensus (Fiske, 1989a, p. 8). This separates Fiske from liberal humanists and procapitalist apologists.
- On "resistance": The products of the cultural industries are not received passively by audiences but are always interpreted so that the resultant meaning either resists or evades the purposes of the cultural industries and dominant classes that provide the products. Madonna fans interpret her in ways opposed to forces of social domination (Fiske, 1987, pp. 232-264; 1989a, pp. 95-113); surfers evade the forces of dominant society (1989a, pp. 43-76). This distinguishes Fiske from the assumption that cultural industries automatically

dominate, incorporate, or contain the minds and mass behavior of the public, an assumption especially associated with the Frankfurt school, mass culture, and political economy critiques.

- On "popular culture": For Fiske, popular culture exists only in the act of popular resistance to and reappropriation of the cultural materials provided. "There can be no popular dominant culture, for popular culture is formed always in reaction to, and never as part of, the forces of domination" (1989b, p. 43). Jeans worn and interpreted, not jeans as standard product, make jeans operative as popular culture (1989b, pp. 1-22). By positing the central activity within a resisting audience rather than the producers of media, Fiske redefines popular culture as something other than mere widespread consumption of mass-produced cultural goods.

- On "cultural economy": To avoid econometric and "bottom-line" reductionism in the analysis of popular culture and media, Fiske posits a "cultural economy" as well as a financial economy in the cultural industries. While in the financial economy the producers make a show, which in turn produces an audience, which is sold to advertisers, in the cultural economy the audience produces meaning and pleasure. This, for example, prevents television from narrowly monopolizing meaning because the success of television "in the financial economy depends on its ability to serve and promote the diverse and often oppositional interests of its audiences" in the cultural economy (Fiske, 1987, p. 326). Moreover, cultural economy requires studying jeans, surfing, and shopping malls—any form of cultural expression, materials, and interpretations—and not only the products and processes of mass media of communication. This separates Fiske's object of study from that of the mass communication science specialists.

- On "method": Semiotics, polysemy, intertextuality, gender, and other interpretive tools facilitate the identification and analysis of audience meanings created from cultural industries. Turning away from classic process models of sending a message, Fiske (1982) adds what he terms a radically different approach to the study of communication: "Here the emphasis is not so much on communication as a process, but on communication as the generation of meaning" (p. 42).

With this emphasis, Fiske has delineated a fresh and promising perspective for communication research and has avoided several dead ends. In his positioning, he does not completely reject the traditional celebratory approaches to popular culture, approaches that failed to situate popular culture in a model of power. Nor does he directly reject political economy and mass culture, with their emphasis on and, at times, obsession with structures of domination. But, in contrast, he labels his approach a "third direction." In this new direction, "It, too, sees popular culture as a site of struggle, but while accepting the power of the forces of domination, it focuses rather upon the popular tactics by which these forces are coped with, are evaded or resisted" (Fiske, 1989b, p. 20). He shifts his emphasis away from the insidious practices of dominant ideology and the processes of incorporation, without denying the reality of either, in order to concentrate on the everyday resistances and evasions that force ideology and incorporation to work so hard to maintain themselves. Within the structures of late capitalism, he creates a space for populism, participation, and democratization of communication: "This approach sees popular culture as potentially, and often actually, progressive (though not radical), and it is essentially optimistic, for it finds in the vigor and vitality of the people evidence both of the possibility of social change and the motivation to drive it" (Fiske, 1989b, p. 21).

To those trained in communication science, the weakness of Fiske's approach is in the subjectivity of method and the absence of measures of significance and validity. For example, in one case study he observes the irony that Australian aborigines and American Indians commonly prefer country and western music, which is generally associated with a reactionary consciousness. The same oddity in popular music preference can be observed in Liberia, West Africa (Real, 1985). On a visit to a Cherokee reservation, Fiske (1989b) sensed that the obvious bastardized westernization of Indian culture was countered by an Indianizing process at work, an Indianization of western culture:

> I felt, but could not prove, that the performance was not just a masquerade for the tourists, but that the Cherokee musicians had, in some ironically contradictory way, made this anti-Indian music into a cultural form that could carry elements of Indianness. I felt, too, that the young Indians clog dancing to it were not only performing for the whites (and encouraging them to join in) but were also, as a subtext, dancing for and with each other. (pp. 166-167)

Such analysis is subjective and impressionistic to the point of lacking fixed points of reference associated with objective scientific evidence and conclusions. In Fiske's defense, of course, cultural studies epistemologically rejects claims of objectivity and scientism. But the analysis, however perceptive, at times leaves critics seeming to debate no more than personal opinions and impressions.

To those concerned with critical theory, a distinct but related concern arises with Fiske's position. Is cultural domination nine-tenths of the picture and popular resistance a marginal one-tenth, as traditional political economy has implied? Or is the people's reappropriation and generation of countermeanings nine-tenths of the picture and dominating cultural structures only one-tenth, as Fiske seems to suggest? Fiske (1989a) concedes that capitalism's control of the production and distribution of resources "is well nigh unchallengeable" (p. 213), but in his own work he is preoccupied with popular powers of resistance. Should communication research turn all its attention to themes of popular resistance, or is Fiske merely trying to correct an imbalance, to open a new possibility that will coexist alongside other thriving forms of research on media, culture, and the popular? The concluding chapter, "Politics," in his theoretically oriented *Understanding Popular Culture* points toward the latter. He argues that the people's semiotic power is micropolitical power on the everyday level. This is his cause for optimism and for portraying popular culture positively. However, there is controversy concerning whether this does or should lead to macropolitical change of a more radical sort. Fiske (1989b) asserts that progressivism and radicalism are compatible: "The two models of social change should not be at odds" (p. 193). In Fiske's view, new knowledge arises not by evolution but as adversary, so he concludes with a challenge:

> I do wish to contest the variety of views that, in their different ways, judge the popular to be a negative social influence, for, in the final analysis, I believe the popular forces to be a positive influence in our society and that failing to take proper account of their progressive elements is academically and politically disabling. (p. 194)

Whether one sees the optimism of Fiske and some other reception theorists as a choice based on wishful thinking (Evans, 1990, p. 162) or evidence or both, we still have a great deal yet to learn about the precise linkages between the meaning generated by audiences and the political economy that shapes the messages conveyed to them. For political economy, as much as it has been attacked politically since its inception and academically in the last decade, remains a foundation stone of any comprehensive culture-centered paradigm.

DEBATES ON POLITICAL ECONOMY:
ECONOMICS VERSUS CULTURE

Much as political economy and cultural studies may draw from a common heritage of critical theory indebted to Marx and the Frankfurt school, is it not stretching it to attempt to unite them in any integral way no matter which is given ascendancy? In Great Britain a long-standing conflict has pitted "culturalists" against "economic determinists," stressing the polarities rather than the commonalities of approach. Yet one of the great promises of a culture-centered paradigm is the reconciliation of the more deterministic approaches of political economy to the more interpretive analyses of culture studies and reception theory.

Political economy, to return to its founding text, sees communication media as contemporary instruments of class domination, protecting the interests of the privileged:

> The ideas of the ruling class are in every epoch the ruling ideas: i.e. the class which is the ruling *material* force in society is at the same time its ruling *intel-*

lectual force. The class which has the means of material production at its disposal has control at the same time over the means of mental production, so that thereby, generally speaking, the ideas of those who lack the means of mental production are subject to it. (Marx & Engels, 1970, p. 64)

Yet even in this most absolute of texts, there is the qualifying phrase "generally speaking." Subordinate classes are not always automatically, absolutely, and necessarily subject to the ruling class's control of the means of mental production, even in the writings of Marx and Lenin. How much variation occurs away from economic determinism is a recurring debate. As a more or less typical example of an American political economist, Stuart Ewen (1988) acknowledges Fiske's notion of the audience's generating its own meaning, but refuses to underestimate the power of media managers to convey, magnify, refract, and influence popular notions of style. As Barbara Welch Breder (1989) summarizes it, "The individual may pick and choose, mix and match; but the menu is set, the palette prepared, by those whose first commitment is to corporate profit, to selling not only products but ways of being and seeing that are profoundly acquisitive" (p. 18).

An influential classificatory system by James Curran, Michael Gurevitch, and Janet Woollacott (1982) distinguishes structuralist, political economy, and culturalist approaches to media analysis, all occurring more or less within a Marxist framework. Structuralism combines continental work of Saussure, Lévi-Strauss, Barthes, Lacan, and especially Althusser, with an emphasis on structures of ideology and the state, especially as these occur within film studies. Political economy charges that structuralism is "a top-heavy analysis in which an elaborate autonomy of cultural forms balances insecurely on a schematic account of economic forces shaping their product" (Murdock & Golding, 1977, p. 17). Culturalism, in turn, rejects any economic reductionism on the part of political economy, rejects structural autonomies in favor of humanist experience, and places media and other social practices within a society conceived of as a complex expressive totality (Curran et al., 1982, pp. 24-27).

Ian Connell has extended this conflict between structuralism and political economy in a series of attacks on first Graham Murdock and Peter Golding (Connell, 1978, 1980-1981) and then Nicholas Garnham (Connell, 1983, 1985; Connell & Curti, 1986). Connell (1983) charges political economists with wrongly viewing "the proposed technologies as functions of economic processes" (p. 73). For Connell, Garnham's work is marred by its overestimation of the economic, its exclusive preoccupation with media corporations and industries, and its assumption of opposition between commercialization and cultural democracy. As an alternative, Connell offers little more than a celebratory account of the effects of privatization, multinationals, and commercial competition. But, supporting Connell's attack, Carl Gardner (1984) writes, "Privileging the moment of production and the commercial intentions of the producers, ignoring any politics of representation, this leads to the notion of the total hegemonic effectivity of commercial products and a massive cultural pessimism" (p. 45).

Kevin Robins and Frank Webster (1987) step back from this debate and suggest that at its heart is an "unjustified (and unjustifiable) separation of culture and economy" (p. 88). Connell's version of cultural studies ignores the influence of capitalist and commodity forms of culture production; Garnham's (1986) political economy remains narrowly economic, with inadequate attention to the politics of representation and the complexity of cultural practices. Robins and Webster, following Jameson, Brenkman, and others, argue that culture and economy are not externally related as separate spheres with the result that either culture or economics can be considered autonomously. They reason that "the dichotomization of economic and superstructural analysis provides only partial truths about, and insights into, the 'communications revolution'—a 'revolution' that is, simultaneously and integrally, cultural, political and economic in its scale and impact" (p. 87). What remains, they suggest, is to establish a common framework and vocabulary that will address communication and social practice in their totality—political, cultural, and economic—in order to address issues of liberation and control in postmodern cultural forms. It is precisely this search for a larger frame that is the attraction of the "culture-centered paradigm" proposed in general terms by Davis and Puckett.

CRITICISMS AND LIMITATIONS
OF INTERPRETIVE AUDIENCE THEORY

Criticisms of Fiske's reception theory, like those of Garnham's political economy, have been numerous and emphatic. Budd, Entman, and Steinman (1990) have argued that U.S. cultural studies have overestimated the freedom of audiences in reception, have confused active reception with political activity, and have taken the exceptional situation of progressive readings promoted within oppositional subcultures as the norm. Gitlin (1990) traces this to a desire to find radical potential, absent in current political parties or mass movements, in popular styles. Demanding clarification of what kind of resistance and opposition these variant readings represent and connect with, he warns:

> "Resistance"—meaning all sorts of grumbling, multiple interpretation, semiological inversion, pleasure, rage, friction, numbness, what have you—is accorded dignity, even glory, by stamping these not-so-great refusals with a vocabulary derived from life-threatening political work against fascism—as if the same concept should serve for the Chinese student uprising and cable TV grazing. (p. 191)

Lembo and Tucker (1990) likewise argue that text-reception approaches miss much of television viewing's complexity by reducing all interpretation to struggles between dominant and subordinate groups, preferred and oppositional readings.

Two of the finest critiques of polysemic texts and oppositional audience interpretations have attempted to identify limits to such approaches and linkages to other approaches. Celeste Michelle Condit (1989) has argued that if the text is not closed it is also not limitless. The ability of some receivers to experience pleasure in producing oppositional codings does not justify isolating the audience from the communication process. In examining interpretations of a *Cagney & Lacey* episode involving abortion, Condit found that different viewer interpretations occurred in valuation of textual elements more than in the denotation of the text itself; that is, viewers understood the story similarly, but liked opposite sides. This "polyvalence" is distinct from polysemy in the text and occurs when audience members share understandings of the denotation of the text but disagree about the valuation of those denotations. Condit's critique of interpretive reception theory is specific. She finds that audience members have varied access to and ability with oppositional codes, that the work required to decode a text oppositionally varies and may conflict with pleasure produced, that the repertoire of available texts is specific, and that both the text and the historical occasion will position the relative pleasures and empowerment of dominant and marginal audiences. She calls for a larger frame: "I conclude that mass media research should replace totalized theories of polysemy and audience power with interactive theories that assess audience reactions as part of the full communication process occurring in particular rhetorical configurations" (p. 104).

Kevin Carragee (1990) likewise decries the "growing tendency to romanticize audience members as semiological guerrillas who consistently construct oppositional readings of media texts" (p. 93). The polysemic interpretive reception theory, in his view, is not superior to the work of critical audience research, which employs concepts of hegemony and demonstrates through close readings the degree to which media messages express meanings and values in the interests of established power. The role of textual characteristics in shaping audience interpretations and the location of social actors within historical, social, and cultural contexts cannot be slighted in attempting to identify media reception and the generation of meaning.

TOWARD A CULTURE-CENTERED RECONCILIATION

What the emerging culture-centered paradigm offers is a larger frame for sustaining and interrelating the often conflicting elements in newer understandings of audiences, industries, power, and meanings in human communication and postmodern culture. The culture-centered paradigm is at heart "constructivist" rather than "objectivist." As Walter Anderson (1990) says of cognitive scientists, there are two camps in social research. The *objectivists* see the human mind as mirroring external nonhuman reality and achieving truth in an absolute, unchanging correspondence between the fixed external world and the internal reflection of that world. In contrast, the *constructivists* see human understanding as a symbolic construct, a social reality that many people construct together and experience as the "real world." Constructivists see existence not as a *single* symbolic world but as a universe of multiple realities constructed through differing perceptions, experiences, languages, and cultures. Therapists, according to Anderson, find subjects mistakenly seeking objectivist solutions to a constructivist existence: "The shift to postmodernism is far more likely to be traumatic if you are convinced that there can be no truth without absolutes, no science without objectivity, no morality without rules, no society without uniform values and beliefs, no religion without a church" (p. 254)

Conflicts between constructivist and objectivist assumptions may be the rocks upon which Davis and Puckett's culture-centered reconciliation runs aground. The willingness to seek truth without absolutes and science without objectivity is a mark of cultural studies, whether in reception theory, critical analysis, or, to a lesser extent, political economy. The communication science perspective, especially to the extent that it retains the mechanical style that predates Einstein's theory of relativity, may stumble on these points and insist on an objectivist universe. For this reason, the culture-centered paradigm offers greater hope of reconciling conflicts within semiotic, cultural, qualitative, interpretive, and critical work than between such work and a communication science approach, despite the larger ecumenical goals of Davis and Puckett.

As this review has attempted to draw out, there is, first, a need for such reconciliation among the various members of the broad cultural studies family and then, second, a possibility for forging deeper kinships with sympathetic members of the communication science family. Within the cultural studies family, siblings must recall that to attack a particular point in reception theory or political economy is not to destroy the legitimacy of the entire approach. To forge ties with communication science, both sides must recall that human truth is not one-dimensional; to approach truth as if it were is to distort the nature of human symbol making and symbol using and doom the effort of research and teaching to failure. The traditional preoccupation of communication science with measures of individual behavior can carve out a larger space to include culture and interpretation as well. Media may claim to mirror society, but, more important, media "construct" society. People may be influenced by media messages, but, more significantly, people "generate meaning."

In Giddens's concept of structuration between social practices and social institutions there is a potential meeting point between macro- and micro-analysis, between the findings of cultural studies and communication science. Likewise, in Martin-Barbero's (1987) account of "mediations" there is a point of articulation between the hegemonic pressures of media production and its popular reappropriation by people rooted in family, community, temporal rhythms, previous narrative memory, media genres, and other elements of the popular consciousness. Curiously, with the fragmentation of knowledge and the simulation of substance in the postmodern world, synthetic conciliatory thinking may contribute as much as precise critiques, especially in the effort of critical thinking to identify, evaluate, and develop a productive culture-centered paradigm for communication theory and research.

This effort may call to mind that in *Nice Work*, David Lodge's satirical novel mentioned above, the progress of the relationship between Robyn, the feminist academic, and Vic, the plant manager, evolves with difficulty to work itself out psychologically and symbolically. They begin as strangers. As they come to know the conflicting worlds and attitudes each assumes—radical versus reactionary, idealist versus materialist, and so on—they grow into enemies. Then thesis and antithesis skid precariously into momentary synthesis and they become one-shot lovers. Finally, recovering from their polarized reactions to this intimacy, the two find reconciliation, and they become mutually respectful collaborators and friends. Perhaps a similar complex dynamic works for contending scholarly positions.

REFERENCES

Anderson, W. (1990). *Reality isn't what it used to be: Theatrical politics, ready-to-wear religion, global myths, primitive chic, and other wonders of the postmodern world.* New York: Harper & Row.

Ang, I. (1985). *Watching* Dallas: *Soap opera and the melodramatic imagination.* London: Methuen.

Ang, I. (1990a). Culture and communication: Towards an ethnographic critique of media consumption in the transnational media system. *European Journal of Communication, 5,* 239-260.

Ang, I. (1990b). The nature of the audience. In J. Downing, A. Mohammadi, & A. Sreberny-Mohammadi (Eds.), *Questioning the media: A critical introduction* (pp. 155-165). Newbury Park, CA: Sage.

Breder, B. (1989). Kaleidoscopic mode [Review of *All consuming images: the politics of style in contemporary culture*]. *Journal of Communication, 39*(4), 17-20.

Budd, M., Entman, R., & Steinman, C. (1990). The affirmative character of U.S. cultural studies. *Critical Studies in Mass Communication, 7,* 169-184.

Carragee, K. (1990). Interpretive media study and interpretive social science. *Critical Studies in Mass Communication, 7,* 81-96.

Condit, C. (1989). The rhetorical limits of polysemy. *Critical Studies in Mass Communication, 6,* 103-122.

Connell, I. (1978). Monopoly capitalism and the media. In S. Hibbin (Ed.), *Politics, ideology and the state.* London: Lawrence & Wishart.

Connell, I. (1980-1981). The political economy of broadcasting: Some questions. *Screen Education, 37,* 89-100.

Connell, I. (1983). Commercial broadcasting and the British left. *Screen, 24*(6), 70-80.

Connell, I. (1985, May). Auntie shows her age. *Marxism Today,* pp. 14-17.

Connell, I., & Curti, L. (1986). Popular broadcasting in Italy and Britain: Some issues and problems. In P. Drummond & R. Paterson (Eds.), *Television in transition.* London: British Film Institute.

Curran, J., Gurevitch, M., & Woollacott, J. (1982). The study of the media: Theoretical approaches. In M. Gurevitch, T. Bennett, J. Curran, & J. Woollacott (Eds.), *Culture, society and the media.* New York: Methuen.

de Certeau, M. (1984). *The practice of everyday life* (S. Rendall, Trans.). Berkeley: University of California Press.

Evans, W. (1990). The interpretive turn in media research: Innovation, iteration, or illusion? *Critical Studies in Mass Communication, 7,* 147-168.

Ewen, S. (1988). *All consuming image: The politics of style in contemporary culture.* New York: Basic Books.

Fiske, J. (1982). *Introduction to communication studies.* New York: Methuen.

Fiske, J. (1987). *Television culture.* New York: Methuen.

Fiske, J. (1989a). *Reading the popular.* Winchester, MA: Unwin Hyman.

Fiske, J. (1989b). *Understanding popular culture.* Winchester, MA: Unwin Hyman.

Gardner, C. (1984). Populism, relativism and left strategy. *Screen, 25*(1), 45-52.

Garnham, N. (1986). Contribution to a political economy of mass communication. In R. Collins, J. Curran, N. Garnham, P. Scannell, P. Schlesinger, & C. Sparks (Eds.), *Media, culture and society: A critical reader* (pp. 9-33). Newbury Park, CA: Sage.

Gitlin, T. (1990). Commentary: Who communicates what to whom, in what voice and why, about the study of mass communication? *Critical Studies in Mass Communication, 7,* 185-196.

Lembo, R., & Tucker, K. H., Jr. (1990). Culture, television, and opposition: Rethinking cultural studies. *Critical Studies in Mass Communication, 7,* 97-116.

Liebes, T., & Katz, E. (1986). Patterns of involvement in television fiction: A comparative analysis. *European Journal of Communication, 1,* 151-171.

Lodge, D. (1989). *Nice work.* New York: Penguin.

Lull, J. (1988). *World families watch television.* Newbury Park, CA: Sage.

Martin-Barbero, J. (1987). *De los medios a las mediaciones: Comunicacion, cultura y hegemonia.* Mexico City: Ediciones Gustavo Gili.

Marx, K., & Engels, F. (1970). *The German ideology.* London: Lawrence & Wishart.

Morley, D. (1980). *The "Nationwide" audience: Structure and decoding.* London: British Film Institute.

Morley, D. (1986). *Family television: Cultural power and domestic leisure.* London: Comedia.

Murdock, G., & Golding, P. (1977). Capitalism, communication and class relations. In J. Curran, M. Gurevitch, & J. Woollacott (Eds.), *Mass communication and society.* London: Edward Arnold.

Radway, J. (1984). *Reading the romance: Women, patriarchy and popular literature.* Chapel Hill: University of North Carolina Press.

Real, M. (1985). Broadcast music in Nigeria and Liberia: A comparative note. In F. Ugbuoajah (Ed.), *Mass communication, culture and society in West Africa.* New York: Hans Zell.

Robins, K., & Webster, F. (1987). The communications revolution: New media, old problems. *Communication, 10,* 71-89.

Some Good News-Bad News About a Culture-Centered Paradigm

LANA F. RAKOW
University of Wisconsin—Parkside

EVERY writing of a history, every attempt at making a map, is a political act. The position—physical, social, intellectual, experiential—of the person doing the recording and mapmaking gives that person a standpoint from which to see the world. The words and deeds of some people and not others will stand out and be recorded, some signposts and markers will seem more relevant. Other people, other events will go unseen and, hence, undocumented.

The essay by Dennis Davis and Thomas Puckett is an act of writing a history and making a map. They have described the state of communication theory and research as seen from their standpoint. As the view from any one standpoint is limited, their account is partial, reflecting their own situatedness in the historical developments of the field and their own subjectivities. For just as Davis and Puckett explain that the "average person" is continuously engaged in meaning-making, so too are academics. And just as "average persons" typically lose sight of their own authorship of meanings, so too do academics often lose sight of their own part in inventing the worlds within which we take up residence.

Davis and Puckett begin by describing what has now become a standard history of the criticism of the development of U.S. mass-produced culture. Moving into contemporary theory and research on mass entertainment, they argue for the need to bridge the estrangement between communication science and cultural studies with the common ground to be found in what they call a culture-centered paradigm (although it is unclear why the already quite well developed paradigm of culture studies is not suited). This new paradigm would be characterized by an understanding of such phenomena as the connection between the individual and institutions, the social

Correspondence and requests for reprints: Lana F. Rakow, Communication Department, University of Wisconsin—Parkside, Wood Road, Box 2000, Kenosha, WI 53141-2331.

Communication Yearbook 15, pp. 47-57

production of meaning, the social construction of reality, the acculturation of individuals into the social order, the role of media rituals in providing meaning for individuals, and the possibility of community replacing bureaucratic structure. They identify theories and theorists who offer contributions to this understanding—Giddens's theory of structuration, Goffman's notion of frames that provide social rules for action, Real's analysis of media rituals—perhaps with the intention of introducing newcomers to these already fairly well known approaches. Davis and Puckett point out the problems left unresolved by these approaches, and end by suggesting the directions to which research could best be pointed in the years to come. As stated strongly in the beginning, their main goal in identifying and asserting this culture-centered paradigm is to provide a unifying framework for scholarship.

Davis and Puckett are among a number of others who have been examining the benefits and pitfalls of a cultural or interpretive approach to the study of communication. The articles in the June 1990 issue of *Critical Studies in Mass Communication* all deal with the state of this approach, particularly as it relates to media studies. The authors of these articles, as well as others, disagree about what approach within cultural studies is the most fruitful. While most seem to believe something is wrong with other people's "brand" of cultural studies, their interpretations of the state of things vary. Who *is* the "enemy"? Communication science? Those who emphasize audiences and texts while ignoring production? Those who emphasize meaning without accounting for power? Those who do nothing but account for power? (Ironically, two articles in this issue make opposite interpretations of the same phenomenon: Lembo & Tucker, 1990, criticize cultural studies for reducing all cultural activity to struggles over power; Budd, Entman, & Steinman, 1990, criticize cultural studies for its retreat from politics and its cheery optimism about audience resistance.) Or is the enemy "us," as Todd Gitlin (1990) argues, because we have splintered into our specialized journals and jargons while failing to engage in a public discourse about our concerns?

I do not stand in quite the same place as Davis and Puckett or the authors of these others'articles. I have arrived at my place by a different route, a different set of circumstances, additional authors read, different influences encountered, and different subjectivities experienced. While I can claim an identification with this tradition of cultural studies, I do not read the history and state of communication studies in the same way. Other names, other issues, other landmark events constitute my map of the field. But, troublingly, these "others" have not entered the increasingly solidified canon of the field. While interpretations vary, those engaged in these discussions evoke the same father figures, recount the same histories, and reiterate the same debates. To enter into my map of the field, one would have to raise other questions. For example, who else besides the self-appointed critics of the Right and the Left, now reified by our histories, have had something to say about the development of mass media and entertainment? My frustration with precisely this absence of other critics led to the uncovering of a variety of women critics in the twentieth century (Rakow, 1986a). An awareness of other voices such as these makes clear that the manner in which these historical debates have been constructed has privileged a class analysis to the exclusion of an analysis of race and gender. The debate over a "mass" society made of up "atomized" individuals suffering from a loss of community would not look the same—then or now—if we accounted for the experiences of African Americans and native peoples, who were segregated into their own communities, and of white women, who were presumed to have no identity other than through their relationships to others. The concern over the "privatization of discourse" supposedly brought about with the rise of mass media does not capture the exclusion of people of color and white women from discourse when it was supposedly "public," or their exclusion from even everyday conversations and other nonmedia institutional practices.

It is precisely because of the absence even of these few questions in the ongoing discussions about cultural studies that I cannot share Davis and Puckett's urgency for establishing a unifying paradigm for our field. I sense only another "master's narrative" in the making. Somehow, when the boundaries get put on the paradigms and the field is mapped "once and for all," many of us are once again excluded, despite the fact that the questions we are asking should be of paramount importance to the future. It is usually only an economic and class analysis that gets included, without even attention to the impact of race and gender as a mediator of and contributor to class differences. It happened blatantly in the special *Journal of Communication* issue, "Ferment in the Field" (Gerbner, 1983). It happened again in the above-mentioned issue of *Critical Studies in Mass Communication.* And, despite Davis and Puckett's good intentions to bridge boundaries and find commonalities rather than divisions, these authors, too, have replicated the same power relations that have thus far characterized the field.

Feminist and ethnic study scholars are often accused or excused on the basis of their "partiality"; the special interests they bring to the topics of race and gender are seen as narrow and specialized compared with the broad and general theorizing and research that others—such as those engaged in these discussions of cultural studies—are presumed to be doing. Yet the greatest insight that feminist and ethnic study scholars have had is that *all* of us speak from a position of race and gender, that what has been passed off as broad and general theory and research is not only partial and narrow, but flawed for its claim to universality.[1] The side references to the same few pieces of feminist scholarship made in these discussions does little to change the thinking and approach of the writers. (Ethnic studies literature is almost completely left out of the histories and maps, or, where race and ethnicity are discussed, a faulty conceptualization is used, as Nakayama, 1990, documents.) Feminist scholarship is seen as a sideshow, a special interest cause, one of many strands of a rapidly fragmenting field.

Not so. In fact, if indeed a unifying paradigm is a good idea, feminist scholarship could provide its basis rather than the work of Anthony Giddens, as suggested by Davis and Puckett. Perhaps no other area of thinking and research has been so fruitful in challenging assumptions and providing insights into the very questions of individuals and institutions, meanings and resistance, community and bureaucracy that Davis and Puckett identify as critical to a common paradigm.[2] Feminist scholarship continuously engages in core questions about the nature of knowledge and the knower, about the connection between theory and activism, about the concepts of difference and identity, about the bifurcation of rationality and emotion, and about the politics of silencing and marginalizing. And rather than borrowing from other areas of cultural studies, as Davis and Puckett assume, feminist scholarship has paved the way in many of these areas. However, the trail is generally swept clean by those pacing off the map of the field.[3]

Certainly some of what Davis and Puckett argue about the nature of social life and the role of communication in it is shared by many feminist scholars. Yet, there are areas in which feminist scholarship goes beyond these observations and raises different concerns and different solutions and other areas in which feminists such as myself are in complete disagreement. In the following pages I would like to set forth an alternative to Davis and Puckett's description of the process by which communication— and hence social life—works, taking up some of these concerns and disagreements along the way. My conceptualization of communication and culture involves what I think of as the "good news and bad news" about communication.

FIRST, THE GOOD NEWS

The world is of our own making. Perhaps no other idea is as profound, as resisted, or as potentially liberating as this. This "good news" provides the fundamental—epistemological—distinction between communication science and cultural studies. Those theorists and researchers who are based in positivistic science claim to be neutral observers of a world "out there," a world that exists apart from our knowing of it. To come to terms with the realization that *both* the physical and the social world are products of human creation, called into existence through the act of naming, is to release us from the determinism (and tyranny) of physical and social "laws" and biological and material "givens."

But even those who profess an interpretive approach do not always grasp the profundity of the claim that humans make their own worlds. They may recognize that humans would have no access even to what is tangible in the physical world without language, and that it is language that makes order out of what would otherwise be nothing but physical sensation without meaning or differentiation. They may agree that the dominant mode of knowing in Western culture—science—is but one way of understanding the world, as made up of properties governed by laws of physics. They may even go so far as to recognize that the individual is not a precultural entity whose essential humanness is modified by particular cultural formations, but is rather someone who *becomes* human by the very entrance into culture, by taking up the human identity assigned by those who preceded him or her (the process Davis and Puckett call "acculturation"). But human biology has tended to remain an intractable given, not only for most members of society but also for nearly all communication theorists except feminist scholars. Even Berger and Luckmann, whose book *The Social Construction of Reality* (1967) has become a canonized landmark of cultural studies history, fail to recognize that gender is as much a human construction as every other linguistic category. Just as we see the world that language has called into existence for us, we see a world populated by two and only two genders because that is what we believe "really" exists. The physical differences (of genitals, reproductive capacity, skin color, hair texture, and so on) that are presumed to divide people into natural categories of gender and race are in fact the products of our social vision, overlaid as it is with a gridwork of politically motivated categories (see Rakow, 1986b).

If we accept the notion that humans make their own worlds—from the ground up, as it were—we must recognize all humans as fundamentally "meaning-makers," despite the fact that humans occupy worlds that are already made to mean. The trick to understanding what might otherwise be seen as a sleight of hand here is to account for the historical dimension of the social construction of reality. Humans make cultures over time, so that each new human enters a world already made, meanings made external and institutionalized in routinized practices and patterns through the likes of cars and highways, factories, families living together in houses, churches, crops and livestock, and news reports. And for each new human, human authorship of these meanings has faded; the "naturalness," the "givenness" of the particular way of understanding the world upon which this external evidence is predicated takes its place.

But meanings are not static, fortunately, or there would be no accounting for the changes that occur in cultures. Meanings get added and modified as more and different phenomena need to be accounted for and made sense of. Discrepancies open the possibility for new interpretations. Realities can be thought of as "generative"; that is, as the structure of language permits novel combinations of elements into an infinite possibility of sentences, so too is it possible for humans to generate new meanings out of the old. In this way, humans are at the same time occupants of a world they have not personally made while being actively engaged in making sense of it, sometimes with quite different meanings from those intended by others. How else can we account for social movements, whose members refuse the definition of things as given to argue for an alternative definition? For example, feminism is the result of women seeing the discrepancies between the way things are said to be (e.g., women are less intelligent and able than men, women can count on the protection of men) and the way they experience these things (e.g., they see they are more intelligent and competent than many men, they know that women are beaten and raped by men).

It should come as no surprise that media audiences also engage in active meaning-making. Feminist scholars have had no difficulty rejecting notions of a passive media audience. We have uncovered a long history of women rejecting and criticizing media content as well as meanings given to them by other interpersonal and institutional sources. If people of color accepted the meanings provided for them by the dominant culture, they would long ago have given up any sense of self-worth and cultural pride. Patricia Hill Collins (1989) examines how black women use an alternative knowledge system for understanding themselves because they have been able to create a self-defined standpoint for making sense of their experiences.

The notion that humans make their own realities is truly a liberating one. If we are living in a product of our own making, it can be changed. There is nothing—not genes, hormones, instincts, natural laws, the unconscious, operant conditioning, or gods—to prevent us from becoming something other than what we are now, except the failure of our own imaginations.

NOW, THE BAD NEWS

We have not done a very good job of it—or, more precisely, someone has not done a very good job of it. One has only to glance briefly around at the state of local and global affairs to recognize that the world that has been made is in a disastrous state. How did this happen? What went wrong? Surely something fundamental must have gone wrong to produce a world characterized by so much conflict and violence, such unequal distribution of material goods, so much disregard for the humanness of others, such life-threatening disruption of the planet's equilibrium. Was it the loss of community and the rise of bureaucracy in the nineteenth century? Was it a displacement of other sources of meaning by the mass media? Was it a failure of appropriate "symbiosis" between individuals and institutions? A weakening of individual acculturation?

None of these areas identified by Davis and Puckett seems appropriate for the magnitude of the problem when seen from this global perspective. In fact, Davis and Puckett seem most worried about the social control of people, particularly large-scale populations, implying that the problem is (in the tradition of past media debates) really the *audiences* of the media, not the media themselves.[4] If people have the appropriate "symbiotic relationship" with institutions, then all is potentially well, and social stability will be ensured. It is not clear whether Davis and Puckett fully appreciate the frightening implications of what they are saying, even though they recognize the dangers of such arrangements as Nazi Germany. Feminists are not in favor of the stability of current institutions, but of their instability. Institutions have not historically been the friends of people of color and white women in the United States, or, for that matter, women in most times and places. The institutions of religion, the family, and the law have all been sources of women's oppression.[5] Did the development of the mass media, another oppressive institution, change things all that much? (And why don't we know the answer to the question?)

It is not clear from their chapter what it is Davis and Puckett think is the problem, if indeed they do think there is one. I would propose that the problem is one of our model of communication. Only a mentality of domination, exploitation, and competition could justify the pathological relations between men and women, colonizer and colonized, white people and people of color, religions, and countries that now permeate most of the world. We have, I can only conclude, a pathological model of "the other" that underlies the rest of human activity.

The importance of feminist scholarship to the foundation of communication theory is most apparent in the model of "the other." Feminist scholarship has focused its theoretical attention on understanding "the other," since women are the quintessential "other" in nearly every cultural group, regardless of the position of "otherness" occupied by the larger cultural group.[6] Women are defined by their difference—their difference relative to what is taken as the given, men. Just so are colonized people of color defined by their difference relative to what is assumed as the norm, white Anglo-Europeans. Similarly, the tastes and values and meanings of poor and working-class people are judged by their difference relative to a professional and middle-class norm. But difference is not innocuous, for difference in dominant cultural terms means less than, not as good as, inferior, less than fully human (see MacKinnon, 1987). Enter a model of communication that establishes a relationship of dominant to subordinate, subject to object, sender to receiver, producer to consumer, and symbol-maker to symbolized. The "bad news" part of the communication coin makes us qualify the good news that humans make their own worlds with the realization that, despite the creative capacities of all to do so, not all of us are allowed to do so. Those of us who are excluded are intended to be restricted to making meaning in our individual lives out of, or in response to, the tools—pregiven definitions and categories—supplied to us.

Dorothy Smith (1978) uses the metaphor of a circle to describe how women are excluded from the making of culture by men. Women (and men from nondominant cultural groups) are outside the circle of those who produce the general currency of thought. Ironically in a field that purports to be interested in understanding how knowledge is made and how culture is created, communication as a discipline replicates the same practices it should be studying. The ideas of those outside the circle rarely become part of the general currency of thought in the field. Anyone who doubts this need only look at the reference lists for almost all the published pieces in the field of communication—Davis and Puckett's included. Smith's (1978) description of the circle effect seems appropriate again here:

> Men attend to and treat as significant only what men say. The circle of men whose writing and talk was significant to each other extends backwards in time as far as our records reach. What men were doing was relevant to men, was written by men about men for men. Men listened and listen to what one another said. (p. 281)

The condition of feminist scholarship's exclusion from the general currency of thought in the field suggests that white women and people of color have a bigger bone to pick with the general state of affairs than past and current discussions about mass culture have led us to. The question that we who have been part of "them," "the other," have to pose is not whether the mass media are supplying the appropriate meanings to people, or even what role people have in actively making meanings from what is supplied. In other words, the question is neither, What do the media do to people? nor What is it people do with the media? These have been the two prevailing— and sterile—sides of the debate thus far. The real question to be asked is, What *could* people do with the media? The problem is not a *lack* of meaning in people's lives (Davis and Puckett make a sound argument that all people live meaningful lives), but rather *what* meaning and *whose* meaning. Davis and Puckett imply that replacing bureaucracies with communities as suppliers of meaning will somehow make things better. However, as long as someone else gets to do it, the problem will remain.

Feminists are likely to agree that some notion of community should be part of a re-visioned cultural process. Certainly bureaucracies and most of our present institutional arrangements will have to go.[7] But the key to change will be instituting a process by which *all* people in a society are fully participating members. Everyone should have the opportunity to contribute to making the meanings that are the general currency of thought. This necessitates redefining "the other" and rearranging our models. Can we envision a *true* model of dialogue in which "oppressive ways of knowing and being known," the hallmark of our current model of communication, are replaced with speaking subjects with the capacity for respectful listening?[8] In doing so, we will have to unlearn our racism, our sexism, our anti-Semitism, our elitism, our ageism, our ableism, and our heterosexism—

all of those justifications for relegating people to categories of "other" that deny them their humanness. That does not mean that everyone should then be thought of as the "same," or that differences should be ignored. As Tom Nakayama (1990) argues, the concept of "diversity" is preferable to that of difference, because it recognizes a multiplicity of differences rather than the binary opposition of "other" compared against the dominant group. "So long as there is an Other, it needs to be managed in some way. Binary oppositions lend themselves to hierarchies," he observes (p. 9).

What would the media look like in a culture modeled on an egalitarian relationship of speaking subjects? They certainly would not be the closed system they make up now, with a majority of people consigned to the status of object and receiver. The media will have to be restructured to accommodate the telling of stories, the making of meaning by the many rather than the few. It is strange that the insights of the Women's Institute for Freedom of the Press have never been grasped by the field of communication at large:

> In a century as intellectually and technologically creative as ours, we know a way to provide a means of communication to all who need it can be devised. . . . We know that changes in the structure of mass communications are going to come; too many people are now being left out. The question is: on what principles will restructuring be made? As women, we intend to have a voice in how the communications systems of the future will develop. (M. L. Allen, 1988, p. 68)

I said earlier that nothing was stopping humans from becoming other than what they are except a failure of imagination. Now I would like to propose that this same failure of imagination has been at work in our own field. The same histories, the same debates, and the same points of view continue to be repeated with little new insight because we have failed to apply our theories about meaning-making to an analysis of our own field. Meanings change, as I explained earlier, when new phenomena need to be accounted for or when discrepancies generate new interpretations. Those who are in the best position to rename and reinterpret are those who have been silenced and marginalized, those who see the world as the dominant group sees it as well as from their own standpoint as "other." We are the ones who are most likely to resist pregiven meanings in favor of our own novel combinations. Perhaps that is why I have heard and read many who have said that feminist scholarship is currently the most exciting enterprise in the field. This will become even more the case as feminist scholarship comes to transform itself through its own inevitable (if initially painful) relationship with the discourses of other "others."

But how can feminist scholarship make its revolutionary contribution to the field of communication when no one else pays attention to it? I mean, *reads* it and is *transformed* by it? That is the final good news-bad news we must contemplate. The good news is that the imagination to think our way out of the serious problems of communication, culture, and community exists right in our own field. The bad news is that no one seems to want to listen.

NOTES

1. One corrective to this problem would be to rename what is usually called simply "cultural studies" with the qualifier "white male cultural studies," not because *only* white males engage in it (though most are white and male) but because that is the standpoint one is standing in when seeing the world this way. Naming one's partiality is a good way to become conscious of it.

2. At the same time I make these laudatory claims about feminist scholarship, I want to point out that women of color have had to challenge many of the assumptions and claims of feminist scholarship because of its overriding whiteness. The struggle of white feminist scholars to decenter themselves in their theories to account for and appreciate women's differences is a forerunner to what white males will need to do to decenter themselves from their universe.

3. Ann Balsamo (1987), to give one example, gives postmodernism a good thumping when she suggests that feminism anticipated the agenda of postmodernism. Rather than considering feminism an "instance of postmodern thought," she implies, postmodernism might be thought of as another instance of patriarchal thought.

4. The excessive attention to audience by both communication science and cultural studies (see, for example, Allor, 1988, and critical responses to his essay in the same issue) implies the same nervous concern about *them,* whether writers and researchers are trying to redeem them or not. After having demonstrated quite thoroughly that audiences are active meaning-makers who sometimes resist ready-made meanings, why has the field not moved on? Whom are we trying to convince?

5. The oppressive nature of these institutions varies by cultural group, however. Church and family have traditionally been sources of strength and solidarity for black women, for example.

6. This is not intended to "whitewash" important differences among women, all of whom are part of some other cultural—and more or less privileged—group. Bell Hooks (1981) is instructive on the point that black women are still "other" to black men, in spite of a shared racial identity and experience. Paula Gunn Allen (1986) reminds us that the original gender system of Native Americans did not include an oppressive notion of women as "other," or alien, until the enforcement of an Anglo-European system that introduced patriarchy to the tribes.

7. See Kathy Ferguson's (1984) critique of bureaucracies as masculine institutions for a better understanding.

8. See Elizabeth Ellsworth (1989) for a discussion of the difficulties associated with trying to create a place for dialogue and with resisting oppressive discourses.

REFERENCES

Allen, M. L. (Ed.). (1988). *1988 directory of women's media.* Washington, DC: Women's Institute for Freedom of the Press.

Allen, P. G. (1986). *The sacred hoop: Recovering the feminine in American Indian traditions.* Boston: Beacon.

Allor, M. (1988). Relocating the site of the audience. *Critical Studies in Mass Communication, 5,* 217-233.

Balsamo, A. (1987). Un-wrapping the postmodern: A feminist glance. *Journal of Communication Inquiry, 11*(1), 64-72.

Berger, P., & Luckmann, T. (1967). *The social construction of reality: A treatise in the sociology of knowledge.* Garden City, NY: Anchor.

Budd, M., Entman, R. M., & Steinman, C. (1990). The affirmative character of U.S. cultural studies. *Critical Studies in Mass Communication, 7*, 169-184.

Collins, P. H. (1989). The social construction of Black feminist thought. *Signs, 14*, 745-773.

Ellsworth, E. (1989). Why doesn't this feel empowering? Working through the repressive myths of critical pedagogy. *Harvard Educational Review, 59*, 297-324.

Ferguson, K. E. (1984). *The feminist cast against bureaucracy.* Philadelphia: Temple University Press.

Gerbner, G. (Ed.). (1983). Ferment in the field [Special issue]. *Journal of Communication, 33*(3).

Gitlin, T. (1990). Commentary: Who communicates what to whom, in what voice and why, about the study of mass communication? *Critical Studies in Mass Communication, 7*, 185-196.

Hooks, B. (1981). *Ain't I a woman? Black women and feminism.* Boston: South End.

Lembo, R., & Tucker, K. H., Jr. (1990). Culture, television, and opposition: Rethinking cultural studies. *Critical Studies in Mass Communication, 7*, 97-116.

MacKinnon, C. A. (1987). *Feminism unmodified: Discourses on life and law.* Cambridge, MA: Harvard University Press.

Nakayama, T. K. (1990, June). *From racial differences to diversity in critical communication studies.* Paper presented at the annual meeting of the International Communication Association, Dublin.

Rakow, L. F. (1986a). Feminist approaches to popular culture: Giving patriarchy its due. *Communication, 9*, 19-41.

Rakow, L. F. (1986b). Rethinking gender research in communication. *Journal of Communication, 36*(4), 11-26.

Smith, D. (1978). A peculiar eclipsing: Women's exclusion from man's culture. *Women's Studies International Quarterly, 1*, 281-295.

2 The Resourceful Reader: Interpreting Television Characters and Narratives

SONIA M. LIVINGSTONE
London School of Economics

The television viewer is an active interpreter, not a passive recipient, of programs. Viewers' interpretations of programs mediate television effects. The "active viewer" is accepted by both traditional and critical mass communication scholars, allowing for a possible convergence between these two schools through a more sophisticated theory of the relation between text and reader. Recent empirical research within the reader-reception theory tradition is discussed. An original research program is described in which the "role of the reader" is explored, using both quantitative and qualitative methods to show how viewers' interpretations of programs depend on their sociocognitive resources (a summary of experiences and understandings of everyday life) as well as on program structure. Theoretical problems with reception research are considered, focusing on the differences between comprehension and interpretation and between consensus and divergence, and the nature of the preferred reading and the active viewer.

THE ACTIVE AUDIENCE

New ways of conceptualizing the television audience may be seen in mass communication concepts such as the introduction of the active viewer, the implied reader, the interpretive community, critical distance, and divergent readings. The audience is no longer "disappearing" (Fejes, 1984); on the contrary, it is flourishing. The audience is now widely seen as an active interpreter of television programs rather than as a passive recipient. In addition, the audience is now seen as occupying specific and diverse cultural contexts rather than as homogeneous and isolated. The meanings of television programs, as interpreted by viewers, are now seen

AUTHOR'S NOTE: My thanks to Nuffield College Oxford for financial support and to Michael Argyle and Peter K. Lunt for helpful comments on earlier versions of this chapter.

Correspondence and requests for reprints: Sonia M. Livingstone, Department of Social Psychology, London School of Economics, London WC2A 2AE, England.

Communication Yearbook 15, pp. 58-90

as a subject for empirical investigation rather than to be presumed through textual analysis. Most important for the present essay is the assumption that the audience brings its own experiences and knowledge to bear on the task of making sense of television; the audience is no longer considered ignorant.

Researching the Television Audience

Recent research on the television audience has centered on the role of interpretation in processes of viewing and effects. Mass communication researchers from both the traditional and critical schools have come together in debating issues of audience reception (Blumler, Gurevitch, & Katz, 1985; Schroder, 1987), and a growing body of empirical work has resulted (Ang, 1985; Hodge & Tripp, 1986; Katz & Liebes, 1986; Radway, 1985). This work has been conducted in different ways—with critical researchers drawing on reader-response theory through ethnographic methods and traditional researchers drawing on sociocognitive psychology through quantitative methods. However, the convergence of researchers on problems of audience reception and interpretation has raised a range of new questions and challenges for audience research. After nearly a decade of this research, we are now in a position to consider some tentative conclusions and to identify remaining research questions. This chapter will attempt to do this through the presentation of a specific body of work on audience interpretations—both theoretical and empirical—that has bridged the traditional and critical approaches.

I have conducted a series of studies on viewers' reception of popular soap operas, focusing on the ways in which viewers make sense of and represent characters and narratives. As the title of this chapter, "The Resourceful Reader," indicates, I will focus mainly on the reconceptualization of the television viewer as a knowledgeable and informed interpreter of meaning, rather than on related changes in views of the text and of media effects. To ground this approach, I will draw on empirical and theoretical links between research on interpretation in social psychology and in mass communication, focusing on parallel developments in these two domains.

The Convergence on Audience Interpretation

In studies of media effects, production, and content, researchers typically make implicit assumptions about the interpretations that viewers make of programs: that the audience is homogeneous, that viewers interpret programs in the same way as researchers, that meanings are obvious and given, and that prior social knowledge and experience are relatively unimportant. This is often true for both schools of mass communication—traditional or "administrative" (Lazarsfeld, 1941) and critical, for neither tends to focus on audience interpretations. In general, traditional scholars have focused on audience effects but have neglected the structure of programs or texts, resulting in an underestimation of the complexity of program meanings. Thus little recognition is given to the interpretive work required to make sense of television, whether theories conceive of the audience as passive, as in behavioral learning theory, cultivation theory (Gerbner & Gross, 1976), and "hypodermic" theories, or as active, selecting from the media according to their motivations, as in uses and gratifications theory (Blumler & Katz, 1974).

On the other hand, critical scholars have neglected audiences by focusing on the text. While textual analyses of programs have resulted in an awareness of the interpretive complexities required in making sense of programs, these analyses have been conducted largely from the analyst's point of view (Fiske, 1987; Rowland & Watkins, 1984). It is not known whether viewers make the same interpretations, either compared with researchers or with each other, or whether their social knowledge and experiences are unimportant in the interpretive process (effective only in generating trivial individual differences). Text analysts often require assumptions to be made about viewers' interests and experiences for their analyses of the pleasures or impacts of texts (Fiske, 1987; Mander, 1983; Newcomb, 1982). Until recently these assumptions have not been seen as a subject for empirical investigation.

The above is, of course, a simplified characterization of a vast and diverse body of mass communication research. Yet there is concern about the relation between the traditional critical schools. Together with others (Fry & Fry, 1986; Katz & Liebes, 1986; Morley, 1980; Schroder, 1987), my research has proposed that we address the interrelation between viewers and programs (or readers and texts). How do people actively make sense of programs? How does their social knowledge direct and inform the interpretive process? How do texts guide and restrict the interpretive process?

Recent empirical research on audience reception of television programs shows that common assumptions about the television audience are questionable—the audience has been found to be heterogeneous (Liebes & Katz, 1986; Morley, 1980), to interpret programs differently from researchers (Hodge & Tripp, 1986; Radway, 1985), and to play an active, constructive role in the reception of meaning (Drabman et al., 1981; Pingree et al., 1984; Reeves, Chaffee, & Tims, 1982). We can no longer infer audience interpretations or media effects from semiotic or content-analytic findings, nor can we assume the meanings of experimental materials in effects studies (van Dijk, 1987).

We must consider both the roles of programs in inviting an interpretive contribution from the reader/viewer and of the social knowledge of the viewer in fulfilling this role. Research must investigate the meanings that viewers actually construct from programs, and the ways in which prior social knowledge and experience guide and inform this constructive process. To do this, we must also explore different methodologies for studying audience interpretations. There has been some debate about the possibility of convergence between the critical and traditional schools over the empirical study of audience interpretation of texts. Some traditional scholars welcome this move (e.g., Blumler et al., 1985), while critical scholars are more uncertain. For example, Hall (1980) and Schroder (1987) are cautiously optimistic, while Carey (1985) and Allen (1985) seem more resistant. Notwithstanding these doubts, research is going ahead and should, perhaps, be judged on its results.

The Role of Interpretation in Mediating Effects

There has been a certain disappointment over the failure of traditional mass communication research to provide clear evidence for the effects of television on its audience. For example, despite considerable funding and research effort, Hawkins and Pingree (1983) and Durkin (1985b) argue that the evidence for effects is weak and problematic. Roberts and Bachen (1981) blame the "problem orientation" of research on the neglect of theoretical innovation and integration. Many researchers are now reconceptualizing the effects of the media in terms of gradual, cumulative cognitive effects on people's frameworks for thinking, and on the content of their thoughts (Katz, 1980; Reeves et al., 1982; Roberts & Bachen, 1981). According to the sociocognitive formulation, cognitive frameworks and representations are held to mediate or buffer the effects of television.

Before we can study the effects of television, we must ask how viewers have interpreted the programs whose effects are being questioned. When interpreting television, viewers must, on the sociocognitive account, integrate the information in the program with their own knowledge—of the program, its genre, and the real-world phenomena to which the program makes reference. This process of integration itself depends on the viewer's cognitive habits, processing heuristics, and motivations. Presumably, the effects of a program must surely depend on viewers' personal interpretations and transformations of the program.

For example, if viewers of *Dynasty* saw the heroine, Alexis Carrington Colby, as a successful and powerful older woman, those older women in the audience may have gained an increase in self-esteem through watching such a relatively rare positive image of older women on television. If, however, they saw her as an unattainable ideal, she may have simply depressed them and increased their feelings of helplessness. If they saw her power as inevitably linked to her wickedness, they may have ended up with a diminished desire for public power. If they saw her as externalizing her inner loneliness and neurosis through manipulation of others, they may have pitied her and striven instead for alternative sources of self-esteem. One could go on, for such a character was deliberately formulated so as to be read in multiple ways and to appeal to diverse audiences. The point is that character interpretation is the mediator of effects.

The presumption of particular interpretations in order to hypothesize about particular effects is a recipe for exactly the minor, confused, and contradictory results so common in the effects literature. For example, in light of Noble's (1975) argument that western films are primarily interpreted as portrayals of loyalty and cooperation rather than aggression and individualism, should we be surprised that research has found only weak and inconsistent evidence for increased aggressiveness, or "fear of crime," following viewing of supposedly aggressive programs? If a text is open to different readings, then it may also generate different, possibly contrasting, effects.

Not only may different readings or interpretations give rise to different effects, but the same effect may have different implications or be a product of different processes, depending on the interpretation made. For example, Tan (1979) conducted a study that showed that watching advertisements for beauty products increased ratings of the importance of beauty in popularity with men among adolescent girls, but how should we understand the observed effect? Did the girls consider women more powerful than previously so, having interpreted the advertisements as showing how women can manipulate men's vulnerabilities, or did they consider women less powerful than previously, having interpreted the advertisements as saying that beauty is women's major, if not only, source of power, so that in all other areas they are inferior?

I have been arguing that we should study the television audience's interpretations of programs because it is these that mediate any effects of television. Any study of interpretations may clarify predictions about types of effects (e.g., direction of effect, implications of effect), about the nature of texts (e.g., genre, openness) that produce different effects, and about processes of effects (e.g., the use of heuristics for consistency, parsimony, coherence, relevance, and selectivity, the use of social knowledge representations in interpretation). There is also a phenomenological reason to study viewers' interpretations—they are of interest themselves. Viewers' interpretations inform us about the nature of the viewing experience—the ideas, images, and concepts with which viewers can and do engage, the pleasures and emotions that fill their leisure time, and, consequently, the repertoire of representations on which they may draw in their everyday interactions with others.

The Interpretive Process

How, then, should we theorize the process of interpreting television? Thus far, I have made use of the "text-reader" metaphor of audience interpretation in place of the more traditional "sender-message-receiver" model. Treating television programs as texts focuses attention on the symbolic and structural nature of program meanings, on the cultural practices and contexts within which they are constructed, and on the interpretive demands that they impose upon their readers. The reader (or viewer) is, on this account, an active and informed participant in the construction of meaning. Just as the text is to be conceived in terms of the reader's interpretive strategies and resources, so too is the reader to be conceived in terms of the structural demands of the text. This contrasts with the strict separation of sender, message, and receiver in traditional communication theory—in which the message is seen as fixed, acontextual, and unitary in meaning and the receiver is typically a passive and powerless pawn in the communication process.

Reader-oriented textual theories have focused on the relationship between texts and readers (Holub, 1984). Specifically, in Germany there has arisen a school of reception aesthetics (Iser, 1980; Jauss, 1982); in Italy, Eco (1979) has theorized the "role of the reader"; and in the United States, various literary critics offer the "reader-response" approach to texts (Suleiman & Crosman, 1980; Tompkins, 1980). Reader-oriented theories begin by recognizing the twin problems of unlimited semiosis and divergent readings. In neither theory nor practice can one identify a unique and fixed meaning in a text. Consequently, different readers can make different but meaningful and coherent readings of the same text, and so the communicative process is inherently plural.

The text can be split, according to Eco (1979), into the "virtual" or as yet unread, nonmeaningful text and the "realized" or interpreted (and thus plural and context-dependent) text that participates in communication. Ingarden (1973) discusses the text as a "schematized structure" to be concretized by the reader. In this, he draws upon the similar, Gestalt-based imagery of the cognitive psychologist, who talks of knowledge structures as schemata—abstract and incomplete representational systems that require completion by concrete and contingent circumstances in order to generate meaning.

The text, then, cannot be said to be meaningful independent of an interpreting or "implied reader" (Iser, 1980) or "model reader" (Eco, 1979), a reader whose own knowledge or "horizon of expectations" (Jauss, 1982) provides the contingent circumstances against which the text is realized. The text anticipates, or presupposes, a competence in the reader and at the same time constructs that competence through the process of reading. Developing the structuralist tradition, Eco's model reader can be conceived of as a set of textual codes that constitute the competence or interpretive resources of the reader. The model reader is discoverable by analyzing the textual codes of stereotyped overcoding, coreference, rhetoric, inference, frames, and genre. These codes are the means by which the text invites the knowledge and interpretive strategies of the reader to inform the reading process and thus to realize the virtual text. Textual analyses should thus reveal the "role of the reader," or the demands that the text places on the reader in order for it to make sense.

A further distinction relevant to mass communication is Eco's opposition of open and closed texts. For Eco, popular culture texts are typically closed, insofar as they aim for a specific, predetermined reading, presuming a particular set of codes or resources on which the reader must draw to make sense of the text. Open texts, on the other hand, typify the texts of high culture, for they envisage a variety of interpretations and play on the relations between the different possible readings that they invite their readers to make. Through the notion of the open text, we may escape the assumptions of traditional message analysis and focus instead on the multiplicity of meanings in a text, on the interplay among meanings, and on the conventions—generic, cultural, or ideological—that constrain the range of possible meanings.

Regarding programs as texts rather than stimuli or messages allows us to accommodate their complexity more easily. Contrary to being unitary and given, and multiple yet bounded, as in the stimulus-based assumptions of traditional psychology and mass communication, texts should be expected to be multilayered, conventionally constrained, open, and incomplete. This complexity, then, need not be regarded as "noise" or miscommunication or a source of problems, and we need not design measures to eliminate it. Similarly, diversity in audience interpretations, or interpretations that differ from those of the text analyst, need not be regarded as instances of inaccuracy or miscommunication, but should instead raise questions about the role of the audiences' resources and circumstances that produce the observed interpretations.

This approach moves us away from conducting text analysis or content analysis as a way of studying the meanings that circulate in society as a result of watching television. In relation to content analysis, Durkin (1985a) notes that "frequency of message has yet to be demonstrated to be isomorphic with viewers' receptive processes" (p. 203). In relation to semiotic analysis, we must also study the activities of empirical audiences, unless the implied reader is held to be so strongly inscribed in the text that actual readers have no option but to follow instructions. If the meanings that result from television viewing depend on the actual realization or instantiation of virtual texts, we are directed toward an investigation of the knowledge, experience, and viewing contexts of the audience. Thus reception analysis becomes an empirical project.

A further move treats popular culture texts such as television programs as open rather than closed texts (Allen, 1985; Seiter, 1981). Certain popular genres, especially the soap opera, can be seen as open to some degree because they resist closure through their conventional absence of beginnings and endings. They present a never-ending and interweaving cluster of narrative strands. The soap opera constructs multiple viewpoints of the events portrayed, as personified by the characters, and thus the interactions among characters represent the interplay among diverse perspectives. By appealing to a wide audience, and by anticipating a wide variety of interests and experiences, the soap opera invites its audience to construct actively any of a range of possible and coherent readings. The very familiarity and perceived realism of the characterizations permits the audience to become involved with or to interrogate the text, undermining any passive or fantasy-based reception of closed meanings. Hence we must study actual interpretations as a function of the mode of interaction with the text, this mode of interaction being itself influenced by the conventions of the genre.

The social rather than the literary concerns of mass communication research are, consequently, transforming the reader-oriented approach in a manner possibly unanticipated, or even disapproved of, by its originators (Holub, 1984). In short, the concept of the role of the reader is being treated not simply as an analytic category but as one that may raise empirical questions (Liebes, 1986b; Livingstone, 1990; Schroder, 1987), and that may be applied to popular culture texts as well as high culture.

The kinds of empirical questions one might raise concerning the interpretation of television programs may be illustrated by a consideration of the task facing viewers when they must make sense of characters portrayed in a drama. The range of personality traits perceived by viewers must be inferred from the interactions among the characters, as revealed through the concrete details of the narrative as these unfold over time. As characters are typically used by writers as vehicles to personify key themes, the conflicts and allegiances among characters can be read as carrying underlying messages about the relations among moral or social themes. Characters may be stereotyped according to gender, class, occupation, or whatever, so as to facilitate the inference process by simplifying the required inferences and by making salient the relevant social knowledge resources of the viewer. On the other hand, characters may also be drawn ambiguously, so as to appeal to diverse viewers, who must realize their own "preferred" versions of the characters, according to their own interests and experiences. The perceived realism of the characters (Livingstone, 1988) is enhanced by the complexity of the portrayals, and most of the pleasure in viewing lies in having to work out for oneself what the characters are like and what the meaning is of the narratives enacted. Viewers come to a program equipped with considerable interpretive resources for making sense of people in everyday life, and they exploit the openness of television drama programs in constructing their own motivated and informed interpretations of the characters they see.

Consequently, we need a theory of the viewer's interpretive resources. The present approach to the "active viewer" reconstructs theories of social knowledge—of people and of episodes—as theories of interpretive resources—of characters and of narratives. This social knowledge should be conceived of as dynamic and integrative, directing and informing interpretations of television, rather than as a static and disjointed set of facts that television may simply replace with its own given set of meanings. *Social cognition* (Fiske & Taylor, 1984; Reeves et al., 1982) involves, for example, people's biases toward seeking confirmatory rather than falsifying evidence to fit their preconceptions, their knowledge of standard event sequences, or "scripts" (Schank & Abelson, 1977), their use of story grammars (Mandler, 1984) to interpret narrative, and their use of implicit personality theories (Bruner & Tagiuri, 1954; Schneider, Hastorf, & Ellsworth, 1979) in making sense of people in their everyday lives.

Researchers have examined the interpretive heuristics that people draw upon, based on considerations such as salience, availability, recency, relevance, and prototypicality (Kahneman, Slovic, & Tversky, 1982). A theory of viewers' interpretations of the media may be found at least in part within theories of social cognition. For example, what do viewers find salient in programs and according to what criteria are they selective? How do they integrate "new" program information with "old" social knowledge? How perceptive are they of underlying messages? When and to what extent do they impose standard knowledge structures such as schemata, story grammars, and implicit personality theories onto the programs they view?

Social Psychology and the Role of the Reader

Readers approach a text with a range of interpretive resources in addition to the role that is provided for them by the text. Readers—or viewers—have expectations, knowledge, experiences, and motivations that, in order to prevent the "disappearing audience," we must study. The role of the empirical reader should not be underestimated. Nor need it be investigated from scratch. In his study of the reception of *EastEnders* (a popular British soap opera), Buckingham (1987) argues that viewers draw upon three categories of knowledge: Viewers require knowledge of people, so as to identify the different perspectives from which to interpret the programs; they require knowledge of narrative, in order to piece together sequences of events and make inferences and predictions about past and future events; and they require commonsense knowledge of everyday life, so as to relate the program to their ordinary experiences and fill out their interpretations of the program. This is, of course, a fairly basic specification of the resources required by the reader, and is intended as only a beginning point in the project of theorizing the role of the reader in more complex terms.

My point is that theories of personality, narrative, and commonsense knowledge (encompassing attributional explanations, moral judgments, prejudice and stereotyping, sociolinguistic rules and practices, and so forth) fall within the domain of social cognition. Thus, far from beginning at the beginning, there is a large literature on which we can draw (e.g., Fiske & Taylor, 1984; Heider, 1958). The field of developmental psychology is, necessarily, relevant for theorizing the role of the child reader, as children do not share adults' knowledge of narrative (Collins, 1983), moral judgment (Kohlberg, 1964), or media conventions (Rice, Huston, &

Wright, 1987). Furthermore, so that the role of the reader is not conceived of in the disjointed manner implicit in text-oriented approaches—here filling in a gap, there making an inference, later elaborating an example—we need to consider the broader cognitive goals of the reader: attempting coherence and order in episode sequencing, constructing a "mental model" (Johnson-Laird, 1983), and aiming for parsimony and consistency in the relation between text and social knowledge.

Several theoretical and methodological advantages result from the use of social psychology to study the interpretations made by the television audience. On the level of theory, there are a number of parallels between social cognition theories and reception theories that can be exploited in theorizing the empirical role of the reader.

First, the semantic representation approach to social knowledge parallels the binary opposition approach to text analysis. As the social world is presumed too complex and varied for adaptive action based on complete and veridical perception, the person is seen as selective, constructing abstract representations for organizing perceptions in meaningful ways. These abstract summaries of past experiences then also frame people's understandings of new experiences. The analysis of the emergent underlying themes of organization resembles the approach of the text analyst who, seeking to reveal the order underlying a complex and multilayered text, identifies key organizing themes with binary poles according to which different aspects of the text may be arranged in a meaningful way. For example, Dyer et al. (1981) analyze the soap opera *Coronation Street* on the basis that their "method of analysis examines the oppositions operative in the serial. This approach, which owes much to Lévi-Strauss . . . seeks to uncover the concealed structures of the text within its cultural framework" (p. 84). For both approaches, a domain is in an important sense understood once the basic themes—described as dimensions or oppositions—have been revealed beneath the surface diversity, for then relations among domains and transformations of the themes are readily identified. Both the study of semantic representations and the oppositional analysis of textual structures depend on the "spatial metaphor of meaning" (Livingstone, 1990). This proposes that meaning lies in the similarities and differences among semantic units rather than in the relations between signs and real-world referents, where semantic relations are conceptualized by analogy with physical relations (closeness, distance, orthogonality, opposition, clusters, and so forth).

For example, in the domain of perceiving other people in daily life, researchers have discovered that people use a common semantic representation organized around the independent abstract themes of evaluation (positive:negative), activity (active:passive), and potency (weak:strong). On meeting a new person, people seek to locate that person on each of these dimensions, and then to use this knowledge to generate expectations about the person's other traits and to make comparisons between one person and another (Ashmore & Del Boca, 1986; Osgood, Suci, & Tannenbaum, 1957; Schneider et al., 1979).

Similarly, the domain of gender stereotyping has been studied in terms of two competing semantic representations: One opposes masculinity and femininity, and relates all personality traits to this basic dimension (Ashmore & Del Boca, 1986; Broverman, Vogel, Broverman, Clarkson, & Rosenkrantz, 1972); the other conceives of masculinity and femininity as two separate dimensions along which individuals may be perceived to vary independently (Bem, 1984). Under the former scheme but not the latter, one would expect people to draw inferences or generate predictions about, for example, a target person's warmth or kindness on the basis of knowing how decisive or assertive he or she is.

A second parallel between sociocognitive and text-reader approaches to interpretation concerns the focus on narrative. Psychologists have studied people's interpretations of narrative in terms of "story grammars" (Mandler, 1984). By analogy with linguistic grammars, these representational structures are organized by culturally accepted rules that serve to generate expectations, legitimate inferences, and make possible comparisons between stories. These story grammars resemble the episode sequences studied, for example, by Propp (1968) in his literary analysis of the underlying structure of folktales. They comprise distinct, ordered parts, each subdivided (for example, summary, setting, orientation, complication, resolution, evaluation, conclusion; van Dijk, 1987); they provide for set roles (characters, settings, goals, and so forth); they determine what counts as the beginning and ending of a narrative; and they define out any contraventions of these rules as ungrammatical.

Third, both social cognition and reception theory use the notion of the schema to conceptualize strategies for interpretation. The schema, deriving originally from German Gestalt theory, is a representational structure that is dynamic and process oriented. It is flexible, adaptive, efficient, and holistic in its processing (Bartlett, 1932; Piaget, 1968). It operates by balancing assimilative and accommodative forces in integrating past and present experiences. In social cognition, the person is held to operate a set of abstract but adaptive schemata that provide general interpretive guidelines, but provide for gaps to be filled by particular environmental contingencies (Fiske & Taylor, 1984). Reception theory reverses this (Holub, 1984), conceiving of the interpretive process as one in which the skeletal structures of the text provide for gaps in which the reader may insert his or her social knowledge to realize the hitherto virtual text. Unfortunately, each focuses on the nature of the schema and each neglects the ways in which gaps are filled and the resources with which this is achieved—yet each awaits a theory of the other. Clearly, both the knowledge of the person and the structures of the text are schematic, organized, incomplete, abstract, and awaiting instantiation in specific contexts of interpretation.

There are, no doubt, other ways in which theories of readers and of texts parallel each other. For example, both are concerned with ideological biases, such as theories of prejudice and stereotyping and theories of preferred or dominant readings. Both must deal with the balance between openness and closure in representations. Both acknowledge the role of sociostructural factors in determining the construction of knowledge representations or text structures. While differences will naturally exist also, these parallels seem sufficiently sound to provide a basis for using social cognition as a theory for the interpretive resources used by television viewers in their active role of making sense of programs.

Finally, let us consider the methodological advantages of drawing on social psychology to investigate the active viewer of television. Social psychology has developed a range of methodologies for studying the ways in which people make sense of their everyday lives, and these can be applied to the study of the ways people make sense of television. Those audience researchers who have begun to study audience reception clearly indicate uncertainty about methodology (Ang, 1985; Morley, 1980, 1981). *How* should we discover the interpretations that people make of television, and what criteria should we use to assess the results (e.g., reliability, validity, generalizability)? One problem is how to aggregate data from many viewers in a meaningful way, without either losing the differences between individuals and groups or claiming false generalities on the basis of single cases. Researchers using qualitative methods tend to provide illustrative or suggestive quotations from viewers, with the implicit suggestion that these illustrative cases are typical of the sample. Other qualitatively oriented researchers provide summary statistics on the frequencies with which certain characteristics were found in their samples (e.g., Hodge & Tripp, 1986; Liebes & Katz, 1986). Although some psychological methods involve the imposition onto the data of a priori categories of interest to the researcher, other methods are concerned with discovering data structures or principles of cognitive perception and organization.

Bartlett's (1932) study on dynamic remembering processes, using a version of the children's game "Chinese whispers," shows the operation of Gestalt principles (Kohler, 1930) of coherence over disconnected text, of meaningfulness over incomprehension, of the familiar over the unfamiliar, of the gist over trivia, of narrative sequence over temporal inconsistency, and of causal over associative linkages. By studying either the ways in which people recall a text or the elements of a text that they recognize when shown them later, we can reveal the schematic structures by which people organize material. For example, finding false intrusions in the recall paradigm reveals the knowledge structures that inform interpretation, showing the statements that people falsely believe were present in the text because, to them, it is more meaningful for them to be included. Similarly, omissions or failures to recognize certain statements reveal the parts of the text that do not fit knowledge structures. We can also learn about readers' interpretive structures or story grammars from their reordering of narratives, from the elements of the text that they foreground, and from the inferences they insert or the connotations they add to their recall of the narrative (see, for example, Liebes, 1986a, on cultural differences in "retellings" of episodes from *Dallas*; and Owens, Bower, & Black, 1979, on the "soap opera effect" in narrative recall).

Another method that aims to reveal implicit and spontaneous knowledge structures used by people to make sense of their everyday worlds is that of multidimensional scaling (Kruskal & Wish, 1978). Multidimensional scaling operationalizes the spatial metaphor of meaning, discussed earlier, by exploiting the analogy between conceptual and physical space. Premised on the notion that meaning lies in the relations among semantic units, rather than in the relations between units and their referents, multidimensional scaling obtains measures of conceptual similarity and difference among the units of interest and then transforms these conceptual relations into physical ones, so that conceptual similarity may be expressed as physical distance. Thus a model is fitted to the data rather than imposing a preexisting model upon the data. Oppositions underlying these judgments of similarities may then emerge as the polar dimensions of a multidimensional space. Multidimensional scaling discovers the implicit themes by which people make sense of a set of concepts and the structural relations (e.g., clusters, circumplex) perceived to hold among the concepts. From this, we can test hypotheses about the number and identity of the dimensions.

In the research reported in the next section, the concepts used were television characters (see also Reeves & Greenberg, 1977; Reeves & Lometti, 1978). Here, the analysis of viewers' judgments of similarities and differences among characters reveals the implicit, underlying themes by which viewers make sense of characters. This opens the way to theoretically informed investigations of the active viewer, for the dimensions of a scaling space parallel both the dimensional theories of social knowledge (e.g., person perception and stereotyping; Schneider et al., 1979) and the oppositional approach of textual analysis. As Forgas (1979) notes, multidimensional scaling can be used as a discovery method, as "an excellent alternative to the qualitative journalistic, descriptive methodologies currently being advocated by some critics" (p. 254).

Viewers of soap operas discuss the characters with the familiarity and involvement with which they discuss real people, and they describe the experience of viewing as one of engaging with people they know well, as if dropping in to catch up on gossip with the neighbors (Livingstone, 1988). Consequently, theories of person perception, and methods of multidimensional scaling, can reasonably be applied to the representation of television characters so as to reveal the underlying processes of perception and judgment that guide the construction of these representations.

THE RESEARCH PROGRAM

The program of research to be described in this section is an investigation into the television audience's interpretations of characters and narrative in soap opera. The research aims were as follows:

(1) to discover and describe the nature and structure of viewers' interpretations of characters and narrative and to compare these with the interpretations made by text analyses of the same programs, in order to determine how viewers may diverge from the text in their interpretations

(2) to reveal the relationship between social knowledge structures of persons and narratives and the viewers' representations, in order to determine the role of social knowledge in interpretations of television

(3) to examine the extent of divergence or consensus among viewers' interpretations

(4) to examine the relationships among different aspects of interpretation, specifically between characterization and narrative

On a more general level, the project is an attempt to study empirically the role of the reader in mass communication, with a focus on the role of social knowledge as a resource for informing the interpretive process. While one may analyze both texts and readers separately, empirical study is required to discover what happens when they come together. This represents a break from theoretical analyses of texts alone, or of ideal rather than actual readers, and from simply inferring about interpretations when studying the effects of viewing. On a still more general level, the research aims to facilitate convergences between the domains of traditional and critical mass communication and between mass communication and social psychology.

There are, of course, many ways to study the negotiation between text and reader, although little empirical research has been conducted thus far. This research examines the representations that result from and mediate people's interpretations, rather than the process of interpretation itself. To study representations that are both relatively stable and naturally available, a domain was used with which people have become familiar as part of their daily routines over many years. Soap opera characters and narratives were selected because viewers have long-term, complex, naturally acquired, and involved relationships with them. Soap opera also raises theoretical challenges through its portrayal of relatively dominant women (contrasting with viewers' stereotypes) and through the relative openness of its texts.

Viewers' Representation of Characters

Television characters mediate a range of television effects, through the processes of imitation, identification, role modeling, and parasocial interaction. Especially in soap operas, viewers become acquainted with the relatively constant set of characters and feel involved with them. Characters carry the narrative, so that narrative or genre themes should be reflected in viewers' representations of the characters. Arguably, the openness of soap opera, where the role for the reader is maximized, is located especially in the characters rather than in the narratives (Allen, 1985). As the characters in soap opera offer multiple possibilities, and as the viewers must be aware of the paradigm of possibilities from which any one choice is made, considerable demands are placed on viewers' interpretive efforts. The research on character representation used multidimensional scaling to discover the nature of viewers' representations of the characters in an American prime-time soap opera, *Dallas*, and two popular British soap operas, *Coronation Street* and *EastEnders*. Predictions made by theories of social perception were compared with cultural studies' research on program structure, so as to examine the relative importance of and roles of viewer and program determinants, as reflected in the representations. Subjects were regular and long-term viewers of the programs. They varied in age, occupation (few students), and sex.

Literary analysis of *Dallas* suggests that the program is structured around two major themes (Ang, 1985; Arlen, 1981; Mander, 1983). The viewers' interest is derived from the conflict between and ambiguity in these themes as they are repeatedly enacted through various characters and plots. The first theme is that of morality, closely related to the unifying symbol of the family (implying loyalty, honesty, and durability). The second theme is the morally corrupting power of organizations, business, and money.

In the study of audience reception of *Dallas*, viewers were found to discriminate among characters using two general themes or dimensions (see Livingstone, 1987a, for details). These were morality (aligned with warmth and valuing the family) and, almost orthogonal, power (dominance:submissiveness, active:passive, valuing power and business, hard:soft). The morality dimension polarized the characters (e.g., Miss Ellie versus J.R.), with few characters in between (e.g., Sue Ellen). The power dimension was highly gender stereotyped, with no male characters in the soft/submissive portion of the space. Certain women were perceived as counterstereotyped (e.g., Donna) and, generally, the women were perceived to occupy a greater range of positions than the more rigidly stereotyped men. The character representation is shown in Figure 1. Conceptual similarities and differences among characters, as judged by viewers, have been transformed into closeness and distance in two-dimensional space. The attribute vectors superimposed on this space were generated by a second sample of viewers who rated each character on a range of attributes. These were regressed onto the space to aid in interpretation of the original implicit similarity judgments. Each vector represents a linear increase in a character's ratings on the attribute. As the vectors are shown in one direction only, for clarity one must imagine each attribute extending in opposite directions. For example, in the

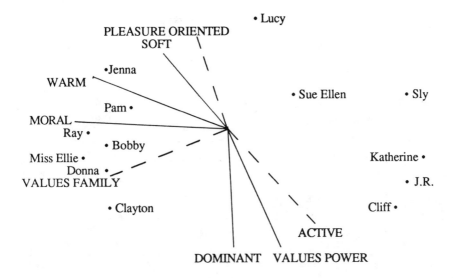

Figure 1. Character representation: *Dallas*. Solid lines, $p < .05$; dashed lines, $p < .01$.

case of morality, as one moves through the space to the left, the characters are perceived by viewers as increasing in morality (e.g., Miss Ellie is more moral than Sue Ellen), and as one moves to the right, the characters become increasingly immoral (e.g., J.R. is more immoral than Lucy or Bobby).

Dallas is seen to contrast a (mainly female) world of pleasure, weakness, and femininity with a (mainly male) world of organizational power and hardheaded business. The former, hedonistic world is not seen to differ in morality from the business world, for the morality vector is orthogonal to the potency cluster of vectors. With power split equally between the "goodies" and the "baddies," the fight between good and bad in *Dallas* will be equal and endless.

One might have expected that morality would be associated with business and immorality with pleasure, or that immorality would be associated with dominance (Ang, 1985). As these themes were orthogonal, characters may occupy any of four positions. Narratives are tied to these themes, for characterization is in part reification of characters' past narrative involvements. For example, in different plots, harmony in the Ewing home may be divided according to business issues, while at other times characters realign to divide according to moral issues. Interestingly, the character representation provided a variety of female positions. While the men were seen simply as either moral and powerful or immoral and powerful, the women occupied all four possible combinations permitted by these two oppositional themes.

The characters in the British soap operas were seen rather differently, though quite similarly to each other, indicating a basic difference in genre

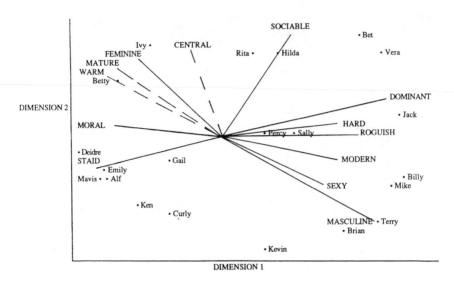

Figure 2. Viewers' representation of the characters in *Coronation Street*. Solid lines, $p < .05$; dashed lines, $p < .01$.

conventions. *Coronation Street* concerns everyday events in a small, urban, working-class street in Northern England. It is noted for its strong women. Paterson and Stewart (1981) conclude that "it is possible to see the major oppositions of *Coronation Street* as Inside:Outside and Male:Female" (p. 84). Generally, narratives are set within a class framework, so that inside:outside is frequently aligned with working-class:middle-class. Like *Coronation Street, EastEnders* conforms to the genre conventions for British soap opera in the social realist tradition (Dyer et al., 1981), containing strong women, a nostalgic concern with traditional, working-class life, and a focus on contemporary social issues (Buckingham, 1987).

In the study of viewers' representations, the characters in the British soap operas were, as for *Dallas*, represented in terms of the basic themes of morality, power, and gender (for details, see Livingstone, 1989, 1990). However, these were differently related to each other and they carried different connotative meanings. See, for example, the viewers' representations of the characters in *Coronation Street* (Figures 2 and 3). Morality (here meaning staid versus roguish, rather than good versus evil) was opposed to power in viewers' representations. Characters seen as moral were lacking in power; immoral characters were powerful. Unlike in *Dallas*, the moral battle is an unequal one here. The spaces show how the generation of certain inferences and expectations by viewers is valid. For example, if a moral character in *Coronation Street* is portrayed in an argument with an immoral character, viewers may assume that the moral character is more

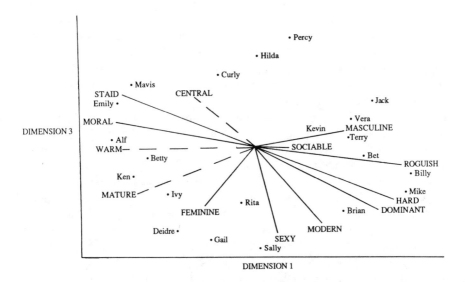

Figure 3. Viewers' representation of the characters in *Coronation Street*. Solid lines, $p < .05$; dashed lines, $p < .01$.

likely to be defending a traditional issue, to be emotionally warm, and to lose the argument, compared with the immoral character.

The main arena for conflicts in British soap operas is not morality but gender. Female and male characters are not differentiated by their potency; rather, they are equally matched. Moreover, gender is interpreted in this genre as having a matriarchal flavor, for it does not relate femininity to passivity, irrationality, or submissiveness, but to maturity, warmth, and centrality to the community. On the other hand, masculinity is strongly related to immaturity, coldness, and a peripheral role in the community. A third dimension, of traditional versus modern approach to life, suggests that many narratives are construed in terms of a conflict between traditional, nostalgic, domestic stability and the exciting and seductive challenges of a new and changing way of life.

While only the representation for *Coronation Street* is shown here, that for *EastEnders* is very similar, suggesting basic differences of genre between British and American programs (Livingstone, 1990). These character representations have proved reliable across and within samples, and over different methods of data collection. They seem durable insofar as the replacement of old by new characters in a soap opera is often achieved without altering the basic dimensional structure of the program (Livingstone, 1990).

The character representations were examined for differences among viewers as a function of age and gender. The representations from different subgroups were remarkably similar. There were only slight and inconsistent differences by gender, so that men differed slightly from some women in the third dimensions. Although there seem to be few differences in representation for different groups, caution is required because the samples were rather small once subdivided, and, further, one might subdivide viewers in different ways, according to social class, for instance, or their identification with different characters.

The studies of viewers' reception of soap opera characters show that viewers construct coherent representations of the characters in television programs. These representations throw light on viewers' experiences and understandings of the programs. The nature of the representations provided evidence for the constructive use of person knowledge as the social knowledge resources of interpretive viewers. This is exemplified by the common importance of the themes of potency, gender, and social evaluation in the character representations, for these are central to the perception of people in daily life (Ashmore & Del Boca, 1986; Bem, 1984; Osgood et al., 1957). Social knowledge also overrides the themes foregrounded in the program structure. This may be observed in the clarity of the moral and immoral clusters (supposedly ambiguous in the texts; Ang, 1985; Arlen, 1981; Mander, 1983) and in the independence, rather than the opposition, of the themes of morality/family and power/business (Ang, 1985).

Certain themes central to the textual analyses proved irrelevant to character representations—they could not be fitted to the spaces without excessive error—most notably, the theme of social class. A subsequent content analysis of the interactions among characters in *Coronation Street*, which was scaled as pairwise frequency of interactions, showed that characters interact more with those of similar social class (Livingstone, 1989). Thus Dyer et al.'s theme of class did seem to be present within the program, but it was nonetheless not salient to the viewers. The viewers' representations focused on alternative themes, guided by their strategies for perceiving and representing people in everyday life. It was not that the viewers could not identify the characters in terms of their social class, for they did, but rather that they did not when asked for their spontaneous and implicit character perceptions.

While the concept of insider:outsider (or central:peripheral to the community) was important to viewers, as suggested by Dyer et al. (1981), it was not related to working-class:middle-class, as they had argued, but instead was related more to gender, at least for *Coronation Street*. Men were seen to threaten the stability and security of a primarily female and domestic community, rather than the middle classes being seen as threatening to disrupt a working-class way of life.

The research also revealed ways in which viewers are receptive to the structure of the text in precedence to the dictates of abstract social knowledge. For example, themes central to textual analyses of soap operas, but not relevant to person perception (Schneider et al., 1979), were found to structure the character representations—morality, centrality to the community, and matriarchal femininity. Similarly, certain person perception dimensions (e.g., intelligence and rationality) were neglected, and the relations predicted to hold between these dimensions were modified. For example, the general prediction (Osgood et al., 1957) that evaluation, potency, and activity would all be independent of each other was not supported. This social knowledge schema was variously "overwritten" by the text structure, depending on the nature of the program being represented. Again, the opposition of masculinity and femininity in the representations does not fit with gender schema theories (Bem, 1984), suggesting a receptivity to the basic gender stereotyping of the programs.

The existence of differences between the representations for the British and American programs also suggests that viewers are receptive to different program structures. Such findings argue against a heavily top-down or overly constructivist approach that holds that viewers see what they want to see, presumably according to prior knowledge of other people in the case of character representation, or that they reduce all information to a standard formula. Clearly, social knowledge and text structure are both determinants of viewers' representations, and each serves to modify or buffer the influence of the other. The resultant representation depends on the input of each, and on the nature of the interaction or negotiation between the two.

Viewers have been shown here to be sensitive to messages concerning nontraditional images of gender. These images may be found within the counterstereotyped images of *Dallas* or in the matriarchal images of the British programs (see Modleski, 1982, on women's pleasure in watching dominant women). One might predict that viewing soap opera would increase viewers' nontraditional conceptions of women (Pingree, 1978). But, conversely, the neglect by viewers of messages concerning social class suggests that viewing may not increase beliefs about social class distinctions, despite the apparent emphasis on such distinctions by programs.

Viewers may generate particular expectancies about narrative development, make predictions about the course of events, and readily identify the issues at stake, all on the basis of their more permanent knowledge of the characters involved. From the relationships among characters in the scaling representations, one can see an operationalization of the concept of paradigm: If all characters are potentially available for a particular narrative role, then the selection of a specific character gains its significance for the viewer through its relations to other, nonselected characters. The reader or viewer must follow the developing thematic contrasts for equivalences established among characters during the course of the narrative.

From comparing the personality space with the interaction space for the same characters, it seems that characters perceived as similar are less likely to interact than are personality opposites—indeed, they may serve as functional equivalents in interactions. Interactions occur between personality opposites on the dimensions central to the program. These interaction patterns are likely to be institutionalized in the narratives through work relationships or long-standing friendships, and, of course, the latter may lead to marital or other family relationships that make permanent the enactment of a particular opposition. This makes sense, as it is through the enactment of the thematic oppositions, with each pole personified by a particular character, that the narratives gain interest, involve conflict, and explore culturally important oppositions. The opposition on which a particular character pair differ is likely to be the one on which their interactions are based.

Viewers' Representations of Narrative

Following Bartlett (1932) and his more recent proponents (Mandler, 1984) on the ways in which memory distortions create divergences in recall, several studies have examined narrative interpretation. In the first exploratory study (Livingstone, 1990), viewers were asked to retell narratives involving a popular and central character, Rita Fairclough, in *Coronation Street.* Much attention focused on Rita's friendship and work relationship with Mavis Riley, both popular, middle-aged women who are less working-class than most of the program's other characters. From the multidimensional scaling character representation (Figures 2 and 3), it appeared that viewers represented Rita and Mavis as quite different in personality on the dimensions of sociability, morality, power, and approach to life. Thus Rita is seen as more dominant, modern, and sociable than Mavis, who is in turn seen as more moral, traditional, and staid. The two are fairly equivalent in femininity.

Consequently, narratives that center on their relationship often concern Rita's teasing dominance, bossiness, or modern approach to life—conflicting either harmoniously or more acrimoniously with Mavis's old-fashioned, staid, and weak personality. Narratives, thus, concern the areas of personality conflict or contrast rather than those of consonance, such as their femininity or warmth. Being based on salient oppositions, their apparently trivial gossip about the others in the community ensures the expression of two contrasting viewpoints on events, establishing a range of perspectives for viewers.

Divergence in retelling lay in how viewers used these consensual personality representations. Some viewers evaluated Rita's dominance positively—she teases and supports Mavis; others saw her as domineering—"giving trouble" to Mavis and manipulating her. Specific events were thus given different interpretations: Compare "Rita badgered Mavis into learning to drive, she was devious about it by the way she had Mavis's flat decorated in exchange" with "She persuaded Mavis to have driving lessons and told her that she would pay for them, and have her flat painted and decorated for her. This shows she can be very kind and generous."

Viewers differed in the complexity of their interpretations and in the social rhetoric that they drew upon to support their interpretations. In this, they varied in their use of the open aspects of the text. The closed aspects also gave rise to divergence, through inaccuracies in recall, when actions were misremembered and then woven into a meaningful story. In both cases, viewers made various kinds of inferential connections to make their stories coherent. Thus they fitted the narratives to their perceptions of the characters by, for example, making different attributions of motivations to lie behind the events.

Certain viewers exhibited Liebes and Katz's (1986) referential mode of viewing, showing themselves as involved in the events and talking of Rita as they might of someone they knew. Others appeared to stand back and admire, assessing the quality of the events as fictional construction (the critical mode of viewing).

In sum, narratives were interpreted as involving conflict between characters along the themes found to be salient discriminators of those characters in studies of character representation. Viewers draw their own inferences about the significance of events observed. These inferences involve motivations, feelings, and intentions that serve to fill out the interpretations. Often viewers draw upon more general mythic or culturally consensual knowledge frames, concerning, for instance, rhetoric about maternal feelings, the nature of relationships, or ways of helping or influencing others. Viewers may misremember certain aspects of a narrative, but all interpretations are nonetheless made coherent and contain the gist of the events that occurred.

A second study examined in more detail the narrative structure of viewers' retold versions of a single story from *Coronation Street* (Livingstone, 1990, in press-b). Viewers' treatment of areas of openness and closure within the text were analyzed. The story concerned potential adultery between a secretary and the husband in a long-standing and popular marriage in the program. This analysis reveals ways in which the structure of viewers' interpretive schemata and their past knowledge of the genre and program served to guide their readings of the narrative. The openness of the text posed a particular problem for them, as it conflicted with the closed and familiar structures of social knowledge. The various resolutions that viewers adopted, resulting in divergent readings of the same text, illustrate the roles of social knowledge and expectations in constructing the meanings of television programs. Viewers focus on different events or make different inferences according to their evaluations of the characters or their introduction of cultural knowledge. Further, the narratives told by viewers depend on viewers' recognition of textual openness, which they resolve through the application of story grammars.

First, viewers' accounts were compared with both the text itself and the abstract structure of a story grammar, with which viewers presumably make sense of specific narratives on television (Mandler, 1984; van Dijk, 1987). While the text contained various inconsistencies or indeterminacies in its sequencing of events, these were often "clarified" by viewers, who imposed a determinate and commonsense story grammar onto the events seen. For example, while the married couple in the program went on holiday during the period in which their marriage was under threat, many viewers recalled that the holiday took place at the end of their accounts, where it gained added meaning as the celebratory conclusion to the eventual reconciliation. In general, events that fitted key places in the story grammar—disruptive events, complications, resolutions, conclusions—were well recalled, while intervening or incidental events were more often forgotten.

The text offered a range of explanations for the occurrence of adultery (Livingstone, 1987b, 1990), each personified in a different character. This textual openness was also "read" according to viewers' prior knowledge of the characters or their expectations of the program. The "preferred reading" (Hall, 1980), or that most advocated and validated by the text, namely, that men commit adultery as a result of fears of lost virility (the "male menopause"), was not favored by viewers. Instead they emphasized psychological motives such as revenge and jealousy. The former explanation was particularly interesting, as it depended upon viewers' recalling a story from long ago in which the wife in this marriage herself committed adultery. Textual explanations for adultery that identify the husband as the agent but that avoid responsibility attributions are resisted by viewers in favor of explanations that identify female agents (either the wife or the secretary) and that attribute clear responsibility for the events that take place.

Soap opera stories do not so much begin and end as they emerge from previous stories and feed into future stories, with numerous intertwining links across time and events (Allen, 1985). Story grammars, on the other hand, place considerable emphasis on the beginning and ending of a narrative as fixed points around which the events may be organized and to emphasize the goal toward which events are directed. As a similar vagueness about boundaries existed for the text under study here, one can ask how the viewers coped with the conflict between text and interpretive resources in their readings. Most viewers, interestingly, were receptive to the conventions of the genre, reflecting the vague beginnings of the narrative in their accounts. A few viewers, however, imposed a clear closure on the narrative, eliminating all uncertainty. Compare "we had weeks of Ken being worried about his feelings for Sally changing from those of a boss to those of a potential lover, and it eventually culminated in him kissing her and embracing her in the office" with "It started with a kiss in the office." Despite the typical absence of an ending to this narrative, as the reconciliation scene was marred by a lingering uncertainty never to be clarified, many viewers inserted endings of their own to resolve the marital conflict. They variously referred to a second honeymoon holiday, a "happy ever after," an agreement to try again, a realization of the temporary nature of the infatuation, and so forth. Fewer viewers than for the beginning of the narrative were able to leave their accounts unresolved, and all told stories that fitted with the genre conventions and that "made sense," irrespective of their accuracy.

How can we account for viewers' divergence in their interpretations of narrative? Although uses and gratifications research has pointed to the importance of viewers' relationships with soap opera characters (Carveth & Alexander, 1985; Livingstone, 1988), little attention has been paid to the importance of these relationships in affecting interpretations. Various psychological factors could affect interpretive divergence (Eisenstock, 1984; Jose & Brewer, 1984; Noble, 1975; Potkay & Potkay, 1984) by influencing the viewers' experienced relationships with the characters—through identification, recognition or "parasocial interaction" (Horton & Wohl, 1956), or character evaluation.

These relationships were examined in a study of narrative recall (Livingstone, in press-a). A narrative was selected from *Coronation Street* that concerned a father's opposition to the marriage to an older man of his young daughter by his first marriage because this man had previously had an affair with the father's present wife. At least two readings were potentially available in this narrative: Either love triumphs over prejudice, where the young daughter represents love or naïveté, or naïveté triumphs over wisdom, where the father represents prejudice or wisdom. The text provided various types of support for both of these readings. Viewers were asked to say how much they agreed with a series of interpretive statements that indexed both textual readings. By cluster analyzing viewers according to their responses, it was found that viewers fell into one of four categories.

The *cynics* saw the father as having acted reasonably; they considered that he was right to oppose the marriage, for they did not believe that the couple really loved each other, each being deluded about the character of the other. They were especially critical of the daughter, seeing her as a gold digger who was also fulfilling her need for a father figure. The *romantics* interpreted the father's actions as unreasonable, vindictive, and possessive, seeing him putting his hostility to the bridegroom before his feelings for his daughter, and seeing her as right to disappoint her father. They believed that the couple were right for each other, that they could overcome any problems that they might encounter, and that the marriage would last. The *negotiated cynics* and the *negotiated romantics* took coherent intermediate positions, making less judgmental, more straightforward assessments about the characters, and making inferences that fitted their own perspectives.

In general, the cynics comprised a relatively large number of male viewers. They were more likely to identify with the father, evaluate him positively, and perceive the narrative sympathetically from his viewpoint. The two romantic clusters, who formed the majority, considered themselves highly unlike the father, and they disliked him. These viewers saw events from the viewpoint of the couple and could not sympathize with the father's position. The negotiated cynics were in an interesting position, for while their interpretation of events was closest to that of the cynics and they too disliked the couple, they nonetheless sympathized with the daughter and were less critical of her in their inferences about her thoughts and motives.

The relationships experienced by the characters proved important in determining the perspective taken on interpreting the narrative, with identification (or perceived similarity of characters to oneself), evaluation or liking/disliking, and, to a lesser extent, recognition (or perceived similarity of characters to people one knows in daily life) all influencing interpretation. Given viewers' often considerable involvement in soap opera, it seems plausible that character evaluation, identification, and perspective taking should become interrelated over time. As shown here, an individual's response to just one major character—here, the father—can significantly affect his or her perspective on the narrative as a whole.

The narrative opposed young/female (daughter) against old/male (father), yet viewers' ages made no difference to their interpretations, and the women did not especially side with the daughter; indeed, the female cluster (negotiated cynics) merely sided less strongly with the father than did the viewers to whom they are otherwise closest (cynics). One cannot make straightforward assumptions about interpretations from a knowledge of the viewers' sociostructural position, but one must know how viewers relate to the characters. This is especially true for soap opera, where regular viewers build up substantial relationships over the years with the characters.

ISSUES IN AUDIENCE RESEARCH

While we no longer see audiences as passive, mindless, and homogeneous, there is a danger in too wholeheartedly adopting the opposite stance. To see people simply as initiators, constructors, or creators is to replace one polemic with another. If we see the media as all-powerful creators of meaning, we neglect the role of audiences. If we see people as all-powerful creators of meaning, we neglect program structure. Instead, we should ask how people actively make sense of structured texts and how texts guide and restrict interpretations. Through the analysis of these processes, traditional conceptions of both texts and readers may require rethinking.

Comprehension and Interpretation

The concept of the "reader" contrasts with the concept of the "information processor," which traditionally implies consensual responses. The "information" to be processed is unitary and given, and "processing" implies a single, linear set of automatic transformations by which information is comprehended. These two ways of conceptualizing the person carry different implications. For example, the information-processing approach tends to treat communication as information transfer, thus raising questions of miscommunication or inaccurate transfer, in contrast to the questions of divergence among interpretations resulting from the constructivist account of the reader. Only if it were easy to specify a correct and unique message, if people generally agreed on this message, and if, further, we had a semantic theory that avoided intuitive identification of meanings might the information-processing approach serve us well. Unfortunately, we lack a theory to identify the "correct" meaning of a message, falling back on an implicit consensus among researchers. Moreover, people commonly and routinely disagree both among themselves and with researchers about the meanings of messages. Thus an approach that anticipates and theorizes divergence, that sees texts as multiple rather than as singular in meaning, and that conceives of texts and readers as related rather than as independent is preferable.

Interpretation is a variable process rather than an automatic function of the nature of the "information," and it is constrained by the structure of the text and is socially located so that the experience and knowledge of the reader plays a central role. This is not to say, however, that texts do not contain information, or that questions of accuracy or miscommunication are irrelevant; the viewer who hears that 40 people instead of 14 were killed in a plane crash or the child who thinks the detective committed the crime because she or he sees the detective reenact the crime to establish the means are clearly wrong or have missed the point. However, much research on the comprehension of television has confined itself to those aspects of texts that can be assessed in terms of correct or incorrect understandings, focusing on the denotational level of texts and considering texts insofar as they are closed. Thus research may be discouraging and invalidating divergent or creative interpretations. Interpretation concerns ways of understanding texts through their relation to mythic or ideological meanings, narrative or conventional frames, and cultural resonances. Interpretation implies a contribution of the reader, and so is not to be judged correct or incorrect, but rather should be seen as a product of the reader's experience, as more or less plausible given normative assumptions, or as more or less creative, critical, or interesting. As interpretations are specifically invited by textual openness, they are very likely to diverge from one another.

Researchers can easily talk at cross-purposes by referring ambiguously to understanding or sense-making without distinguishing between comprehension and interpretation. Traditionally, psychologists have found comprehension more interesting, for it reveals viewers' dependence on basic knowledge structures, while critical media researchers focus on interpretation because this reveals the cultural and contextual factors that differentiate among viewers. Each approach has addressed itself to a different aspect of the sense-making process. The questions for research must concern the relationship between comprehension and interpretation, the relations among different aspects of texts, the development of increasingly sophisticated social knowledge structures, the importance of divergence and consensus (for some divergence is trivial and other divergence critically functional), and so forth.

The analysis of programs and their audiences is ultimately concerned with the power of the media to influence and the power of the audience to resist or enhance that influence. Not only do interpretive processes mediate effects, but different modes of relationships between audience and program also mediate different types of effects. One can suggest that critical readings offer resistance to influence; passive, comprehension-oriented, or referential readings encourage reinforcement or consolidation of past effects; active, creative readings allow for the introduction of new ideas or validation of uncertain associations, while mindless viewing may enhance mainstreaming effects (Gerbner, Gross, Morgan, & Signorielli, 1982). Maybe active viewing is more typical of relatively open texts, where divergence is meaningful, for active processing of closed texts may simply lead to aberrant readings.

Consensus and Divergence

Much television programming, especially the soap opera, is designed to engage and involve the viewer. The more open and diverse programs are, the better they may implicate the viewers in the construction of meaning and thus enhance their interest both cognitively and emotionally. We can assume neither complete consensus nor complete divergence interpretations, but instead should begin to investigate the areas of consensus and divergence. For this, we should anticipate variations in the experienced relation between viewer and text. Viewers may identify with particular characters, seeing themselves as in that character's shoes; they may regard a character as a role model, imitating that character's behavior in order to gain some of the rewards the character is shown to enjoy; or they may engage in parasocial interaction (Horton & Wohl, 1956), watching the action as if playing opposite the character. Different genres invite different viewer positions—and this affects the viewer's response in terms of involvement and interpretation.

Katz, Iwao, and Liebes (1988) suggest a typology of interpretive modes deriving from basic distinctions between referential and critical modes and hot and cool modes. Alternatively, we may distinguish between readings that diverge on the level of denotation (as studied by the information-processing and developmental psychology of Collins, 1983, or Pingree et al., 1984), on the level of connotation (focusing on the different horizons of expectation of reception theory, social knowledge structures, or Piagetian schemata), on the level of ideology (accepting or opposing preferred readings, making oppositional, dominant, or negotiated readings), or on the level of contextual relevance (with reference to different interpretive communities and social uses; Ang, 1985; Modleski, 1982; Radway, 1985). Doubtless there are yet further ways of subdividing varieties of readings.

This raises several empirical questions. To take the case of the study on divergent interpretations discussed earlier, the parasocial relationships that viewers experience with characters appear to generate divergence, possibly more so than the viewers' sociostructural position. How are the multiple readings related to diversity in the audience? For example, do the interpretive clusterings found in that study represent permanent or temporary divergences (i.e., do some viewers consistently adopt a romantic view of events in all drama or even in all of their lives, while others are consistently cynical)? Do these divergences derive from the viewers' own experiences or, for example, personal relationships? If not, how freely do viewers fluctuate, adopting different interpretive positions on different occasions? We can also ask about the kinds of divergence to be expected. While all would agree that in the retelling study discussed earlier, the father opposed the couple's marriage, viewers disagreed over the connotative issues of whether one side was in the right and why the characters acted as they did, and presumably they would also disagree over the deeper ideological themes of, for example, whether the program is saying that young women should not marry much older men or that fathers always oppose their daughters' fiancés, or that the patriarchal fabric of modern society is disintegrating. Can different theories of textual analysis predict the nature and loci of divergence? How should we assess not only the degree but also the types of divergence in interpretations?

The research presented on viewers' representations of television characters generally found consensus in interpretations. Other researchers have identified areas of divergence (Ang, 1985; Katz & Liebes, 1986; Morley, 1980). Discovering divergence in interpretations may be an artifact of methodology, for while the research presented in the previous section uses a quantitative approach, other researchers use qualitative methods that, while often highly suggestive in their findings, leave one with doubts concerning the representativeness of the illustrations provided and the reliability of the findings. Further research using multiple methods for convergent validity is now needed.

Additionally, while consensus exists in relatively abstract meanings, divergence may be found at a more concrete level. The multidimensional scaling studies indexed fairly general and abstract representations of characters and summaries of general program themes, as the viewers perceive them, which provide a resource for the interpretation of particular narratives. Yet the viewers' character representations do not solely determine the interpretation of particular narratives. The retelling research suggests that divergence in interpretation occurs in narrative interpretation, when the application of general knowledge structures is varied as a function of the viewers' experienced relationships with familiar characters.

The Preferred Reading

Drawing on the concept of preferred readings, which have "the institutional/political/ideological order imprinted in them" (Hall, 1980, p. 134), allows for divergence in interpretation yet avoids pluralism by retaining some notion of textual determination or guidance by which certain readings are made easier, specifically those that fit with the dominant ideology. However, the studies of the reception of preferred readings have confounded the idea of a majority reading by the audience with the idea of an ideologically normative reading (Morley, 1980). A text may contain two normative, although opposed, readings. In the retelling study, while the romantics clearly endorse a dominant romantic ideology, idealizing love and predicting a "happy ever after" ending for the characters, the cynics do not fit the oppositional category, for they endorse another, concerning notions of the patriarchal father, of daughters as property, the alignment of age and wisdom, and the corrupting influence of an adulterous older man. Neither reading appears critical in the political sense of oppositional, challenging the authority of the text, intended by Morley; both groups viewed the program referentially (Liebes & Katz, 1986).

Further, the majority of viewers may make a different interpretation from the preferred reading. This is illustrated in the retelling study, where most viewers made a romantic reading of an arguably cynical narrative (for content analysis has repeatedly demonstrated that soap opera marriages frequently end in divorce and that "true love" is often illusory, deceitful, and temporary; Cantor & Pingree, 1983).

Allen (1985) suggests that the involvement of viewers lies not in predicting *what* will happen, but in seeing *how* it happens (a concern with the paradigmatic, not the syntagmatic). The present research suggests that viewers may not perceive the predictability in narrative that researchers identify, but that, alternatively, they suspend this knowledge and enter into the certainty or uncertainty of the characters themselves.

A number of normative alternatives can be encoded in the text, and different viewers may select different readings and yet remain within a dominant framework. Hence the negotiated readings may be a compromise between two dominant but contradictory discourses. Divergence is not simply a function of critical distance from the text, for the text is open to a number of referential readings. Despite interest in subversive or feminist interpretations of soap opera (Ang, 1985; Seiter, 1981), it is apparent when analyzing empirical data that much interpretive divergence will represent conventional rather than radical positions.

The Active Viewer

The term *activity* is the source of much confusion, for an active viewer need not be alert, attentive, and original. *Activity* may refer to creative reading—making new meanings of the text—but it may also refer to the more mindless process of fitting the text into familiar frameworks or habits. Here the person is active in the sense of changing the context for and associations of the text ("doing" something with it), but not creative in the sense of doing something original or novel with the text. The notion of active, creative readings may be further divided into readings invited by the text (as a function of openness) and those made despite the text (which we would term *aberrant* if they deny denotational aspects of the text, and *oppositional* if they oppose ideological aspects of the text). As a term, *active* has become fashionable; it has been used in many, often contradictory, ways that need to be clarified on use.

To reject the tool-kit, do-what-you-will-with-the-text model is not necessarily to reject a vigilant, attentive, and creative reader or viewer, but neither is it to reject a habitual, schematic, unimaginative one. Rather, the point is that viewers must inevitably "do" something with the text, but that they are likely to draw upon their formidable resources of knowledge and experience to do so, and whether viewers are creative or habitual in their responses will depend on the relationships among the structures of the text, the social knowledge of the viewers, and the mode of interaction between the two.

REFERENCES

Allen, R. C. (1985). *Speaking of soap operas.* Chapel Hill: University of North Carolina Press.

Ang, I. (1985). *Watching* Dallas: *Soap opera and the melodramatic imagination.* London: Methuen.

Arlen, M. (1981). Smooth pebbles at Southfork. In R. P. Adler (Ed.), *Understanding television: Essays on television as a social and cultural force* (pp. 173-181). New York: Praeger.

Ashmore, R. D., & Del Boca, F. K. (1986). *The social psychology of female-male relations: A critical analysis of central concepts.* Orlando, FL: Academic Press.

Bartlett, F. C. (1932). *Remembering: A study in experimental and social psychology.* Cambridge: Cambridge University Press.

Bem, S. L. (1984). Androgyny and gender schema theory: A conceptual and empirical investigation. In *Nebraska Symposium on Motivation, 32,* (pp. 179-226). Lincoln: University of Nebraska Press.

Blumler, J. G., Gurevitch, M., & Katz, E. (1985). Reaching out: A future for gratifications research. In K. E. Rosengren, L. A. Wenner, & P. Palmgreen (Eds.), *Media gratifications research: Current perspectives* (pp. 255-273). Beverly Hills, CA: Sage.

Blumler, J. G., & Katz, E. (Eds.). (1974). *The uses of mass communications: Current perspectives on gratifications research.* Beverly Hills, CA: Sage.

Broverman, I., Vogel, S., Broverman, D., Clarkson, F., & Rosenkrantz, P. (1972). Sex-role stereotypes: A current appraisal. *Journal of Social Issues, 28*(2), 59-78.

Bruner, J. S., & Tagiuri, R. (1954). The perception of people. In G. Lindzey (Ed.), *Handbook of social psychology* (Vol. 2). Cambridge, MA: Addison-Wesley.

Buckingham, D. (1987). *Public secrets: EastEnders and its audience.* London: British Film Institute.

Cantor, M., & Pingree, S. (1983). *The soap opera.* Beverly Hills, CA: Sage.

Carey, J. W. (1985). Overcoming resistance to cultural studies. In M. Gurevitch & M. R. Levy (Eds.), *Mass communication review yearbook* (Vol. 5, pp. 27-40). Beverly Hills, CA: Sage.

Carveth, R., & Alexander, A. (1985). Soap opera viewing motivations and the cultivation process. *Journal of Broadcasting and Electronic Media, 29*, 259-273.

Collins, W. A. (1983). Interpretation and inference in children's television viewing. In J. Bryant & D. A. Anderson (Eds.), *Children's understanding of television* (pp. 125-150). New York: Academic Press.

Drabman, R. S., Robertson, S. J., Patterson, J. N., Jarvie, G. J., Hammer, D., & Cordua, G. (1981). Children's perception of media-portrayed sex roles. *Sex Roles, 7*, 379-389.

Durkin, K. (1985a). Television and sex-role acquisition 1: Content. *British Journal of Social Psychology, 24*, 101-113.

Durkin, K. (1985b). Television and sex-role acquisition. 2: Effects. *British Journal of Social Psychology, 24*, 191-210.

Dyer, R., Geraghty, C., Jordan, M., Lovell, T., Paterson, R., & Stewart, J. (1981). *Coronation Street*. London: British Film Institute.

Eco, U. (1979). *The role of the reader: Explorations in the semiotics of texts*. Bloomington: Indiana University Press.

Eisenstock, B. (1984). Sex-role differences in children's identification with counterstereotypical televised portrayals. *Sex Roles, 10*, 417-430.

Fejes, F. (1984). Critical mass communications research and media effects: The problem of the disappearing audience. *Media, Culture and Society, 6*, 219-232.

Fiske, J. (1987). *Television culture*. London: Methuen.

Fiske, S. T., & Taylor, S. E. (1984). *Social cognition*. New York: Random House.

Forgas, J. P. (1979). Multidimensional scaling: A discovery method in social psychology. In G. P. Ginsberg (Ed.), *Emerging strategies in social psychological research*. New York: John Wiley.

Fry, D. L., & Fry, V. H. (1986). A semiotic model for the study of mass communication. In M. L. McLaughlin (Ed.), *Communication yearbook 9* (pp. 463-479). Beverly Hills, CA: Sage.

Gerbner, G., & Gross, L. (1979). Living with television: The violence profile. *Journal of Communication, 26*(2), 173-199.

Gerbner, G., Gross, L., Morgan, M., & Signorielli, N. (1982). Charting the mainstream: Television's contributions to political orientations. *Journal of Communication, 32*(2), 100-127.

Hall, S. (1980). Encoding/decoding. In S. Hall, D. Hobson, A. Lowe, & P. Willis (Eds.), *Culture, media, language: Working papers in cultural studies 1972-1979* (pp. 128-138). London: Hutchinson.

Hawkins, R. P., & Pingree, S. (1983). Television's influence on social reality. In E. Wartella & D. C. Whitney (Eds.), *Mass communication review yearbook* (Vol. 4, pp. 53-76). Beverly Hills, CA: Sage.

Heider, F. (1958). *The psychology of interpersonal relations*. New York: Wiley.

Hodge, R., & Tripp, D. (1986). *Children and television: A semiotic approach*. Cambridge: Polity.

Holub, R. C. (1984). *Reception theory: A critical introduction*. London: Methuen.

Horton, D., & Wohl, R. R. (1956). Mass communication and para-social interaction. *Psychiatry, 19*, 215-229.

Ingarden, R. (1973). *The cognition of the literary work of art*. Evanston, IL: Northwestern University Press.

Iser, W. (1980). The reading process: A phenomenological approach. In J. P. Tompkins (Ed.), *Reader-response criticism: From formalism to post-structuralism*. Baltimore: Johns Hopkins University Press.

Jauss, H. R. (1982). *Towards an aesthetic of reception*. Minneapolis: University of Minnesota Press.

Johnson-Laird, P. N. (1983). *Mental models: Towards a cognitive science of language, inference and consciousness*. Cambridge: Cambridge University Press.

Jose, P. E., & Brewer, W. F. (1984). Development of story liking: Character identification, suspense, and outcome resolution. *Developmental Psychology, 20,* 911-924.

Kahneman, D., Slovic, P., & Tversky, A. (Eds.), (1982). *Judgment under uncertainty: Heuristics and biases.* New York: Cambridge University Press.

Katz, E. (1980). On conceptualizing media effects. *Studies in Communication, 1,* 119-141.

Katz, E., Iwao, S., & Liebes, T. (1988). *On the limits of diffusion of American television: A study of the critical abilities of Japanese, Israeli and American viewers.* Report to the Hoso Bunka Foundation, Tokyo.

Katz, E., & Liebes, T. (1986). Mutual aid in the decoding of *Dallas*: Preliminary notes from a cross-cultural study. In P. Drummond & R. Paterson (Eds.), *Television in transition.* London: British Film Institute.

Kohlberg, L. (1964). Development of moral character and moral ideology. In M. L. Hoffman & L. W. Hoffman (Eds.), *Review of child development research* (Vol. 1). New York: Russell Sage Foundation.

Kohler, W. (1930). *Gestalt psychology.* London: Bell & Sons.

Kruskal, J. B., & Wish, M. (1978). *Multidimensional scaling.* Beverly Hills, CA: Sage.

Lazarsfeld, P. F. (1941). Remarks on administrative and critical communications research. *Studies in Philosophy and Science, 9,* 3-16.

Liebes, T. (1986a, May). *Cultural differences in the retelling of television fiction.* Paper presented at the annual meeting of the International Communication Association, Chicago.

Liebes, T. (1986b, October). *On the convergence of theories of mass communication and literature regarding the role of the "reader."* Paper presented at the Conference on Culture and Communication, Philadelphia.

Liebes, T., & Katz, E. (1986). Patterns of involvement in television fiction: A comparative analysis. *European Journal of Communication, 1,* 151-171.

Livingstone, S. M. (1987a). The implicit representation of characters in *Dallas*: A multidimensional scaling approach. *Human Communication Research, 13,* 399-420.

Livingstone, S. M. (1987b). The representation of personal relationships in television drama: Realism, convention and morality. In R. Burnett, P. McGhee, & D. D. Clarke (Eds.), *Accounting for relationships: Explanation, representation and knowledge* (pp. 248-268). London: Methuen.

Livingstone, S. M. (1988). Why people watch soap opera: An analysis of the explanations of British viewers. *European Journal of Communication, 3,* 55-80.

Livingstone, S. M. (1989). Interpretive viewers and structured programs: The implicit representation of soap opera characters. *Communication Research, 16*(1), 25-57.

Livingstone, S. M. (1990). *Making sense of television: The psychology of audience interpretation.* Oxford: Pergamon.

Livingstone, S. M. (in press-a). Interpreting television narrative: How viewers see a story. *Journal of Communication.*

Livingstone, S. M. (in press-b). The role of the viewer in audience research: A case study in retelling romantic drama. In M. Gurevitch & J. Curran (Eds.), *Mass communication and society.* London: Routledge.

Mander, M. S. (1983). "Dallas": The mythology of crime and the moral occult. *Journal of Popular Culture, 17*(2), 44-50.

Mandler, J. M. (1984). *Stories, scripts, and scenes: Aspects of schema theory.* Hillsdale, NJ: Lawrence Erlbaum.

Modleski, T. (1982). *Loving with a vengeance: Mass-produced fantasies for women.* New York: Methuen.

Morley, D. (1980). *The "Nationwide" audience: Structure and decoding.* London: British Film Institute.

Morley, D. (1981). The "Nationwide" audience: A critical postscript. *Screen Education, 39,* 3-14.

Newcomb, H. (Ed.). (1982). *Television: The critical view* (3rd ed.). Oxford: Oxford University Press.

Noble, G. (1975). *Children in front of the small screen.* London: Sage.

Osgood, C. E., Suci, G. J., & Tannenbaum, P. H. (1957). *The measurement of meaning.* Urbana: University of Illinois Press.

Owens, J., Bower, G. H., & Black, J. B. (1979). The "soap opera" effect in story recall. *Memory and Cognition, 7*(3), 185-191.

Paterson, R., & Stewart, J. (1981). *Street* life. In R. Dyer, C. Geraghty, M. Jordan, T. Lovell, R. Paterson, & J. Stewart (Eds.), *Coronation Street.* London: British Film Institute.

Piaget, J. (1968). *Structuralism.* London: Routledge & Kegan Paul.

Pingree, S. (1978). The effects of nonsexist television commercials and perceptions of reality on children's attitudes about women. *Psychology of Women Quarterly, 2,* 262-277.

Pingree, S., Hawkins, R. P., Rouner, D., Burns, J., Gikonyo, W., & Neuwirth, C. (1984). Another look at children's comprehension of television. *Communication Research, 11,* 477-496.

Potkay, C. R., & Potkay, C. E. (1984). Perceptions of female and male comic strip characters II: Favorability and identification are different dimensions. *Sex Roles, 10,* 119-128.

Propp, V. (1968). *The morphology of the folktale.* Austin: University of Texas Press.

Radway, J. (1985). Interpretive communities and variable literacies: The functions of romance reading. In M. Gurevitch & M. R. Levy (Eds.), *Mass communication review yearbook* (Vol. 5, pp. 337-361). Beverly Hills, CA: Sage.

Reeves, B., Chaffee, S. H., & Tims, A. (1982). Social cognition and mass communication research. In M. E. Roloff & C. R. Berger (Eds.), *Social cognition and communication.* London: Sage.

Reeves, B., & Greenberg, B. (1977). Children's perceptions of television characters. *Human Communication Research, 3,* 113-127.

Reeves, B., & Lometti, G. (1978). The dimensional structure of children's perceptions of television characters: A replication. *Human Communication Research, 5,* 247-256.

Rice, M., Huston, A., & Wright, J. (1987). The forms of television: Effects on children's attention, comprehension and social behaviour. In O. Boyd-Barrett & P. Braham (Eds.), *Media, knowledge and power.* London: Croom Helm.

Roberts, D. F., & Bachen, C. M. (1981). Mass communication effects. *Annual Review of Psychology, 32,* 307-356.

Rowland, W. D., & Watkins, B. (1984). *Interpreting television: Current research perspectives.* Beverly Hills, CA: Sage.

Schank, R. C., & Abelson, R. P. (1977). *Scripts, plans, goals, and understanding: An inquiry into human knowledge structures.* Hillsdale, NJ: Lawrence Erlbaum.

Schneider, D. J., Hastorf, A. H., & Ellsworth, P. C. (1979). *Person perception.* Reading, MA: Addison-Wesley.

Schroder, K. C. (1987). The convergence of antagonistic traditions? The case of audience research. *European Journal of Communication, 2,* 7-31.

Seiter, E. (1981). The role of the woman reader: Eco's narrative theory and soap operas. *Tabloid, 6.*

Suleiman, S., & Crosman, I. (Eds.). (1980). *The reader in the text.* Princeton, NJ: Princeton University Press.

Tan, A. S. (1979). TV beauty ads and role expectations of adolescent female viewers. *Journalism Quarterly, 56,* 283-288.

Tompkins, J. P. (Ed.). (1980). *Reader-response criticism: From formalism to post-structuralism.* Baltimore: Johns Hopkins University Press.

van Dijk, T. A. (1987). *Communicating racism: Ethnic prejudice in thought and talk.* Newbury Park, CA: Sage.

The Active Viewer and the Problem of Interpretation: Reconciling Traditional and Critical Research

ANDREA L. PRESS
University of Michigan

L IVINGSTONE'S essay is centrally concerned with a rather distinctive problem that we face in the communication field. Comparatively young, our discipline is in a position to benefit from methods developed in a number of diverse social science and humanistic disciplines. We have been able to apply different methodologies developed in these fields toward investigating the questions that have become central to our own. Yet, in doing so, we sometimes attempt to aggregate data that have been collected in noncomparable ways. More serious, in some cases the methodologies used to collect these data have themselves been developed in noncomparable contexts, in the attempts of different academic disciplines to answer questions that have been spawned by noncomparable concerns, questions, and slants. In the case of data about the mass media audience, in particular, this has made it very difficult to bring together into one coherent field the different bodies of literature that exist concerning media effects and audience reception.

Livingstone focuses on the problem of the audience. She offers an admirably exhaustive review of the types of literature about audiences that have been developed in our field. Livingstone makes the claim that these different bodies of literature can indeed be brought together. In fact, the problem

AUTHOR'S NOTE: I would like to thank Bruce A. Williams and Kenneth H. Tucker, Jr., for criticisms and comments on an earlier draft of this commentary.

Correspondence and requests for reprints: Andrea L. Press, Department of Communication, 2020 Frieze Building, University of Michigan, Ann Arbor, MI 48109-1285.

Communication Yearbook 15, pp. 91-106

of the "active" audience, in particular, has been researched with vastly differing methodologies, ranging from journalistic investigations and qualitative studies to more social psychological surveys, and from vastly differing vantage points, ranging from traditional to critical. Traditional and critical methodologies have converged, she argues, if rather unconsciously, on the theory of the "active audience." Both have thrown aside their earlier assumptions that media simply inject audiences on a mass scale with a particular perspective. The approach that is favored emphasizes the openness of the possible meanings of media texts and the role audience activity and interpretation play in determining whatever impact texts have.

Livingstone, like many in our field at present, is concerned with emphasizing the similarities between current traditional and critical audience study, rather than their differences. In particular, she mentions the possibility of bringing together more traditional social cognition theories, used within social psychology to study media reception, with the more critical reception theories in our field, originating in the British and American cultural studies traditions. To this end, Livingstone draws parallels at the theoretical level between the two traditions. She mentions in particular that (a) the semantic representation approach to social knowledge in social psychology parallels the binary opposition approach to text analysis in critical text analysis, (b) both focus on the mechanics of the narrative or "story grammars," and (c) both use the notion of the "schema" to conceptualize strategies for interpretation. She concludes this discussion by cautiously arguing in favor of the methodological advantages to drawing on social psychology in investigating the active viewer of television. The type of qualitative research that has been employed by those beginning to study the audience in the critical tradition (Livingstone cites in particular here Ang, 1985; Morley, 1980, 1981) often relies, she argues, on haphazard, single quotes that suggest, if only implicitly, that we can generalize from the very few cases presented. Actually, Livingstone argues, we cannot generalize from these types of studies at all. Such methods, she maintains, are then of limited usefulness to us. Social psychological methods, on the other hand, address similar questions and give us data that can be aggregated and presented as representative of different groups of people. This method holds more promise for those interested in future knowledge of the active audience.

Livingstone proceeds to illustrate these claims with examples drawn from her own very interesting work on viewer responses to British and American prime-time soap opera narratives and characters, in which she uses a multidimensional scaling approach to gathering and organizing her data (Livingstone, 1987a, 1987b, 1988, 1989, 1990). In one study she looks at the way viewers categorize various characters on *Dallas* along the dimensions of morality and gender. This she compares to the way viewers used these dimensions differently to represent characters in the British soap operas *Coronation Street* and *EastEnders*. In other studies, Livingstone looks at the way different viewers relate specific narratives shown in British soap operas. One narrative used concerned a central character, Rita Fairclough, and her friendship and work relationship with Mavis Riley. Another narrative concerned a potential adulterous relationship between a long-married central character and his secretary in *Coronation Street*. Livingstone relies primarily on psychological explanations to account for differences in the way viewers retell each of these narratives. She concludes with a warning that is equally valid for those working in critical and noncritical traditions: that we not "replace one polemic with another" in substituting too active a theory of the audience for our earlier passive characterization, and that we remember those influences that intrude on audience activity.

IRRECONCILABLE DIFFERENCES:
THE PROBLEM OF METHODOLOGY

While Livingstone seeks to draw together the audience research that has been spawned by the critical and noncritical traditions, she overlooks some of the most important dissimilarities between the two bodies of work. In her comparison, Livingstone focuses on the issue of methodology. Critical research has only recently moved from considering texts to actually studying the audience, she argues; and most of the audience study it has spawned uses qualitative research. With the term *qualitative research*, Livingstone refers to the type of in-depth individual interviews some have conducted (Ang, 1985) or the group interviews others have organized (Morley, 1980, 1981). Both are flawed by the idiosyncratic nature of their data and argument: it is difficult to get accurate aggregate measures using data collected in this way, due to the problems of small numbers and the imprecise ways in which most questions are asked and answered. Primarily because of this problem of aggregation, Livingstone recommends that we turn to the methods more common to social psychological research, primarily sample surveys or highly structured interviews, that yield data more amenable to meaningful aggregation and analysis. These methods will allow us to investigate the same questions much more effectively, giving us more accurate and less misleading information than current critical methods will allow.

Livingstone is certainly not alone in raising the problem of the commensurability of critical and noncritical research.[1] Others have noticed the similarities between the current emphasis on the active audience in critical audience research and mainstream research such as Katz and Lazarsfeld's (1955) early theory of the two-step flow or the uses and gratifications tradition (Rosengren, Wenner, & Palmgreen, 1985) (e.g., Carragee, 1990; Press, 1991; Schroder, 1987). Critical researchers are not sure what to make of this unlikely alliance. As Livingstone herself mentions, there is disagreement even within the critical camp itself concerning the question of whether reunification is possible or even desirable. In the wake of Gitlin's (1978) much-publicized critique of what he terms the "dominant paradigm" in mass communications research (an article often used to introduce and exemplify critical research in communication theory courses and in which Gitlin considers Katz & Lazarsfeld, 1955, a prime example of the sort of mainstream research he would like to critique), this apparent return to the mainstream among new critical audience researchers has been something of an embarrassment. Those of us doing "active audience" research in the critical camp, myself among them, are at best confused: It is increasingly difficult to figure out which "side" we are on, a question that is often posed in a field as visibly polarized as our own.

However, in the attempt to depolarize our field, Livingstone and others have overlooked some of the basic factors that initially gave rise to our differences. At this point, it is not simply a matter of substituting one methodology for another; before the issue of methodology can be meaningfully addressed, the theoretical paradigms that have given rise to different sets of questions, typically served by certain methodologies to the exclusion of others, must themselves be examined. Critical audience researchers embraced qualitative methods for particular political reasons, which are directly tied to their broader theoretical, as well as political, convictions. These remain to be addressed before critical researchers can begin to work with those whose work originates in other theoretical paradigms, which have given rise to other basic questions. Of course, those first in line to address these issues are critical researchers themselves; yet, this is a task we have effectively shirked in many current discussions and debates. This is due in part to the diversity of disciplinary backgrounds and the resulting difficulties involved in bringing to consciousness our collective questions within the critical cultural studies field itself. Still, this sort of dialogue within the critical research community is necessary before we can reach an agreement on the question of how strong our links with more mainstream research methodologies and traditions can be.

THE DOMINANT PARADIGM TEN YEARS LATER: THE PROBLEM OF MEANING

In a much-cited work, Fejes (1984) notes the paucity of audience research characterizing the critical tradition. In the time since Fejes's critique, however, critical audience research has experienced a resurgence. Originating in the United States primarily from researchers who have come to communication from their training in the humanities (Fish, 1980; Fiske, 1986, 1990; Holland, 1985; Newcomb, 1979; Radway, 1984), the new audience researchers moved from an open meaning theory of texts to the study of meaning-making itself. Influenced by new theories of text analysis, these researchers became interested in how mass media audiences make sense of mass media texts, in different ways that are perhaps distinctive of different social groups. Some studies were extremely small scale and subjective (Fiske, 1990; Holland, 1985), others somewhat larger, but most embraced the qualitative methods of anthropology and sociology, primarily the in-depth interview, in their investigations.

The new critical audience researchers, then, have rather a different background than the critical communications researchers Fejes mentions as representative of critical research. Actually, the two groups are separated by more than their interest, or lack of interest, in the audience. The critical social scientists were rooted in a critical Marxist social science framework that stressed the need to examine those aspects of social institutions that contribute to continuing oppression in capitalist society by suppressing critical social movements. In contrast, the new audience researchers are only loosely touched by this version of Marxism. They are more firmly rooted in a humanistic tradition that deemphasizes the importance of the directly political study of institutions and social movements.

Gitlin's work exemplifies the first group. His early book on the mass media discusses the representation of radical social movements in dominant news media. In this work, Gitlin (1980) sets forth a theory of hegemony, borrowed from Gramsci (1971), with which he argues that the news media promote certain dominant viewpoints in our society while functionally suppressing alternatives. His next book continues this frame by focusing on the underlying functioning of social hegemony in the consciousness of those who make executive decisions concerning the business of prime-time television (Gitlin, 1983). Although in most of Gitlin's work his argument is explicitly about media content rather than audience behavior and thought, Gitlin argues, or at least implies, that media exert powerful effects on society.

Critical audience researchers in the United States, in trying to rectify the paucity of data specifically about the audience in the works of Gitlin and others in his tradition, in some respects do end up substituting one polemic for another, thus falling into the trap of which Livingstone warns. In their zest at rediscovering the audience, researchers in this school have sometimes overemphasized the tendencies and abilities of audiences to resist ideas that are presented in the media or to use them in critical ways, even those ideas representing dominant or, in Gitlin's terms, "hegemonic" values. Thus Radway (1984) argues that women romance readers actually identify with strong defiant heroines rather than simply succumbing to an oppressive ideology of romance.[2] Fiske (1986, pp. 209-210) emphasizes that the contradictions within popular culture mandate that its meanings not be exclusively those of the dominant culture, but are fought over in struggles resembling those of "guerrilla war," with victories never clear-cut and continually claimed by both dominant and subordinate sides.[3] The result is that, in this literature, media consumption often becomes identified as a terrain of resistance against the status quo; its role in promoting the hegemony of different social groups is deemphasized and at times completely denied.[4]

The cultural studies spawned by the work of the Birmingham school in Great Britain provide a middle ground to the more polarized American situation (Hall, Critcher, Jefferson, Clarke, & Roberts, 1978; Hebdige, 1979; McRobbie, 1978a, 1978b, 1984; Willis, 1977, 1978). Carried out primarily by researchers trained in the social sciences, the work produced by this group uses the Marxist theory that inspired Gitlin and other critical social science researchers in the United States, but takes this tradition in a slightly different direction. Gramsci's theory of hegemony was developed to bridge the gap between those determinist strands within Marx that paint social movements as resulting from mechanistic laws and less materialist versions of Marxism that emphasize the importance of the critical action of the subject in initiating and effecting social change. Gitlin's Marxism is often interpreted by communication researchers as mechanistic and deterministic; yet, in fact, in borrowing from Gramsci, it is precisely the opposite. As Gramsci intended it, hegemony theory fully acknowledges, and respects, the active nature of subjects (Adamson, 1980; Boggs, 1976; Cammett, 1967; Gramsci, 1971); it goes beyond this, however, and combines its subject theory with a structural analysis of capitalist society, the formation of orthodoxies of opinion within it and the way in which such orthodoxies aid, or prevent, social transformations. Hegemony theory concedes the power of the active, transformative subject, but it finds that this power may at times be co-opted, muted, or misdirected.

The aspect of Gramsci's work in which theories of the active subject are stressed comes through more strongly in the work of the Birmingham school than it does in the work of American Marxist researchers. The latter seem to downplay the openings the system of hegemony leaves for resistance, and the places in which the system inevitably breaks down—these are an integral part of Gramsci's theory. The Birmingham researchers, on the other hand, document audience activity in a way that leaves open the possibility for true resistance. Their focus on resistance differs from that in the American cultural studies tradition. They differ in that the Birmingham school helps give us the tools with which to tell the difference between truly political, effective resistance and resistance that is by nature ineffective or co-opted. So Willis (1977) is convincing when he describes the pseudoresistance of British working-class lads as they develop a culture of noncompliance in their schools. McRobbie (1978b) is equally impressive in describing the intimate worlds of working-class girls as they prepare for working-class marriage by learning the ideology of romance, and learning it well. Both researchers paint pictures of working-class life that leave openings for political movements by telling us the places where such resistance

might occur. Yet, at the same time, they document its overwhelming absence in these contexts. Their focus on social groups contrasts markedly
with the more individual focus of the American cultural studies researchers; the latter tend to locate resistance within individuals or at the individual level of action, where, if resistance does exist, it is inevitably
politically ineffective.[5] In the United States, we need to broaden our focus,
by tracing actual political resistance to the places in the real world where
political movements have made some headway. We must also explain the
genesis and presence of such movements, where they do exist, as well as
their almost overwhelming absence from the daily lives of most of us.

TOWARD A THEORY OF THE POLITICAL

Others have pointed recently to the lack of an adequate theory of the political in much current critical audience research. Delli-Carpini and Williams (1989, 1990a, 1990b), Lembo and Tucker (1990), and Budd, Entman,
and Steinman (1990) all discuss the need for critical communication researchers to foreground questions concerning the possibility of democratic
oppositional movements in our society, and to adopt a perspective on
media effects and/or the active audience that highlights this question. There
is, then, an incipient debate on these issues within the critical tradition itself; alongside Livingstone, we too are questioning the active audience polemic. Yet not all of us are willing to move in the direction of taking
seriously the issue of politics, a movement that in my view is the question
around which our tradition could once again cohere. In part we remain divided still by our diversity of academic and theoretical backgrounds. As
Raymond Williams (1959) noted in his early investigations into cultural
studies, the question of the political has historically taken a very different
form in the humanities than in critical social science; we are as yet hesitant
to bridge the gap, although the direction in which rapidly expanding communication departments, with their large numbers of students, are moving
is certainly one factor encouraging this reconciliation.

Others in our field have recently suggested that the lack of attention to
explicitly political issues is a key problem in our current critical literature.
The "Reading Recent Revisionism" issue of *Critical Studies in Mass Communication* (June 1990) offers several discussions that highlight precisely
this problem in our literature. Lembo and Tucker (1990), in particular,
mention the lack of political sophistication in contemporary cultural studies
works in the United States. For them, the key problem is the fact that cultural studies theorists operate with a highly individualized model of reception, which stresses that widespread opposition to dominant meanings
occurs at the individual level. The individual focus of this model precludes
a theory of the formation of shared meanings, which are the inevitable

basis of any politically effective oppositional movement; politics is reduced to the aggregate thoughts and activities of discrete individuals. Budd
et al. (1990) make a similar point in their criticism of the affirmative character of U.S. cultural studies. They note the lack of discussion in current
works of the way in which politically organized subcultures (rather than individuals or simple aggregates of individuals) do or do not actively appropriate subversive readings in ways concretely promoting political change.
They urge us toward a more politically focused field of study.

Delli-Carpini and Williams (1990b) take the critique of cultural studies a
step further. In their work, they identify three levels of politics—institutions and processes, substance, and foundations[6]—and recommend that reception be considered in relation to its interaction with each. Their work
foregrounds the vague, unspecific manner in which the topic of politics enters current discussions about media reception. It argues that closer examination of this concept is an important next step for those working in the
critical tradition. Like Lembo and Tucker (1990) and Budd et al. (1990),
they argue that perhaps the most important and most neglected area of
study is the way people communally use the media as they collectively
form their ideas and beliefs about each level of politics.

If we in the critical tradition could reach some unity around giving due
importance to questions of the political, what implications would this have
for Livingstone's recommendations urging a more far-ranging unity in audience research? Unfortunately, the direction she recommends has been
and will remain a difficult one for us to travel. Social psychology has remained one of the social sciences most isolated from critical perspectives
(Adorno, 1967, 1968; Billig, 1982; Rosnow, 1981; Wexler, 1983) precisely
because of its affinity for large-scale survey research that ultimately is
premised on a conception of the individual somewhat at odds with more
politically critical notions. In fact, social psychology has been one of the
disciplines most widely examined by critical social scientists, both internally (Gergen, 1973; Harre & Secord, 1972; McGuire, 1973) and externally
(Archibald, 1978; Armistead, 1974; Larsen, 1980). While they differ as to
the remedies offered, the thrust of these critiques is the asocial and
ahistorical nature of the knowledge that the discipline gathers.

The real barrier to bringing together fully the two modes of audience research lies in the questions posited by each. Social psychology remains
committed to investigating what is—to documenting how viewers describe
and group characters, how they retell specific narratives, what they remember and what they do not. These questions are intrinsically interesting to
most of us doing audience research, but to critical researchers they are not
the whole story, or even the most interesting part of the story. Critical research, as Adorno (1967, 1968) explained so well in his early critiques of
psychology, must put a premium on the question of what might be, continually questioning what is and asking why things are the way they are, and

how they might be changed. These questions are much more difficult and sometimes, indeed, impossible to answer in measured, quantifiable terms. For example, Livingstone calls upon cognitive schema theory to help her investigate the resources viewers use to make sense of the television programs they watch. While this is certainly an interesting question to audience researchers in both traditions, more critical researchers might attempt to go beyond the question of what the schema is, to ask how particular cognitive schemata are produced within a specific sociological, economic, and political context, what their political effects are, and what alternatives we might envision to the schemata currently produced.

These sorts of questions are not always easily amenable to scientific investigation in the traditional sense. In part, they call for speculation by the researcher, which can be inspired by one nonrepresentative, fragmentary quote, by the researcher's own experience, or by nothing research related at all. Our scientific training tells us that this mere "exploratory" stage of research then leads to more concrete, limited, documentable questions, which in turn can be investigated using more aggregate methods. However, some questions cannot be investigated in this way at all. Often and for precisely this reason, these are the questions shirked in the more scientifically faithful disciplines such as social psychology.

Researchers working in more critical traditions cannot afford to shirk such questions, however, particularly not on the grounds that they are difficult or even impossible to investigate with scientific accuracy. Difficult, speculative, politically motivated questions about what might be define our tradition as critical by allowing us to challenge the implicit political premises of other fields. They will also ensure, I fear, that our work will be viewed with continuing suspicion and criticism by those concerned with questions of scientific reliability and generalizability. Our interest—indeed, our central interest—in questions that by definition are not easily investigated will keep us, I suspect, from merging entirely our questions and investigations with those characteristic of the more scientific, or mainstream, end of the social sciences. There can be and already has been a merger of sorts, but these differences in our concerns mandate that its scope remain limited. In the end, it will be difficult to agree on our central concerns, which ultimately define what our investigations are all about.

THE POLITICAL TRADITION: NEW BEGINNINGS

In fact, critical audience researchers are increasingly coming to recognize the primacy of the political, and the importance of paying closer, more specific attention to defining its place within our work. Some have even incorporated these issues into their research questions and paradigms. We are, by some measures, entering a new era in audience research in which it seems that critical researchers will engage in dialogue more freely and fully with one another, and with those in the mainstream as well. This will aid in identifying with new clarity the issues upon which we can reach at least paradigmatic agreement and those that will continue to separate us.

I would like to take this opportunity to discuss briefly my own work, both past and future. I do not in any way offer this work as paradigmatic, but this discussion will help me to spell out some of the difficulties involved in practicing what I have perhaps too literally preached in this commentary. In my past work I, too, have attempted to grapple with the problem of the relative absence of politically effective working-class movements in the United States (Katznelson, 1981; see Press, 1989, 1990, 1991). Using the in-depth interview method, I compare the ways working-class and middle-class women of two generations talked about entertainment television. Like Livingstone and Delli-Carpini and Williams, I take the position that television reception is a complicated process, one that cannot be adequately summarized by the term *resistance* or by the terms *passivity* and *accommodation* (e.g., that we should not substitute one polemic for another). With the open-ended interviewing method I employ in the study, women are able to express elements of both, and often do, in their responses to my questions and in their discussions overall. Specifically, I frame my research as an argument within the critical tradition for a truce between proponents of the active audience and theorists emphasizing hegemonic theories of media influence.

In my work, I have found that it is much too simplistic to argue that women resist domination when they watch and talk about television.[7] While in many respects television texts are open to competing interpretations, in others they bear the unmistakable marks of the hegemonic culture that creates them. It is wishful thinking, I fear, to believe that viewers are unaffected by these ideas as they are present in mass media texts and, concomitantly, in our culture at large. Further, such thinking ignores the obvious political situation of the American working class that sociologists, political scientists, and historians have widely documented.

On the other hand, it is also simplistic to argue that television viewers are simply passive recipients of the medium's hegemonic messages, or that members of a culture simply imbibe, passively, the ideological messages of that culture. Individuals and groups show themselves capable of creativity and independence both in thought and in strategies of action.[8] In many ways in our culture, people often express, both verbally and in practice, resistance to dominant ideas, and realize the contradictions among competing aspects of our cultural ideologies. Women watching television, the object of my analysis, are no different. Often they find themselves frustrated with their family and/or work situations, and are dissatisfied with the ideas that our culture makes available for expression of this frustration. The process of receiving television may include strategies for expressing, as well as for coping with, this frustration. Evidence of this abounds in women's responses to my interviews.

In my discussion, however, rather than making an overarching claim as to the ends television watching serves in our society, I emphasize the different forms in which these responses to questions about television occur between class- and age-differentiated groups. I find that working-class women resist television, but, paradoxically, the standards of critique they use are not their own. In large part, working-class women criticize television content for its lack of reality, yet the concept of reality they use corresponds to television's portrayal of middle-class life. The potential resistant thrust of their critique of television, therefore, is blunted by television's hegemonic impact itself. My findings lead me to conclude that the hegemonic aspects of the way in which television operates are more gender specific for middle-class women (e.g., are related to the operation and perpetuation of patriarchy), and that television's hegemonic function works in more class-specific ways for working-class women (e.g., in ways related to the organization of the class system in our society). I certainly do not mean to suggest that working-class women are not oppressed by their gender. Rather, I argue that the manner in which they interact with television culturally is more a function of their social class membership than of their membership in a particular gender group. In comparing the remarks of women of different social classes, I find that television contributes to their oppression, both as women and as members of the working class. While women criticize television, and resist much of its impact, it is clear that television contributes to these two dimensions of women's oppression. Currently, in addition, women of different age groups experience television's political impact differently; both older and younger women are at once critical of and compelled by pictures of television women in the family and at work.

In my current project, I work along with Delli-Carpini and Williams, using focus groups to illustrate the ways in which television structures group discourse about specific political and moral issues. In our work, we find television reception to be an immensely more complex process than the minimal effects, hegemonic reinforcement, or open-meanings arguments are able in themselves to explain (Delli-Carpini, Williams, & Press, 1989). Focus group discussions allow researchers to observe the context within which attitude change, reinforcement, or lack of change occurs. This allows us more insight into the interaction between viewing and attitudes than is possible with either more traditional methods or other critical methods. In particular, of course, groups allow preliminary examination of discursive interactions among viewers; this is of central interest to those concerned with television's impact on political discourse and collective movements in our society. It can be used to supplement both the quantitative data of traditional researchers and the other qualitative methods critical researchers are using. Currently I am using this method to research the way women of different social classes or races invoke characteristic discourses to discuss the issue of abortion. Preliminary findings indicate that this method can be used to illustrate the ways in which television treatments of the abortion issue interweave with the discourse of different social groups (Press & Cole, 1990).

I hope that my discussion here will serve to further debate and potentially have some practical implications as well regarding these issues, particularly as they affect women in our society. The political motivations of these studies are, I hope, only thinly, if at all, disguised. The earlier study originated out of a concern with both gender and class oppression in our society; these concerns gave rise to its questions. They influenced its research design and choice of methodology as well. My concern was to figure out how women use television to illuminate their own lives. In-depth interviews, while not yielding particularly generalizable data, at least provided me with the opportunity to probe this question—insofar as it was possible to answer it through probing the consciousness of actual living subjects. I was less interested in the generalizability of my results than in shedding theoretical light on the political questions that motivated the investigation in the first place. In the future, I plan to continue incorporating the more collective method of focus groups into my research, thus giving further content to the claims I seek to make about the political relevance of the collective responses to television that characterize different social groups of women.

Perhaps Gitlin best sums up the methodological dilemma researchers in the critical school face when he quotes a former student of Lazarsfeld's in his dominant paradigm article more than a decade ago:

> One of my favorite fantasies is a dialogue between Mills and Lazarsfeld in which the former reads to the latter the first sentence of *The Sociological Imagination*: "Nowadays men often feel that their private lives are a series of traps." Lazarsfeld immediately replies: "How many men, which men, how long have they felt this way, which aspects of their private lives bother them, do their public lives bother them, when do they feel free rather than trapped, what kinds of traps do they experience, etc., etc., etc." If Mills succumbed, the two of them would have to apply to the National Institute of Mental Health for a million-dollar grant to check out and elaborate that first sentence. They would need a staff of hundreds, and when they finished they would have written *Americans View Their Mental Health* rather than *The Sociological Imagination*, provided that they finished at all, and provided that either of them cared enough at the end to bother writing anything. (Stein, 1964; quoted in Gitlin, 1978, p. 223)

Of course this quote exaggerates the problem, since over the last decade traditional researchers have been forced to confront some of the issues—the whys of their research—that inspired this quotation. Yet the problem of where we spend our time and where we place our limited resources demands further attention from all of us, particularly in this age of declining resources and consequently threatened academic careers. It is one each of us has had to confront as we make the decisions that guide our future research and consequently determine the types of knowledge we gather and shape the course of our field. Too often, our decisions are determined by the contours of the field that already exists. We write research proposals directed toward what "they" in the scientific establishment want to fund; questions are chosen because they are the most easily answered using the latest and more impressive methodological tools. Critical researchers don't have a prayer of maintaining our critical edge if we give in too easily to these influences, overwhelming as they often are. As we proceed to define and debate the contours of our field, we must continue to struggle not to lose sight of the broader concerns informing our research.

NOTES

1. At a recent conference titled "Toward a Comprehensive Theory of the Audience," held at the University of Illinois at Champaign-Urbana in September 1990, this topic was a central issue for discussion. There was much controversy and little agreement regarding its proper resolution.

2. Of course, Radway offers a feminist critique of romances as well, and is quite conscious of the contradictions between these two perspectives in her book. The book has become paradigmatic of the new audience research in the United States and abroad.

3. Fiske (1986) offers an early, paradigmatic statement of the active subject theory:

A discourse theory of reading leads us to the formation of the reader's liberation movement, which asserts the reader's right to make out of the program text that connects the discourses of the program with the discourses through which he or she lives out social experience, and thus for program, society and subject to come together in an active, creative living of culture in the moment of reading. The reading subject is no longer totally at the mercy of the text or the inherited discourse, but can play an active role, however limited, in creating a text for self and meanings for self out of the discursive resources available to the reader to bring to bear on the discourses of the program. (pp. 207-208).

See also Fiske (1989a, 1989b).

4. See Carey (1989) for a good definition of the school and its roots.

5. Of course, these contrasting foci correspond in some respects to actual differences between the two societies. Scholars have noted the virtual lack of overt class consciousness in the United States vis-à-vis Great Britain (Katznelson, 1981).

6. By "institutions and processes" of politics, Delli-Carpini and Williams mean the formal channels of politics and government—elections, the presidency, and so on. The "substance" of politics, their second level, includes issues, policies, and the like, that are on the political agenda or that are becoming part of the agenda (e.g., social security, AIDS, drug testing, criminal rights). The third level, the "foundations" of politics, includes the processes and concepts upon which the very idea of politics and government is based—authority, power, equality, freedom, justice, community, and so on. Delli-Carpini and Williams argue that this level is the one most neglected by students of the media, and perhaps is the area of discussion most important for those interested in critical media research. See Delli-Carpini and Williams (1989, 1990a, 1990b).

7. See Gitlin (1980) and Lembo and Tucker (1990) for a critical review of the way in which this argument has become widespread in the literature.

8. See Swidler (1986) for an interesting description of the way in which culture operates as a set of practical strategies.

REFERENCES

Adamson, W. L. (1980). *Hegemony and revolution.* Berkeley: University of California Press.

Adorno, T. W. (1967). Sociology and psychology. *New Left Review, 46,* 67-80.

Adorno, T. W. (1968). Sociology and psychology II. *New Left Review, 47,* 79-97.

Ang, I. (1985). *Watching* Dallas: *Soap opera and the melodramatic imagination.* London: Methuen.

Archibald, W. P. (1978). *Social psychology as political economy.* Toronto: McGraw-Hill Ryerson.

Armistead, N. (Ed.). (1974). *Reconstructing social psychology.* Baltimore: Penguin.

Billig, M. (1982). *Ideology and social psychology: Extremism, moderation and contradiction.* New York: St. Martin's.

Boggs, C. (1976). *Gramsci's Marxism.* London: Pluto.

Budd, M., Entman, R., & Steinman, C. (1990). The affirmative character of U.S. cultural studies. *Critical Studies in Mass Communication, 7,* 169-184.

Cammett, J. M. (1967). *Antonio Gramsci and the origins of Italian communism.* Stanford, CA: Stanford University Press.

Carey, J. W. (1989). *Communication as culture: Essays on media and society.* London: Unwin Hyman.

Carragee, K. M. (1990). Interpretive media study and interpretive social science. *Critical Studies in Mass Communication, 7,* 81-96.

Delli-Carpini, M. X., & Williams, B. A. (1989). *Defining the public sphere: Television and political discourse.* Paper presented at the annual meeting of the American Political Science Association, Atlanta, GA.

Delli-Carpini, M. X., & Williams, B. A. (1990a). "Fictional" and "non-fictional" television celebrate Earth Day, or politics is comedy plus pretense. Paper presented at the annual meeting of the American Political Science Association, San Francisco.

Delli-Carpini, M. X., & Williams, B. A. (1990b). *The method is the message: Focus groups as a means for uncovering the impact of television on political discourse.* Paper presented at the annual meeting of the International Society of Political Psychology, Washington, DC.

Delli-Carpini, M. X., Williams, B. A., & Press, A. L. (1989). *Television and the socialization of political meaning.* Paper presented at the annual meeting of the International Society of Political Psychology, Tel Aviv.

Fejes, F. (1984). Critical mass communication research and media effects: The problem of the disappearing audience. *Media, Culture and Society, 6,* 219-232.

Fish, S. (1980). *Is there a text in this class? The authority of interpretive communities.* Cambridge, MA: Harvard University Press.

Fiske, J. (1986). Television and popular culture: Reflections on British and Australian critical practice. *Critical Studies in Mass Communication, 3,* 200-216.

Fiske, J. (1989a). *Reading the popular.* Winchester, MA: Unwin Hyman.

Fiske, J. (1989b). *Understanding popular culture.* Winchester, MA: Unwin Hyman.

Fiske, J. (1990). Ethnosemiotics: Some personal and theoretical reflections. *Cultural Studies, 4*(1), 85-99.

Gergen, K. J. (1973). Social psychology as history. *Journal of Personality and Psychology, 26,* 309-320.

Gitlin, T. (1978). Media sociology: The dominant paradigm. *Theory and Society, 6,* 205-254.
Gitlin, T. (1980). *The whole world is watching: Mass media in the making and unmaking of the New Left.* Berkeley: University of California Press.
Gitlin, T. (1983). *Inside prime time.* New York: Pantheon.
Gramsci, A. (1971). *Selections from the prison notebooks* (Q. Hoare & G. N. Smith, Eds. & Trans.). London: Lawrence & Wishart.
Hall, S., Critcher, C., Jefferson, T., Clarke, J., & Roberts, B. (1978). *Policing the crisis: Mugging, the state, and law and order.* London: Macmillan.
Harre, T., & Secord, P. F. (1972). *The explanation of social behavior.* Totowa, NJ: Rowman & Littlefield.
Hebdige, D. (1979). *Subculture: The meaning of style.* London: Methuen.
Holland, N. (1985). *The I.* New Haven, CT: Yale University Press.
Katz, E., & Lazarsfeld, P. F. (1955). *Personal influence: The part played by people in the flow of mass communications.* Glencoe, IL: Free Press.
Katznelson, I. (1981), *City trenches: Urban politics and the patterning of class in the U.S.* Chicago: University of Chicago Press.
Larsen, K. S. (Ed.). (1980). *Social psychology: Crisis or failure.* Monmouth, OR: Institute for Theoretical History.
Lembo, R., & Tucker, K. H., Jr. (1990). Culture, television, and opposition: Rethinking cultural studies. *Critical Studies in Mass Communication, 7,* 97-116.
Livingstone, S. M. (1987a). The implicit representation of characters in *Dallas*: A multidimensional scaling approach. *Human Communication Research, 13,* 399-420.
Livingstone, S. M. (1987b). The representation of personal relationships in television drama: Realism, convention and morality. In R. Burnett, P. McGhee, & D. D. Clarke (Eds.), *Accounting for relationships: Explanation, representation and knowledge* (pp. 248-268). London: Methuen.
Livingstone, S. M. (1988). Why people watch soap opera: An analysis of the explanations of British viewers. *European Journal of Communications, 3,* 55-80.
Livingstone, S. M. (1989). Interpretive viewers and structured programs: The implicit representation of soap opera characters. *Communication Research, 16,* 25-57.
Livingstone, S. M. (1990). *Making sense of television: The psychology of audience interpretation.* Oxford: Pergamon.
McGuire, W. (1973). The yin and yang of progress in social psychology. *Journal of Personality and Social Psychology, 26,* 446-456.
McRobbie, A. (1978a). *Jackie: An ideology of adolescent femininity.* Birmingham, England: Centre for Contemporary Cultural Studies.
McRobbie, A. (1978b). Working-class girls and the culture of femininity. In Women's Studies Group (Ed.), *Women take issue* (pp. 96-108). London: Hutchinson.
McRobbie, A. (1984). Dance and social fantasy. In A. McRobbie & M. Nava (Eds.), *Gender and generation* (pp. 130-223). New York: Macmillan.
Morley, D. (1980). *The "Nationwide" audience: Structure and decoding.* London: British Film Institute.
Morley, D. (1981). The "Nationwide" audience: A critical postscript. *Screen Education, 39,* 3-14.
Newcomb, H. (Ed.). (1979). *Television: The critical view* (2nd ed.). New York: Oxford University Press.
Press, A. L. (1989). Class and gender in the hegemonic process: Class differences in women's perceptions of realism and identification with television characters. *Media, Culture and Society, 11,* 229-252.
Press, A. L. (1990). Class, gender, and the female viewer: Women's responses to *Dynasty.* In M. E. Brown (Ed.), *Television and women's culture* (pp. 158-182). Newbury Park, CA: Sage.
Press, A. L. (1991). *Women watching television: Gender, class, and generation in the American television experience.* Philadelphia: University of Pennsylvania Press.

Press, A. L., & Cole, E. (1990, August). *Mass media and moral discourse: The impact of tele-vision on modes of reasoning about abortion.* Paper presented at the annual meeting of the American Sociological Association, Washington, DC.

Radway, J. A. (1984). *Reading the romance: Women, patriarchy, and popular literature.* Chapel Hill: University of North Carolina Press.

Rosengren, K. E., Wenner, L. A., & Palmgreen, P. (Eds.). (1985). *Media gratifications research: Current perspectives.* Beverly Hills, CA: Sage.

Rosnow, R. L. (1981). *Paradigms in transition: The methodology of social inquiry.* New York: Oxford University Press.

Schroder, K. C. (1987). The convergence of antagonistic traditions? The case of audience research. *European Journal of Communication, 2,* 7-31.

Stein, M. (1964). The eclipse of community: Some glances at the education of a sociologist. In A. Vidich, J. Bensman, & M. Stein (Eds.), *Reflections on community power* (pp. 215-216). New York: John Wiley.

Swidler, A. (1986). Culture in action: Symbols and strategies. *American Sociological Review, 51,* 273-286.

Wexler, P. (1983). *Critical social psychology.* Boston: Routledge & Kegan Paul.

Williams, R. (1959). *Culture and society 1780-1950.* Garden City, NY: Doubleday.

Willis, P. (1977). *Learning to labor: How working-class kids get working-class jobs.* New York: Columbia University Press.

Willis, P. (1978). *Profane culture.* London: Routledge & Kegan Paul.

At the Intersection of Messages and Receivers: Enriching Communication Theory

SUZANNE PINGREE
University of Wisconsin—Madison

W HAT has brought audience interpretive activity to the forefront for me is the generally weak relationships we consistently (and sometimes inconsistently) find between television viewing and beliefs. While there are other explanations as well, it does seem a fruitful line of research to suggest that effects questions based on manifest content analysis of television texts may not be as useful in exploring the consequences of media use as effects questions based on more sophisticated critical reader-response analysis, which in turn may not be as useful as questions based on audience readings.

Reading Sonia Livingstone's work is a pleasure and a relief. She clarifies the potential for assumption breaking and theory construction of studying a genre such as soap operas. As I have written elsewhere, soap operas are very different from the rest of television, and many of our assumptions about television content do not apply to them; their viewers behave very differently with them, behavior that is quite at odds with behaviors assumed to be normative for the rest of television (Cantor & Pingree, 1983; Pingree & Thompson, 1990). These peculiarities of the genre drew my attention to my own assumptions about television effects research, assumptions that bolster the core of the research tradition. Studying soap operas made me look again at what we have meant by television content, television viewing, and television effects, and these reassessments have shaped my research on television effects more generally. Livingstone has apparently selected soap operas to work with for some of these reasons as well, because her research is about theory, not about soaps.

Correspondence and requests for reprints: Suzanne Pingree, Department of Agricultural Journalism, University of Wisconsin, Madison, WI 53706.

Communication Yearbook 15, pp. 107-114

Livingstone's approach to research represents a new and important set of insights about television viewers, and is an ambitious program that attempts to integrate sociocognitive psychology with empirical mass communication research and qualitative critical reader-response theory. The focus of the work is on how viewers actively interpret and make sense of television messages, an area that has only recently become a subject of interest to effects researchers, according to Livingstone.

While I would agree that mainstream effects research is beginning to focus on viewer interpretations of television messages in understanding television viewing processes and effects, Livingstone contrasts her approach to a characterization of "traditional" empirical research that is misleading and unnecessary. That is, she presents the critique that empirical research has until recently assumed homogeneous, passive audiences all reacting similarly to messages (the "magic bullet"), when in fact recognizing the audience as an active participant in the effects process is not a recent phenomenon.

Mass communication research has long conceived of the audience as heterogeneous and active, taking different meanings from the same message. Studies of "who won" political debates have reported different perceptions by partisans of opposing candidates (Kraus, 1980). Viewers of *All in the Family* have been shown to judge the humor and success of characters according to their own political ideologies (Vidmar & Rokeach, 1974). Wilbur Schramm, in his essay "The Nature of Communication Between Humans" (1971), argues that meanings do not reside in messages but are always constructed by individuals. Raymond Bauer found the audience "obstinate" in 1964, arguing that communication should be understood as a transaction between senders and receivers. In fact, the whole "limited effects" tradition of research represents such variation, from Hastorf and Cantril's (1954) "They Saw a Game" study (in which fans of Dartmouth and Princeton might as well have seen two entirely different games) to the frustrations of trying to fight prejudice with the "Mr. Biggott" cartoons (Cooper & Jahoda, 1947; see also the excellent summary of selective perception by Krech & Crutchfield, 1948). And the Payne Fund studies of the effects of motion pictures phrased those effects as highly conditional on such things as competing opinions and audience background and knowledge (Charters, 1933).

In fact, it is much harder to come up with research examples of the homogeneous, passive audience and massive direct effects (Sproule, 1989). There are exceptions, such as the cultivation hypothesis, that television's portrayals of social relations form a coherent whole (i.e., as the product of many, many messages) affecting audience perceptions of social reality so as to dampen social change and reinforce societal norms (Gerbner & Gross, 1976). But this characterization of cultivation research as within the magic bullet paradigm is not really fair either. The cultivation hypothesis is ultimately sociological, about whether "society" is shaped and controlled by mass communication, and is not really a theory of individual behavior.

More generally, whenever effects research has addressed "only" questions about the "existence" or nonexistence of effect, or even occasionally when it has addressed conditions for the existence of effects, variations in interpretation have been neglected. But these activities have been neglected not because researchers were blinded to their own assumptions so much as because the questions addressed were not "about" the interpretive processes of viewers or readers. Thus, although audience activity was certainly recognized, it was sometimes treated as irrelevant to the issues at hand, as noise in the equation. But ignoring audience interpretation as outside the scope of a given study is not the same thing as assuming homogeneity, passivity, and so on.

So it is not that empirical research has just discovered that audiences are heterogeneous, active, and constructive. Empirical researchers have known (or should have known) this all along, though we all seem to take delight in tarring the previous generation with the magic bullet brush to celebrate how much smarter we all are now. Maybe it is time to lay that received history to rest.

At any rate, if empirical research has seen audiences as heterogeneous and constructive all along, do Livingstone's proposals fall when deprived of their straw man? The answer is no, because what Livingstone is proposing is indeed something new and does not need a magic bullet to which to oppose itself. By and large, empirical mass communication research has conceived its active audience members as differing in their responses to what have been conceived of as "unitary" messages. That is, individuals or subgroups differed in their gratifications sought, needs experienced, cognitive development, schemata, social roles and positions, ideologies, and so on, and these differences led to variation in selective perception and attention, the making of differing inferences, emphases on different parts of the message, and so forth. *But,* conceptually, it was the audience members or their behaviors or their cognitions that varied, not the message. The message, as a set of signs and symbols, was a given they all shared.

What Livingstone proposes is that another research tradition, that of text analysis and reception, poses a complementary and opposite conception of messages and audiences, one in which messages are as open and "active" as the audience in empirical cognitive research (and in which the potential complexity of audience members has been generally ignored). Livingstone proposes that theory be constructed at the intersection of these two research traditions, each of which preaches activity and heterogeneity for its subject. What is new, then, is the proposal that we go beyond active, interpreting audiences *and* beyond rich and textured messages, and develop theories of the *interaction* of messages and receivers.

This is not a trivial or mundane proposal; it asks that we change some fundamental assumptions. Speaking from within the empirical/cognitive tradition Livingstone identifies, I can address primarily what is novel and surprising to me. Consider the following quotes from Livingstone's chapter: "Just as the text is to be conceived in terms of the reader's interpretive strategies and resources, so too is the reader to be conceived in terms of the structural demands of the text" (p. 63). "Clearly, both the knowledge of the person and the structures of the text are schematic, organized, incomplete, abstract, and awaiting instantiation in specific contexts of interpretation" (p. 68). "The resultant representation depends on the input of each, and on the nature of the interaction or negotiation between the two" (p. 77).

These statements intentionally put the text on an equal footing with the reader, and this is not something most of us are used to. Of course, we know that print texts and television programs are the product of the cognitive processes of an author or authors, drawing on cultural knowledge and media formulae, intending more or less openness or directedness in reading. But Livingstone is not talking about texts as simply representing their authors; she has something much more radical in mind. Just as readers'/viewers' knowledge is schematic and provides interpretive guidelines for reading, the text too is schematic and provides its own guidelines for the encounter.

While the text is not literally "active," in the sense of behaving and thinking, the term is useful, metaphorically, to express its equal standing in interactions with readers/viewers. Another metaphor for what Livingstone proposes might be the tug-of-war, in that interpretation is a negotiation or dynamic tension between two evenly matched adversaries (not a struggle by the reader to extract interpretation from a recalcitrant message).

That interpretation emerges from the interaction and tension between readers and texts can be illustrated in several of the studies Livingstone reports. Most simply, it should be readily apparent that neither the reader nor the text is entirely in control in these interpretations of soap operas. Many viewers in one study reordered the timing of a vacation to provide a neater resolution of a story; on the other hand, Livingstone argues that the different character representation spaces for the British and American programs demonstrate that viewers are receptive to the program structures. At a deeper, more interesting level, Livingstone describes several ways viewers adopt and use structures available in the text of the soap operas instead of applying structures they would normally apply in person perception. But she also reports two studies in which viewers' representations bypassed the "preferred reading" advocated by the program to apply their own schemes (although I will disagree with her over whether the cynical reading of the romance in *Coronation Street* is actually preferred—despite the fact that she cites me in support of the cynical reading; any cynicism about romance is in the long run, and an alternative preferred reading of soap opera is "There's always hope for romance").

Livingstone is not alone in this research area; more and more research on audiences is taking a closer look at the message too. Discourse analysis and story grammar analysis are directing experimental design, measurement, and stimulus construction in a growing number of mass communication research programs (e.g., Meadowcroft & Reeves, 1989). And a recent volume in the Annual Reviews of Communication Research, *Message Effects in Communication Science* (Bradac, 1989), was at one point tentatively titled *The Interaction of Messages and Receivers*. Nonetheless, Livingstone is unique in two senses: She incorporates qualitative analysis techniques into her research, and she explicitly proposes what this interaction means as a research focus.

The implication of the research program is a call for research on "how people actively make sense of structured texts and how texts guide and restrict interpretations," which clearly leads to many exciting and interesting lines of inquiry, as Livingstone suggests in her final section on issues in audience research. At the same time, she implicitly poses a serious problem for mass communication research: If we believe it is crucial to understand the intersection of reader and text—that reader interpretations and text structures are no longer controllable irrelevancies, but may even be very central questions—then how do we get from these microstudies of narratives from one plot line and character relationships from one show back up to the level of programs, genres, and television as a whole? How do we go from interpretation back out to effects? And if we take the whole argument about active, interpreting viewers seriously, does this question make any sense?

To answer the last question first: Yes, it does make sense, because active, structuring texts are also a central part of the argument. Viewers are not completely free to make meanings from texts; texts vary in their ability to guide the reader, but they limit and shape the readings to be made. The exception might be Livingstone's denying-the-text readers, but the text may shape even them, since they were moved by something in the text to interpret the meanings they did. Thus the first question—about moving from the micro back up to the whole—does need an answer.

How do we generalize from rich and detailed analysis of viewer interpretations of television narratives? Perhaps some clues lie in Livingstone's studies. As she suggests, narratives re-created by long-term program viewers may tell us more than how the viewers interpreted the specific story, and how those interpretations vary with the open versus closed nature of the text. Livingstone shows that interpretations are clusterable, that they are not all idiosyncratic. In other words, it seems that powerful and more abstract variables may be derived from these microstudies of viewer interpretation that can then be used in effects research.

We have also been working on developing abstract variables in several studies of viewer interpretation of television narratives (Pingree & Thompson, 1989). Like Livingstone, we worked with soap operas in one study. However, the structure of U.S. television presented us with a problem that Livingstone does not have to deal with to such an extent: U.S. audiences have 12 different soaps to choose from, while I suspect the range is some-what narrower for British viewers. Because of this, we did not select a sin-gle popular soap and probe for reactions to a particular story line. Instead, we asked college students to "tell us a story that interests you" from a cur-rent soap they were watching. We asked them to predict what would hap-pen next, and to tell us why.

That we had stories from 12 different soaps (potentially)—and that the stories selected by viewers from the same soap were not necessarily the same ones—presented us with both disadvantages and advantages. We were disadvantaged in being unable to do the sort of narrative analysis that Livingstone conducted. But being forced to move up a level of abstraction at the very beginning proved to be an advantage as well. Instead of looking for categories of viewer interpretation, we looked for viewer strategies. We used an approach suggested by Liebes and Katz (1986) and coded the students' stories for metalinguistic (relying on genre structure) or referen-tial (relying on the story) strategies in their predictions for the stories. About half of the stories were metalinguistic. When we looked more closely at the students' responses to survey measures of attention and parasocial activity, we found that metalinguistic viewers paid more atten-tion and were more engaged with their soaps than were referential viewers. While this is counterintuitive and interesting in and of itself, the point here is that it may be possible to move from very small-scale and local interpre-tations of unique parts of specific programs to more abstract levels of anal-ysis that cut across stories and programs and still maintain some sense of the process of viewing.

In another study, we showed college students selections from movies in-volving couple interactions (Hawkins, Pingree, Fitzpatrick, Thompson, & Bauman, 1991). The students signaled with a soundless button when they saw something that was either meaningful or significant. Button pushes were computer recorded and matched with seconds of elapsed time on the video, so that the action of the movie could be matched against viewer ac-tivity (as indexed by button pushes). Our results suggested that viewers found common points of meaning in the video—places where many sig-naled and that had some internal consistency with both video content and paper-and-pencil measures taken after the viewing.

This approach only indirectly tells us about how viewers are interpreting television content; we plan next to use signaled sites in the video as places to stop the action after an initial viewing and ask viewers to write down their thoughts. With a supplementary critical reading of the text, it should be fascinating to see whether or not viewers are thinking along the lines of a "preferred reading," what else they are thinking, and which viewers re-port thinking of any kind. These thoughts would then be a source of the sort of analyses described above, and we would eventually move back up to more abstract measures of viewer interpretation and activity that could be used in research on effects. Birgitta Hoijer and Lillian Nowak of Swedish Radio have also been experimenting with this "thought listing" technique in an effort to describe ongoing cognitive interpretations of television. They are conducting in-depth interviews following presentation of programs from different genres, with an eye toward developing more abstract categories of thoughts that could suggest different sorts of processing by genre.

It is immediately apparent that when we move above the level of specific stories and characters, we lose some valuable richness of detail and elaboration. But we gain in our ability to move beyond a clearer understanding of viewer interpretations and their relationships with text structure toward a better understanding of how television is used by society and shapes individuals in society. If we were interested only in how viewers make meaning of television narratives—if the focus of the research were on sociocognitive processes at the intersection of theories of text structure—then we should be content to continue exploring with qualitative and quantitative convergent approaches in this arena: It is both very interesting and very rewarding theoretically. But interpretations are not the end point in the program, they are an intermediate stage in looking at how television viewing as a whole leads people to have certain beliefs, attitudes, and behaviors. As Livingstone says:

> I have been arguing that we should study the television audience's interpretations of programs because it is these that mediate any effects of television. Any study of interpretations may clarify predictions about types of effects (e.g., direction of effect, implications of effect), about the nature of texts (e.g., genre, openness) that produce different effects, and about processes of effects (e.g., the use of heuristics for consistency, parsimony, coherence, relevance, and selectivity, the use of social knowledge representations in interpretation). (p. 62)

Thus, while these interpretations in the context of text structure may be of interest for themselves, we must search for ways to preserve their integrity while moving them up levels of analysis so that they may enrich and elaborate research on the effects of television.

REFERENCES

Bauer, R. (1964). The obstinate audience: The influence process from the point of view of social communication. *American Psychologist, 19*, 319-328.

Bradac. J. (1989). *Message effects in communication science.* Newbury Park, CA: Sage.

Cantor, M., & Pingree, S. (1983). *The soap opera.* Beverly Hills, CA: Sage.

Charters, W. W. (1933). *Motion pictures and youth: The Payne Fund studies.* New York: Macmillan.

Cooper, E., & Jahoda, M. (1947). The evasion of propaganda: How prejudiced people respond to anti-prejudice propaganda. *Journal of Psychology, 23*, 15-25.

Gerbner, G., & Gross, L. (1976). The violence profile. *Journal of Communication, 26*, 173-199.

Hastorf, A. H., & Cantril, H. (1954). They saw a game: A case study. *Journal of Abnormal and Social Psychology, 49*, 129-134.

Hawkins, R. P., Pingree, S., Fitzpatrick, M. A., Thompson, M., & Bauman, I. (1991). Implications of concurrent measures of viewer behavior. *Human Communication Research, 17*, 485-504.

Kraus, S. (1980). *The great debates, 1976*. Bloomington: Indiana University Press.

Krech, D., & Crutchfield, R. S. (1948). Perceiving the world. In D. Krech & R. S. Crutchfield, *Theory and problems of social psychology*. New York: McGraw-Hill.

Liebes, T., & Katz, E. (1986). Patterns of involvement in television fiction: A comparative analysis. *European Journal of Communication, 1*, 151-171.

Meadowcroft, J., & Reeves, B. (1989). Influence of story schema development on children's attention to television. *Communication Research, 16*, 352-374.

Pingree, S., & Thompson, M. (1989). *Soap stories and real stories*. Paper presented at the annual meeting of the International Communication Association, San Francisco.

Pingree, S., & Thompson, M. (1990). The family in daytime serials. In J. Bryant (Ed.), *Television and the American family* (pp. 113-128). Hillsdale, NJ: Lawrence Erlbaum.

Schramm, W. (1971). The nature of communication between humans. In W. Schramm & D. F. Roberts (Eds.), *The process and effects of mass communication* (pp. 3-53). Urbana: University of Illinois Press.

Sproule, J. M. (1989). Progressive propaganda critics and the magic bullet myth. *Critical Studies in Mass Communication, 6*, 225-246.

Vidmar, N., & Rokeach, M. (1974). Archie Bunker's bigotry: A study in selective perception and exposure. *Journal of Communication, 24*, 36-47.

3 Schema Theory and Measurement in Mass Communication Research: Theoretical and Methodological Issues in News Information Processing

ROBERT H. WICKS
Indiana University

The schema construct has received considerable attention in the mass communication literature during the last decade because it has helped to explain the cognitive processes associated with information processing. However, the fuzziness of the concept and difficulties associated with schema measurement may have prevented it from blossoming into a more widely used theoretical construct. This chapter endeavors to explicate the schema construct as it applies to mass communication research. It concludes with recent examples of schema measurement strategies that have been employed by social psychologists and communication researchers.

WHAT causes a person to decide to read one article in a newspaper rather than another? Why does a person attend to several news items on the *World News Tonight* while apparently selectively "tuning out" others? What prompts a person to decide to subscribe to *Sports Illustrated* over *Redbook* or the *Ladies Home Journal?*

The answer seems simple. Different people are interested in different types of information. Certainly people living in Detroit will generally have more use for a news item pertaining to crime in that city than a story on crime in San Antonio. Likewise, the college football quarterback will generally find stories appearing in *Sports Illustrated* more interesting and useful than most articles that typically appear in *Redbook.*

Specialty media such as magazines and cable television supply specific types of information and programming to identifiable audience segments,

Correspondence and requests for reprints: Robert H. Wicks, School of Journalism, Ernie Pyle Hall, Indiana University, Bloomington, IN 47405.

Communication Yearbook 15, pp. 115-145

but when it comes to daily newspapers, radio newscasts, or the evening television news, a much more diverse audience must be satisfied. These media have historically sought broad-based appeal. Television newscasts and daily newspapers have traditionally attracted an audience that is highly diverse in terms of both demographics and psychographics (Frank & Greenberg, 1980).

Gatekeepers select information they believe is relevant, useful, and interesting to the audience. Editors and reporters structure messages to be processed easily and *assimilated* by receivers into a broader context. Editors presume that people weave old and new information together. Only the latest facts about an ongoing news story, such as a sensational murder or an investigation into the factors leading to a major airline disaster, are typically reported. Interrelated bits of knowledge on a particular topic constitute the *schema* for that domain. The associations among these related bits of information form a higher-level cohesive knowledge structure. Receivers of information thus pick up only what they have *schemata* for "and willy-nilly ignore the rest" (Neisser, 1979, p. 80).

Social scientists from psychology and communication have used the schema construct to help explain how the mind copes with the daily onslaught of new information (Crocker, Fiske, & Taylor, 1984; Crockett, 1988; Fiske & Taylor, 1984; Graber, 1988; Reeves, Chaffee, & Tims, 1982; Wicks, 1986). Recent studies designed to test the construct empirically suggest that it will continue to play an important role in mass communication research for some time to come (Garramone, Steele, & Pinkleton, 1989; Meadowcroft & Reeves, 1989; Wicks, 1990; Wicks & Drew, 1991).

But what, specifically, are schemata? A schema may be viewed as a "cognitive structure that represents organized knowledge about a given concept or type of stimulus" abstracted from prior experience (Fiske & Taylor, 1984, p. 139). For any given news topic, such as politics, economics, or social welfare, people have from zero to many schemata upon which to draw. Research suggests, however, that most people use relatively few schemata in the course of information processing. Terms such as *prototypes* (Cantor & Mischel, 1977, 1979), *frames* (Minsky, 1975), *stereotypes* (Lippmann, 1922), *social scripts* (Schank & Abelson, 1977), and *cognitive maps* all share a basic theme with the schema concept. While subtle differences exist among these concepts, each refers to a categorization plan by which an individual summons a concrete image of the so-called average category member (Rosch, 1978; Rosch, Mervis, Gray, Johnson, & Boyes-Braem, 1975).

The concept of the "average category member" stems from work begun four decades ago. Solomon Asch (1946) found that people combine personality traits of another person in developing an overall impression. He discovered that people tend to classify the picture by adding information not provided (Tesser, 1978). This gap-filling or *inference function* may explain, for example, why people might automatically think of Palestinian terrorists when the words *airplane hijacking* are mentioned. In thinking of a "chair," most people would summon a mental picture of a four-legged object used for sitting upon, rather than a king's throne or a dollhouse chair, even though all three qualify.

Schema theory presumes that people are forced to be "cognitive misers" because of limited processing abilities; people simply cannot hope to hold in memory every discrete item of information encountered (Lippmann, 1922). To cope with this "information tide," people classify and organize information as it is received to make living more manageable (Graber, 1988). Schemata provide a means by which the world can be efficiently classified and organized.

Researchers have expressed a decided preference for experiments rather than surveys to assess the presence, type, and complexity of cognitive schemata. Lau (1986) notes that surveys inevitably "must include a good deal of random noise, which will decrease the power of the analyses to find significant effects." Common sense provides most people with something to say about a topic when provided with a subject category—if for no reason other than to avoid creating the impression that they are uninformed.

Schema theory rests on the assumption that general knowledge structures guide the processing of specific information. In order to test this proposition, specific information must be provided to the respondent and then followed up with measures believed to assess information-processing capabilities (Graber, 1988). Accurate and articulate responses to survey questions may indeed demonstrate the presence of a well-developed schema. However, researchers must once again resort to assuming that it is the schema (and not specific knowledge) that has been tapped.

Experimental approaches permit manipulation of messages. Many of the past studies have involved instructions to subjects designed to invoke a specific schema. Stimulus materials, often in the form of a topical text concerning the hypothesized schema, are introduced to the subjects. The subjects are then tested to evaluate presumed script guidance of message processing. Measures of processing commonly used include (a) recall tests, (b) the ability of subjects to infer from the knowledge set, and (c) clustering of related concepts. Descriptions of the experimental designs and examples of how these measures are used will be provided shortly. The experimental designs and measurement approaches presented in this chapter may serve as models for future research on the schema construct.

LITERATURE REVIEW

Schema Theory Background

Three strains of thought processes dominate the social psychology literature: "consistency seekers," "naive scientists," and "cognitive misers" (Lau, 1986; Taylor, 1981). Consistency seekers are motivated to minimize inconsistencies by revising an element of a belief system such as an attitude to permit cognitive consistency, thereby reducing or eliminating dissonance (Festinger, 1957; Heider, 1946, 1958). The naive scientist approach suggests that people methodically and rationally solve problems and deduce answers from careful analysis (Jones & Davis, 1965). Recent research suggests that people rarely utilize such precision in problem solving (Nisbett & Ross, 1980).

The third major strain of thinking and perceiving suggests that people are cognitive misers, forced to economize in processing new information (Crocker et al., 1984; O'Sullivan & Durso, 1984; Tesser, 1978; Tesser & Leone, 1977; Valenti & Tesser, 1981). This concept stems from work beginning with Bartlett (1932), who suggested that "organized knowledge structures," which he called schemata, develop and grow as people develop expertise in a given topical area.

The chief objective in schematic thinking is ease and efficiency in handling information, so that the essence of the information can be used quickly for ordinary human interactions and judgments (Cohen, 1981). Social schemata help us to "structure, organize, and interpret new information; they facilitate encoding, storage, and retrieval of relevant information; they can affect the time it takes to process information, and the speed with which problems can be solved. Schemata also serve interpretive and inferential functions" (Crocker et al., 1984, p. 197).

When new information is deposited into a schema, the structure grows in complexity (Taylor & Crocker, 1981). Complexity implies cohesive linkages among a wide variety of concepts. To visualize the concept, consider an example from the physical sciences. Bohr's model of the helium atom, with a pair of neutrons, protons, and electrons, will suffice. This may be viewed as the physical science equivalent of a simple schema. Alternatively, gold, with 70 protons and electrons and 118 neutrons, is a highly complex structure. A complex schema, like gold, is highly compact and hard to alter. Each electron may be viewed as a discrete piece of information, but the collective atom is the most important unit.

One might wonder if shared belief systems and the schema concept are semantic equivalents. Although the two overlap, differences do exist. Shared belief systems provide avenues whereby people may "communicate thoughts and ideas" (DeFleur & Ball-Rokeach, 1982, p. 138). Rokeach (1960) suggests that people utilize a highly organized belief-attitude-value system that guides the behavior of the individual: "All of these conceptually distinct components—the countless beliefs, their organization into thousands of attitudes, the several dozens of hierarchically arranged terminal values—are organized to form a single, functionally interconnected belief system" (p. 215). Near the core of the belief system is a set of relatively stable and unchangeable beliefs. At the perimeter of the system lie many unimportant and changeable beliefs.

As with theories associated with shared belief systems, schema theory suggests that highly evolved schemata are much more difficult to alter than are simple schemata. And shared schematic concepts, of a "chair" or "democracy," for example, permit people to communicate and exchange ideas easily. For Rokeach (1960), certain "primitive beliefs" are learned by direct contact with the object of belief and are reinforced by general agreement by one's peers. These indisputable truisms, such as "The sun sets in the west" and "Nothing is certain but death and taxes," tend to be located at the center of the belief system. They are also probably a part of well-defined schemata for "the solar system" and "the tax system."

Schema theory suggests that people are active processors of information and that schematic thinking derives from the need to organize thinking for the purpose of cognitive economy. As such, it may serve as an appropriate modification to Rokeach's approach, despite inherent differences underlying assumptions associated with schema and consistency theories. Consistency theories presume that people try to make information consistent with their belief systems. But, contrary to cognitive consistency theories, schema theory rests on the assumption that people are not highly motivated to make their thinking consistent with general principles, such as values and attitudes stored in the mind.

Social cognition researchers propose that people identify categories of object stimuli and apply appropriate schemata to them. Thus a schema for a bird is applied to a blue jay rather than an airplane even though both have wings and fly through the air. People assess similarities among objects and then derive an average or central tendency for the category (Rosch, 1978). They then make a cognitive comparison between the available schemata prototypes before assigning an object to a specific category. This process utilizes both prior experience and inference (Hayes-Roth & Hayes-Roth, 1977).

Schema theory also rests on the assumption that old information affects the manner in which we "interpret new information in social settings" and elsewhere (Fiske & Dyer, 1985). Knowledge about others and ourselves guides our responses to new information. This has been studied in work on stereotyping (Allport, 1954; Lippmann, 1922), impression information (Asch, 1946; Bruner & Tagiuri, 1954), and attribution (Heider, 1958). Social schema researchers have built upon this foundation in order to explain how prior knowledge guides attention, memory, and interpretation of social information (Fiske & Taylor, 1984).

A Social Schemata Typology

Social psychology researchers have devoted an abundance of time to studying four types of "social schemata." Fiske and Taylor (1984, p. 149) have defined these content schemata in the following manner:

(1) *Person schemata:* People's understanding of the psychology of typical or specific individuals, composed of traits and goals, helps them to categorize others and to remember schema-relevant behavior.

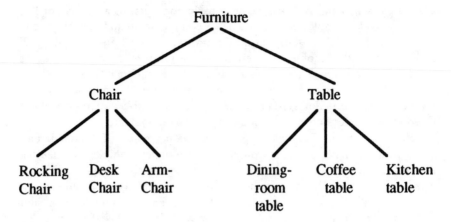

Figure 1. Hierarchy of object categories in levels of abstraction.
SOURCE: S. T. Fiske and S. E. Taylor, *Social Cognition.* Copyright 1984 by McGraw-Hill Publishing Company. Reprinted by permission.

(2) *Self-schemata:* General information about one's own psychology makes up a complex, easily accessible verbal self-concept that guides information processing about the self.

(3) *Role schemata:* Intergroup perception and stereotyping are affected by role schemata that describe the appropriate norms and behavior for broad social categories, based on age, race, sex, and occupation.

(4) *Event schemata:* People's prior knowledge of the typical sequence of events in standard social occasions helps them to understand ambiguous information, to remember relevant information, and to infer consistent information where it is missing. Schank and Abelson (1977) have called these "action-based" or "event schemata scripts."

This social schema typology offers a useful starting point in the study of individual schemata utilized in the course of assessing news and media information. Most news stories possess elements of a particular "event." Scripts are perhaps the single most important consideration for media researchers, as news and information is presented in these terms. Other schemata, such as person schemata, are also important, however, because people play major roles in most news stories.

Levels of Abstraction

Schemata exist at differing levels of abstraction, but people tend to operate at the middle level of abstraction. The illustration of a schema for furniture shown in Figure 1 may help clarify this concept. The upper level is the most abstract schema. The second and third levels represent more precise levels of the schema (Fiske & Taylor, 1984, p. 147).

Schema theory suggests that people typically develop a schema for each of the items listed in the figure. The highest level is the most abstract level, in this case, "furniture." However, the concept lacks clarity and precision. Unless a house is entirely unfurnished, it is doubtful that a person would say that he or she needs to go to the store to purchase a new "chair" or "table" in the near future. When queried on the specifics, the individual may report that a "rocking chair" or a "kitchen table" is the specific type of furniture to be purchased.

However, the second level of abstraction tends to be utilized with the greatest regularity. Scholars suggest that the optimal level of abstraction is the middle level, as it provides for broad and inclusive categorization while permitting a degree of descriptive richness (Rosch, 1978; Rosch et al., 1975).

Schema Activation

But what causes the development and activation of schemata? A schema begins when a person comes in contact with a new idea or concept. There is nothing mysterious about the process—it is simply the basic root of social learning. Abelson (1976) has demonstrated that as people encounter information that is in harmony with or compatible to an established schema, the structure grows in complexity, which is defined here as more abstract and more general. Schemata grow from concrete to general until they are highly sophisticated.

Consider the child who watches a television newscast and sees Palestinian terrorists hijacking a plane. The schema constructed—in this case the *script*—may be that bearded men steal planes. More information, however, will lead the child to alter the schema. Eventually, the child will develop a schema that incorporates other essential elements of the story, such as the political motivations associated with terrorism and a general connection to political and economic issues in the Middle East.

Schema theory suggests that a concrete example forms an impression that serves as a foundation. Links between concepts contained within a schema develop as the individual makes connections between concepts. As the person develops expertise in a topic, the schema grows in complexity, abstraction, and compactness. A tight or compact schema is one that is highly developed and is relatively unwavering (Fiske & Pavelchak, 1984).

But if individuals possess many schemata, what dictates which will be activated when a person comes in contact with information provided through the media? Incoming information typically invokes either the most developed or the most recently activated schema. As of yet, it is unclear which will be activated, although researchers continue to probe this question (Higgins & King, 1981; Wyer & Srull, 1981). Recent studies have focused on what is known as the "priming" effect. One view of priming is that when a concept is placed at the top of the mental heap or "storage bin," it displaces others in a downward direction (Srull & Wyer, 1979; Wyer & Srull, 1980, 1981). If, for example, a person learns of five airplane hijackings in a month, that person is likely to activate a Middle East hijack schema if he or she hears only a portion of newscast such as ". . . passengers arrived safely."

Schema Change

The literature suggests three models of schema change:

(1) The *bookkeeping model* proposes that each discrepant encounter changes the schema gradually (Fiske & Taylor, 1984).

(2) The *conversion model* proposes that a single concentrated encounter with incongruous information can change a schema totally (Rothbart, 1981).

(3) The *subtyping model* suggests that incongruence causes the perceiver to form subcategories within the overall schema (Taylor, 1981).

The subtyping model has received empirical support when these models have been pitted against one another (Weber & Crocker, 1983). Specifically, people apparently have little difficulty making an exception to the rule when it comes to a schema. Suppose a person reads of a Palestinian "terrorist" who forcibly took over an airplane and then passed out flowers and released his hostages. While the incident clearly contains elements of the prototypical hijacking situation, an "exception" makes this "script" strikingly different from what one would expect. In this case, it is possible that a moderate change might take place in the schema. However, it also seems clear that the incident might simply be filed away as a nonprototypical occurrence.

Level of Expertise

Schemata may be used in different ways, according to levels of development. For example, novices in a topical domain tend to rely most heavily on information that is consistent with a particular schema. Chi and Koeske (1983) propose that knowledge possessed by experts in a given topical domain is denser—they possess more knowledge and the concepts are better integrated—than knowledge possessed by novices in that domain. Their work reflects a basic underpinning of schema theory—that "experts" may be expected to draw on more schemata when processing information than will "novices." When a new piece of information reinforces old knowledge, it tends to be easily accessible in recall tests. By contrast, "experts" use "schema-discrepant" as well as "schema-consistent" information (Fiske, Kinder, & Larter, 1983). Experts tend to be less willing to alter schemata when confronted with discrepant information, because they apparently have more invested in their schemata than do novices (Crocker et al., 1984). These people, with well-developed schemata, seem willing to accept "exceptions to the rule" without dramatically altering the schemata. However, well-reasoned arguments are capable of causing individuals with considerable expertise to adjust their schemata as a result of the new information encountered.

Expertise on a topic may be associated with many factors. Innate intelligence or curiosity about certain people, institutions, themes, or events can lead to expertise. The amount of effort devoted to learning about a topic can contribute. The role of the media in setting topical agendas can also lead to expertise (McCombs & Shaw, 1972), and the uses and gratifications approach can explain why people choose to attend to certain types of messages (Blumler & Katz, 1974; Rosengren, Wenner, & Palmgreen, 1985). In short, expertise is associated with numerous factors. In any event, an "expert" on a subject would be expected to have not only more schemata but also more complex schemata upon which to draw.

Assimilation and Accommodation

Piaget (1970) characterized assimilation as interpretation of information in the context of an existing schema. *Assimilation* thus refers to the process by which discrete units of information become a part of or absorbed into the schema. Information assimilated into a schema will tend to reinforce the schema. Conversely, information inconsistent with an established schema will be accommodated by the schema. *Accommodation* refers to the process of either initiating a new schema or giving up attempts to interpret the information.

Schemata resist change even though people rarely find a precise fit between a schema and a piece of information (Crocker et al., 1984). Discrepant information can cause a schema to change when the message is irrefutable or undeniable. A moderate mismatch between the schema and the message typically leads to message assimilation. And if the discrepant information may be viewed as situational, or as an exception to the schema, it clearly will have little impact (Crocker, Hannah, & Weber, 1983).

What transpires when the individual has an ill-defined schema upon which to draw? Typically, a weak or ambiguous image will be summoned. And what occurs when an individual lacks confidence in the schema selected? In similar fashion, the individual may then search for another schema (Fiske & Taylor, 1984) or alter the schema originally summoned (Rothbart, Evans, & Fulero, 1979). If information is inconsistent with an established schema, an individual may simply assume that the new information is "an exception" to the established schema. So what transpires if an individual is told that "a Norwegian organization was responsible for the hijacking of an American jet"? Individuals with limited "hijack" schemata may begin forming a schema connecting Norwegians with hijackings. People with well-defined hijack schemata would likely challenge the credibility of the source or conclude that the incident was nontypical.

Individuals may change their schemata when they are forced to develop counterarguments for those schemata (Fiske & Taylor, 1984). Existing schemata may be expanded and refined when direct and indirect experiences challenge their accuracy and completeness. However, major alterations or revisions of a well-defined schema based on a single discrepant item seem to be the exception rather than the rule. Verification of the schema selected is thus based on a thorough evaluation of the schema that is first invoked.

Summary

The external information environment largely determines what schemata are developed. In view of this, agenda-setting theories seem to complement the schema concept. That is, schemata will develop and grow based largely on what is selected for presentation by media gatekeepers. Yet random exposure to banner headlines or the lead story on the evening news can hardly be considered the sole determinant of what schemata will evolve. Information availability is also related to schema formation—those with access to modern communication tools such as radio and television have a greater opportunity to receive information (Dizard, 1989). Innate intelligence, individual effort or motivation, and perceived gratifications associated with information gain all have effects. Additionally relevant are the expectations of peers and colleagues in the workplace that intelligent persons keep well informed. The so-called civic obligation of people to keep abreast of current affairs may also serve as a motivation to obtain information. Indeed, the list of reasons for schema development may be nearly endless. The basic point is that while some changes are clearly a function of random information encounters, a wide variety of factors are involved in schema growth and development.

In summary, the term *schema* refers to an organized knowledge structure based on a subjective theory that guides a person in processing information (Fiske & Linville, 1980; Tesser, 1978). In guiding thought processes, schemata grow and develop from moment to moment because of the addition and incorporation of new inputs of information (Bartlett, 1932; Fiske & Linville, 1980). Schemata contain networks of associations that provide rules for making inferences about various stimuli (Fiske & Taylor, 1984).

SCHEMA PROCESSING MODELS

A good model is simple and relies on a limited number of assumptions. It provides the possibility of generating a large number of predictions, and it generally makes a statement about a process. A good model suggests outcomes with important social and scholarly implications (Lave & March, 1975). Furthermore, a good model produces interesting implications that surprise us and suggest new directions for research.

A good information-processing model should seek to explain not only *how* information is processed, but also *if* information is effectively and efficiently processed by the receiver. In this case, processing may be associated with effective information transmission and retention between mass communicators and individuals.

Information-processing models specify the steps intervening between stimulus and response. Broadbent (1958) breaks information processing into several key components. Initially, a statement or question will be attended to. An individual may then engage in a search for relevant information on the topic. The person may then search for additional reinforcing information. Finally, the person will respond with an appropriate statement or answer.

Attention and encoding are the first steps in social information processing (Kahneman, 1973). Before any information processing can occur, the stimuli outside the person must be brought to the mind. Whether attention is directed outward, toward encoding external objects, or inward, toward memory, it usually is seen as having two components: direction (selectivity) and intensity (effort) (Burnkrandt & Sawyer, 1983). The processes associated with searching for an appropriate response represent the schema activation process.

Two models illustrating the process of schematic thinking are introduced below. Conspicuous in their absence are models that separate the long-term and short-term memory stores (Atkinson & Shiffrin, 1968). This is because schema theory operates from the assumption that short-term memory is merely that portion of the long-term memory that is currently accessible or activated (Norman & Bobrow, 1975, 1976).

The "data-pool" model (Norman & Bobrow, 1976) outlines a course by which physical signals reach the sensory organs and are perceived. The new information is condensed and simplified for brief storage in short-term memory.

> It then becomes part of the *datapool* which is checked against the reservoir of "memory schemata" to determine whether it can be appropriately integrated. If assimilation is achieved, the information becomes part of the individual's repertoire of schemata. Failing integration, either because no suitable schema is available or because an overload of information prevents preliminary processing, the information passes quickly from consciousness. (Graber, 1988, p. 123)

The data-pool model presumes that cognitive processing is based on several properties (Norman & Bobrow, 1976, pp. 123-125):

(1) There is a single, limited pool of resources from which processes must draw.

(2) Memory is constructed of active units—schemata—that use the data available in a common pool, perform computations upon these data, and then send new results back (into the common pool or to other schemata) and/or

request specific information from other schemata. Schemata communicate with one another either directly or through the data pool.

(3) Schemata are required. A schema consists of a framework for tying together the information about any given concept or event, with specifications about the types of interrelations and restrictions upon the way things fit together. Schemata can activate procedures capable of operating upon local information and the common pool of data.

(4) Schemata can be invoked by the occurrence of data in the common data base relevant to their operations, or by requests from either other schemata or the central communication mechanism.

(5) There are no fixed memory locations in the head; therefore, memory structures must refer to one another by means of descriptions of the information that they seek.

The model suggests that people respond to the environment they encounter firsthand or through the media by selecting appropriate schemata. For example, the introduction to a political television news item might prime schemata associated with issues. But as the piece unfolds and it becomes clear that it will deal with a political candidate, the issues schema might be retired and another, more appropriate, schema may be activated, such as one associated with personality traits.

As illustrated in Figure 2, the process of moving from schema to schema is quite fluid. And a good number of schemata might be linked at any given time. The selected schemata provide conceptual guidance in determining both where else to seek new data and how to interpret current data. The Norman and Bobrow model provides a useful overarching framework concerning information processing.

The data-pool model offered by Norman and Bobrow serves as an appropriate illustrative model, clearly tracing the process by which schemata are activated. However, it fails to explain adequately the precise channels through which specific types of information must pass during the processing of information. Other scholars, such as Hastie (1981), have offered models that trace the process of schematic thinking in detail. Figure 3 suggests that schemata are activated to give structure to information. At the core of the Hastie model is the belief that the individual is active, goal seeking, and purposeful (Bower, 1975). Hence people use schemata to comprehend news and information, leading to sensible interpretations of day-to-day events and personal connections between themselves and the new information.

The Hastie model, when applied to news and information acquisition, may offer clues on the connection between the uses and gratifications approach and agenda-setting. Fruitful theories provide predictive capability, heuristic value, links to the observable, parsimony, and generalizability. Implicit to the Hastie model is the idea that people using more schemata (in

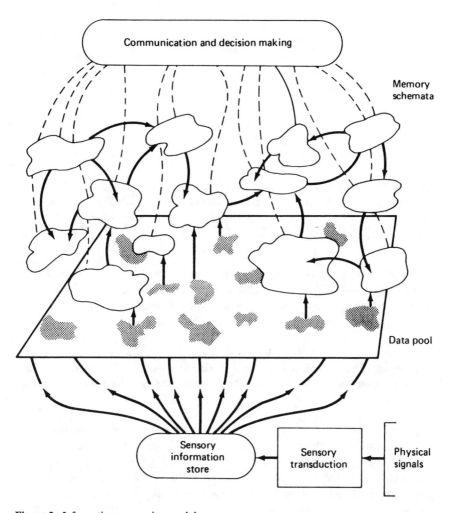

Figure 2. Information-processing model.
SOURCE: Donald R. Norman and David G. Bobrow, "On the Role of Active Memory Processes in Perception and Cognition," in Charles Cofer (Ed.), *The Structure of Human Memory* (p. 118). Copyright 1976 by W. H. Freeman and Company. Reprinted by permission.

absolute terms), as well as more sophisticated schemata, will be better equipped to process new information related to existing schemata.

The Hastie model suggests that people must react to an event in one of two ways: They must find an appropriate schema and assimilate the new information, or accommodate the new information by either beginning a new schema or accepting the new information as an exception to the rule. Consider a point concerning processing of television news information. Graber (1988) notes that, of "the 15 or 18 stories presented in a television newscast,

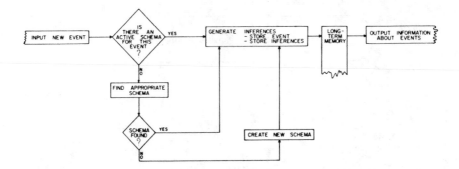

Figure 3. Flowchart diagram to represent a schematic perception and memory information-processing system. Arrows indicate the flow of information among subparts cf the system.

SOURCE: R. Hastie, "Schematic Principles in Human Memory," in E. T. Higgins, C. P. Herman, & M. P. Zanna (Eds.), *Social Cognition: The Ontario Symposium* (p. 45). Copyright 1981 by Lawrence Erlbaum Associates. Reprinted by permission.

no more than one is retained sufficiently well so that it can be recalled a short time afterward" (p. 250). One might conclude that most of the stories failed to activate an appropriate schema and simply exited without interpretation, but Graber provides an alternative explanation:

> [Use of schemata] allow[s] individuals to extract only those limited amounts of information from news stories that they consider important for incorporation into their thinking. The Schema process also facilitates integration of new information into existing knowledge. (p. 250)

In other words, a person may fail to recall a news item shortly after exposure because he or she already knew the information. Or, to put it another way, the new information simply confirmed what was already filed away and therefore failed to create a lasting impression. This interpretation suggests that the items conformed to a developed schema and did not provoke the development of a new schema.

The models by Norman and Bobrow and Hastie agree that schemata will inevitably be used when an individual comes in contact with specific types of information. For example, by conducting experiments with different categories of subjects, it is possible to evaluate processing operations that are carried out as information passes through the formal model. The models are helpful in providing a clear explanation of the process of human cognition as it pertains to information acquisition through the mass media.

Although these models are elegant in their simplicity, they are merely plausible explanations of the schema activation and usage process. Models must be tested empirically to gain widespread acceptance. Some recent studies have been conducted to measure cognitive schemata; several are described below in the interest of reinforcing the bedrock upon which these models stand.

Schema Measurement

The communication field has a rich research tradition in measuring and evaluating the effects of media messages on audiences and the society. Research has focused on topics such as the impact of television on children and potential for media-inspired social behavior. Schema theory and measurement offer the promise of putting this past research into context. They promise explanations as to *why* certain messages have effects on certain people that lead to specific responses and behavior.

The abstractness of the schema concept prompted early researchers in this area simply to assume the presence of schemata in information processing. This assumption stemmed from the lack of techniques available for "getting inside people's minds" to evaluate the presence or sophistication of a particular schema. During the last two decades, however, several approaches to schema measurement have been employed that to some degree circumvent this problem. While less precise than measuring column inches in a newspaper or counting stories on the evening news, schema measurement provides an avenue by which the schema notion may progress as a useful theoretical construct.

Cognition researchers believe that high *recall* of information is related to well-developed schemata. This is because new information will either (a) reinforce old knowledge or (b) obtrude because it is not consistent with a developed schema. *Inferential* abilities are assumed to designate schemata presence and sophistication, because people with well-developed schemata in a particular domain typically find it easier to draw on past experience to fill in missing information. Finally, *conceptual clustering* measures the manner in which people group related concepts. Researchers typically use several measures concurrently to test the validity of the scores obtained.

Experimental Versus Survey Strategies

The bulk of the literature on schema measurement comes from social psychology, a science deeply rooted in the experimental tradition. It thus comes as no surprise that most studies have employed experimental techniques. However, it is more than tradition that has prompted psychologists to favor experiments over surveys. Most schema research designs query individuals on a specific set of information or a "knowledge set" that has been provided by the experimenter. This enables the researcher to evaluate recall based upon the specifics of the information provided; it presumably guards against purely conjectural or impromptu subject responses. As opposed to experiments, the survey approach would fail to guard against this systematic bias.

Experimenters typically present subjects with an unfamiliar "knowledge set" and then ask them to answer questions or make inferences about it. The knowledge set may be a new message, such as information on the mating habits of the South American ant bear, or it may be new, surprising, information; for example, the researcher may suggest that forest fires are beneficial for forests, irrespective of what Smoky the Bear has been preaching for several decades (Wicks & Drew, 1991).

Schema theory suggests that an individual possessing a well-defined schema in a particular topical domain will have more success at recalling information accurately, will infer more confidently, and will tend to group or cluster related concepts more so than will an individual with an ill-defined schema. It is this introduction of the knowledge set that makes the experimental approach generally superior to the survey approach. Experimenters can test what "stuck" with the subjects.

In recent years, researchers have employed survey strategies to evaluate schema complexity, drawing upon a more general kind of knowledge. As Lau (1986) has noted, the survey approach inevitably must include a good deal of random noise, which will decrease the power of the analyses to find significant effects. Hence experimental approaches tend to be superior as an analytical tool.

Schema Measurement Techniques

Topics presented in video form, or as text or symbols, have served as the materials designed to invoke cognitive schemata in many studies. The amounts of recall, inferential abilities, and clustering of concepts have served as the dependent measures. A review of some of the work along these lines may illustrate the range of approaches employed.

Much of this work has focused on shared knowledge of routine activities (e.g., eating in a restaurant or visiting a dentist) and how that knowledge is organized and used to understand and remember narrative texts. Bower, Black, and Turner (1979) suggest we use cognitive scripts to anchor these action stereotypes. Schank and Abelson (1977) propose that part of our knowledge is organized around hundreds of stereotypical situations based on routine activities. A series of recent studies have suggested that stereotyping is common (Anderson & Pichert, 1978; Bower et al., 1979; Cantor & Mischel, 1979; Conover & Feldman, 1981; Fiske et al., 1983; Fiske, Taylor, Etcoff, & Laufer, 1979; Markus & Smith, 1981; Ostrom, Pryor, & Simpson, 1981).

Assessing Shared Script Schemata Using Recall Tests

Bower et al. (1979) investigated whether a "cultural uniformity" was responsible for shared scripts. Students at Stanford University were asked to generate events or actions for one of five situations: attending a lecture, visiting a doctor, shopping at a grocery store, eating at a fancy restaurant, or getting up in the morning and getting off to school.[1] The study found a great deal of agreement in the "basic action" descriptive language used. A total of 161 subjects participated in the study, and out of 730 statements they made associated with the restaurant script, only 4 were unique. The pattern was similar for the other four stories. In effect, the agreed-upon social norms learned in early childhood and reinforced throughout the years prompted the subjects to conjure up similar mental pictures of given events.

Bower et al. (1979) also demonstrated that script recall is enhanced when people are provided with several related stories. The researchers tested recall on implied information by asking 18 respondents to read a series of 18 short stories. Each story was different, but many were related in terms of general themes. For example, stories titled "The Doctor," "The Dentist," and "The Chiropractor" were among those included. However, each respondent was asked to read from one to three of these stories.[2] The subjects then wrote down all of the information they could recall about certain stories. The results were subjected to an ANOVA in which stated actions were compared to unstated script actions and finally to other actions. The researchers concluded that reading more than one version of a story increased the percentage of unstated script actions that a subject recorded. They explain that "multi-instance texts create more intrusions, there are more opportunities for 'output interference,' whereby output of an intrusion causes forgetting of a not-yet-recalled stated action" (p. 193). To summarize, subjects falsely recall actions that are in underlying scripts but not necessarily in the text, especially if two or more related texts are presented.

In another set of experiments, Anderson and Pichert (1978) looked at the processing of goal-directed social events. The dependent measure was level of processing based on information salience rooted in the directives of the researcher. The independent variable was goal-directed processing, which was operationalized by asking respondents to assume a given perspective. A group of 32 student subjects read a story about the behavior of two boys who skipped school. The action in the text was set in the home of one of the boys. The passage contained information of interest to a prospective home buyer and to a burglar. A knowledge set containing 72 facts was provided.

Half of the students were assigned to a group that was asked to read the text from the perspective of a burglar (burglar schema) and the other half read it from the perspective of a home buyer (home buyer schema). They then wrote down all they could recall about the story. After a distracter test, the students were again asked to recall facts from the story, but half of each group was told to do so from the other perspective. The researchers then tallied the recalled facts from the differing perspectives to evaluate whether or not processing varied depending upon the perspective of the individual attempting to retrieve the information. An ANOVA performed on the data suggested that instructions to take a new perspective led subjects to invoke a schema that provided cues for processing of different categories of story information.

Fiske et al. (1979) explicitly instructed 50 student subjects to take the points of view of individuals in a text they had provided. The researchers told the students to imagine an accident from the point of view of the motorcyclist or of the cabbie involved in the accident, or from the perspective of a spectator. This set of experiments was designed to test recall based on visual point-of-view influences. The students answered a series of questions based on a text they had read about the mishap. The questions probed specific details, such as memory of the events leading up to the accident. The students then assessed responsibility for the accident to one of the drivers involved. The recall and attribution data were analyzed separately.

The independent variable in this experiment was the perspective of the person reading the text. The dependent measures were drawn from the answers to the open-ended questions. An ANOVA involving recall suggested that recall is enhanced based on visual perspective and goal orientation. Of prime concern in this study is that people selectively processed visual cues when all of the information was semantically equal. Specific groups of people processed information in a similar manner based on a point-of-view schema invoked by the researchers.

Assessing Shared Story Schemata Using Recall Tests

Meadowcroft and Reeves (1989) suggest a measure of "story schema" in children. According to these researchers, a story schema is, similar to a script, a hierarchical memory clustering that represents prototypical story structure, including typical story elements and information about how the elements are interrelated (Mandler & Johnson, 1977; Thorndyke & Yekovich, 1980). Meadowcroft and Reeves hypothesized that story schema development would influence how children attend to and process television story content. Noting that most television programs tell stories, they suggest schemata may be important in influencing children's processing and comprehension of television programs. In their study, they predicted that story schemata would affect information attended to, how children organized incoming information while watching television stories, how children related story events, and what story content would be remembered.

A two-session testing method was utilized. In the first testing session, children saw two children's stories on videotape and were then given seven still pictures depicting the action in these videotapes. In the sequencing task (the first assessment measure) children were asked to sequence these pictures in the proper order. In the sorting task (the second assessment measure) children were asked which of the seven pictures from the story represented important story content. Performance on these two tasks was used to assign children to either low or high story schema groups for the next phase of the experiment.

In the experimental session, children in the low and high story schema groups were randomly assigned to view a story on television that was structured like a typical story or to view a story that had no underlying story structure (events not related). Recall data were submitted to an ANOVA on story schema development (low/high) by story content (central/incidental) and by story structure (story/nonstory). The measure of story schema was based on the children's performance on the two assessment tasks. Dependent variables were the amount of attention allocated to central and incidental story content and memory of story content.

Consistent with the hypotheses, the experiment demonstrated that story schema development was associated with (a) more efficient patterns (children with high story schema skills allocated less cognitive effort when attempting to tell the story), (b) greater flexibility in attention allocation (these children allocated attention differently to the same content between program structure condition, indicating flexibility in allocation decisions), and (c) greater coordination between attention and memory processing. The results indicate that it is important to consider differences in terms of an individual's strategies for processing and making sense of information from television programs. As this study and others (e.g., Collins, 1983) have shown, interpretation is likely influenced by existing memory structures in organizing, interpreting, and storing program content.

Assessing Schemata Related to Expertise Using Recall Tests

The work by Meadowcroft and Reeves dovetails with a study conducted by Fiske et al. (1983) that suggests that political information processing vitally depends on past experience and that individuals will vary enormously in both the availability of schemata and how schemata are used. The politically involved should differ from the uninvolved in their processing of information about politics, in the nature of schemata available to them, in the ease with which such schemata are invoked, and in the facility with which such schemata are employed in information processing. As such, assimilation of information should be facilitated if an individual is politically astute.

Fiske et al. (1983) designed a series of experiments intended to evaluate specific differences in political information processing. They assembled a group of political "experts" and a group of political "novices." They operationalized this concept by evaluating individual levels of political knowledge using standard measures provided by the Center for Political Studies at the University of Michigan. The researchers predicted that both the political experts and the novices would use information consistent with their shared prior knowledge set, but they hypothesized that the experts would also use information inconsistent within the knowledge set provided. They tested this by asking 82 student subjects to participate in a media study. The researchers prepared a text about Mauritius, a little-known country in the Indian Ocean. The text was laden with concepts tending toward democratic and communist ideologies. The independent variable was manipulated in the opening sentence of the text by suggesting that the country was communist, democratic, or neither.

The students read the text and then were asked to recall as many facts as possible. Amount of recall was measured by counting the facts recalled and by submitting the recall data to an ANOVA. Fiske and Kinder (1981) concluded from this study that "through practice, experts acquire more-and-more complexly organized knowledge, which includes strategies for dealing with particular domains. These knowledge structures in our theoretical vocabulary, schemata, encompass both declarative knowledge (descriptions of attributes) and procedural knowledge (rules or strategies for the use of that knowledge)" (p. 177).

These experiments collectively suggest that people tend to conceptualize action-based routines in a similar fashion based in large part on cultural norms dictated by the society. Yet differing social roles, level of expertise, interest, motivation to learn about a topic, and agendas set by media gatekeepers explain why people process information differently.

Garramone et al. (1989) investigated the role of "image" and "issue" schemata in political information processing. They suggest that people may tend to be motivated more by one or the other. They hypothesized that those characterized as *image processors* would focus on visual aspects of media messages more than would those characterized as *issue processors*. In the first phase of the study, 239 subjects were sorted into one of the two categories. Those who were neither issue nor image dominated were removed, leaving a sample of 200.

The stimulus materials were manipulated by presenting attractive or unattractive candidates in two commercials. Students were then asked to recall all they could from the commercials. Responses were coded based on visual or auditory aspects of the message. The researchers report that image processors encoded more visual information from the political commercials than did the issue processors.

Wicks and Drew (1991) used the schema construct to investigate the effect of consistent versus inconsistent news on schema development. A total of 178 experimental subjects were presented with information designed to invoke schemata on two different topics—forest fires and population growth.[3] This information was presented in text form. Subjects were then given additional information on these topics that was consistent, inconsistent, or unrelated to the first story. The second set was issue specific to either the Yellowstone fires of 1988 or concerns about lack of population growth in Quebec. In other words, the second story gave a concrete example refuting or reinforcing the information provided in the initial general story that was provided in order to establish the schemata.

Those in the inconsistent group that had read that forest fires were basically harmful to the environment but had then read, viewed, or listened to a second story suggesting that fires have long-term cleansing effects recalled more facts than those who had received consistent sets of information. The authors suggest that the ubiquitous nature of the Yellowstone story provided a complex knowledge set for the subjects. Hence inconsistencies obtruded, leading to enhanced recall of the news story. A recall difference for the population story was not found, and the researchers suggest that the obscurity of the issue had not provided a knowledge base upon which subjects could build. Hence inconsistencies did not obtrude as they had for the Yellowstone story.

In a follow-up study, Wicks (1990) predicted (a) that people would recall more facts when a message with a high degree of personal relevance was presented on television rather than in newspapers, and (b) that television leads to more accurate recall of facts when the information contained in the message is personally relevant. A two-phase factorial design was used. Randomly assigned subjects were exposed to two sets of news stories. The first part of the experiment was intended to provide baseline knowledge about three topics by invoking schemata for certain common topics and then adding additional reinforcing information. An initial set of three newspaper stories was presented in text form, and then a second set of four stories was presented in either television or newspaper form. The experimental story was titled "Sunglasses: The Pros and Cons." This story explained that most sunglasses fail to block out enough harmful ultraviolet radiation from the sun. As a result, exposure to the sun could lead to cataracts and other injuries to the eyes. ANOVA suggested that television appears to have an edge in facilitating recall of facts for personally relevant information and tends to aid in accuracy or recall as well.

Inferential Testing

Several of the studies described thus far suggest that people apparently conceptualize simple action-based routines in similar fashion. But a good deal of work has focused on individual difference factors, such as education, innate intelligence, and motivation. Recent work suggests that individual differences provide for substantially different levels of processing of information (Fiske et al., 1983; Graber, 1988; Markus, 1977). This variation in processing can be analyzed by investigating differences among people in their inference-making capabilities.

A number of studies suggest that people tend to use beliefs and attitudes to make inferences about others. Mintz (1956) found a positive relationship between children's ages and how old they believed Peter Pan to be. Golding (1954) suggests that people perceive the happiness of others in relation to their own happiness. Katz and Allport (1931) reported that the likelihood of one's own cheating behavior is related to what one believes about the cheating of others. And Sherif and Hovland (1961) suggest that people interpret others' stands on issues in the context of their own attitudes and beliefs.

Markus (1977; Markus & Smith, 1981) addressed the issue of self-schemata in her classic work on individual differences. She demonstrated that people process information differently depending upon the degree to which a particular stimulus domain is salient. Markus uses the term *schematic* to refer to individuals with significant interest or knowledge in a particular stimulus domain; conversely, *aschematic* describes individuals with little or no knowledge or interest in a particular domain. People predicting their own future behavior will usually extrapolate from their past behavior and attitudes.

Markus hypothesized that self-schema would determine the type of self-judgments that subjects would make and that these judgments would vary in latency depending on the presence and content of self-schemata. She also predicted that individuals with self-schemata (operationalized as highly dependent or independent) should find it easier to describe specific behavior related to their schemata. Further, she proposed that people with well-developed self-schemata would be more certain about their self-judgments.

Bower et al. (1979) suggest that shared scripts are rooted in a form of "cultural uniformity" that tends to cause people to share perceptual stereotypes concerning the manner in which certain typical or routine events unfold. They hypothesized that subjects presented with a hypothetical scenario would add information or misremember facts from a story based on what they expected to transpire. The researchers operationalized their hypothesis by asking 161 student subjects to generate a script (the dependent variable) based on their expectations of how a series of common events such as "ordering a meal in a restaurant" (the independent variables) should unfold. They then assessed the consensual agreement on characters, props, the action contained in the stories, and the elements of the stories that were generated.

Fiske et al. (1983) also used inference measures in the study described earlier. As noted, that study dealt with perceptions of political orientation of the island of Mauritius. The political experts and novices were asked to make decisions about a set of items not included in the text. The researchers asked questions such as "How easy or difficult do you think it would be for a citizen to emigrate from Mauritius?" A 9-point anchored scale with varying degrees of perceived difficulty associated with emigrating was employed. Inferences were analyzed based on the knowledge set using ANOVA (communist/democratic/neither) by expertise (high/low). The subjects also made inferences about the country by providing answers to questions not included in the text. Answers by political novices reflected consistent information. Experts, by contrast, focused more on inconsistencies. Given more information, their inferences were more moderate than were those of the novices.

Wicks and Drew (1991) used inferential testing in their study. Recall that a knowledge set for two news items (forest fires and population growth) had been established. Issue-specific information on the Yellowstone fires and Quebec's population growth was added. The result was that one-third of the subjects had received two consistent stories, one-third had received two inconsistent stories, and one-third had received only one story, combined with an unrelated story.[4]

ANOVA produced significant results for each of the six inference statements based on treatment condition—schema consistent, schema inconsistent, or control. Those who were told that population growth was good and who were then provided a concrete example, as in the Quebec story, inferred that anything that disrupts population growth is bad. The results were similar for the fire story—those who were told that fire is beneficial and then were provided with a concrete example, as in the Yellowstone story, inferred that other natural disasters such as floods and tornadoes are, in fact, beneficial to the environment.

The schema-inconsistent subjects were noncommittal in their responses. The subjects apparently were not able to reconcile quickly the differences in the information. After having been told that fires have a long-term destructive impact, and then been presented with contrary evidence suggesting that the Yellowstone fire was beneficial in certain ways, subjects were unable to infer with much certainty. Hence they tended to waffle by sticking to the middle of the scale. The schema-consistent group, with more complex population and fire schemata, were more willing to take chances even at the risk of being wrong. The control group acted as one might expect—they split the difference between the schema-consistent and schema-inconsistent groups.

Clustering in Free Recall

The adjusted ratio of clustering (ARC) method (Bousfield & Bousfield, 1966; Ostrom et al., 1981; Roenker, Thompson, & Brown, 1971) indexes the deviation of clustering of ideas from levels based on chance. Clustering in free recall identifies the presence of schemata by demonstrating that items within similar categories tend to group together.

Schema theory suggests that this clustering occurs as an economy measure to organize social information. Suppose, for example, that a group of subjects is read a list of words that contains the names of animals randomly interspersed among the names of flowers. Researchers have found that the order in which items are listed in free recall reflects their association in organized memory. Specifically, subjects with well-defined animal and flower schemata will cluster the animals in one part of the recall sequence and flowers in another.

A number of indices for clustering of free recall have been proposed. The relative advantages and disadvantages of many of the early clustering methods have been outlined by Shuell (1969). But one method—the ARC technique—has correlated highly (.90) with other measures (Ostrom et al., 1981). To employ this technique, adjacent pairs of items must be tallied. Since the raw number of adjacent pairs is confounded with total recall of each type, the clustering scores have to be adjusted for the number of pairs expected by chance, which in turn is a function of the number of items in a given topical domain (Fiske et al., 1983).[5]

Reliability and Validity

The fuzziness of the schema construct makes measurement reliability an important concern. Most studies have employed experimental approaches, and college students have typically served as the subject pool. It certainly seems possible that a subject pool composed of students from major research institutions may produce unrepresentative results. In addition, the experimental environment may prompt people to pay attention to facts and details that they may ignore in their homes.

Given these caveats, the empirical research described here collectively suggests that the schema construct is worth pursuing as a theoretical approach. However, it also suggests that several scales should be used concurrently to cross-check the reliability of the results. Several measures reflecting similar patterns of processing are believed to validate each other. Social science research is generally trusted only when several measures agree, especially when the focus of the research is relatively new (Simon & Burnstein, 1985), as is the case with the schema measurement domain.

The measure that permeates virtually all of the literature on schema measurement is that of recall testing. Recall tests have been employed in most of the classic studies during the last decade (Anderson & Pichert, 1978; Bower et al., 1979; Fiske et al., 1979, 1983; O'Sullivan & Durso, 1984; Rothbart et al., 1979; Snyder & Cantor, 1978). The early work in schema measurement relied almost exclusively on recall testing. More recent work has tended to employ other approaches (Fiske et al., 1983; Wicks & Drew, 1991). It should be noted that many of the studies cited were carried out within the last decade. New measurement approaches will likely continue to emerge, but it is impossible at this point to assess with any degree of certainty whether any of these approaches are clearly superior to any others.

Content Validity

Content validity is a system of using logic, common sense, and previous work in the interest of specifying which variables represent an abstract concept. Schema theory suggests that information can be more easily assimilated when a developed schema is available. A person would also be expected to infer more from a set of information if he or she possesses a well-developed schema on that topic. Such an individual simply has a greater knowledge base upon which to draw and will find it easier to find parallel situations in memory that serve as models for current incoming information.

Individuals well versed in a given topical domain will logically cluster related concepts when asked to do so, based upon their enhanced appreciation of the boundaries for a given concept. The professional baseball player, for example, will be able to cluster all major league teams. The less interested observer may include several football teams in the list and fail to include several baseball teams.

Criterion Validity

Criterion validity is established when the strength between a scale and a variable can be reasonably gauged. It is the degree to which the operational measure corresponds to the theoretical construct (Carmines & Zeller, 1979). Criterion validity is normally gauged through the use of a correlation coefficient to determine the degree of association between the new measurement and the criterion variable (Phillips, 1985).

Schema measures typically ask people to recall facts based upon a knowledge set provided by the researcher. Coders must then sort the responses to assess the degree to which people recalled or grouped certain conceptual items. If the sorting categories are too similar, for example, coders may fail to sort the responses in a similar fashion. High intercoder reliability demonstrates appropriate analysis of the data. Criterion validity then refers to the highly specific elements of a research design rather than broad concepts assessed in the area of content or face validity. If an experiment is set up in such a manner that people comprehend and perform a given task properly and the data are analyzed such that agreement is strong between coders, then criterion validity is high.

Standardized tests such as the Graduate Record Exam (GRE) typically predict the ability of an individual to perform (in graduate school, in the case of the GRE) reasonably well. Tests of schema presence may ultimately serve a similar predictive function by giving guidance to information providers concerning shared processing abilities. However, standardized tests such as the GRE have had the luxury of use over time, which has proven their validity with reasonable certainty.

Unlike the GRE, schema measures have a limited research tradition upon which to draw, hence they are especially vulnerable with regard to criterion validity. Concerning schema measurement, the stimulus or knowledge set will ideally be provided to all respondents under similar conditions. Each experimental subject must understand the directions provided by the experimenter. But it is not essential that the stimulus messages be comprehended equally by all subjects. Ultimately, it will be the differences in comprehension and retrieval that will serve as evidence of schema presence (or lack of presence); hence criterion validity hinges vitally upon intercoder agreement, development of an unambiguous data collection instrument, and clear articulation of the task to be performed.

Construct Validity

Schema theory and measurement constitute a relatively new frontier for communication and social cognition researchers. One may certainly make the case that schemata do not exist—that the variables measured simply reflect memory or chance clustering. Construct validity is present if the researcher can demonstrate that a scale measuring an abstract concept is related to other scales. This typically begins with a hypothesis on how a set of ideas or concepts may be related. Scales must then be developed to measure concepts. Results consistent with predictions tend to suggest that construct validity is present.

It is this point that has often been addressed by researchers during the last decade. Scholars of cognition, such as Fiske et al. (1983), have provided several measures on the same responses to demonstrate that the results agree. One may argue that clustering of concepts is hopelessly entangled with recall of facts, since facts must be recalled before they can be clustered. But the cluster scores obtained using the ARC measures will be considerably lower if the individual recalls a great deal but fails to cluster related concepts. The scales used to measure schemata—including recall, inference, and clustering—have tended to yield the anticipated results based on formal hypotheses. Agreement among scales, or results tending in the same direction, suggests that the schema notion possesses construct validity when proper measurement techniques are employed.

Internal and External Validity

Internal validity is rarely a problem in properly conducted experimental research. Problems associated with factors such as history, maturation, testing, instrumentation, regression, and mortality are insignificant in the designs described above. However, without internal validity, experiments can become uninterpretable (Campbell & Stanley, 1963). Critical to the concept of internal validity is the question of whether or not measurement is able to determine if the experimental manipulation made a difference in a particular instance.

External validity pertains to the generalizability of the results of an experiment, or to what populations, settings, treatment variables, and measurement variables the effects can be generalized (Campbell & Stanley, 1963). Most of the work on schema measurement has been conducted in the laboratory, using stimulus materials specifically designed to evaluate schemata. More experiments demonstrating "real-world" applications of schemata measurement will help buttress the schema construct.

The specific threat to external validity centers on the types of experiments that have been carried out. People have typically been tested on shared scripts of simple events such as ordering a meal in a restaurant. Or they have been tested on recall of facts pertaining to powerful concepts such as democracy or communism. Hence the time is right to begin assessing the degree to which these measures may be considered externally valid. The path to be followed in this regard involves continued use of "real" news and information for stimulus materials. The measurement approaches described in this chapter will serve as a foundation for more elegant approaches. The schema concept still needs to mature, and measurement approaches will aid in this area. However, as Fiske and Linville (1980) eloquently state, "The most clear-headed overall view of the schema concept—or of any other newcomer—is to let a thousand conceptual flowers bloom." In this respect, the schema construct is evolving as an important construct for mass communication research.

NOTES

1. The instructions for eliciting the lecture script were as follows: "Write a list of actions describing what people generally do when they go to a lecture in a course. We are interested in the common actions of a routine lecture stereotype. Start the list with arriving at the lecture and end it with leaving after the lecture. Include about 20 actions or events and put them in the order in which they would occur."

2. The story pool contained nine clusters of three stories per cluster: attending a symphony, play, or movie; visiting a doctor, dentist, or chiropractor; playing a game of football, baseball, or golf; going swimming, skin diving, or surfing; and so on. Each subject read one story each for three of the nine scripts, two stories each for another three scripts (i.e., six stories), and three stories each for the other three scripts (i.e., nine stories). Hence each subject read a total of eighteen stories presented in random order. Which story fell into which category was balanced across subjects.

3. The initial stimuli determined the manipulation of the knowledge set. For example, one-third of the subjects read that forest fires have a long-term negative effect, one-third read that forest fires have beneficial effects, and one-third read a control story unrelated to fires. Similarly, one-third of the subjects read that population growth is beneficial because it leads to a strengthened international economy, one-third read that it places a strain on available resources, and one-third read an unrelated control story. The first measure taken was unaided recall. Subjects were asked to recall facts from all of the stories. A pretest had suggested that most could finish the task in 12 minutes. Aided recall was then employed. Subjects were asked to recall facts from only the population and fire stories. A pretest had suggested that most could finish the task in 5 minutes.

4. The inference scale was developed during several pretests. The instructions read as follows: "Now we would like you to think about the news stories. These statements are designed to find out *WHAT YOU THINK* ABOUT THE ISSUES—not to assess accuracy. In other words, we want to find out what you would guess about these issues having learned from these news stories." A 9-point anchored scale ranging from "strongly agree" through "strongly disagree" was used.

The statements were related to forest fires and population growth, but none had been expressly or implicitly stated during the experiment. Following are examples of the inference statements:

The new birth control for men will have a positive impact on global population trends.

The scientific community is concerned that population growth is bad for societies around the world since there just is not enough room on the planet to dispose of all of the refuse.

It will be increasingly difficult for most societies to provide basic social services such as public transportation and medical care as population growth continues to escalate worldwide.

As with forest fires, floods and tornadoes probably have a devastating long-term impact on the environment and regions they affect.

Forest fires can permanently ruin all hope of future farming in a region.

A forest fire can upset the ecological balance of nature by destroying certain insect populations.

5. Specific examples have not been provided because the technique has rarely been used. For an excellent example of this measurement strategy, see Fiske et al. (1983).

REFERENCES

Abelson, R. P. (1976). Script processing in attitude formation and decision making. In J. S. Carroll & J. W. Payne (Eds.), *Cognition and social behavior* (pp. 33-46). Hillsdale, NJ: Lawrence Erlbaum.

Allport, G. W. (1954). *The nature of prejudice.* Reading, MA: Addison-Wesley.

Anderson, R. C., & Pichert, J. W. (1978). Recall of previously unrecallable information following a shift in perspective. *Journal of Verbal Learning and Verbal Behavior, 17,* 1-12.

Asch, S. E. (1946). Forming impressions of personality. *Journal of Abnormal and Social Psychology, 41,* 258-290.

Atkinson, R. C., & Shiffrin, R. M. (1968). Human memory: A proposed system and its control processes. In K. W. Spence & J. T. Spence (Eds.), *Advances in the psychology of learning and motivation: Research and theory* (Vol. 2, p. 195). New York: Academic Press.

Bartlett, F. C. (1932). *Remembering: A study in experimental and social psychology.* London: Cambridge University Press.

Blumler, J. G., & Katz, E. (1974). *The uses of mass communications: Current perspectives.* Beverly Hills, CA: Sage.

Bousfield, A. K., & Bousfield, W. A. (1966). Measurement of clustering and of sequential constancies in repeated free recall. *Psychological Reports, 19,* 935-942.

Bower, G. H. (1975). Cognitive psychology: An introduction. In W. K. Estes (Ed.), *Handbook of learning and cognitive processes* (Vol. 1, pp. 25-80). Hillsdale, NJ: Lawrence Erlbaum.

Bower, G. H., Black, J. B., & Turner, T. J. (1979). Scripts in memory text. *Cognitive Psychology, 11,* 177-220.

Broadbent, D. E. (1958). *Perception and communication.* London: Pergamon.

Bruner, J. S., & Tagiuri, R. (1954). The perception of people. In G. Lindzey (Ed.), *Handbook of social psychology* (Vol. 2, pp. 634-654). Reading, MA: Addison-Wesley.

Burnkrandt, R. E., & Sawyer, A. G. (1983). Effects of involvement and message content on information-processing intensity. In R. J. Harris (Ed.), *Information processing research in advertising.* Hillsdale, NJ: Lawrence Erlbaum.

Campbell, D. T., & Stanley, J. C. (1963). *Experimental and quasi-experimental designs for research.* Chicago: Rand McNally.

Cantor, N., & Mischel, W. (1977). Traits as prototypes: Effects on recognition memory. *Journal of Personality and Social Psychology, 35,* 38-48.

Cantor, N., & Mischel, W. (1979). Prototypes in person perception. In L. Berkowitz (Ed.), *Advances in experimental social psychology* (Vol. 12, pp. 3-52). New York: Academic Press.

Carmines, E. G., & Zeller, R. A. (1979). *Reliability and validity assessment.* Beverly Hills, CA: Sage.

Chi, M. T. H., & Koeske, R. (1983). Network representation of a child's dinosaur knowledge. *Development Psychology, 19,* 29-39.

Cohen, C. E. (1981). Goals and schemata in person perception: Making sense from the stream of behavior. In N. Cantor & J. F. Kihlstrom (Eds.), *Personality, cognition, and social interaction* (pp. 45-68). Hillsdale, NJ: Lawrence Erlbaum.

Collins, W. A. (1983). Interpretation and inference in children's television viewing. In J. Bryant & D. R. Anderson (Eds.), *Children's understanding of television: Research on attention and comprehension* (pp. 221-240). New York: Academic Press.

Conover, P. J., & Feldman, S. (1981). The origins and meaning of liberal/conservative self-identification. *American Journal of Political Science, 25,* 617-645.

Crocker, J., Fiske, S. T., & Taylor, S. E. (1984). Schematic bases of belief change. In J. R. Eiser (Ed.), *Attitudinal judgment* (pp. 197-226). New York: Springer-Verlag.

Crocker, J., Hannah, D. B., & Weber, R. (1983). Person memory and causal attributions. *Journal of Personality and Social Psychology, 44,* 55-66.

Crockett, W. H. (1988). Schemas, affect, and communication. In L. Donohew, H. E. Sypher, & E. T. Higgins (Eds.), *Communication, social cognition, and affect* (pp. 33-51). Hillsdale, NJ: Lawrence Erlbaum.

DeFleur, M., & Ball-Rokeach, S. (1982). *Theories of mass communication* (4th ed.). New York: Longman.

Dizard, W. P. (1989). *The coming information age: An overview of technology, economics, and politics.* New York: Longman.

Festinger, L. A. (1957). *A theory of cognitive dissonance.* Stanford, CA: Stanford University Press.

Fiske, S. T., & Dyer, L. M. (1985). Structure and development of social schemata: Evidence from positive and negative transfer effects. *Journal of Personality and Social Psychology, 48,* 839-852.

Fiske, S. T., & Kinder, D. (1981). Involvement, expertise, and schema use: Evidence from political cognition. In N. Cantor & J. F. Kihlstrom (Eds.), *Personality, cognition, and social interaction* (pp. 131-140). Hillsdale, NJ: Lawrence Erlbaum.

Fiske, S. T., Kinder, D., & Larter, W. M. (1983). The novice and the expert: Knowledge-based strategies in political cognition. *Journal of Experimental and Social Psychology, 19,* 318-400.

Fiske, S. T., & Linville, P. T. (1980). What does the schema concept buy us? *Personality and Social Psychology Bulletin, 6,* 543-557.

Fiske, S. T., & Pavelchak, M. A. (1984). Category-based versus piecemeal-based affective responses: Developments in schema-triggered affect. In R. U. Sorrentino & E. T. Higgins (Eds.), *The handbook of motivation and cognition* (pp. 167-203). New York: Guilford.

Fiske, S. T., & Taylor, S. E. (1984). *Social cognition.* Reading, MA: Addison-Wesley.

Fiske, S. T., Taylor, S. E., Etcoff, N. L., & Laufer, J. K. (1979). Imaging, empathy, and causal attribution. *Journal of Experimental Social Psychology, 15,* 356-377.

Frank, R. E., & Greenberg, M. G. (1980). *The public's use of television: Who watches and why.* Beverly Hills, CA: Sage.

Garramone, G. M., Steele, M. E., & Pinkleton, B. E. (1989, August). *The role of cognitive schemata in determining candidate characteristic effects.* Paper presented at the annual meeting of the Association for Education in Journalism and Mass Communication, Washington, DC.

Golding, H. J. (1954). On the avowal of projection of happiness. *Journal of Personality, 23,* 30-47.

Graber, D. A. (1988). *Processing the news.* New York: Longman.

Hastie, R. (1981). Schematic principles in human memory. In E. T. Higgins, C. P. Herman, & M. P. Zanna (Eds.), *Social cognition: The Ontario Symposium* (Vol. 1, pp. 39-88). Hillsdale, NJ: Lawrence Erlbaum.

Hayes-Roth, B., & Hayes-Roth, F. (1977). Concept learning and the recognition and classification of exemplars. *Journal of Verbal Learning and Verbal Behavior, 16,* 321-338.

Heider, F. (1946). Attitudes and cognitive organization. *Journal of Psychology, 21,* 107-112.

Heider, F. (1958). *The psychology of interpersonal relations.* New York: John Wiley.

Higgins, E. T., & King, G. A. (1981). Accessibility of social constructs: Information-processing consequences of individual and contextual variability. In N. Cantor & J. F. Kihlstrom (Eds.), *Personality, cognition, and social interaction* (pp. 69-122). Hillsdale, NJ: Lawrence Erlbaum.

Jones, E. E., & Davis, K. E. (1965). From acts to dispositions: The attribution process in person perception. In L. Berkowitz (Ed.), *Advances in experimental social psychology* (Vol. 2, pp. 220-266). New York: Academic Press.

Kahneman, D. (1973). *Attention and effort.* Englewood Cliffs, NJ: Prentice-Hall.

Katz, D., & Allport, F. (1931). *Student attitudes.* Syracuse: Craftsman.

Lau, R. R. (1986). Political schemata, candidate evaluations, and voting behavior. In R. R. Lau & D. O. Sears, *Political cognition* (pp. 95-126). Hillsdale, NJ: Lawrence Erlbaum.

Lave, C. A., & March, J. G. (1975). Three rules of thumb for model building. In C. A. Lave & J. G. March (Eds.), *An introduction to models in the social sciences.* New York: Harper & Row.

Lippmann, W. (1922). *Public opinion.* New York: Macmillan.

Mandler, J., & Johnson, N. (1977). Remembrance of things parsed: Story structure and recall. *Cognitive Psychology, 9,* 111-151.

Markus, H. (1977). Self-schemata and processing information about the self. *Journal of Personality and Social Psychology, 35,* 63-78.

Markus, H., & Smith, J. (1981). The influence of self-schema on the perception of others. In N. Cantor & J. F. Kihlstrom (Eds.), *Personality, cognition, and social interaction* (pp. 233-262). Hillsdale, NJ: Lawrence Erlbaum.

McCombs, M. E., & Shaw, D. L. (1972). The agenda-setting function of mass media. *Public Opinion Quarterly, 36,* 176-187.

Meadowcroft, J. M., & Reeves, B. (1989). Influence of story schema development on children's attention to television. *Communication Research, 16,* 352-374.

Minsky, M. A. (1975). Framework for representing knowledge. In P. H. Winston (Ed.), *The psychology of computer vision.* New York: McGraw-Hill.

Mintz, E. (1956). An example of assimilative projection. *Journal of Abnormal and Social Psychology, 52,* 270-280.

Neisser, U. (1979). *Cognition and reality: Principles and implications of cognitive psychology.* San Francisco: W. H. Freeman.

Nisbett, R., & Ross, L. (1980). *Human inference: Strategies and shortcomings of social judgment.* Englewood Cliffs, NJ: Prentice-Hall.

Norman, D. A., & Bobrow, D. G. (1975). On data-limited and resource-limited processing. *Cognitive Psychology, 7,* 44-64.

Norman, D. A., & Bobrow, D. G. (1976). On the role of active memory processes. In C. Cofer (Ed.), *The structure of human memory* (pp. 114-132). San Francisco: W. H. Freeman.

Ostrom, T. M., Pryor, J. B., & Simpson, D. D. (1981). The organization of social information. In E. T. Higgins, C. P. Herman, & M. P. Zanna (Eds.), *Social cognition: The Ontario Symposium* (Vol. 1, pp. 3-38). Hillsdale, NJ: Lawrence Erlbaum.

O'Sullivan, C., & Durso, F. T. (1984). Effect of schemata-incongruent information on memory for stereotypical attributes. *Journal of Personality and Social Psychology, 47,* 55-70.

Phillips, B. (1985). *Sociological research methods: An introduction.* Homewood, IL: Dorsey.

Piaget, J. (1970). Piaget's theory. In P. Mussen (Ed.), *Carmichael's manual of child psychology* (Vol. 1). London: Routledge & Kegan Paul.

Reeves, B., Chaffee, S., & Tims, A. (1982). Social cognition and mass communication research. In M. Roloff & C. Berger (Eds.), *Social cognition and communication* (pp. 9-32). Beverly Hills, CA: Sage.

Roenker, D. L., Thompson, C. P., & Brown, S. C. (1971). Comparison of measures for the estimation of clustering in free recall. *Psychological Bulletin, 76,* 45-48.

Rokeach, M. (1960). *The open and closed mind: Investigations into the nature of belief systems.* New York: Basic Books.

Rosch, E. (1978). Principles of categorization. In E. Rosch & B. B. Lloyd (Eds.), *Cognition and categorization.* Hillsdale, NJ: Lawrence Erlbaum.

Rosch, E., Mervis, C., Gray, W., Johnson, D., & Boyes-Braem, P. (1975). Basic objects in natural categories. *Cognitive Psychology, 7,* 573-605.

Rosengren, K. E., Wenner, L. A., & Palmgreen, P. (Eds.). (1985). *Media gratifications research: Current perspectives.* Beverly Hills, CA: Sage.

Rothbart, M. (1981). Memory processes and social beliefs. In D. Hamilton (Ed.), *Cognitive processes in stereotyping and intergroup behavior* (pp. 145-182). Hillsdale, NJ: Lawrence Erlbaum.

Rothbart, M., Evans, M., & Fulero, S. (1979). Recall for confirming events: Memory processes and the maintenance of social stereotypes. *Journal of Experimental Social Psychology, 15,* 343-355.

Schank, R. C., & Abelson, R. P. (1977). *Scripts, plans, goals, and understanding: An inquiry into human knowledge structures.* Hillsdale, NJ: Lawrence Erlbaum.

Sherif, M., & Hovland, C. I. (1961). *Social judgment: Assimilation and contrast effects in communication and attitude change.* New Haven, CT: Yale University Press.

Shuell, T. J. (1969). Clustering and organization in free recall. *Psychological Bulletin, 72,* 353-374.

Simon, J. L., & Burnstein, P. (1985). *Basic research methods in social science* (3rd ed.). New York: Random House.

Snyder, M., & Cantor, N. (1978). Testing hypotheses about other people: The use of historical knowledge. *Journal of Experimental Social Psychology, 15,* 330-342.

Srull, T. K., & Wyer, R. S. (1979). The role of category accessibility in the interpretation of information about persons: Some determinants and implications. *Journal of Personality and Social Psychology, 37,* 1660-1672.

Taylor, S. E. (1981). The interface of cognitive and social psychology. In J. Harvey (Ed.), *Cognition, social behavior, and the environment* (pp. 189-211). Hillsdale, NJ: Lawrence Erlbaum.

Taylor, S. E., & Crocker, J. (1981). Schematic bases of social information processing. In E. T. Higgins, C. P. Herman, & M. P. Zanna (Eds.), *Social cognition: The Ontario Symposium* (Vol. 1, pp. 89-134). Hillsdale, NJ: Lawrence Erlbaum.

Tesser, A. (1978). Self-generated attitude change. In L. Berkowitz (Ed.), *Advances in experimental social psychology* (Vol. 11, pp. 289-333). New York: Academic Press.

Tesser, A., & Leone, C. (1977). Cognitive schemas and thought as determinants of attitude change. *Journal of Experimental Psychology, 13,* 340-356.

Thorndyke, P. W., & Yekovich, F. R. (1980). A critique of schema-based theories of human story memory. *Poetics, 9,* 23-49.

Valenti, A. C., & Tesser, A. (1981). On the mechanism of thought-induced attitude change. *Social Behavior and Personality, 9,* 17-22.

Weber, R., & Crocker, J. (1983). Cognitive processing in the revision of stereotypic beliefs. *Journal of Personality and Social Psychology, 45,* 961-977.

Wicks, R. H. (1986, May). *Applying schema theory to news information processing.* Paper presented at the 36th Annual Convention of the International Communication Association, Chicago.

Wicks, R. H. (1990, August). *The relationship between involvement and medium in news information processing.* Paper presented at the 73rd Annual Convention of the Association for Education in Journalism and Mass Communication, Minneapolis.

Wicks, R. H., & Drew, D. G. (1991). Learning from the news: Effects of message consistency and medium on recall and inference making. *Journalism Quarterly, 68*(1-2), 155-164.

Wyer, R. S., & Srull, T. K. (1980). The processing of social stimulus information: A conceptual integration. In R. Hastie, T. M. Ostrom, E. B. Ebbesen, R. S. Wyer, D. Hamilton, & D. E. Carlston (Eds.), *Person memory: The cognitive basis of social perception* (pp. 227-300). Hillsdale, NJ: Lawrence Erlbaum.

Wyer, R. S., & Srull, T. K. (1981). Category accessibility: Some theoretical and empirical issues concerning the processing of social stimulus information. In E. T. Higgins, C. P. Herman, & M. P. Zanna (Eds.), *Social cognition: The Ontario Symposium* (Vol. 1, pp. 161-197). Hillsdale, NJ: Lawrence Erlbaum.

A Broader and "Warmer"
Approach to Schema Theory

GINA M. GARRAMONE
Michigan State University

W ICKS advocates the application of schema theory and measurement to mass communication research problems, specifically to news information processing. The strategy of couching established mass communication conceptualizations in terms of schema theory may well enrich the original conceptualizations and instigate new lines of research. However, the full measure of heuristic potential is not adequately represented by the Wicks essay. This critique will attempt to elaborate the heuristic possibilities by highlighting additional contributions to the schema and mass communication research literatures.

"COLD" VERSUS "HOT" INFORMATION PROCESSING

Wicks's review of the schema literature reflects the predominant "cold" perspective of social cognition psychologists in the 1970s, whereby a concerted effort was made to explain all the variance in cognitive terms without invoking such "hot" factors as motives, values, affect, or goals. The idea was that all behavior could be explained entirely by its "cold" information-processing antecedents (Markus & Zajonc, 1985). Wicks does describe social psychology studies that include perceiver goals as a variable (Anderson & Pichert, 1978; Fiske, Taylor, Etcoff, & Laufer, 1979), but reviews them in terms of their dependent variables ("assessing shared script schemata using recall tests"), rather than in terms of the role of perceiver goals. Similarly, Wicks does mention "perceived gratifications associated with information gain" and "civic obligation" as motivations for information gain, and states that at the core of the Hastie (1981) model is the belief

Correspondence and requests for reprints: Gina M. Garramone, Department of Advertising, Michigan State University, East Lansing, MI 48824-1212.

Communication Yearbook 15, pp. 146-154

that the individual is active, goal-seeking, and purposive. However, his description of schema activation neglects the role of the perceiver. And, while he notes the potential relationship between schema theory and the uses and gratifications approach to mass communication, that relationship could be explicated in much greater depth and breadth.

In social psychology, a swing toward "hot" cognition is already in progress (Markus & Zajonc, 1985). A "warmer" approach to the application of schema theory to mass communication research would increase its heuristic value and provide new insights regarding some established mass communication research perspectives. The significance of "hot" factors is perhaps best appreciated when placed in the context of the various factors determining schema influence. According to Markus and Zajonc (1985), to specify more precisely the nature of a schema's likely influence,

> one must know something about each of the following five factors: (1) the nature or content of the schema; (2) the nature or content of the input or stimulus information; (3) the fit between the schema and the stimulus information; (4) the state of the perceiver; and (5) the context of the information processing situation or task. (p. 163)

These same factors may be used to outline possible applications of schema theory to mass communication research. The present analysis will focus on schema content, stimulus content, and the state of the perceiver. However, it is important to note that the five factors are interrelated. For example, *context* may determine the immediate state of the perceiver—particularly which processing goals are being served. Similarly, whether or not a schema will *fit* a particular stimulus depends on both the perceiver's goals and the context within which the perceiver is processing the stimulus (Markus & Zajonc, 1985).

MASS COMMUNICATION AND SCHEMA CONTENT

Only limited research has attempted to describe schemata that may be particularly relevant to the processing of media messages. Most of this research has been in the area of political information processing (Fiske & Kinder, 1981; Graber, 1984; Kraus & Perloff, 1985; Lau & Sears, 1986; Lodge & Hamill, 1986). Wicks suggests that event schemata or scripts may be especially important for media researchers, as news and information are presented in these terms. Thus researchers might attempt to explore people's scripts for such recurring news events as racial conflicts, medical advances, or natural disasters. For example, when considering the prototypical "racial conflict," what do people perceive as the likely causes, consequences, and actors/groups involved (Fiske & Taylor, 1984; Schank & Abelson, 1977)?

McLeod, Kosicki, Pan, and Allen (1987) investigated the nature and content of respondents' schemata for a specific issue—the Tax Reform Bill. Schema descriptions were based on survey participants' free responses to open-ended questions regarding the issue. The researchers measured schema *complexity* in terms of the number of codable words, facts, areas, causes, and motives as well as whether a time frame was used and whether both positive and negative consequences were reported.

They also measured schema *content* in terms of "frames," defined as "non-hierarchical categories that serve as forms or major headings into which any future news content can be filled." They analyzed four dimensions of frames: time frame of anticipated consequences; group schema, party, and class; the locus of anticipated effects in the person, the economy, or the society; and cynicism about serving the actors' own interests and their activity benefiting society. McLeod et al. suggest that this set of frames varies from issue to issue. This latter observation acknowledges another of the five factors determining schema influence—fit between the schema and the stimulus information.

Perhaps uniquely pertinent to media message processing are schemata regarding the media themselves. In another innovative program of research, McLeod and his colleagues have sought to identify and describe the "images" or schemata that people hold for the media (see Amor, McLeod, & Kosicki, 1987; McLeod, Kosicki, Amor, Allen, & Philps, 1986). They conceptualize media schemata to include beliefs and attitudes regarding news content, the role of journalists in the news-gathering process, and the role of the news media in society. Their research has identified empirically a core of five media images or schemata: quality, patterning of news, negative affect, special interests, and dependency and control.

Their research also indicates that media schemata influence how people use, cognitively process, and evaluate media, and what they learn as a consequence (Fredin & Kosicki, 1989; Kosicki, McLeod, & Amor, 1987). For example, Fredin and Kosicki (1989) found that people compensate for distortions they think occur in the news because of the ways the news media operate. Thus media schemata were employed by adjusting outcomes of the media to compensate for the distortions that were implied by the media schemata. Fredin and Kosicki note that what media schemata are "pertinent" varies from "situation to situation." This notion suggests another of the five factors determining schema influence—context.

MASS COMMUNICATION AND STIMULUS CONTENT

There are at least two ways in which stimulus content such as media messages may determine schema influence. First, messages are to some extent constraining in the schemata that are applicable. Blumler, Gurevitch, and Katz (1985) present a similar argument in their discussion of the interpretation or "reading" of "texts." They state that "texts are not infinitely open and may allow a limited number of possible readings. Perhaps the *New York Times* can be read as pornography, but that is unlikely to be its statistically dominant use" (p. 260). Similarly, particular news items, commercials, or programs may be more likely to be represented in certain ways than in others. For example, while a schema regarding political candidate personality factors may frequently be used to interpret political commercials, it will be used less frequently to interpret commercials for disposable diapers. Media messages also vary in the *number* of schemata that are applicable. Thus mass communication researchers might investigate how media message attributes facilitate many versus few schematic interpretations.

A second, more active, influence of the stimulus on schema selection is schema activation via priming. The priming effect is based on the fact that, for some time after a concept is activated, there is an increased probably that it and associated thought elements will come to mind again (Berkowitz & Rogers, 1986). Since schema selection is influenced by the relative accessibility of different schemata that could be used to represent the message (Higgins, Rholes, & Jones, 1977), message content itself may activate schemata that are used in subsequent processing. Such an effect can operate automatically and even without awareness (Bargh & Pietromonaco, 1982).

The priming effects of television news programs have been clearly demonstrated by Iyengar and his colleagues (Iyengar, Kinder, Peters, & Krosnick, 1984; Iyengar, Peters, & Kinder, 1982). Their work has concentrated on the consequences of accessibility for evaluation. Specifically, they asked whether television news programs, by calling attention to some aspects of presidential performance while ignoring others, might affect the standards by which presidents are judged. They reasoned that coverage of a particular problem provides new information that is accessible by its recency and that coverage may also influence viewers to consider what they already know about the problem (thereby activating relevant schemata). Consequently, both newly acquired information and relevant schemata may be made highly available and therefore perhaps particularly influential. The results of their series of experiments support this hypothesis.

The notion that schemata may be activated by messages themselves has some interesting implications for message construction. Blumler et al. (1985) describe a scenario that derives from a view of the journalistic function as providing "sweeteners" to get people involved in politics. Paraphrasing their conceptualization in schema terminology, by embedding bits of information in dramatic reporting forms, apparently catering to a "spectator" schema expected to be activated initially, audience members might be induced to invoke some different schemata—perhaps schemata more useful for acquiring the knowledge necessary for voter decision making. Thus messages may be constructed that attempt "to lead the reader by the hand from one mind-set to another."

Purposive schema activation via message construction would appear to call for knowledge of the audience's likely relevant schema set and of the likely consequences of processing subsequent information with a particular schema. For example, prior to addressing the public regarding the 1990 Persian Gulf crisis, President Bush may have sensed that Americans might interpret the crisis with a "Vietnam" schema. Personal experience, news media reports, and, more recently, a number of movies have provided most Americans with Vietnam schemata that include evaluations of both the morality and the likely success of such military endeavors. Interpretations of the Gulf crisis and of possible U.S. involvement with a "Vietnam" schema would be detrimental to public support for U.S. intervention. Instead, Bush chose to prime, through rhetoric and analogy, an alternate relevant schema—that of "Hitler and World War II." The implications of a "Hitler" schema for public support of U.S. intervention were clearly more favorable than the implications of a "Vietnam" schema.

Knowledge of the information-processing implications of candidate issue versus candidate image schemata may lead campaign media managers to attempt to prime one schema over the other via message construction. For example, there is some evidence that the effect of candidate attractiveness on vote likelihood is greater for males processing political commercials with an "image" schema than for those processing with an "issue" schema (Garramone, Steele, & Pinkleton, 1990). Consequently, extremely attractive candidates might want to capitalize on their good looks by priming viewers to process their commercials with an image schema. Conversely, unattractive candidates may prefer to prime an issue schema. How to prime schemata via message construction is an empirical question awaiting research.

MASS COMMUNICATION AND
THE STATE OF THE PERCEIVER

A "warm" approach to schema theory suggests that the state of the perceiver—including his or her needs, desires, and motives—influences the nature and course of schematic thinking (Markus & Zajonc, 1985). Such an approach should be ringing bells with gratifications researchers, who contend that much media use can be conceived as goal directed (Palmgreen, Wenner, & Rosengren, 1985) and that audience members are active processors rather than passive receivers of media messages (McLeod & Becker, 1981). Yet gratifications researchers have been accused of neglecting this premise of active message processing (Blumler et al., 1985; Garramone, 1983, 1984, 1985, 1987; Palmgreen, 1984; Rubin, 1986; Swanson, 1977). Swanson (1977) notes that "the typical uses and gratifications research design investigates nearly every stage in the process—need, goal or expectations, media exposure, consequences of exposure—*except* the perceptual activity of interpreting or creating meaning for messages" (p. 220). By applying a "warm" schema theory to media message processing, gratifications researchers are provided several directions for pursuing the active message-processing premise.

A substantial body of research indicates that motives or goals are instrumental in determining which schemata are activated in a particular situation (Cohen, 1981; Higgins, McCann, & Fondacaro, 1982; Jeffery & Mischel, 1979; Wyer, Srull, Gordon, & Hartwick, 1982; Zajonc, 1960). If gratifications sought from the media are conceptualized as motives or goals for media message processing, then when people approach a media message to attain particular gratifications, appropriate schemata may be activated (Garramone, 1987). The activated schemata, in turn, should influence the encoding and organization of the message, its recall, and the inferences drawn.

To understand how a goal determines the influence of schemata on information processing, one must know both the goal and the nature of the schema that is activated (Markus & Zajonc, 1985). Gratifications researchers have identified many goals for attending to media messages: the next step may be to explore the corresponding schemata and their effects on message processing. For example, motives for viewing a televised presidential debate may include forming impressions of the candidates' personalities, learning the candidates' stands on issues, gathering information to be used in later interpersonal discussions, and enjoying the conflict as a spectator sport.

Schema research provides indications of the likely nature of the schemata activated by such goals. For example, individuals with personality analysis goals are more likely than those with "memory" goals to encode a target's behavior in terms of personality trait concepts (Wyer & Gordon, 1982). Thus "image-motivated" individuals may be more likely than "issue-motivated" individuals to process debate information with personality trait schemata. The activated schemata will, in turn, influence message processing. For example, if people attend to and encode those aspects of stimulus information that are particularly relevant to activated schemata, and if information channels are perceived to differ in the amount of such information they contain, then perhaps individuals will differentially attend to channels based on their activated schemata. Although candidate issue information may be contained largely in the audio portion of a political commercial, candidate personality trait information is present in both audio and video portions. Thus one might predict that individuals viewing political commercials to form an impression of the candidate's personality would pay more attention to and recall more information from the video portion of the commercials than would individuals viewing to learn issue stands. Both experimental and survey research support this hypothesis (Garramone, 1983, 1984).

Schema research also indicates that individuals expecting to "transmit" information to others are more likely than those expecting only to "receive" information to assimilate the new information into a single schema, so as to absorb the main information as accurately as possible (Zajonc, 1960). Thus individuals viewing a debate in order to have fuel for later discussions may be particularly likely to encode the information in a streamlined or unified manner. Debate viewing with a "conflict" schema may result in message processing and subsequent inferences that are very different from those generated by debate viewing with some other schema. The research of Massad, Hubbard, and Newton (1979) found that activating a schema involving an aggressor results in impressions of the participants that are different from those that result from activating a schema involving a guardian, and that subjects unitized the stimulus film (divided it into segments) in very different ways depending on which of the two schemata was activated.

Research questions concerning the relationships between media use goals/motives and schemata, and between schemata and media message processing, may be approached using various methods and research designs. Media use goals may be experimentally manipulated via instruction sets, subjects presented with stimulus messages, and then effects on message processing and their consequences measured (see Garramone, 1983). Or schemata may be measured and their effects on message processing evaluated in an experimental setting (see Garramone et al., 1990). Survey designs are also possible—both motives for media use and processing consequences may be measured in naturalistic settings (see Garramone, 1984). Blumler et al. (1985) suggest the usefulness of an ethnographic approach.

The application of a "warm" schema theory to mass communication questions might also involve investigating the relationships among affect, schemata, and media message processing. Affective orientations influence the kinds of schemata applied to stimuli, and strong arousal appears to interfere with the effective employment of complex schemata (Crockett, 1988). If "experts" in a given topical area have more complex schemata than do "novices" (Chi & Koeske, 1983), then perhaps the media message processing of experts suffers more from strong arousal than does the processing of novices. Producing news stories for maximum emotional impact, therefore, may actually interfere with their processing by experts.

As these examples illustrate, mass communication researchers will find many research questions generated by a "warm" approach to schema theory. If "the most clear-headed overall view of the schema concept . . . is to let a thousand conceptual flowers bloom" (Fiske & Linville, 1980), then by expanding our view of the schema concept, we can only be enriching our garden.

REFERENCES

Amor, D. L., McLeod, J. M., & Kosicki, G. M. (1987, May). *Images of the media, orientations to the world: Where do public images of mass media come from?* Paper presented at the annual meeting of the International Communication Association, Montreal.

Anderson, R. C., & Pichert, J. W. (1978). Recall of previously unrecallable information following a shift in perspective. *Journal of Verbal Learning and Verbal Behavior, 17*, 1-12.

Bargh, J. A., & Pietromonaco, P. (1982). Automatic information processing and social perception: The influence of trait information presented outside of conscious awareness on impression formation. *Journal of Personality and Social Psychology, 43*, 437-449.

Berkowitz, L., & Rogers, K. H. (1986). A priming effect analysis of media influences. In J. Bryant & D. Zillman (Eds.), *Perspectives on media effects* (pp. 57-81). Hillsdale, NJ: Lawrence Erlbaum.

Blumler, J. G., Gurevitch, M., & Katz, E. (1985). Reaching out: A future for gratifications research. In K. E. Rosengren, L. A. Wenner, & P. Palmgreen (Eds.), *Media gratifications research: Current perspectives* (pp. 255-273). Beverly Hills, CA: Sage.

Chi, M. T. H., & Koeske, R. (1983). Network representation of a child's dinosaur knowledge. *Developmental Psychology, 19*, 29-39.

Cohen, C. E. (1981). Goals and schemata in person perception: Making sense from the stream of behavior. In N. Cantor & J. F. Kihlstrom (Eds.), *Personality, cognition, and social interaction* (pp. 45-68). Hillsdale, NJ: Lawrence Erlbaum.

Crockett, W. H. (1988). Schemas, affect, and communications. In L. Donohew, H. E. Sypher, & E. T. Higgins (Eds.), *Communication, social cognition, and affect* (pp. 33-51). Hillsdale, NJ: Lawrence Erlbaum.

Fiske, S. T., & Kinder, D. K. (1981). Involvement, expertise, and schema use: Evidence from political cognition. In N. Cantor & J. F. Kihlstrom (Eds.), *Personality, cognition, and social interaction* (pp. 131-140). Hillsdale, NJ: Lawrence Erlbaum.

Fiske, S. T., & Linville, P. T. (1980). What does the schema concept buy us? *Personality and Social Psychology Bulletin, 6*, 543-557.

Fiske, S. T., & Taylor, S. E. (1984). *Social cognition.* Reading, MA: Addison-Wesley.

Fiske, S. T., Taylor, S. E., Etcoff, N. L., & Laufer, J. K. (1979). Imaging, empathy, and causal attribution. *Journal of Experimental Social Psychology, 15*, 356-377.

Fredin, E. S., & Kosicki, G. M. (1989). Cognitions and attitudes about community: Compensating for media images. *Journalism Quarterly, 66*, 571-578.

Garramone, G. M. (1983). Issue versus image orientation and effects of political advertising. *Communication Research, 10*, 59-76.

Garramone, G. M. (1984). Audience motivation effects: More evidence. *Communication Research, 11*, 79-96.

Garramone, G. M. (1985). Motives and political information processing. In S. Kraus & R. Perloff (Eds.), *Mass media and political thought: An information-processing approach* (pp. 201-219). Beverly Hills, CA: Sage.

Garramone, G. M. (1987, May). *Active message processing: The neglected premise.* Paper presented at the annual meeting of the International Communication Association, Montreal.

Garramone, G. M., Steele, M. E., & Pinkleton, B. E. (1990). The role of cognitive schemata in determining candidate characteristic effects. In F. Biocca (Ed.), *Television and political advertising* (Vol. 1). Hillsdale, NJ: Lawrence Erlbaum.

Graber, D. (1984). *Processing the news: How people tame the information tide.* New York: Longman.

Hastie, R. (1981). Schematic principles in human memory. In E. T. Higgins, C. P. Herman, & M. P. Zanna (Eds.), *Social cognition: The Ontario Symposium* (Vol. 1, pp. 39-88). Hillsdale, NJ: Lawrence Erlbaum.

Higgins, E. T., McCann, C. D., & Fondacaro, R. (1982). The "communication game": Goal directed encoding and cognitive consequences. *Social Cognition, 1*, 21-37.

Higgins, E. T., Rholes, W. S., & Jones, C. R. (1977). Category accessibility and impression formation. *Journal of Experimental Social Psychology, 13*, 141-154.

Iyengar, S., Kinder, D. R., Peters, M. D., & Krosnick, J. A. (1984). The evening news and presidential evaluations. *Journal of Personality and Social Psychology, 46*, 778-787.

Iyengar, S., Peters, M. D., & Kinder, D. R. (1982). Experimental demonstrations of the not-so-minimal consequences of television news programs. *American Political Science Review, 81*, 848-858.

Jeffery, K. M., & Mischel, W. (1979). Effects of purpose on the organization and recall of information in person perception. *Journal of Personality, 47*, 397-419.

Kosicki, G. M., McLeod, J. M., & Amor, D. L. (1987, May). *Processing the news: Some individual strategies for selecting, sense-making and integrating.* Paper presented at the annual meeting of the International Communication Association, Montreal.

Kraus, S., & Perloff, R. (Eds.). (1985). *Mass media and political thought: An information-processing approach.* Beverly Hills, CA: Sage.

Lau, R. R., & Sears, D. O. (1986). *Political cognition.* Hillsdale, NJ: Lawrence Erlbaum.

Lodge, M., & Hamill, R. (1986). A partisan schema for political information processing. *American Political Science Review, 80*, 505-519.

Markus, H., & Zajonc, R. B. (1985). The cognitive perspective in social psychology. In G. Lindzey & E. Aronson (Eds.), *The handbook of social psychology* (Vol. 1, 3rd ed., pp. 137-230). New York: Random House.

Massad, C. M., Hubbard, M., & Newton, D. (1979). Selective perception of events. *Journal of Experimental Social Psychology, 15*, 513-530.

McLeod, J. M., & Becker, L. B. (1981). The uses and gratifications approach. In D. Nimmo & K. R. Sanders (Eds.), *Handbook of political communication* (pp. 67-99). Beverly Hills, CA: Sage.

McLeod, J. M., Kosicki, G. M., Amor, D. L., Allen, S. G., & Philps, D. M. (1986, August). *Images of mass media news: What they are and does it matter?* Paper presented at the annual meeting of the Association for Education in Journalism and Mass Communications, Norman, OK.

McLeod, J. M., Kosicki, G. M., Pan, Z., & Allen, S. G. (1987, August). *Audience perspectives on the news: Assessing their complexity and conceptual frames.* Paper presented at the annual meeting of the Association for Education in Journalism and Mass Communication, San Antonio, TX.

Palmgreen, P. (1984). Uses and gratifications: A theoretical perspective. In R. N. Bostrom (Ed.), *Communication yearbook 8* (pp. 20-55). Beverly Hills, CA: Sage.

Palmgreen, P., Wenner, L. A., & Rosengren, K. E. (1985). Uses and gratifications research: The past ten years. In K. E. Rosengren, L. A. Wenner, & P. Palmgreen (Eds.), *Media gratifications research: Current perspectives* (pp. 11-37). Beverly Hills, CA: Sage.

Rubin, A. M. (1986). Uses, gratifications, and media effects research. In J. Bryant & D. Zillman (Eds.), *Perspectives on media effects* (pp. 281-301). Hillsdale, NJ: Lawrence Erlbaum.

Schank, R. C., & Abelson, R. P. (1977). *Scripts, plans, goals, and understanding: An inquiry into human knowledge structures.* Hillsdale, NJ: Lawrence Erlbaum.

Swanson, D. L. (1977). The uses and misuses of uses and gratifications. *Human Communication Research, 3*, 214-221.

Wyer, R. S., & Gordon, S. E. (1982). The recall of information about persons and groups. *Journal of Experimental Social Psychology, 18*, 128-169.

Wyer, R. S., Srull, T. K., Gordon, S. E., & Hartwick, J. (1982). Effects of processing objectives on the recall of prose material. *Journal of Personality and Social Psychology, 43*, 674-688.

Zajonc, R. B. (1960). The process of cognitive tuning in communication. *Journal of Abnormal Social Psychology, 61*, 159-167.

4 Insights into Soviet Life Provided by Soviet Movies: Political Actors and Their Ideologies in the 1970s and 1980s

VLADIMIR SHLAPENTOKH
Michigan State University

DMITRY SHLAPENTOKH
Harvard University

Because Soviet movies reflect the ideological processes and psychological atmosphere dominant during specific periods, an analysis of these movies can provide
a broad understanding of major developments in the objective and subjective dimensions of Soviet life during those periods. Soviet films of the 1970s and 1980s
reflect the deeply rooted malaise and moral decay of the Soviet people. In addition, they present a portrait of the Soviet bureaucracy, and they help to illustrate
the nature of the country's resistance to the dominant regime, offering a vivid portrait of the Soviet people's alienation from the state, public life, and official political activity.

L IKE novels and other creative works, movies provide an invaluable
source of information regarding the society and the time in which
they are created. Of course, no single source of information, whether
films or sociological studies, can claim to offer complete and reliable coverage of any given social issue. All sources, including those declared "objective," are vulnerable to the subtle influences of the examiner's own
personal ideology. Even the most sophisticated quantitative methodology is

AUTHORS' NOTE: The authors express their deep gratitude to Neil F. O'Donnell for his
thoughtful comments and careful editing, which significantly improved this chapter.

Correspondence and requests for reprints: Vladimir Shlapentokh, Department of Community
Health Sciences, 547 West Fee Hall, Michigan State University, East Lansing, MI 48824.

Communication Yearbook 15, pp. 155-193

susceptible to what Alvin Gouldner (1979) calls the influence of the "the domain of the sociologist," that is, his or her ideology, past experiences, individual tastes, and so on (about the influence of ideologies on Soviet sociologists, see Shlapentokh, 1987).

Given their dependence on intuition and imagination, however, movies are even more susceptible to the influences of their creators' personal ideologies than are "scientific" sources, and are therefore less likely to provide "objective" pictures of reality.[1] Similarly, the interpretation of fictional movies is more readily influenced by the views of the examiner than is the interpretation of "hard" sociological data.

Still, despite these "limitations" (in a positivistic sense; see Hughes, 1976, pp. 53-54), movies and other visual media, which provide a multidimensional reconstruction of life, have an advantage over literature and the social sciences, which tend to use a linear/consecutive mode of reporting. Unlike sociological data, which by definition can provide only relatively abstract, composite information regarding the "average member" of a certain social group or institution (e.g., an average party apparatchik or an average member of the Young Communist League), movies present concrete, individualized cases that often convey a richer variety of information than do "scientifically" collected and processed data.

Although movies, particularly documentaries, are being used increasingly often as sources of historical and sociological data (see, for instance, Grenville, 1971; Smith, 1976), they have yet to be used as sources of data for so-called area studies, that is, studies of foreign countries. Although American social scientists studying Soviet and Chinese cultures regularly cite books and articles published in the countries studied, they rarely mention movies or television programs. This avoidance of audiovisual sources is related, in part, to their relative novelty, as well as to the comparative difficulties of nonnative speakers in understanding oral versus written texts.

Whatever the reason, a survey of leading Western periodicals devoted to the Soviet Union (e.g., *Slavic Review* and *Soviet Studies*) reveals that the authors of articles published in these journals in 1988-1989 totally ignored audiovisual sources of information. One objective of this chapter, then, is to demonstrate to social scientists the utility of using movies as a source of information about a given society.

THEORETICAL CONSIDERATIONS

The major theme of this chapter—the importance of Soviet movies as a source of information about Soviet society—is predicated on our basic assumption that subjective realities (e.g., individual or institutional perceptions of the world) and ideologies differ in the extent to which they reflect "objective" or "true" reality. Given the centrality of this assumption, it is important to clarify several major concepts, including "reality" and "ideology." [2]

In our analysis of Soviet movies, we will differentiate between objective reality and subjective reality in the following way: *objective*, or *ontological*, reality is the objective world faced by all people and institutions, whereas *subjective* reality is the reflection or representation of objective reality held in the psyches and documents of those same people and institutions. This approach differs from the conceptions of objective and subjective realities proposed by Berger and Luckmann (1966), who argue that objective reality is the image of the world accepted in a given social milieu and used as the basis for socialization and resocialization. Our approach more closely matches that of Richard Quinney (1982), who argues that objective social reality is that with which people are presented, even if they then act to change that reality in various ways (p. 46).

While we maintain that there exists only one ontological, objective reality—an implicit assumption made, in fact, by all social actors—there exist as many subjective realities as there are individuals and institutions holding perceptions of the world. As such, it is only by using a typology of social actors and their realities that we can reduce their numbers to a level conducive to analysis. Our approach includes the following five types, or classes, of reality:

(1) *ontological reality:* objectively existing, or "true," reality
(2) *individual reality:* ontological reality as reflected in individual psyches
(3) *institutional reality:* reality as created by social institutions (especially the mass media and educative, religious, and political institutions)
(4) *artistic reality:* reality as it is created in literature and the arts
(5) *scientific reality:* reality as it is created through the use of current scientific methods

Like all movies, Soviet movies include each of these types of reality: subjective reality, as held by the characters in, as well as the viewers of, the movies: institutional reality, which to some degree influences all social actors, whether imaginary or real (e.g., filmmakers of the Stalin era received directives regarding every element of their movies); artistic reality, which is created by every movie; and scientific reality, which is used in assessing a movie's accuracy in reflecting ontological reality.

The interactions among the types of reality mentioned above are quite extensive and are of crucial importance for this chapter. In examining these interactions, it is reasonable to make a distinction between consumers and producers of various subjective realities (about this distinction, see Anderson, 1990, p. 9).

Individuals are, for the most part, consumers of realities produced by social institutions, figures in literature and the arts, and, to a limited degree, scholars. Individuals are especially susceptible to the influence of outside, subjective realities in facets of their lives that are beyond the scope of their everyday experience (e.g., subjective realities presented by the mass media regarding events in foreign countries). However, individuals also produce realities for others, especially when they attempt to impress others in order to increase their status or to reach specific objectives (Goffman, 1959). Filmmakers are, of course, producers of subjective realities, while their audiences are the consumers.

Theories regarding alternative realities are crucially important to moviemakers, even though individual moviemakers may not deliberately follow, or even be aware of, the tenets of a given theory. For this discussion, it is important to distinguish between filmmakers best considered realists and those best considered nonrealists, or formalists. These two groups are also referred to as *objectivists* and *constructivists*, respectively, since the first group objectivizes (i.e., recognizes and conforms to) ontological reality, whereas the second group constructs reality.[3]

The distinction between realist and nonrealist movies is often blurred; numerous movies combine both approaches (see such recent Soviet movies as Manin's *Fountain*, 1988, or Soloviev's *Assa*, 1988). This combined approach is particularly prominent in comedies (see, for example, Bazhanov's *The Most Attractive*, 1985, or Riasanov's *Office Romance*, 1977).

Realists are those who approach film as a medium for reflecting "real life," either as it objectively exists or as it is reflected in the minds of their films' protagonists (Italian neorealist movies of the 1940s are perhaps the best examples of realist movies). Makers of representational movies are slightly further away from the goal of total realism than are the realists.

Nonrealists, by comparison, try to present the world in a manner free of the constraints of objective reality, although they do so under different banners (e.g., entertainment, surrealism, expressionism, escapism, propaganda). Included in the nonrealist category are the advocates of social realism in Soviet films and the creators of the prescriptive "political films" found in the Third World and in Western countries. Although films by nonrealists always reflect the "objective world" to a certain extent, it is difficult to extract the realistic elements. As a result, decoding these films requires great effort, and often, although not always, provides dubious results (see, for instance, the analysis of utopian and realistic elements in the article about American entertainment movies by Richard Dyer, 1985).[4]

Of course, the distinction between realist and nonrealist approaches in no way implies that one approach is preferable or inherently "more artistic" than the other, as some have argued (Kracauer, 1960). Artists and artistic works have many goals, most of which are independent of whether realism is attained (about distinctions among filmmakers and their attitudes toward reality, see Braudy, 1976; Dyer, 1985; Kracauer, 1960; Mitry, 1963; Ogle, 1985).

Soviet Movies in the Fight for Truth in Soviet Society

In the 1960s and 1970s, while several Western experts were attacking the idea of objective reality in filmmaking, Soviet filmmakers were attacking countless official beliefs and images of Soviet society, both past and present. With the first signs of liberalization during Khrushchev's thaw, film directors began producing movies that reflected, although rather timidly, several real issues of Soviet life and that contained allusions to the Stalin era and its remnants.

One of these movies (of which there were few), *Rumiantsev's Case* (Kheifets, 1956), depicted a villainous police prosecutor wanting to jail an honest driver. This film aroused excitement because, for the first time, a prosecutor, albeit from the police and not the KGB, was presented as a vile person. *Rumiantsev's Case* was followed by other movies—such as *Man Was Born* (Ordynskii, 1956), *Cranes Fly* (Kalatozov, 1957), *Nine Days of One Year* (Romm, 1962), *Ordinary Fascism* (Romm, 1966), and *I Am Twenty Years Old* (Khutsiev, 1965)—that overflowed with allusions to and barbs against official ideology. Filmmakers were also involved in the exposure of official mythology. Films such as *Chairman* (Saltykov, 1964) revealed the realities of rural life, while *Your Contemporary* (Raizman, 1968) unmasked the activities and hypocrisy of Soviet officials.

Filmmakers of the 1960s also attacked the official images of the past. Grigori Chukhrai, in his film *The Forty-First* (1956), was the first to describe White Army officers not as scoundrels but as normal and even noble people. The contribution made by Soviet film directors in portraying the real lives and the history of the Soviet people during this period was enormous.

What Is the Best Approximation of Objective Reality?

In everyday life, people make judgments regarding the accuracy of information they receive about the external world. In doing so, they assume that they have some criteria about objective reality to use as reference points or standards against which to compare the information (i.e., the alternative reality) they have received. We maintain that the best, but certainly not the only, approximation of objective reality is the subjective reality based on consensual scientific reality. At its best, consensual scientific reality incorporates as many sources of information as are available and, whenever possible, uses scientific methods to support the representativeness of this information. As such, we suggest that artistic realities, as they are presented in narrative movies or novels, should be critically analyzed from the viewpoint of scientific reality. At the same time, movies and novels should be included as sources of information to be used by scholars in their construction of scientific realities regarding the Soviet Union. Such efforts would contribute to the consensual scientific Soviet reality that resulted from the joint efforts of Soviet and Western social scientists up to the end of the 1980s.

Of course, consensual scientific reality is at best only an approximation of ontological reality, and the scholarly community has often failed to create a realistic picture of a given society (often because of either lack of information or ideological bias). Examples include the failure of Western scholars to comprehend the actual conditions of life in the Soviet Union under Stalin, or to understand the implications of China's Cultural Revolution.

While proclaiming consensual scientific reality to be the best approximation of ontological reality, we are aware that our own evaluation of scientific and artistic reality is unavoidably influenced by our domain, which is that of supporters of liberal ideologies in the Soviet Union. This domain will, of course, affect all of our judgments and conclusions.

Ideology and Soviet Movies

Another concept central to this chapter is that of ideology (or "conceptual machinery"; Berger & Luckmann, 1966). An ideology, defined rather broadly, is a more or less coherent set of values and beliefs that influence judgments of the external world and determine the behavior of individuals, groups, institutions, and societies (Geertz, 1973; Kluckhohn, 1951; about Soviet ideology, see Shlapentokh, 1986, 1988; White, 1988).

Each of the realities discussed above (with the exception, of course, of ontological reality) is influenced to a greater or lesser extent by one or more ideologies, which shape all of the signs and symbols used to describe and maintain images of the world. Among the most important functions of an ideology is control over image management—that is, control over subjective reality. This image-management function was central to all official Soviet ideologies before the late 1980s. The Soviet ideological apparatuses paid far more attention to the maintenance of certain world images than to the propagation of Soviet values, and movies played a prominent role in the Soviet propaganda machine's efforts (see Shlapentokh, 1986).

Of radical importance to this chapter is the way in which ideologies are institutionally controlled and the extent to which institutions (e.g., state or religious sects) try to monopolize the imposition of reality on the people within their spheres of influence. Although social control is sometimes imposed through "therapeutic" devices used to combat deviance (see Berger & Luckmann, 1966, pp. 112-113), the primary means of social control have always been coercive. George Orwell was one of the first Western authors to recognize the role of state violence in imposing "necessary reality" on citizens.

Several Soviet filmmakers, especially those active during the Stalin era, were concerned only with the political elite's reaction to their movies, and, disregarding the everyday experiences of their mass audiences, produced movies totally removed from ontological reality. The famous film *The Don Cossacks* (Pyr'iev, 1950) is a typical example. This film presents the lives of collective farmers as nearly paradisiacal; in reality, their lives had been devastated by collectivization and the war.

We do not want to imply, however, that such movies did not enjoy some (and occasionally even great) popularity among the Soviet people. Many Soviets used such movies to help them escape their grisly everyday concerns and to maintain some hope for the future, much as Americans used movies about the "high life" to help them through the Great Depression (although, unlike those in Soviet movies, the people and images depicted in American movies had some limited equivalents in real life). During the period of glasnost, an interesting discussion developed regarding *The Don Cossacks.* Although many critics lambasted the movie as a typical product of Stalinist distortion, if not outright falsification, of reality, some intellectuals defended the movie as having helped many Soviet people survive a grim time.

With the advent of glasnost, Soviet film directors were finally able to expose the role of physical fear in their lives and their creative work. Speaking (rather philosophically) about his life across the last five decades, Gabrilovich, a famous film director, commented:

> As a close witness of those years, I can contend that the Academies of Sciences, Arts, and Marxism, in establishing the moving forces of history, have neglected a crucial, and perhaps even the most important, mainspring: fear. In order to understand so many of the puzzles, secrets, and absurdities of our complicated life, it is necessary to comprehend, most of all, the real significance of fear. (quoted in *Sovietskaia Kul'tura,* June 17, 1989)[5]

In addition, glasnost allowed filmmakers to discuss the extent to which the authorities controlled their activities, often shelving movies for years.[6] Among the forbidden movies of the Brezhnev era were *Andrei Rublev* (Tarkovski, 1971), *Agony* (Klimov, 1971), *Komissar* (Askol'dov, 1989), and *Check at Roadblock* (German, 1987) (about these movies and others, see *Iskusstvo Kino,* September 1988, p. 67).[7]

In some cases, the ideology followed by a filmmaker has been "imposed" by his or her environment during the natural process of socialization. This was the case with liberal Soviet filmmakers such as El'dar Riasanov, who, regardless of political circumstances, tried to make movies according to his own internalized values and beliefs (compare, for instance, his *Carnival Night,* 1956, made during the Khrushchev era, with *Garage,* 1980, made during the Brezhnev era, and with his *The Forgotten Melody for Flute and Orchestra,* 1987, made during Gorbachev's glasnost, each of which reveals the same sympathies and antipathies).

In contrast, a filmmaker may also choose a particular ideology for conformist and opportunistic reasons and then may abandon this ideology as soon as it is convenient to do so. This approach was taken by directors such as Alexander Alov and Vladimir Naumov, whose movies include *Worried Youth* (1955), which followed the dictates of Soviet Marxism, and *Shore* (1984), which was clearly inspired by Russophile ideology. Similarly, Sergei Soloviev, who in 1988 made *Assa*, a film denouncing the fundamentals of the Soviet system, was also the director of *Hundred Days After Childhood* (1975). The latter film, made during the worst days of the Brezhnev era, was loyal to the system and, in turn, was highly praised by the regime.[8]

We hold that as both access to and opportunities to use varied sources of information decrease, and as institutional control over ideology increases, individuals have fewer opportunities to use their cognitive skills freely and are less able to create subjective realities that accurately reflect ontological reality. Of course, this proposition has clear implications for state control over the movie industry (about ideology and propaganda in movies, see Berger, 1972; Fiske, 1982; Maynard, 1975; Neale, 1985; Nichols, 1985; Taylor, 1971; Turner, 1988).

As Orwellian, totalitarian control over ideology decreases (as in democratic societies) and the variety of available information increases, there exists a greater chance that individuals can create subjective realities that more closely resemble ontological reality. Of course, in relatively free societies, radical ideologists on both the left and the right are able to, and often do, distort ontological reality more actively than do apologists of the dominant system (see MacBean, 1975). We maintain that the more an ideology criticizes the institutionalized, dominant beliefs and values of a given society, the more likely it is to spur cognitive activity regarding ontological reality.

Our approach is also similar to the old Marxist tradition that considers the dominant ideology to be a "false conscience" that impedes cognitive processing. According to this view, the effect of this false conscience is especially strong during times when the ideology is bolstered by mass terror.

Ideologies shape subjective realities primarily through influencing the selection of information and the "weight" given to single facts and processes (i.e., the degree of correctness and authority ascribed to the information). Ideologies also shape subjective realities by affecting the interpretation of cause-effect relationships.

The concept of ideology, as it has been presented here, is central to our recommendation of Soviet films as a source of information regarding Soviet society. In studies of specific cultures and/or time periods, films offer a unique vision of specific ideologies and the ways in which those ideologies influence the reflection of ontological reality.

The vision of the world offered by any ideology consists of countless elements, some of which may be understood through works of art and literature. Soviet movies provide countless reflections of the worldviews propagated by both official and unofficial ideologies active in Soviet society.

METHODOLOGY

In this chapter, we attempt to use Soviet movies reflecting several different prevalent ideologies as a source of information about those ideologies and about the lives of the Soviet people (similar publications on American movies include May, 1980; Steven, 1985; White & Averson, 1972). Our examination of Soviet movies will almost entirely disregard their artistic quality, the specific circumstances of their creation, their evaluation by critics, their influence on audiences, the role of filmmakers in Soviet society, the use of movies for propaganda, and popular attitudes toward movies. For information about the Soviet movie industry, we refer the reader to American publications by MacDonald (1938a, 1938b), Rimberg (1973), Cohen (1974), and Golovskoy and Rimberg (1986), and Soviet publications by Kogan (1968), Volkov (1974), Iutkevich (1986), Lawton (1987), and (in English) Zorkaya (1989).

In order to capture the complexity of Soviet life as presented in Soviet movies, the current study will use a relatively unstructured content analysis that uses social groups, as they are presented in Soviet movies, as its major unit. Since our sample of movies is technically unrepresentative of the universe of Soviet movies produced in the last two decades (about 6,000 movies; see TsSU USSR, 1987, p. 572), we will by and large avoid presenting frequencies and other statistics that would also be unrepresentative.[9]

In addition, we will use elementary decoding techniques to uncover the meaning of some Soviet movies. Because of censorship, Soviet film directors have resorted to the use of allegories, allusions, and historical parallels to convey certain messages. Decoding these elements in movies requires knowledge of the symbolic language widely used by Soviet intellectuals (including movie directors) to convey their messages to the audience.

Because of the tendency of artists to embed secret messages in their works, many literary and artistic works are virtually incomprehensible to those lacking either the intellectual sophistication or the knowledge of history and politics necessary to decode these works (i.e., those outside the Soviet intellectual scene). Coding and decoding artistic works is an important element of intellectual activity in the Soviet Union, and is a common topic of conversation at social gatherings. Film director Andrei Tarkovski was particularly skilled at such encoding, and his films, such as *Andrei Rublev* (1971), *Soliaris* (1973), and *Mirror* (1975), require considerable intellectual effort in order to interpret the hidden messages. (In 1975, Leonid Batkin, a prominent intellectual, spent two hours at a special seminar analyzing *Mirror* and explaining all its metaphors. This analysis was published in the November 1988 issue of *Iskusstvo Kino*.)[10]

Of course, even with our own experiences of living in the Soviet Union (50 years for the senior author and 30 years for the junior author) and of watching Soviet movies from the inside, we concede that our interpretation of specific Soviet movies, especially those that are particularly complex and allegoric, may be assailable in light of modern structuralist semiotics. However, we are confident that our interpretations are similar to those of the majority of Soviet liberal intellectuals, with whom we share not only a history, but a set of values and beliefs. As such, we leave unaddressed any possible differences in the ways others might perceive the movies under examination and assume that our perceptions are shared by the average Soviet liberal intellectual (about Soviet liberal intellectuals, see Shlapentokh, 1990).

The Social Groups in Question

The following social groups in Soviet society, as they are portrayed in Soviet movies, are used as the major units of analysis in this chapter: the bureaucracy, the intelligentsia (with the intellectuals as its core), the masses (both Russians and non-Russians), and society as a whole. Each of these groups is described below.

By the end of the 1980s, the bureaucracy of the Soviet Union consisted primarily of party apparatchiks, figures in various official public organizations (e.g., the Young Communist League, the trade unions, the Union of Soviet Writers), officials in government bodies, and directors of large enterprises. All of these people are part of the Nomenclature, which means that they are appointed by party committees at various levels. Although estimates of the size of the late 1980s Soviet bureaucracy vary, a widely accepted number is about 18 million (for more about Soviet bureaucracy, see Voslenski, 1980).

There are two approaches to defining the intelligentsia and the intellectuals. The first approach, which is normative and therefore somewhat more subjective, supposes that a member of the intelligentsia (or an intellectual) is one who possesses a cluster of intellectual, cultural, and (most important) moral virtues, such as kindness and altruism, and who serves as a model for the rest of society. This approach was dominant in prerevolutionary Russia and continues to be very popular in the Soviet Union (e.g., Dudintsev, 1987; Granin, 1987, 1988; Pomerants, 1985; Solzhenitsyn, 1974; see also the discussions in *Literaturnaia Gazeta*, August 17, 1988; September 21, 1988; November 23, 1988). By utilizing such formal criteria, it is estimated that there are approximately 700,000 highly educated people formally engaged in creative activity in the Soviet Union. Of these, probably about 10% are highly qualified (for more about Soviet intellectuals in the post-Stalin era, see Shlapentokh, 1990). Soviet film directors would clearly be included in this latter group.

The second approach to defining the intelligentsia and intellectuals uses formal criteria, such as level of education and involvement in creative work (that is, the production of either new ideas or new things). This approach is accepted by official Soviet statisticians and by Soviet sociologists (e.g., Shkaratan, 1982; Zaslavskaia, 1988, p. 17).

The masses, as they are presented in Soviet movies, consist primarily of workers and peasants with relatively little education. Soviet movie directors rarely use clerks or technical personnel as representatives of the masses, preferring instead to have their protagonists work in factories or on collective farms.

The analysis of each of these social groups will begin with an examination of its "central tendency" (i.e., the predominant image of the social group as presented in Soviet movies), and will then examine other trends in the presentation of that group. Thus any given ideology might figure heavily in the depiction of one social group, but only secondarily in the portrayal of other groups.

The Era in Question

As mentioned earlier, a movie's portrayal of any facet of life is determined in part by the ideological context in which the movie is made. Thus it is necessary to consider the era in which a movie was created, the degree of institutional and ideological pressure on the movie's director, and the ideology chosen by the director (regardless of whether the director considered him- or herself to be a propagandist for the ruling elite).

Soviet society went through two distinct periods during the 1970s and 1980s. Pre-1985 regimes were repressive (albeit mildly so, in comparison with Stalin's time) and strongly hostile to intellectuals as well as to ideologies that encouraged even modest forms of liberalization. As a result, film directors were essentially unable to make movies that overtly confronted or criticized these regimes. By using allegories and other forms of Aesopian language, however, film directors were able to portray some segments of Soviet life and Soviet society in ways that more accurately reflected ontological reality.[11]

Filmmakers unwilling to follow the dictates of the official ideology were able to develop facets of other ideologies that, although at odds with the ideology supported by the regime, were not considered totally hostile. It is noteworthy that most of these mildly oppositional ideologies had advocates in the highest echelons of power, which accounts in part for the emergence of a few critical movies during the Brezhnev era.

Since 1986, the Gorbachev regime has given movie directors substantially more freedom, and many directors have approached Soviet life from a new democratic, antisocialist ideological perspective.

MAJOR IDEOLOGICAL TRENDS: SUMMARY OF CHARACTERISTICS

In the 1970s and the first half of the 1980s, Soviet movies were influenced by several main ideological trends that differed from one another in several respects. First, some of them (e.g., Brezhnevian and Russophile) were conservative and static, whereas others (e.g., neo-Stalinist, neo-Leninist, and democratic) were dynamic and critical of the current state of affairs in Soviet society. Each had its own central value: For the Brezhnevian and neo-Stalinist ideologies, it was the might of state; for Russophile ideology, it was Russian patriotism and tradition; for neo-Leninist ideology, social progress; for democratic ideology, individual freedom.

The democratic ideology stood alone in its hostility to the basic principles of socialism and the Soviet system. Neo-Leninist ideology, although similar in many ways to democratic ideology, still assumed the possibility of improving Soviet socialism according to Leninist precepts. The two ideologies were most similar in their portrayals of the bureaucracy, and least similar in their presentations of society as a whole (particularly of the masses).

Each of the various ideologies offered its own explanation for the unsatisfactory condition of Soviet society. Russophiles pointed to Western moral decadence and the obliteration of Russian tradition and religion, neo-Stalinists implicated the low labor ethics of the masses, neo-Leninists blamed bureaucratization, and democrats denounced "the system" and its lack of democracy (for more about Soviet ideologies, see Shlapentokh, 1988, 1989).

Of course, each ideology also had its own vision of a better future. Russophiles looked to a resurgence of Russian traditions, neo-Stalinists sought a restoration of order, neo-Leninists favored the active participation of the masses in economic and political activity, and democrats called for a radical transformation of Soviet society to a Western-type system.

Of all the competing ideologies in the Soviet Union, the neo-Leninist and Russophile ideologies exerted the strongest influence on the Soviet movie industry in the 1970s and the early 1980s. Although both ideologies were critical of Soviet life, neither demonstrated hostility to the essence of the Soviet system. As such, filmmakers from these schools were allowed a measure of nonconformity, which they could exercise without seriously jeopardizing their official position in the movie industry.

Neo-Stalinist ideology was dominant for a short period in 1983-1985, and democratic ideology was the most influential from 1986 to 1989. Of all the ideologies discussed, the democratic and neo-Leninist ideologies have been the most critical of Soviet society. Because the proponents of these ideologies have not been controlled by any institution or coerced to propagate institutional values, they have been able to combat many official dogmas and beliefs. Thus, despite their own biases, they have been perhaps most able to depict the ontological realities of Soviet life.

SAMPLE

The current study is based on an analysis of about 110 films. The composition of the sample (which is admittedly nonrandom) was dictated primarily by the availability of Soviet films in the U.S. market. The selection of films from those available was then affected by other factors, including the popularity of each film. Since the popularity of any given film reflects the extent to which its ideology is shared by Soviet viewers, movies that were popular in the Soviet Union were given priority. Thus, for example, the sample includes all of the films of El'dar Riasanov and Vladimir Men'shov, probably two of the most popular Soviet film directors.

Reflecting the general trend toward privatization in Soviet life, 61% of the films deal exclusively or primarily with the private lives of their contemporary characters, 17% focus primarily on contemporary public life, and 22% deal with public and private life in the past. Similarly, 42% of the films have plots that unfold mainly in private homes, 15% in places of entertainment or vacation resorts, 5% in hospitals, and 28% at the workplace.

Of course, the ideological character of several of the films is absolutely clear. Films such as *Shore* (Alov & Naumov, 1984) and *Do Not Shoot the White Swans* (Nakhapetov, 1982) are clearly representative of Russophile ideology; *We, the Undersigned* (Lioznova, 1979), *Repentance* (Abuladze, 1984), and *My Friend Lapshin* (German, 1985) express neo-Leninist ideology; and *Confrontation* (Aranovich, 1985) reveals a neo-Stalinist perspective.

Most of the films, however, despite having prevailing political lines, are mixtures of various ideological perspectives. Examples include *Children's Home* (Mosenko, 1982) and *The Blonde Around the Corner* (Bortko, 1984). Thus a film's particular ideological label does not exclude its use in a discussion of another ideology.

Finally, it is likely that some filmmakers who have produced films reflecting particular ideologies would have actually preferred them to reflect altogether different ideologies. For example, the makers of *My Dear Edison* (Fridberg, 1986) and *Repentance* (Abuladze, 1984) probably would have preferred to adopt a clear stance in favor of democracy rather than neo-Leninism, but were constrained from doing so by the political climate dominant during the films' production.

THE CHARACTERIZATION OF
VARIOUS SOCIAL GROUPS IN SOVIET FILMS

The Bureaucracy

Party bosses or state officials are the focus of the majority of Soviet movies, regardless of the movies' ideological orientations. With the exception of a few films reflecting official Brezhnev-era ideology, Soviet movies of the 1970s are generally hostile to bureaucrats. Of the various ideologies, neo-Leninism is most preoccupied with the bureaucracy. Movies reflecting Russophile and democratic ideologies tend to portray bureaucrats in the same light as do neo-Leninist movies.

Two images of the bureaucracy are developed in Soviet movies. Although both denounce bureaucrats as those most responsible for the defects of Soviet life, the images differ in their respective theories regarding the origins of existing problems. The first theory, referred to as the "extermination theory," suggests that the Soviet Union's current problems are rooted in the Stalin era, during which time the best of the apparatchiks were exterminated. The second theory, referred to as the "degeneration theory," sees the present bureaucracy as a product of the degeneration of the party apparatus, a process that started almost immediately after the civil war of 1917-1921.

The extinction theory, which emerged during Khrushchev's time, clearly distinguishes between the revolutionary regime (which extended from the beginning of the Bolshevik revolution to the time of the great purges) and the Stalin era. Those who participated in the revolution and the civil war are presented as honest and unselfish people devoted to the cause of communism, whereas those who followed are deemed cynical, despotic, and totally lacking in concern for the public good. The Stalinists' ascension to power is seen as a conspiracy, and any fundamental continuity between the regimes of Lenin and Stalin is denied. The distinction between the two regimes is supported by the fact that Lenin's old guard, the generation of the revolution, was physically exterminated by the Stalinists.

The film *My Friend Lapshin* (German, 1985), which provides a clear example of perceived discontinuities between the regimes of Lenin and Stalin, portrays life in 1935, when the mass terror had just begun. Lapshin, the film's protagonist, is the chief of the criminal investigation department in a small provincial town. He is endowed with positive characteristics that clearly distinguish him from the present bureaucracy. He and his friends have no interest in careers or material goods and live in a small, crowded apartment. He is democratically oriented and intensely dedicated to his job of defending the people.

It is clear that the filmmaker wants to present Lapshin, his friends, and his colleagues as ideal personalities. Interestingly, the film ignores the repressions against peasants and other "enemies of the people" in which Lapshin has to participate. Only once is the word *Solovki*—the name of a notorious concentration camp created in the 1920s—mentioned, and even then it comes up in a rather facetious way. Although we are told that Lapshin was wounded in the civil war and that he suffers as a result of his wound, we hear nothing about the sufferings of others (e.g., the "class enemies"), who are depicted as criminals and cruel rural bandits.

The same idealization of the purged party apparatus is seen in *Repentance* (Abuladze, 1984). Those sent to their deaths by Varlam, the head of the city, are depicted as noble and devoted party members. Similar themes are apparent in *War Romance* (Todorovskii, 1984).

Other films reflect a somewhat different vision of Soviet bureaucrats and apparatchiks. *And Life, and Tears, and Love* (Gubenko, 1983), *Sibiriada*

(Mikhalkov-Konchalovskii, 1979), and *Declaration of Love* (Averbakh, 1978) are good examples of such films. The author of the first of these films, like that of *Lapshin* (German, 1985), juxtaposes different generations of apparatchiks. Unlike the author of *Lapshin*, however, he sees basic continuity between the bureaucrats of the first period and those of the second. *And Life* presents the revolutionary protagonists with some irony, and generally rather positively, despite their occasional cruelty when fighting for their ideals (the script compares the terrors of the Russian Revolution with those of the French Revolution). The bureaucrats of the 1930s, however, are presented as cruel, unprincipled brutes. The 1930s bureaucrats—now residents of the nursing home in which the film unfolds—are the most negative characters in the film. One old lady is portrayed as a fanatic who admires power, even when it is used for the persecution of honest people (as was the case in the period of the purges). The woman excitedly tells of her infatuation with a political scoundrel who was active in the mass repressions. Although it does not deny differences between the apparatchiks of the 1920s and those of the 1930s, the film suggests that both were created by the same political system. Even the old revolutionary song "We Boldly Will March Forward Fighting for Soviet Power and We Will All Die Fighting for It" is used in a clearly ironic way, implying that the revolution devoured its children.

According to *Sibiriada*, the 1950s and 1960s marked a new phase in the degeneration of Soviet society and bureaucracy. In the film, this degeneration is seen in a general who becomes the first secretary of the regional party committee after the war. Although the character is not totally without merit—it is clear that his professional work is extremely important to him—he nonetheless violates the example set by his visionary predecessors and pursues the narrow, parochial interests of his region, with little concern for the country. The film depicts the regional party secretary, already very far from the ordinary people, as surrounded by obsequious assistants and lacking regular contact with the masses. Flying about his region like a demigod, he descends to earth for occasional conversations with the common people, who are insincere with him. Only a few very old people, by taking the role of court jester, can speak freely with him. His own boss, a secretary of the Central Committee, is even more arrogant: he does not even invite him to sit down when speaking with him in his Moscow office.

Although bureaucrats in some neo-Leninist-oriented films such as *Sibiriada* still care about their professional obligations, bureaucrats in other films are portrayed as almost entirely devoid of any genuine sense of responsibility toward society. Films such as *The Top Guy* (Sirenko, 1986), *We, the Undersigned* (Lioznova, 1979), *My Dear Edison* (Fridberg, 1986), *Fell in Love at My Own Request* (Popov, 1982), *The Individual from the Entourage* (Rozenberg, 1989), and *Cold Summer of 1953* (Proshkin, 1987) are particularly interesting in this regard. Bureaucrats in these films are concerned primarily with their privileges, and are not above engaging in semicriminal or even criminal activity if it can improve their well-being (see, for example, *We, the Undersigned*). Striving to preserve their privileges and their prestigious jobs, these bureaucrats become quite cynical, resourceful, and cunning. The films provide detailed descriptions of three primary methods used by today's Soviet bureaucrats to survive and to satisfy their own ambitions. Each of these—accommodation, repression, and demagoguery—will be discussed below.

Accommodation

In their portrayal of the Soviet bureaucracy as the main culprit behind Soviet problems, neo-Leninist films criticize the apparatchiks' abilities to adjust to new policies and new trends without forfeiting their positions or their privileges. *Encounter with My Youth* (Popov, 1982) shows how easily a bureaucrat can undermine a positive policy (in this case, the expansion of worker participation in management) by only pretending to implement it. In the film, a shrewd but corrupt bureaucrat advises his old friend, the director of a large plant, how to adapt to the new campaign without relinquishing his old, paternalistic style of management.

In *My Dear Edison*, the director of a research institute is forced to adapt to a post-Brezhnev-era campaign that promotes a modest life-style. The director is building a resort house for the institute, replete with special rooms sumptuously decorated for the director and his guests—big shots from the capital who come to inspect the institute's activities. Amid the campaign against corruption, the director decides that to keep these rooms would be dangerous. With no qualms whatsoever, he orders that everything hinting of luxury, including furniture and rugs, be destroyed in order to hide his intentions. *My Dear Edison*, like other films, portrays bureaucrats as interdependent, mutually supportive criminals able to adapt their behavior to almost any political situation. As *My Dear Edison* suggests, any attempt to remove corrupt and indifferent bureaucrats through the use of bureaucratic means is futile.

Repression

The theme of the bureaucrat ready to use any means to destroy a potential enemy was rather muted in films released prior to 1985, but is becoming increasingly prevalent. The director of the research institute in *My Dear Edison* perpetrates numerous misdeeds: He falsifies statistics, thwarts progress, and ignores the masses. Bureaucrats threaten him, pointing out that his words and deeds are anti-Soviet and that he could be in trouble. An extremely talented new research worker (humorously named Edison), determined to divulge the real state of affairs at the institute, becomes the target of merciless persecution. He is removed from research work, deprived of a separate room in his dormitory, and shunned by his colleagues. It is clear that the director will stop at nothing to punish the young scholar. The terror dominating the landscape at the institute demoralizes everyone, including an old professor who tries valiantly to resist the director but finally capitulates and agrees to write a doctoral dissertation for the director, who is totally ignorant of science.

Demagoguery

Soviet films are especially attentive to bureaucrats' use of sophistry, obfuscation, and propaganda in defense of their position and privileges. *The Top Guy* is particularly powerful in exposing this facet of bureaucratic activity. The film's portrayal of the terrible plight of agriculture is accompanied by an extremely optimistic radio broadcast enumerating various achievements by workers in the countryside.

Along with directly distorting the truth, bureaucrats are often depicted as recognizing various problems and as demonstrating a certain level of objectivity and sensitivity to human needs, only to forget their promises the next moment, as is the case with the high officials depicted in *Director of a Children's Home* (Olshanskii & Olshanskii, 1980).

Bureaucrats are portrayed as having developed a complex system of arguments to justify their unlawful behavior and their failures. One such argument is that of Russian chauvinism. This argument—"We are all Russians"—is used in *We, the Undersigned* when it is necessary to persuade the chief of the commission to sign fake papers regarding the completion of a construction project. Similar nationalistic arguments are used by the journalists in *The Top Guy*, who prepare an inaccurate report on life in the village.

Bureaucrats are also depicted in several films as spreading anti-Semitic feelings. One of the protagonists of *My Dear Edison*, an extremely able scholar, is a Jew. It is obvious to Soviet viewers that his ethnic origin is behind many of the troubles in his life (in particular, finding a different job). He is deftly exploited by the institute's director, who, as mentioned above, pressures the protagonist into preparing a dissertation for him.

Anti-Western propaganda is also portrayed as being central to the ideological arsenal of the bureaucrats. Using a blend of Russophilism and Marxism, they present the West as inhumane and depraved. The corrupt West is juxtaposed with the benign and moral Soviet Russia in order to dupe the masses and hide the bureaucrats' incompetence and corruption. *My Dear Edison* openly mocks officials who rail against the corruption of the West, but who are, in fact, its admirers. A despicable bureaucrat in this film, quite proud to have visited various Western countries, brandishes a Japanese pen as a symbol of his high social position and success.

Bureaucrats as the Enemies of Perestroika

The advent of glasnost heralded the emergence of numerous movies that depict bureaucrats as committed enemies of perestroika, liberalization, and economic reform. The party and state officials in these democratically oriented movies hate the new regime, gloat over its difficulties, and anxiously await its failure and the subsequent restoration of the ancient regime.

In *Because of the Change of Job* (Linkov, 1986), party apparatchiks are depicted as so hostile to perestroika that they kill one of their own. The victim, having recanted his past, wanted to start a new life and participate actively in the renewal of socialist society.

An official in *The Actress from Gribov* (Kvanikhidze, 1989) promises that "our time will come, and it will be thrust under the noses of all reluctant people." A similar hope is held by Kropotov, the director of a large Leningrad enterprise in *Red Arrow* (Sheshukov, 1986). Rude, power hungry, and practiced in the art of demagoguery, Kropotov hates perestroika with all his heart and longs for its demise. The party officials in *Nadia Rodionova* (Soviet TV, 1989) obstruct democratization in their city by trying to use their old ways to corrupt the election of a deputy of the Soviet parliament, all the while ignoring the real mood of the masses.

Positive Images of the Bureaucracy

As mentioned above, negative presentations of bureaucrats are central to most Soviet movies. In neo-Stalinist-oriented movies, however, bureaucrats, especially those active in the repressive apparatus (i.e., the KGB, the police, and the army), are treated differently.

Like neo-Leninism, neo-Stalinism appeared as a response to the economic stagnation and total corruption of the Brezhnev era. Although similar to neo-Leninism in its critique of bureaucracy, neo-Stalinism favors a different approach to change. While neo-Leninist (as well as democratic) movies assume that the bureaucracy should be controlled from below, neo-Stalinist movies trust neither the intellectuals nor the masses, considering them, like the bureaucracy, to be in need of control from above. Because the neo-Stalinist political design implies a strong central power, neo-Stalinist movies approach the state mechanism more conservatively than do neo-Leninist movies. As a result, neo-Stalinists have failed to elaborate a strongly negative image of bureaucracy similar to that presented by the neo-Leninists. Instead, the neo-Stalinists concentrate their attention on portraying positive images of Russia's rulers (e.g., representatives of security forces, the militia, the army), whom they view as central to the rejuvenation of the country. The positive qualities of these rulers are emphasized, thereby distinguishing them from members of Brezhnev's bureaucracy.

In *Confrontation* (Aranovich, 1985) a KGB man is presented as a national hero and as a potential savior of society. Because neo-Stalinists wish to preserve the authority of the state, they are less openly critical of the bureaucracy—although the film's protagonist is clearly displeased with the bureaucracy, he rarely directly criticizes party officials. During the segments of the film concerned with the pursuit of a traitor, a party bureaucrat appears only once, and then as a negative character who actually obstructs the search. The protagonist appeals to practically every segment of Soviet society for assistance in his search, but fails to solicit help from the party apparatus.

Confrontation clearly emphasizes the positive characteristics of KGB members. According to the film, KGB agents oppose criminal and semi-criminal activity and are thus quite different from the corrupt, Brezhnev-type party bureaucrats. The secret police, particularly those at the top, are never portrayed as using their position to obtain privileges. One of the film's main characters, a Georgian KGB man who, because of his nationality, is stereotypically expected to be prone to quasi-illegal activities, points out that the meat he purchased for a party was obtained absolutely legally. Another of the film's protagonists is a high-ranking KGB officer who stays in a hotel together with common citizens. His apartment is modest, and a lower-ranking provincial KGB man is heard bragging that he enjoys a better apartment than does his superior. The protagonist's clothes are quite modest; a tailor contemptuously remarks about his unstylish manner of dress. Viewers do not see him shopping at any special store, and the canteen where he entertains a female journalist apparently contains no special products or reduced prices. While in the provinces, he dines at a colleague's apartment.

The KGB officer is also portrayed as a good family man. He calls his wife regularly and rejects the sexual advances of a young girl. He exhibits great physical courage and appears to have no nationalistic prejudices. Although one Jew in the film is presented as a negative character, the protagonist refers to another Jew in glowing terms. The fact that the traitor being tracked is a Russian further demonstrates that *Confrontation*'s creator had no intention of catering to Russian chauvinism.

Neo-Stalinist films such as *Confrontation* also portray bureaucrats as educated individuals who respect intellectuals. *Confrontation*'s protagonist, for example, demonstrates his respect through his knowledge of and regard for Mandel'shtam, the famous elitist Russian poet. KGB men also demonstrate their appreciation for intellectuals through their free thinking. *Confrontation*'s protagonist, for example, clashes with party officials who try to stop a journalist's activity on the grounds that her publications will provide fuel for bourgeois propaganda. He also demonstrates his appreciation for Vladimir Vysotskii, the famous semiofficial bard of the Brezhnev era. The protagonist's affinity for the intellectuals is further highlighted through contrast with the main villain's disdain for literature.

Unlike classic Stalinism, neo-Stalinist films portray Soviet apparatchiks as humane and compassionate toward ordinary people, and direct comparisons are sometimes made between the two groups of Stalinists. In *Confrontation*, for example, the protagonist often disagrees with those who idealize Stalin's time and who complain about the excessive humanism of the present regime. The protagonist is also extremely polite to a suspected criminal who complains that the Stalin era has returned. Since this complainer is clearly a negative character, it is evident that his complaints are baseless. The protagonist points out that the neo-Stalinist ruling elite will not repeat the Stalin-era practice of spying on citizens, and he states that he does not care about citizens' correspondence with foreign countries, including Israel.

Because the army and the militia are also included in the repressive apparatus, they enjoy treatment similar to that given the KGB in neo-Stalinist films. In films such as *I Took Control Over the City* (Soviet TV, 1979), *Railway Station for Two* (Riasanov, 1982), *Night Accident* (Dunaiaeva, 1981), *Passing Twice* (Gordon, 1979), *Black Castle* (Ptashuk, 1980), and *Sunday, Eight O'Clock* (Zlobin, 1988), militia members are presented as honest and courageous.

"Democratic Bureaucrats" in Gorbachev's Time

In the spirit of Gorbachev's reforms, such as privatization in the economy and liberalization of the political system, neo-Leninist and democratically oriented movies began to present officials and managers who heartily support the ideas of the new regime and who are willing to combat their conservative colleagues. Such pro-Gorbachev apparatchiks appear in Brovkin's *The Three People on the Red Rug* (1989), in which Mikhail Soshkin, the new chairman of a collective farm, fervently argues in defense of privatization in the countryside with his opponent, an old party apparatchik. He denounces the existing economic relations as being responsible for the deterioration of agriculture. He even refers to the ancient Roman Empire, which "perished because of the wrong attitudes toward work."

The Intellectuals

Intellectuals are presented dualistically in Soviet movies. On one hand, most Soviet movies depict members of the intellectual community as devoted to their professional work and to some social ideals, and try, albeit moderately and inconsistently, to defend the intellectuals. On the other hand, Soviet movies also tend to denounce the intellectuals' depravity, which is presented as similar to the apparatchiks' corruption. The tenor in portraying the intellectuals is set, once again, by the neo-Leninists and is supported by the neo-Stalinists and democrats, but is supported only partially by the Russophiles. The two dominant representations of the Soviet intellectuals will be discussed separately.

The Positive Features of Intellectuals

True intellectuals are the only valuable characters in these movies. Great emphasis is placed on the intellectuals' creativity and dedication to their professional duties, traits that are depicted as absent among ordinary people.

Praise for creative intellectuals is found in such movies as *Engineer Berezhkov* (Beck, 1988), in which an engineer, despite the obstacles created by the Soviet system, continues his activities as an inventor. Similarly, *The Everyday Life and Holidays of Serafimy Gliukina* (Goriaev, 1988) describes the selfless activity of the female cultural worker from whom the movie derives its name. In *Fast Train* (Iashin, 1989) an intellectual in a remote city risks running a semiprivate theater in order to keep Russian liberal cultural traditions alive. Similar treatment of intellectuals is seen in *Grasshopper* (Grigoriev, 1986), in which a young noble scholar absorbed with his work permits himself to be fooled by an opportunistic woman. He succumbs to her trap and they marry, but eventually divorce. He gives her his car as well as his apartment, which are invaluable assets in Moscow.

Kind People (Shakhnazarov, 1980) portrays a historian committed to his job; in *The Blonde Around the Corner* (Bortko, 1984) we meet a similarly dedicated scientist. The image of an honest and sympathetic musician is portrayed in *Railway Station for Two* (Riasanov, 1982). Even apparently corrupt intellectuals can be dedicated to their jobs, as seen in *Garage* (Riasanov, 1980).

According to neo-Leninist and neo-Stalinist films, intellectuals also have another positive characteristic: They generally lack any national prejudice. Filmmakers identify minorities either through their places of origin and accents or through other identifiable national traits. Residents of Caucasus, for example, are often presented as temperamental (*Vanity of Vanities*, Surikova, 1979), as hospitable (*The Kidnapping of the Century*, Makarov, 1981), or as having a patriarchal approach to life (*Married Bachelor*, Rogov, 1983). According to neo-Leninist films, the national characteristics of minorities do not cause them problems when they deal with Russian intellectuals. In fact, these relationships, as manifested in liaisons and intermarriages between Russian intellectuals and minorities, are presented as being quite harmonious.

Intellectuals as Fighters Against Bureaucracy

When portraying the fight against bureaucracy, films with neo-Leninist and democratic tendencies focus not on the masses, and certainly not on the moral recovery of the apparatchiks, but on single, brave individuals, usually intellectuals. These heroes in the fight against bureaucracy are likened to the revolutionaries of the past—kind, concerned about others, and deeply devoted to their professional work (see Mosenko's *Children's Home*, 1982; Fridberg's *My Dear Edison*, 1986; Sirenko's *The Top Guy*, 1986; Troshchenko's *The Long Road to Herself*, 1983; Bykov's *Leveret*, 1985; Gubenko's *And Life, and Tears, and Love*, 1983; and Averbakh's *Declaration of Love*, 1978). In many cases, such heroes are romantic and have great respect for love (Nakhapetov's *Valentine and Valentina*, 1983;

Popov's *Fell in Love at My Own Request*, 1982; Riasanov's *Railway Station for Two*, 1982; Troshchenko's *The Long Road to Herself*, 1983; and Goriaev's *The Everyday Life and Holidays of Serafimy Gliukina*, 1988).

Intellectual heroes follow almost the same pattern of behavior in all neo-Leninist films. First, they try to improve bad situations by turning to party officials for help, only to receive either open animosity (*My Dear Edison, The Top Guy*) or a bureaucratic response that implies no real action (*Leveret, Director of a Children's Home*). Although such protagonists occasionally find positively responsive bureaucrats, these bureaucrats usually urge the protagonists to stop their activity and concentrate on some minor local improvements (e.g., *The Top Guy*). Disenchanted with bureaucracy, the protagonists then appeal to ordinary people, assuming that they will be eager to support the protagonists' noble goals.

Movies of the Brezhnev era (and even a few years thereafter), when corruption and conformity had peaked, praise not only those intellectuals who defy the system, but also those who abandon public activity (which could only benefit the party) in order to pursue private life (where they preserve their honesty). This is the case with Gushchin, the protagonist of *Late Date* (Grigoriev, 1986).

Intellectuals in Russophile Movies

Although Russophile movies resemble neo-Leninist and democratic movies in their praise of intellectuals, the characteristics they praise are quite different. Whereas neo-Leninist and democratic movies laud intellectuals for their nonconformity and their readiness to fight the bureaucrats, Russophile films emphasize the intellectuals' support for Russian values. Even if these intellectuals go astray, they are easily brought back to traditional tenets.

In several films, good intellectuals demonstrate their inclination to make sacrifices for the sake of the Russian people (Nakhapetov's *Do Not Shoot the White Swans*, 1982; Holov's *Married for the First Time*, 1978). In *Do Not Shoot the White Swans*, a young female teacher reveals her allegiance to Russian values in various ways, including prominently displaying a book on medieval Russian art with a picture of an icon, and demonstrating her strong interest in Russian classical literature, with its obvious religious overtones. Most important, her self-effacing behavior and selfless service reveal her allegiance to Russian values. In *Married for the First Time*, the protagonist is a self-taught countryside intellectual who works to create a museum in the local church and to spread Russian culture throughout the village.

An intellectual's repentance is shown in the film *Turn* (Abrashidov, 1979), which is explicitly influenced by Dostoevsky's *Crime and Punishment* and imbued with high religious overtones. The film's protagonist, a prosperous, middle-aged intellectual, neglects Russian Christian values and becomes absorbed with vain and petty issues, such as his scientific career and prestigious vacations. An accident, in which an old woman is hit by the protagonist's car, becomes a turning point in his life. At the beginning of the ordeal, he remains involved in his career and desperately tries to avoid imprisonment. As events unfold, however, he concludes that he is guilty not only of hitting the woman, but in a broader sense as well. He begins to realize that his life has been emotionally cold and meaningless, and, like Raskolnikov, he is ready to go to prison, in hopes that suffering will purify him. The protagonist is acquitted by the court, however, and seems to return to his old life-style. Still, the spiritual awakening triggered by his time of trial and uncertainty is not completely lost, and the film implies that he is on the path of moral rehabilitation. This theme of the moral recuperation of an intellectual gone astray in a life full of temptation is seen in other films as well, such as *Relatives* (Mikhalkov, 1982).

Russophile movies present the Western life-style as the major threat to the Russian intelligentsia and youth. In *Relatives*, Western values are blamed for destroying the life of a young girl who, like her mother, is completely under the influence of the West. The girl is too absorbed with the roaring sounds of a Western song and its constant refrain of "I love you" to take the time to react to her mother's worries.

In Russophile films, Western culture is primarily identified with consumerism and sexual promiscuity. Although these movies do not ignore the efficiency of the Western economy and science, such achievements receive no praise. Moreover, in portraying village life as more virtuous than urban life, Russophiles imply that technological progress is an enemy of high moral values. For this reason, it is ultimately not intellectuals, with their close links to science and to the West, who emerge as the true bastions of Russian values and the hope of the country, but rather the common people. The author of *A Few Days from the Life of Oblomov* (Mikhalkov, 1980) changes the classic interpretation of Goncharov's novel portraying Oblomov, who avoids any professional activity or career, as a positive protagonist. Oblomov is contrasted with Shtolz, who is condemned as a hustler, unable to appreciate lofty and sublime ideas as can his friend.

The Negative Features of Intellectuals

Although some film directors try to emphasize the noble features of the intellectuals, others are much more critical of the intellectual community (of which filmmakers are members). In some cases, critical filmmakers present intellectuals as no better than bureaucrats or the masses. Intellectuals are shown yearning for the same things as bureaucrats (i.e., material comfort and prestige), and as cynical, conformist, and engaged in a perennial hunt for pleasures and Western goods.

In their depictions of modern Soviet intellectuals, neo-Leninist films, especially those made prior to 1986, strongly emphasize the sexual permissiveness of the intellectuals. A major reason for this focus is that filmmakers, intending to portray the complete cynicism of modern educated individuals and their contempt for any principles and ideals, are prohibited by censorship from discussing the political attitudes of their characters. Filmmakers therefore focus on their characters' total disregard for moral principles in sexual relations in order to make their point.

Love affairs are not always presented as symbols of cynicism, however. Reasons for involvement in romance range from the characters' boredom with provincial life and a woman's compassion for a loser (Kheifets's *The Only One*, 1976), to the younger generation's rebellion against parental domination (Lapshin's *Prolong the Enchantment*, 1977), to the desire for real passion (Manasarova's *A Fantasy on Love Themes*, 1981; Lebedev's *Accuse Klava for My Death*, 1980). In most cases, however, promiscuity and cheating serve as symbols for the total cynicism of Soviet intellectuals and of society in general.

For the most part, libertinism is regarded by filmmakers as a product of Soviet society, not of cultural traditions. Thus filmmakers always try to avoid national stereotypes, such as presenting philanderers as Caucasians, who have a reputation in the Soviet Union for a proclivity toward a sexually loose lifestyle. In fact, Caucasian men are quite often presented as exemplary family men (Surikova's *Vanity of Vanities*, 1979; Rogov's *Married Bachelor*, 1984).

In these films, women are rarely presented as victims of lecherous men (Olshanskii & Olshanskii's *Director of a Children's Home*, 1980, is one exception)—females are portrayed as just as cynically promiscuous as males. The intellectuals and party officials in all of these films are generally rather tolerant of the love affairs of their colleagues, friends, and relatives. They apparently accept lying as well, except when done in excess or to friends. Intellectuals view moral degeneration and cynicism not as aberrations, but as normal behavior, and sometimes even as positive traits.

The Most Attractive (Bazhanov, 1985) portrays two intellectuals in a marriage in which the husband openly cheats on his wife. Although the wife apparently knows about her husband's behavior, this knowledge does not spoil their relationship. The viewer can easily imagine that she is similarly involved. The film's other heroine, also an intellectual, marries a man she does not love. Enchanted by eighteenth-century French culture (known for its erotic tastes), she quotes La Rochefoucauld. The reference to eighteenth-century French culture by the heroine, who is apparently of dubious reputation, implies that she is not opposed to cheating on her husband. She assumes that by cheating on him she would be imitating the great courtesans of the French court. In *Vanity of Vanities* (Surikova, 1979), the female friend of a lonely divorced woman finds a lover to console her, and the lover turns out to be married. *Valentine and Valentina* (Nakhapetov, 1983) also depicts a liaison between a female intellectual and a married man.

Intellectuals and their offspring boast about their privileges in comparison with ordinary people. Higher education (especially in such prestigious establishments as Moscow University), knowledge of foreign languages and cultures (as in *Valentine and Valentina*), and possession of highly coveted foreign goods are symbols of their privileges. Their contempt for the masses is even greater than their distaste for the bureaucracy. They mock their intellectual forefathers, the Populists, who sacrificed their careers to serve the people (Sirenko's *The Top Guy*).

The majority of intellectuals seem to be as attached to their privileges as are the bureaucrats. A protagonist in *My Dear Edison* is informed that entrance to prestigious universities and colleges is made possible only by the connections and high position of one's parents. Only a few representatives of the common people are fortunate enough to be accepted along with the intellectual elite. Edison, the bright, positive main character, is one of these select few. Deprived of a strong and influential parental hand, however, he cannot prevent his eventual failure.

Intellectuals are not only happy with their privileged positions in Soviet society, but they are intent on passing them along to their children. In *Director of a Children's Home*, one protagonist is convinced that higher education is reserved only for privileged groups, and that orphans, for example, are destined only for factory benches. The movie's main character, though otherwise seemingly likable, sees nothing wrong with this type of caste stratification.

Whereas neo-Leninist and democratic movies tend to denounce intellectuals for their vices and try to appeal to their consciences, neo-Stalinist movies portray intellectuals as children who, unable to manage even their own affairs, require a strong power placed above them. An example of this perceived relationship between the ruling elite and the intellectuals is provided in *Railway Station for Two* (Riasanov, 1982). The protagonist is an intellectual who is placed in a camp after having taken the blame for a crime committed by his wife. He eventually comes to resent his wife for visiting so infrequently. When he hears that she has arrived and awaits him in a nearby village, the protagonist refuses to visit her. The camp chief, however, understands that the protagonist's decision could irreversibly damage his family life. He also understands that the protagonist, a musician and a very emotional person, is incapable of reason, even in dealing with his own personal problems. The camp's chief therefore orders the man to see his wife. The visit, which is not actually from his wife, but from another woman who loves him, is a great consolation for the imprisoned musician. The film implies that he should thank the strong but paternalistic militia man for compelling him to do what is best for him.

The Masses

Soviet movies differ more in their portrayals of the masses than in their portrayals of any other group. Russophile movies present a picture of the masses that is very different from that presented in movies influenced by the other three ideologies. With few exceptions, the Rusophiles consider only true ethnic Russians eligible for membership in "the masses," and Rusophile movies generally describe ethnic Russians very positively. By contrast, filmmakers with other ideological orientations do not distinguish between Russians and non-Russians, and tend to describe all of their fellow country people rather disparagingly. The Rusophile's sympathetic approach to depicting the "ordinary people" will be examined first.

Ethnic Russians as a Distinct Group

Russophiles place a strong emphasis on the basic differences between Russia and the rest of the world, particularly the West. Russophiles view ethnic Russians as the only Christian people able to demonstrate the qualities of meekness, natural nobility, devotion to lofty spiritual principles, and self-sacrifice (see Melentiev, 1986; Nesterov, 1984). Endowed with such characteristics, Russians have no need of technological progress and economic growth in order to lead happy lives. This explains why Russophilism was so eagerly accepted by the Brezhnev regime in the 1970s, and was, to a certain extent, incorporated into official ideology as a rationale for stagnation.

Although war provides the most frequent opportunities for Russians to manifest their noble and spiritual values, Russophile movies portray most Russians as behaving in accordance with Christian morals during peacetime as well. There are, however, numerous Russians who abandon their Christian standards, and it is the task of society to help them regain their Russian values.

The true repository of the highest national virtues is, of course, the countryside. As a result, Russophile movies directly or, more often, indirectly praise the technological backwardness of the countryside. The protagonist of *Do Not Shoot the White Swans* (Nakhapetov, 1982) is a village resident with no formal education beyond elementary school. He does not work hard, achieve, read books, go to movies, or, in general, show an interest in the outside world. Although he is not without creative skills, he exercises them only when he is in a good mood and when he likes his job. If both of these conditions are not met, his professional performance is abysmal. He can neither perform any official job adequately nor sustain his family, the poorest in the village. Still, he is endowed with several very positive qualities, and, like Karataev in Tolstoy's *War and Peace*, is absolutely content with his daily life. He loves all living creatures, is extremely generous, and is absolutely free of vanity and ambition. He possesses artistic talents but does not exploit them, not because of his resistance to bureaucratic routine, but mostly because of his absolute carelessness and childlike irresponsibility.

This man, a "noble fool," is portrayed as the sole defender of nature against the offenses of civilization. Having been appointed forester, he decides to repopulate a lake with the swans that left it many years earlier. Using money given to him to attend an ecological conference, he buys swans for his lake and dies defending them from poachers. His death, full of religious overtones, is not in vain; civilization retreats, and the lake, as in the remote past, is once again filled with life.

In *Love and Pigeons* (Menshov, 1984), the protagonist, a member of the masses so highly regarded by the Russophiles, also displays the Russians' characteristic low level of education, discomfort with modern life, and passionate love of nature and living things—in this case, of pigeons. Both the protagonist and his equally unsophisticated wife are depicted as happy, in contrast to those who try to live by Western standards.

The Masses in Non-Russophile Movies

The neo-Leninist, neo-Stalinist, and democratic ideologies are even more unanimous in their attitudes toward the masses than they are toward the intellectuals. The movies influenced by these three ideologies all reveal a high level of contempt for ordinary people, portraying them as lazy individuals deprived of elementary moral virtues.

Workers and peasants in these films display a weak work ethic (Popov's *Fell in Love At My Own Request*; Sirenko's *The Top Guy*) and are often involved in consumerism (Ibragimov's *Business of the Heart*, 1974). Members of the public become involved in fraudulent activity, secure positions for which they are not qualified (Riasanov's *Railway Station for Two*; Shakhnazarov's *Kind People*), obtain material and equipment for their businesses through illegal channels, and hoard scarce goods to obtain useful connections (Bortko's *The Blonde Around the Corner*).

The films show that the involvement of the masses in private activity interferes with their performance on the job. In *The Top Guy*, for example, the peasantry neglect the collective farms while becoming intensely involved in the cultivation of private plots. Similarly, private activity is regularly portrayed as being connected with semilegal, if not openly illegal, activity. The protagonists of *The Kidnapping of the Century* (Makarov, 1981), for example, must occasionally resort to illegal means to obtain the services required for them to operate their private business. Those involved in private activity are also shown dabbling in speculation (Gaidai's *Sports Lotto*, 1982), gold and currency trading (Aranovich's *Confrontation*, 1985), and using state equipment to accomplish their speculative ventures.

Like bureaucrats and intellectuals, the masses crave Western consumer goods and are often sexually promiscuous (*My Dear Edison, Sibiriada, The Only One, Valentine and Valentina, Railway Station for Two,* and Gubenko's *The Life of Vacationers*, 1980). In addition, the masses are plagued by drunkenness (Daneliia's *Autumn Marathon*, 1979; Dosortsev's *A Foreign Case*, 1985; and *Fell in Love at My Own Request*).

The public's quest for foreign goods and sexual adventure seems to provide further inducement to illegal activity. Desire for videocassettes (*Railway Station for Two*), Western clothes (*Railway Station for Two, Sports Lotto*), and other Western goods often leads ordinary people to participate in the black market.

The masses are depicted as having a weak sense of social solidarity (*The Only One, Fell in Love at My Own Request*) and little social prestige (*Married Bachelor, Fell in Love at My Own Request*). They apparently loathe the bureaucracy and the intellectuals because of the privileges enjoyed by these two groups. These feelings are prompted not by egalitarian ideals, however, but by envy, and the common people are portrayed as being equally susceptible to corruption (*My Dear Edison*). The masses demonstrate little interest in democracy, and are quite content to have their superiors appointed from above (*The Top Guy*).

Those employed in the service industry receive equally cold treatment in Soviet movies. Films portraying kind and industrious service workers usually also present their negative counterparts—workers who are rude, lazy, or both (*Children's Home, The Blonde Around the Corner, And Life, and Tears, and Love, Married Bachelor*). The service workers in *We, the Undersigned* display extreme rudeness in dealing with clients. In addition, it is implied that these workers, particularly salespersons, are involved in theft and the hoarding of scarce goods. Private activity in general, such as renting apartments in resort areas (Surikova, *Please Be My Husband*, 1981) and distributing hotel beds through bribery, is also depicted negatively. It is implied that people's indulgence in private activity fills them with greed and alienates them from others.

Society as a Whole

The emergence of democratically oriented movies in 1986-1989 allowed filmmakers to express their views about the Soviet people as a whole (see Woll, 1987; see also the highly liberal Soviet magazine *Iskusstvo Kino* [The Art of Movies] for 1987-1989). The rejection of Soviet socialism is manifested particularly strongly in movies that present the Soviet people as a demoralized entity, with no distinctions made among different groups. The movies of the glasnost era portray the Soviet people as hostile to conscientious and hard work, and as prone to alcoholism and violence.

The contempt for ordinary people, especially the workers, seen in *Dog's Heart* (Bortko, 1989), the recent movie version of the Bulgakov novel of the same name (1925/1968), is typical of the treatment given to the masses in glasnost-era films. The movie presents the masses as cruel, lazy, and immoral—little better than beasts—and depicts the intelligentsia as self-deluded and irresponsible. The people fare no better in *Humble Cemetery* (Shtygilov, 1988), where those involved in the business of interment are seen as devoid of almost any moral values, including any respect for death.

Piotr, the protagonist of *Sinner* (Popkov, 1989), is seen as a violator of moral norms. He is persecuted and even beaten by both his supervisors and his colleagues because he refuses to work slowly, and easily completes a full day's quota of work in one hour.

Glasnost-era film directors are able to explore aspects of Soviet life considered taboo since the October revolution—including social hypocrisy, violence, and sex. A whole series of Soviet movies deal with the subject of violence in everyday Soviet life (e.g., Soloviev's *Assa*, 1988; Kara's *Legal Thieves*, 1986), and filmmakers have been equally tenacious in describing, often in detail, the sex lives of the Soviet people. The sexual involvement of a female teacher and her secondary school student in *Little Doll* (Fridberg, 1989) and the exotic intercourse seen between the apparatchik and his mistress in *The Extraordinary Event of the District Scope* (Snezhkin, 1988) are presented as violent and immoral (see also Tregubov's *Tower*, 1989; Alexadrovich's *They Could Not Get Along*, 1989; about sexual themes in Soviet movies in 1987-1989 see *Pravda*, November 21, 1989; *Literaturnaia Gazeta*, September 29, 1989).

The desolate picture of Soviet life presented in the movies of 1986-1989 offers no hope that socialist society in the Soviet Union will be rejuvenated. Even the positive characters express doubts about the future of perestroika. *The Forgotten Melody for Flute and Orchestra* (Riasanov, 1987) suggests that the Soviet people have become so corrupt that they are simply unable to change their life-style, which includes total indifference to their jobs and a permanent interest in promotion. The protagonist, representing Soviet society in general, is an able flutist who marries the daughter of a high official and becomes an apparatchik involved in the meaningless activities of the Ministry of Free Time. His mistress, who symbolizes the opportunity for radical perestroika in his life and in society, fails to convince him to start a new life. Having saved him several times from heart attacks (symbolizing the crises in society), she leaves him, suggesting that both the protagonist and society are doomed.

The director of *The Fountain* (Manin, 1988), using a large multiunit apartment building to symbolize the country, paints a tragic picture of a decaying socialist society. The residents of the building are obedient citizens willing to tolerate and rationalize any and all suffering imposed on them by their superiors. When the heating system fails they submissively accept the cold; they react similarly when they lose their electricity. The building's residents are portrayed as sheep, patiently awaiting their building's (i.e., their country's) collapse.

Other movies appearing in the glasnost era also contribute to this negative image of the Soviet people. In *Jubilee Tango* (Azernikov, 1989), a restaurant waitress who is very pessimistic about the future complains that her life has deteriorated since glasnost, and that the authorities are only repeating the promises of the last 70 years. Her complaints are seconded by her customer, a manager, who insists that the changes wrought by glasnost are illusory. The characters in *Young Man from a Good Family* (Gusarov, 1988) are equally pessimistic about perestroika.

In the 1970s and early 1980s, filmmakers wishing to portray the gloomy state of the Soviet Union sent their characters into private life, the single refuge from decaying society (e.g., *Fell in Love at My Own Request*). By 1987-1989, due to the revelations of glasnost, the mood of the country had changed so much that even family and friends no longer provided a haven for people disappointed with social activity. The Soviet family is presented very negatively in films produced in 1987-1989, with spouses often portrayed as being unfaithful and cruel.

Family life appears nightmarish in movies such as *Little Vera* (Pichula, 1988) and *The Extraordinary Event of the District Scope* (Snezhkin, 1988). In the former, violence is seen as a normal part of everyday life. In the latter, the protagonist, the secretary of the Young Communist League, dreams of his wife's instant death as he makes love to her. This would eliminate the danger of her reporting his affairs to his party boss. The collapse of the family figures prominently in other movies of the late 1980s as well (see, for example, Liubimov's *School Waltz*, 1989).

CONCLUSION

The analysis of Soviet movies can provide a broader understanding of the major developments in the objective and subjective dimensions of Soviet life during specific periods of time. Soviet movies can, for example, illuminate the roles played by various actors in Soviet social and political life during the Brezhnev era, as outlined below.

Soviet films of the 1970s and 1980s reflect the deeply rooted malaise of Soviet society, suggesting that Gorbachev's reforms are likely merely to scratch the surface, leaving intact the fundamental, chronic problems of Soviet society. These films help us understand why so many Soviet people view the post-1985 developments in their country with great skepticism, in contrast to the enthusiasm that many in the West feel for Gorbachev's activity. The majority of the films, regardless of their ideological perspectives, portray such total moral decay among the Soviet people that a moral revival of society, and with it radical economic and social progress, seems extremely unlikely.

These movies also provide a rather profound portrait of the Soviet bureaucracy. The movies, examined collectively, trace the degeneration of Soviet bureaucrats from Stalin's time to the end of the Brezhnev era. Soviet films are particularly attentive to the use of sophistry, obfuscation, and propaganda by bureaucrats in defense of their positions and privileges. No Soviet sociological data exist that can provide as comprehensive a description of this stratum as movies can. As such, no serious student of Soviet society can afford to ignore Soviet movies as a source of information.

It should be noted also that Soviet movies are second only to the mass media in detailing the special role played by Soviet intellectuals in criticizing Brezhnev's regime.

Soviet movies help to illustrate the nature of the country's resistance to the dominant regime. Specifically, they depict a few courageous individuals, prepared to fight for the interests of society, facing off against hostile or, at best, passive bureaucrats, intellectuals, and ordinary people whose attitudes doom any heroic efforts.

In addition to providing information on the objective and subjective dimensions of Soviet life, Soviet movies also reflect the ideological processes and psychological atmosphere dominant during specific periods. The analysis of Soviet films can facilitate a better grasp, both intellectual and emotional, of the essence of the four major ideological trends in the Soviet Union: Russophile, neo-Leninist, neo-Stalinist, and democratic.

The inclusion of emotional elements in this analysis helps to highlight the most significant outcome of this study—a more comprehensive understanding of the deep impasse at which Russia found itself, both during "the period of stagnation" and later, when the country entered a new era that promised economic and spiritual resurrection. As depicted in the films and represented by the characters, adherents of all four of the ideologies are in fact quite pessimistic and dubious of the possibility of radical change in Soviet society.

Characters representing Russophile ideology emerge as opponents of modernization, of technological progress, and of active, energetic, and professionally competent individuals. They would prefer that Russians be motivated by religious and other traditional values. The positive characters in neo-Stalinist, neo-Leninist, and democratic movies are unable to persuade viewers that their reform programs can be implemented in the present-day Soviet Union. If the films suggest any hope for the Soviet Union, it lies in the unleashing of the individualistic, egotistical instincts of the Soviet people, and in a widening of the scope of their private activity.

The films—including those representing official ideology—unanimously describe the strong alienation of the Soviet people from the state, public life, and official political activity. These films also seem unable, despite the exhortations of official ideologues, to portray the image of hard workers devoted to the cause. Even Russophile movies have failed to produce protagonists inspired in their professional activities by their love of the motherland.

Even if readers agree with the results of our analysis of Soviet films, we do not wish to suggest that we share the pessimistic views of Gorbachev's perestroika that are presented in Soviet films. Even optimists, however, cannot ignore this analysis in their assessment of the situation in the Soviet Union in the mid-1980s. The films underscore the fact that the task of transforming Soviet society is extremely difficult and that there is still no evidence that a socialist society of the Soviet type is able to change its structure in the direction of democracy and peaceful reform.

NOTES

1. Our use of terms such as *objective reality* and *subjective reality* will be clarified in the following section.

2. It is noteworthy that the postmodernist trend in epistemology is nearly identical to the Marxist "class approach" in social science, literature, and the arts, which was strictly enforced by the Soviet political elite from the 1930s through the 1950s. The class approach resolutely rejected the possibility of a single objective picture of the world—there were both "bourgeois" and "socialist" visions. Followers of the class approach found terms such as *objectivity* and *objectivism* as naive and misguided as do contemporary postmodernists (compare the Soviet definition of *objectivism* in Prokhorov, 1983, p. 911, with that of Anderson, 1990, pp. 60-64).

3. The concept of "representation" is not very useful for the current analysis, since it goes without saying that each filmmaker (like any other figure in literature and the arts) presents his or her own version of reality. However, unlike some advocates of representational theory, such as Nelson Goodman (1978), we suggest that comparing the "movie world" with the "real world" is reasonable and useful for those movies that claim to reflect reality, but is less justified for intentionally formalist movies (see also Andrews, 1984, pp. 39-40).

4. Even movies that stray widely from objective reality contain "real-life" details. Before 1987, the Soviet people were permitted to watch only those American movies that concentrated on the grim side of life in the United States, such as *The Godfather* or *The French Connection*. Still, Soviet critics assessed American life positively, because the movies contained details (such as the number of rooms in an apartment or the assortment of food available) that suggested that, despite its grisly aspects, life in the United States was still far better than that in the Soviet Union.

5. During Stalin's time, and to a lesser extent later, any act of benevolence on the part of the authorities was perceived as a sign of "salvation" from arrest or dismissal from one's job. Raizman, a prominent film director, recounts what happened when his friend Mikhail Romm, the famous Soviet film director, was awarded a medal in 1937: Romm ran upstairs, shouting, "I got the Order of Lenin, they will not arrest me now" (*Sovietskaia Kul'tura*, June 4, 1988). Memoirs discussing the 1949 anticosmopolitan campaign (which were unpublishable until the period of glasnost) graphically depicted the fear that plagued the intellectuals, and the numerous cases of betrayal between friends and colleagues. Sergei Iutkevich (1988, p. 106), a prominent film director, has recounted how his friend Mark Donskoi, the famous film figure, ardently attacked him at a public meeting devoted to the denunciation of cosmopolites. The fear subsided only partially after Stalin's death. Alexei German, a famous film director, described how, when his movies started to be shelved in the 1970s, his circle of friends became smaller and smaller, until he had no one left to invite to his birthday party (see Kornilov, 1988).

6. Stalin's intervention in the moviemaking process can be seen in a transcript of a 1947 meeting between him and two great Soviet intellectuals—the famous film director Sergei Eisenstein, and the brilliant actor Nikolai Cherkasov—regarding their film *Ivan the Terrible*. The transcript, published 31 years later, shows that the world-famous author of *Battleship Potemkin* asked Stalin for directions regarding the length of Ivan's beard, and that the actor sought approval for various scenes in the movie (*Moskovskie Novosti*, August 7, 1988). Official interference in Soviet filmmaking did not stop following Stalin's death. In a 1988 article Klimov recounted what he was told by a high-ranking party official who demanded that he remove a scene from a film. After the official had exhausted all of his arguments, he told

Klimov, "You argue to no purpose. Under Stalin emerged an all-pervasive system of power which none of the absolute monarchies had. You will never win" (our translation).

7. The Soviet establishment not only refused, for anti-Semitic reasons, to release Alexander Askol'dov's movie *Komissar* (1989), which sympathetically described the life of Jews during the civil war, but ordered all copies of the film destroyed and punished the film director with many years of poverty (about this incident, see *Novoye Russkoye Slovo*, June 21, 1988).

8. Soviet filmmakers' attitudes before Stalin's death in 1953 present a special case. Ideologies supported by mass terror are extremely complex phenomena, and it is difficult to find unambiguous data for any position. Filmmakers who appeared to be ideologically committed during Stalin's lifetime were often very different from those who acted similarly after Stalin's death. During Stalin's reign a filmmaker could easily be executed for producing a nonconformist film, whereas during later periods, all that was at stake was a filmmaker's career (this was similar to the situation in Hollywood during the McCarthy era).

During the first decade after the revolution, a number of film directors, including Sergei Eisenstein and Lev Kuleshov, appeared to be revolutionary enthusiasts and true believers in the cause. Their films *Battleship Potemkin* (1925), *October* (1927), and *The Extraordinary Adventures of Mr. West in the Land of the Bolsheviks* (1923) all appear to be accurate reflections of the era as it was perceived by the authors at the time.

Interestingly, later disappointment with the revolution failed to cause these filmmakers to change their views. Growing terror forced them to maintain their ties with the official ideology. Eisenstein's overt behavior, for example, was that of a true zealot, although his actual convictions are as yet unknown. His movies, such as *Alexander Nevski* (1938) and *Ivan the Terrible* (1945), display both his great talent and his blatant submission to Stalin's dictates (see the debate about Eisenstein's conformism in *Iskusstvo Kino*, April 1990, pp. 58-62).

During the 1930s and 1940s, young filmmakers such as Mikhail Romm, Sergei Gerasimov, Friedrich Ermler, Abram Room, Grigori Kozintsev, and Sergei Iutkevich, most of whom were very talented, produced scores of movies praising Stalin's regime. How did these people ignore the suffering and death of millions of their compatriots and support an ideology so clearly at odds with ontological reality? Most likely, rationalization and a strong instinct for survival turned them into true believers of a special kind. In any case, when those lucky enough to make it to the era of glasnost reflected about their ideological convictions during Stalin's times, they offered several different explanations for their behavior.

In 1987, the famous filmmaker Iosif Kheifets contended that he was proud of the movies he had made during the Stalin era, such as *A Member of the Government* (1940) and *A Deputy of the Baltic Navy* (1937), both of which were typical products of rude propagandists. He defended his actions by saying that he believed then and now in the cause of the revolution (Kheifets, 1987).

Alexander Shtein, a prominent scriptwriter, referred to "the music of the revolution" and "the revolutionary conviction" of his generation to avoid condemnation of his activities. Although he did renounce his film *The Court of Honor* (Room, 1949), one of the worst Stalinist films, he suggested that he and his colleagues were able to find explanations for the mass repressions (Shtein, 1987, 1988, pp. 178-179). Shtein's sentiments were seconded by the famous movie actress Tamara Makarova, who said that, despite the repression of members of her family, "there was full trust . . . in the party and her tasks" and that she was proud of the "heroic movies" of the times (*Sovietskaia Kul'tura*, July 30, 1987).

Other filmmakers have suggested that they successfully avoided politics during the Stalin era—a barely tenable contention. Still, the argument that "politics was not my business" was used by Iulii Raizman (1988), the famous film director who was awarded six Stalin prizes, to vindicate his work.

Several filmmakers, such as Evgeni Gabrilovich, have claimed that they "understood and saw everything" and that they did the best they could under the terrible conditions

(Gabrilovich, 1987; see also Sergei Bondarchuk's defense of his past in *Sovietskaia Kul'tura*, July 28, 1987).

9. Even if it were possible to obtain a random sample of movies (which would require that we have thousands of movies at our disposal—a practical impossibility, even using the Moscow film archives), the variety of movies thus obtained (i.e., movies produced by directors with a wide range of statuses for a wide range of audiences) would, using purely quantitative methods of analysis, hardly produce results in keeping with the Herculean efforts necessary to obtain them.

10. In the late 1980s, liberalization significantly changed many aspects of the intellectuals' cultural life. Coding and decoding literary works and movies almost disappeared from the intellectual life of the country. The most popular movies of this period, such as *Repentance* (1984) and *Fountain* (1988) (not to mention Govorukhin's documentary *It Is Impossible to Live in This Way*, 1990, which describes Soviet society as a hell), contained nothing between the lines. Instead of resorting to associations, they bluntly revealed their hostile attitudes toward Stalinist society both past and present.

11. Movies that reflect ideologies only moderately critical of the current political and social order, as well as movies that are pure "entertainment" and reflect the dominant value system (such as those to come out of Hollywood in the 1930s and 1940s, and Soviet comedies before 1985; see Hughes, 1976, pp. 65-66), tend to concentrate on facets of life that are of less importance in movies adopting stronger ideological stances. Specifically, entertainment-oriented movies tend to emphasize the concrete details of their characters' lives: their interpersonal relationships, their life-styles (clothing, apartment, transportation), the regions in which they live, and so on.

FILMS INCLUDED IN THE STUDY

Abrashidov, V. (Director), & Mindadze, A. (Scriptwriter). (1979). *Turn* [Povorot].
Abuladze, T. (Director, Scriptwriter). (1984). *Repentance* [Pokaianie].
Alexadrovich, N. (Director). (1989). *They could not get along* [Ne soshlis' kharakterami].
Alov, A., & Naumov, V. (Directors). (1955). *Worried youth* [Trevozhnkia molodost].
Alov, A., & Naumov, V. (Directors), & Bondarev, I. (Scriptwriter). (1984). *Shore* [Bereg].
Aranovich, S. (Director), & Semenov, I. (Scriptwriter). (1985). *Confrontation* [Protivostoainie].
Askol'dov, A. (Director). (1989). *Komissar*.
Averbakh, I. (Director), & Gabrilovich, E. (Scriptwriter). (1978). *Declaration of love* [Ob'iasnenii v lubvi].
Azernikov, V. (Director, Scriptwriter). (1989). *Jubilee tango* [Iubileinnoie tango].
Bazhanov, G. (Director), & Eidel'man, A. (Scriptwriter). (1985). *The most attractive* [Samaia privlekatel'naia].
Beck, A. (Scriptwriter), & Misharin, A. (Scriptwriter) [Director unknown]. (1988). *Engineer Berezhkov* [Enzhener Berezhkov].
Bortko, V. (Director, Scriptwriter). (1989). *Dog's heart* [Sobachie sertse].
Bortko, V. (Director), & Chervinskii, A. (Scriptwriter). (1984). *The blonde around the corner* [Blondinka za uglom].
Brovkin (Director), & Solntsev (Scriptwriter). (1989). *The three people on the red rug* [Tri cheloveka na krasnom kovre].
Bykov, L. (Director), & Ginn, M. (Scriptwriter). (1985). *Leveret* [Zaichik].
Chukhrai, G. (Director). (1956). *The forty-first* [Sorok pervyi].
Daneliia, G. (Director), & Volodin, A. (Scriptwriter). (1979). *Autumn marathon* [Osenii marafon].

Dosortsev, V. (Director, Scriptwriter). (1985). *A foreign case* [Chuzhoi sluchai].
Dunaiaeva, B. (Director), & Bakhnov, V. (Scriptwriter). (1981). *Night accident* [Nochnoiie proisshestviie].
Eisenstein, S. (Director). (1925). *Battleship Potemkin* [Bronenosets Potemkin].
Eisenstein, S. (Director). (1927). *October* [Oktiabr].
Eisenstein, S. (Director). (1938). *Alexander Nevski* [Alexander Nevski].
Eisenstein, S. (Director). (1945). *Ivan the Terrible* [Ivan Groznyi].
Eisenstein, S. (Director), & Kuleshov, L. (Scriptwriter). (1923). *The extraordinary adventures of Mr. West in the land of the Bolsheviks* [Chrezvchainye prikluchenia Mistera West vstrane Bolshevikov].
Fridberg, I. (Director, Scriptwriter). (1986). *My dear Edison* [Dorogoi Edison].
Fridberg, I. (Director, Scriptwriter). (1989). *Little doll* [Kukolka].
Gaidai, L. (Director), & Bakhnov, V. (Scriptwriter). (1982). *Sports Lotto* [Sportloto].
German, A. (Director, Scriptwriter). (1987). *Check at roadblock* [Proverka na dorogakh].
German, A. (Director), & Volodarskii, E. (Scriptwriter). (1985). *My friend Lapshin* [Moi drug Lapshin].
Gordon, A. (Director), & Bulganon, A. (Scriptwriter). (1979). *Passing twice* [Dvoinoi obgon].
Goriaev, R. (Director, Scriptwriter). (1988). *The everyday life and holidays of Serafimy Gliukina* [Budni i prazdniki Serafimy Gliukinoi].
Govorukhin, S. (Director). (1990). *It is impossible to live in this way* [Tak zhit nel' zia].
Grigoriev, V. (Director, Scriptwriter). (1986). *Grasshopper* [Kuznechik].
Grigoriev, V. (Director), Gabrilovich, E., & Gabrilovich, A. (Scriptwriters). (1986). *Late date* [Pozdnee svidanie].
Gubenko, N. (Director, Scriptwriter). (1980). *The life of vacationers* [Iz zhizni otdykhaiushchikh].
Gubenko, N. (Director, Scriptwriter). (1983). *And life, and tears, and love* [I zhizn', i slezy, i lubov].
Gusarov, N. (Director, Scriptwriter). (1988). *Young man from a good family* [Molodoi chelovek iz khoroshei sem'i].
Holov, G. (Director), & Nilin, P. (Scriptwriter). (1978). *Married for the first time* [Vpervyie zamuzhem].
Iashin, B. (Director, Scriptwriter). (1989). *Fast train* [Skoryi poezd].
Ibragimov, A. (Director), & Kulin, V. (Scriptwriter). (1974). *Business of the heart* [Dela serdechnyie].
Kalatozov, M. (Director). (1957). *Cranes fly* [Letiat zhuravli].
Kara, I. (Director, Scriptwriter). (1986). *Legal thieves* [Vory v zakone].
Kheifets, I. (Director). (1937). *A deputy of the Baltic Navy* [Deputat Baltiki].
Kheifets, I. (Director). (1940). *A member of the government* [Chlen pravitelstva].
Kheifets, I. (Director). (1965). *Rumiantsev's case* [Delo Rumiantseva].
Kheifets, I. (Director), & Nilin, P. (Scriptwriter). (1976). *The only one* [Edistvennaia].
Khutsiev, M. (Director). (1956). *I am twenty years old* [Mne dvadtsat let].
Klimov, E. (Director). (1971). *Agony* [Agonia].
Kvanikhidze, L. (Director, Scriptwriter). (1989). *The actress from Gribov* [Artistka iz Gribova].
Lapshin, I. (Director), & Chervinskii, A. (Scriptwriter). (1977). *Prolong the enchantment* [Prodlis mgnoveniie].
Lebedev, N. (Director), & Iasan, E. (Scriptwriter). (1980). *Accuse Klava for my death* [V moiei smerti vinit' Klavu].
Linkov, S. (Director), & Misharin, A. (Scriptwriter). (1986). *Because of the change of job* [V sviazi s perekhodom na druguiu rabotu].
Lioznova, T. (Director), & Gel'man, A. (Scriptwriter). (1979). *We, the undersigned* [My, nizhe podpisavshiiesia].
Liubimov, P. (Director, Scriptwriter). (1989). *School waltz* [Shkol'nyi val's].

Makarov, V. (Director), & Bakhnov, V. (Scriptwriter). (1981). *The kidnapping of the century* [Pokhishcheniie veka].

Manasarova, A. (Director), & Mariamov, A. (Scriptwriter). (1981). *A fantasy on love themes* [Fantasiia na temu lubvi].

Manin, I (Director, Scriptwriter). (1988). *Fountain* [Fontan].

Menshov, V. (Director). (1984). *Love and pigeons* [Lubov i golubi].

Mikhalkov, N. (Director). (1980). *A few days from the life of Oblomov* [Neskol'ko knei iz zhizni Oblomova].

Mikhalkov, N. (Director), & Merezhko, V. (Scriptwriter). (1982). *Relatives* [Rodnia].

Mikhalkov-Konchalovskii, A. (Director), & Ezhov, V. (Scriptwriter). (1979). *Sibiriada* [Sibiriade].

Mosenko, V. (Director), & Evtushenko (Scriptwriter). (1982). *Children's home* [Detskii dom].

Nakhapetov, R. (Director), & Rapoport, V. (Scriptwriter). (1982). *Do not shoot the white swans* [Ne streliaite v belykh lebedei].

Nakhapetov, R. (Director), & Roshchin, V. (Scriptwriter). (1983). *Valentine and Valentina* [Valentine i Valentina].

Olshanskii, I., & Olshanskii, V. (Directors, Scriptwriters). (1980). *Director of a children's home* [Khosian detskogo doma].

Ordynskii, V. (Director). (1956). *Man was born* [Chelovek rodlsia].

Pichula, V. (Director, Scriptwriter). (1988). *Little Vera* [Malen'kaia Vera].

Popkov, V. (Director, Scriptwriter). (1989). *Sinner* [Greshnik].

Popov, V. (Director), & Evdokimov, N. (Scriptwriter). (1982). *Encounter with my youth* [Svidaniie s molodost'iu].

Popov, V. (Director), & Evdokimov, N. (Scriptwriter). (1982). *Fell in love at my own request* [Vliublen po sobstvennomu zhelaniie].

Proshkin, A. (Director). (1987). *Cold summer of 1953* [Kholodnoie leto 1953].

Ptashuk, M. (Director), & Korotkevich, V. (Scriptwriter). (1980). *Black castle* [Chernyi zamok].

Pyr'iev, I. (Director). (1950). *The Don Cossacks* [Kubanski Kazaki].

Raizman, U. (Director). (1968). *Your contemporary* [Tvoi sovremennik].

Riasanov, E. (Director). (1956). *Carnival night* [Karnavalnaia noch].

Riasanov, E. (Director, Scriptwriter). (1987). *The forgotten melody for flute and orchestra* [Zabytaia melodia dlia fleity s orkestrom].

Riasanov, E. (Director), & Braginskii, E. (Scriptwriter). (1977). *Office romance* [Sluzhebnyi roman].

Riasanov, E. (Director), & Braginskii, E. (Scriptwriter). (1980). *Garage* [Garazh].

Riasanov, E. (Director), & Braginskii, E. (Scriptwriter). (1982). *Railway station for two* [Vokzal na dvoikh].

Rogov, V. (Director), & Shaikevich, A. (Scriptwriter). (1983). *Married bachelor* [Zhenatyi kholostiak].

Romm, M. (Director). (1962). *Nine days of one year* [Deviat dnei odnogo goda].

Romm, M. (Director). (1966). *Ordinary fascism* [Ofyknovennyi fashizm].

Room, A. (Director), & Shtein, A. (Scriptwriter). (1949). *The court of honor* [Sud chesti].

Rozenberg, A. (Director, Scriptwriter). (1989). *The individual from the entourage* [Chelovek svity].

Saltykov, A. (Director). (1964). *Chairman* [Predsedatel].

Shakhnazarov, K. (Director), & Zorin, L. (Scriptwriter). (1980). *Kind people* [Dobriaki].

Sheshukov, I. (Director), & Khamraiev, I. (Scriptwriter). (1986). *Red arrow* [Krasnaia strela].

Shtygilov, A. (Director, Scriptwriter). (1988). *Humble cemetery* [Smirennoie kladbishche].

Sirenko, A. (Director), & Grigoriev, E. (Scriptwriter). (1986). *The top guy* [Pervyi paren].

Snezhkin, S. (Director, Scriptwriter). (1988). *The extraordinary event of the district scope* [Chrezvychainoie sobyitie raionnogo masshtaba].

Soloviev, S. (Director). (1975). *Hundred days after childhood* [Sto dnei posle detstva].
Soloviev, S. (Director, Scriptwriter). (1988). *Assa.*
Soviet TV. (1979). *I took control over the city* [Vzial komandu nad gorodom].
Soviet TV. (1989). *Nadia Rodionova.*
Surikova, A. (Director), & Akopov, E. (Scriptwriter). (1981). *Please be my husband* [Pozhaluista, bud'te moim muzhem].
Surikova, A. (Director), & Braginskii, E. (Scriptwriter). (1979). *Vanity of vanities* [Sueta suet].
Tarkovski, A. (Director). (1971). *Andrei Rublev.*
Tarkovski, A. (Director). (1973). *Soliaris.*
Tarkovski, A. (Director). (1975). *Mirror* [Zerkalo].
Todorovskii, P. (Director). (1984). *War romance* [Voenno-polevoi zoman].
Tregubov, V. (Director, Scriptwriter). (1989). *Tower* [Bashnia].
Troshchenko, N. (Director), & Gabrilovich, E. (Scriptwriter). (1983). *The long road to herself* [Dolgaia doroga k sebe].
Zlobin, V. (Director, Scriptwriter). (1988). *Sunday, eight o'clock* [Voskresenie v polovine vos'mogo].

REFERENCES

Anderson, W. (1990). *Reality isn't what it used to be.* New York: Harper.
Andrews, D. (1984). *Concepts in film theory.* Oxford: Oxford University Press.
Berger, J. (1972). *Ways of seeing.* London: BBC and Penguin.
Berger, P., & Luckmann, T. (1966). *The social construction of reality.* Garden City, NY: Doubleday.
Braudy, L. (1976). *The world in a frame: What we see in films.* Garden City, NY: Anchor.
Bulgakov, M. (1925/1968). *Dog's heart.* New York: Harcourt, Brace & Wolff.
Cohen, L. (1974). *The cultural-political traditions and developments of the Soviet cinema, 1917-1972.* New York: Arno.
Dudintsev, V. (1987, February 17). Genetika sovesti [Genetics of the conscience]. *Sovietskaia Kul'tura,* p. 3.
Dyer, R. (1985). Entertainment and utopia. In B. Nichols (Ed.), *Movies and methods: An anthology* (Vol. 2, pp. 220-232). Berkeley: University of California Press.
Fiske, J. (1982). *Introduction to communication studies.* New York: Methuen.
Gabrilovich, E. (1987, October 11). Tragedii i dramy shchastlivogo kontsa [Tragedies and dramas with happy endings]. *Moskovskie Novosti,* p. 16.
Geertz, C. (1973). *The interpretation of cultures.* New York: Basic Books.
Goffman, E. (1959). *The presentation of self in everyday life.* Garden City, NY: Doubleday.
Golovskoy, V., & Rimberg, J. (1986). *Behind the Soviet screen: The motion picture industry in the USSR, 1972-1982.* Ann Arbor, MI: Ardis.
Goodman, N. (1978). *Ways of worldmaking.* Indianapolis: Hacket.
Gouldner, A. (1979). *The future of the intellectuals and the future of the new class.* New York: Seabury.
Granin, D. (1987, May 27). Ekho dal'neie i blizkoie [Remote and near echoes]. *Literaturnaia Gazeta,* p. 9.
Granin, D. (1988). Kak stat' dobreie [How to become kinder]. *Nedelia, 3,* 11.
Grenville, J. A. S. (1971). *Film as history: The nature of film evidence.* Birmingham, England: University of Birmingham.
Hughes, W. (1976). The evaluation of film as evidence. In P. Smith (Ed.), *The historian and film* (pp. 49-80). Cambridge: Cambridge University Press.

Iutkevich, S. (1986). *Kino. Entsiklopedicheski Slovar* [Soviet encyclopedia and dictionary]. Moscow: Sovietskaia Entsiklopedia.

Iutkevich, S. (1988). My s uvlecheniem nachali s'iemki. *Iskusstvo Kino, 2*, 94-108.

Kheifets, I. (1987, October 20). O druziakh-tovarishchakh [About friends and comrades]. *Sovietskaia Kul'tura*, p. 3.

Klimov, E. (1988, June 19). Vlast'—vot v chem vopros [About power—here there is a question]. *Moskovskie Novosti*, p. 3.

Kluckhohn, C. (1951). Values and value orientations in the theory of action. In T. Parsons & E. Shils (Eds.), *Toward a general theory of action.* Cambridge, MA: Harvard University Press.

Kogan, L. (Ed.). (1968). *Kino i zritel* [Movie and spectator]. Moscow: Iskusstvo.

Kornilov, V. (1988, July 13). Pol'za vpechatlenii [Benefits of expression]. *Literaturnaia Gazeta*, p. 7.

Kracauer, S. (1960). *Theory of film: The redemption of physical reality.* New York: Oxford University Press.

Lawton, A. (Ed.). (1987). *An Introduction to Soviet cinema.* Washington, DC: Kennan Institute for Advanced Russian Studies.

MacBean, J. R. (1975). *Film and revolution* Bloomington: Indiana University Press.

MacDonald, D. (1938a, July). The Soviet cinema: 1930-1939. *Partisan Review*, pp. 37-50.

MacDonald, D. (1938b, August/September). The Soviet cinema: 1930-1939. *Partisan Review*, pp. 35-61.

May, L. (1980). *Screening out the past: The birth of mass culture and the motion picture industry.* New York: Oxford University Press.

Maynard, R. A. (Ed.). (1975). *Propaganda on film: A nation at war.* Rochelle Park, NJ: Hayden.

Melentiev, I. (1986). *Glazami naroda* [In the people's eyes]. Moscow: Sovremennik.

Mitry, J. (1963). *Esthetique et psychologie du cinema* [The aesthetics and psychology of movies]. Paris: Editions Universitaires.

Neale, S. (1985). *Cinema and technology: Image, sound, and color.* Bloomington: Indiana University Press.

Nesterov, F. (1984). *Sviaz' vremen* (2nd ed.). Moscow: Molodaia Gvardia.

Nichols, B. (Ed.). (1985). *Movies and methods: An anthology.* Berkeley: University of California Press.

Ogle, P. (1985). Technological and aesthetic influence on the development of deep-focus cinematography in the United States. In B. Nichols (Ed.), *Movies and methods: An anthology* (Vol. 2, pp. 58-82). Berkeley: University of California Press.

Pomerants, G. (1985). Zhazhda dobra [Yearning for goodness]. *Strana i Mir, 9*, 83-96; *10*, 66-79.

Prokhorov, A. (Ed.). (1983). *Sovietski entsiklopedicheski Slovar'* [Soviet encyclopedia and dictionary]. Moscow: Sovietskaia Entsiklopedia.

Quinney, R. (1982). *Social existence: Metaphysics, Marxism, and the social sciences.* Beverly Hills, CA: Sage.

Raizman, I. (1988, June 4). Ia niaogda ne byl politikom [I was never a politician]. *Sovietskaia Kul'tura.*

Rimberg, J. D. (1973). *The motion picture in the Soviet Union 1918-1952: A sociological analysis.* New York: Arno.

Shkaratan, O. (1982). Peremeny v sotsial'nom oblike gorozhan [Changes in the social aspects of townspeople]. In T. Riabushkin & G. Osipov (Eds.), *Sovietskaia sotsiologia* (Vol. 2, pp. 39-52). Moscow: Nauka.

Shlapentokh, V. (1986). *Soviet public opinion and ideology: Mythology and pragmatism in interaction.* New York: Praeger.

Shlapentokh, V. (1987). *The politics of sociology in the Soviet Union.* Boulder: Westview Press.

Shlapentokh, V. (1988). *Soviet ideologies in the period of glasnost: Response to Brezhnev's stagnation.* New York: Praeger.

Shlapentokh, V. (1990). *Soviet intellectuals and political power.* Princeton, NJ: Princeton University Press.

Shtein, A. (1987, May 23). Moie pokoleniie [My generation]. *Sovietskaia Kul'tura*, p. 3.

Shtein, A. (1988). I ne tol'ko o nem [And not only about him]. *Teatr, 3,* 169-187.

Smith, P. (Ed.). (1976). *The historian and film.* Cambridge: Cambridge University Press.

Solzhenitsyn, A. (Ed.). (1974). *Iz-pod glyb* [From under the rubble]. Paris: Imka.

Steven, P. (Ed.). (1985). *Jump cut: Hollywood, politics, and counter-cinema.* New York: Praeger.

Taylor, R. (1971, April). A medium for the masses: Agitation in the Soviet civil war. *Soviet Studies,* pp. 562-574.

TsSU USSR. (1987). *Narodonie khosiastvo SSSR za 79 Let* [The national economy of the USSR for 20 years]. Moscow: Finansy i Statistika.

Turner, G. (1988). *Film as social practice.* London: Routledge.

Volkov, V. (1974). Film i iego auditoriia [Movies and their audiences]. In L. Kogan & V. Volkov (Eds.), *Sotsiologicheskiie issledovaniia problem dukhovnoi zhizni trudiashchikhsia Urala* [Sociological analysis of the problems of the spiritual lives of the Ural's workers] (pp. 94-131). Sverdlovsk: Ural'skii Zentr AN SSR.

Voslenski, M. (1980). *La nomenclature: Les privileges en URSS* [The Nomenclature: Privileges in the USSR]. Paris: Pierre Belfon.

White, D. M., & Averson, R. (1972). *The celluloid weapon.* Boston: Beacon.

White, S. (1988). Ideology and Soviet politics. In S. White & A. Pravada (Eds.), *Ideology and Soviet politics.* New York: St. Martin's.

Woll, J. (1987). Daring voices in Soviet films. *Dissent, 34,* 159-162.

Zaslavskaia, T. (1988). O strategii sotsial'nogo upravlenia perestroikoi [About strategies of social management in perestroika]. In I. Afanasiev (Ed.), *Inogo ne dano* [There is no alternative] (pp. 9-50). Moscow: Progress.

Zorkaya, N. M. (1989). *The illustrated history of the Soviet cinema.* New York: Hippocrene.

Politics and Aesthetics in the Cinema of Postrevolutionary Societies

ANNA BANKS
University of Idaho

I N their essay Shlapentokh and Shlapentokh set out to show how narrative cinema in the Soviet Union provides a unique window into the "true reality" of Soviet life. The authors argue that because of the multifaceted nature of the film medium, films provide an important— and all too frequently ignored—source of information about the society that produced them. I too believe that a society's film industry and its products are a valuable source of information about the sociocultural and political practices of that country. I differ from Shlapentokh and Shlapentokh, however, in my understanding of the theoretical relationship between film and culture.

I view film as a discursive practice, borrowing from Foucault's (1972) definition of discursive practices as "not purely and simply ways of producing discourse. They are embodied in technical processes, in institutions, in patterns of social behavior, in forms for transmission and diffusion, and in pedagogical forms which, at once, impose and maintain them" (p. 200). In addition, I understand films as semiotic systems composed of sequences of photographic and verbal messages.

On this point Stuart Hall (1980) makes an important observation about analyzing television, and his comments are also relevant to film and photography. To Hall, visual images are products or commodities, and the object of the practice of creating visual images is to produce "meanings and messages in the form of sign vehicles" (p. 128). Hall describes the process of producing an image as one in which the sign vehicles must be made meaningful to an audience:

Correspondence and requests for reprints: Anna Banks, School of Communication, University of Idaho, Moscow, ID 83843.

Communication Yearbook 15, pp. 194-205

> The process thus requires, at the production end, its material instruments—its *means*—as well as its own sets of social (production) relations—the organization and combination of practices within media apparatuses. But it is in the discursive form that the circulation of the product takes place, as well as its distribution to different audiences. Once accomplished, the discourse must be translated—transformed, again—into social practices if the circuit is to be both complete and effective. If no meaning is taken, there can be no consumption. If the meaning is not articulated in practice, it has no effect. (p. 128)

At an even more fundamental level, I take films to be composed of mediated messages. Following Eco (1976), I define a mediated message as one "capable of producing multiple levels of meaning" (p. 57). In a similar vein, Fry and Fry (1986) adopt a semiotic approach to the study of mass communication, in which they postulate:

> Mass media messages are textual resources capable of engendering multiple levels of potential meanings. . . . a media text, then, is not simply a transmitter of a particulated meaning from source to receiver; instead, a text is a resource or a matrix of possible meanings. An audience, drawing from textual and nontextual sources, reduces the range of potential meanings (or contents) by selecting definitive interpretations from the matrix. (p. 445)

Moreover, each image in a film incorporates a "way of seeing" (Berger, 1972) that is informed by and embodies the perceptions of the viewer. In other words, from within the range of possible meanings, the individual viewer selects the one that holds true for his or her understanding of the social-cultural-historical environment.

Consequently, I differ from Shlapentokh and Shlapentokh when they state, "Because of the tendency of artists to embed secret messages in their works, many literary and artistic works are virtually incomprehensible to those lacking either the intellectual sophistication or the knowledge of history and politics necessary to decode these works" (p. 163). In my view, our ability to read photographs is cultural, not technical; that is, our understanding of visual images is "part of the social stock at hand" (Hall, 1973, p. 177). Thus I find myself aligned with the intellectual camp that Shlapentokh and Shlapentokh oppose in that I do not believe objective social reality "is that with which people are presented, even if they then act to change reality in various ways" (p. 157, citing Quinney, 1982, p. 46). Rather, I find it more useful to approach film analysis from the perspective that asserts that films are made by people and that reality is socially constructed (Berger & Luckmann, 1966; Templin, 1982).

For my own analysis of the relationship between film and culture, I appeal to the theoretical principles of praxis theory, in particular the form of praxis theory expounded by Michel Foucault. I find a praxis perspective especially useful in analyzing films because it is concerned with a central problem, namely, how sociocultural forms express the structure of domination in human society (Sulkunen, 1982). Foucault is primarily concerned with how institutions actively influence the common practices of individuals. His emphasis is on the reproduction of social practices and their effects on the structure of society. Thus, from Foucault's perspective, cinema is a tool manipulated by institutions and, at the same time, a way of revealing the hidden power structures within those institutions. The emphasis that praxis theory places on power is particularly useful in analyzing films from countries such as the Soviet Union because it allows the critic to address the "important socialist legacy of assigning to film a larger political and sociocultural status than it typically enjoys in the West" (Goulding, 1989, p. xii).

Before presenting my analysis of the relationship between film and culture, it is necessary to establish a theoretical framework and to demonstrate where my understanding of key terms such as *reality, truth,* and *ideology* differs from that presented by Shlapentokh and Shlapentokh.

FOUCAULT'S PRAXIS PERSPECTIVE

In his works, Foucault insists on the need for social theorists and critics to reconceptualize traditional approaches to power. Most significant is that Foucault rejects the traditional understanding of power as a wholly repressive force within society. Foucault's call is for a more positive and productive approach to power. Tagg (1988), paraphrasing Foucault, writes:

> We must cease once and for all to describe the effects of power in negative terms—as exclusion, repression, censorship, concealment, eradication. In fact, power produces. It produces reality. It produces domains of objects, institutions of language, rituals of truth. (p. 87)

Thus, for Foucault, power takes on a far more complex, multifaceted, and subsequently ambiguous role within human social interactions. Foucault conceives of power as participating in a circular relationship. Moreover, he views the relationship among the various facets of power as one in which power is one component of a triangular set:

> I have tried, that is, to relate its mechanisms to two points of reference, two limits: on the one hand to the rules of right that provide a formal delimitation of power; on the other, to the effects of truth that this power produces and transmits, and which in their turn reproduce this power. Hence we have a triangle: power, truth, right. (Foucault, 1980a, p. 93)

Shlapentokh and Shlapentokh define ideology "rather broadly" as "a more or less coherent set of values and beliefs that influence judgments of the external world and determine the behavior of individuals, groups, institutions, and societies" (p. 160). Foucault rejects ideology as a concept in and of itself for three reasons: (a) Ideology always stands in virtual opposition to something else that purports to stand for the truth; (b) ideology refers to something of the order of a subject; and (c) ideology stands in a secondary position relative to something that functions in its infrastructure, as its material, economic determinant (Foucault, 1980b, p. 118). While Foucault rejects the notion of ideology, however, he elaborates on notions of truth and right that function within his theory as a form of ideology.

Truth

Foucault's use of the term *truth* varies from the commonly understood meaning of the term. In a long discussion of the concept of truth, Foucault (1980b) demonstrates the relationship of power and truth and the nature of his understanding of truth:

> Truth isn't outside power or lacking in power. . . . Truth is a thing of this world; it is produced only by virtue of multiple forms of constraint. And it induces regular effects of power. Each society has its regime of truth, its *general politics* of truth: that is, the types of discourse which it accepts and makes function as true; the mechanisms and instances which enable one to distinguish true and false statements, the means by which each is sanctioned; the techniques and procedures accorded value in the acquisition of truth; the status of those who are charged with saying what counts as true. (pp. 131-132)

He further emphasizes his belief about the nature of truth, comparing it with rules of social interaction:

> There is a battle *for truth,* or at least around truth, it being understood once again that by truth I do not mean *the ensemble of truths which are to be discovered and accepted,* but rather *the ensemble of rules according to which the true and the false are separated and specific effects of power attached to be true.* (p. 132)

I have quoted this passage at length because an analysis of Foucault's notion of truth is key to an understanding of his theory of praxis, and because it demonstrates how I (following Foucault) differ in my concept of truth and reality from that offered by Shlapentokh and Shlapentokh. From this perspective, truth is an integral part of power. In any one of the many forms in which power may manifest itself one will find truth. Implicitly, Foucault indicates that truth exists at a less than conscious level. Such a view does violence to Shlapentokh and Shlapentokh's notion of five types of reality—ontological, individual, institutional, artistic, and scientific—since *truth* informs and influences the way we behave in our society, although we are not fully cognizant of how or why our social institutions take the forms they do.

From Foucault's perspective, the notion of truth is allotted the status of a metaconcept. He tells us that truths are not out there waiting to be discovered; rather, they are evident only in the forms of rules embedded in our social structure. One obvious way truth is made manifest is through public statements (including forms of mass communication such as film). In his analysis of photographs depicting the New Deal in the 1930s United States, Tagg (1988) uses Foucault's concept of truth to evaluate the institutionalized role of photography in creating and/or maintaining truth:

> What defines and creates truth in any society is a system of more or less ordered procedures for the production, regulation, distribution and circulation of statements. Through these procedures truth is bound in a circular relation to systems of power which produce and sustain it, and to the effects of power which it induces and which, in turn, redirect it. (p. 172)

From this perspective, truth is carried in practices such as film and photography. Consequently, the role of the social critic who wishes to analyze issues of truth and, by implication, power must do so by analyzing the social practices that manifest truth. Further, the critic not only must investigate practices, but within those practices must reveal and understand the rules embedded in them.

Knowledge

Like the concepts of power and truth, the concept of knowledge is multifaceted. Foucault (1972) describes knowledge as "a group of elements, formed in a regular manner by a discursive practice, and which are dispensable to the constitution of a science" (p. 182). In other words, there is a mutually influencing relationship between discursive practices and knowledge; the one cannot function without the other. Consequently, knowledge cannot exist without a particular discursive practice, such as the medium of film. Foucault suggests that knowledge can be made manifest only through practices that define and carry it. Knowledge is transferred from one source to another through these practices. So, for example, knowledge of Soviet society is made manifest in Soviet film and carried to audiences both in the Soviet Union and abroad. In addition, knowledge acts as a mediating force that breaks down the dichotomy of subject to object and facilitates the kind of circular relationship described previously. Thus knowledge is a dynamic concept and should more accurately be used in the plural—*knowledges*—for the specific form of knowledge is determined by the spatial and historical context in which it operates.

In my discussion of knowledge I have used the verbs *operate* and *carry* and other verbs of motion. This choice represents a deliberate attempt to emphasize the dynamic nature of Foucault's conceptualization of knowledge. However, in order for knowledge to be made mobile it must be generated in some manner. The two primary generating principles found in Foucault's thought are discourse and visualization. These principles not only allow knowledge to function in a fluid manner, but make possible the operation of both truth and power.

Visualization and Discourse

For Foucault, discourse and visualization are different but related modes of production in any given practice. Both discourse and visualization provide evidence or, as Foucault would prefer, evidences. Foucault distinguishes at least two forms of evidence: evidence and self-evidence. In keeping with his theory of historical discontinuities (see Foucault, 1972), Foucault is most interested in the phenomenon he calls a *rupture d'evidence*, or a break with self-evidence. That is, a break with "those evidences on which our knowledges, our agreements, our practices, rest" (Foucault, quoted in Rajchman, 1988, p. 94).

The role of evidences is important to Foucault because revealing the evidence is related to the acceptability of a given practice. It is part of what makes a strategy of power tolerable (Rajchman, 1988, p. 94). According to Foucault, power strategies are acceptable only because of what they are able to hide. In other words, "Power is only tolerable on the condition that it mask a substantial part of itself" (quoted in Rajchman, 1988, p. 105). Consequently, for Foucault, the role of a social critic is that of a seer, "someone who sees something not seen" (Deleuze, quoted in Rajchman, 1988, p. 95). That is, the social critic should reveal the hidden power strategies that prevent us from seeing the truth and from understanding the knowledge that we are presented with in its partial form. Thus the purpose of a social critic in examining or creating discursive practices such as film is to reveal, either verbally through discourse or by making visible what cannot readily be seen. This is the role of the filmmaker commenting on his or her society and of the film critic reflecting on the film produced.

Shlapentokh and Shlapentokh severely limit their analysis of Soviet films by stating:

> Our examination of Soviet movies will almost entirely disregard their artistic quality, the specific circumstances of their creation, their evaluation by critics, their influence on audiences, the role of filmmakers in Soviet society, the use of movies for propaganda, and popular attitudes toward movies. (p. 163)

From the theoretical perspective I have presented I would argue that the elements Shlapentokh and Shlapentokh have elected to disregard are crucial to an understanding of the role of film in Soviet society and to a critic who wishes to learn about that society through its films. Moreover, these elements, rather than having a negligible role, actually constitute the essence of film.

John Tagg (1988) has applied Foucault's theories in an examination of the roles that means of representation (such as photographic images) have played in the development of modern social regulation. In order to understand the representative power of visual images, Tagg (1988) asserts, we must "look not to some magic of the medium, but to the conscious and unconscious processes, the practices and institutions through which the [images] can incite a phantasy, take on meaning, and exercise an effect" (p. 4). In a similar manner I believe that a social critic examining the ways in which films reflect society must look not only at the content of the film but at the interrelated elements of production.

Each of the elements disregarded by Shlapentokh and Shlapentokh can provide valuable insight into the relationship between film and any given culture. Moreover, because film is a discursive practice and constitutes a semiotic system, all the elements of its production, messages, consumption, and effects are inextricably linked. Thus Tagg (1988) points out:

> We cannot think of abstracting experience from the signifying systems in which it is structured, or of decoding cultural languages to reach a given and determinant level of material interest, since it is the discursive structures and material processes of these languages that articulate interest and define sociality in the first place. (p. 23)

In the next section I will analyze the relationship between film and culture, drawing examples primarily from the Soviet experience, but also from Latin America and China. I focus on these cultures because they are all—in different but related ways—postrevolutionary societies. In each country the role of film has either played a major part in the restructuring of society or provides a clear illustration of the repressive conditions under which artists are forced to work.

THE RELATIONSHIP OF FILM AND CULTURE

Shlapentokh and Shlapentokh choose to disregard the "specific circumstances" of the creation of a movie. I argue that the circumstances of production are instrumental in determining the conception of the film and the final product viewed by the audience.

In 1978 China reopened the Beijing Film Academy, which had been closed for more than a decade following the Cultural Revolution. The Beijing Academy brought together a group of young directors whose formative experiences had been the circumstances of the Cultural Revolution and their own personal experiences of that time. Known as the Fifth Generation filmmakers, the directors who emerged from their training at the Beijing Academy rejected the traditions of urban melodrama that had prevailed in

China before 1949 and "reopened important questions about the relations among art, ideology, and popular cinema" (Kaige, 1990, p. 28). The films produced by the Fifth Generation reflected a keen interest in history, an interest in the marginal cultures of the border regions of China—such as Mongolia and Tibet—a desire to deal with social issues, and a wish to provide the viewer with a form of political knowledge that empowers him or her (Ning, 1990, pp. 33-34). Such goals were frequently incompatible with those of the Chinese authorities, even within the brief period of openness that developed in the mid-1980s. Chen Kaige, one of the leading figures in the Fifth Generation of filmmakers, described how he and other directors had to make changes in their films in order for their works to be distributed. For example, the first important film produced by the Fifth Generation, *The One and the Eight* (1983), a film set in the anti-Japanese war, was previewed by the Propaganda Department of the Central Committee, which subsequently banned the film for two years. A total of 46 separate changes were made to *The One and the Eight* before it was released. The release of another Fifth Generation film, *The Big Parade* (1985), directed by Chen Kaige, was blocked for a year until the ending was altered to suit the government. *The Big Parade* tells the story of an army squadron and its members as they train for the opportunity to take part in the 1984 National Day Parade in Tiananmen Square. In the original version the preparations were shown, but not the actual parade itself. Kaige (1990) describes the reaction his film received:

> At the film bureau I was told that some military officers in charge of training had not liked the film. They said it was not a true film—that the characters in the film were not Chinese, that they were like Japanese soldiers. They thought I was dangerous. (p. 30)

After much thought and pressure from various sources, Kaige changed the ending of the film so that it culminates in documentary footage of the National Day Parade. When the film was released in its altered form, the Chinese government awarded it a prize "because it shows strong spirits, to prove China is a great country and the soldiers have great character" (Kaige, 1990, p. 31).

The Chinese examples listed here demonstrate my objection to the form of analysis used by Shlapentokh and Shlapentokh in their discussion of Soviet films and their relationship to Soviet society. Among the elements of film disregarded by the authors are "the use of movies for propaganda" (p. 163). In the cases of *The One and the Eight* and *The Big Parade*, this element played a definite role in the final content of the films. Significant changes were made to both films because of the circumstances of their production, and, in the case of *The Big Parade*, the film was altered to such a degree that the government awarded it a prize because it reflected "the right values"; in essence, therefore, it became a form of propaganda despite the director's original intent.

In the Soviet Union, Gorbachev's policies of glasnost and perestroika have brought significant changes not only in the content of the films produced, but in the circumstances under which these works are created. In her evaluation of Soviet cinema between 1976 and 1987, Lawton (1989) notes that "Soviet cinema from its inception has been strictly connected with the national political reality. It has been a sensitive recorder of socioeconomic changes and shifts in cultural politics" (p. 1). Following the Fifth Congress of the Filmmakers Union in May 1984, there was a radical shakeup of the film industry in the Soviet Union. Many leading figures were replaced, and film studios and centers of production found themselves under new and very different leadership. The major change has been a decentralization of filmmaking away from Moscow, giving greater independence to the filmmakers themselves and to smaller studios in the republics (see Golovskoy, 1986; Lawton, 1989). These changes directly reflect Gorbachev's policies of glasnost and perestroika, which have "provoked challenges to established verities in every corner of Soviet life" (Foner, 1990, p. 70). These challenges are clearly reflected in the content of contemporary Soviet films. Similarly, the decentralization of the film industry has yielded such ethnic productions as *The Needle* (1988) from Kazakhfilm Studios and *Little Man in a Big War* (1989) from Uzbekfilm Studios. *Little Man in a Big War* is a particularly political film in which Uzbekistan serves as a metaphor for the Soviet Union during World War II and the rise of Stalinism.

Another element Shlapentokh and Shlapentokh choose to avoid in their analysis is the "artistic quality" of a film. I take this to mean not only the evaluated quality of the images, but the aesthetics of a film. Again, I find artistic quality to be one of the constituent elements of film and therefore one that must be included in any serious commentary.

Only three months after the Cuban Revolution, Cuba's revolutionary leaders founded the country's national film institute—Instituto Cubano del Arte y Industria Cinematograficos, or ICAIC—because Fidel Castro and others recognized the tremendous political and ideological potential of the film medium. The March 24, 1959, decree establishing ICAIC called for the "reeducation" of the tastes of moviegoers and urged filmmakers to use Cuban historical themes "to make of our cinema a fount of revolutionary inspiration, of culture and information" (West, 1986, p. 50). This reeducation was to retrain Cuban moviegoers accustomed to Hollywood fare. Consequently, a key issue for ICAIC and its founding filmmakers was "how to wed revolutionary themes, esthetic innovation and entertainment" (West, 1987, p. 20). Thus the artistic qualities of postrevolutionary Cuban cinema directly reflect the political goals of the culture. Cuban films are experimental, often blurring genres of documentary and narrative cinema, and typically contain self-reflexive devices that mock Hollywood conventions and fulfill ICAIC's goal of decolonizing the taste of the moviegoing public. In *Memories of Underdevelopment* (1968), for example, director Thomas Gutierrez Alea himself appears at ICAIC reviewing films censored prior to the revolution. The clips we are shown are from pornographic movies, where a young couple make love on a sun-drenched beach, with the sound of waves behind them. The image is a cliché in cinematic language, so Alea plays the short scene over and over again until it appears comic. The eroticism of the moment is gone and the triteness of the image is revealed. Similarly, a strong theoretical base has developed around Cuban cinema; books of film theory such as Michael Chanan's *The Cuban Image* (1985) and Julio Garcia Espinosa's *An Image Circles the Globe* (1979) clearly demonstrate the relationship between stylistic and political aspects of film.

Soviet cinema too reflects a form of postrevolutionary consciousness. The revolution of the glasnost era can be termed an "organic revolution," that is, one that builds on existing institutions rather than destroying them (Foner, 1990, p. 71). Contemporary Soviet cinema is stylistically experimental. Critics in the United States and elsewhere have noted:

> *Glasnost* and *perestroika* have fostered a period of widespread experimentation in Soviet film, embracing the avant-garde and non-narrative forms. . . . the *new model* cinema made possible by increased artistic freedom is fitfully emerging, and film artists must explore all the possibilities. (Ciesol, 1989, p. 48)

Some 50 years earlier, Soviet filmmakers like Sergei Eisenstein and Vsevolod Podovkin were producing revolutionary films that influenced filmmakers throughout the rest of the century. Eisenstein developed a theory of montage that was in itself inherently political. For Eisenstein, meaning was created through a collision or conflict of images. In addition, he attempted to create an image of collective action on the film screen, obviously reflecting the new Soviet belief in the power and strength of the masses (see Eisenstein, 1942, 1949; Leyda, 1970).

Shlapentokh and Shlapentokh also disregard the influence of films on their audiences and on popular attitudes toward film in the Soviet Union. Again examples from Cuba and the Soviet Union itself show the problems of such omissions. Following the 1917 revolution in the Soviet Union, Lenin declared that the most important of all arts is the cinema. Thus film achieved an elevated status within the country. Eisenstein's (1942) theory of film was one in which the meaning of an image is created by the spectator:

> The desired image is not fixed or ready-made, but arises—is born. The image planned by the author, director and actor is concertized by them in separate representational elements, and is assembled—again and finally—in the spectator's perception. (p. 31)

Thus to disregard the influence of films on their audience is to deny spectators their role in the creation of the film's meaning. Or, as Hall (1980, p. 128) suggests, it is to deny the part of the consumer in the process of meaning consumption.

In Cuba, ICAIC has played a central role in the development of a "radical cultural consciousness . . . and the institute's films have come to represent both the collective memory of the nation's people as well as a major force for social cohesion and social debate" (West, 1986, p. 50). Film has the potential to play a similar role in the Soviet Union. Movies about contemporary life and historical reexamination dominate Soviet cinema today.

Foner (1990) notes that, in the Soviet Union today, "slowly and chaotically, a new history is emerging—a history interesting, provocative, and less *political* than the old" (p. 71). It is apparent that films are a reflection and a constituent part of the new history developing in the Soviet Union. Films are not abstract forms, but "a material product of a material apparatus set up to work in specific contexts, by specific forces, for more or less defined purposes" (Tagg, 1988, p. 3). Therefore, the analysis of film and its usefulness to decode cultural messages requires a theoretical approach that insists on the political nature of the medium and its role in society.

REFERENCES

Berger, K. (1972). *Ways of seeing.* London: Penguin.

Berger, P., & Luckmann, T. (1966). *The social construction of reality.* Garden City, NY: Doubleday.

Chanan, M. (1985). *The Cuban image: Cinema and cultural politics in Cuba.* Bloomington: Indiana University Press.

Ciesol, F. S. (1989). Cinema of the Soviet Union. In *Catalogue of the Eighth Vancouver International Film Festival* (pp. 48-51). Vancouver: Greater Vancouver International Film Festival Society.

Eco, U. (1976). *A theory of semiotics.* Bloomington: Indiana University Press.

Eisenstein, S. (1942). *The film sense* (J. Leyda, Trans.). New York: Harcourt, Brace.

Eisenstein, S. (1949). *Film form* (J. Leyda, Trans.). New York: Harcourt, Brace & World.

Foner, E. (1990). Restructuring yesterday's news: The Russians write a new history. *Harper's, 281*(1687), 70-76, 78.

Foucault, M. (1972). *The archaeology of knowledge* (A. M. S. Smith, Trans.). New York: Pantheon.

Foucault, M. (1980a). Two lectures. In C. Gordon (Ed.), *Power/knowledge: Selected interviews and other writings 1972-1977* (C. Gordon et al., Trans.) (pp. 78-108). New York: Pantheon.

Foucault, M. (1980b). Truth and power. In C. Gordon (Ed.), *Power/knowledge: Selected interviews and other writings 1972-1977* (C. Gordon et al., Trans.) (pp. 109-133). New York: Pantheon.

Fry, D. L., & Fry, V. H. (1986). A semiotic model for the study of mass communication. In M. L. McLaughlin (Ed.), *Communication yearbook 9* (pp. 443-462). Beverly Hills, CA: Sage.

Garcia Espinosa, J. (1979). *Una imagen recorre el mundo* [An image circles the globe]. Havana: Editorial Letras Cubanas.

Golovskoy, V. S. (1986). *Behind the Soviet screen* (S. Hill, Trans.) Ann Arbor, MI: Ardis.

Goulding, D. J. (Ed.). (1989). *Post new wave cinema in the Soviet Union and Eastern Europe.* Bloomington: Indiana University Press.

Hall, S. (1973). The determination of news photographs. In J. Young (Ed.), *The manufacture of news: Social problems, deviance and the mass media* (pp. 176-190). London: Constable.

Hall, S. (1980). Encoding/decoding. In S. Hall, D. Hobson, A. Lowe, & P. Willis (Eds.), *Culture, media, language: Working papers in cultural studies 1972-1979* (pp. 128-138). London: Hutchinson.

Kaige, C. (1990). Breaking the circle: The cinema and cultural change in China. *Cineaste, 17,* 25-31.

Lawton, A. (1989). Toward a new openness in Soviet cinema, 1976-1987. In D. J. Goulding (Ed.), *Post new wave cinema in the Soviet Union and Eastern Europe* (pp. 1-50). Bloomington: Indiana University Press.

Leyda, J. (1970). *Film essays and a lecture by Sergei Eisenstein.* New York: Praeger.

Ning, M. (1990). New Chinese cinema: A critical account of the Fifth Generation. *Cineaste, 17,* 32-35.

Quinney, R. (1982). *Social existence: Metaphysics, Marxism, and the social sciences.* Beverly Hills, CA: Sage.

Rajchman, J. (1988). Foucault's art of seeing. *October, 44,* 89-117.

Sulkunen, P. (1982). Society made visible: On the cultural sociology of Pierre Bourdieu. *Acta Sociologica, 25,* 103-115.

Tagg, J. (1988). *The burden of representation: Essays on photographies and histories.* Amherst: University of Massachusetts Press.

Templin, P. (1982). Still photography in evaluation. In N. L. Smith (Ed.), *Communication strategies in evaluation* (pp. 121-174). Beverly Hills, CA: Sage.

West, D. (1986). *The Cuban image: Cinema and cultural politics in Cuba,* a review. *Cineaste, 15,* 50-51.

West, D. (1987). Reconciling entertainment and thought: An interview with Julio Garcia Espinosa. *Cineaste, 16,* 20-26, 89.

SECTION 2

MASS MEDIA MESSAGES AND INFLUENCE

5 Encounters with the Television Image: Thirty Years of Encoding Research

DAVID BARKER
University of Missouri—Columbia

BERNARD M. TIMBERG
Radford University

This chapter surveys 30 years of research on the audiovisual codes of television. This research centers on close readings of encoded texts and the processes and practices of television encoding. The chapter discusses the humanist precursors of encoding research (McLuhan, Ong, Carpenter); the first phase of educational research on individual production variables; the next phase, in which scholars of literary texts applied their methodologies to television studies; and finally the phase in which forms of critical theory and cultural studies were related to the study of the audiovisual codes of television. Forefront work of leading scholars (Horace Newcomb, Herbert Zettl, Stuart Hall) is discussed as it has affected this newly emerging field.

T HE medium is the message. It *was* a catchy phrase and one that, not so long ago, seemed not just insightful but visionary. Yet its hold on the collective psyche was fleeting; soon the phrase sounded contrived, superficial, and decidedly passé. Still, a question lingered: Is there an ongoing need to explore our encounters with the aural/visual codes of the television image? Did the scholarly community move too hastily in its retreat from a technologically deterministic focus on the medium itself to speculations about the effects of the medium's content?

Mindful of McLuhanesque rhetorical excess, it is encouraging nonetheless to realize, first, even if mass communication research as a whole shifted the preponderance of its collective focus to effects, a committed number of scholars insisted on focusing their efforts on television's

Correspondence and requests for reprints: David Barker, Department of Communication, 115 Switzler Hall, University of Missouri, Columbia, MO 65211.

Communication Yearbook 15, pp. 209-238

aural/visual codes and, second, that this work has continued to grow in scope and complexity. Thus, although this research has demonstrated a particular vitality since its infusion by critical and cultural studies, it is not merely a recent phenomenon: It has a 30-year history of some complexity. Nor is this work the exclusive province of any one group of researchers. Although comparatively small in number, this group at various times has been extraordinarily diverse, encompassing scholars of every theoretical and methodological stripe. Early work on television codes had roots in the most traditional, empirically based approaches to educational and children's television; later work, influenced by art history and literary criticism, moved toward a generalized television aesthetic at the same time it distinguished television from film, drama, and literature; finally, a newly emerging body of work, influenced by critical theory and cultural studies, has provided new directions in research concerning television production processes, texts, and audiences, and their relationship to the specific aural/visual codes of television.

Such theoretical and methodological diversity suggests that research of this kind is not always easily categorized. Accordingly, drawing conclusions about this work based upon either the number of scholars involved with it or their positions within the discipline as a whole is potentially quite problematic. Two things about this research are certain, however. Over its 30-year history, and particularly in the last decade or so, this growing body of work has provided significant insight into the role of television's aural/visual codes with increasing degrees of specificity and, in the process, insights into the workings of television discourse in general. Furthermore, the successes as well as failures of this kind of research underscore the necessity of approaching all manifestations of television studies holistically. As scholars, we can accept or ignore any component of the television apparatus only at the risk of seriously diminishing our understanding of both the apparatus itself and its multiple sites of engagement. The purpose of this chapter, therefore, is to survey the evolution of research into television's aural/visual codes, assess its significance, and outline four potentially fruitful directions we see it moving in the future.

DEFINITIONS

One problem in dealing with research into the aural/visual codes of television is a semantic one: What does one call this kind of research? *Production research* is troublesome because it suggests analysis of the process of production when, in fact, much of the research focuses on the end result of the process, the text itself. *Textual research* is also troublesome, because it suggests, among other things, structural analysis of narrative, which is often beyond the scope of this research, though intimately related to it, and because it excludes the production process. *Visual analysis* is both too broad and too narrow a term, suggesting other visual arts without suggesting the importance of aural/visual relationships. Most research in this area simply avoids the problem by identifying itself according to the set of assumptions from which it operates: *semiotic analysis, structural analysis, ideological analysis,* and so on. While expressing the diversity of theoretical approaches at work, such labeling only exacerbates the lack of a sense of cohesion among different studies and within the field of research as a whole.

Encoding research strikes us as an appropriate alternative for several reasons. First, and perhaps most important, to the extent the term *encoding* suggests the necessity of transforming the "raw material" of television's discourses into forms appropriate for those discourses, the importance of the medium itself is underscored. Second, the term encompasses the apparatus of television as a mode of production (routines, skills, strategies), a division of labor to staff that mode (producers, writers, directors, and so on), and a technological and economic system to plan, structure, and disseminate the end product (broadcast and cable networks, affiliates, independents). Third, *encoding* necessarily suggests *decoding*. This underscores our contention that every act of encoding is also and always an act of decoding. In turn, this suggests the viewer occupies a position of equality relative both to the text and to the producers of the text in the negotiation and construction of meaning. Finally, the notion of "code" inherent in *encoding* suggests the overarching influence of culture and ideology: The aural and visual codes of television are culturally based and, as such, ideologically motivated.

Providing encoding research with a name does not put an end to semantic difficulties, however. We are now faced with a problem of definition: What, precisely, is *encoding research*? First, it must be recognized that *all* television research is, to some degree, encoding research. After all, television researchers of necessity must at some point and on some level engage television's aural/visual codes. Having said this, however, we are quick to point out that obviously not all television research deals *explicitly* with the medium's aural/visual codes. The research we are concerned with does deal explicitly, formally, and centrally with television's aural/visual codes, engaging in analysis of the encoding process at the sites of text production (encoding) or reception (decoding) or at a combination of the two.

What is meant precisely by the term *television codes*? Definitions of *code* are numerous (see Corner, 1986) and, when articulated relative to a visual medium such as television, often derived from semiotics. We suggest that encoding research, however, does not necessarily utilize the notion of code in the semiotic sense of an arrangement of signs. Instead, encoding research more commonly defines *code* as a specific component of one of television's representational forms. One therefore encounters codes relative to lighting, camera, and performer blocking, set design, music and sound effects, switching, editing and montage, and so on. These codes, combined in particular ways, result in, for instance, the representational form of multiple-camera, proscenium-staged, live-on-tape situation comedy (this includes the filmed or pretaped introductions that serve as "signatures" of the show). This conceptualization of code also suggests the inherent presence and power of the viewer. Each code (and, by extension, each representational form) is the product of an unstated reciprocal contract between producer and viewer (that is, between encoder and decoder) such that the producer can utilize a given code with some sense that the viewer will negotiate the code more or less as the producer intended. Emphasizing the reciprocity of the process in turn suggests that any given code can most productively be conceptualized as the site of intersection of numerous forces: aesthetic, institutional, narrative, economic, ideological. As defined by Fiske (1987), "Codes are links between producers, texts, and audiences, and are the agents of intertextuality through which texts interrelate in a network of meanings that constitutes our cultural world" (p. 4).

Having defined *code*, we can now define encoding research as *analysis of the aural and visual codes making up the representational forms of television and the roles they play in the articulation of the multiple intersecting discourses of television texts.* Notice that our definition gives equal weight to both the aural and visual codes of television. Obviously, the communication of television discourse can be most productively analyzed if done so holistically, by looking at all components of television's representational forms. More important, however, television's status as an information-poor medium and its typical regimes of viewing result in the responsibility for communicating much of the discourse necessarily being shouldered by the audio portion of the text.

ORIGINS

Tracing the 30-year evolution of encoding research requires some sense of its theoretical and methodological roots within the field of mass communication research as a whole. We can begin by considering yet another basic question: In light of the precedent set by film studies' long tradition of aesthetic analysis of cinematic codes of representation, why has television yet to receive analysis of a similar scope and complexity?

One rather familiar reason is that the field of film studies historically tended to make its academic home in the humanities, often playing a curricular role in departments of English or art. This in part led to the development of theories and methodologies that borrowed heavily from literary criticism, art history, and aesthetics. Television studies, such as it was, traditionally resided in the social sciences, where it was informed by a methodological tradition grounded in empiricism and behaviorism and infused with a concern for psychological impact and persuasion. The result as often as not was industry-oriented, often industry-sponsored, institutional research. Although arguably of some utility for the consideration of "effects," such a tradition was fundamentally ill suited for close analysis of aural/visual codes. Indeed, as will become clear, encoding research did not see its potential unfold until television studies converged with the more humanistic traditions of aesthetic film analysis and literary criticism.

For us, however, the single most important reason television has failed to establish the body of aesthetic research amassed by film is a basic theoretical failure to recognize the distinction between television as *an industry* and television as *a mode of communication*. Television has long labored under the perception that it is best suited for the commercialized, profit-driven endeavor of mating audiences with advertisers. Indeed, with its immediate reach into millions of homes, television was in some ways ideally suited for this task. However, taken as a blanket characterization of the medium, this identification has proven singularly unfortunate. The sweeping strokes of such a generalization have obfuscated the fact that we experience television first and foremost as a commercial, capitalistic enterprise not because television must be this way, but because of the peculiar institutional, economic, and ideological forces that intersected in the 1920s and 1930s to shape a television industry in the image of network radio.

Compounded by the sheer efficiency and ubiquitousness of commercial television, an equation persists in the public mind of television-as-mode-of-communication with television-as-industry. This marriage of mode and industry is so complete, in fact, that efforts to articulate and exploit those dynamics of television that do not lend themselves to commercialization— video art, experimental video, television as a dynamic for social change and/or a tool for critical awareness—have dropped the mantle of "television" altogether in favor of "video." Nonetheless, it has been assumed (and, admittedly, with some justification) that "television" as it is most commonly conceptualized is the product of profligate capitalist enterprise, that richness of text and expression have been sacrificed for the sake of delivering audiences to advertisers. Coupled with the well-heeled metaphor of Hollywood as programming machine, spitting out series clone after series clone from a narrative and aesthetic cookie cutter, it is not difficult to understand why the role of encoding has been not just taken for granted but openly ridiculed as a valid subject for analysis in the first place. It perhaps is no surprise, therefore, that the first attempts at encoding research dealt almost exclusively with the one province of television that has consistently managed to avoid significant derision by arbiters of culture and social policy: educational television. Equally significant is the fact encoding research achieved scholarly respectability only when the shift in television studies to textual analysis effectively argued that close reading of television's programming was as worthy an academic pursuit as speculation on its broad social effects.

PRECURSORS TO AND
CATEGORIES OF ENCODING RESEARCH

In our view, research into the aural/visual codes of television can be grouped into three categories preceded by the work of several scholars that, collectively, set the stage for encoding research as a whole. These "precursors" were a small group of humanists (e.g., Marshall McLuhan, Edmund Carpenter, and Walter Ong) who, while not dealing explicitly with television's aural/visual codes, nonetheless argued that these codes altered the sensorium of the individuals who engaged with them.

The first category of encoding research is that undertaken by individuals (often working within the framework of educational television) interested in determining the effect of various production techniques on the comprehension of televised instruction. This work, typically operating within a "hard" sciences framework, tends to be informed by cause-and-effect empirical methodologies and characterized by a distinct theoretical insularity. In some cases, research in this category broadens its scope to consider how manipulation of specific production variables influences audience decoding in general (e.g., the influence of camera angle on generalized perceived credibility of a newscaster or sincerity of a political candidate). This work was complemented by a series of content analysis studies that examined not the aural/visual codes of television but the themes (incidents of violence, for instance, or the kinds of domination/subordination relationships in different forms of programming). "Form" was radically separated from "content," and each was studied separately. What lingered in each of these kinds of studies, however, was the influence of cause-and-effect empiricism, theoretical insularity, and the investigative procedures of the physical sciences as a methodological model.

Work in the second category of research we have identified reflects a distinct shift in the paradigm away from empirically based studies of the influence of single production variables or elements of thematic content to an engagement with the television "text" as a whole. Empirical studies of the audience here are abandoned in favor of textual analysis that attempts to factor in all components of a production strategy. Often energized by the work of literary and film scholars who turned their attention to television, research in this category typically adopts a methodology borrowed from literary criticism: close textual analysis.

The third (and most contemporary) category sees research moving increasingly into the realm of cultural studies combined with more sophisticated approaches, empirical as well as theoretical, to the role of the audience. Work in this category is characterized less by adherence to any one methodological approach than by attempts to reconceptualize the notion of television texts and the role of aural/visual codes within them in terms of, among other things, semiotics, structuralism, poststructuralism, and feminist criticism.

Precursors: McLuhan, Carpenter, and Ong

The precursors of encoding research were a small group of humanists— Marshall McLuhan, Edmund Carpenter, and Walter Ong foremost among them—who argued, each in a different way, that the codes of the new electronic media altered the sensorium of the individuals who experienced them and ultimately affected the culture in profound and permanent ways. McLuhan became the publicist and signpost for the movement, and *Explorations*, the journal he coedited with Carpenter in Toronto in the late 1950s and early 1960s, was a sounding board for the movement.

The media theorists' positions on television were an extension of research and theorizing they had done on the shifts between oral/aural and written (chirographic) cultures, most notably in the work of Walter Ong (1967) and Eric Havelock (1963), and in the shifts between chirographic and typographic cultures (again with Ong and McLuhan himself, in *The Gutenberg Galaxy*, 1965, leading the way). Unfortunately, none of the scholars knew, understood, or embraced the products of the new electronic culture in terms of textual analysis. Their years of training in the print media disposed them to understand and articulate traditional discourses of literature and criticism, and though a number of interesting insights came out of this work, most scholars considered it too broad and sketchy, even at its peak of popularity in the 1960s and 1970s, to be of much use.

In spite of the tenuousness of their work, the media theorists did draw attention to the phenomenological impact of the medium of television and raised serious questions about that impact. Though they did not look at the play of codes within individual texts (or, if they did so, only incidentally or anecdotally), they set the stage for subsequent encoding research through their intense interest in the new aural/visual codes ("new languages," Carpenter put it) and their presumed importance. At the same time, these theorists may have delayed or retarded text-centered investigations in academia. It was McLuhan, of all the media theorists, who became by far the most well known. The publicity was the result of a combination of a genuinely distinctive personality— McLuhan had a knack for publicity and an effusive scholarly sociability with a wide range of people inside and outside academia—and a colorful epigrammatic style with apocalyptic overtones that seemed exactly right for the counterculture *Zeitgeist* of the 1960s (Marchand, 1989). But McLuhan's popularity and, in the eyes of much of the academy, his rhetorical excess tended to make television studies a taboo in the most prestigious university departments. This perhaps was particularly so in the very departments that were traditional bastions of text-centered scholarship. Graduate students and junior professors who might overcome other forms of prejudice against pursuing close studies of television now had to contend with particular animosity (and sometimes outright jealousy) from senior faculty members as McLuhan moved rapidly into the position of America's first academic superstar.

What is more intriguing is why McLuhan himself did not engage television texts in their specificity once this became his major area of concern. After all, he received his postgraduate education in Cambridge in the mid-1930s from people like I. A. Richards, William Empson, and F. R. Leavis, the "fathers" of what would come to be known as New Criticism (Marchand, 1989, pp. 30-41). New Criticism focused on the precise verbal analysis of literary texts in all levels of complexity, ambiguity, and meaning. In his early work McLuhan did critique specific texts. *The Mechanical Bride* (1967) was developed out of a series of slide presentations, and his analysis, piecemeal but insightful, is full of examples. Perhaps McLuhan's broad media determinism and focus on audience effects was in part a reaction to what he perceived to be the increasing insularity of New Criticism's focus on autonomous texts. Carpenter (1973) used numerous examples in his cross-cultural discussion of media decoding, but he did not investigate the aural/visual codes of television in any systematic way, either. Ong, who began his career as a student of McLuhan's at St. Louis University and maintained a lifetime correspondence with him (Molinaro, 1987), was more careful in his generalizations about the influence of electronic communication and the "secondary orality" he saw it occasioning. He dealt with the issue in a much more tentative way, realizing that he never did the kind of systematic work with television texts that would enable him to make more fundamental claims about the shift from chirographic/typographic culture to the electronic culture now in ascendancy.

The fact was that McLuhan did not watch television very much, nor did Carpenter or Ong, and when they did watch it was not in a way that concentrated on the imagery. Though Ampex had a working system for videotape as early as 1957, it was not available for use by scholars and critics in the formative years of media theory, and, more crucially, it would not have been used even if it had existed. (It is worth noting that videotape was available and not used by Horace Newcomb some 10 years after McLuhan's *Understanding Media* appeared in 1964; Newcomb's bold step of claiming television texts as literary texts that could be explored and understood using the methods of literary criticism concentrated on television narratives, with scant reference to their aural/visual encoding.) McLuhan shared the prejudices of his class, educational background, and generation, and the idea of studying a television program as one would study a poem or a short story was as foreign to McLuhan as it was to most of his colleagues. Indeed, his most famous empirical study (he promoted and attempted to do others) was the comparison of a lecture, a television program, and a radio program for student recall of information presented in a classroom setting—a classic example of the kind of work we place in the first category of encoding research.

The First Category:
Single Production Variable Research

Work in the first category of encoding research typically has been carried out by individuals working within the framework of educational television. This work, exemplified by the efforts of Baggaley and Duck (1974a, 1974b, 1975a, 1975b, 1975c, 1975d, 1975e), Coldevin (1976, 1978a, 1978b, 1980), and Schlater (1968, 1969, 1970), is concerned with determining the effects of various production techniques on the comprehension of televised instruction. Much of Baggaley and Duck's work, for instance, has consisted of a series of experiments in which they studied the impact on comprehension made by the manipulation of background, camera, angle, use of cutaway shots, and editing patterns, concluding that presentation methods in educational television can have significant impact on information retention (see specifically 1974b, 1975a, 1975b, 1975c, 1975d).

This is important work to the extent it both recognizes the role of encoding in communication through television and makes a systematic attempt to analyze that role. Ultimately, however, this research is problematic for several reasons. First, the empirical, cause-and-effect assumptions upon which this research is based, while understandable in light of its roots in educational psychology, is nonetheless significantly reductionist. Schlater (1969), for example, begins his article by commenting:

> The development of techniques for achieving predictably strong effects of messages on viewers is of continuing concern. Notably lacking are television production techniques developed and verified by rigorous scientific research. Producers and directors follow "rules" of production that have been developed largely through intuition. The time has arrived when these "rules" should be subjected to precise scientific testing if the medium is to improve its ability to make a desired impact upon viewers. (p. 63)

Such cause-and-effect empiricism is equally evident in the methodology of the Schlater study. Seeking to "establish base lines for a variety of television production variables," Schlater developed six different "message treatments" utilizing fives types of "irrelevant stimuli" (superimposure of words, boom shadow, ornate frames, letters or numbers on visuals, and the shadow of a gesturing hand) and "exposed" 485 "subjects" to each treatment. As the ratio of irrelevant to relevant cues was "manipulated" by increasing the number of irrelevant cues per 30 seconds of message, Schlater measured subject response to the "interference."

The difficulty with such reductionism, of course, is that it works against the remarkably complex processes of, on the one hand, the encoding of television discourse and, on the other, engagement between work and viewer in the work of text construction. Even if one could discuss the aural/visual codes of television in terms of "effects," one must allow for the cumulative, symbiotic nature of the representational forms arising from the codes. These forms are the sum of all production variables utilized in the encoding process as well as the history and state of mind of the decoders at the moment of decoding. Drawing conclusions relative to the role of one variable when it is excised from all others is no more tenable than observing an amputated leg to deduce how human beings walk. Similarly, approaching the relationship between text and viewer in television discourse in terms of the "desired impact" of one on the other ignores the indisputable power exercised by the viewer in negotiating the codes making up the text.

The final reason research in this first category is troublesome arises directly from the shortcomings of the theoretical assumptions and methodologies upon which it is based. Research straitjacketed by such an insular approach to its object of study almost necessarily results in data and conclusions that simply are not particularly useful. This is seen both in the conclusions themselves (again, Schlater, 1969, is typical: "The data in this study suggest that television viewers may be able to tolerate more irrelevant visual information than professional television producers and directors would intuitively expect"; p. 69) and in their low external validity: Results tend to hold true for one set of students at one point in time under one set of circumstances, making extrapolation to other instructional settings— much less to television in general—very difficult.

The theoretical and methodological problems arising from the insularity of these studies of educational television likewise plague the single production variable studies of other forms of television. There are studies concerning image size (Acker & Tiemens, 1976), the extent to which one side of the television frame is perceived as "heavier" than the other (Avery & Tiemens, 1976), the impact of the television frame on perceptions of material contained within its confines (Herbener, Tubergen, & Whitlow, 1979), whether or not variations in camera angle affect perceived credibility or attractiveness of televised subjects (McCain, Chilberg, & Wakshlag, 1977; Tiemens, 1970), and the relationship between acting style and shot selection relative to the perceived impact of a television drama (Wurtzel & Dominick, 1971).

Although it is encouraging to note that work in this category expands beyond the parameters of televised instruction, these studies remain problematic nonetheless. The continued inappropriateness of a hard-sciences, empirical methodology still misleads researchers into isolating a single production variable for controlled study, thereby undercutting the internal dynamics of television's representational forms. In addition, the role of the viewer in negotiating meaning is still reduced to passive consumption (or ignored altogether), and results and conclusions lack extrapolative ability and are tentative to the point of being virtually useless (particularly in light of the fact that studies claiming to be initial research are rarely followed up with further research that could refine or extend the initial results).

Whatever the ultimate shortcomings of work in this category, to the extent it tended to be among the first systematic encoding research undertaken, it underscored the importance of articulating an aesthetic for television. Indeed, shortly after much of this work was first published, encoding research received its first attempts at aesthetic theory. Antin (1979) argues that the aesthetics of television are defined largely by the social and economic distribution of technological resources. Hanhardt (1979) suggests that television aesthetics must account for regimes of viewing, the fact that television is a site of domiciliary consumption. Schroeder (1979) argues that television aesthetics are best understood as rooted in the serial nature of most television narratives. Tarroni (1979) posits an aesthetic theory of television grounded in the medium's ontology of a constant state of becoming. All of these authors argue that an aesthetic for television must be grounded in the uniqueness of the medium itself rather than conceptualized as a hybrid bastardization of cinema and radio. Toogood (1978) and Zettl (1968) are particularly explicit on this point; in Toogood's words, "Film and video are clearly different forms of expression," each of which "has a distinctive contribution to make to our visual language" (p. 15).

Although recognizing the importance of articulating television aesthetics relative to the uniqueness of the medium, these initial, tentative forays into theory were often defensive, reflecting a need to justify why it was necessary even to outline an aesthetic for a medium as crass as television. In 1973, however, Herbert Zettl (who can rightly lay claim to being the founder of an aesthetic theory for television codes) produced his seminal text, *Sight-Sound-Motion: Applied Media Aesthetics*. In the preface to the book, Zettl forthrightly declares:

> A thorough understanding of aesthetic principles, and their prudent use, is no longer a matter of choice; it has become an essential prerequisite for the responsible communicator. In the midst of the extreme pollution of our senses and widespread perceptual insensitivity, if not illiteracy, aesthetics may well emerge as one of the most important and effective means for personal and social stability, if not survival.

Having thrown down the gauntlet, Zettl goes on to provide the most rigorous articulation of television aesthetics yet produced; indeed, *Sight-Sound-Motion* remains the central work of television aesthetic theory to this day. Zettl divides television aesthetics into five "aesthetic fields" (light and color, space:area, space:volume, time-motion, and sound), which he chooses to discuss in terms of "vectors." Vectors are defined as "forces that push or pull in certain directions or simply exert energy" (p. 2). Perhaps the single greatest contribution of Zettl's work at this stage was in providing a way for media scholars to talk precisely about a significant component of television that up until that point had been approached largely through intuition.

One "knew" that, visually, something on television "worked," yet one was at something of a loss to explain *why* it worked.

The Second Category:
The Shift to Textual Analysis

Work in the second category of encoding research is characterized by a recognition of the necessity of moving away from empirically based studies of the influence of a single production variable to holistic engagement with an entire television "text." This idea arose as a result of the general shift in television studies toward textual analysis. American studies scholar Horace Newcomb constructed a theory of narrative aesthetics for television at about the same time Zettl produced his description of the phenomenological basis of television's codes. Newcomb's *TV: The Most Popular Art* (1974) engaged in "humanistic analysis" (p. 19), the purpose of which was "to find out where the aesthetic qualities of television come from in the culture that produces them" (p. 24). Although Newcomb defines "aesthetic qualities" broadly, including narrative, institutional, and cultural factors in his analysis, his insistence on television's formulas as the most productive point of entry into television discourse naturally suggests the significance of—without explicitly dealing with—the aural/visual formulas accompanying those of story and setting as traditionally conceived in literature and drama. Suggesting that a television program, like a novel or play, is most appropriately engaged as a text, and drawing upon the tools of textual analysis long utilized in literary criticism, work in this category of television research sets aside the notion of television programming as a mere vehicle for the delivery of an audience to an advertiser in favor of a conceptualization emphasizing the layers of meaning embedded within the text.

A wide array of work followed that centered on television texts. Allen (1983), utilizing the tenets of reader-response criticism, studied the television soap opera as cultural document (and, in the process, delivered a broadside to empiricist research). Alley (1982) explored the fit between imperatives within society as a whole and their manifestation in television drama, dealing specifically with violence and police-detective shows. Anderson (1987) explored the use of memory in *Magnum, P.I.* and the extent to which a past experience—in this case, the Vietnam War—can come to define present reality. Blair (1982) assessed the cult appeal of *Star Trek* in terms of the search for a culturally stereotypical paradise. Craft (1982) analyzed *Mary Hartman, Mary Hartman* in terms of the series' playing against the genre conventions of the soap opera at the same time it parodied the "joys" of life in a capitalist/consumerist culture. Aristotelian dramatic theory was applied to the television commercial by Esslin (1982), while Marc (1984) underscored the influence of the theater on television in helping to define it first and foremost as a comic medium. Dennis Porter (1982), resonating with Allen's work on the soap opera, highlighted the parallels between television text as cultural document and television text as commodity. Real (1982), in focusing on the yearly spectacle of the Super Bowl, argued for a conceptualization of the television text as myth. Rosenblatt (1979) argued that television's use of the family unit as an organizing structure for much of its narrative must be seen in light of television's consistent undermining of authority figures. Schatz (1987), utilizing *St. Elsewhere* as a case study, traced the evolution of the ensemble series as a reflection of broader narrative, aesthetic, institutional, and ideological changes within the television industry as a whole in the 1970s and 1980s. Sklar (1982) argued that *Happy Days* and *Laverne & Shirley* are best understood not as situation comedies but as microcosms of socioeconomic class struggle. Thorburn (1979), in contrast to Marc's assertion that television is primarily a comic medium, posited melodrama as the narrative form best suited to the economic and aesthetic exigencies of American commercial television. Williams (1979) argued that the *Mary Tyler Moore Show* suggests the importance of the production company as auteur in producing a text capable of humanizing pertinent social issues.

As these studies suggest, emphasizing the layers of meaning embedded within the television text necessarily means engagement with all dimensions of the text. This includes analysis of television's representational forms—as crucial to the communication of television discourse as language is to written discourse—in their entirety, as integrated, ordered systems of aural and visual codes. As encoding research embraced this realization, the study of isolated production variables was spurned.

At the same time encoding research turned its back on single production variable studies, its traditional focus on the codes themselves broadened to include attempts at engagement with their narrative function. Many working in encoding research argued that accurate articulation of the role of television's aural/visual codes in the communication of its discourses can be achieved only through recognition of the symbiotic relationship between narrative structure and representational form (e.g., Barker, 1985; M. Porter, 1983; Timberg, 1982, 1987). The idea of television's narrative formulas as an entry point into its texts is again useful. Situation comedy, for example, is predicated on both narrative and aural/visual formulas such that, at any given time, a majority of sitcoms work from a narrative structure defined by either a centripetal figure (e.g., *All in the Family*) or an ensemble (e.g., *M*A*S*H*) and a representational form defined, respectively, by multiple-camera proscenium shooting or single-camera film-style shooting. Closer analysis, however, suggests that the relationship between narrative structure and representational form is not necessarily coincidental. Very often, though certainly not exclusively, the centripetal (and often patriarchal) position of a single character is most felicitously communicated through proscenium staging, whereas the more egalitarian nature of an ensemble is better handled with a single camera and multiple setups (see Barker, 1985). This is not to suggest that the relationship between narrative structure and representational form is a function of just those two components, however. Increasingly, encoding research is attempting to account simultaneously for the roles of economic, institutional, cultural, and ideological forces in constructing this relationship.

The conceptualization of television as text is reinforced by another of the significant developments of work in this category of encoding research, the convergence—albeit an uneasy one at times—of television with film studies. One can perhaps mark the beginnings of this convergence with the appearance in *Screen* in 1977 of an article by Gillian Skirrow and Stephen Heath on *World in Action,* in which an attempt was made to open a discourse with television in terms of subjectivity and the language of narrative, issues that up until that point had remained within the realm of film theory and analysis (see Caughie, 1984). Increasingly, a number of film scholars began turning their attention to television, bringing with them a diverse set of theoretical assumptions that encouraged television scholars to consider the subject of their endeavors in new ways.

This influx of film scholarship has been particularly important for encoding research because it further invigorated the retreat from the theoretical reductionism of earlier work by tapping into the long tradition of aesthetic film theory. Indeed, many of the early attempts to deal holistically with the aural/visual codes of television are obviously beholden to early work in film theory (see Altman, 1986; Barker, 1985; Hilmes, 1985; M. Porter, 1980, 1981, 1983; Pryluck, Teddlie, & Sands, 1982; Timberg, 1982, 1987).

As previous work in film studies has opened encoding research to new possibilities, scholars have been reminded that, in spite of similarities, the aural/visual codes of television and film are fundamentally different. (We use the word *reminded* advisedly because, in fact, this realization is nothing new. As early as the 1920s, once television technology had developed to the point where its commercial introduction was being actively considered, motion picture aesthetics were often utilized as a point of comparison for television.) Simultaneously, it has been recognized that the basic ontological differences between the two media correspond to differences between their respective aural/visual repertoires. Television is "live" in a way the motion picture never can be, and parameters for its engagement have traditionally been affected by its low-definition characteristics and smaller, more intimate screen size.

To say this shift toward television as text has proven to be a turning point in scholarly analysis and criticism of television is not to overstate its significance. However, the emphasis on a holistic approach to texts does not mean that all television scholarship since the shift has dealt explicitly with aural/visual codes. Similarly, the speed and degree of completeness with which the shift has ultimately occurred within encoding research itself does not mean that other, particularly empirical, methodologies have given way altogether. Nikos Metallinos (1979a, 1979b, 1982, 1984, 1985), for example, continues to refine his efforts to analyze the aural/visual codes of television through specifically quantitative and neurophysiological methodologies. Further, Tiemens (1990) has developed a computer software program that enables the encoding researcher to quantify and thus more easily manage the daunting amounts of data that often amass as the result of close textual readings of encoding strategies. Nonetheless, recognition of the role played by all components of a television text and the importance of holistic engagement with each component has been of singular importance in moving encoding research beyond single production variable studies.

The Third Category:
Shift from "Text" to "Textuality"

Although close textual analysis continues to be perhaps the primary critical approach in television studies today, work in the third category of encoding research is moving increasingly into the realm of cultural studies, with a renewed, more individuated interest in the role of the audience. "Text" becomes "textuality" in these most recent studies, and, on the decoding side, audience survey research is replaced by a movement toward an audience ethnography.

By way of introduction to our discussion of work in this category, the relationship between encoding research and cultural studies deserves comment. We take as our point of departure for these comments the notion of "culture," and here reaffirm one of our earlier arguments for naming aural/visual code analysis in television *encoding research*: The idea of "code," being inherent in "encoding," suggests the overarching influence of culture and ideology on television's representational forms. A concern with culture, therefore, has necessarily existed throughout all phases of encoding research's evolution even if that concern was neither voiced nor overt. Scholars making the earliest attempts at encoding research by looking at educational television or, later, by isolating a single production variable for controlled study were dealing nonetheless with objects of study generated by and firmly rooted in culture. Indeed, Schlater's contention that "producers and directors follow 'rules' of production that have been developed largely through intuition" alludes to the fact that even the standard industry practices of Hollywood television production are the products of a specific institutional appropriation of the perceptual rules of a specific culture at a specific point in that culture's evolution. Furthermore, the shift to textual analysis that defined encoding research's second phase made the presence of culture overt, in the narrative of the texts if not always in the representational forms that communicated them. It would be incorrect, therefore, to assume that the weight of culture was not brought to bear on encoding research until the research itself was affected by the tenets of formalized cultural studies.

Perhaps the single most significant contribution cultural studies has made to encoding research has been the recognition of the necessity of a truly holistic approach to the analysis of television's representational forms. An accurate assessment of the role of television's aural/visual codes in the communication of its discourses can be achieved only if the codes are analyzed relative to the narrative content they manifest, the specific forces—historical, cultural, economic, technological, institutional, ideological—that intersect within them, and the regimes of viewing that encompass their decoding. By looking at how this recognition has manifested itself in work in this third category, we can appreciate the impact cultural studies has had on encoding research.

Many of the questions that would ultimately define both cultural studies and encoding research were first posed by an anthropologist with little aesthetic interest in television, Sol Worth. Worth's interest was film, particularly as a form of visual anthropology; he did not extend his ideas to television and certainly never wrote in terms of "cultural studies" or "encoding research." His importance to the latter has been significant nonetheless, and, because encoding research (and cultural studies, for that matter) has yet to acknowledge the debt it owes Worth, some discussion of his work is appropriate.

As early as 1956, Worth was beginning to articulate questions that not only would inform encoding research throughout its evolution but also would come to assume a role of absolute centrality in much of the work in this third category. At their most basic, Worth's concerns centered on how meaning is communicated through visual images. Gradually, however, through his teaching, his anthropological film research with John Adair among the Navajo, and an assimilation of ideas from psychology, linguistics, and semiotics, Worth shifted his focus to film as *cultural* communication that reflected "the value systems, coding patterns, and cognitive processes of the maker" (Worth, 1981, p. 16). Worth was soon making statements that, among other things, anticipated Stuart Hall's encoding/decoding model and concept of "naturalized codes," the notion of multiple (e.g., dominant, negotiated, oppositional) viewer decoding positions, and, nearly a decade before cultural studies turned Marxist criticism upon the media, the notion that encoding processes are unavoidably ideological processes. While Worth's short life prevented him from articulating many of his positions in more definitive terms, he asked the right questions. He recognized the necessity of engaging the production and reception of visual texts—not to mention the texts themselves—as cultural documents with much to say about those who simultaneously elaborated and were enmeshed in their webs of meaning.

After Sol Worth, any discussion of how encoding research has been enriched by its engagement with what has come to be known as "cultural studies" must start with Stuart Hall's "Encoding/Decoding" (1980; it should be noted that the actual writing and initial circulation of this work

as a number in the Centre for Contemporary Cultural Studies' stenciled occasional paper series predates this publication date by several years), which provides the most cogent early expression of what a cultural studies approach to
media texts could mean to encoding research. Indeed, in our view, Hall's ideas
in "Encoding/Decoding" have been as seminal in their own way as Zettl's
Sight-Sound-Motion and Newcomb's *TV: The Most Popular Art.*

Two points in Hall's article have proven to be of particular significance.
First, the very articulation of the encoding/decoding model elevated encoding
to a homologous position within the structure of television discourse. To the
extent that television's representational forms embrace television's narratives,
rigorous analysis must account for both. This was an extremely important
point at the time it was made and served to redress the imbalance of decades
of mass communication research that took television's representational forms
for granted. Up to that point the first phases of encoding research had too often
erred in the opposite direction, focusing exclusively on representational forms
and their encoding processes. Hall argued that television must be seen not as
an assemblage of discrete moments that can be isolated, as the exigencies of
academic research dictated, but as a discourse system of interrelated moments.
Hall's point likewise had significant ramifications for conceptualizations of
the role of the viewer. Audience analysis must address not just how viewers
negotiate content but how they first negotiate representational form in the process of negotiating content: in short, study of encoding must necessarily encompass the study of decoding.

The second of Hall's points, that the often "mundane" or "commonplace"
nature of television's aural/visual codes (so-called naturalized codes) does not
preclude their analysis but demands it, was important because it assailed the
argument that television's cookie-cutter sameness made it unworthy of serious
aesthetic analysis. More important, however, this stressed that any process of
signification (including the most "invisible") is also and always an ideological
process. Accordingly, naturalized codes did not become naturalized by accident. They are structured via specific ideological, economic, and institutional
forces, appearing "natural" because that is the way Western capitalist society
prefers its representations of the world. This made it quite clear that hence-
forth encoding research must not only account for the relationships among encoding, text, and decoding as they affect television's representational forms,
but also work to situate that project within the larger ideological matrix of
television culture as a whole.

Altman (1986), recognizing that the regimes of television viewing are
such that television sound plays a crucial role in the maintenance of its discourses, offers the first (and, as of the date of this writing, only) systematic
analysis of the medium's aural codes. Caughie (1981), borrowing notions
of visual and narrative pleasure from psychoanalytic film criticism, argues
that television produces a number of specific pleasures as opposed to an already existing reservoir of pleasure that is "somehow natural to spectators

and which television simply taps" (p. 11). Ellis (1982) compares cinema
and "broadcast TV," arguing they are "divergent and complementary, having developed distinctive aesthetic and commodity forms . . . and divergent
forms of narration and representation of events and people" (p. 1). Feuer,
Kerr, and Vahimagi (1984) provide a critical/analytical study of the rise of
MTM Productions, treating MTM products as economic, cultural, aesthetic,
and ideological documents, the complexity of which raises the question of
"quality" television. Fiske (1984) offers a structuralist analysis of the British science-fiction series *Dr. Who* in an attempt to explore the connection
between the world of television drama and the social world of the audience.
Flitterman-Lewis (1985) and Nowell-Smith (1978) both explore issues of
ideology, with the former analyzing patriarchy and male bonding in *Magnum, P.I.* and the latter exploring the relationships among television, politics, and sport as a terrain for ideological struggle. Likewise, Timberg and
Himmelstein (1989) address the question of signifying processes as ideological processes by analyzing the decoding positions of students asked to
engage with a specific television text, the Kodak *America* commercial.

To the extent cultural studies focused on "the general ideological nature
of mass communication and the complexity of the . . . structuration of its
forms" (S. Hall, 1980, p. 118), it turned with increasing frequency to semiotics. Not surprisingly, encoding research found that many of the assumptions of semiotics fit comfortably within its heuristic agenda (see Eco,
1972; Heck, 1980; M. Porter, 1980, 1981, 1983). Encoding research's appropriations from semiotics have not been total, however. Encoding research has resisted much semiotic terminology and, as we have suggested,
even in those places where terminology tends to overlap (e.g., *codes*) encoding research often utilizes terms in a different way. More troubling,
however, is semiotics' focusing of its efforts almost exclusively at the level
of the text. Because of semiotics' concern with signs and sign systems,
such a focus, while understandable, can create difficulties. There is a tendency to elevate the importance of the text to a level where forces working
to construct the text's representational forms are obscured. Mindful of
needing to account for the broader historical cultural matrix within which
television discourse is enmeshed, encoding research has carried on an uneasy relationship with semiotics, attempting to use some of its theoretical
insights while avoiding the methodological pitfalls of its ahistoricism.

As central as semiotics has been to cultural studies, cultural studies scholars
have fearlessly raided other disciplines as well. Borrowing from such diverse
fields as anthropology, sociology, literary criticism, economics, and history, as
well as bodies of theory that cut across disciplines (feminism, structuralism,
psychoanalysis, postmodernism, and so on), cultural studies has drawn its theoretical parameters broadly, finding strength in an interdisciplinary approach
that refused to limit the range of its endeavors (see S. Hall, 1980). In a similar
fashion, encoding research in this third category has drawn upon all these

fields and theories, utilizing whatever seems to offer the most efficacious point of entry into the analysis of some aspect of television's representational forms. Whereas work in the first and second categories of encoding research is characterized by a general theoretical and methodological uniformity, work in the third category, like that of cultural studies in general, is best characterized by its diversity.

This tradition of theoretical diversity is conspicuously represented in Fiske and Hartley's *Reading Television* (1978), a ground-breaking work in television studies that articulates the points of intersection between many of the theoretical appropriations made by cultural studies and manifestations of television critical practice. In arguing that television texts are "read" and that, therefore, television's representational forms are to television discourse as language is to written discourse, Fiske and Hartley provide encoding research scholars with a significant example of how the agenda advanced by Stuart Hall in "Encoding/Decoding" can be engaged from a diversity of theoretical positions.

With some swiftness in the years after the publication of *Reading Television*, television textual analysis—much of it dealing in part, some exclusively, with aural/visual codes—became informed by bodies of theory that, at best, existed only tangentially to television studies before: structuralism (e.g., Barbatsis, n.d.; Barbatsis & Kenney, 1985; Fiske, 1984), Marxist ideological analysis (e.g., Connell, 1980; Hartley, 1983; Heck, 1980; Schulze, 1986), psychoanalytic criticism (e.g., Deming, 1985; Flitterman-Lewis, 1987; Morse, 1983; Stam, 1983), feminist criticism (e.g., Byars, 1987; Flitterman-Lewis, 1988; Schwictenberg, 1987), and so on.

The most recent work undertaken in encoding research reveals the extent to which scholars have assimilated both the theoretical plurality of cultural studies and the significance of a truly holistic approach to the analysis of television's representational forms: Barker's (1989) analysis of the power of multiple histories in television discourse in general and in *St. Elsewhere* in particular; Butler's (1986) and Corcoran's (1984) analysis of television as representational, technological, and ideological apparatus; Campbell and Reeves's (1989) and Himmelstein's (1989) critique of the ideological agenda advanced by and through aural/visual coding; Timberg and Himmelstein's (1989) analysis of the ideological complexity of the decoding process; Freeman's (1989) synthesis of the numerous points of intersection among industry, aesthetics, and new technologies in the creation of HDTV programming; and Plasketes's (1989) articulation of the multiple forces intersecting within the editing stage of the encoding process.

FUTURE DIRECTIONS FOR ENCODING RESEARCH

As the foregoing discussion suggests, encoding research has moved from a narrowly focused endeavor beset by theoretical and methodological shortcomings to a place where, conscious of its position relative to the broader parameters of television critical practice in particular and cultural studies in general, it has begun to produce work offering significant insight into the complexities of television discourse. Building upon its gains achieved through interfacing with close textual analysis and cultural studies, encoding research seems ready to enter yet another phase in its development. While it is early yet to be able to categorize this new work easily, it seems to us that the immediate future of encoding research lies in articulating a history of television encoding, the development of what might be termed *production ethnography*, studies that address questions of encoding from the position of decoding, and cross-cultural analysis of representational forms.

A History of Television Encoding

In arguing that the absence of history from academic television criticism is "critical," John Caughie (1984) has suggested that "to write about television is almost always to write about now, the current. . . . But to understand television properly, or to understand anything properly, we need to be able to take it out of its frozen historical moment and see the formative shifts and transformations and ask why they happen" (pp. 199-120). Aesthetic film analysis has long been informed by the sense that film's aesthetic development exists in and is subject to the multitudinous forces of history. Encoding research, on the other hand, has been decidedly ahistorical, typically taking the form of a close reading of the aural/visual codes at work in a single text or genre. Thus documentation of television's rich aesthetic development too often must be read off of separate analyses of seemingly autonomous texts. It is almost as if the strategies into which television's aural/visual codes are arranged leaped, Athenalike, from laboratories where the technology of television was first developed, to a program production industry, and, finally, into the arena of television critical practice.

We suggest that to the extent television's aural/visual codes are as central to its dialogic work as film's are to its work, such forms demand a documented history. Furthermore, this history must account for the multitude of forces resonating within it, so that the evolution of television's forms of representation are placed within the broader framework of a developing television practice. There are basic questions to be asked: How did television move from the invention of a single, workable camera to a multiple-camera-with-video switcher configuration? When and where was the first instantaneous cut between two cameras? To what degree did the rules of classic Hollywood continuity editing affect television's evolving representational forms? To what degree have television's representational forms been affected by ideological as well as technological forces? What impact did the assimilation of television production into the Hollywood studio system in the 1950s have on television's representational forms? Barker

(1991), in his most recent work, is attempting to address many of these questions.

The Development of Production Ethnography

The spirit of pursuing encoding research within a framework that is both holistic and historical is particularly evident in the work of *production ethnography*, the term we have adopted to describe the study of all the forces intersecting within the production of a specific narrative and representational form. As defined by Timberg (n.d.), production ethnography strives to "articulate, through a thoroughly and consistently detailed close study of production processes on-site, a culture of production: the principal participants, the decision-making structure, the formative influences of genre and discourse practice, the economic, organizational, and political constraints that govern the encoding process." To a significant degree, production ethnography is similar to a cultural anthropologist's work in a culture or society he or she comes to know from within, and is usually obtained from a combination of sustained, long-term participant observation and in-depth interviews with informants whose judgments and opinions form the center of the production culture.

A number of works fulfill the fourfold requirements of scholarly production ethnography: that it be comprehensive (based on months of on-site work), that it be an inside view (giving what anthropologists term an *emic* view of the production community, through the words and eyewitness reports of the professionals at the center of production), that it build a theoretical model out of its observations, and that it complement, rather than duplicate, other production studies. Some ethnographies are retrospective accounts (Gitlin, 1983; Himmelstein, 1989); others are direct observations of production (Intintoli, 1984; Plasketes, 1989; Schlesinger, 1987).

The Relationship Between Encoding and Decoding

Shaun Moores (1990), in an overview of audience studies, argues, "The time has come to consolidate our theoretical and methodological advances by refusing to see texts, readers and contexts as separable elements and by bringing together ethnographic studies with textual analyses" (p. 24). Ironically, Hall's articulation of encoding and decoding as "determinate moments" has tended to perpetuate their separation as objects of analysis: One studies either the moment of encoding or the moment of decoding, though one recognizes their interrelationship. But to the extent that a moment of encoding is also and always a moment of decoding, it strikes us as more a series of sites at which forces of encoding continually intersect with forces of decoding.

This sort of conceptualization has significant ramifications for encoding research. First, it reflects a much more accurate articulation of how the process of encoding itself works. Almost without exception, encoding decisions are considered and executed in terms of potential decoding, which is to say, in terms of the audience. Here, *audience* might be better capitalized, for, as we use the term, *Audience* refers to a somewhat mythical entity. Certainly, a television series delivers to an advertiser a statistically defined number of individuals who can be profiled demographically. However, they remain faceless quantifications with little or no chance for substantive interaction with series producers. In terms of the daily routines of television production, the Audience exists primarily as a collection of assumptions. Yet, through what might be termed a process of textual "preengagement," these assumptions inform virtually every production decision made by the producers at the moment of encoding. This process of preengagement effectively results in the Audience being structured into the text itself.

Equally important here is Roland Barthes's notion that a work does not become a text until it is engaged by a viewer, such that the forces embedded within the work intersect those making up the discursive history of the viewer in the process of the negotiation of meaning. In a very real sense, therefore, the moment of encoding is given meaning only when the encoded text is engaged by a viewer in decoding—thus the notion of the inscribed Audience.

Second, reconceptualizing the encoding/decoding process as we have suggested hits at the very heart of a basic question that has yet to be addressed in any substantive way: How do people negotiate television's representational forms? Typically, any concern with this question is either subsumed in analyses of how people negotiate content (e.g., Brunsdon & Morley's *Nationwide* study, 1978) or talked to death—as is sometimes the case in film studies—through countless theories of the text/viewer relationship. This is unfortunate, because if (as is generally the case) it is accepted that no message can be communicated on television in its raw form, then, as Barker (1988) has argued elsewhere, there is no "degree zero" in television's representational forms: At some level, all manifestations of television content must first be engaged via aural/visual codes.

It therefore seems prudent that high on encoding research's future agenda should be empirically sound ethnographic analysis of the multitudinous ways in which television's representational forms may be negotiated. Much of the groundwork for such an endeavor has already been put in place through content analysis. Admittedly, we are uncomfortable with a methodological approach that, in effect, attempts to postulate meaning through codification: In place of ethnographic study that asks viewers what sense they make of a given text, content analysis substitutes a shopping list of categories of manifest content, each of which represents potential interpretations. Nonetheless, content analysis seeks to identify the layers of meaning embedded within yet often obscured by the television text and, at its best (e.g., the cultural indicators studies of Gerbner & Gross, 1976), it can offer powerful—if conjectural—insights into the relationships among text, viewer, and culture.

The type of analysis of the encoding/decoding relationship we envision borrows from content analysis (not to mention reader-response criticism and reception theory) the fundamental notion that meaning cannot be "read off" the text by the researcher and then ascribed to a hypothetical audience. We are suggesting the necessity of an ethnographic methodology that asserts both a viewer's ability to articulate the sense he or she makes of television and an awareness on the part of the viewer of the aural/visual codes through which television communicates. As recent work by Porter, Moeder, and Deering (1990) concerning viewer negotiation of reaction shots in television drama suggests, audiences are not only aware of the potential for aural/visual codes to suggest a given reading of the narrative, but also can readily identify instances of and articulate their responses to such instances. The relationship between encoding and decoding must therefore be explored through a combination of empirical, ethnographic, and textual analysis that relates specific moments of encoding within a given text to equally specific moments of viewer engagement and decoding. Furthermore, this analysis must account for regimes of viewing, the existence of multiple sites of textual engagement, and the impact of sociocultural and cross-cultural factors such as class, gender, and ethnicity. Several scholars have begun moving in this direction in their work (e.g., Lull, 1988; Morley, 1986), a direction echoed by a recent symposium in *Critical Studies in Mass Communication* titled "Reading Recent Revisionism" (see Carragee, 1990; Gripsrud, 1990; Jensen, 1990; Lembo & Tucker, 1990).

Cross-Cultural Analysis of Aural/Visual Codes

As Worth and Adair (1972) discovered in their work in "teaching" Navajo people to make films, representational forms are also cultural forms. This premise is as operable in television as it is in any media. To take but one example: The construction of screen space according to the familiar classic Hollywood formulas of continuity editing is rooted in Western (specifically American) notions of interpersonal space. Anthropologist Edward Hall (1966) has identified four types of distance in Western culture, pointing out that, as we encounter people, we typically move through each of these four proxemic categories, maintaining a distance appropriate to the intimacy of a given relationship. In the closest of these proxemic categories, "intimate distance," one has peripheral vision of about 30 degrees, enough to see the outline of a person's head and shoulders, and a clear vision of about 15 degrees, enough to see a person's face (p. 117). Significantly, this corresponds closely to the horizontal field of view of a television close-up. It is no coincidence, then, that continuity editing's movement from establishing shot through increasingly tighter shots to close-ups mimics this proxemic hierarchy.

The cultural dimensions of television's representational forms do more than raise issues of ideology for the culture that produces them. To the extent that the United States exports significant amounts of media material to every corner of the globe, encoding researchers have the opportunity to explore what texts are created when a work encoded within the parameters of one culture is decoded by viewers within the parameters of a different culture (see Ang, 1985; Liebes & Katz, 1990).

In making a statement such as this, it is not our intention to minimize the cultural diversity at work in virtually any act of decoding, nor are we ignoring the fact that the hegemony Hollywood production practices exercise over media production industries worldwide makes it difficult to escape the representational forms preferred by Western capitalist culture. What we are emphasizing is the necessity of ascertaining—to utilize the above example—what happens when a viewer working from a distinctly non-Western sense of interpersonal space negotiates screen space as it is constructed through classic Hollywood continuity editing.

In a real sense, we are suggesting that cross-cultural analysis of the encoding and decoding of representational forms can—and should—be an exercise in defamiliarization. If one is concerned about the ideological masking value of naturalized codes, for example, what better way to lift the mask than through the eyes of someone for whom the codes are not "natural"? If Sol Worth was correct in arguing that much of the cultural work embedded within representational forms is hidden, taken for granted, assumed as somehow "correct" or "normal," cross-cultural analysis provides a tool for excavation.

CONCLUSION

In this chapter we have argued that research into the aural/visual codes of television can be grouped into three categories preceded by the work of several scholars that, collectively, set the stage for encoding research as a whole. These "precursors" were a small but influential group of humanists (e.g., Marshall McLuhan, Edmund Carpenter, and Walter Ong) who, while rarely dealing explicitly with television's aural/visual codes, nonetheless argued that these codes altered the sensorium of the individuals who engaged them. The first category of encoding research contains work by individuals typically operating within the framework of educational television and interested in determining the effects of various production techniques on the comprehension of televised instruction. This work, usually operating within a "hard-sciences" framework, is informed by cause-and-effect empirical methodologies and characterized by a distinct theoretical insularity. Some research in this category broadened its scope to consider how manipulation of production techniques influences audience decoding in other forms of television (e.g., the effect of camera angle on generalized perceived credibility of a newscaster or sincerity of a candidate for political office). However, the influence of cause-and-effect empiricism and theoretical insularity remained intact.

Work in the second category reflects a shift in the research paradigm away from empirically based studies of the influence of single production variables to an engagement with the television "text" as a whole. Empirical studies of the audience here are abandoned in favor of textual analysis that attempts to factor in all components of a production strategy. Energized by the work of film scholars who turned their attention to television, research in this category adopts a methodology borrowed from literary criticism: close textual analysis.

The third category, which includes much current work in encoding research, sees scholars moving increasingly into the realm of cultural studies, combining more sophisticated approaches to audience, ideology, and decoding processes. This phase is characterized less by adherence to any one methodological approach than by attempts to reconceptualize the notion of television texts and the role of aural/visual codes within them in terms of, among other things, semiotics, structuralism, poststructuralism, and feminist criticism. Throughout our discussion of these categories, and in our suggestions for further research, we have attempted to stress the shift toward a holistic approach to the analysis of television's representational forms, one that accounts for all aspects of the television apparatus and regimes of viewing.

Encoding research in television, by whatever terms it has been known, has always suggested the necessity of critical analysis of television's aural/visual codes to any program of systematic study. Yet, until recently, this research could offer no comprehensive rationale for its importance to television studies. But when the aural/visual codes of television are seen as the very points of entrance into the text for the viewer and theorized as sites of institutional, narrative, aesthetic, economic, technological, ideological, and gendered work, they take on new significance. Indeed, their analysis—no longer an option—becomes an imperative.

REFERENCES

Acker, S., & Tiemens, R. (1976). *Image size as an element of visual language.* Unpublished manuscript.

Allen, R. (1983). *The Guiding Light:* Soap opera as economic product and cultural document. In J. O'Connor (Ed.), *American history/American television* (pp. 306-327). New York: Frederick Ungar.

Alley, R. (1982). Television drama. In H. Newcomb (Ed.), *Television: The critical view* (3rd ed., pp. 89-121). New York: Oxford University Press.

Altman, R. (1986). Television/sound. In T. Modleski (Ed.), *Studies in entertainment: Critical approaches to mass culture* (pp. 39-54). Bloomington: Indiana University Press.

Anderson, C. (1987). Reflections on *Magnum, P.I.* In H. Newcomb (Ed.), *Television: The critical view* (4th ed., pp. 112-125). New York: Oxford University Press.

Ang, I. (1985). *Watching Dallas: Soap opera and the melodramatic imagination.* London: Methuen.

Antin, D. (1979). Video: The distinctive features of the medium. In H. Newcomb (Ed.), *Television: The critical view* (2nd ed., pp. 494-516). New York: Oxford University Press.

Avery, R., & Tiemens, R. (1976). *The syntax of visual messages: An empirical investigation of the asymmetry of the frame theory.* Unpublished manuscript.

Baggaley, J., & Duck, S. (1974a). ETV production methods versus educational intention: Some unintended biases. *Educational Broadcasting International, 7,* 158-159.

Baggaley, J., & Duck, S. (1974b). Experiments in ETV: Effects of adding background. *Educational Broadcasting International, 7,* 208-209.

Baggaley, J., & Duck, S. (1975a). Experiments in ETV: Effects of camera angle. *Educational Broadcasting International, 8,* 134.

Baggaley, J., & Duck, S. (1975b). Experiments in ETV: Effects of edited cutaways. *Educational Broadcasting International, 8,* 36-37.

Baggaley, J., & Duck, S. (1975c). Experiments in ETV: Further effects of camera angle. *Educational Broadcasting International, 8,* 183-184.

Baggaley, J., & Duck, S. (1975d). Experiments in ETV: Interviews and edited structure. *Educational Broadcasting International, 8,* 93-94.

Baggaley, J., & Duck, S. (1975e). Psychological effects of image variations. *Video and Film Communication, 8,* 11-17.

Barbatsis, G. (n.d.). *Pictorial communication: Exchanges with social coins of unknown value.* Unpublished manuscript.

Barbatsis, G., & Kenney, K. (1985). *Pictorial language: Meaning in form.* Unpublished manuscript.

Barker, D. (1985). Television production techniques as communication. *Critical Studies in Mass Communication, 2,* 234-246.

Barker, D. (1988). "It's been real": Forms of television representation. *Critical Studies in Mass Communication, 5,* 42-56.

Barker, D. (1989). *St. Elsewhere:* The power of history. *Wide Angle, 11,* 32-47.

Barker, D. (1991). The emergence of television's repertoire of representation, 1920-1935. *Journal of Broadcasting and Electronic Media, 35,* 305-318.

Blair, K. (1982). The garden in the machine: The why of *Star Trek.* In H. Newcomb (Ed.), *Television: The critical view* (3rd ed., pp. 181-197). New York: Oxford University Press.

Brunsdon, C., & Morley, D. (1978). *Everyday television: "Nationwide."* London: British Film Institute.

Butler, J. (1986). Notes on the soap opera apparatus: Televisual style and *As the World Turns. Cinema Journal, 25,* 53-70.

Byars, J. (1987). Reading feminine discourse: Prime-time television in the U.S. *Communication, 9,* 289-304.

Campbell, R., & Reeves, J. (1989). TV news narration and common sense: Updating the soviet threat. *Journal of Film and Video, 41,* 58-74.

Carpenter, E. (1973). *Oh! What a blow that phantom gave me!* New York: Bantam.

Carragee, K. (1990). Interpretive media study and interpretive social science. *Critical Studies in Mass Communication, 7,* 81-96.

Caughie, J. (1981). Rhetoric, pleasure and "art television": Dreams of leaving. *Screen, 22,* 9-31.

Caughie, J. (1984). Television criticism. *Screen, 25,* 109-121.

Coldevin, G. (1976). Comparative effectiveness of TV production variables. *Journal of Educational Television, 2,* 21-24.

Coldevin, G. (1978a). Experiments in TV presentation strategies. *Educational Broadcasting International, 11,* 17-18.

Coldevin, G. (1978b). Experiments in TV presentation strategies: Number 2. *Educational Broadcasting International, 11,* 158-159.

Coldevin, G. (1980). Experimental research in television production techniques and presentation strategies: Current directions. *Educational Technology and Communications Journal, 26,* 65-78.

Connell, I. (1980). Television news and the social contract. In S. Hall, D. Hobson, A. Lowe, & P. Willis (Eds.), *Culture, media, language: Working papers in cultural studies 1972-1979* (pp. 139-156). London: Hutchinson.

Corcoran, F. (1984). Television as ideological apparatus: The power and the pleasure. *Critical Studies in Mass Communication, 1*, 131-145.

Corner, J. (1986). Codes and cultural analysis. In R. Collins, J. Curran, N. Garnham, P. Scannell, P. Schlesinger, & C. Sparks (Eds.), *Media, culture, and society: A critical reader* (pp. 49-62). Newbury Park, CA: Sage.

Craft, R. (1982). Elegy for *Mary Hartman*. In H. Newcomb (Ed.), *Television: The critical view* (3rd ed., pp. 148-157). New York: Oxford University Press.

Deming, R. (1985). The television spectator-subject. *Journal of Film and Video, 37*, 49-63.

Eco, U. (1972). Towards a semiotic inquiry into the television message. *Working Papers in Cultural Studies, 3*, 103-121.

Ellis, J. (1982). *Visible fictions.* London: Routledge & Kegan Paul.

Esslin, M. (1982). Aristotle and the advertisers: The television commercial considered as a form of drama. In H. Newcomb (Ed.), *Television: The critical view* (3rd ed., pp. 260-276). New York: Oxford University Press.

Feuer, J., Kerr, P., & Vahimagi, T. (1984). *MTM: "Quality television."* London: British Film Institute.

Fiske, J. (1984). Popularity and ideology: A structuralist reading of *Doctor Who.* In W. Rowland & B. Watkins (Eds.), *Interpreting television: Current research perspectives* (pp. 165-198). Beverly Hills, CA: Sage.

Fiske, J. (1987). *Television culture.* London: Methuen.

Fiske, J., & Hartley, J. (1978). *Reading television.* London: Methuen.

Flitterman-Lewis, S. (1985). Thighs and whiskers: The fascination of *Magnum, P.I. Screen, 26*, 42-59.

Flitterman-Lewis, S. (1987). Psychoanalysis, film, and television. In R. Allen (Ed.), *Channels of discourse* (pp. 172-210). Chapel Hill: University of North Carolina Press.

Flitterman-Lewis, S. (1988). All's well that doesn't end: Soap operas and the marriage motif. *Camera Obscura, 16*, 119-128.

Freeman, J. (1989). Evolving production strategies for high-definition television: A study of *Julia and Julia. Journal of Film and Video, 41*, 25-41.

Gerbner, G., & Gross, L. (1976). Living with television: The violence profile. *Journal of Communication, 26*, 173-199.

Gitlin, T. (1983). *Inside prime time.* New York: Pantheon.

Gripsrud, J. (1990). Toward a flexible methodology in studying media meaning: *Dynasty* in Norway. *Critical Studies in Mass Communication, 7*, 117-128.

Hall, E. (1966). *The hidden dimension.* Garden City, NY: Doubleday.

Hall, S. (1980). Encoding/decoding. In S. Hall, D. Hobson, A. Lowe, & P. Willis (Eds.), *Culture, media, language: Working papers in cultural studies 1972-1979* (pp. 128-138). London: Hutchinson.

Hanhardt, J. (1979). Video/television space. In H. Newcomb (Ed.), *Television: The critical view* (2nd ed., pp. 238-246). New York: Oxford University Press.

Hartley, J. (1983). *Understanding news.* London: Methuen.

Havelock, E. (1963). *Preface to Plato.* Cambridge, MA: Harvard University Press.

Heath, S., & Skirrow, G. (1977). Television, a world in action. *Screen, 18*, 7-60.

Heck, M. (1980). The ideological dimension of media messages. In S. Hall, D. Hobson, A. Lowe, & P. Willis (Eds.), *Culture, media, language: Working papers in cultural studies 1972-1979* (pp. 122-127). London: Hutchinson.

Herbener, G., Tubergen, N., & Whitlow, S. (1979). Dynamics of the frame in visual composition. *Educational Technology and Communications Journal, 27*, 83-88.

Hilmes, M. (1985). The television apparatus: Direct address. *Journal of Film and Video, 37*, 27-36.

Himmelstein, H. (1989). Kodak's "America": Images from the American Eden. *Journal of Film and Video, 41*, 75-94.

Intintoli, M. (1984). *Taking soaps seriously: The world of Guiding Light.* New York: Praeger.

Jensen, K. (1990). Television futures: A social action methodology for studying interpretive communities. *Critical Studies in Mass Communication, 7*, 129-146.

Lembo, R., & Tucker, K. H., Jr. (1990). Culture, television, and opposition: Rethinking cultural studies. *Critical Studies in Mass Communication, 7*, 97-116.

Liebes, T., & Katz, E. (1990). *The export of meaning: Cross-cultural readings of "Dallas."* New York: Oxford University Press.

Lull, J. (Ed.). (1988). *World families watch television.* Newbury Park, CA: Sage.

Marc, D. (1984). *Demographic vistas: Television in American culture.* Philadelphia: University of Pennsylvania Press.

Marchand, P. (1989). *Marshall McLuhan: The medium and the messenger.* New York: Ticknor & Fields.

McCain, T., Chilberg, J., & Wakshlag, J. (1977). The effects of camera angle on source credibility and attraction. *Journal of Broadcasting, 21*, 35-46.

McLuhan, M. (1964). *Understanding media: The extensions of man.* New York: Mentor.

McLuhan, M. (1965). *The Gutenberg galaxy: The making of typographic man.* Toronto: University of Toronto Press.

McLuhan, M. (1967). *The mechanical bride: Folklore of industrial man.* Boston: Beacon.

Metallinos, N. (1979a). Composition of the TV picture: Some hypotheses to test the forces operating within the television screen. *Educational Technology and Communications Journal, 27*, 205-214.

Metallinos, N. (1979b). Looking to new areas for research in broadcasting. *Feedback, 21*, 18-22.

Metallinos, N. (1982). Children's perception, retention, and preference of asymmetrical composition in pictures. In R. Braden & A. Walker (Eds.), *Television and visual literacy: Readings from the 13th Annual Conference of I.V.L.A.* (pp. 33-34). Bloomington: Indiana University Press.

Metallinos, N. (1984). *Visual space: Empirical research in z-axis staging.* Unpublished manuscript.

Metallinos, N. (1985). Empirical studies of television composition. In J. Dominick & J. Fletcher (Eds.), *Broadcasting research methods* (pp. 297-311). Boston: Allyn & Bacon.

Molinaro, M. (Ed.) (1987). *Letters of Marshall McLuhan.* New York: Oxford University Press.

Moores, S. (1990). Texts, readers and contexts of reading: Developments in the study of media audiences. *Media, Culture and Society, 12*, 9-29.

Morley, D. (1986). *Family television: Cultural power and domestic leisure.* London: Comedia.

Morse, M. (1983). Sport on television: Replay and display. In E. Kaplan (Ed.), *Regarding television* (pp. 44-66). Los Angeles: American Film Institute.

Newcomb, H. (1974). *TV: The most popular art.* Garden City, NY: Anchor.

Nowell-Smith, G. (1978). Television — football — the world. *Screen, 19*, 45-59.

Ong, W. (1967). *The presence of the word.* New Haven, CT: Yale University Press.

Plasketes, G. (1989). The videotape editor as sculptor: Paul Simon's *Graceland in Africa,* a case study. *Journal of Film and Video, 41*, 42-57.

Porter, D. (1982). Soap time: Thoughts on a commodity art form. In H. Newcomb (Ed.), *Television: The critical view* (3rd ed., pp. 122-131). New York: Oxford University Press.

Porter, M. (1980). *Two studies of Lou Grant: Montage style and the dominance of dialogue.* Unpublished manuscript.

Porter, M. (1981). *The montage structure of adventure and dramatic prime time programming.* Unpublished manuscript.

Porter, M. (1983). Applying semiotics to the study of selected prime time television programming. *Journal of Broadcasting, 27*, 69-75.

Porter, M., Moeder, M., & Deering, B. (1990, November). *The influence of close-up reaction shots on viewers' understanding of the television text.* Paper presented at the annual meeting of the Speech Communication Association, Chicago.

Pryluck, C., Teddlie, C., & Sands, R. (1982). Meaning in film/video: Order, time and ambiguity. *Journal of Broadcasting, 26,* 685-695.

Real, M. (1982). The Super Bowl: Mythic spectacle. In H. Newcomb (Ed.), *Television: The critical view* (3rd ed., pp. 206-239). New York: Oxford University Press.

Rosenblatt, R. (1979). Growing up on television. In H. Newcomb (Ed.), *Television: The critical view* (2nd ed., pp. 350-362). New York: Oxford University Press.

Schatz, T. (1987). *St. Elsewhere* and the evolution of the ensemble series. In H. Newcomb (Ed.), *Television: The critical view* (4th ed., pp. 85-100). New York: Oxford University Press.

Schlater, R. (1968). Would you believe: The medium is half the message. *Educational Broadcasting Review, 2,* 24-28.

Schlater, R. (1969). Effect of irrelevant visual cues on recall of television messages. *Journal of Broadcasting, 14,* 63-69.

Schlater, R. (1970). Effect of speed of presentation on recall of television messages. *Journal of Broadcasting, 15,* 207-214.

Schlesinger, P. (1987). *Putting "reality" together.* London: Methuen.

Schroeder, F. (1979). Video aesthetics and serial art. In H. Newcomb (Ed.), *Television: The critical view* (2nd ed., pp. 407-419). New York: Oxford University Press.

Schulze, L. (1986). *Getting Physical*: Text/context/reading and the made-for-television movie. *Cinema Journal, 25,* 35-50.

Schwichtenberg, C. (1987). *The Love Boat*: The packaging and selling of love, heterosexual romance, and family. In H. Newcomb (Ed.), *Television: The critical view* (4th ed.), (pp. 126-140). New York: Oxford University Press.

Sklar, R. (1982). The Fonz, Laverne, Shirley, and the great American class struggle. In H. Newcomb (Ed.), *Television: The critical view* (3rd ed., pp. 77-88). New York: Oxford University Press.

Stam, R. (1983). Television news and its spectator. In E. Kaplan (Ed.), *Regarding television* (pp. 23-43). Los Angeles: American Film Institute.

Tarroni, E. (1979). The aesthetics of television. In H. Newcomb (Ed.), *Television: The critical view* (2nd ed., pp. 437-461). New York: Oxford University Press.

Thorburn, D. (1979). Television melodrama. In H. Newcomb (Ed.), *Television: The critical view* (2nd ed., pp. 536-554). New York: Oxford University Press.

Tiemens, R. (1970). Some relationships of camera angle to communicator credibility. *Journal of Broadcasting, 15,* 483-490.

Tiemens, R. (1990, November). *Analyzing visual content: Managing mountains of data.* Paper presented at the annual meeting of the Speech Communication Association, Chicago.

Timberg, B. (1982). The rhetoric of the camera in television soap opera. In H. Newcomb (Ed.), *Television: The critical view* (3rd ed., pp. 132-147). New York: Oxford University Press.

Timberg, B. (1987). Television talk and ritual space: Carson and Letterman. *Southern Speech Communication Journal, 52,* 390-402.

Timberg, B. (n.d.). *Letterman and company: An analysis of late night television talk.* Unpublished manuscript.

Timberg, B., & Himmelstein, H. (1989). Television commercials and everyday life: A follow-up to Himmelstein's production study of the Kodak "America" commercial. *Journal of Film and Video, 41,* 67-79.

Toogood, A. (1978). A framework for the exploration of video as a unique art form. *Journal of the University Film Association, 30,* 15-19.

Williams, C. (1979). It's not so much "You've come a long way baby" as "You're gonna make it after all." In H. Newcomb (Ed.), *Television: The critical view* (2nd ed., pp. 64-73). New York: Oxford University Press.

Worth, S. (1981). *Studying visual communication.* Philadelphia: University of Pennsylvania Press.

Worth, S., & Adair, J. (1972). *Through Navajo eyes.* Bloomington: Indiana University Press.

Wurtzel, A., & Dominick, J. (1971). Evaluation of television drama: Interaction of acting styles and shot selection. *Journal of Broadcasting, 16,* 103-111.

Zettl, H. (1968). The study of television aesthetics. *Educational Broadcasting Review, 2,* 36-40.

Zettl, H. (1973). *Sight-sound-motion: Applied media aesthetics.* Belmont, CA: Wadsworth.

Closer Encounters
with Television:
Incorporating the Medium

CAREN J. DEMING
University of Arizona

D AVID Barker and Bernard Timberg's review of what they term *encoding research* identifies significant research strands that have not been integrated adequately into critical television research. Their attempt to award the work of such authors as McLuhan, Worth, Ong, and Zettl rightful places in mainstream critical theory is both necessary and timely. They sense, correctly, that the burgeoning of cultural studies has created an opening into the television criticism arena through which this laudable early work might take its rightful place in the history of television studies.

The outcome of Barker and Timberg's historical view of several research strands is an agenda for the future that also brings production research and cross-cultural research into play. The resultant vision of the future of television studies, built upon basic tenets of cultural studies, points to an integrating framework for understanding television and a variety of ways in which it is legitimately studied.

Curiously absent from Barker and Timberg's formulation of how the field might zero in on the role of aural and visual codes in television's discourses is express attention to the physical apparatus of television and the physical apparatus of the television auditor (viewer). More specifically, Barker and Timberg's conceptualization of encoding research—as revealed in their reliance upon Fiske's definition of codes—for the future is articulated strictly in cultural terms. As a result, they do not take the medium itself into account explicitly in their envisioned research agenda. This occurs despite their stated desire to "underscore" the importance of "the medium

Correspondence and requests for reprints: Caren J. Deming, Department of Media Arts, MLB 265, University of Arizona, Tucson, AZ 85721.

Communication Yearbook 15, pp. 239-250

itself" and despite the importance of physical factors in some of the research they aim to recuperate (especially Zettl).

This apparent contradiction in Barker and Timberg's formulation need not deter the progress of their agenda. Rather, the accommodation of the physics of image production and perception requires some adjustments in their formulation of encoding. This suggestion not only recognizes the overarching influence of culture on encoding and decoding; it also takes the physical bases of the processes into account. The incorporation of the medium in this manner strengthens, rather than weakens, the cultural critique of television. The ways in which a cultural studies formulation might accommodate physical aspects of image production and reception are what I will attempt to show in the remainder of this essay.

Barker and Timberg get into some related difficulties in their eagerness to embrace cultural studies as a "holistic" approach to television study. Seizing the works of John Fiske and Stuart Hall as primary exemplars, they uncritically assume an emphasis on narrative and the equality of text and audience. However, they neglect to explicate the value (and, by implication, limitations) of such assumptions in cultural studies research to their project. As a result, they fail to provide a holistic model of encoding specific to their thesis.

In basic agreement with the authors in regard to their direction, I will use these pages to suggest a conceptual model appropriate to the integration of physical and cultural properties and practices in encoding/decoding. I will then explore the utility of that model with regard to specific elements of some cultural studies agendas recently articulated by its practitioners and (some) critics.

THE REALITY MATRIX

A model that has apparent application to the variables of central concern in the study of television encoding is one I developed with Billie Wahlstrom some years ago. The notion of a "reality matrix" developed primarily out of a pedagogical impulse. Wahlstrom and I were seeking a way for students to comprehend in accessible, communication-based terms the physically and culturally constructed (and, thereby, limited) nature of what humans experience, or know, as reality. The model is, above all, an attempt to employ knowledge of cognitive and cultural processes in the service of critical thinking about the media.

The reality matrix posits the assumptive nature of reality as apprehended by the senses, as well as through sociocultural filters. Sensory data are understood to be incomplete, abstracted, and limited in range, although improvable through training or specialization. Sensory data also are understood to undergo further abstraction as they are transmitted to the brain for yet further processing. Human physiology is thus the first contributor to the assumptive reality. In this conception, culture is the second major contributor. A third contributor is the individual, with his or her unique physiology and life history. The assumptive reality of any individual is thus an amalgam of species-specific assumptions, culture-specific assumptions, and idiosyncratic assumptions. It is the product of physical properties, culture, and an individual life history.

Assumptive reality, derivative of the interaction of complex information systems, is the underlying principle of the reality matrix. Assumptive reality is thus the product of the information megasystem through which humans encounter and create their worlds. In mathematics, a matrix is a pattern for arranging numbers or terms to facilitate the study of relationships. The word *matrix* (Latin for womb) refers to a place where something originates and from which it takes its shape. (*Matrix* is used in printing and in the manufacture of phonograph records, referring to the models from which type or records are produced.) The reality matrix organizes people's conscious and unconscious experiences with assumptive realities, whether social or physical. By organizing those realities, it also shapes them. The reality matrix subsumes consciousness because it includes the information stored in the unconscious as well as that in the conscious mind and because it incorporates the physical mechanisms of the brain and central nervous system.

In order to apprehend and comprehend physical reality, humans employ various physiological and symbolic communication systems. These systems process information to create the assumptive reality, which, in turn, acts as both filter and lens for the incorporation of new information into the reality matrix.

Any mass communication medium, such as television, also may be understood in terms of the reality matrix. The medium is bound first by the physics of its production, the operation of physical equipment that encodes and decodes. Although it may be argued that cultures have *more* to do with shaping television information than physics, the presence and limiting function of the physics must be acknowledged. Likewise, although it may be argued that cultures have *more* to do with shaping television's reception than its physical properties or the physiological properties of viewers, the presence and interpretive function of the individual viewer with a unique life history must be acknowledged if we are to have an adequate concept of television encoding/decoding (Wahlstrom & Deming, 1977).

ISSUES IN CULTURAL STUDIES

In the remainder of this commentary, I will explore some advantages of the reality matrix as a model for incorporating key preoccupations of critical studies into the television encoding research agenda advanced by Barker and Timberg.

The Construction of Reality

First, the physical base of encoding/decoding in the reality matrix extends the idea of worldview beyond the cultural sphere. The tacit knowledge forming the basis for communicative action known in Habermasian
terms as the *lifeworld* is strictly ideological. It is " 'culturally transmitted,
prereflexively certain, intuitively available background knowledge' that
provides taken-for-granted interpretive patterns as well as resources that
sustain social life" (Lembo & Tucker, 1990, p. 102; quoting Habermas,
1982, p. 211). The reality matrix expresses the role of physical image production and perception in the formation of assumptive reality.

The reality matrix is distinguished from a Habermasian focus on strictly
ideological constructions by its attempt to mediate between empiricism and
cultural determinism as applied to the processes by which humans construct
their worlds. The reality matrix accounts for the existence of physical matter
(whirling or oscillating molecules, pressure waves, light waves, and so on) as
factors deployed by humans in the construction of reality. In contrast to social
formations, these physical phenomena have a kind of existence outside of our
ability to perceive them. As soon as they are noticed, measured, or comprehended in some way, however, they have been conditioned ("formed") by the
reality matrix. They are independent, or "objective," only in this strictly limited way. Thus the physical world is not construed as a "fixed" reality in the
common empirical sense, but as a remote, elusive, dynamic—yet decidedly
physical—world. We require the reality matrix to make sense of (to construct)
this world every bit as much as we require it to make sense of the social world.
This is what I mean by "incorporating the medium" into a discussion of television encoding and decoding.

In other words, the reality matrix provides physical and cognitive analogues
to naturalization, the process by which the symbolic work of re-representation
is effaced. Schwichtenberg's (1989) study of the Farrah Fawcett phenomenon
of the late 1970s illustrates this process. Drawing upon Barthes's formulation
of myth as a second-order semiological system, Schwichtenberg demonstrates
how beauty culture, or the ideology of beauty, displaces the concept of natural
hair and replaces it with a constructed image based on the cut, dyed, conditioned, and sprayed hair of Farrah Fawcett. The new construction then is taken
up as the meaning of *natural* as applied to hair.

In the physiological analogue, the human perceptual systems respond to
other physical matter in forms such as light, sound, and pressure waves,
process received information, and persuade us that we are sensing the outer
world directly. The "work" of perception produces an involved set of abstractions, interpretations, and hunches. Rather than acknowledging these
processes taking place within our own bodies, we happily ascribe to "nature" the characteristics of the universe manufactured by our own perceptual systems. The fictions we create in this manner—that grass is green and

the sky is up, for example—are as necessary to our getting through life as are more clearly social constructions. Like social constructions, too, these physiological constructions are subject to deconstruction.

One theoretical use of this physiological analogue to symbolic naturalization is that it provides a way of dealing with behaviors and constructions that tap funds of memory and knowledge independent of narrative engagement with a text. Such a conceptualization could allow for the understanding of subliminal suggestion, for example, as both a physical and a cultural phenomenon, one that takes advantage of the constructedness of images both physically and culturally.

Also, incorporating the physics of sound and picture production could help to integrate research on television aesthetics into the critical agenda in a variety of ways. For example, Barker and Timberg assert their interest in giving aural and visual codes equal weight in the formulation of an encoding research agenda. One of the strands they identify in their history of encoding research, that dealing with the efficacy of television as an instructional medium, contains a debate over which channel is dominant. As the term reflects, a number of studies were done in an effort to establish the validity of "picture primacy" as a precept of educational television. Judging simply by the relative attention paid to picture and sound in Zettl's *Sight-Sound-Motion: Applied Media Aesthetics* (1990), one might conclude that he too is more fascinated by the power of pictures. By contrast, scholars who turned to television analysis after extensive work in film saw things the other way around. Working from a critical base, Altman (1986) may have been the first to assert the dominance of sound in television, as opposed to pictures in film. Ellis (1982) makes a similar assertion in his comparative analysis of film and television as narrative media. The point is that we have little basis for deciding who is right in this debate, let alone under what circumstances or in what sort of context.

A conceptualization of the critical study of television that pays attention to how the medium works physically, as well as discursively, to produce images (and how people decode them perceptually) could help to unravel the complexities of what it means to "listen to television," as many people report doing, and other responses to the presence of television in one's environment. At the least, such a focus would remind us that the picture primacy debate never was resolved. Better, it could show us numerous other assumptions about how television functions that have not been articulated sufficiently for debate.

The Role of Narrative

More immediately important to cultural studies is the opening of viewing behaviors that are not narrative based to critical scrutiny by taking into account physical characteristics of both apparatus and viewer. Cognitive processes such as image recognition and pattern formation are basic to what

Lembo and Tucker (1990) describe as viewers relating to television at the level of movable images rather than at fictional levels of meaning. In connection with channel-switching behavior, their subjects revealed their recognition of formulas as patterns of images derived from commercial requirements. Lembo and Tucker characterize this behavior and its interpretation by those engaging in it as "an opposition to commodification of meaning, not to individual ideologies as embodied in texts" (p. 106). According to Lembo and Tucker, this "decentered, nondiscursive viewing relation, this disengagement, leads to more emotionally laden forms of image-play" (p. 107) than does narrative engagement. Among these forms of image-play are fantasy and creative uses of individual memory. In their conclusion, the authors posit a "variety of viewing relations that are *cultural* but that do not rely for their meaning on a correspondence between text and the act of interpretation" (p. 111). Employing the reality matrix would allow Lembo and Tucker also to explore meanings made in relation to the physicality of the television image and to idiosyncratic features of responses to those images in relation to the cultural viewing relations they observed. Further explorations along this line could result in methods of dealing with fantasy, memory, and even the unconscious more harmonious with critical agendas than psychoanalytic approaches have been.

In their repeated reference to codes of *representation* as the focus of interest in their research agenda, Barker and Timberg reveal a preoccupation with narrative forms that has characterized much cultural studies research. The foregoing paragraphs suggest that the notion of representation is too limited to accomplish the goals they set for the analysis of television encoding. But beyond nondiscursive engagement with television by decoders, one must recognize the presence of many television offerings that are presentational rather than representational. Of course, it always can be said that television news, game shows and other "reality" genres, comedy, and many commercials depend upon narrative through mythic speech (see Schwichtenberg, 1989) if they are not themselves narrative in form. However, the work of Lembo and Tucker suggests that cultural studies already may be breaking free of the concentration on narrative that has characterized so much work to date.

The Dominance of Culture

As such illustrations suggest, a conceptual model that gives the physical properties of the medium their due is advantageous to the agenda Barker and Timberg set out because it anchors research in the medium rather than in culture. Thus asserted, such a notion requires immediate qualification. That qualification brings us to the second advantage of the reality matrix as a device for aligning Barker and Timberg's encoding/decoding agenda with cultural studies. The reality matrix—dependent as it is on assumptions— acknowledges that culture influences both cognition and the formation of the self. Thus culture is recognized as overarching and overdetermining with regard to the other two levels of the model (species-specific/medium-specific elements and idiosyncratic elements of individual people or television artifacts).

Meehan's (1986) summary definition of culture demonstrates the unequal relationship of cultural factors in relation to physical and idiosyncratic factors:

> Culture is both relations of diversity and shared webs of meaning. Culture exists as a fund of meanings, images, understandings, etc., which human collectivities construct within the constraints of social structure, economic structure, concrete experience, socialization, overdetermination and random error. (p. 453)

The physical properties of humans and television equipment evoked by the reality matrix are part of "concrete experience" in Meehan's list. Culture thus can be seen as the greatest determiner of assumptive realities, subsuming and interpreting presumably more "raw" data of experience. Culture has much to do with the sense we make of sensory data and with building the life histories Americans like to think are so individual. For Meehan, division of labor based on gender is the most important cultural constraint. Second, in capitalist cultures, is the hierarchical structure of class. Seen in proper perspective, then, the reality matrix is consonant with generally held conceptions of culture and with views of culture posited in critical studies and, as advanced by Meehan, political economy.

Autonomy of Text and Viewer

A related issue receiving attention from critical scholars is the relative autonomy of the encoding and decoding processes and, by extension, the freedom of the decoder to make meanings from texts. Barker and Timberg contend that the television viewer "occupies a position of equality relative both to the text and to the producers of the text in the negotiation and construction of meaning." Budd, Entman, and Steinman (1990) recently have taken American cultural studies practitioners to task for their "misleading affirmation of the power and independence of media audiences" derived in part from an overestimation of the freedom of audiences in reception (p. 169). Carragee (1990), in his critique of recent interpretive audience research, enunciates the more temperate view characteristic of critical studies: "Individual viewers do negotiate the meanings of the television texts they view, but their definitions do not match the discursive power of a centralized storytelling institution" (p. 88).

Carragee goes on to chastise researchers who assume the polysemic nature of texts, siding instead with Condit's (1989) rendering of the relationship:

> The claim perhaps needs to be scaled back to indicate that responses and interpretations are generally polyvalent, and texts themselves are occasionally or partially polysemic. It is not that texts routinely feature unstable denotation but that instability of connotation requires viewers to judge texts from their own value systems. (p. 107; quoted in Carragee, 1990, p. 89)

Condit's reference to viewers' own value systems recognizes that viewers are individuals without losing sight of the generally greater power of culture in the creation of text and interpretation.

In Barker and Timberg's work, the assumption that viewer and text are equal stems from the interconnectedness of coding and decoding processes. The inseparability of encoding and decoding is a tenet of cultural studies, readerly theories in particular. However, that concept does not imply the equality of the viewer for most scholars. Comparing television to the folktale, Silverstone (1986) points out that

> the argument that the text in the final analysis only exists in the act of reading it does not preclude the assumption that all texts (and especially television texts) are constructed to be read and must presume their readership. These presumptions are built into both their form and their content. Analysis which seeks to establish what these presumptions are, and how they are operationalized, is, therefore, I submit, entirely legitimate and epistemologically supportable. (p. 7)

The situation of viewers in the reality matrix conception is that viewers negotiate from a position of fairly severe handicap (via the constraints of physiology and culture) but that they can be empowered and can empower themselves through the cultivation of critical awareness. Without its critical edge, the scholarly practice of cultural studies loses the potential that drew so many excellent scholars to its arena in the first place, namely, its capacity to advance its empowering political agendas.

The Importance of History

In contrast to their position on the viewer's power in relation to the text, Barker and Timberg's call for a history of encoding/decoding research that includes a history of representational forms is less controversial. Cultural studies' preoccupation with the historical context of interpretation and political action is well established. Grossberg (1989) summarizes this position:

> At any moment, the project of cultural studies involves locating "culture" by defining the specificity of both cultural struggle and the historical context within and against which such struggles are functioning. . . . In other words, the point of cultural studies is that the relations between culture and society, or between culture and power, are always historically constituted. (p. 416)

Antihumanism

The concern for specificity evokes the presence of the individual in the reality matrix. Yet, as Angus, Jhally, Lewis, and Schwichtenberg (1989) have pointed out, in contrast to liberal pluralism, cultural studies scholars do not assume that individuals constitute social relations. From a cultural studies point of view, the argument for the political significance of "individuality" in an ethical sense is a central component of a contemporary critical theory of communications; however, if one attempts to return to individuals as the *basis* of social analysis, rather than the *articulation* of many determinations, one has slipped into apologetic mode: One does not investigate the *constitution* of individuality but assumes it as given. Thus it can neither be regarded as *endangered*, requiring political practices for its new formation, nor can the social formation as a whole be understood, since it is always reduced back into the actions of individuals. (p. 448)

For cultural studies, a focus on individualism is a sure way back to mainstream American ideology. The adoption of such a perspective reflects co-optation of cultural studies' critical agenda.

Concomitantly, cultural studies also is antihumanist in the sense that the search for universals is regarded as intellectually and politically counterproductive. Cultural studies aims, rather, at a moving target. It "has no pretensions to totality or universality; it seeks only to give us a better understanding of where we are so that we can get somewhere else" (Grossberg, 1989, p. 415). Such a position emphasizes the power of the cultural components of assumptive reality without denying that the reality matrix contains aspects originating in human physiology in relation to other physical objects and phenomena. The point is that these species-specific elements do not express themselves in humans or artifacts they create, except through culturally determined lenses and filters. Grossberg (1989) expresses such an idea in the terms of cultural studies:

Antihumanism does not deny individuality, subjectivity, experience, or agency; it simply historicizes and politicizes them, their construction, and their relationships. If there is no essential human nature, we are always struggling to produce its boundaries, to constitute an effective (and hence real) human nature, but one which is different in different social formations. In other words, human nature is always real but never universal, singular or fixed. (p. 418)

The dynamic variability and fluidity of the reality matrix make it amenable to social and political action.

Moreover, the collection of universal traits without their cultural specificities is an intellectual dead end. A vivid expression of this principle in Marx is called up by Gripsrud (1990): "Hunger is hunger, but the hunger gratified by cooked meat eaten by knife and fork is a different hunger from that which bolts down raw meat with the aid of hand, nail and tooth" (p. 118; quoting Marx, 1973, p. 92). Gripsrud uses Marx to bolster his point that *Dynasty*'s reception by audiences in Norway is determined partly by its American production. More pertinent to this discussion, the quotation underscores the relative importance of culture-specific, epoch-specific, and class-specific traits over universal ones.

To add complication to complexity, in an age of rampant global media circulation, the location of individual cultures is as difficult to certify as human nature or individuality. As characterized by Ang (1990), the hegemonic and the popular interpenetrate one another: "In the increasingly integrated world system there is no such thing as an independent cultural identity; every identity must define and position itself in relation to the cultural frames affirmed by the world system" (p. 253). The task for the researcher, in order to understand cultural phenomena in such a context, is to "trace the global in the local and the local in the global" (p. 252). And because the way people deal with media is always particular and always changing, Ang recommends that an ethnographic approach is best for understanding audience behaviors in "their concrete multi-facetedness" (p. 257).

Summary

In summary, cultural studies provides a variety of approaches in answer to Barker and Timberg's call for holistic analysis of television encoding/decoding. As Silverstone (1986) suggests, part of the task is the analysis of the economics and politics of capitalist society, part is analysis of the relationship of states and multinational industry to the products of the mass media, and part is

> analysis of the complexities and subtleties of cultural work: the production, textuality and reception of television in this case, theoretically informed to be sure, but sensitive enough both to the core processes which are likely to have a universal character, and to the uniqueness and ambiguities of everyday cultural experience. (p. 11)

Therefore, as well as antihumanist, cultural studies also is antireductionist.

From their various methodological perspectives, cultural studies scholars agree on the necessity of contextualizing audiences, media, and their texts historically, socially, culturally, and economically. This imperative, in the words of Grossberg (1989), "requires us to recognize the active complexity in which people live their lives. . . . Only on this messy terrain can we begin to sort out how people recognize and transform themselves and their world within and through popular cultural practices" (p. 419). It is the same "messy" and fertile terrain on which Barker and Timberg have situated their agenda for the future of television research.

CONCLUSION

In closing, I will reiterate the agenda Barker and Timberg set forth while indulging in certain liberties with it. I take these liberties in order to account for concerns articulated recently in the cultural studies debate and (by employing the reality matrix as a conceptual model) to sharpen the focus on the medium that a study of television encoding/decoding requires. First, television studies needs histories of televisual forms. I use *televisual* in place of Barker and Timberg's *representational* in order to include television's presentational forms explicitly and to broaden the field from a too emphatic stress on narrative. Implied in this item, nonetheless, is the need for voluminous close textual analysis.

Second, television studies requires not only greater study of the culture of production, including specific production ethnographies, but also greater understanding of the historical context of such cultures. Among other things, the resulting body of work would allow for more comprehensive knowledge of the role of technological innovation in television—the contexts of invention, adoption, exploitation, and impediments thereto.

Third, the study of encoding and decoding needs to be carried out with regard to a multitude of sites at which these processes interact. Such a project requires study as eclectic and as interdisciplinary as cultural studies itself. In addition to accounting for cultural and social determiners, care must be taken to account for the physics and chemistry involved in human perception and in television's technical apparatus if we are to have an adequate understanding of medium-specific processes. No level of the reality matrix—physical, cultural, or idiosyncratic—should escape scrutiny or contextualization.

Fourth, the extensive role of culture in encoding/decoding television needs the benefit of what is to be learned from cross-cultural analysis. Such study must take cognizance of the extent to which the traffic in television images is transnational and, in a growing number of cases, global in scope.

The pursuit of such an agenda promises to situate important work on television images that tended to be anomalous before cultural studies provided a comprehensive framework for the critical study of television. More important, however, that agenda portends the maturation of television study. Such an observation—as indeed it should—produces feelings almost as ambivalent as those produced by the encounter with television itself. Ambivalent feelings are not known to keep people from watching television, and they are even less likely to deter scholars from ever closer, more critical scrutiny of the medium and the cultures through which it is created and experienced.

REFERENCES

Altman, R. (1986). Television/sound. In T. Modleski (Ed.), *Studies in entertainment: Critical approaches to mass culture* (pp. 39-54). Bloomington: Indiana University Press.

Ang, I. (1990). Culture and communication: Towards an ethnographic critique of media consumption in the transnational media system. *European Journal of Communication, 5,* 239-260.

Angus, I., Jhally, S., Lewis, J., & Schwichtenberg, C. (1989). Commentary: On pluralist apology. *Critical Studies in Mass Communication, 6,* 441-448.

Budd, M., Entman, R. M., & Steinman, C. (1990). The affirmative character of U.S. cultural studies. *Critical Studies in Mass Communication, 7,* 169-184.

Carragee, K. M. (1990). Interpretive media study and interpretive social science. *Critical Studies in Mass Communication, 7,* 81-96.

Condit, C. (1989). The rhetorical limits of polysemy. *Critical Studies in Mass Communication, 6,* 103-122.

Ellis, J. (1982). *Visible fictions: Cinema, television, video.* London: Routledge & Kegan Paul.

Gripsrud, J. (1990). Toward a flexible methodology in studying media meaning: *Dynasty* in Norway. *Critical Studies in Mass Communication 7,* 117-128.

Grossberg, L. (1989). The circulation of cultural studies. *Critical Studies in Mass Communication 6,* 413-420.

Habermas, J. (1982). A reply to my critics. In J. Thompson & D. Held (Eds.), *Habermas: Critical debates* (pp. 192-216). Cambridge: MIT Press.

Lembo, R., & Tucker, K. H., Jr. (1990). Culture, television, and opposition: Rethinking cultural studies. *Critical Studies in Mass Communication 7,* 97-116.

Marx, K. (1973). *Grundrisse.* Harmondsworth, England: Penguin.

Meehan, E. R. (1986). Conceptualizing culture as commodity: The problem of television. *Critical Studies in Mass Communication 3,* 448-457.

Schwichtenberg, C. (1989). The "mother lode" of feminist research: Congruent paradigms in the analysis of beauty culture. In B. Dervin, L. Grossberg, B. J. O'Keefe, & E. Wartella (Eds.), *Rethinking communication: Vol. 2. Paradigm exemplars* (pp. 291-306). Newbury Park, CA: Sage.

Silverstone, R. (1986, May). *Television: Myth, science, commonsense.* Paper presented at the annual meeting of the International Communication Association, Chicago.

Wahlstrom, B. J., & Deming, C. J. (1977). *The reality matrix: Culture, media, and the individual mind.* Unpublished manuscript.

Zettl, H. (1990). *Sight-sound-motion: Applied media aesthetics* (2nd ed.). Belmont, CA: Wadsworth.

Cultural Studies and the Politics of Encoding Research

MIKE BUDD
Florida Atlantic University

CLAY STEINMAN
California State University, Bakersfield

BARKER and Timberg's history of what they call encoding research usefully organizes some of the most interesting recent scholarship on television. In particular, it synthesizes contemporary work in ways that show clearly productive avenues for the future. But it also ignores crucial dimensions of much of the work it summarizes, especially the political stakes in television research and for viewers as well. Like much recent U.S. mass communication research on television, it borrows from poststructuralism, film studies, and cultural studies, taking socially critical theories and approaches out of context, replacing them within the seemingly neutral, objectivist discourse of social science research. So in the space available to us here, we will sketch some of the context for issues of encoding and decoding, and some of the consequences of ignoring that context in an overview that represents itself as comprehensive.

For more than 20 years now, a whole range of U.S. academic disciplines in the humanities, arts, and social sciences has been increasingly influenced, even in some cases transformed, by interrelated bodies of twentieth-century European theory. Amid a variety of influences, these have become prominent: French semiotics, structuralism, and poststructuralism (Belsey, 1980; Silverman, 1983; Weedon, 1987); German neo-Marxist critical theory, especially the Frankfurt school (Buck-Morss, 1977; Held, 1980; Kellner, 1989); and the analyses of hegemony of the Italian Communist theorist Antonio Gramsci (1971, 1985). Challenging the objectivist, positivist, and behaviorist traditions of many U.S. (and other) researchers, this and other

Correspondence and requests for reprints: Mike Budd, Communication Department, Florida Atlantic University, PO Box 3091, Boca Raton, FL 33431.

Communication Yearbook 15, pp. 251-262

work, developed in the more overtly political context of European intellectual life, has been taken up in complex ways, often by feminist and leftist scholars, to produce an enormously productive ferment in many established fields. As African-American, women's, Native American, Chicana and Chicano, and gay and lesbian studies programs develop in U.S. universities, the new theory and its diverse uses in different disciplines have contributed significantly to the conceptual foundations of these new fields as well (Butler, 1990; Gates, 1988).

While theoretical and political issues are most often still institutionally marginalized, older, more traditional disciplines change as well. Both the vitality and the contentiousness of much contemporary literary study come largely from this interaction of theory and politics: Fundamental debates over who and what will be included in the canon, over the status of literature, even over how to read and to write now derive in substantial part from the radical theoretical and political questions posed by Roland Barthes (1972, 1977), Jacques Derrida (1976), Edward Said (1989), Eve Kosofsky Sedgewick (1990), and others. Historians are challenged by Michel Foucault (1980), Lynn Hunt (1989), Hayden White (1987), and others to question their assumed objectivity, and to incorporate issues of discourse (their own included) into their research. In the arts, the problems around postmodernism frequently center on Fredric Jameson's (1984) critique based on stages of capitalist development. Anthropologists such as James Clifford and George E. Marcus (1986) problematize the scientific assumptions of ethnography by treating it as literature or rhetoric. And these developments spill over onto one another: The confluence of new theories and new politics is generating whole new areas and possibilities of study (and change) for which "interdisciplinary" is an inadequate description. More accurately, scholars conscious of the connections between knowledge and power critique the disciplining of knowledge itself; disciplines and their relations are being redefined, and objects, subjects, and methods of study revised (Heller, 1990b).

These changes in the internal dynamics of the disciplines are part of larger developments. Many liberal arts faculty members feel increasingly peripheral in U.S. universities. With students continuing to choose business and other professional majors in large numbers, professors in the more traditional disciplines become more alienated, are more likely to recognize that their function is no longer central to their institutions but a service to more technical and instrumental forms of higher education. Following Allan Bloom (1987) and E. D. Hirsch (1987), conservatives adopt a defensive posture, reinforcing disciplinary boundaries and a pseudoreligious, affirmative conception of Eurocentric moral values. Others, however, may be drawn by the shrinking relative size and importance of the liberal arts to recognize their underlying connections and unity, not as a fortress to be defended against the vocationalist barbarians, but as a more integrated set of discourses. Coming out of the social and political movements of the 1960s and 1970s into an increasingly contested institutional position, younger professors, especially women, have often taken up the socially critical new cross-disciplinary theories.

A related but much broader development is multiculturalism. Educators at many levels call for greater attention to cultural diversity in an increasingly multicultural society. The feminist movement continues to press for more proportional representation of women and women's concerns in what are still almost entirely male institutions of power. Even policymakers with both eyes on the bottom line acknowledge that a future U.S. work force composed largely of women and people of color has to be educated in different ways. Even more important, with the United States no longer dominating the world economy, understanding international relations and foreign cultures seems more important. Many universities are considering changes to their core curricula to incorporate issues of gender, ethnicity, and non-European cultures and histories.

These and other large social and institutional forces ground the new theory and politics in the disciplines mentioned earlier. But this new theory has its own dynamic as well, complicated by its travels from Europe to North America, often through Britain. As it appears in universities, it is above all a theory and politics of discourse, of representation and signification: It assumes that human discourse and the production of meaning are hardly natural processes, but cultural constructions based in the social hierarchies of gender, race, class, nationality, and sexual orientation. Showing how signs are divided into signifiers (physical form) and signifieds (meaning) that culture only seems to unify, semiotics opens a whole new realm: Since the relation of signifier and signified is culturally contingent rather than logical or natural, it can be changed—indeed, is constantly changing as part of larger historical shifts in language and other meaning systems. Coming from the structural linguistics of Ferdinand de Saussure (1966) and others, semiotics is often a technical and formalist exercise, but it always holds critical potential in its insistence that meaning is a process rather than a product, a construction rather than a reified thing, and that, following the model of language, all kinds of ordinary cultural practices (advertising, dress, gestures, movies, and television) are coded and conventionalized to generate meanings. Joined to an institutional and political critique, semiotics becomes a powerful way of analyzing both the reproduction of ideological domination through the control of meanings and the struggles that go on around meaning as articulations of political interest.

As the closest intellectual relative of semiotics, structuralism understands codes, discourses, and signification as institutional structures that are not only made by humans but make us in return. We do not come to the codes of television and other cultural structures fully formed; rather, the matrix of institutional forces, of which meaning production is a major dimension, actually constitutes our subjectivity, the identity from which individual agency proceeds (Hawkes, 1977). In the 1970s, film and other scholars influenced by Louis Althusser (1971) argued that readers and spectators are ideologically hailed or positioned by the address of texts. Feminist critics, responding to the psychoanalytic theories of Jacques Lacan (1970), argued that patriarchal ways of seeing and reading were deeply structured into texts as well (see, e.g., Kuhn, 1982; Mulvey, 1975). Taking the arguments of structuralism and semiotics about the arbitrariness of the sign one step further, Jacques Derrida and other poststructuralists pointed out that the relation between signifier and signified in a sign always depends on other relations of difference around that sign: Meaning is not just coded but context-bound, not substantive but relational. But since the meanings of those other signifiers also depend on our first sign, and still others, meaning can never be ultimately fixed, is always endlessly deferred, in free play, despite efforts of authority to limit its range. In literary and cultural theory, such relativist arguments have been usefully subversive of traditional aesthetics and dominant interpretations, even though sometimes hampered by a linguistic or semiotic determinism that limits the visibility of social forces and movements.

All these traveling continental theories, arriving one on top of another in the 1970s, both generated and sublimated political energies on U.S. campuses. The late 1970s culminated as a moment of "high theory" for many, synthesized best perhaps in *Language and Materialism* by Rosalind Coward and John Ellis (1977). In film studies the synthesis even became the dominant paradigm, later called screen theory or "*Screen* theory," after the influential British journal that promulgated it.

Such theory (and its associated focus on texts) remains persuasive today, but its internal dynamic has focused more attention on reception. Poststructuralism's deconstructive play with signifiers already emphasizes that texts are open, with multiple signifieds. And reception theory suggests a reader who "activates" the potential codes of the text rather than being entirely constituted in ideology (Tompkins, 1980). Language and other signifying systems are always dimensions of social systems, so receivers would have different relations to them, and different discourses for varying social groups.

In the 1980s, sympathetic scholars in the United States have not so much turned away from theory as applied it, tested and revised it in the encounter with concrete social and historical questions. Literary theory became the basis of the New Historicism (Veeser, 1989), film study turned partly to a history of modes of discourse and of reception, and "the American study of media [was] increasingly integrated into 'cultural sociology' (the American term for what the British call 'cultural studies')" (Tuchman, 1988, p. 619). Certainly the internal dynamic of the theory, especially the shift in focus toward decoding and reception, helped carry it toward what has now become known as cultural studies. The relatively benign political climate of the 1970s also made possible the speculative theory of that period, partly as a substitute for increasingly difficult political work; the hostility of the

Reagan-Thatcher "counterreformation" (Heller, 1990a, p. A8) helped bring many back to more concrete problems.

A complex of poststructuralist, feminist, neo-Marxist, and other theories existing in tension with practical progressive politics, both inside and outside universities, within changing institutional and disciplinary boundaries—these make U.S. cultural studies possible (Brantlinger, 1990). A politics and theory of representation, focusing increasingly on the social bases of cultural forms and articulations of power, on what Gramsci called the war of position over meaning and pleasure and reception of ordinary cultural products, and thus on a new, more critical ethnography sensitive to the power and subjectivity of the ethnographer—these give some shape to a loose grouping of approaches spanning a dozen disciplines. Cultural studies critiques claims to scientific objectivity (Haraway, 1989) or to realism and the natural (Barthes, 1972) by demonstrating the cultural and other politics within such claims. It often begins with the scholar's own personal experience. At a recent conference on cultural studies at the University of Illinois, one speaker argued that cultural studies scholars should work only on topics in which they are personally implicated.

The personal is political: The roots of cultural studies in feminism are strong. A related, more specific influence, especially for communication, is British cultural studies, from Raymond Williams (1966, 1977), Richard Hoggart (1961), and E. P. Thompson (1963) to the Centre for Contemporary Cultural Studies at the University of Birmingham, especially the work of Stuart Hall (1980; see also Turner, 1990). Describing the CCCS in the 1960s and 1970s, Hall (1990) shows the necessary role of personal experience and engagement:

> Therefore, if someone came to me asking me to suggest an interesting project that could be done in cultural studies, that person would not be a good candidate for us at the Center, because it was not someone who had already engaged with and become committed to a field of inquiry which seemed, to that person, to matter. . . . So, from the start we said: What are you interested in? What really bugs you about questions of culture and society right now? What do you really think is a problem you don't understand out there in the terrible interconnection between culture and politics? What is it about the way in which British culture is now living through its kind of postcolonial, posthegemonic crisis that really bites into your experience? And then we will find a way of studying that seriously. (p. 17)

Transgressing and exploring those boundaries enforced by our culture and economy—private/public, psychological/social, personal/political boundaries—constitutes a central task of cultural studies.

The Birmingham Centre developed or influenced an exemplary series of studies on subcultures (Hebdige, 1979; McRobbie & Nava, 1984), encoding and decoding (Hall, 1980), television audiences (Morley, 1986), and a variety of other topics. These emerged in significant part from concrete elaboration of Antonio Gramsci's (1971) theory of hegemony, from the attempt to make intellectual work organic to progressive social movements, from a productive tension between theory and practical politics. In particular, the collective work *Policing the Crisis: Mugging, the State, and Law and Order* (Hall, Critcher, Jefferson, Clarke, & Roberts, 1978) links racist media coverage of London muggings in the early 1970s to issues of the social production of news and of explanations of crime, and finally to the rise of the Right in Britain around "problems" of law and order. Central to this study is

> a quite novel concern with 'the popular' in a radically new sense: national-popular cultural traditions, popular ideologies, the popular as the ground of common sense in which more developed and organized 'philosophies' intervene, the popular as the stake in the struggle for hegemony and consent (populist/popular democratic elements in political discourses and their articulation with different class practices, for example). (Hall et al., 1978, p. 40)

It is worth noting the critique as well as the affirmation of the popular here, since some in U.S. cultural studies often collapse the popular into a one-dimensional affirmation of the power and independence of media audiences (Budd, Entman, & Steinman, 1990).

Not always able to make explicit links with social movements, cultural studies has nevertheless produced original syntheses of the various traditions mentioned earlier. One of the best of these is *Bond and Beyond: The Political Career of a Popular Hero,* by Tony Bennett and Janet Woollacott (1987). Surveying the construction of the figure of James Bond across novels, films, advertising, reviewing, commentary, fanzines, and soft-core pornography, the book traces the historical changes in the coding of this intertextual figure over three decades. Bennett and Woollacott combine sophisticated literary and film theory and insightful textual analysis within a history of gender, class, racial, and national ideologies and pleasures, and show how "Bond" condenses and helps transform popular ideas of British national identity, the Cold War and détente, and the rise of the women's movement. In its integration of social, political, economic, and textual elements into a cultural history of encoding and decoding—into production, texts, and reception—*Bond and Beyond* demonstrates the continuing importance of British cultural studies.

In the United States as well as in Britain, much of the strength of cultural studies lies in its continuing sympathetic conversation with contemporary and historical movements for social change. Neither a collapse of some imaginary scholarly neutrality and objectivity nor a utopian fusion of theory and practice, this conversation helps maintain the critical, negative edge to cultural studies' focus on the politics of everyday life. For example, Linda Williams's *Hard Core: Power, Pleasure, and the "Frenzy of the*

Visible " (1989) speaks both to feminist film theory and to a larger feminist community debating the violent and misogynistic dimensions of pornography. In a history of the hard-core genre of film and video pornography centered on its attempts to represent female desire (usually for male viewers), Williams explores the power of gendered pleasure and knowledge in the spectacle of sexuality. The study analyzes rather than condemns or glorifies its object, and so can speak to and even for an even larger group of women now experiencing pornography for the first time.

In this encapsulated summary, we have emphasized the broad history and politics of cultural studies and related developments because it is this context that is largely missing from Barker and Timberg's construction of a tradition of encoding research. These authors offer a three-decade history of research into the significance of television's specific representational forms (of camera, editing, sound, setting, and so forth). Constructing a narrative of progress, they move first through behaviorist studies of educational television, then to aesthetic studies, seeking to name the particularities of the medium, and "finally, [into] a newly emerging body of work, influenced by critical theory and cultural studies" (p. 210). Their quest is for the most "accurate" analysis, "one that accounts for all aspects of the television apparatus and regimes of viewing" (p. 233). For them, the goal of the most valuable television scholarship has been "to grow in scope and complexity" (p. 210) toward the "holistic" (pp. 210, 212, 222, 223, 233) or, even better, the "truly holistic" (pp. 224, 227).

Although they find that much empirical research has been narrow and reductionist, seeking isolated cause-effect relations, still infusing their work is the empiricist fantasy that the world can be holistically known. Schroyer (1973) calls this fantasy a "copy theory of reality," the "belief that knowledge in a sense copies reality" and that the most rigorous work will offer the best copy (p. 119). Such a theory denies how all thinkers construct the world they seek to understand, as it abjures the inevitable partiality of knowledge in whatever form. It ignores as well the politics of theory, how power and resources shape strategies of research. And it tends to construct a theoretical *telos*, ending, not surprisingly, in work just like its own.

Whatever their intentions and personal politics, Barker and Timberg have put together a history unconsciously marked by the same partiality as the scholarship they extol. Just as they seem to have missed completely the North American tradition of political-economic analysis of communication (see, e.g. Smythe, 1977), they treat feminist work only as an afterthought, at the end of lists of other theories informing the work they admire (pp. 226, 227, 231, 233).[1] They discuss Stuart Hall extensively, but from their treatment one would never know the connection of his work to Marxism, the pertinence of "decoding" to the principal question for the twentieth-century socialist movement: the character of the revolutionary subject. Overall, the partiality of their history betrays an antipathy to politically committed work. This antipathy is itself structural: As Gitlin (1990) points out, starting at least with Max Weber, the well-behaved social scientist has forsworn explicit political activity on the job; that is the professional code. Ironically, it is precisely political commitment that drives the work in cultural studies that Barker and Timberg find so energizing to television research.

The absence of concern with politics or power seems clearest in their discussion of relations between viewers and texts. Following the work of Fiske (1987) and others, Barker and Timberg suggest that "the viewer occupies a position of equality relative both to the text and to the producers of the text in the negotiation and construction of meaning" (p. 211). They write of the "power of the viewer" (p. 212), who has an "unstated reciprocal contract [with the television text's producer] . . . such that the producer can utilize a given code with some sense that the viewer will negotiate the code more or less as the producer intended" (p. 212). They say "the viewer" exercises "indisputable power . . . in negotiating the codes making up the text" (p. 218). They speak of the "role of the viewer in negotiating meaning," and they oppose the notion that watching television is "passive consumption." But who is "the viewer"? For more than a decade, feminists and representatives of other disempowered groups have been arguing that viewers *differ* in crucial ways, and that each viewer oscillates between social psychological positions from moment to moment.

Barker and Timberg write as if there were an ideal viewer who comes to the set preformed, ready to deal. Indeed, the viewer they imagine is the ideal type of market-democratic society, protagonists of the "chamber of commerce" scenario: the rational actors who, conscious of and pursuing their own interests, ultimately serve the interests of all. *Negotiation, contract, equality,* and *reciprocity*—these are the terms of a commercial relationship whose fairness is guaranteed, as if unequal power relations were not built into communication in hierarchical societies. It is as if the high school graduate in rural California were normally prepared to evaluate the appeal of ads for the Army Reserve, as if the senior citizen in New York were normally able to fathom her way through the medical insurance sales pitch, as if the suburban mother of the 1950s normally stood on equal ground measuring herself against Jane Wyatt as a role model for her unpaid household work.

Where audiences are significantly empowered against television, the cause can more likely be traced to a contingent intersection of events and discourses than to the market-democratic social formation Barker and Timberg seem to take as a fixture of contemporary life. For Hall and others in British cultural studies, television viewers are envisioned not in isolation, and not for always, but as they are situated in a specific historical social formation that oppresses them, a social formation many fight in the streets and in the workplace (which also means the home), as well as in electoral campaigns. Cultural studies in Britain has an *interest* in viewers' resistance to television encoding: It is concerned with its relation to the struggle for socialism. The model for "negotiation" is the struggle between labor and capital, not the search for the lowest price. Viewers are already (unevenly) empowered by working-class culture; their decoding extends the struggle by other means.

In U.S. media studies, viewer empowerment all too easily slides into a uses and gratifications argument that, like classical economics, validates the interests of everyone. Television cannot be that bad—people make their own meanings. Class and culture have disappeared; viewers are consumers, making their best deals in front of the set. Emancipation in theory comes to substitute for emancipation in practice (see Budd et al., 1990; Budd & Steinman, 1989).

Without an interest in power relations, communication can easily be seen as a harmonious ensemble of interactions, of reciprocal relations. But hierarchical social relations (between workers and their bosses, between women and men, between ethnic groups) tend to seem harmonious only to those at the long end of the stick. And it is they whom communication studies in the United States has tended to serve. Paul Lazarsfeld (1941) clarified the distinction 50 years ago between administrative research that serves the powerful, who want compliance or sales or service from the disempowered, and critical research that analyzes power within communication relations with an interest in change. For decades the separation held, as practitioners on both sides had little to do with each other.

Since the early 1980s, however, Lazarsfeld's dichotomy has broken down. Partly because of its rigor and persuasiveness, particularly in its critique of unreflective empiricism, critical communication research has changed the face of what many mainstream communication scholars do (see Gerbner, 1983). This has had contradictory implications.

On the one hand, as Barker and Timberg say (and as their scholarship shows), critical communication research and, more recently, British cultural studies have led to a reinvigoration of much work in the field. The authors' emphasis on the limitations of empirical research, on the problems of taking representational forms for granted, on the inadequacy of the old sender-receiver models of communication and reception, on the importance of looking at the material qualities of text, on the complexities of television's development—these all can be traced to paradigms opposed to conventional administrative work. Between administrative and critical research, then, a hybrid category has developed, appropriating terms of critical research within the avowedly apolitical boundaries of conventional scholarship.

This stretching of traditional communication studies (of which there remains far, far more than there is of critical work) would seem to be in everyone's interest: scholars of all points of view, students, the public at large to the extent that new knowledge becomes diffused. Yet much has been lost. This is especially evident in the hollowing out that has taken place in British cultural studies as it has been taken up in the United States (O'Connor, 1989). Increasingly, graduate students at the major research universities have been hearing cover versions of cultural studies, critiques severed of connection to their original project of radical social change. Not knowing how elements of critical and cultural studies have been expurgated and decontextualized, these students—now beginning professors—have begun teaching others and publishing their own work, unself-conscious about the evisceration of politics in their sense of their source material, or perhaps unconcerned about the exnomination of what might in the mainstream seem to be oddball ideas in any case.

This is, perhaps, a testament to audience power, to the inability of texts or their writers to control meaning and use. If so, it is a sign just as much of the power of institutions in this culture to diminish the communication of ideas that criticize them at their roots. As becomes terribly clear in times of offensive war, there remains an unavoidable difference between academic work aimed at studying the system for knowledge in itself and work studying the system in order to change it. Revising critical and cultural studies away from their interest in social change removes them from the shelf of resources that could be used to contest unequal relations of communication, to write new contracts, and to fight for institutions of genuine reciprocity and democratic engagement.

NOTE

1. The chapter also makes scant mention of issues of ethnicity and class, or psychoanalysis and poststructuralism, and is silent on gay studies and the important work of the Frankfurt school and of deconstruction. Indeed, the authors seem disinclined to read psychoanalytic film theory (the major area of feminist work in the field in the last decade in such first-rank film journals as *Camera Obscura* and *Screen*). Film studies, they say, has sometimes "talked to death . . . countless theories of the text/viewer relationship" (p. 230).

REFERENCES

Althusser, L. (1971). Ideology and ideological state apparatuses (Notes toward an investigation). In L. Althusser, *Lenin and philosophy and other essays* (B. Brewster, Trans.) (pp. 127-186). New York: Monthly Review Press.
Barthes, R. (1972). *Mythologies* (A. Lavers, Trans.). New York: Hill & Wang.
Barthes, R. (1977). *Image-music-text* (S. Heath, Trans.). New York: Hill & Wang.
Belsey, C. (1980). *Critical practice.* London: Methuen.
Bennett, T., & Woollacott, J. (1987). *Bond and beyond: The political career of a popular hero.* London: Methuen.
Bloom, A. (1987). *The closing of the American mind.* New York: Simon & Schuster.
Brantlinger, P. (1990). *Crusoe's footprints: Cultural studies in Britain and America.* New York: Routledge.
Buck-Morss, S. (1977). *The origin of negative dialectics: Theodor W. Adorno, Walter Benjamin, and the Frankfurt Institute.* New York: Free Press.

Budd, M., Entman, R. M., & Steinman, C. (1990). The affirmative character of U.S. cultural studies. *Critical Studies in Mass Communication, 7*, 169-184.

Budd, M., & Steinman, C. (1989). Television, cultural studies, and the "blind spot" debate in critical communications research. In G. Burns & R. Thompson (Eds.), *Television studies: Textual analysis* (pp. 9-20). New York: Praeger.

Butler, J. (1990). *Gender trouble: Feminism and the subversion of identity.* New York: Routledge.

Clifford, J., & Marcus, G. E. (Eds.). (1986). *Writing culture: The poetics and politics of ethnography.* Berkeley: University of California Press.

Coward, R., & Ellis, J. (1977). *Language and materialism: Developments in semiology and the theory of the subject.* London: Routledge & Kegan Paul.

Derrida, J. (1976). *Of grammatology* (G. C. Spivak, Trans.). Baltimore: Johns Hopkins University Press.

Fiske, J. (1987). *Television culture.* London: Methuen.

Foucault, M. (1980). *Power/knowledge: Selected interviews and other writings, 1972-1977* (C. Gordon et al., Trans.). New York: Pantheon.

Gates, H. (1988). *The signifying monkey: A theory of African-American literary criticism.* New York: Oxford University Press.

Gerbner, G. (Ed.). (1983). Ferment in the field [Special issue]. *Journal of Communication, 33*(3).

Gitlin, T. (1990). Commentary: Who communicates what to whom, in what voice and why, about the study of mass communication? *Critical Studies in Mass Communication, 7*, 185-196.

Gramsci, A. (1971). *Selections from the prison notebooks* (Q. Hoare & G. Nowell-Smith, Eds. and Trans.). New York: International.

Gramsci, A. (1985). *Selections from cultural writings* (D. Forgacs & G. Nowell-Smith, Eds.; W. Boelhower, Trans.). Cambridge, MA: Harvard University Press.

Hall, S. (1980). Encoding/decoding. In S. Hall, D. Hobson, A. Lowe, & P. Willis (Eds.), *Culture, media, language: Working papers in cultural studies 1972-1979* (pp. 128-138). London: Hutchinson.

Hall, S. (1990). The emergence of cultural studies and the crisis of the humanities. *October, 53*, 11-23.

Hall, S., Critcher, C., Jefferson, T., Clarke, J., & Roberts, B. (1978). *Policing the crisis: Mugging, the state, and law and order.* London: Macmillan.

Haraway, D. (1989). *Primate visions: Gender, race, and nature in the world of modern science.* New York: Routledge.

Hawkes, T. (1977). *Structuralism and semiotics.* Berkeley: University of California Press.

Hebdige, D. (1979). *Subculture: The meaning of style.* London: Methuen.

Held, D. (1980). *Introduction to critical theory: Horkheimer to Habermas.* Berkeley: University of California Press.

Heller, S. (1990a, January 31). Cultural studies: Eclectic and controversial mix of research sparks a growing movement. *Chronicle of Higher Education*, pp. A6-A8.

Heller, S. (1990b, May 2). Protest at cultural-studies meeting sparked by debate over new field. *Chronicle of Higher Education*, pp. A10-A11.

Hirsch, E. D. (1987). *Cultural literacy: What every American needs to know.* Boston: Houghton Mifflin.

Hoggart, R. (1961). *The uses of literacy: Changing patterns in English mass culture.* Boston: Beacon.

Hunt, L. (Ed.). (1989). *The new cultural history.* Berkeley: University of California Press.

Jameson, F. (1984). Postmodernism, or the cultural logic of late capitalism. *New Left Review, 146*, 53-92.

Kellner, D. (1989). *Critical theory, Marxism and modernity.* Baltimore: Johns Hopkins University Press.

Kuhn, A. (1982). *Women's pictures: Feminism and cinema*. London: Routledge & Kegan Paul.

Lacan, J. (1970). The insistence of the letter in the unconscious. In J. Ehrmann (Ed.), *Structuralis* (pp. 101-137). Garden City, NY: Anchor.

Lazarsfeld, P. F. (1941). Remarks on administrative and critical communications research. *Studies in Philosophy and Social Science, 9*, 2-11.

McRobbie, A., & Nava, M. (Eds.). (1984). *Gender and generation*. London: Macmillan.

Morley, D. (1986). *Family television*. London: Comedia.

Mulvey, L. (1975). Visual pleasure and narrative cinema. *Screen, 16*(3), 6-18.

O'Connor, A. (1989). The problem of American cultural studies. *Critical Studies in Mass Communication, 6*, 405-413.

Said, E. (1989). *The world, the text, and the critic*. Cambridge, MA: Harvard University Press.

Saussure, F. de. (1966). *Course in general linguistics*. (W. Baskin, Trans.). New York: McGraw-Hill.

Schroyer, T. (1973). *The critique of domination: The origins and development of critical theory*. Boston: Beacon.

Sedgewick, E. K. (1990). *Epistemology of the closet*. Berkeley: University of California Press.

Silverman, K. (1983). *The subject of semiotics*. New York: Oxford University Press.

Smythe, D. (1977). Communications: Blindspot of Western Marxism. *Canadian Journal of Political and Social Theory, 1*(3), 1-27.

Thompson, E. P. (1963). *The making of the English working class*. New York: Vintage.

Tompkins, J. (Ed.). (1980). *Reader-response criticism from formalism to post-structuralism*. Baltimore: Johns Hopkins University Press.

Tuchman, G. (1988). Mass media institutions. In N. J. Smelser (Ed.), *Handbook of sociology* (pp. 601-626). Newbury Park, CA: Sage.

Turner, G. (1990). *British cultural studies: An introduction*. Winchester, MA: Unwin Hyman.

Veeser, H. A. (1989). *The new historicism*. New York: Routledge.

Weedon, C. (1987). *Feminist practice and poststructuralist theory*. Oxford: Basil Blackwell.

White, H. (1987). *The context in the text: Narrative discourse and historical representation*. Baltimore: Johns Hopkins University Press.

Williams, L. (1989). *Hard core: Power, pleasure, and the "frenzy of the visible."* Berkeley: University of California Press.

Williams, R. (1966). *Culture and society, 1780-1950*. New York: Harper & Row.

Williams, R. (1977). *Marxism and literature*. New York: Oxford University Press.

6 A Theory of Belief, Attitude, Intention, and Behavior Extended to the Domain of Corrective Advertising

MICHAEL BURGOON
DEBORAH A. NEWTON
THOMAS S. BIRK
University of Arizona

The literature on corrective advertising is replete with conflicting reports on its effectiveness in changing attitudes and/or behavior. Part of the ambiguity in the published literature is due to lack of theoretical specificity and conceptual clarity about the potential outcomes associated with mass media efforts to correct deception in commercial advertisements. Moreover, the published research suffers from methodological imprecision in measuring the social impacts of corrective advertisements that make cross-study comparisons difficult, if not impossible. This chapter develops a propositional calculus to explain corrective advertising effects based upon a significantly modified version of Fishbein's theory of belief, attitude, intention, and behavior. It is argued that while Fishbein's theory provides impetus for a theoretical formulation of corrective advertising effects, the model suffers from a major logical deficiency in explaining how corrective advertisers attempt to have limited impact in revising attitudes about previously misrepresented products, which demonstrates the inadequacy of a modified Fishbein model as a predictor of the social effects of corrective advertising. A new theoretic model, specifically developed for the corrective advertising situation, dramatically alters the predictions made in prior research and offers propositions about a new component of source sequence deception that cannot be derived from the original or extended Fishbein models. Implications are discussed for corrective advertising research, regulatory agencies, and theoretical development in the general area of social influence.

C ORRECTIVE advertising was developed by a government regulatory agency, the Federal Trade Commission (FTC), as a mechanism for more efficiently regulating false or deceptive advertising. Debates

Correspondence and requests for reprints: Michael Burgoon, Department of Communication, University of Arizona, Tucson, AZ 85721.

Communication Yearbook 15, pp. 263-286

over the use and effectiveness of such a strategy have been articulated by several sources (Armstrong, Gurol, & Russ, 1983a; Maddox & Zanot, 1979; Wilkie, 1974; Wilkie, McNeill, & Mazis, 1984). In brief, the concept was developed and originally advanced by a group of George Washington University law students who sought to intervene in an FTC proceeding against the Campbell Soup Company. A case was brought against Campbell Soup when its advertiser used clear marbles placed in the bottom of soup bowls to force solid ingredients to the surface for photographs. It was argued that traditional use of cease and desist orders did not adequately protect the public interest and that a corrective remedy was needed to inform consumers of the deception (Maddox & Zanot, 1979). Since that original intervention, major corrective advertising campaigns have been ordered against several products, two of which (Listerine and STP oil additive) have captured the attention of media effects researchers.

A number of policy decisions by government regulatory agencies have attempted to reverse the effects of deceptive advertising by forcing advertisers to make "corrective" statements in future advertisements. Such a penalty is seen to deprive advertisers of any benefits from the use of misleading advertising. The primary objective of corrective advertising is to dispel the "residual effects" of deceptive advertisements, thereby presumably restoring consumers to the beliefs they held prior to the deception. Regulatory agencies are not interested in destroying products or companies; instead, they desire limited impact resulting from a corrective mass media campaign. In other words, they are interested in rectifying beliefs about a product by affecting people's attitudes in a short-term, restrictive manner, without causing permanent behavioral changes in the form of purchasing products.

Because the outcomes of any corrective campaign are complicated, the specification of limited impacts is particularly troublesome for regulators, message producers, and researchers. Public admission of deception may produce multifaceted and potentially grave affects in (a) consumers' attitudes toward the product, (b) the credibility of the company, (c) consumers' future purchase intentions, and (d) actual buying behavior. Moreover, in some segments of the market, it is possible that one company's use of corrective advertising for a product may change attitudes toward or buying behavior associated with similar products, thereby bringing substantial harm to companies not guilty of wrongdoing (see Dyer & Kuehl, 1978). Thus whenever a corrective advertising campaign is ordered, unintended effects are a source of concern.

EMPIRICAL FINDINGS

It is apparent that the Federal Trade Commission believes that corrective advertising can "undo" the negative consequences of deceptive advertising

(Scammon, McNeil, & Preston, 1980). However, research is inconclusive as to whether or not corrective advertising in fact dissipates misleading effects about a product or service and reconstructs beliefs. To address this issue, Armstrong, Gurol, and Russ (1983b) conducted a longitudinal study of Listerine's 1978 corrective advertising campaign and found a reduction of only 20% in the level of beliefs about falsely advertised attributes of the product. Though this was seen by the researchers as a relatively successful campaign, they suggest that corrective advertising remains difficult, especially when long-term beliefs or personal experience supports a false belief. This particular study lends support to one notion of a limited effects view of corrective advertising in that the false beliefs about the product were not changed in a large majority of the people studied. Lamb and Stutts (1979) similarly believe that corrective advertising via the mass media neither significantly influences consumers' false impressions nor brings brand impressions into equilibrium with normative impressions.

In 1976, Mazis and Adkinson claimed that corrective advertising messages had a significant impact on brand belief. However, seven years later, Mazis changed his opinion and concluded that people could remember little about corrective advertising or disputed claims without prompting (Mazis, McNeill, & Bernhardt, 1983). Sawyer and Semenik (1978) found that when subjects were exposed to corrective advertisement on only one occasion, brand beliefs were not influenced. A later study by Semenik (1980) also showed that the content of a corrective advertisement did not produce the desired effect of altering beliefs about product performance. No support for even a limited effects view of corrective advertising was found by Dyer and Kuehl (1978), who contend that limited exposure to a corrective message may not remove falsely based beliefs about a product.

Other researchers report equally confounding results. Jacoby, Nelson, and Hoyer (1982) found that remedial advertising claims may be miscomprehended as much or more than the advertising they are supposed to remedy. Hence, these researchers claim, rather than undoing negative consequences of deceptive advertising, corrective efforts result in confused consumers. A report on consumers' ability to comprehend the purpose and content of corrective advertising in two mandated corrective campaigns revealed that consumers are somewhat naive as to the purpose of corrective advertising (Belch, Belch, Settle, & DeLucchi, 1981). Kinnear, Taylor, and Gur-Arie (1983) take strong exception to this confusion hypothesis and provide evidence of a 50% increase in awareness of product attributes in a corrective advertising campaign involving Hawaiian Fruit Punch.

The research on the impact of corrective advertising runs the gamut from no effects to limited effects to evidence suggesting very dramatic effects. Some researchers are convinced of the efficacy of corrective advertising in dispelling false beliefs; others remain skeptical. Though research is inconclusive as to whether or not deceptive claims made in commercial advertising can be reversed with additional information, what cannot be ignored by investigators are critical issues about the potential long-term damage a corrective campaign may cause a company or product image.

Conflicting findings in the literature surround the issue of whether or not corrective advertising harms company image and affects purchase intent. In a controlled field study on Listerine's corrective campaign, Mizerski, Allison, and Calvert (1980) found no significant changes in subjects' perceptions of Listerine's honesty or their intentions to purchase Listerine. Similarly, Semenik (1980) found that corrective advertising did not have a significant adverse effect on the brand or firm image tested. Conversely, Armstrong, Franke, and Russ (1982) found that the Listerine corrective advertising campaign produced a deterioration in Warner-Lambert's (the manufacturer's) image.

Part of the problem in the research on corrective advertising may be caused by the inaccessibility of much of the data collected by the FTC or by errors in representation. Bernhardt, Kinnear, Mazis, and Reece (1980) have published an interpretation of secondary data that concludes that the STP campaign had *marked effects on awareness of a problem* with STP that resulted in decreased intention to purchase STP, but *did not negatively impact attitudes* about the STP Corporation. In fact, as will be discussed later, the credibility of the corporation and attitudes about its financial future were dramatically degenerated by the corrective advertising campaign. It is possible that since Mazis was an employee of the FTC at the time of this data collection, he interpreted the data as he did based on criteria that differed significantly from those used by the independent researchers who actually conducted the investigation (Burgoon & Burgoon, 1978).

Hunt (1973) warns that corrective advertisements indeed reduce favorable attitudes toward the company or manufacturer and can produce significant adverse effects. He cautions advertisers to consider the risk of deceptive advertising carefully because of the possibility of mandated corrective campaigns. Dyer and Kuehl (1974) found that intention to buy decreased when the FTC was identified as the source of the order for corrective advertising but was not affected when a company was the presumed source. Moreover, company image suffered in some conditions where the FTC was seen as the source of the order for the corrective campaign. Interestingly, when a company was seen as mounting a campaign to correct false beliefs it helped foster, it was actually seen as more trustworthy. Thus the source sequence (company/FTC versus company/company) appears to be a crucial variable in determining the impact of corrective advertising on source credibility.

The methodological adequacy of research on corrective advertising has also received the attention of a number of critics (Aaker, 1974; Allison & Mizerski, 1981; Belch et al., 1981; Burke, DeSarbo, Oliver, & Robertson, 1988; Kuehl & Dyer, 1978; Nkonge, 1984). Studies conducted in field environments or in laboratories have been criticized for not considering publicity and news coverage that typically precedes or accompanies a real corrective campaign (Tyebjee, 1982). That is due, in some part, to the data not being collected while the corrective advertising campaign was actually being conducted. An examination of the entire body of corrective advertising research indicates that much of the research involves samples of college students. The generalizability of such results calls into question the bulk of the published research findings, particularly when student samples are unlikely to have been exposed to either the original advertisements or the corrective attempts. Measurement issues, such as aided versus unaided recall, have also contributed to conflicting findings. In addition, the interrelationships among variables have not been assessed in research efforts—the focus of some studies is only on recall of arguments; others measure only attitudes toward the product. A dearth of studies exist that have adequately measured issues, product attitudes, credibility, purchase intent, and actual behavior. The resulting enigma surrounding corrective advertising effects can be attributed in part to inadequate research design, methodological problems, and misinterpretations of secondary data.

Rather than rendering this body of research uninterpretable, what is needed is a theoretical model that allows for both limited effects in the form of simple belief reversal on specific claims and the possibility of complex, multiple outcomes in the form of concomitant covariation in beliefs, credibility, intention, and behavior. Without such an explanatory, and therefore predictive, propositional framework, little progress can be made in understanding the morass of research in corrective advertising/media effects.

This chapter attempts to lay such a foundation by further modifying Fishbein's (1967; Fishbein & Ajzen, 1974) model of belief and attitude formation and extending it to the domain of corrective advertising. Expansion of the model provides a means of predicting and explaining attitudes, intentions, and behaviors that result from a corrective advertising campaign. The modified model is adequate to address the following questions empirically:

(1) Does corrective advertising work in dispelling false beliefs?
(2) Does corrective advertising harm company or brand image?
(3) Does corrective advertising affect purchase intent?

EXPLANATORY FRAMEWORK:
ATTITUDE/BELIEF FORMATION MODEL

Working from a behavioral perspective, Fishbein (1967) derived a model based upon principles of mediated (secondary or conditioned) generalization. According to Fishbein, beliefs are attributions people make about the world; cognitions about the existence of things, events, ideas, and/or persons; the perceived probability of relationships between them; and characteristics of them. Attitudes are the products of beliefs that cluster together to form preferences for or against an object or an idea. Beliefs and attitudes are formed from either direct observation or data received from external sources.

The central proposition of Fishbein's original model is that an attitude toward an object is a summative unit made up of an individual's belief that the object is associated with certain attributes, the individual's evaluations of those attributes, and the number of salient beliefs the individual possesses regarding the object. Thus beliefs are derived from information received from outside sources and through the inferential and attributional processes and serve as fundamental building blocks in our conceptual structure (Fishbein, 1967). Beliefs assist humans in making judgments, forming evaluations, and arriving at decisions about themselves, other people, institutions, behaviors, events, objects, concepts, and the like (Fishbein & Ajzen, 1974).

Fishbein's theory of attitude/belief formation can be summarized in the following manner:

(1) Information is received from external sources;
(2) an individual forms many beliefs about an object—that is, many different characteristics, attributes, values, goals, and concepts are positively or negatively associated with the object;
(3) associated with each of these "related objects" is a mediating evaluative response—an attitude;
(4) these evaluative responses summate;
(5) through the mediation process, the summated evaluative response becomes associated with the attitude object; and thus
(6) on future occasions the attitude object will elicit this summated evaluative response—this attitude. (Fishbein & Ajzen, 1974)

It was initially assumed that people's attitudes toward an object could be used to predict their subsequent behaviors toward that object. Such an assumption is made by many researchers interested in corrective advertising who directly measure only beliefs and attitudes and not purchase intents and actual purchases of a product. The inability of this model to withstand empirical test and its consistent falsification caused Fishbein to modify the original model, a course of action that similarly might be wise for corrective advertising researchers.

THE EXTENDED MODEL

Fishbein's extended model suggests that the performance or nonperformance of a behavior cannot be predicted from knowledge of a person's attitude toward an object. Instead, behavior is determined by the person's *intention* to perform or not perform a behavior. The prediction of consumers' behavioral intentions involves assessments of both their attitudes toward a behavior and normative pressures regarding the behavior. This attitude toward performing a given behavior is a function of beliefs about the attributes or consequences of the behavior as well as an evaluation of those consequences. Other beliefs relevant to the prediction of consumers' behavioral intentions are those of a normative nature—that is, beliefs about whether referents think they should perform a specific behavior.

According to the model, an individual's beliefs about a referent's expectations concerning a behavior and the motivation to comply with the referent lead to normative pressures. The totality of these normative pressures may be termed an individual's *subjective norm*. Like the individual's attitude toward the behavior, subjective norms are major determinants of a person's intentions to perform a behavior. Thus behavioral intentions are a function of two factors: a person's attitude toward the behavior and the extent of normative pressures. As noted, this intention is viewed as the immediate determinant of corresponding behavior. Fishbein's extended model is unique in that it has an explanatory mechanism for predicting both the attitude toward and the behavioral intention toward the object.

The extended Fishbein model has been adopted as the foundation for developing a theory of corrective advertising because it offers a means to assess consumer beliefs, attitudes, intentions, and behavior. Three arguments exist for initially working with this model. First, it is conceptually isomorphic with the FTC's view of belief and attitude formation in the domain of deceptive and corrective advertising. Second, it provides promise for explaining and predicting consumer attitudes and behavior. Third, it provides a framework for devising behavioral change strategies that are central to the corrective advertising remedy.

APPLICATION OF THE MODEL
TO CORRECTIVE ADVERTISING

Advertisements are external sources of information that contain various informational cues, from explicit verbal claims of product performance or effectiveness to implicit nonverbal claims in pictures, illustrations, and symbols. If consumers are exposed to advertisements and attend to them, they may acquire and comprehend some of these cues. During comprehension, the cues are encoded, or converted to an internal symbolic or cognitive code. Then, if appropriate cognitive effort is exerted, consumers will make certain attributions and form systems of beliefs concerning objects related to the advertisement. Beliefs about an object will be hierarchically arranged according to belief strength, and each will have a corresponding evaluative dimension. These dimensions summate and through secondary reinforcement become attached to the attitude object.

Corrective advertising is a sequential message strategy involving a minimum of two advertisements. The first concerns a claim that is deceptive in nature. The second involves refutation of the deceptive claim. Most corrective campaigns involve multiple messages disseminated via multiple media. The definition of corrective advertising as a *sequential* message strategy specifies the minimum criteria necessary for inclusion in the set of message strategies called corrective advertising. Given exposure to corrective advertising and adequate cognitive effort, a person will make attributions about the objects associated with the sequential message strategy.

The attributions crucial to understanding and explaining the domain of corrective advertising are attributions about (a) the source of the deceptive advertisement; (b) the source of the corrective advertisement; (c) the product, brand, or service; and (d) the purchase of the product, brand, or service. The prediction of a consumer's attitude toward these objects can be explained by the central proposition of Fishbein's model. Simply stated, an attitude toward any object (company, brand, product, behavior) is a function of the sum of the strength of each belief times the corresponding evaluation of each belief. It will be argued later in this chapter that the Fishbein model is inadequate to predict and explain the full impact of corrective advertising because of the summative method used to combine attributions concerning the source of a deceptive message and the source of the corrective advertisement to arrive at the overall component of attitude toward the product.

The development of a deductive theory of corrective advertising has been systematically approached by (a) delineating the boundary conditions under which the explanatory model will hold, (b) conceptualizing the relevant units that constitute the theory, and (c) defining the laws of interaction among the units of the theory.

SPECIFICATION OF THE RANGE OF PHENOMENA

The relationships set forth in the theory apply to average consumers within a reasonable market segment who have been exposed to corrective advertising. These consumers must also have exerted sufficient cognitive effort to form beliefs about objects related to the sequential messages. These necessary conditions serve to limit the external boundaries of the theory in four important ways. First, the theory focuses on the average consumer; impressions and/or beliefs of consumers that fall beyond what two-thirds of the population would normally believe to be true are extraneous factors. Second, the theory assumes that consumers who are clearly not included in any reasonable market segment cannot be used to judge the effects of a deceptive or corrective advertising claim. For example, a 67-year-old widow who has never ridden or is unlikely ever to ride an all-terrain vehicle, and who has no interest in ATVs, would not be a credible source for determining the effects of a corrective campaign. Third, the theory holds *only* for those consumers who have been exposed to sequential advertisements involving first a claim and then a refutation of that claim. Fourth, only those consumers who have exerted the cognitive effort necessary to form beliefs about objects related to the sequential advertisements fall within the boundary of the theory. If, and only if, the above boundary conditions are satisfied are consumers considered within the explanatory range of the model.

UNITS OF THE THEORY
AND EXPLANATORY MECHANISMS

(1) $Aa = BE$

where Aa = the attitude toward some attribute of an object, O

         B = the subjective probability that the object is related to the attribute

         E = an evaluation of that attribute

(2) $Ao = \sum_{i=1}^{N} Bi\,Ei$

where Ao = the individual's attitude toward some object, O

         Bi = the individual's belief i about O

         Ei = the individual's evaluation of attribute i

         N = the number of salient beliefs

         If O equals performance of a behavior, then $Ac = BE$.

(3) $Ac = BE$

where Ac = the attitude toward some consequence of behavior, B

         B = the subjective probability that the behavior is related to the consequence

         E = an evaluation of that consequence

(4) $Ab = \sum_{i=1}^{N} Bi\,Ei$

where Ab = an individual's attitude toward performing a behavior

         Bi = the individual's belief that performing the behavior B leads to some consequence i

         Ei = the individual's evaluation of consequence i

         N = the number of salient beliefs

(5)   If Ab, then NP.

         $NP = bm$

where NP = the normative pressure of a referent

         b = the subjective probability that a referent believes the individual should or should not perform a behavior

         m = the motivation to comply with referent

(6) $Sn = \sum_{j=1}^{N} bj\,mj$

where Sn = the subjective norm with respect to the behavior (i.e., the influence of the social environment on behavior B) bj = the normative belief regarding referent j's expectations as to whether the individual should or should not perform the behavior

mj = the individual's motivation to comply with referent j

N = the number of salient referents

(7) $B = I = (Ab)w1 + (Sn)w2$

where   B = the behavior under study

I = the individual's intention to perform the behavior

Ab = the individual's attitude toward performing a behavior

Sn = the subjective norm with respect to the behavior (i.e., the influence of the social environment on behavior B)

w1, w2 = empirically derived weights

PROPOSITIONS LOGICALLY DERIVED FROM THE EXPLANATORY MECHANISM

Fishbein's extended model has been incorporated with the previously reviewed research on corrective advertising in order to delineate a set of logically related propositions. The following propositions are based on relationships among the units of the theory and are deduced from the laws of interaction previously defined above. Outcomes in the form of behavior are specified in relation to corrective advertising.

- P1: A consumer's attitude toward the product, brand, or service (Ao) in a corrective advertisement is a function of his or her belief that the product, brand, or service is associated with some attribute, the consumer's evaluation of that attribute, and the number of salient object-attribute linkages in the consumer's belief hierarchy.

- P2: A consumer's attitude toward purchasing the product, brand, or service (Ab) in a corrective advertisement is a function of his or her belief that the purchase of the product, brand, or service is associated with some consequence, the consumer's evaluation of that consequence, and the number of salient purchase-consequence linkages in the consumer's belief hierarchy.

- P3: A consumer's subjective norm toward purchasing the product, brand, or service (Sn) in a corrective advertisement is a function of his or her belief that certain referents think he or she should or should not purchase the product, brand, or service, the consumer's motivation to comply with the referents, and the number of salient referents.

- P4: A consumer's purchase intentions toward a product, brand, or service (I) are a function of his or her attitude toward purchasing the product, brand, or service and the subjective norm surrounding its purchase. Purchase intentions are positively associated with purchases (B).

TABLE 1
Hypothetical Attitude Toward the Attributes of Brand X

Time	Attribute	B	E	Aa
Time 1	freshens breath	.90	+2	1.80
	hygienic	.60	+1	.60
	curative	.90	+2	1.80
Total				4.20
Corrective advertising				
Time 2	freshens breath	.90	+2	1.80
	hygienic	.60	+1	.60
	curative	.20	+2	.40
Total				2.80

Given: **Aa** = BE
where **Aa** = the attitude toward some attribute Brand X
  B = the subjective probability that Brand X is related to the attribute
  E = an evaluation of that attribute
Then: The consumer's attitudes toward the attributes of Brand X at Time 1 are "freshens breath" = 1.80; "hygienic" = .60; "curative" = 1.80.

Given: $Ao = \sum_{i=1}^{N} Bi\,Ei$
where Ao = the individual's attitude toward Brand X
  Bi = the probability that Brand X has the attribute i
  Ei = the individual's evaluation of attribute i
  N = the number of salient beliefs
Result: The consumer's attitude toward the product Brand X at Time 1 is 4.20.

AN ILLUSTRATION

The following hypothetical example is offered to illustrate how a corrective advertising campaign could lead to inferential belief formation and to predict and explain the outcomes of consumer attributions.

Theoretically, consumers use the information they obtain from outside sources, such as advertising, to form beliefs and make attributions that lead to attitudes about products, goods, or services. If average consumers from reasonable market segments have been exposed to advertising about Brand X mouthwash and have expended adequate cognitive effort, they might make the following object-attribute associations: Brand X freshens breath, is hygienic, and is curative. Linked with each belief are probabilities that the product indeed possesses these attributes as well as evaluations of the attributes. In Table 1, Time 1 provides a numerical computation of these belief structures.

Following the dissemination of the original message, it is determined that the curative claim in the Brand X advertisement is fallacious and a corrective advertising remedy is needed. If a message is designed and disseminated that refutes the curative claim, we would expect a weakening of the subjective probability that the attribute is associated with the object in Time 2 (see Table 1: reduction from Time 1 to Time 2 in *probability* of

TABLE 2
Hypothetical Attitude Toward the Consequences of Using Brand X

Time	Consequence	B	E	Ac
Time 1	social benefits	.90	+2	1.80
	fights plaque	.60	+1	.60
	prevents colds	.90	+2	1.80
Total				4.20
Corrective Advertising				
Time 2	social benefits	.90	+2	1.80
	fights plaque	.60	+1	.60
	prevents colds	.20	+2	.40
Total				2.80

Given: Ac = BE
where   Ac = the attitude toward some consequence of behavior B
        B = the subjective probability that the behavior is related to the consequence
        E = the evaluation of that consequence

Given: $Ab = \sum_{i=1}^{N} Bi\,Ei$

where   Ab = an individual's attitude toward performing a behavior
        Bi = the individual's belief that performing the behavior B leads to some consequence i
        Ei = the individual's evaluation of the consequence i
        N = the number of salient beliefs
Then: The consumer's attitude toward the expected consequences of using Brand X at Time 1 are "social benefits" = 1.80; "fights plaque" = .60; "prevents colds" = 1.80.
Then: The consumer's attitude toward the expected consequence of using Brand X at Time 2 are "social benefits" = 1.80; "fights plaque" = .60; "prevents colds" = .40.

curative attribute at B). In addition, the *attitude* toward the curative attribute (Aa) is affected by corrective advertising. Because of the summative nature of salient attitudes about the product after a corrective remedy, we would expect an overall negative change in beliefs about the product at Time 2. Thus *the consumer's attitude toward the product Brand X at Time 2 is 2.80.*

Because advertisements often deal with claims about the benefits of products, brands, or services, we would expect beliefs about the consequences, purchase, and use of a product to be strongly associated with attitudes about its attributes. That is, there should be a strong subjective probability that the behavior is related to the consequence. An advertisement at Time 1 and a correction in the curative attribute at Time 2 may cause the object-consequence probabilities and associations shown in Table 2.

When the consequences of attitudes are taken into account, in this case the intent to purchase and use a product, consumers' attitudes toward the behavior of purchasing and using Brand X before and after corrective advertising should produce a negative net outcome. The result in this case is a reduction from 4.20 to 2.80 in the overall attitude about the consequences of purchasing and using this product.

To the extent that normative pressures are important in predicting and explaining behaviors, Fishbein's attempt to model the relationships among

TABLE 3

Hypothetical Subjective Norm Toward the Purchasing of Brand X

Time	Referent	Belief	D	b	m	NP
Time 1	R1	should purchase	+	.90	+2	1.80
	R2	should purchase	+	.80	+2	1.60
	R3	should not purchase	−	.60	+1	−.60
	R4	should not purchase	−	.50	−3	1.50
Total						4.30
Corrective Advertising						
Time 2	R1	should purchase	+	.90	+2	1.80
	R2	should purchase	+	.80	+2	1.60
	R3	should not purchase	−	.60	+1	−.60
	R4	should not purchase	−	.50	−3	1.50
Total						4.30

The following is a summary of logical steps necessary to include a precise estimate of normative pressures (Sn) in the model:

Given: If Ab, then NP

Given: Ac = BE

Given: NP = bm

where   NP = the normative pressure of a referent

   b = the subjective probability that a referent believes the individual should or should not perform a behavior

   m = the motivation to comply with referent

Then: The normative pressure of the consumer's first referent in the hierarchy equals 1.80.

Given: $Sn = \sum_{j-1}^{N} bj\, mj\, D$

where   Sn = the subjective norm with respect to the behavior (i.e., the influence of the social environment on behavior B)

   bj = the normative belief regarding referent j's expectations as to whether the individual should or should not perform the behavior

   mj = the individual's motivation to comply with referent j

   N = the number of salient references

   D = the direction of advocacy (added)

Result: the consumer's subjective norm concerning the behavior of purchasing Brand X at Time 1 and Time 2 = 4.30.

beliefs, intentions, and behaviors had to account for the influence of such normative pressures on the final outcomes of concern. Thus, in developing the extended model, he attempted to quantify the impact of social pressures on behavioral intent in a relatively precise manner. It is important to note that the direction of advocacy must be reflected in the model such that referents with competing claims about whether an individual should or should not perform a behavior counterbalance each other. Table 3 provides an illustration of the kinds of subjective norms that might operate in this hypothetical example. Not included in Fishbein's model is column D, which reflects the direction of advocacy. In this case, if a referent tells an individual not to purchase a product, but the person's motivation to comply with the referent is negatively valued, we would expect this to lead to positive pressure to purchase the product.

Given the boundary conditions of this theory, we would not posit a corrective advertising campaign necessarily to have a direct effect on a consumer's normative pressures. Although there would likely be some modification in purchase intent if a consumer hears a referent criticize, or infers that a referent would criticize, the product or source of the product, such information derived from interpersonal channels is out of the domain of this media effects model. Thus no significant changes in a consumer's normative pressures are predicted based on the corrective advertisements alone.

In sum, a final formulation of the model predicts consumer behavior from the following weighted model:

Given: $B = I = (Ab)w1 + (Sn)w2$
where B = the behavior under study
         I = the individual's intention to perform the behavior
        Ab = an individual's attitude toward performing a behavior
        Sn = the subjective norm with respect to the behavior (i.e., the influence of the social environment on behavior B)
    $w1, w2$ = empirically derived weights

Inconsistent with the goals of those responsible for devising and enforcing corrective advertising policy (simply restoring attitudes to their level prior to exposure to deceptive advertising), this model posits that a consumer's purchase intentions at Time 2 would decrease as a result of corrective advertising. The exact calculations of B require w1 and w2 to be computed from multiple regression analyses. This hypothetical example illustrates that though there is some impact on purchase intent, the major impact is on the attitude component. The limited effects model presumably desired by regulatory agencies is fairly isomorphic with the results of the research suggesting minimal behavioral change, yet there are logical deficiencies in this extended model that must be repaired to explain and predict corrective advertising as it actually works.

AN EMPIRICAL TEST OF
CORRECTIVE ADVERTISING RESEARCH QUESTIONS
USING THE MODIFIED FISHBEIN MODEL

Burgoon and Burgoon (1978), under contract to Louis Harris and Associates for the Federal Trade Commission, conducted a field experiment of the effects of the STP corrective advertising campaign, providing a test of the modified Fishbein model. This study improved upon much of the corrective advertising research because a field experiment was conducted while the actual corrective advertisements were appearing in national publications.

The study involved a large sample of adults who voluntarily exposed themselves to the corrective advertisements as they appeared in publications, providing the independent variable within the design. Most corrective advertising studies cannot claim high ecological validity because they utilize student samples, data are collected in contrived environments, and researchers typically have inadequate funding actually to produce advertisements and test their social effects.

Several basic questions, phrased in a more abbreviated, general form earlier, were of interest in the study; the modified Fishbein model should be able to answer these:

(1) Did the corrective advertising campaign dispel false beliefs about the product (STP, specifically)?

(2) Did the advertising campaign affect attitudes toward other oil additives?

(3) Did the advertising campaign decrease intention to purchase STP?

(4) Did the corrective advertising adversely affect the overall image and credibility of the STP Corporation?

(5) Did the corrective advertising campaign negatively affect the public's attitudes toward the financial prospects and/or the publicly traded stock of the STP Corporation?

Method

A pretest-posttest design was used to provide answers to the research questions. As part of a consent order signed by the STP Corporation, $200,000 was to be spent by the company to place a public notice advertisement in 14 widely distributed periodicals. This notice was actually the corrective advertising, which suggested that previous claims made by the company were not true. The publications in which the agreed-upon advertisement appeared included the *Wall Street Journal, New York Times, Washington Post, Barron's, Newsweek, U.S. News & World Report, People,* and *Business Week.* In addition, *Screw Magazine* ran the advertisement on its own. Prior to the corrective advertising campaign, a quota sample with a 60:40 ratio of general public to business-related occupations was drawn and contacted for interviews by telephone from centralized phone banks. All calls were monitored by supervisors and the interviews were conducted by trained interviewers. A total of 823 adults completed the interviews and served as the baseline for subsequent data analyses.

A second wave of data collection, using identical procedures, was conducted seven days after the last advertisement appeared. The sample size of the Time 2 measurement was 845. Thus the power of this particular field experiment is substantial, and, as previously claimed, the entire process allowed controls and a degree of ecological validity that has not been achieved in much of the prior research on the effects of corrective advertising.

Data Analyses

Tests of significance were conducted using analysis of variance on all attitude items. Chi-square tests were also conducted on the few nominal-level measures used in the interview. If people had not been exposed to any of the periodicals during the time period the advertisements appeared, they were put in the No Exposure group. If people had read one or more of the print sources, they were put in the Exposed group and analyses were done on exposure. On each of the research questions, there was a main effect for potential exposure ($p < .05$), indicating (a) that the corrective advertising campaign had a significant impact, and (b) that the procedures used in this research were capable of detecting that impact.

Moreover, there was a statistically significant negative effect on all dependent measures in the Exposed group, not just a dispelling of previously stated false claims about the product in the advertisements ($p < .05$). In addition, there were no significant differences between the No Exposure group in Wave 2 and the control group of 823 people collected prior to the campaign ($p < .05$). This provides further evidence of the impact of the campaign. The effect sizes in all tests were substantial, indicating that the corrective advertising campaign had dramatic negative impacts that were not only statistically significant but socially important on all attitudes, beliefs, and intents measured.

Discussion

Obviously, the results provide rather compelling evidence about the questions addressed by the modified Fishbein model. Since the data produced far more negative results than the modified Fishbein model would have predicted, one must conclude that the modified Fishbein model is not an adequate predictor of the effects of corrective advertising. In fact, the results were so dramatically negative concerning the impact on a variety of attitudes, beliefs, and intentions, one policy implication discussed was that it would be difficult to get corporations to sign consent orders, rather than litigate, if they knew how negative the results of corrective advertising campaigns could be. Such a discrepancy between data collected in a well-controlled field study indicates a need for further refinement and alterations in the modified Fishbein model, if it is to be useful in the domain of corrective advertising. This need for refinement and theoretical development is also especially pressing given the confounded, confusing nature of the extant research literature. Given the failure of the modified Fishbein model to withstand empirical scrutiny, the remainder of this chapter will attempt to provide additional alternative approaches to explaining and predicting the effects of corrective advertising campaigns.

A MODIFIED MODEL
OF CORRECTIVE ADVERTISING EFFECTS

A major problem with Fishbein's extended model is that source evaluations and product evaluations are summed to become a part of the overall attitude measure (Ao). In that much prior research clearly establishes a causal path from evaluations of credibility to formation of attitudes, it is quite possible in the case of corrective advertising that the credibility of the company may actually be enhanced in a company/company sequence (Jolly & Mowen, 1985; Lammers, 1985). Indeed, some research reveals that people perceive the company as more "trustworthy" when it corrects past mistakes. Conversely, when the sequence is company/FTC, deception is implied by the presence of the FTC, and consumers may make judgments about the company that override any attitudes they have about the product. By way of example, a person may never have purchased Brand X and may have a neutral to favorable attitude about its attributes. Once a corrective remedy is in place, particularly with the attribution of FTC enforcement, the consumer may determine never to purchase the product because of the deceptive practices of the company. If the Fishbein model were implemented to explain the outcome of this case, it would mathematically support a limited effects interpretation because the positive product attributes and the negative source attributes are summed, resulting in a relatively minor decrease in overall attitude (Ao). This could be the case even though the person has resolved never to purchase the product again. In most corrective advertising research, source evaluation and sequencing variables are left uncontrolled; the fact that at least source evaluations were measured by Burgoon and Burgoon (1978) may explain part of the discrepancy between their findings and those that would have been predicted by the modified Fishbein model.

Obviously, negative source evaluations such as those found in some empirical work (Burgoon & Burgoon, 1978; Hunt, 1973) can supersede any product evaluations and have direct impact on intent and behavior; such evaluations must be built into the model if it is to have explanatory power. The following modifications in the extended model add theoretical specificity and predictive precision:

- P5: Evaluations of the original source and the source of the corrective advertisement are causally related to and antecedent to evaluations of those beliefs related to intentions and behaviors.

- P5a: A company/company condition is associated with decreases in a consumer's

  Aa = attitude toward some attribute of a product, brand, or service

  Ac = attitude toward some consequence of purchasing a product, brand, or service

    I = intention to purchase a product, brand, or service

    B = purchase of a product, brand, or service

- P5b: A company/company sequence condition may lead to an increase in

  As = attitude toward some attribute of the source of the deceptive advertisement

- P6: In all cases, a company/FTC sequence condition rather than a com-
  pany/company sequence condition is associated with greater decreases in

  attitude toward the product, brand, or service

  attitude toward the source of the deceptive advertisement

  attitude toward purchasing the product, brand, or service

  purchase intentions

  purchases

- P7: A consumer's attitude toward the source of the deceptive advertisement
  (As) is a function of his or her belief that the source of the deception is associated with some attribute, the consumer's evaluation of that attribute, and the
  number of salient object-attribute linkages in the consumer's belief hierarchy.

- P8: A company/FTC sequence can cause such negative evaluations to be made of
  a company that purchase intent (I) and actual purchasing behavior (B) are significantly decreased even without a change in the evaluation of the product attributes
  (Aa) or the overall attitude toward the object of correct advertising (Ao).

Table 4 illustrates how the addition of these propositions (P5 to P8) can
alter the predictions made about the final outcomes of a corrective advertising campaign. Clearly, the introduction of corrective advertising brings
about a new salient belief concerning deception at Time 2 that significantly
alters beliefs about the source formed at Time 1.

Thus the consumer's attitude toward the intent of the source of the deceptive advertisement at Time 1 = 3.10. However, the attitude at Time 2,
which has a high probability of occurring in a company/FTC sequence,
would be −4.40.

The following formula better represents what happens in the sequential
message condition of corrective advertising:

Given: $B2 = I = (As)w3 + (Ab)w1 + (Sn)w2$

where $B2$ = the behavior under study after corrective advertising

        I = the individual's intention to perform the behavior

        As = the individual's evaluation of the source after corrective advertising

        Ab = the individual's attitude toward performing the behavior

        Sn = the subjective norm with respect to the behavior

$w1, w2, w3$ = empirically derived weights

This model is an improvement over the extended Fishbein model in that
the summative procedures give an independent and critical weight derived
from regression analyses to the source/sequence. This allows the weighted

TABLE 4

Hypothetical Attitude Toward the Source of an Advertisement

Time	Belief	B	E	As
Time 1	competent	.90	+3	2.70
	trustworthy	.30	+1	.30
	dynamic	.10	+1	.10
	deceptive	n/a	n/a	n/a
Corrective Advertising				
Time 2	competent	.00	+3	.00
	trustworthy	.00	+1	.00
	dynamic	.10	+1	.10
	deceptive	.90	−5	−4.50

Given: As = BE
where   As = the attitude toward some attribute of the source of the deceptive advertisement
       B = the subjective probability that the source is related to the attribute
       E = an evaluation of that attribute
Then: The consumer's attitudes toward the attributes at Time 1 are competent = 2.70; trustworthy = .30;
       dynamic = .10; deceptive = .00.

       The consumer's attitudes toward the attributes at Time 2 are competent = .00; trustworthy = .00;
       dynamic = .10; deceptive = −4.50.

Given $As = \sum_{i=1}^{N} B_i E_i$
where   As = the attitude toward the intent of the source of the deceptive advertisement
       Bi = the probability that the intent of the source has attribute i
       Ei = the evaluation of attribute i
       N = the number of salient beliefs

source evaluation term to have more impact in the determination of intent (I) and subsequent behavior (B2) than the summative process, which allows As to become a part of Ab and then become weighted. Although this model represents a significant improvement in the extended Fishbein model, it is not the optimal model if one conceptualizes prior attitudes/behaviors and source evaluation as antecedent to, and causally related to, the behavior after a corrective advertising campaign. The path model depicted in Figure 1 more clearly demonstrates the possible causal links among the elements in the extended Fishbein model and the modified corrective advertising model developed in this chapter.

This path model suggests that prior behavior affects the perceived credibility of the company in different ways. The attitude toward a source during a corrective campaign is particularly dependent on the source sequence (company/company or company/FTC) and whether or not the path continues such that source evaluation affects product evaluation or bypasses all evaluative responses to the product and has direct impact on intent to purchase and, ultimately, purchase decisions. Such precision in prediction, especially when each term is modified by empirically determined weights (w) or path coefficients, allows for a great deal of predictive ability and explanatory

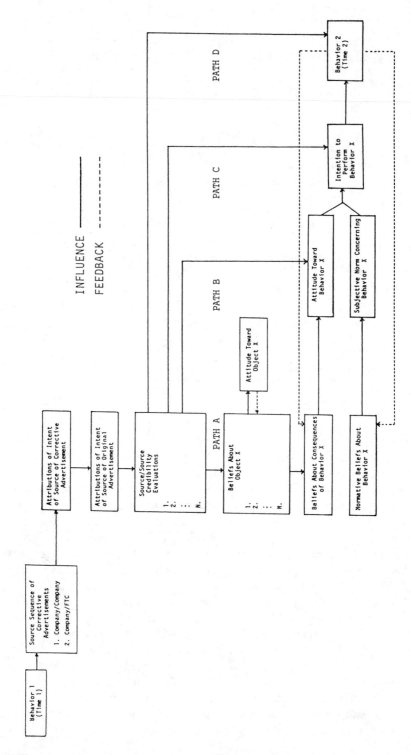

Figure 1. Path model of the possible causal links among the elements in the extended Fishbein model and the modified corrective advertising model.

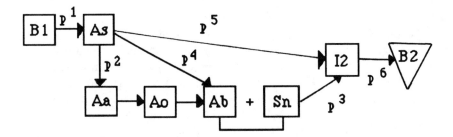

Figure 2. Modified corrective advertising model of belief, attitude, intention, and behavior.

validity not afforded in the additive models previously used in attitude/behavior research. Figure 2 presents a more complete visual representation of the modified corrective advertising model.

DISCUSSION AND IMPLICATIONS

Implications for Research in Corrective Advertising

It has been argued that research in corrective advertising is needlessly confusing and confounded by lack of theoretical precision and methodological sophistication. As an alternative to the variable-analytic approach most often used by survey researchers who analyze an ordered corrective remedy, a theoretical model has been developed that adds precision to the prediction of the multiple effects of a corrective advertising campaign. This chapter provides a propositional framework with an explanatory calculus that specifies antecedent conditions and possible outcomes that may obtain under varying conditions. Initially, Fishbein's extended model was used to derive a small number of propositions that apply to the corrective advertising situation. Original research, conducted in a controlled field study, has been reported that indicates the modified model has problems in predicting the impact of a corrective advertising campaign. Logical deficiencies in that model were corrected by adding propositions applicable to corrective advertising. As a result, several new propositions were derived that allowed the addition of a weighted term for the source sequence and formulation of a summative model of media effects. A causal path model elucidating possible relationships among original beliefs, source of a corrective advertisement, attitudes toward a product or service, consequences of behavior, and norm components has been offered as the optimal analytic framework. This predictive path model is superior to the Fishbein formulation because, unlike the extended model, which is summative, this causal model specifies time order and alternative paths that allow for a range in media effects from maximal to very limited changes in attitudes and behaviors.

Implications for Regulatory Agencies

The theoretical model suggests that regulators such as the FTC may be enforcing policies that militate against the limited media effects outcomes they appear to embrace. Specifically, if all the regulatory agency desires is the restoration of beliefs to a level equal to that existing prior to the deceptive advertising, such an outcome is least likely if a company/FTC sequence is employed. A consumer's belief that an advertiser has been deceptive makes more likely the causal path from source evaluation directly to intent. Even when attribute evaluations are positive, the resulting decision is to discontinue prior purchasing behavior or to resolve never to try the product.

Though the research remains unclear on the magnitude of harm corrective advertising may bring company image and product purchase intent, it is manifest that some corrective advertising campaigns have resulted in significant damage to the corporate image and/or credibility of the producer. Unless models can be developed that predict rather precisely how likely changes are in attitudes toward the product, credibility of the company, and, ultimately, purchasing of the product, it is quite probable that organizations are going to be less willing to sign consent orders and initiate corrective advertising campaigns without first exhausting lengthy litigation processes. The modified model of corrective advertising presented here allows a more precise test of the relations among multiple variables and provides a heuristic base for research that can inform policy in both regulatory agencies and organizations involved in corrective advertising decision making.

Implications for General
Theoretical Development in Social Influence

In addition to having policy implications for regulators, this derived model also could apply to a variety of social influence situations and contribute to theoretical models of persuasion in general. Since the Fishbein model has been used in general persuasion research in contexts ranging from interpersonal influence attempts to the social effects of the mass media, the proposed alterations offered in this chapter should have applicability to those social influence situations in which the Fishbein model (in whatever iteration) has previously been used. However, the proposed alternative propositional framework and attendant causal model should have more predictive precision, in general, than the previously used Fishbein model. Moreover, the explanatory calculus offered in support of the alternative framework should have wide applicability in providing theoretical support about all kinds of attacks, refutations, and arguments that occur when individuals attempt to persuade or to undo the effects of prior persuasive efforts. For example, in the area of argumentation the proposed model adds theoretical specificity to cases in which an individual is attempting to refute previously stated claims he or she may believe to be untrue but that have been accepted. The path model should explain how an individual can get an audience or an individual to *reverse* attitudes toward previously accepted arguments and/or claims.

The proposed theoretical schema has great potential value in such contexts as political communication, health campaigns, organizational public affairs, and other situations in which policy or action claims are being advanced to alter public opinion at the sociological level. This utility stems from its systematically incorporating source characteristics, attributional intent, and norms, and adding a stochastic element that produces predictions about *sequences* of persuasive efforts. To date, in too many instances attempts to change the beliefs and behaviors of heterogeneous audiences have been variable-analytic and atheoretical. This chapter has examined the theoretically critical elements in terms of logical structure and content that will lead to desired outcomes in altering beliefs, intentions, attitudes, and behaviors for researchers interested in mass persuasion.

REFERENCES

Aaker, D. A. (1974). Deceptive advertising. In D. A. Aaker & G. S. Day (Eds.), *Consumerism: Search for the consumer interest* (2nd ed., pp. 137-156). New York: Free Press.

Allison, N. K., & Mizerski, R. W. (1981). The effects of recall on belief change: The corrective advertising case. In K. B. Monroe (Ed.), *Advances in consumer research* (Vol. 8, pp. 419-422). Arlington, VA: Association for Consumer Research.

Armstrong, G. M., Franke, G. R., & Russ, F. A. (1982). The effects of corrective advertising on company image. *Journal of Advertising, 11*, 39-47.

Armstrong, G. M., Gurol, M. N., & Russ, F. A. (1983a). Corrective advertising: A review and evaluation. In J. H. Leigh & C. R. Martin, Jr. (Eds.), *Current issues and research in advertising* (pp. 93-113). Ann Arbor: University of Michigan, Graduate School of Business Administration, Division of Research.

Armstrong, G. M., Gurol, M. N., & Russ, F. A. (1983b). A longitudinal evaluation of the Listerine corrective advertising campaign. *Journal of Public Policy and Marketing, 2*, 16-28.

Belch, G. E., Belch, M. A., Settle, R. B., & DeLucchi, L. M. (1981). An examination of consumers' perception of purpose and content of corrective advertising. In A. Mitchell (Ed.), *Advances in consumer research* (Vol. 9, pp. 327-332). St. Louis, MO: Association for Consumer Research.

Bernhardt, K. L., Kinnear, T. C., Mazis, M. B., & Reece, B. B. (1980). Impact of publicity on corrective advertising effects. In K. B. Monroe (Ed.), *Advances in consumer research* (Vol. 8, pp. 414-415). Washington, DC: Association for Consumer Research.

Burgoon, J. K., & Burgoon, M. (1978). *The effects of the STP corrective advertising campaign.* Unpublished research report.

Burke, R. R., DeSarbo, W. S., Oliver, R. L., & Robertson, T. S. (1988). Deception by implication: An experimental investigation. *Journal of Consumer Research, 14*, 483-494.

Dyer, R. F., & Kuehl, P. G. (1974). Source and strength effects in corrective advertising. In S. Ward & P. Wright (Eds.), *Advances in consumer research* (Vol. 1, pp. 85-86). Urbana, IL: Association for Consumer Research.

Dyer, R. F., & Kuehl, P. G. (1978). A longitudinal study of corrective advertising. *Journal of Marketing Research, 15*, 39-48.

Fishbein, M. (1967). A behavior theory approach to the relations between beliefs about an object and the attitude toward the object. In M. Fishbein (Ed.), *Readings in attitude theory and measurement* (pp. 389-399). New York: John Wiley.

Fishbein, M., & Ajzen, I. (1974). *Belief, attitude, intention and behavior: An introduction to theory and research.* Reading, MA: Addison-Wesley.

Hunt, H. K. (1973). Effects of corrective advertising. *Journal of Advertising Research, 13,* 15-22.

Jacoby, J., Nelson, M. C., & Hoyer, W. D. (1982). Corrective advertising and affirmative disclosure statements: Their potential for confusing and misleading the consumer. *Journal of Marketing, 46,* 61-72.

Jolly, D. W., & Mowen, J. C. (1985). Product recall communications: The effects of source, media and social responsibility information. *Advances in Consumer Research, 12,* 471-475.

Kinnear, T. C., Taylor, J. R., & Gur-Arie, O. (1983). Affirmative disclosure: Long-term monitoring of residual effects. *Journal of Public Policy and Marketing, 2,* 38-45.

Kuehl, P. G., & Dyer, R. F. (1978). Brand belief measures in deceptive corrective advertising: An experimental assessment. In H. K. Hunt (Ed.), *Advances in consumer research* (Vol. 5, pp. 373-397). Chapel Hill, NC: Association for Consumer Research.

Lamb, C. W., Jr., & Stutts, M. A. (1979). The impact of corrective advertising upon consumers' attitudes, beliefs and behavior. *Journal of the Academy of Marketing Science, 7,* 307-315.

Lammers, H. B. (1985). The overkill effect of corrective advertising: An Heiderian perspective on the influence of corrective advertisement sponsorship on cognitive responses toward the company. *Advances in Consumer Research, 12,* 426-431.

Maddox, L. M., & Zanot, E. J. (1979). Corrective advertising: Review and prognosis. In J. H. Leigh & C. R. Martin, Jr. (Eds.), *Current issues and research in advertising* (pp. 53-63). Ann Arbor: University of Michigan, Graduate School of Business Administration, Division of Research.

Mazis, M. B., & Adkinson, J. E. (1976). An experimental evaluation of a proposed corrective advertising remedy. *Journal of Marketing Research, 13,* 178-183.

Mazis, M. B., McNeill, D. L., & Bernhardt, K. L. (1983). Day-after recall of Listerine corrective commercials. *Journal of Public Policy and Marketing, 2,* 29-37.

Mizerski, R. W., Allison, N. K., & Calvert, S. (1980). A controlled field study of corrective advertising using multiple exposures and a commercial medium. *Journal of Marketing Research, 17,* 341-358.

Nkonge, J. H. (1984). How communication medium and message format affect corrective advertising. *Journal of Academy of Marketing Science, 12,* 58-68.

Sawyer, A. G., & Semenik, R. J. (1978). Carryover effects of corrective advertising. In H. K. Hunt (Ed.), *Advances in consumer research* (Vol. 5, pp. 343-351). Ann Arbor, MI: Association for Consumer Research.

Scammon, D. L., McNeil, D., & Preston, I. (1980). The FTC's emerging theory of consumer protection via increased information. In *Proceedings, American Marketing Association Theory Conference.*

Semenik, R. J. (1980). Corrective advertising: An experimental evaluation of alternative television messages. *Journal of Advertising, 9,* 21-30.

Tyebjee, T. T. (1982). The role of publicity in FTC corrective advertising remedies. *Journal of Marketing & Public Policy, 1,* 111-121.

Wilkie, W. L. (1974). Research on counter and corrective advertising. In S. F. Divita (Ed.), *Advertising and the public interest* (pp. 189-202). Chicago: American Marketing Association.

Wilkie, W. L., McNeill, D. L., & Mazis, M. B. (1984). Marketing's "scarlet letter": The theory and practice of corrective advertising. *Journal of Marketing, 48,* 11-31.

Deception, Accountability, and Theoretical Refinement

RICHARD E. CRABLE
California State University, Sacramento

HE social and economic importance of deceptive advertising justi-
fies its serious study, and Burgoon, Newton, and Birk add much to
our understanding. In addition, the methodology they use is worthy
of further comment, and the modifications or alterations of Fishbein's theorizing have implications far beyond the subject of this commentary. Indeed,
even though my own research is critical/theoretical and focuses more generally on political rhetoric, argumentation, public relations, and issue management, the Burgoon, Newton, and Birk chapter provides the opportunity
for a discussion of some mutual concerns.

As readers undoubtedly have judged, the chapter ultimately revolves
around a method of determining whether or not "corrective" advertising
accomplishes too much. To readers not acquainted with the specific content
of the chapter, that may seem to be a very strange sort of "ultimate" concern. Communicators in general worry less about achieving too much impact than about achieving too little; advertisers, I think, seldom worry
about creating too much demand for a product; and public relations people
infrequently feel that they have helped generate too much goodwill toward
an organization. One might speculate that corrective advertising is an interestingly deviant sort of communication. It is.

In order to assess the essay, readers should understand the relative
stances of the participants when corrective advertising is begun. Potential
or actual customers of a product or service have been misled or "deceived"
by an advertisement or (more typically) an advertising campaign. When
such deception is clearly established (by whom the deception is established
is a topic taken up later in this commentary), the Federal Trade Commission may initiate action aimed at securing the correction of the false or

Correspondence and requests for reprints: Richard E. Crable, Department of Communication
Studies, California State University, Sacramento, CA 95819.

Communication Yearbook 15, pp. 287-298

misleading statements. Organizations "caught" engaging in deceptive advertising may choose to deny the allegations, even if this means a costly and time-consuming court action.

Alternatively, the organization and the FTC may enter into an agreement or "consent decree" affirming that "corrective" messages will be issued at the expense of the organization. In essence, as a reward for saving the regulatory agency (and taxpayers) a lengthy and costly court action, the organization is supposed to "correct" the deceptive conceptions possibly created. *No punishment is intended.* The new messages simply are supposed to "restore" the situation to what it was prior to the dissemination of the deceptive message(s), to return audience beliefs to what they were before the deception occurred. In the *maximally* successful corrective advertising campaign, the negative impacts of the new messages on the organization and its products/services are intended to be truly *minimal*.

Burgoon, Newton, and Birk have provided an interesting, useful, and thought-provoking study about the more precisely stated and measured effects of corrective advertising. I find the study interesting on three increasingly broad levels. Specifically in this commentary, those levels are reflected in three areas of concern: the chapter itself, the conceptual issues it raises for me, and (as a part of my concluding remarks) the regulatory policy discussion it seems to invite.

ISSUES PRESENTED IN THE CHAPTER

From their abstract onward, Burgoon, Newton, and Birk make it clear that their chapter is at least in part a response to the current lack of clarity and specificity about the results of efforts to "correct" instances of deceptive advertising. They acknowledge the inconsistent findings of such research and propose an intellectual means not necessarily of resolving the inconsistencies but of explaining why such findings have arisen. In essence, they argue that the inconsistent findings may be explained by theoretical difficulties that have given way to problematic research results. What they succeed in doing in this chapter is to intertwine theoretical concepts and assumptions with research in ways such that both present theory and future research may be enhanced. This intertwining can be seen in a brief review of the issues raised in the essay.

First, Burgoon and his colleagues demonstrate that Fishbein's earlier model presumed that behavior toward an object could be predicted on the basis of attitude toward that object. In general the problem with such an assumption is that it fails to account for the complexity of the situation; that is, as Fishbein came to specify in his extended model, behavior is determined by the individual's intention to perform or not perform some behavior. The authors provide an excellent rationale for why a modified Fishbein model might *seem* to be an entirely appropriate base for research into corrective advertising. Despite a foreshadowing that "summative judgments" may make even a modified model inadequate, they list clearly the predicted outcomes in corrective advertising as implied in the extended theory.

Having now the (presumably but not actually) adequate theory, the authors then engage in a treatment of that theory that I think clearly is the key to understanding the strength of the chapter. The treatment is based on the results of the Burgoon and Burgoon (1978) study of the impact of STP's corrective advertising. That study, strong by such measures as ecological validity, indicates that the corrective advertising did far more than simply "restore" the situation to what it was prior to the transmission of deceptive messages. The negative effect on several dependent measures—not simply a dispelling of a previously believed but deceptive claim—leads the authors to advance two critical claims: first, that corrective advertising may generate outcomes far in excess of what the regulatory body wishes, and, second, that even the extended Fishbein model "is not an adequate predictor of the effects of corrective advertising." In what strikes me as a near perfect case of the intelligent interplay of theory and research, Burgoon, Newton, and Birk use what appears to be some fine research as the necessary evidence for claims relating to the task of theory building: In this case, which arguably is not typical, the adequacy of the theory *as applied* (not the research) is called into question by the inconsistency between the anticipated results and the actual outcomes.

As promised, however, a third and final issue I see implied in the chapter concerns what exactly is accomplished as the chapter evolves. Based on the treatment of the theory just reviewed, the alleged inadequacy of the extended Fishbein theory invites further theory refinement. The authors supply one such refinement as they offer ways of measuring the source/sequence variation that eliminate some of the problems with summative measurements. In addition, they generate a path model that they argue is better able to account for the existence of attitudes/behaviors/judgments of source credibility prior to (and causally related to) behavior after a corrective campaign.

What the authors accomplish by the development and presentation of their findings, then, seems to me to require consideration at a number of levels. First, at the level of praxis, the chapter sheds interesting light on what it means to issue a corrective message. That issuance may well mean more than the act of restoring a situation to the one that existed prior to dissemination of a deceptive advertising message. It may mean so much more in terms of attitudes toward products and even companies that (second, at a policy level) regulatory agencies may be reluctant to argue for corrective messages and that (third, at a sociolegal level) companies may be extremely reluctant to consent to issue such messages without a full set of court hearings. Not to be ignored, of course, is the sense in which the results and analysis in the chapter represent accomplishments at the (fourth) theoretical level. The chapter, with its refinements of Fishbein and its created path model, should provide an invitation for others to pursue the research direction begun here. As presented, then, the chapter clearly provides reason to believe that we now know more about corrective advertising than we did before reading it.

My commentary thus far obviously reveals my positive reaction to the chapter as presented, but "the chapter as presented" was identified as simply the first of three areas of comment. Other, more "questioning"—not actually negative—reactions relate to the other two areas: certain conceptual issues and some policy concerns. Some of these reactions relate to matters specified *in* the chapter, some to matters merely suggested *by* the chapter. Most of the remainder of my commentary deals with some concerns I have at the conceptual level.

CONCEPTUAL ISSUES

Burgoon, Newton, and Birk have performed a valuable service by clarifying the concepts relevant to corrective advertising—by perhaps clarifying concepts even more generally relevant to persuasion and argumentation. Yet research is doubly valuable if it stimulates thought and ideas in others as it offers its own conclusions. The remainder of this commentary is less a response to the chapter per se than it is a response to ideas and issues that (for me, at least) seem to arise from it. This section, then, will involve discussions of the concepts of accountability, deception, judgment of deception, message source, and message variability.

Accountability

In commonsense terms, corrective advertising is a means of forcing or allowing organizations to be accountable for their actions—and their messages. The terms *force* and *allow* are both used here because it clearly is possible for organizations to realize after the fact that they have engaged in deceptive advertising and so themselves initiate corrective measures. More typically, one supposes, an organization is faced with some other body's discovery of the deception and the organization signs a consent decree that involves the issuance of corrective messages. This latter case is not, strictly speaking, "force" because the organization has the choice of engaging in a perhaps lengthy and costly legal action, but such action might result in image and purchase impacts far more severe than any that may be associated with corrective messages. Despite distinctions in the situations, it remains the case that any form and any source of corrective advertising is relevant to organizations being accountable for their message effects.

But what then is accountability? Unlike the commonsense understandings just mentioned, accountability *does not* imply that an organization *has been* made to answer for wrongdoing. It means simply that the organization *may be* made to answer for such activity. Organizations, then, face a constant "liability" in that they are "liable" to be called "to account" for their activity at any time (Crable, 1978). While organizations are not sure that they *will* be called to account, the possibility—and the uncertainty prompted by that possibility— will be omnipresent. That uncertain but possible accounting, as Burke (1954) has indicated, is a major way of "regulating" human behavior (p. 269). In the case of accountability represented in this study, the theoretical expectation is that organizations would so wish to avoid any actual accounting for deceptive messages that they would be scrupulously honest in their advertising strategies. For this to happen, one must assume that organizations would view the negative impact of any "amends making" or actual accounting to be so substantial that any possible gains from deception would be clearly overshadowed by the risk of having to make corrections.

As a regulating process, then, accountability—the liability of being called to account, defend, or justify—is an instrument of deterrence based on possible punishment. Yet Burgoon and his colleagues tell us that punishment or *net negative* impact is *not supposed* to be the result of corrective advertising. In saying that, they tell us that corrective advertising (ironically) is essentially irrelevant to societal accountability; that is, since it is supposed simply to restore the situation to what it was before the deception, "successful" corrective advertising (a return to the status quo) scarcely is capable of being a believable deterrent.

I shall return to this question of accountability as it relates to policy matters later, but for now we may consider it one of the interesting conceptual matters to arise in the chapter. Moreover, given that potential accountability relates to deception, it is appropriate that the next concept to be discussed is deception itself.

Deception

The several dictionaries I have consulted are unanimous that *deception* refers to "deceiving or intending to deceive." Though at first reading this may seem to be a near tautology—seemingly as unhelpful as the statement "A horse is a rather horselike animal," the definition is critical to an understanding of some conceptual problems with both corrective advertising and research into corrective advertising. That is, the identification of *deception* as "deceiving or intending to deceive" presents us with at least four substantially different alternative situations. Ignoring at the outset which of these might seem most/least likely or most/least believable, let us consider these four possible cases and then how they each might relate to corrective advertising.

In what I shall call Case 1, an advertiser *attempts but does not succeed* in deceiving. Messages containing false or misleading statements either are not received by market audiences or are not believed by those audiences who do receive/have received the message. The intent to deceive is present, but no one believes the falsehoods or misleading statements. Instances of this first case occur when demonstrably guilty politicians claim innocence but are not believed, or when an advertisement promises social success to audiences who remain aware that social success is based on more than clean breath.

In contrast to the *unsuccessful intent* to deceive just introduced, Case 2 involves *unintentional success* at deception. Not meaning to be playful with the contrast, I refer to instances in which audiences in general and audiences as consumers specifically may come to believe false or misleading statements through unintentionally created misunderstanding. In this case, scientific terms may confuse or accidentally mislead; diagrams may be incorrectly interpreted; qualifiers concerning product performance may be ignored. Were any of these to occur, advertisers accused of "deception" might legitimately claim that while deception occurred, receivers primarily (and unfortunately) deceived themselves. While deception existed, there actually was no villain in the situation.

Case 3 involves what perhaps most typically is thought of as deception: Audiences come to believe messages that contain purposefully false or misleading statements, explanations, or illustrations. *Explicit intentional success* at deceiving others might seem to be the paradigm case of deception: Statements (and so on) known to be untrue are presented as reasons to purchase a product or service.

Arguably more frequent, but more difficult to "police," are instances of *implicit intentional success* in deception. Aftershave advertisements abound with gorgeous women and (in turn) other advertisements abound in which women with newly colored hair are shown surrounded by handsome and admiring men, but no *explicit* deception occurs. Case 4 thus presents situations in which advertisers intentionally generate scenarios predicted to prompt receivers to "deceive themselves." False statements are not made, but message contexts are visualized with the expectation that false impressions almost undoubtedly will be created. Even at this implicit, more subtle level, *deception* is hardly an irrelevant term.

Corrective advertising will not be found to relate equally to these four cases of potential deception, but clearly that is not a criticism to be leveled at Burgoon, Newton, and Birk. Corrective advertising seems oriented toward Case 3, explicit and intentional success in falsifying or misleading. While the policy aspects of that fact will be dealt with later, what is important here is deception at the conceptual level.

The research implications of these four varied conceptions of deception seem obvious. Burgoon, Newton, and Birk's study advances our understanding of corrective advertising, but it (much as with Fishbein's extension) can be refined even more once the complexity of deception as a variable is recognized. While it is possible to consider collectively (and as an undifferentiated whole) any and all instances of what the FTC calls "deceptive," more insight *for the academic field* will arise if better discriminations are built into the research project. Better discriminations among types of deception may provide some relevant additional understanding of corrective advertising per se, but making such discriminations should result in a great deal more insight into communication in general—and this latter realm of implication is a claimed concern of Burgoon and his colleagues. In their additional studies in the area, perhaps they might turn their attention to kinds of deception as a varying situation.

Judgment of Deception

A third concept I find intriguing is the "judgment of deception." Burgoon, Newton, and Birk seem to me to be justified in claiming that their treatment of the issues constitutes an advance in this respect. I find it likely that the audience's judgment of deception arises particularly when the FTC performs the role of source (or at least/even instigator) of the corrective message. The authors make a contribution in arguing that we must consider that judgment (or conclusion) as another and separate element in the situation. With Fishbein, we have our attention turned toward attitudes or evaluations of the messages that obviously are present in the situation. With the authors' help here, we also may focus on and attempt to measure a newly created element: audience belief that deception has occurred. That is no small contribution.

On the other hand, a more complete understanding of the situation— "more complete" here meaning that for the moment we ignore the more specialized concerns of the FTC—would require that we consider the varying senses in which "deception" may be charged. This idea clearly depends on one's beliefs that the four cases of deception mentioned earlier are indeed diverse enough to make a difference. I think they are, and I think that the audiences who might be involved in such different situations probably would feel the same. In interpersonal situations, in public apologies by government officials, and in advertising, I would argue that audiences do in fact perceive real differences among the cases as described. In common parlance, the success of an explicit and intentional effort to deceive likely will lead to a more damning public reaction than deception that occurs merely as a misunderstanding—for which the public may even see itself as partially to blame (Crable, 1978). Those public reactions will be no more alike than the message efforts were in the beginning. Both, however, are instances of the judgment of deception.

Again, ignoring policy considerations for the moment, a more complete understanding of what it means to make a "judgment of deception" requires that we make allowance for those judgments to vary in accordance with the perception of "what kind of" deception has occurred. Those perceptions will vary, and the variance makes the entire situation a great deal more complex and difficult. Yet to ignore that complexity and to avoid that difficulty would be to restrict the validity of future research.

Complexity and difficulty, in fact, have emerged as themes in this discussion of certain conceptual issues. Those themes continue as we turn to an examination of a fourth concept: message source.

Message Source

One of the clear contributions of Burgoon, Newton, and Birk's work is the aforementioned differentiation of the possible sources of deceptive and corrective messages. Intuitively, companies who correct their own messages without outside prompting and companies whose messages are corrected because of intervention by an outside agency such as the FTC seem to constitute crucially different cases. As the authors argue, organizational rhetoricians who correct their own messages actually may enhance their credibility; those whose messages must be corrected by others may be adjudged guilty of deception. One way of viewing the situation is to say that this analysis affirms the importance of what has been discussed about the types of deception and the correspondingly variable judgments of deception.

A second perspective that I would like to develop here, however, is that even the complexity suggested by the authors or by the preceding paragraph fails to reflect the situation clearly. Because of the focused concern of the authors, a concentration so exclusively on a particular company and the FTC is reasonable. Such a concentration is what allowed Burgoon, Newton, and Birk to generate the insight they do into the importance of the source of corrective messages: I am convinced that a company/FTC sequence of messages (deceptive/corrective) probably will result in greater negative effects than will a company/company sequence. The authors' path model helps us to understand, plot, and measure those differences.

On the other hand, the age of investigative reporting and consumer advocacy suggests that any model and any approach that presumes the exclusive importance of a company and the FTC fails to appreciate the reality of the media environment in which we live at the very end of the twentieth century. A survey of newspapers in the last 20 or so years will confirm personal reflection: Instances of deception are not always discovered by the FTC or originally admitted by the company responsible. While Burgoon, Newton, and Birk write realistically of "media coverage" as a factor in how audiences may respond to messages, it also seems fair to say that media or interest groups themselves may be the discoverers, announcers, and publicizers of alleged deception.

If that were found to be the case, then the model and discussion presented by Burgoon and his colleagues would need expanding. The importance of message source would remain and indeed would be seen as even more important. But the list of potential sources of the corrective message would have to be elongated. Moreover and more important, as that list is seen to grow, so also would the variations in levels of credibility attached by audiences to the various sources. The chapter discussed here improves Fishbein's model by adding the possibility of two different sources, with different implications for judgments of corrective messages from them. But that variability is simply the beginning. A more exacting study of the possibilities would include potentially different judgments as consumer groups or members of Congress or members of the American Medical Association or others seem to engage in what amount to "other-generated" corrective messages. An example may serve to illustrate.

As 1990 closed, Converse had been arguing in advertisements that the technology of the company's newly developed athletic shoes would "return" about 50% of the "energy you exert" (Milkey, 1990). Not only was this the latest in a very long line of athletic shoe developments, but also it was clearly suspect. Note, however, that among the sources of (unofficial) corrective advertising was the chairperson of the Athletic Footwear Committee of the American Society of Testing and Materials, who asked, "How can you measure something [referring to energy return] for which no standard definition exists?" (Burfoot; quoted in Milkey, 1990). Burfoot implies that, while "energy return" began with validity in the 1970s, it was an outgrowth of research on characteristics of *tracks*, not the shoes used upon them. Any *valid* adaptation of the concept to shoes remains to be made.

Regardless of the ultimate outcome of that case, the point perhaps is clear. Various bodies and individuals—not merely the company or the FTC—can become engaged in what amounts to the "correction of deceptive advertising." Those concerns may not equal the narrower technical concept of corrective advertising discussed here. On the other hand, those concerns might indicate areas of concentration for someone's future research; though the FTC may not be interested in any except its own efforts to "correct," communication scholars and citizens in general cannot afford such an exclusive arena of interest. The consideration of the range of variability in sources—and the corresponding judgment of those sources—might be a means for Burgoon and his colleagues to argue the broader implications of their study even more effectively. As it stands, they suggest that what they develop may help us understand other situations in which someone attempts to replace a previously held belief with a new one. I believe what the authors have done may have some relevance to those more diverse concerns. Yet, more useful for such general concerns than the model presented in the chapter would be one that acknowledges that in our society a number of varying and simultaneously competing voices vie for hearing—and some of those voices concern deceptive advertising. Some concern other issues, of course, but the understanding of all the voices would be improved by more attention to the varying sources of messages.

Message Variability

A final conceptual concern is for the nature of the corrective message it-self. Not accidentally have I left this concern for last: Given the complexity of issues of accountability, the variations in deception, the variable judg-ments of deception, and (finally) the diverse potential sources of messages, the *discourse of the message*—what actually is said in the message in order to correct a deception—is a pivotal concern for me. The attempt to general-ize about the effects of messages clearly is a laudable effort; in one way or another, communication scholars have been engaged in that behavior since before Aristotle's time. The utility of that generality is obvious in both re-search and regulatory policy arenas.

On the other hand, generalizations can be either the desired goal or, iron-ically, a beginning point for better understanding. Though its analogical utility is obviously limited, we might benefit from considering what the rhetorical critic would call *apologia*. Ware and Linkugel's (1973) treatment of this genre or type of discourse is not absolutely irrelevant to the topic under discussion. As rhetoricians seek to explain or justify their possible or alleged wrongdoing, they engage in somewhat related strategies. Thus Nixon's "Checkers speech" shares some similarities with Ted Kennedy's message to the people of Massachusetts concerning Chappaquidick or with one or another of Gary Hart's speeches of defense. For the purposes of this commentary, what are more interesting than the similarities among these speeches are the differences. One speech intended for atonement is not identical to any other one in form, in substance, or in apparent effect. In comparatively general senses, similarities exist in situations, options, and viable responses. Those similarities formed the basis of Black's (1965) seminal critique of neo-Aristotelianism and permitted the development of what we know as generic criticism. Yet speeches containing the same (sorts of) elements will be adjudged vastly differently by audiences.

Where Burgoon, Newton, and Birk have worked needs to be the starting point for understanding corrective messages in their complexity. Just as there are variations in deceptions, judgments of deceptions, and sources of messages, we also must presume that we need better means of differentiat-ing among corrective messages. The authors use a case study of sorts to argue that corrective advertising *in that case* produced more far-reaching results than perhaps would have been predicted. That other corrective mes-sages would share some similarities with this one case is obvious; that we can use one case with one message as a basis for generality is obviously fallacious. The authors have given us reason to encourage more research in this area. Perhaps at some point far into the future we may be able to gener-alize about what a *particular* corrective message might accomplish based on scores of studies such as this one. But what we have now is a case study that tells us about the case under consideration. While that study makes some theoretical advances, it clearly cannot be used to talk of corrective messages in general or (even less) argumentation and persuasion in general.

Burgoon, Newton, and Birk have sparked our interest in a more sophisticated approach to studying a kind of message; it is up to these authors and others to continue to enhance the realism of further studies so that we begin to understand corrective messages even more adequately.

CONCLUSION

In concluding my commentary, I wish finally to turn to policy issues. As indicated very early on, the concept of corrective advertising may strike the reader as strange. For the FTC purposely to avoid seeking *punishment* even for a deliberate attempt to deceive audiences and customers is indeed strange. "Regulation" in that sense will not "fit" any other situation with which I am familiar. In the admittedly imperfect analogue of apologia, speakers do not enter the situation expecting to achieve a total restoration of a situation prior to an infidelity, an indiscretion, or the commission of a crime. People committing fraud, when discovered, cannot normally expect to admit their fraud and then "go back" to the "way it used to be." Any number of other examples would demonstrate what political scientist Murray Edelman (1964) suggested decades ago: Regulatory bodies exist to protect the regulated organizations instead of the public or the consumer. Without the FTC, we might be tempted to see purposely deceptive advertising as what it is: an attempt to gain advantage through fraud. Such fraud should be prosecutable and often prosecuted by the public, and organizations found guilty should be punished. That, of course, does not occur with any regularity. We have regulatory agencies for protection; unfortunately, they tend to protect the regulated from action by the public (Crable & Vibbert, 1986).

It is from that cynical, and yet I think realistic, perspective that I am most disturbed by the chapter. The authors advisedly worry that if organizations discover that corrective advertising may result in more negative results than typically thought, they may not agree to settlements such as we have seen in the past. First, I am disturbed that this one case study of STP might be used for any sort of generalization (given my concern for a number of conceptual issues). Second, however, as a communication scholar, I am disturbed that anyone would study a process such as corrective advertising *without noting how completely questionable* the FTC's goal of "nothing but restoration" is. Clearly, researchers can study the strangest of processes and even focus on how such processes can be studied more adequately. At some point, however, it seems to me that the social responsibility of the researcher arises. The alternative is that researchers themselves become partially responsible for questionable practices that they have made better, more efficient, more exact, or more effective.

Clearly, not every commentator will see Burgoon, Newton, and Birk's chapter in the same way, nor reach the same conclusions, as I do. I think the chapter makes a contribution to our understanding of corrective advertising, and I think it helps develop and clarify some theoretical issues. Its conclusions, for me, are overstated, and, again for me, the authors fail to address the study in its conceptual complexity and in its societal ramifications. But the chapter does what good (not necessarily perfect) research papers do: It has presented clearly some things the authors have been thinking about, and it catalyzes an additional set of thoughts in the reader. Every research paper should do so much.

REFERENCES

Black, E. (1965). *Rhetorical criticism: A study in method.* Madison: University of Wisconsin Press.

Burgoon, J. K., & Burgoon, M. (1978). *The effects of the STP corrective advertising campaign.* Unpublished research report.

Burke, K. (1954). *Permanence and change* (2nd rev. ed.). Los Altos, CA: Hermes.

Crable, R. E. (1978). Ethical codes, accountability, and argumentation. *Quarterly Journal of Speech, 64,* 23-32.

Crable, R. E., & Vibbert, S. L. (1986). *Public relations as communication management.* Edina, MN: Bellwether.

Edelman, M. (1964). *The symbolic uses of politics.* Urbana: University of Illinois Press.

Milkey, C. (1990). *The Converse energy wave.* Paper presented at California State University, Sacramento.

Ware, B. L., & Linkugel, A. W. (1973). They spoke in defense of themselves: On the generic criticism of apologia. *Quarterly Journal of Speech, 59,* 273-283.

Effects and Effectiveness of Corrective Advertising: Assumptions and Errors in Regulation Research

HERBERT J. ROTFELD
Auburn University

W HEN first introduced by the Federal Trade Commission two decades ago, corrective advertising was an aggressive and innovative remedy. Prior FTC orders merely directed users of deceptive advertising claims to "never say that again." Corrective advertising took that directive one step further and required the advertiser to correct consumer misinformation engendered by the years (or, in some cases, decades) of advertising claims.

Using a data base apparently compiled by the senior author while under contract to Louis Harris and Associates, which, in turn, was under contract to the FTC, Burgoon, Newton, and Birk provide a model and analysis of possible persuasion effects of corrective advertising. An assessment of their discussion could refer to attitude theory development and a recent meta-analysis of past research on the Fishbein and Ajzen model (Sheppard, Hartwick, & Warshaw, 1988). However, since the authors do not directly address similar assessments of the extended attitude model, and most discussion delineates legal concerns or regulatory implications, commentary discussion must, of necessity, dwell on the pragmatic ramifications of their model.

From the point of view of FTC policies and programs, Burgoon, Newton, and Birk's proposed model is irrelevant. Their discussion is not atypical for

AUTHOR'S NOTE: I wish to thank FTC consultant Richard Mizerski, professor of marketing at Florida State University, for his suggestions and inspiration for parts of this discussion. I remain responsible for all errors, oversights, and antagonistic comments.

Correspondence and requests for reprints: Herbert J. Rotfeld, Department of Marketing and Transportation, Auburn University, AL 36849-5246.

Communication Yearbook 15, pp. 299-311

scholars whose expertise is not legal, but rather in the realm of communication theory and persuasion research, but the FTC employees and staff would find this model far removed from their pragmatic information needs and decision-making concerns.

ASSUMPTIONS, ERRORS, AND NONLAWYERS' RESEARCH

FTC programs and remedies in the regulation of advertising are defined in terms of communication and are phrased in reference to an expected influence on consumer information. These legal terms and their definitions come from past case decisions, from legal history; their actual communication effects may be assumed and not founded on research data (e.g., Preston, 1975; Rotfeld & Preston, 1981). Regardless, the issues are *legal*. Research by communication scholars on these consumer information issues has drawn heavily on theories and research in psychology, marketing, advertising, and related fields, but often without adequate consideration of the relevant legal literature (Preston, 1980, 1983a).

Not understanding legal rules and requirements, many communication researchers attempt to redefine legal terms to fit their own concerns for experimental design and needs for an "operational definition." Studies based on the cutting edge of communication theory and research often present arguments and issues that ignore the legal priorities that allegedly formed the basis for the study.

This implies three interrelated assumptions and errors in attempts to apply various theories of perception and persuasion to FTC efforts to regulate advertising. The first and basic error is researchers' self-aggrandizing belief that they can redefine the legal issues regardless of legal evidence requirements and the ability of the people involved in enforcing the regulatory program to understand technical concerns of communication theory. Researchers often attempt to redefine legal terms, presuming their terminology will have legal relevance. The regulatory rules or programs are broadly stated in terms of consumer information and persuasion, but the legal definitions of these concepts are the ones that must be applied, regardless of the established details of related communication theories.

Second, and closely allied with the first, researchers and lawyers differ by training, background, and perceptual worldview—and regulatory personnel are mostly lawyers. (President Reagan appointed two economists to the FTC, the only two nonlawyers ever to serve as commissioners.) The proceedings are legal, using economists for advice and insight, sometimes asking communication research experts to provide evidence to assist in making legal decisions or to assess the effects of programs already under way. Regulatory decision makers may not even understand the intricate details of a model of consumer decision processes or those of the extended Fishbein model, but then, it is not required that they do so.

Third and more pragmatic—and potentially insulting to many mass communication researchers—communication, advertising, and marketing journals may publish inaccurate statements of the law. Articles in these journals aim primarily at understanding, explaining, and predicting how consumers respond to various advertising strategies and appeals. The journals' peer reviewers judge the research on that basis because, logically, that is most referees' expertise. Ignorant of regulatory concerns, these journal reviewers allow researchers to state that data and theories apply in legal contexts, even though such statements might be in error. The errors might not be caught, are seldom (if ever) corrected, and are then cited as authoritative applications by other researchers who similarly lack legal expertise.

As a logical result of these three interrelated errors, many researchers have generated theories, explanations, and data that are irrelevant to issues of advertising regulation. While these discussions might extend general understanding of mass communication and persuasion, it is not necessarily valid to expect them to be relevant to legal programs or remedies. By not understanding the goals of the various corrective orders studied and by making errors in their review of the legal requirements, Burgoon, Newton, and Birk have done little to contribute to understanding of the legal issues.

What follows are strong recommendations of cautions that should be used by researchers when pronouncing potential legal implications of behavioral science findings. The material in some sections might already be known to readers who are familiar with the literature on advertising regulation, but the nature of the topic is such that virtually everyone dealing with issues of mass communication and persuasion has a smattering of knowledge and (mis)information on the topic.

FTC REGULATION AND CORRECTIVE ADVERTISING

To understand these errors better, discussion must first point out the FTC's advertising regulation requirements and pragmatic directives about what advertisers can and cannot say. An advertising message can be considered deceptive if it communicates, by statement, implication, or omission, product values or benefits that are at variance with the facts. The FTC need not show that anyone actually believed the claims; there need not be any actual deception or harm to the public for the claims to be stopped. What the advertiser intended to convey is irrelevant, and the claim might be deceptive even if it is literally or technically true (Preston, 1975, 1987, 1989; Preston & Richards, 1986; Richards, 1990; Rotfeld, 1983).

If false claims are communicated, they have a "tendency or capacity to deceive" and can be proscribed. In 1983, President Reagan's appointees introduced an alternate concept called "likeliness to deceive," though asserting that it would not make a particular difference in terms of message considerations. The alternative concept presents the variations in terminology, priorities, and perspectives that could be applied by the FTC leadership, but the established law remains unaltered.

Burden of Proof

As stated by Preston (1987):

> The Commission must first determine what messages are conveyed to consumers, either expressly or implied, following exposure to a challenged communication. Then it bears the burden of showing that the messages conveyed are deceptive in that they falsely depict the advertised object. (pp. 633-634)

He additionally states (in a footnote):

> The relevant evidence is that pertaining to what message, either express or implied, the challenged communication has the capacity, tendency or likelihood to convey to consumers. . . . Evidence of other sorts, such as whether consumers believed what was conveyed, whether they relied justifiably on it, or whether they were actually deceived or damaged is not required [by the law].

FTC actions aim at simply stopping "unfair and deceptive acts and practices." An FTC order does not punish anyone, at least not in the legal sense of the term, which means that it does not issue any fines or send anyone to jail. Its basic remedies, consent decrees and cease and desist orders, direct firms to quit making false claims (Preston, 1975; Stern & Eovaldi, 1984). These orders may include detailed restrictions on types of claims that can be made in the future or may require "affirmative disclosures" of future product information, additional information to be included whenever certain types of claims are made when its omission would make the claims deceptive (Wilkie, 1982, 1985).

An FTC order might cause negative outcomes that firms wish to avoid, such as short-term loss of stock value (e.g., Peltzman, 1981), but, because there are no fines or prison sentences, no one is "punished." Preston (1975) observes: "The seller must stop the message; that's all. . . . The goal is to give maximum aid to consumers at the sacrifice of less than maximum punishment to offenders, rather than the opposite" (pp. 135-136).

After a proposed complaint is issued, the FTC offers the firm the option of signing a consent order by which the firm would be agreeing to stop the deceptive practices. If the advertiser and the FTC are unable to agree, a trial is held before an administrative law judge, who can recommend a cease and desist order. The full Commission can then vote to issue an order against the firm, after which the firm can appeal the decision to the federal court of appeals and, ultimately, if *certiorari* is granted, to the U.S. Supreme Court.

The only pragmatic difference between consent and cease and desist orders is that the former is entered by bargaining and negotiation and the latter is the result of an adversarial process that can be appealed through the federal appellate courts. Anything that might be included in one order may be included in the other, though a firm could "agree" to do things that go beyond FTC powers or that appellate courts might not uphold. Once finalized, both have the same impact on future advertising claims. If the firm later fails to abide by either type of order, the FTC or the Justice Department sues the firm in federal district court and, if guilty, the firm is fined by the court. The fine is for violating a direct order, not for deceptive advertising per se.

As the FTC's regulatory efforts became more active, efficient, and effective in the 1970s, advertising agencies implemented their own internal processes to make certain that proposed campaigns were within the law. An obvious question for advertisers might be, Why bother to screen commercials to make certain they are "FTC-proof"? After all, the FTC orders are not punishments, but merely directives to go and sin no more. Burgoon, Newton, and Birk speculate that firms might not bargain if they perceive corrective outcomes as "too strong."

However, the simple act of responding to an FTC request for claim substantiation is not costless. Litigation itself can be a very expensive endeavor, which is why the overwhelming majority of FTC cases, including those that result in directives for corrective advertising, are settled by consent orders. Beyond the obvious fees paid to lawyers to handle the response, plus costs tied to the preparation and submission of necessary documents, there exist opportunity costs. When a request comes in from the FTC or any other government agency, people must be pulled off their jobs to respond.

Therefore, the firms *must* bargain: The entire aim of negotiation is to attempt to temper the tone of the final order, since the FTC can still issue strong directives after the costly and time-consuming adversary proceeding. Swift agreement would save both the FTC and the firm time and costs of litigation.

Affirmative Disclosures and Corrective Advertising

Besides telling the advertiser to stop specific practices, FTC orders may also require future advertising to include specific statements if failure to do so would be deceptive. Orders for future affirmative disclosures require the firm to offset future claims in one area with additional information (Wilkie, 1982, 1985). The problem arises when the deceptive claims have been made for so long or have been so strongly associated with a brand that *any* future advertising of the product or brand name would trigger the false associations consumers formed from the earlier deceptive messages.

To handle this problem, in the early 1970s the FTC started to require advertisers to include messages in future advertising with the corrected information, even if the corrected message was irrelevant to the new campaign.

In the first corrective advertising order, Profile Bread was required to spend 25% of its budget on saying that the bread is not significantly lower in calories. Ocean Spray had to state that the company's cranberry juice does not contain more vitamins and minerals than tomato or orange juice.

There still exists uncertainty about whether or not the FTC has the power to force corrective advertising actions on unwilling firms. Corrective advertising has, in almost all cases, been part of consent orders; the only directive from a cease and desist order was appealed (Stern & Eovaldi, 1984).

Warner-Lambert argued on appeal for Listerine that the FTC did not have the power to order the firm to spend $10 million over the next two years stating that "Listerine will not help prevent colds or lessen their severity." While the court of appeals did not accept Warner-Lambert's argument, the Supreme Court denied *certiorari*, leaving the case precedent tied to that single type of case in that single appellate jurisdiction. It is unknown if the high court would agree that the FTC has power to force such orders on unwilling advertisers. (For detailed analysis of this issue, see Stern & Eovaldi, 1984, pp. 381-385.)

Regardless of the actual legal status, for several years advertisers accepted corrective advertising requirements without argument. While the legal power might be in question, many firms have tacitly accepted that the FTC could force such disclosures. The consent order from one case (involving STP, the one studied by Burgoon, Newton, and Birk) actually had the corrected messages aimed at the business community, not consumers, as a form of notification to firms that the FTC was willing to require such corrected messages.

Within this context, journals dedicated to mass communication and persuasion theory and research publish a growing body of literature that addresses issues purportedly raised by this remedy. But while the research papers are almost all academically interesting as studies of mass communication and persuasion, because of interrelated errors and assumptions about the FTC's powers and concerns, many of these articles present discussions that are legally irrelevant.

ERROR 1: REGULATION CONCERNS ARE LEGAL

Over the last two decades, the FTC has increased its used of research consultants, experts on mass communication and persuasion, to help provide evidence, insight, and advice on how advertising influences consumers. At the same time, a growing body of literature in communication, advertising, and marketing journals has called for the FTC to do even more to integrate consumer research and behavioral perspectives into its programs and policies of advertising regulation.

The FTC did increase its use of research evidence during this period (Brandt & Preston, 1977; Preston, 1986, 1987, 1989; Rotfeld & Preston,

1981), but the mere increased use of external survey evidence does not mean that policy or case decisions evolved into academic interpretations of communication theory and data (Preston, 1983a, 1987, 1989; Rotfeld, 1978). The regulators' orientation remains tied to the legal system, using recognized procedures and legal definitions of relevant terms.

Researchers cannot demand that the FTC adopt their standards and definitions of deception; rather, they need to understand the legal or regulatory procedures in order to prepare and deliver research that would best serve the FTC or other regulatory agencies' decision needs. Lacking such understanding, many researchers unsuccessfully attempt to impose their perspectives on the commissioners (see discussions in Preston, 1975, 1980, 1983a, 1986, 1987; Richards, 1990; Rotfeld, 1978, 1983).

The number of "behavioral definitions" of deception found in the literature is too lengthy to describe, or even to list. But what many of these discussions miss is that the important legal inquiry in the case of advertising deception is the impression an ad makes on consumers, making the topic one that can be directly researched (e.g., Richards, 1990; Rotfeld & Rotzoll, 1980, 1981). Many legal issues are phrased in terms of consumers' cognitive structures, but it is an error to assume the FTC needs experts in the research of information and persuasion to define it "better." Researchers should not be trying to tell commissioners how to "redefine" terms (Preston, 1980); rather, they should bring an application of research insights to answer legal questions (e.g., Preston, 1986, 1987, 1989; Preston & Richards, 1986). Like any other scientist serving in a legal setting, the researcher is there to provide data that focus on the *legal* decision to be made.

This error of researchers' mistaken perceptions of legal concerns provides the basis for discussions that misunderstand the actual goals the program researchers are allegedly attempting to address. For example, Burgoon, Newton, and Birk discuss the goals of corrective advertising in terms of sales. While such sales effects might be a hope or expectation of a corrective advertising order, the actual goal has to do with consumer knowledge and information.

The law is not based on the extended Fishbein model; many models can assess the nature of consumer reactions and apply them to the legal concerns. The relationship between consumer perceptions and market share alterations requires more awareness of communication theory than any commissioners would ever be required to possess, and greater degrees of research analysis than they are required to conduct.

Legal references to sales or market shares relate solely to the FTC's origins as a body charged with enforcement of antitrust laws. How a remedy is legally or logically argued helps determine whether or not the appellate courts will agree that the Commission possesses a power or whether a certain FTC order would be legally acceptable. The FTC cannot *say* it wishes to use corrective advertising to "punish" firms, or to use it with a stated intent to cause corporate harm. But commissioners and their staff know this and would not make such legal arguments.

Similarly, any speculative possible effects caused by corrective advertising that may be detrimental to the advertiser, such as harm to overall brand image, are legally irrelevant. No one goes to jail, fines are not charged, and so, by legal definition, no one is punished. Economists might discuss various other possible corporate injuries emanating from FTC orders, such as drops in stock value (e.g., Peltzman, 1981), but these, too, are irrelevant to whether a firm is punished by an FTC order.

ERROR 2: WORLDVIEWS—RESEARCHERS ≠ LAWYERS

A law degree is similar to a Ph.D. in that both are certifications of research training. However, they involve different types of research, applying different methods and priorities. For communication researchers, and especially those involved with advertising issues, the "truth" often seems so logical, so intuitively obvious, they find that everyone encountered possesses a self-image as an expert on the relevant issues and concerns of persuasion. Similarly, since the law touches many people's lives, lawyers often find that many people like to consider themselves legal experts.

This conflict is clear to communication researchers who have read one or two law journal articles that purport to address information and persuasion concerns and yet misunderstand material found in any undergraduate communication course. FTC lawyers understand the idea of a target audience, the relevant target public for an advertising campaign, but in terms that many communication researchers or analysts with expertise in marketing science would consider very basic. A Reagan-appointed commissioner once commented to reporters that a danger from strict advertising regulation might be that advertisers will then resort to "greater" (sic) use of subliminal messages.

This is not to assert that lawyers are completely ignorant when dealing with mass communication and persuasion, but their worldview and basic priorities are in terms of legal history and precedent (e.g., Preston, 1975; Rotfeld & Preston, 1981). Communication research can serve only as evidence; communication experts do not write the laws (Preston, 1980).

Similarly, this is not to say that nonlawyers are incapable of understanding the basic concerns of legal regulatory interests. Some mass communication scholars develop a research expertise that includes a thorough understanding of legal views and methods of legal analysis (e.g., Parsons, 1987; Preston, 1975). Others have backgrounds that include legal training or law degrees (e.g., Le Duc, 1987; Richards, 1990). But to present research conclusions and then state probable legal or regulatory relevance, the researcher must first attempt to understand the legal concepts and concerns from the point of view of those who will make the regulatory decisions.

ERROR 3:
CITATIONS OF AUTHORITY DO NOT FACTS MAKE

A person wishing to learn the law should not depend just on communication, advertising, or marketing journals any more than a person wishing to learn attitude theory should depend upon law journals. Communication researchers wishing to address legal issues must include legal resources and analysis in any background study of the issues to develop their own legal expertise. A scholar with "credentials" as a research consultant for the FTC is not necessarily a knowledgeable source on legal issues or concerns.

A communication scholar who depends only upon other communication or marketing sources as a guide, without any prior understanding of legal issues or the lawyer's worldview, ends up repeating the mistakes of the past. Discussing another area of psychological testing, Dershowitz (1971) points out, "It must never be forgotten that . . . [the] unknown mistake of the past becomes the foundation for a confident, but erroneous prediction for the future" (p. 317).

This third error should not be unexpected. Journals that deal primarily with persuasion and consumer behavior concerns seldom use peer referees who are lawyers or legal experts; the focus of the journals is on research and theory development. Once published, for a variety of reasons (as in any area of academic research), errors are seldom caught; when they are caught, authors and editors may resist publication of corrections (Broad & Wade, 1982). For example, Scammon and Semenik (1982) present a summary of cases that engendered FTC use of corrective advertising orders, then state that the FTC's "authority to require corrective advertising has been upheld by the Supreme Court" by its denial of *certiorari* in the case involving Listerine (Preston, 1983b). Actually, denial of *certiorari* only means that the Supreme Court refused to hear the case. Reasons for denial are not known, but it is *never* to indicate approval of lower court decisions. Since the Supreme Court has not heard any appeals on corrective advertising, the FTC's power is still in doubt beyond a single appellate jurisdiction (see discussion in Stern & Eovaldi, 1984, pp. 381-385).

Armstrong, Franke, and Russ (1982) discuss how the FTC could do more to "punish" deceivers, not realizing that the Commission cannot use punitive remedies or what the term means in the legal realm (Preston, 1983b). In another area of advertising regulation concerns, Cutler and Muehling (1989) relied almost totally on marketing journals to develop their own knowledge of advertising regulation and protection of commercial speech under the First Amendment to the U.S. Constitution, and ignored some marketing and advertising journals whose analyses of those issues were based on case law and the legal literature. As a result, misunderstanding the role, nature, and history of advertising regulation pertaining to constitutional issues, their analysis involves several legal errors.

This is not to assert that all legal discussions in communication, advertising, or marketing journals should be ignored. Analysis in these journals presents a fresh perspective that might be valuable and interesting for legal concerns and may subsequently be cited in legal journals. Some of this research provides insightful assessments of the effects of government programs on business activities and resulting impact on consumer information (e.g., Healy & Kassarjian, 1983), regardless of specific use of the data in a legal proceeding. However, lacking legal expertise, researchers cannot validly pronounce the legal significance of their data by the mere review of similar studies in nonlegal sources. They know not of what they speak.

APPLICATION OF THE FISHBEIN MODEL

Burgoon, Newton, and Birk are correct in that, to date, published data on many types of FTC corrective advertising concerns have yielded large amounts of data but minimal conclusions that can be generalized and no solid basis for new intellectual structures. But data in the mass communication literature also have not aided in building an understanding of pragmatic legal concerns. Burgoon, Newton, and Birk might be contributing to the latter problem with their misapplied and misunderstood perspectives of the law, lifted unquestioned from marketing, advertising, and consumer research journals. They play fast and loose with a wide range of literature, use a model that is itself controversial in the literature, and fail to develop their own legal expertise before making pronouncements on legal applications.

At the outset, Burgoon, Newton, and Birk delineate very restrictive goals for corrective advertising, a narrow window of specific influence on buyer behavior that demands a specific, *limited* degree of audience reactions. But it is uncertain why the FTC should (or would) aim at such limited and specific effects on audiences. Consumers' behavior changes, product purchase selections, and potential attitude "fallout" from a corrective order are all irrelevant to the FTC. Strictly speaking, even changes in consumer attitudes or purchase behaviors are irrelevant. The basic goal is to convey information to consumers.

With this in mind, it should not be unexpected to find that research on impact of past corrective advertising orders "runs the gamut from no effect to minimal effects to dramatic effects." This is true of all research that tries to ascertain the effects of advertising in general. Even when the subject of study is the same corrective advertising campaign, such as the studies Burgoon, Newton, and Birk review on Listerine, conflicting findings are to be expected when the studies employ different experimental environments. Each test is limited to how the corrective advertising resulting from FTC orders can be effective or ineffective only in reference to the specific materials and audiences tested.

Of course, this type of research, looking for some general conclusions about what "works," is not atypical (e.g., see the review in Gelb, Hong, & Zinkhan,

1985). Many studies have compared different types of appeals, such as appeals to humor (e.g., Brooker, 1981), to guilt (e.g., Bozinoff & Ghingold, 1983), or to fear (e.g., Ray & Wilkie, 1970; see critical discussion in Rotfeld, 1988). All are seeking some ubiquitous type of overall effect.

Obviously, the valid conclusions are limited: For some groups, in some cases, under some conditions, a corrective advertising order might result in altered consumer beliefs for some communication formats. Burgoon, Newton, and Birk present a theoretical framework for possible copy tests, an approach for selecting a creative strategy and for finding segments with which it is optimal, but it cannot be generalized beyond the narrow context of their discussion. The questions of corrective advertising effects that the authors assert their model can address—potential harm to company or brand image, effects on purchase intention—are interesting, but not legally relevant. All these problems and errors directly relate to reliance on academic communication and persuasion research journals, not FTC cases or the legal literature, for development of their legal expertise.

It should also be pointed out that the FTC's goals for the corrective advertising required for STP make that campaign a much less than optimal subject for a test of consumer impacts of corrective advertising. For a variety of reasons (and covered in various news releases), the order was aimed at the business community, not at consumers. As part of a consent order, commissioners desired that STP's corrective ads serve as an informal statement to the business community of the FTC's willingness to use this remedy.

Regardless, the basic problem with Burgoon, Newton, and Birk's application is that the FTC does not need a research-based communication theory of corrective advertising. Contrary to their assertions, behavioral change strategies are not central to the corrective advertising remedy. Advertising is the consumer's predominant source of market information; thus when an advertiser has communicated deceptive statements in the past, it must now convey the corrected information.

And while the FTC has long recognized the concept of relevant markets, Burgoon, Newton, and Birk's desire to review only consumers exposed to the false claims seems unduly limited and virtually impossible to establish validly and reliably in the sense of who did and did not previously see the ads. As a regulatory goal or burden-of-proof requirement, such a test demands more from the FTC than it is legally required to ascertain, going into micro-research detail that few (if any) advertisers could reliably assess, and requiring research assets for every case that the FTC would not possess.

CONCLUSIONS

The FTC can direct an advertiser to halt an advertising campaign if the messages communicate—by statement, implication, or omission—information that is at variance with the facts of the matter. A corrective advertising order, at its core, presumes that the deceptive claims are so entrenched that the mere mention of the firm, product, or brand will trigger the false claims in consumer's heads.

Scholars of attitude change and persuasion might find some insight in the Burgoon, Newton, and Birk model, but it is hoped that no one takes their proposed applications as valid statements of the law. Their findings are overgeneralized on many counts; the Fishbein model is one of many possible ways to study possible effects.

It is important to remember that the goal of corrective advertising is not a sales effect per se, but rather to provide consumers with honest and correct information. The change is not in terms of "harms" or "drops" in positive evaluations; rather, it is an attempt to make certain that people have the correct information after being provided deceptive information by a firm in the past.

This is not to say that the FTC is not concerned about effects of the orders, nor is it to assert that studies of corrective advertising that are legally irrelevant are to be ignored. Deceptive advertising and corrective advertising both provide research environments with a range of features and concerns that scholars might wish to address (Preston, 1983b; Preston & Richards, 1986; Rotfeld, 1983). But to state legal implications, one must first understand the legal requirements. Lacking such understanding, one only contributes to the overall confusion among communication scholars about the role and applications of their research data in a legal context.

REFERENCES

Armstrong, G. M., Franke, E. R., & Russ, F. A. (1982). The effects of corrective advertising on company image. *Journal of Advertising, 11*(4), 39-47.

Bozinoff, L., & Ghingold, M. (1983). Evaluating guilt arousing marketing communications. *Journal of Business Research, 11*, 243-255.

Brandt, M. T., & Preston, I. L. (1977). The FTC's use of evidence to determine deception. *Journal of Marketing, 41*, 54-62.

Broad, W., & Wade, N. (1982). *Betrayers of the truth: Fraud and deceit in the halls of science*. New York: Simon & Schuster.

Brooker, G. (1981). A comparison of the persuasive effects of mild humor and mild fear appeals. *Journal of Advertising, 10*(4), 29-40.

Cutler, B. D., & Muehling, D. D. (1989). Advocacy advertising and the boundaries of commercial speech. *Journal of Advertising, 18*, 40-50.

Dershowitz, A. M. (1971). Preventing detention. In A. Goldstein & J. Goldstein (Eds.), *Crime, law and society*. New York: Free Press.

Gelb, B. D., Hong, J. W., & Zinkhan, G. M. (1985). Communications effects of specific advertising elements: An update. *Current Issues and Research in Advertising, 2*, 75-98.

Healy, J.S., & Kassarjian, H. H. (1983). Advertising substantiation and advertiser response: A content analysis of magazine advertisements. *Journal of Marketing, 47*, 107-127.

Le Duc, D. R. (1987). *Beyond broadcasting: Patterns in policy and law.* White Plains, NY: Longman.

Parsons, P. (1987). *Cable television and the first amendment.* Lexington, MA: D. C. Heath.

Peltzman, S. (1981). The effects of FTC advertising regulation. *Journal of Law and Economics, 24,* 403-448.

Preston, I. L. (1975). *The great American blow-up: Puffery in advertising and selling.* Madison: University of Wisconsin Press.

Preston, I. L. (1980). Researchers at the Federal Trade Commission: Peril and promise. *Current Issues and Research in Advertising, 3,* 1-15.

Preston, I. L. (1983a). Research on deceptive advertising: Commentary. In R. J. Harris (Ed.), *Information processing research in advertising* (pp. 289-305). Hillsdale, NJ: Lawrence Erlbaum.

Preston, I. L. (1983b). A review of the literature on advertising regulation. *Current Issues and Research in Advertising, 6,* 1-38.

Preston, I. L. (1986). Data-free at the FTC? How the Federal Trade Commission decides whether extrinsic evidence is required. *American Business Law Journal, 24,* 359-376.

Preston, I. L. (1987). Extrinsic evidence and Federal Trade Commission deceptiveness cases. *Columbia Business Law Review, 3,* 633-694.

Preston, I. L. (1989). The Federal Trade Commission's identification of implications as constituting deceptive advertising. *University of Cincinnati Law Review, 57,* 1243-1310.

Preston, I. L., & Richards, J. I. (1986). Consumer miscomprehension as a challenge to FTC prosecutions of deceptive advertising. *John Marshall Law Review, 12,* 605-635.

Ray, M., & Wilkie, W. (1970). Fear: The potential of an appeal neglected by marketing. *Journal of Marketing, 34,* 54-62.

Richards, J. I. (1990). *Deceptive advertising: Behavioral study of a legal concept.* Hillsdale, NJ: Lawrence Erlbaum.

Rotfeld, H. J. (1978). The differing perspectives of researchers and lawyers towards deceptive advertising and puffery. In S. E. Permut (Ed.), *Advances in advertising research and management* (pp. 101-104). New Haven, CT: American Academy of Advertising.

Rotfeld, H. J. (1983). What is misleading? In R. J. Harris (Ed.), *Information processing research in advertising* (pp. 169-174). Hillsdale, NJ: Lawrence Erlbaum.

Rotfeld, H. J. (1988). Fear appeals and persuasion: Assumptions and errors in advertising research. *Current Issues and Research in Advertising, 11,* 21-40.

Rotfeld, H. J., & Preston, I. L. (1981). The potential impact of research on advertising law. *Journal of Advertising Research, 21,* 9-17.

Rotfeld, H. J., & Rotzoll, K. B. (1980). Is advertising puffery believed? *Journal of Advertising, 9*(3), 16-20, 45.

Rotfeld, H. J., & Rotzoll, K. B. (1981). Puffery vs. fact claims: Really different? *Current Issues and Research in Advertising, 4,* 85-103.

Scammon, D. L., & Semenik, R. J. (1982). Corrective advertising: Evolution of the legal theory and application of the remedy. *Journal of Advertising, 11,* 10-20.

Sheppard, B. H., Hartwick, J., & Warshaw, P. R. (1988). The theory of reasoned action: A meta-analysis of past research with recommendations for modifications and future research. *Journal of Consumer Research, 15,* 325-343.

Stern, L. W., & Eovaldi, T. L. (1984). Legal aspects of promotion strategy: Advertising. In L. W. Stern & T. L. Eovaldi, *Legal aspects of marketing strategy: Antitrust and consumer protection issues* (pp. 369-411). Englewood Cliffs, NJ: Prentice-Hall.

Wilkie, W. L. (1982). Affirmative disclosure: Perspectives on FTC orders. *Journal of Public Policy and Marketing, 1,* 95-110.

Wilkie, W. L. (1985). Affirmative disclosure at the FTC: Objectives for the remedy and outcomes of past orders. *Journal of Public Policy and Marketing, 4,* 91-111.

7 Bridging Theory and Praxis: Reexamining Public Health Communication

CLIFFORD W. SCHERER
NAPOLEON K. JUANILLO, JR.
Cornell University

As it examines the theoretical bases of the strategies employed in public health communication programs, this chapter attempts to establish patterns and trends in theory application, to synthesize the lessons learned in public health communication programs, and to draw implications for combining theoretical insights and practical program development. Based on a review of selected public health communication programs conducted between 1970 and 1991, three broad theoretical categories of health communication approaches are discussed: (a) a continuing reliance on the direct effects of mass media, (b) attempts to recapture interpersonal processes, and (c) a synergistic intervention utilizing person-to-person, community support, and mass communication techniques. Issues are raised about the implications of these approaches for communication plans and strategies for the future.

T HE prevention of chronic diseases and accidents is an important focus of modern health care. Preventive action or behavior is emphasized as the primary factor in intervention strategies of public health promotion programs. Health promotion efforts to reduce health risks can be broadly classified as institutional strategies and communication strategies. Institutional strategies involve shaping the public's behavior toward health maintenance through structural changes in the institutional arrangements of society. This includes incentives, improved services and delivery, administrative regulations and standards, technological innovations, and legislative prohibitions. Communication strategies involve the use of mass media and other communication channels to generate positive changes in the awareness, orientation, and behavior of people toward better personal and community health (McGuire, 1984).

Correspondence and requests for reprints: Clifford W. Scherer, Department of Communication, 312 Roberts Hall, Cornell University, Ithaca, NY 14853.

Communication Yearbook 15, pp. 312-345

This chapter focuses on the communication component of health promotion programs. As part of a larger program of action, public health communication represents an organized or programmed set of health intervention strategies that depend exclusively or predominantly on mass communication channels. The channels are used to generate specific outcomes or effects among a relatively large number of individuals within a specified time period. Overall, public health communication is intended to (a) inform the public about health hazards, (b) motivate them to reduce health risks, (c) train them in skills that enable them to adopt more healthful life-styles, and (d) persuade them to assume more effective responsibility for maintaining their own health (McGuire, 1984; Rogers & Storey, 1987).

During the last two decades, public health communication has been increasingly utilized to discharge institutional responsibility for the promotion of desirable health practices and to transmit prevention-related messages to the public. Faith in the potential of the mass media to reach, inform, and motivate large numbers of the population to undertake healthy life-style changes is reflected in the amount of money invested in communication campaigns. It can also be seen in legislation that restricts commercial advertising for products deemed deleterious to public health (Wallack, 1981).

However, evidence of possible gains and effects of public health communication programs on people's health life-styles remains minimal. The research done on such programs has focused on documenting the efficacy of the preventive measures themselves. Little quantitative research has been devoted to assessing the communication interventions utilized to promote the widespread use of preventive measures (Monahan & Scheirer, 1988). Many programs have not been evaluated adequately, and studies conducted on programs that have undergone scrutiny provide either unsatisfactory or marginal impact. Those that indicate some effects on behavior are of limited relevance, because no systematic attempts have been made to determine the relationships between the changes in health behavior and the communication events.

The paucity of records pointing to either the efficacy or lack of impact of health communication programs certainly calls for more systematic research and experimentation as well as an examination of the theoretical underpinnings that guide public health communication efforts. In a study of communication campaigns, Rogers and Storey (1987) found that although there is a substantial body of research in the area of public communication, various components of this research are only tenuously linked by a few general principles, without overarching generalizations or theories. Simpkins and Brenner (1984) likewise suggest the need for more holistic health communication research, which should include the synergistic functions of interpersonal, intrapersonal, and mass media communication upon cognitive, affective, and conative states. This phenomenon clearly manifests a real need for a comprehensive framework to direct research, development, and program strategies in the field.

This chapter, therefore, aims to explore the following questions: Has there been any significant progress in theory application within the context of public health communication? Is there movement toward synthesizing theories that have guided, successfully or at least satisfactorily, public health communication programs? Are there emerging theoretical perspectives resulting from the development and implementation of public health communication programs? This chapter attempts to examine the theoretical bases, whether tacit or explicit, of the strategies and processes employed in public health communication programs, to establish patterns and trends in theory application, to synthesize the lessons learned in public health communication programs, and to draw implications for combining theoretical insights and practical program development.

PUBLIC HEALTH COMMUNICATION PROGRAMS: 1970-1991

Some form of health communication was evident in the United States as early as the colonial era. In 1721, at the onset of a smallpox epidemic, a clergyman named Cotton Mather started a communication campaign that combined pamphleteering and personal persuasion. In spite of the city physicians' opposition, he sought to persuade the citizens of Boston to submit to inoculation. When the epidemic subsided by 1722, Mather showed the city's medical experts that death from smallpox had been nine times more prevalent among the noninoculated who contracted the disease than among those inoculated. In 1784, another public health-related effort was initiated by Benjamin Rush, a Philadelphia physician, who published the first important temperance tract, "Inquiry into the Effects of Spiritous Liquors on the Human Body and Mind." He followed with another publication, "Medical Inquiries and Observations upon the Diseases of the Mind" (Paisley, 1981). By 1839, 15 temperance journals were being published, and the use of mass communication for public health education became particularly prominent in the crusade against alcohol. Temperance movements flooded the American public with pamphlets, novels, newspapers, sermons, and lectures on the evils of alcohol use. As some observers put it, it was "the longest sustained and perhaps the largest organized effort at mass communication about a social issue that the country has ever seen." In the 1840s another health-related movement emerged when Dorothea Dix started the campaign for treatment of the mentally ill (Wallack, 1981).

By the end of the nineteenth century, advances in hygiene and disease control gave health workers further justification to reach out to the public through the use of mass media. Interest groups, cause advocates, and individuals espousing other platforms or areas of social concern likewise utilized public communication in their appeals for participation and reform. The government also found itself administering social change programs that required communication with special interest groups and the general public. Public communication was complemented by strategies involving grass-roots organizing, confrontation, and legislative lobbying. Sociology and psychology, although in their infancy, provided a scientific basis for several of these communication efforts.

Generally, public communication in the nineteenth century viewed the movement for social reform as culminating in the legislature or in the courts. Social issues, which were passionately campaigned for, were considered resolved once a law had been passed. Advocates of change rested on their laurels, as it were, after the amendments were ratified and unfair prohibitions were rectified (Paisley, 1981).

Modern-day public communication, especially as it is utilized in health promotion, is a much more complex process. The objective to change health orientation or life-style, at the individual, family, or community level, through a massive information and education campaign is closely linked with other strategies that "direct" changes through "engineering" and institutionalize them through law enforcement. For example, at the onset of the radon gas problem, the Environmental Protection Agency alerted the public to the hazards of indoor radon exposure via an information campaign. The campaign was complemented by the provision (in some states) of free radon detectors by the state or local government. The prevention of motor vehicle-related injuries through safety belt use is another clear example of a combination of public communication, engineering, and enforcement strategies.

Public communication's vital role in health promotion did not receive much recognition until the mid-1970s. While there was initially a pervasive optimism in the 1930s and 1940s concerning the mass media's "all-powerful hypodermic effect" on message receivers, media studies conducted after World War II led to conclusions pointing to the media's impotence or lack of any significant impact. The resultant pessimism expressed by many public health specialists regarding the improbable success of public communication campaigns generated a search for alternative strategies for health promotion. The 1960s were generally characterized by eager attempts to utilize engineering solutions to social problems, while the early 1970s favored enforcement strategies. At a certain point, public health experts believed that effective serums or low-cost drugs would obviate information campaigns to warn the public about potential dangers and the need for medical testing. The Food and Drug Administration banned possible carcinogenic substances in consumer products and cigarette advertising was prohibited on radio and television. During this period, communication was seen only as support for the so-called direct solutions, which involved laws, new technologies, or both. Communication was employed as an alternative intervention only after an engineering or enforcement strategy had failed to achieve utilization or compliance among its target publics (Paisley, 1981).

Eventually, however, the use of public communication itself as an instrument of change was brought into focus as engineering and enforcement interventions had, by themselves, become infeasible. The marked increase in utilizing mass media for health communication purposes had been particularly conspicuous in the dissemination of information about the negative consequences of cigarette smoking (Flay, 1987). As Paisley (1981) has noted:

> For instance, there are only a few services that directly contribute to heart disease prevention. Checkups can be provided and smoking cessation clinics can be established, but individuals are ultimately responsible for choosing behaviors that reduce the risk of heart disease. . . . the decline in cigarette smoking in the population is not a consequence of engineering or enforcement. After the federal ban on television and radio advertising of cigarettes, there was a marked increase in print advertising. The only strategy that can possibly counteract the advertisement has been public communication in its many forms ranging from school programs to the American Cancer Society's annual "Great American Smoke Out" campaign. (pp. 36-37)

The shift in mood from pessimism to cautious optimism about mass media effects engendered a number of endeavors employing communication as a tool for health awareness and change.

While the efficacy of public health communication programs has yet to be proven through rigorous experimentation, the growing number of health communication undertakings invites some answers to a significant aspect of the issue that revolves around a simple question: Where is public health communication going? This section reexamines major health communication efforts, as well as small-scale programs conducted during the period between 1970 and 1991, tracing the programs from their conceptualizations to evaluations, if any exist. The programs discussed below were culled from a review of articles from journals and other periodicals collected through manual and electronic searches. The cases selected for this study may not represent the best programs in the field of health communication, but they provide the opportunity to discern their contributions to the generation of knowledge in health communication. As we engage in the scientific study of communication, we are confronted with the Herculean task of selecting out of a virtually infinite supply a few assumptions that are deserving of our inquiry. The discussion is followed by an analysis of the theoretical paths of future health communication programs, gleaning insights from emerging issues and drawing implications for communication planning and strategy.

Heart Disease Campaigns

The Stanford Heart Disease Prevention Program (1972-1991)

One large-scale U.S. research endeavor in preventive medicine was the Stanford Heart Disease Prevention Program. It was initiated in 1972 as a means of modifying health life-styles in order to prevent or reduce the risk of fatal or life-threatening premature heart attacks. The program underscored the individual's control over the key determinants of heart disease, such as smoking, consumption of cholesterol-rich foods, tension, high blood pressure, and lack of exercise. In the short term, the program intended (a) to reduce cardiovascular risk significantly, and eventually morbidity and mortality; and (b) to decrease the level of tobacco consumption by 9%, body weight by 2%, blood cholesterol levels by 4%, and blood pressure by 7%. Due to the interactive effects of these risk factors, the overall reduction in cardiovascular disease was expected to be greater than the sum of the reductions in individual risk variables (Maccoby & Solomon, 1981).

The program had two phases: the Three-Community Study and the Five-City Multifactor Risk Reduction Project. The Three-Community Study was started in three small cities in northern California: Gilroy, Watsonville, and Tracy. A communication-education campaign, designed to promote information on heart disease and to teach specific preventive measures, was launched in the two experimental communities, Gilroy (population 12,700) and Watsonville (population 14,500). Information was delivered in both English and Spanish, owing to the large Mexican-American population in the target areas, and was transmitted via a combination of several media that included newspapers, radio, television, posters, calendars, and posted materials. Two-thirds of the subjects in Watsonville who were found to be particularly susceptible to heart disease received supplementary, intensive, face-to-face training. No communication-education campaign activities were conducted in the control site, Tracy (population 14,700).

To gauge the effectiveness and impact of the program, the basic intake interview, the medical examination, and measures of cardiovascular risk were repeated twice at one-year intervals, and the results were analyzed in relation to the baseline data. As a whole, experimental communities posted a 20% reduction in the total risk index, compared with the control community. More specifically, it was observed that knowledge of cardiovascular risk factors increased about 50% in the control city, that knowledge increased almost 400% among those in the intensive-instruction group, that behavior changes followed the increases in knowledge, and that consumption of high-cholesterol foods decreased somewhat in the control city, but more in the experimental cities (Maccoby & Solomon, 1981; Stern, Farquhar, Maccoby, & Russel, 1976). The intensive-instruction group showed even greater improvements. However, weight loss was not found for any group, and cigarette smoking was reduced only among those in the intensive-instruction group (Maccoby & Solomon, 1981; Stern et al., 1976).

The results of the Three-Community Study show that when the expected behavioral change is dependent on the acquisition of knowledge for improving consumption habits, the use of mass media as the sole intervention can be effective. However, when the desired behavior involves other changes, such as cigarette smoking cessation, the intervention necessitates a configuration of media events, skills training, self-monitoring, and feed-back. Likewise, there are cases that need to combine medication with mass media, face-to-face communication, and social support in order to facilitate the transition toward change. Overall, although it cannot be categorically claimed that change is a function of mass media, the general assessment of the Three-Community Study clearly points out the vital role that the mass media play either as a sole factor or as a catalyst in the synergistic interaction of inputs that has effected the process of change in people's health orientation (Maccoby, Farquhar, Wood, & Alexander, 1977).

The second phase of the program, the Five-City Multifactor Risk Reduction Project, was conducted in five California communities: Monterey, Salinas, San Luis Obispo, Modesto, and Santa Maria. Initiated in 1978, the Five-City Project was a consequence of the promising results of the Three-Community Study. Emphasizing generalizability and cost-effectiveness, the goal was to develop a model program that could be adopted by other communities. Building upon the successful elements of the previous study, the Five-City Project had a bigger scope, including larger target sites, a longer time span (five to eight years), and a bigger sample of community participants. It was designed as a quasi-experiment in five communities of moderate size varying in population from 44,000 to 130,000. Monterey and Salinas were the educational program communities, and San Luis Obispo, Modesto, and Santa Maria were the comparison communities. Due to concerns of replicability, the program developers confined themselves to the design of the organizational plan, the production of mass media materials, and the training of indigenous community leaders who would in turn train others to provide direct services (Maccoby & Solomon, 1981).

The key strategy of the Five-City Project was the provision of multiple opportunities, places, and forums for achieving self-directed behavioral change through the mass media, health professionals, community groups, and commercial channels. In-school education constituted a separate dissemination mechanism. This project mobilized various mass media more vigorously than did the Three-Community Study, utilizing public service announcements (PSAs) on radio and television, frequent television documentaries, weekly articles in local newspapers, books, and pamphlets. On the interpersonal level, health professionals were encouraged to discuss heart disease prevention methods with their clients and patients, and their offices were employed as distribution channels for educational materials. Community organizations ranging from medical associations to religious and civic groups were tapped to conduct on-site training and to facilitate community action (Maccoby & Solomon, 1981).

While the behavioral and physiological outcomes of the Five-City Project are still being analyzed, promising interim results have shown favorable effects on smoking, blood pressure, exercise habits, and blood cholesterol levels comparable to the changes achieved in the Three-Community Study.

Final results of the epidemiologic surveillance, however, are not yet known (Flora, Maccoby, & Farquhar, 1989).

El Asesino Silencioso (1978)

A 1977 survey of 2,322 adults from Houston, Texas, revealed that Mexican-Americans exhibited significantly less knowledge than the majority of the population in Texas concerning the impact, nature, and control of cardiovascular disease. Mexican-Americans, in general, lacked an awareness of the risks of heart disease and the measures necessary to reduce or prevent its incidence. The need to inform and educate the Mexican-American population about the risk and prevention of heart disease led to the design of a community health information program called El Asesino Silencioso (The Silent Killer), which used televised public service announcements. The PSAs were aired 224 times over six weeks on all local television stations during daytime and prime-time viewing periods. A three-phase evaluation of the effectiveness of the PSAs consisting of telephone surveys of adults in randomly selected Mexican-American households showed few, though positive, results: (a) More than one-third of the 499 survey subjects expressed an awareness of the PSAs; (b) a significantly greater percentage of the group exposed to the PSAs reportedly discussed their blood pressure with their physician, family, or friends; and (c) almost 17% of those who heard the PSAs said that they started to have regular blood pressure checkups (Ramirez, 1979).

The Minnesota Heart Health Program (1980-1990)

The Minnesota Heart Health Program was launched in July 1980 as a community-based public health communication-education program to prevent the incidence of heart disease in three upper Midwest communities. Designers of the program postulated that since each community generates its own norms, shifts in community standards toward an improved health orientation, as a result of increased awareness and interest, would be expected to engender and reinforce appropriate health behaviors in individuals and families. Thus "educational interventions planned with, through and for communities, could lead to changes in community norms, as well as in individual and family behaviors favorable to heart health." The modification of risk factors related to sociocultural influences and personal health behaviors were likely to decrease heart disease incidence. The program aimed to achieve significant changes in smoking prevalence, eating patterns, physical activity levels, and hypertension management (Carlaw, Mittelmark, Bracht, & Luepker, 1984; Jacobs et al., 1986; Mittelmark, Luepker, Grimm, Kottke, & Blackburn, 1988; Perry & Jessor, 1985).

The first phase of the program was directed at fostering consciousness among members of the target audience concerning the concept of good cardiovascular health, the behaviors that nourish a healthy heart, and the practices that lead to risks. It was expected that raising people's awareness would bring about or modify community norms that could promote health-oriented behavior. The second phase focused on the development of trial behaviors, skills, and sustained behavioral changes consistent with perceived community standards on risk factors. This phase also emphasized direct education for skills development with the assistance of existing social support groups in the communities (Carlaw et al., 1984).

The project was conducted in three successive pairs of similar communities. Each community underwent a planned, intensive, and long-term focused disease prevention and health promotion program. The communities selected for this educational program included a town of 30,000 (community 1a), a city of 110,000 (community 2a), and a suburban area of about 80,000 (community 3a). Matched comparison communities were also identified, and demographic and risk factor data on all six communities were collected annually. The program components included mass media, direct education, and community organization. The mass media component was directed toward raising awareness and generating interest. Newspaper, television, and radio messages were supplemented with booklets, posters, and filmstrips. Annual campaigns of four- to six-weeks' duration were organized sequentially around each of the four risk factors, and these provided a focus for media coverage. The last two interventions were meant to teach health-related skills and to provide local support for community change (Carlaw et al., 1984; Jacobs et al., 1986; Perry & Jessor, 1985).

The Pawtucket Heart Health Program (1983-1991)

Directed at a blue-collar community of 70,000 in southeastern New England, the Pawtucket Heart Health Program (PHHP) was designed to increase smoking cessation, foster healthy eating habits, control blood pressure, and promote beneficial physical activities. It differed from the Stanford and Minnesota heart disease prevention efforts in that it combined the use of the telephone and marketing principles, or the so-called telemarketing approach, in conveying health information and increasing participation among program target beneficiaries. Another important feature of the program was its use of volunteers who served as peer models for cognitive and behavioral change related to heart health and provided a network of support for themselves and for others who were making heart health behavioral changes. Mobilizing volunteers was viewed as a way of generating wide participation from the citizens. These volunteers staffed "Heart Check" stations, performed screening activities, acted as referral counselors, disseminated information on heart health, and conducted awareness-raising activities among the target audience. A volunteer program for "telemarketers" was also organized. This entailed (a) a direct-mail

letter introducing PHHP, practically designed as a self-contained information kit, as not everybody could be a call recipient; (b) volunteer training
and supervision, with each trainee receiving a health information "sales"
kit that included a script and a menu of the items and program to be sold;
and (c) following each calling session, a set of self-help materials or a re-
minder of the starting date and time of the desired program sent to the en-
rollee (Lefebvre, Lasater, Carleton, & Peterson, 1987; Schwertfeger, Elder,
Cooper, Lasater, & Carleton, 1986).

Overall, audience receptivity to the program was noted to be high. The
program's messages were well received by the target audience, particularly
after their receipt of the letter introducing the heart program. Although the
telemarketing volunteers were able to reach directly only 5% of Pawtucket's
population, it was observed that call recipients expressed willingness to listen to the caller's message and to discuss relevant issues, sometimes even
at excessive length. The use of telemarketing particularly resulted in both
direct and indirect program gains. Volunteer staff, who were trained at relatively low cost, stimulated direct program participation by way of group
and self-help kit registration and generated a significant level of awareness
of the heart program among the target audience. In its first three years, the
PHHP had more than 30,000 contacts with people seeking to improve their
heart health. Volunteers have invested more than 30,000 hours in the program (Lefebvre et al., 1987).

Cancer Campaigns

Cancer Quest Line (1974)

In 1974, the Wisconsin Clinical Cancer Center developed a dual program, Steps in the Quest for Cancer and Cancer Quest Line, which employed the telephone as an informational and educational medium for
behavioral change in the area of preventive health. Steps in the Quest for
Cancer was a series of 2-minute public service announcements, each presenting a complete story dealing with cancer. Cancer Quest Line was a 24-
hour toll-free phone service providing cancer information to the public.
These two programs were complemented by a promotional campaign utilizing brochures and 10- and 30-second television spots for Quest Line. Au-
diotapes were also made available over Quest Line (Wilkinson, Mirand, &
Graham, 1976).

In the initial year, the program succeeded in reaching primarily urban
dwellers (65%), the young (54% under 45 years), upper-middle-class (39%)
groups, and those with a high level of education (57% had at least some
college education). Although these populations did not constitute the target
population, they were the ones who expressed needs for information. The
program was subsequently revised during the second year of implementation

in order to reach a high-risk target audience (Butler & Paisley, 1977; Wilkinson & Mirand, 1977; Wilkinson et al., 1976; Wilkinson, Mirand, Graham, Johnson, & Vana, 1977).

Feeling Good (1974-1977)

Feeling Good was a television health series designed and produced by the Children's Television Workshop, which is the producer of the popular children's television show *Sesame Street*. Designed to mix entertainment with informational and motivational messages about a variety of health maintenance and disease prevention behaviors, the series was broadcast for a total of 11 full hours and 13 half hours over the Public Broadcasting System network. The target audience was primarily families, especially those belonging to low-income and minority groups. More specifically, the program aimed to educate and inform the target audience about cancer, particularly cancer of the breast, uterus, and colon-rectum. A parallel promotional campaign was conducted to disseminate information about the television series, through press announcements, information brochures to medical and health officers, posters to schools, and fliers to community groups. Originally intended to air over 26 weeks, the show was stopped by the Children's Television Workshop after only 11 weeks as a result of disappointing ratings. It returned after an 8-week hiatus as a new half-hour show; each program dealt exclusively with a single health topic. Each program in the series is believed to have reached an estimated one million viewers (Butler & Paisley, 1977).

Results of an evaluation of *Feeling Good* conducted by the National Opinion Research Center involving a survey of 237 women in a low-income neighborhood in Dallas, Texas, showed (a) an unexpectedly high proportion of respondents in the control group (23%) watching at least one of the *Feeling Good* shows, and (b) a disappointingly low proportion of subjects in the experimental group (54%) watching half or fewer of the shows. It was, however, observed that (a) the series proved effective in generating some fairly simple behaviors, such as seeking health information, eating more fruit, performing breast self-examination, and writing down the poison control number (at least 15% of the viewers in the experimental group exhibited these behaviors); and (b) knowledge was increased in areas such as proper diet, alcoholism, and cardiovascular disease, with approximately 20% more viewers in the experimental group answering the area-related questions correctly than nonviewers. There was also a reported overall increase in the number of people reading newspaper health articles and discussing health matters with friends (Lau, Kane, Berry, Ware, & Roy, 1980).

A second evaluation of *Feeling Good*, in the form of a correlational and a quasi-experimental study, was conducted via a three-wave panel study in four large cities across the country. The results indicated that viewing particular episodes of *Feeling Good* increased knowledge about high blood pressure, breast and colon-rectum cancer, teenage alcoholism, cigarette smoking, and vision problems. Behaviors such as posting the local poison control center's number, having fresh fruit daily, writing down symptoms before visiting a doctor, and having blood pressure, breasts, and vision checked also increased as a function of watching the show.

However, the series as a whole did not have nearly as much effect as was originally hoped for. Although it was in the top third of popularity among PBS shows, it did not really compete effectively with programming on the commercial networks. Despite the large publicity campaign associated with *Feeling Good*, almost half of those who had never seen any of the shows said that they had never heard about them either (Lau et al., 1980).

The Can-Dial Program (1975)

Working on the assumption that increasing the public's knowledge and awareness of cancer would ultimately contribute to a decrease in the morbidity of and mortality from the disease among the target population, the Can-Dial Program was established as a dial access system to 36 prerecorded short lectures containing simplified and usable information on various aspects of cancer. These minilectures, one to seven minutes in length, were played over the phone in response to calls from target communities.

As a source of health information, Can-Dial had two vital components: an information campaign and access to information on cancer through a toll-free telephone number. To advertise its services, the program used radio and television public service announcements and disseminated brochures via mail, the print media, and public places. Early evaluation results suggested that the telephone could be a novel medium for disseminating health information. It could serve to answer many of the audience's pressing questions, in privacy, at a time and place of their choice, and at no cost to them. It was assumed that if callers had the freedom to choose their own subjects of interest, they would be much more predisposed to listen to and absorb the information being given.

Information about Can-Dial came mainly through brochures, followed by print advertisements, televised PSAs, and personal contact. Interviews conducted a few weeks following telephone inquiries revealed that callers showed greater cancer knowledge than a sample of noncallers, although no clear or definitive conclusions could be drawn because the precall knowledge levels of callers had not been ascertained. However, a two-year evaluation of the Can-Dial Program found a reported positive impact on behavior directly related to physical health for about 40% of a systematic sample of callers interviewed several weeks after their initial contact with the system. Another 20% of the same sample reported some other positive impacts, such as relief of anxiety as a result of listening to one of the prerecorded cancer lectures.

Results showed that approximately 60% of the calls were from individuals who had not phoned previously, 17% were repeat calls, and 7% were hang-up calls. These results indicated that slightly more than three-fourths of the calls received were of a substantive nature, resulting in the transmission of information. Some 95% of those who called requested only one topic. The rest listened to more than one tape during their initial call. The most popular tapes were those concerning cigarette smoking, general aspects of cancer, and breast cancer. With regard to the motivation for using Can-Dial, most respondents cited a desire to quit smoking or stated some curiosity about a cancer problem. About 30% were driven either by their personal experience with cancer or by the experiences of friends or relatives. The remaining 10% reported they were simply interested in a specific type of cancer or in obtaining more knowledge (Wilkinson et al., 1976).

The National Cancer Awareness Program (1984)

Based on strong evidence that cancer is associated with personal behavior choices and that the public's view of cancer is muddled and skeptical, the National Cancer Institute (NCI) began a cancer awareness program in 1984. The program formed part of several other cancer prevention projects by the NCI that aimed to reduce cancer mortality by 50% by the year 2000. The health communication intervention was done via three waves of public service announcements that were meant to create awareness of cancer risk factors, to announce the availability of the new cancer prevention booklet, "Good News, Better News: Cancer Prevention," and to promote the toll-free Cancer Information Service telephone number (1-800-4-CANCER). The PSAs and the booklets were produced in both English and Spanish (Hammond, Freimuth, & Morrison, 1987).

The first set of PSAs ("Hardhat" and "Checkout") was distributed to radio and television stations in March 1984, followed by the second set ("Lifesaver" and "Good News") in July 1984 and the third set ("Aretha I" and "Aretha II") in May 1985. NCI released the PSAs, together with reply postcards, to 1,200 television stations throughout the United States. Some 10-18% of the station managers, or the so-called media gatekeepers, returned the postcards, indicating their intention to air the PSAs. Most of the station managers said that they would run the PSAs fewer than five times a week at no specified time slot and at the station's convenience.

The distribution of the PSAs coincided with a relatively significant rise in cancer prevention calls. After the release of the first set of PSAs, in early March 1984, the total number of prevention calls increased from 323 in February to 6,843 in March and 13,565 in April. The second and third sets of PSAs were also followed by increases in prevention calls, although the increases were not as substantial those found after as the first set. Following the distribution of the second set of PSAs, prevention calls rose from 8,788 to 14,773. Again prevention calls roughly doubled between April and May 1985 after the release of the third set of PSAs.

An analysis of *Broadcast Advertisers Report* (BAR) for the NCI campaign indicated that the PSAs were aired 5,030 times during the 21-month period. BAR estimated that 28% of the total television homes were exposed to the message during the period, which was roughly equivalent to 24,003,720 potential audience members, or only 14% of the total target population of 170,360,000.

With regard to the number of responses by individuals to the message, only 144,442 persons called the Cancer Information Service to request information on cancer prevention during the 21-month period, a mere 0.09% of the target population. Still, there was a possibility that not everyone who called for prevention information was responding directly to the PSAs. However, if the goal of the campaign was to induce information seeking by the public about cancer prevention, then this active audience response is probably the best indicator of the effectiveness of the campaign.

The analysis suggests that only an insignificant percentage of a target population is reached by a public service message. Media gatekeepers play a crucial role in this exposure process. It has been concluded that campaign planners are often naively optimistic about the possible reach of their PSAs, which must go through a narrow "funneling" process, with media gatekeepers controlling the potential exposure of the messages. A PSA must first make it through a gatekeeper's initial screening before it can have any potential impact on its target audience. Therefore, it becomes imperative for those using PSAs to learn more about gatekeepers' selection criteria and the selection process itself (Hammond et al., 1987).

General Preventive Health Campaigns

Radio Novelas for Health Education (1982)

Radio novelas, targeted at Hispanics, were aimed at increasing the levels of knowledge and awareness of, as well as generating positive responses to, the major health problems that affect the Hispanic community, such as hypertension, obesity, and diabetes. The health communication program consisted of five 5-minute radio episodes or novelas, each discussing a major health problem and its corresponding symptoms, diagnosis, treatment, and prevention. The episodes were broadcast twice a day for over five days on a popular Spanish radio station in Richmond and Rosenberg, Texas. Pre- and posttests with groups of adult Hispanics and follow-up conversations with health fair participants indicated that most listeners ranked obesity as a priority health concern over hypertension or diabetes. However, audience awareness of all three problems increased as a result of the radio novelas. It was also noted that 39% of the listeners took action regarding their health, and most of them became more motivated to attend the health fair. Program researchers claim that the radio novela in this case was an effective information-education strategy (Ramirez, 1983).

Alcohol Abuse Prevention Campaign (1980-1982)[1]

A two-year campaign was conducted by the National Institute on Alcohol Abuse and Alcoholism (NIAAA) with the aim of focusing national attention and resources on the prevention of alcohol-related problems. Directed at two target audiences, women and youth, the campaign included messages on drinking patterns of women, especially those from ages 18 to 34; alcohol effects on pregnant women; and drinking and driving among youth.

Program development consisted of the following important steps: (a) use of focus groups, (b) analysis of the media preferences of target audiences, and (c) pretesting of materials for relevance, understandability, realism, and attractiveness. Six focus groups were formed in August 1980 to identify major issues and concerns of youth and women and to explore the participants' attitudes and feelings about drinking and alcohol abuse. The concerns and preferences expressed by group members were then used in the development of educational materials. Each script was presented in storyboard form to small groups of people representative of the target audience. In all, 10 focus groups were probed to elicit reactions to the messages and to determine comprehension and relevance (Maloney & Hersey, 1984).

One campaign effect that had not been fully anticipated was the trigger effect on the broadcast of other spots related to alcohol prevention. Since nationally produced spots could not be provided to cover all local situations, assistance was offered in preparing materials for special groups, and some states developed broadcast materials for special audiences, such as Native Americans or black teenage girls. Other stations aired PSAs that addressed local problems or issues to ensure the interest of the intended viewer, and several others released spots that had been used in other alcohol abuse prevention campaigns. The television PSAs developed by the NIAAA campaign represented 54% of the alcohol spots aired between February and December 1982. In 65% of the Broadcast Advertisers Report cities, the NIAAA spots were the first alcohol abuse prevention PSAs shown. Between February and December 1982, an estimated 17,409 alcohol-related PSAs appeared on television in the major broadcast markets monitored by BAR (Maloney & Hersey, 1984).

After a few months, 2,200 to 2,300 PSAs were being broadcast a month in June and July 1982. While the NIAAA campaign began in earnest in the spring, the level of PSAs remained high throughout the year, with an average of 1,584. In response to concerns about alcohol abuse during the holiday season, 3,639 spots were broadcast in December.

The decentralization of certain aspects of the campaign might have been essential to its success. Based on the assumption that state and local groups

were attuned to special needs of their communities and knew what resources were available to devote to public education, local and state groups
and agencies were allowed to exercise control over the timing of their programs, optimize available resources, and coordinate efforts. This provided
a sense of ownership among those involved, which subsequently triggered
voluntary participation from various groups in many campaign activities.

A Su Salud (1985-1990)

Initiated in 1985 in southwest Texas as a five-year mass media health
promotion program encouraging smoking prevention and cessation among
Hispanic Americans, Programa A Su Salud (To Your Health) was geared to
counteract the explosion of alcohol and tobacco advertisements aimed at
the Hispanic population. In addition, it sought to raise the target audience's
level of concern for the effects of alcohol and tobacco consumption. Utilizing a partially randomized, longitudinal quasi-experimental design, the
study involved the participation of adult residents (18-64 years old) from
approximately 1,200 households in two locations in southwest Texas. It
distinguished itself from other mass media public health promotion programs by its employment of local (in lieu of "professional") role models
within the message design. Using community participation as a framework
for program development, it mobilized target group members in survey administration, formative evaluation sessions, local program promotion activities, and community social service support. A Su Salud likewise involved
focus groups within the target communities in determining people's knowledge and perceptions of health issues, tapped local media professionals in
the design and production of campaign materials, and coproduced television broadcasts with local broadcasting stations.

Initial loci of study during the first year of the program included Eagle Pass
(population 20,000) and Del Rio (population 30,000). A three-tiered experimental activity was established sequentially in different locations in Eagle
Pass: (a) a mass media program aimed at smoking cessation/prevention, (b) a
media program complemented by direct community organization and training,
utilizing existing social networks in order to increase encouragement and reinforcement for responses specifically related to smoking cessation/prevention,
and (c) an additional program of individual attention and support for stress
coping targeted at persons experiencing difficulty in smoking cessation.

To trigger and reinforce the acquisition and performance of desirable
attitudes and behaviors as presented in the media, such as television broadcasts, A Su Salud provided face-to-face communication mechanisms
through simple forms of verbal cuing and mobilizing by volunteers. Volunteers recommended imitation of role models, provided positive feedback
for any behavioral changes, and offered support for maintaining new health
behaviors. Schools were also asked to motivate and instruct students in

ways they might provide cuing and reinforcement. Additional sources of community cooperation included local health care providers (particularly physicians), clerics and lay leadership from community churches, bartenders, shopkeepers, and other persons in key locations (Ramirez & McAlister, 1988).

However, A Su Salud was just one of the numerous antismoking communication campaigns conducted since the first surgeon general's report on the causal relationship between cigarette smoking and disease in 1964. Flay (1987), in reexamining the evaluations of 40 mass media programs or campaigns on smoking cessation, also posits that campaigns designed "to inform or motivate generally produced changes in awareness, knowledge, and attitudes. Extensive national campaigns also produced meaningful behavior change. Programs or campaigns designed to promote some specific smoking-related action produced mixed results, depending on the type of promotion involved" (p. 153). More significantly, he observes that mass media cessation clinics have been found to be effective, with mass media combined with social support programs showing better results than using a single medium or a combination of media. Out of the 40 campaigns, 7 relied on mass media (television) only, 10 combined television and print materials, and 4 campaigns supplemented media with social support.

Citing the experience of the counteradvertising campaign in 1967-1970, Flay also suggests that, given certain conditions, public service announcements may produce some impact. Such conditions include "(a) a number of novel spots, rather than just one or two shown repeatedly; (b) widespread dissemination; (c) high saturation; and (d) endurance" (p. 155). Still, the use of PSAs in campaigns does not guarantee behavioral effects.

An opposing view regarding smoking cessation campaigns has been forwarded by Thompson (1978). In a review of published reports on antismoking campaigns from 1960 to 1976, she notes that none of these campaigns (using various combinations of methods, including mass media advertising, pamphlets and brochures, exhibits, and films) produced significant changes in smoking behavior, and that the reported effects on public attitudes toward smoking were inconsistent. On the other hand, Thompson observes that smoking withdrawal clinics and individual counseling demonstrated the most success, producing abstinence rates of 20-35% one year after treatment.

THEORETICAL DIRECTIONS
OF PUBLIC HEALTH COMMUNICATION

While the cases presented above represent only a small fraction of communication programs directed at changing the public's health life-style and behavior, a closer reexamination of the principles embedded in program components, strategies, and processes can lead us toward definite theoretical paths that they have followed.[2] Overall, three distinct health communication approaches can be noted: first, a continuing reliance on the direct effects of mass media; second, an attempt to recapture interpersonal processes; and third, a synergistic intervention utilizing person-to-person communication, community support, and mass communication.

Continuing Belief in the Direct Effects Model

Drawing assumptions embedded in the direct effects model, or the "hypodermic effects" perspective, the *Feeling Good* series, radio novelas, the El Asesino program, the NIAAA's Alcohol Abuse Prevention Program, and other media-centered antismoking programs have implemented public service announcements, radio spots, or television series as the primary instruments necessary to effect changes in health life-style and behavior. The belief has been that health messages transmitted through mass media would eventually have an impact on the members of the target audience who happened to be exposed to them. A substantial amount of air time has been allotted for broadcasting health information, and campaign success has been measured in terms of the number of times the announcements were aired during a specified period. Based on the estimated population of viewers during that time slot, the campaign extrapolated the number of persons reached by the PSAs or other radio and television spots. In spite of scarce or inadequate evaluation efforts, there have persisted claims of success or effectiveness regarding the sole use of mass media for change-directed endeavors. But, looking at the reports on and evaluations of *Feeling Good*, the El Asesino program, use of radio novelas, and alcohol abuse prevention programs, for instance, results are less than encouraging, with any impact evident among no more than 40% of those who were exposed to the messages.

Indeed, the use of the direct effects model as a framework for health communication programs has long been argued to have limited impact on the intended audience. It is too simple to assume that supplying information through the mass media will have a corresponding impact on the public. Hyman and Sheatsley (1947) argue that several factors must be taken into account, foremost of which is the "importance of motivation in achievement or learning, or in assimilating knowledge" (p. 415). Increasing the supply of information materials or using various mechanisms for information dissemination will be ineffective if it does not consider the public's interest (Hyman & Sheatsley, 1947; Mendelsohn, 1974). Attempts to convey specific information via the mass media in the form of public service announcements do not demonstrate appreciable effects even on self-benefit topics such as antismoking (McGuire, 1986; Warner, 1977). Solomon (1981), Atkin (1981), and McGuire (1986) have concluded that the pervasive or highly exposed PSAs in other areas of health concern, such as drug abuse prevention, seat-belt use, and availability of mental health services, have not shown any tangible proof of awareness, much less compliance or behavioral effects. Even less evidence exists for the behavioral effects of public service announcements.

The contrast between programs that utilize media as the only intervention and programs that combine media with other strategies is particularly apparent in Stanford's Three-Community Study, in which two communities received a variety of media information and persuasion aimed at encouraging smoking cessation while another community received no special communications. A three-year follow-up of smokers from all three communities showed no more than short-term effects of the media campaign. Although overall smoking prevalence rates after three years were still disappointing, those who received face-to-face instruction had more success in smoking cessation than did the smokers who received media and community programs only, and both groups did better than the control community (Flay, 1987).

On the basis of these failures to demonstrate strong and specific communication effects when media-only campaigns are employed, one might conclude that the many informational and persuasive events and campaigns of the last 30 years have had only temporary or limited impacts on health behavior. Given these findings and the successful experiences in the early 1900s of combining mass media with strategies involving local participation, it is therefore surprising to discover present-day health communication programs that continue to rely solely on mass media to encourage complex behavioral change.

Recapturing Interpersonal Processes

Moving from the direct effects model, the Can-Dial, Cancer Quest Line, Pawtucket Heart Health, and National Cancer Awareness programs have utilized the telephone as the medium for conveying health information, combining it with promotion or marketing strategies to introduce the health program to the target audience.[3] These represent information programs that follow an interactive framework for delivering health messages and generating responses or behavioral compliance. This two-way communication process recognizes target audience members as active seekers of information and assumes that there is always some element of motivation and self-interest in what people wish to be informed about. There are practical considerations for designing health communication programs along this framework. The highly personal nature of health concerns such as cancer, drug addiction, or alcohol abuse requires a communication process that can provide information or advice in a manner that approximates the person-to-person mode and ensures the confidentiality of the exchange. Health concerns necessitate conditions of empathy. Communicating health values summons not just a straightforward checklist of simplified health information, but an effort on the part of the communicator to understand the difficulty of the change process. In terms of media strategies, telephone information programs have emerged as a possible means of disseminating preventive health information, especially on cancer prevention. They are considered an economical and accessible mechanism that employs neither scare tactics nor overoptimism. Rather, they provide information that is accurate, straightforward, and sensible. These general observations are posited by Altman (1985), who concludes, in his study on the use of the Cancer Quest Line program, that "health telephone programs . . . combine some of the positive components of mass media—high exposure, convenience, cost-effectiveness, user anonymity—with some of the positive components of face-to-face interaction or personalized attention" (p. 170). In the case of the Pawtucket Heart Health Program, the people who operate the telephone hot lines are the volunteer residents themselves. Their involvement as "telemarketers" of health information is a good indication of the sustainability and replicability of the approach in other target communities.

A requisite element of an information program utilizing the telephone is a promotional activity that generates awareness among the public about the program's existence, through brochures, public service announcements on radio and television, and public service advertisements in local newspapers and newsletters (Wilkinson et al., 1976). The mass media, in this context, are employed to inform the target public about the availability of information that can be obtained through a mode that is much more personalized and "intimate" in orientation. Although there have been some promising indications of success, the impact of using the telephone to transmit health information is an area that remains to be explored fully.

Toward a Synergistic Set of Interventions

From interventions that approximate person-to-person communication, some major present-day health communication programs have moved toward integrated approaches that blend interpersonal mechanisms, social support systems, and mass media in efforts to change health behaviors and life-styles. The Stanford, Minnesota, and Pawtucket heart health programs and the A Su Salud program exemplify such approaches. Common elements or components can be noted in these health communication programs: (a) mass media have both proactive and support functions, (b) the role of the individual and the community as catalysts or as reinforcing agents is underscored, and (c) the audience members are seen as active participants in the change effort. These components do not operate separately, but rather act together to form a holistic intervention. Overall, these programs reflect the theoretical constructs and perspectives of socialization, social learning, salience and pertinence, mass persuasion, and information seeking, and have used them to form a potent framework for individual and community change.

The Role of the Mass Media

The mass media, although they play a vital if not central role in these programs, are not utilized as a fixed and monolithic instrument to generate communicatory inputs to a passive audience on a predetermined schedule. The functions of the mass media in these health communication programs differ not so much in the type of technology used as in the types of messages and information transmitted. On one level, the mass media have been used to promote health programs and their educational and information services. In another context, the mass media have been mobilized to (a) inform target audience members about specific preventive measures they can take in relation to a health problem, (b) motivate audience members to adopt or initiate changes in their health life-styles and behaviors, and (c) teach audience members how to maintain a healthy life-style. Researchers involved in the Stanford Heart Disease Prevention Program even went as far as to view the mass media as a catalyst for behavior change when the skills involved were simple and "teachable," as in the improvement of eating habits. They also speculated that future experiments might be conducted concerning the utilization of mass media to carry messages that focus on the development of more complex skills in health development. The Pawtucket Heart Health Program, while using traditional communication forms to disseminate vital information about the program, attempted to preserve the "personalized" and interactive communication process by using the telephone both as a marketing strategy (telemarketing approach) and as a way of conveying ideas on disease prevention, skills development, and health maintenance.

The manner in which the mass media are employed in these programs contains conceptual elements from the principles of *mass persuasion*. As Cartwright (1949) has suggested, mass behavioral change could be made possible only if communications media are able to activate three psychological processes by creating particular cognitive, motivational, and behavioral structures. In short, behavior is defined by "beliefs, opinions, and facts" a person possesses; by the needs, goals, and values he or she has; and by the momentary control held over his or her behavior by given features of the person's cognitive and motivational structure. Influencing behavior "from the outside" requires the ability to influence these determinants in a particular way. Simply providing the opportunity for mass stimulation of the target audience does not guarantee results in the actual stimulation of any large segment of it (Cartwright, 1949). Of significant importance is that Cartwright's mass persuasion theory also contains principles that operate along the lines of socialization, social learning, salience-pertinence, and interpersonal communication theories and perspectives. Based on a campaign experience in selling U.S. savings bonds, Cartwright suggested that mass media alone were not effective in bolstering sales, but that personal solicitation yielded better results. Thus it was believed that mass media intervention might be enhanced by the addition of an interpersonal element, through face-to-face and group processes, designed to stimulate or trigger specific behavior changes.

Skills Training and Development of Social Support Systems

Many of the objectives related to public health communications depend on more than a positive attitude or a decision to change. Changes in health behavior or life-style happen gradually and are engendered by an environment that is conducive to change and is supportive of newly acquired behaviors. The mass media component may be able to generate interest in a health issue or set the agenda for what has to be learned and why, but it must be strongly supplemented with activities that show the target audience *how* to do these things. Recognizing the importance of social variables or structures in the process of learning exchange or sharing, the Stanford, Minnesota, Pawtucket, and A Su Salud programs have involved complementary activities that included skills development, use of models, and establishment of peer or social support groups. Skills acquisition has been facilitated by training programs that systematically lay down step-by-step measures or actions that work toward better health behaviors. These enable the target audience to *learn how* to cope with new health life-styles and to maintain new health behaviors. This is also accomplished through social modeling, wherein different parts of an action sequence are explicitly identified and repeated by a model. Social modeling, especially if done by peers, is particularly effective when models show realistic standards for self-reinforcement or exhibit self-confidence in trial-and-error learning. In proving that such efforts take time but are not "impossible" to achieve, as in smoking cessation or control of cholesterol intake, programs can encourage audience members to have practical expectations, and thus lessen the pressure they may feel to excel or to make everything right all at once. The creation of an environment favorable to change also entails the formation of self-help and small social support groups. The Pawtucket and Stanford programs are outstanding examples of efforts employing volunteers, community associations, and health professionals as referral counselors and as conveyors of heart health information. Part of their commitment, so to speak, has been to be able to guide and encourage the maintenance of positive health behaviors on an ongoing basis. This underscores the necessity to involve a broad spectrum of people in goal determination and action for effective community change. In the Stanford, Minnesota, and Pawtucket programs, while emphasizing commitment as the real driving force behind health behavioral change, it is worth noting that the application of positive reinforcement for health behaviors also came in the form of token point systems, prizes, and lotteries (Elder, Hovell, Lasater, Wells, & Carleton, 1985).

The provision of training, use of models, and formation of social support groups have a solid basis in the conceptual formulations of the *socialization perspective* and *social learning theory*. As noted by Green and Mc-Alister (1984), "Many of the objectives related to health promotion depend on more than the *decision* to change. They require the learning of challenging new skills of self-control and life-style management. That learning is dependent on more complex aspects of modeling" (p. 333).

The socialization perspective postulates that some form of modeling and reinforcement may be part of the whole dynamics of change. The modeling process prescribes imitation as the key mechanism; that is, a subject is encouraged to emulate the "socialization" agent for specific reasons and the agent's behavior is presented as the most salient alternative open to the person (McLeod & O'Keefe, 1972). Social models, especially those who possess socially desirable characteristics such as attractiveness, perceived social competence, expertise, and credibility, presumably are able to effect changes in attitudes, beliefs, decision making, and acquisition of new patterns of behavior. The process can also be facilitated when models are depicted as sharing the same reality as that of the observer. Hence peers essentially serve as good "models" because they encounter the same pain as they demonstrate the difficult process of change; they fail occasionally, cope with predictable problems, and attain the "ideal" state, as it were, in a gradual manner (McAlister, Ramirez, Galavotti, & Gallion, 1989). Learning becomes easy when models show realistic standards for self-reinforcement and when performance expectations are attainable (Green & McAlister, 1984). Reinforcement plays a part in the socialization process, as the environment provides some form of affirmation or reward for the attainment or maintenance of a desired status. On the other hand, reinforcement may take on a "negative" form, as in the reduction of various barriers and impediments to behavior.

Bandura's (1977) social learning theory presents the idea of "multidirectional interactionism," or the reciprocal interactionist approach. He contends that behavior is determined by expectancies and incentives:

> Individuals who value the perceived effects of changed lifestyles (incentives) will attempt to change if they believe that (a) their current lifestyles pose threats to any personally valued outcomes, such as health or appearance (environmental cues); (b) particular behavioral changes will reduce the threats (outcome expectations); and (c) they are personally capable of adopting new behaviors (efficacy expectations). (Bandura, 1977; as cited by Rosenstock, Stretcher, & Becker, 1988)

Human behavior is regulated by immediate situational influences, a person's performance skills, and his or her anticipations of the consequences of different courses of action, rather than by such global constructs as personality traits. People view the interplay between environment and behavior as a reciprocal influence process in which the environment shapes their behaviors, but they also shape their environment. Social learning theory assumes that people's preferences, choices, and dispositions influence not only their behavior, but their conditions as well, and, in some cases, may even create such conditions. It further posits that behavioral shifts are more tenable if cognitive and motivational foundations exist and are consistent with the new behavior. New knowledge is likewise retained in the absence of any major conflicting experiences, beliefs, attitudes, and behaviors that run contrary to it. Behavioral change is also maximized when explicit directions to attain change are provided, such as appropriate behavioral controls and behavioral skills. The social learning framework is especially evident in the Stanford, Minnesota, and Pawtucket heart health programs, whose interventions promoted what Bandura refers to as "collective efficacy," or bringing together people who are individually high in personal efficacy who then, as a group, can work to effect changes in groups, organizations, and the community at large. The process followed by the Pawtucket Heart Health Program shows the blending of both individual and community-oriented change strategies in planning heart health intervention. In the Stanford program, the social learning model was applied through combined interpersonal communication and mass communication processes (Alcalay, 1983; Lefebvre et al., 1987).

The complementary concepts of interaction, exchange, affirmation, and support within the context of a social environment as advanced by social learning theory and the socialization perspective also bring out elements of *interpersonal communication theory* and *co-orientational concepts*, in which principles of proximity, intimacy, similarities, and "equivalence" are understood. The interpersonal communication process is evident in interventions that employ face-to-face interactions and training of indigenous leaders, health professionals, members of community groups and schools. In the case of the Pawtucket Heart Health Program, volunteers have been used to convey health information. The same intervention activities were used in the Minnesota program, which used social support groups as the mechanisms for transmission. A Su Salud involved the audience in practically all phases of implementation, including the design of the messages. Hence, shifting from the idea of a mass audience as recipient of an information dose, a view of the audience as a group of diverse individuals or communities, functioning within dynamic systems that help shape their individual or communal dispositions, has emerged. Within the context of socialization, this recognizes the necessity of interpersonal contact to supplement the use of mass media, and that attempts to change attitudes and behaviors require personalized communications. Discussion or processing of "mass media program content by teachers or other role models" is an example of a balanced process utilizing interpersonal and mass communication mechanisms (Bettinghaus, 1988). This suggests that interpersonal communications may "perform particular functions at certain stages of the behavioral change process, the most vital of which is the provision of encouragement, feedback, and reinforcement to stimulate learning and performance of the behaviors that are modeled in the mass media" (Green & McAlister, 1984, p. 334).

Audience as Participants in the Change Process

Complementing the basic elements of social learning theory and the socialization perspective, and adding another dimension to the conceptual foundation of public health communication programs, is the idea of *salience and pertinence*. Carter (1965), in proposing a "paradigm of affective relations in an orientation situation," defines pertinence as the relation between two objects (x and y), based on the comparative degree to which each possesses the shared attribute; salience is defined as the value one attaches to an object (x) on the basis of an existing relation with another object (y). Thus, in theory, the more salient the object is, the greater its value. And as the person moves from one situation to another, the salience of an object that occurs in both situations increases as a result of the added experience with it (Chaffee, 1967). This framework has likewise guided the Stanford, Minnesota, and Pawtucket heart health and A Su Salud programs. Individuals and communities jointly assume responsibility with health professionals and community members in planning and carrying out program activities. Both parties engage in discovering culturally appropriate responses to problems related to heart health. The Minnesota program postulated that each community comes up with its own standards of health behavior. Shifts in community norms toward better health were then expected to support and encourage health behaviors in individuals and families. The framework of community participation was particularly evident in A Su Salud. It organized focus groups in the communities, involved local media professionals in the design and production of campaign materials, and mobilized target group members in promotion, formative evaluation activities, and community service support. This phenomenon of change within the salience-pertinence setting may be closely linked with the idea of internalization, wherein an individual consents to influential persuasion because the induced behavior is congruent with his or her value system. Individuals adopt behaviors because they find them useful or important for the solution of an issue, or because the behaviors are congenial to their own orientations. Moreover, people may adopt behaviors because they perceive them as intrinsically conducive to the maximization of their values. The theoretical import of the salience-pertinence concept in the context of public health communication is that it allows the communicator to design programs that are consistent with the value relations that the target audience has placed among objects or situations. It also provides a guide in terms of ensuring that the so-called salience builds up along a "learning" pattern that eventually leads to the desired changes.

The orientation toward a more active and goal-directed audience is best contained in *information-seeking theory*, or the *information-seeking model*, as some communication scholars prefer to call it. Information seeking is essentially a proactive framework in which the audience is seen more as an initiator of information searches. It underscores information *exchanges* between the audience and the so-called information sources, as well as among audience members themselves. The communication agent then catalyzes the group communication processes, encourages the definition of needs, and provides mechanisms for community-initiated solutions (Donohew & Springer, 1980). The information-seeking model views a person's communicatory activities, both mass and interpersonal, as "interwoven in an outgoing system of reciprocal influences" (Chaffee & McLeod, 1973, p. 237), so that the principal effect is further communication. A complementary view is given by the *uses and dependency model* (Rubin & Windhal, 1986), which elaborates the social and psychological origins of individual needs and motives, uses of personal and mediated communication channels, and information-seeking strategies. Both the information-seeking and the uses and dependency conceptual formulations see the process of mass communication as interactive in that there are "combinative effects among media stimuli, media uses and gratifications, and societal structures and events" (Rubin & Windhal, 1986, p. 192). The constant transactions that occur among audience, media, and society affect media coverage and information availability, presentations, and societal or community structures and events. In a health communication setting, this directs program developers toward turning both interpersonal and mass communication into more participative processes that could not only trigger the desired behavioral or life-style changes, but maintain those changes as well.

IMPLICATIONS FOR
COMMUNICATION PLANNING AND STRATEGY

The cases just reviewed reflect three general categories of theoretical movements that have been or are being followed by public health communication programs: (a) a continuing belief in the direct effects model, (b) attempts at recapturing interpersonal processes, and (c) pursuit of methods that aim toward a synergistic set of interventions. While some communication scholars tend to interpret these movements along the "top-down" and "bottom-up" debate (i.e., centralized, change-directed communication programs versus more interactive and participative social change communication programs), our attempt to examine the trends using a phenomenological approach has provided us with a more holistic method of analyzing modern public health communication and drawing the implications for planning and strategy. What lessons can we derive now that we have laid out the general directions of public health communication programs? What gaps can we identify?

Notwithstanding inadequate evaluations of public health communication programs, which make it difficult to ascertain their efficacy in relation to health behavioral change, several generalizations can be made: First, in terms of theoretical assumptions, it is clear that the hypodermic model (almost in a literal sense), as a framework for health communication programs, does not offer much promise in terms of generating shifts in health life-style or behavior, and even the impact on knowledge gain from programs based on this model is minimal (see the above discussions of the National Cancer Awareness Program, the *Feeling Good* series, and the NIAAA's Alcohol Abuse Prevention Campaign). This runs counter to the belief of some communication strategists in the direct gains to be made through the use of mass media—that is, that health change can easily be influenced by increasing inputs through multiple channels of communication. It can be noted that large doses of public service announcements generally do not exhibit any significant contribution toward effecting changes in health life-styles or behaviors. Moreover, it can be said that health communication programs founded on the assumptions of the direct effects model lead to inadequacies in conceptualizing, communicating, and programming health messages, as well as in conceptualizing and communicating with the receivers of these messages. Since the audience is seen as a mere information receiver (the head count as to the number of so-called targeted recipients is usually in terms of television or radio owners, viewers or listeners), it is unlikely that audience members' health information needs are met or that messages are formed on the basis of their general predispositions or perceptions of health issues. This model also does not provide much chance for the audience's feedback to become an input in succeeding communication activities. The need for a more receiver-focused health campaign, compared with a source-oriented one, has been qualified by Dervin (1981) as a "sense-making" approach to mass communication. Dervin views the sense-making approach as a responsive, audience-centered design—one that initially looks at "possible message users and what information they need, and then sees how observations that sources have may serve those needs" (p. 84).

Second, because health is essentially a personal or social value, communicating health concerns necessitates the use of personalized and interactive programming (just as in health care delivery there is a growing clamor for more communication between doctors and patients and between nurses and patients). The recognition of the nature of the issue at hand has already directed numerous health communication scholars and planners toward operationalizing theories that lend themselves to multiple levels of interaction. In the cases we have reviewed, cancer information programs seem to be the forerunner in providing some mechanism for exchange. Although they still use the mass media (mostly to broadcast PSAs), almost as do programs operating under the direct effects model, the emphasis is on the use of the telephone as the major conveyor of information. The idea is to make the telephone a mechanism through which people can seek the health information they need at a time that is convenient for them (which can also be interpreted as "the time when they are predisposed to receive information"). Communication literature, however, does not provide a clear-cut or extensive rationale for the use of the telephone in health information programs. Nonetheless, we can look at it as a commendable attempt to tap the potential of one of the oldest and most widely used electronic, yet interpersonal, means of communication. From the perspective of information seeking, the telephone offers a way to increase, expand, or stimulate information-seeking behavior among the target audience. It preserves the person-to-person mode and allows it to happen regardless of the physical distance. The "neighborhood friend" or "acquaintance" may actually need to be redefined in terms of the people one could call for inquiry, assistance, or simple company. The proliferation of telephone hot lines attests to a growing recognition of this phenomenon. The telephone has now come to serve as a possible conveyor of information, with the audience as the active seeker. Audience members are not held captive, as with television commercials or public service advertisements; rather, they initiate the process of communication. The issue of salience is also resolved by the very fact that there is somehow an element of congruence between audience members' expectations and the messages they are likely to receive. If one dials a breast cancer information hot line, for instance, it is unlikely that one would expect to receive information about a totally unrelated health concern. Messages or information, whether recorded or given by a counselor, are specifically tailored to a specific audience and fulfill their purpose only when the audience is prepared to receive the information. Given the highly targeted nature of the telephone information program, it holds some promise in facilitating follow-up as well as evaluation of impact, areas that have long eluded other public communication programs. Initial attempts of telephone information programs show relative success. However, as a medium of information, it remains to be optimized and opens up the search for other media that can lend themselves to accuracy and uniformity of information, confidentiality, accessibility, and intimacy.

The question, however, as to whether communication strategists should endeavor only to approximate person-to-person exchanges or combine mass media interventions with other strategies that utilize interpersonal exchanges leads us to the third generalization. While emphasizing the personal nature of health and the need for "personalized" interactions, most major health communication programs, which tackle more complex health issues and have larger program scopes, now place an equal importance on the social dimension. They particularly focus on the role of community support systems in stimulating, reinforcing, and nourishing changes in health knowledge, behaviors, and attitudes. We can observe the preponderance of theoretical frameworks in which individual change is seen as a function of the social environment. We can also note a more audience-oriented programming of communication activities, that is, a regard for the audience as an information-seeker and as a participant in the communication process itself. There are efforts to formulate program messages based on audience needs and perceptions of salience, as well as attempts to reformat communication inputs depending on the feedback given. We can also see a movement toward utilizing volunteer community groups both as disseminators of health information and as reinforcers of changed behaviors. While the mass media still play a central role in these programs, their efficacy is seen only in relation to complementary face-to-face communication activities. Recent health communication attempts have forwarded the notion that in some areas, as in the teaching of simple skills, mass media can be utilized as the sole intervention. But, with the ongoing search for more personalized, interactive media, it could happen that the scope of influence that mass media can have in teaching skills and knowledge formation may expand.

Overall, we can see that public health communication programs that have operated under the combined conceptual frameworks of mass persuasion, social learning, socialization, salience and pertinence, and information seeking have shown more success than have those that have emphasized either the role of the media or that of person-to-person communication as the sole intervention for health change. An interesting observation, however, is that initial gains of public health communication programs following this synergistic framework practically reaffirm experiences of early public health communication programs in the late nineteenth century. At that time there was a heavy reliance on social support in addition to mass communication. The major difference is that current programs advocate long-term effects in terms of both individual change and community change, whereas earlier programs ended as soon as legislation was passed.

The Stanford, Minnesota, Pawtucket, and A Su Salud programs are excellent examples of this changing shift in health communication programming. Looking at these cases, however, we could also identify some gaps that may have to be addressed in other public health communication programs. First, "community" has been conventionally operationalized as the existing organized groups or support systems in a particular area. In the Stanford program, viewing "individual change as a function of strong community support" interprets change as made possible only by groups who could help the individual cope with the demands of new behavior and the skills to be learned. As in the case of the Minnesota program, it posits that shifts in community norms of health knowledge, attitudes, and behaviors are likely to put pressure on individual knowledge, attitudes, and behaviors. In both respects, a strong emphasis is put on the viability of change in the individual and the community of which he or she is a part. While there is some validity to this view, defining the community largely in a geographical sense has strategy implications. We wish to point out the supporting role that the individual's immediate community—the family—can offer. Research studies on social relationships conclude that family relationships are particularly instrumental in protecting individual health. Family ties, like other communal relationships, involve elements of meaning and obligations that contribute to social control, which is one avenue through which social relationships affect health behaviors (Umberson, 1987). The mechanisms by which the relationship can be operationalized and enhanced remain largely unexplored. A few of the areas of research concern that need to be looked into in order to aid in strategy planning with a focus on family as a social support include health information sources, perceptions of health issues (as a measure of salience) and control, patterns of information use, and indicators of information processing. A considerable amount of planning would also have to go into preparing and training families for their role as reinforcers of health change. In the long term, even the theoretical constructs of social learning and socialization, which have not really used or viewed the family as a reinforcing environment, may gain from possible theoretical modifications. There may also be a need to consider family communication theories as an additional framework for program conceptualization and planning.

Second, there is still the question of what *full community participation* means in the health change process. The Minnesota, Stanford, Pawtucket, and A Su Salud programs were all "community-based" efforts, with the aim of activating the involvement of community members in changing people's health behaviors and life-styles. Many social communication planners believe that merely involving people in message information and media programming, as well as in providing social support to the target audience, does not constitute full community participation. And if a more acceptable role comes about for the communities, to what extent are they prepared to carry on these responsibilities? What strategies ought to be developed to gear these communities for their roles? The concerns pertaining to long-term community involvement even after the expiration of the program are as vital as those pertaining to how the community's role is defined during the program's lifetime. This then implies further studies of various perspectives on "community participation" or involvement and how best this can be operationalized to obtain optimum changes in people's health life-styles.

Third, another unexplored area in public health communication is the aspect of communicating health risks. Clearly there are emerging health communication concerns that go beyond chronic health risks. The literature seems to be particularly weak when it comes to studies of environmental health risks and the public's reaction to them (Scherer, 1988). Informing the public about health risk in general has proven to be more complex than anticipated. As in the case of indoor radon, individuals are not required to initiate everyday behavioral changes, and there are no requirements for making personal investments to learn new behaviors to shield oneself from future harm. If a problem is detected in the home, remediation consists of a simple one-time investment that may even increase the value of the home. Yet, in spite of evidence that radon exposure poses a health hazard and that remediation is not complex, public health concerns such as these continue to be in need of strategies to overcome public ignorance and possible apathy.

Risk assessment is a complex discipline that is not fully understood by the experts, much less the public. A number of risk researchers have observed, for example, that risk experts focus on "hazard," a combination of how bad a risk is and how likely it is to happen. Technical risk experts often refer to this as "objective" risk, as opposed to "subjective" risk. They note that objective risks are the products of statistics, experimental studies, and risk analysis. Subjective risks can be described as nonexpert perceptions of objective risks, embellished by other considerations (Scherer, 1990). While the experts often argue that the public focuses on subjective, emotional judgments of risk, research has suggested that the public determines risk through a completely different set of criteria. Yet, even with the knowledge that the public and the experts focus on different aspects of risk, the question remains: How do we create an informed public as well as informed experts and policymakers? How do we increase people's concerns for high health risk issues and temper people's overreaction to low health risks? The public, the experts, and the policymakers must all understand and appreciate the different perspectives present in risk communication. The inclusion of health risks in the agenda of public health communicators would certainly change the configuration of theories and perspectives that are guiding present health change interventions.

NOTES

1. Prior to instituting this program, the National Institute on Alcohol Abuse and Alcoholism initiated a three-stage program in March 1972. The first stage sought to point out dangerous drinking patterns, to present the early warning signs and symptoms of alcoholism, and to address the myths of alcohol use and abuse. Subsequent stages in the fall of 1972 addressed the health hazards of alcohol and conveyed the message that alcohol is a drug. The final stage in January 1973 focused on the epidemic of alcoholism and the serious and problematic nature of drunkenness (Wallack, 1981).

2. Other public health communication programs have certainly been conducted in the last 20 years. For instance, Flay (1987) has reviewed 40 mass media programs on smoking cessation over the last 30 years, and other research has been conducted that has discovered that the

impact on adult smoking, particularly among middle-aged males and professional groups, can be attributed largely to the effectiveness of information and educational campaigns, which affirms an earlier finding by Warner (1977), who notes that "the cumulative effect of persistent publicity [on antismoking], supported by other public policies, has been substantial," suggesting a reduction in cigarette consumption in the United States by 20-30%. An update in 1989 claims a higher reduction, of 79-89%, and "campaign-induced decisions not to smoke made prior to 1986 will result in the postponement or avoidance of an estimated 2.1 million smoking-related deaths between 1986 and the year 2000" (Warner, 1989, p. 144).

3. There are at least 21 different cancer information programs in the United States, according to an observation made by Altman (1985).

REFERENCES

Alcalay, R. (1983). The impact of mass communication campaigns in the health field. *Social Science Medicine, 17*(2), 87-94.

Altman, D. G. (1985). Utilization of a telephone cancer information program by symptomatic people. *Journal of Community Health, 10*, 156-171.

Atkin, C. K. (1981). Mass media information campaign effectiveness. In R. E. Rice & W. J. Paisley (Eds.), *Public communication campaigns* (pp. 265-280). Beverly Hills, CA: Sage.

Bandura, A. (1977). *Social learning theory.* Englewood Cliffs, NJ: Prentice-Hall.

Bettinghaus, E. P. (1988). Using the mass media in smoking prevention and cessation programs: An introduction to five studies. *Preventive Medicine, 17*, 503-509.

Butler, M., & Paisley, W. (1977). Communicating cancer control to the public. *Health Education Monographs, 5*(1), 5-24.

Carlaw, R. W., Mittelmark, M. B., Bracht, N., & Luepker, R. (1984). Organization for a community cardiovascular health program: Experiences from the Minnesota Heart Health Program. *Health Education Quarterly, 11*, 243-252.

Carter, R. F. (1965). Communication and affective relations. *Journalism Quarterly, 42*, 203-212.

Cartwright, D. (1949). Some principles of mass persuasion: Selected findings of research on the sale of United States war bonds. *Human Relations, 2*, 253-267.

Chaffee, S. H. (1967). Salience and pertinence as sources of value change. *Journal of Communication, 17*(1), 25-37.

Chaffee, S. H., & McLeod, J. M. (1973). Individual vs. social predictors of information seeking. *Journalism Quarterly, 15*(2).

Dervin, B. (1981). Mass communicating: Changing conceptions of the audience. In R. E. Rice & W. J. Paisley (Eds.), *Public communication campaigns* (pp. 71-87). Beverly Hills, CA: Sage.

Donohew, L., & Springer, E. P. (1980). Information seeking versus information diffusion: Implications for the change agent of an alternative paradigm. *Community Development Journal, 15*, 208-213.

Elder, J. P., Hovell, M. F., Lasater, T. M., Wells, B. L., & Carleton, R. A. (1985). Applications of behavior modification to community health education: The case of heart disease prevention. *Health Education Quarterly, 12*, 151-168.

Flay, B. R. (1987). Mass media and smoking cessation: A critical review. *American Journal of Public Health, 77*, 153-160.

Flora, J. A., Maccoby, N., & Farquhar, J. (1989). Communication campaigns to prevent cardiovascular disease: The Stanford community studies. In R. E. Rice & C. K. Atkin (Eds.), *Public communication campaigns* (2nd ed., pp. 233-252). Newbury Park, CA: Sage.

Green, L. W., & McAlister, A. L. (1984). Macro-intervention to support health behavior: Some theoretical perspectives and practical reflections. *Health Education Quarterly, 11*, 322-339.

Hammond, S. L., Freimuth, V. S., & Morrison, W. (1987). The gatekeeping funnel: Tracking a major PSA campaign from distribution through gatekeepers to target audience. *Health Education Quarterly, 14*, 153-166.

Hyman, H. H., & Sheatsley, P. B. (1947). Some reasons why information campaigns fail. *Public Opinion Quarterly, 11*, 412-423.

Jacobs, D. R., Luepker, R. V., Mittelmark, M. B., Folsom, A. R., Pirie, P. L., Mascioli, S. R., Hannan, P. J., Pechacek, T. F., Bracht, N. F., Carlaw, R. W., Kline, F. G., & Blackburn, H. (1986). Community-wide prevention strategies: Evaluation design of the Minnesota Heart Health Program. *Journal of Chronic Diseases, 39*, 750-788.

Lau, R., Kane, R., Berry, S., Ware, J., & Roy, D. (1980). Channeling health: A review of the evaluation of televised health campaigns. *Health Education Quarterly, 7*, 56-89.

Lefebvre, R. C., Lasater, T. M., Carleton, R. A., & Peterson, G. (1987). Theory and delivery of health programming in the community: The Pawtucket Heart Health Program. *Preventive Medicine, 16*, 80-95.

Maccoby, N., Farquhar, J. W., Wood, P. D., & Alexander, J. (1977). Reducing the risk of cardiovascular disease: Effects of a community-based campaign on knowledge and behavior. *Journal of Community Health, 3*, 100-114.

Maccoby, N., & Solomon, D. S. (1981). Heart disease prevention: Community studies. In R. E. Rice & W. J. Paisley (Eds.), *Public communication campaigns* (pp. 105-125). Beverly Hills, CA: Sage.

Maloney, S. K., & Hersey, J. C. (1984). Getting messages on the air: Findings from the 1982 Alcohol Abuse Prevention Campaign. *Health Education Quarterly, 11*, 273-292.

McAlister, A., Ramirez, A. G., Galavotti, C., & Gallion, K. J. (1989). Antismoking campaigns: Progress in the application of the social learning theory. In R. E. Rice & C. K. Atkin (Eds.), *Public communication campaigns* (2nd ed., pp. 291-307). Newbury Park, CA: Sage.

McGuire, W. J. (1984). Public communication as a strategy for inducing health-promoting behavioral change. *Preventive Medicine, 13*, 299-319.

McGuire, W. J. (1986). The myth of massive media impact: Savings and salvagings. In G. Comstock (Ed.), *Public communication and behavior* (pp. 175-234). New York: Academic Press.

McLeod, J. M., & O'Keefe, G. J. (1972). The socialization perspective and communication behavior. In F. G. Kline & P. J. Tichenor (Eds.), *Current perspectives in mass communication research.* Beverly Hills, CA: Sage.

Mendelsohn, H. (1974). Some reasons why information campaigns can succeed. *Public Opinion Quarterly, 37*, 50-61.

Mittelmark, M. B., Luepker, R. V., Grimm, R., Kottke, T. E., & Blackburn, H. (1988). The role of physicians in a community-wide program for prevention of cardiovascular disease: The Minnesota Heart Health Program. *Public Health Reports, 103*, 360-365.

Monahan, J. L., & Scheirer, M. A. (1988). The role of linking agents in the diffusion of health promotion programs. *Health Education Quarterly, 15*, 417-433.

Paisley, W. J. (1981). Public communication campaigns: The American experience. In R. E. Rice & W. J. Paisley (Eds). *Public communication campaigns.* Beverly Hills, CA: Sage.

Perry, C. L., & Jessor, R. (1985). The concept of health promotion and the prevention of adolescent drug abuse. *Health Education Quarterly, 12*, 169-184.

Ramirez, A. G. (1979, September). *El Asesino Silencioso: A methodology for alerting the Spanish-speaking community.* Paper presented at the Hispanic Health Services Research Conference, Albuquerque.

Ramirez, A. G. (1983, November). *Vivir o morir? The effects of radio on health education for Hispanics.* Paper presented at the annual meeting of the American Public Health Association, Dallas.

Ramirez, A. G., & McAlister, A. L. (1988). Mass media campaign: A Su Salud. *Preventive Medicine, 7*, 608-621.

Rogers, E. M., & Storey, J. D. (1987). Communication campaigns. In C. R. Berger & S. H. Chaffee (Eds.), *Handbook of communication science* (pp. 817-846). Newbury Park, CA: Sage.

Rosenstock, I. M., Stretcher, V. J., & Becker, M. H. (1988). Social learning and the health belief model. *Health Education Quarterly, 15*, 175-183.

Rubin, A. M., & Windhal, S. (1986). The uses and dependency model of mass communication. *Critical Studies in Mass Communication, 3*, 194-199.

Scherer, C. W. (1988, November). *Adoption of health risk reduction behaviors: The case of geologic radon.* Unpublished manuscript, Cornell University, Department of Communication.

Scherer, C. W. (1990). Communicating water quality risk. *Journal of Soil and Water Conservation, 45*, 198-200.

Schwertfeger, R., Elder, J. P., Cooper, R., Lasater, T. M., & Carleton, R. (1986). The use of telemarketing in the community-wide prevention of heart disease: The Pawtucket Heart Health Program. *Journal of Community Health, 11*, 172-180.

Simpkins, J. D., & Brenner, D. J. (1984). Mass media communication and health. In B. Dervin & M. J. Voight (Eds.), *Progress in communication sciences.* Norwood, NJ: Ablex.

Solomon, D. S. (1981). A social marketing perspective on campaign. In R. E. Rice & W. J. Paisley (Eds.), *Public communication campaigns* (pp. 281-292). Beverly Hills, CA: Sage.

Stern, M., Farquhar, J., Maccoby, N., & Russel, S. (1976). Results of a two-year health education campaign on dietary behavior: The Stanford Three-Community Study. *Circulation, 54*, 826-833.

Thompson, E. L. (1978). Smoking education programs 1960-1976. *American Journal of Public Health, 68*, 250-257.

Umberson, D. (1987). Family status and health behaviors: Social control as a dimension of social integration. *Journal of Health and Social Behavior, 28*, 306-319.

Wallack, L. M. (1981). Mass media campaigns: The odds against finding behavior change. *Health Education Quarterly, 8*, 209-259.

Warner, K. E. (1977). The effects of anti-smoking campaign on cigarette consumption. *American Journal of Public Health, 67*, 645-649.

Warner, K. E. (1989). Effects of the antismoking campaign: An update. *American Journal of Public Health, 79*, 144-151.

Wilkinson, G., & Mirand, E. A. (1977). Cancer information by telephone: A two-year evaluation. *Health Education Monographs, 5*, 251-263.

Wilkinson, G., Mirand, E. A., & Graham, S. (1976). Can-Dial: An experiment in health education and cancer control. *Public Health Reports, 91*, 218-222.

Wilkinson, G., Mirand, E. A., Graham, S., Johnson, C. R., & Vana, J. (1977). Can-Dial: A dial access cancer education service. *International Journal of Health Education, 20*(3), 158-163.

Bridging Theory "of" and Theory "for" Communication Campaigns: An Essay on Ideology and Public Policy

CHARLES T. SALMON
University of Wisconsin—Madison

THE bridging of theory and praxis in the domain of health communication campaigns is an important goal. Academics have long decried the absence of explicit theoretical precepts and the avoidance of stringent evaluation procedures characterizing many of the campaigns emanating from the public health sector. At the same time, campaign planners, frequently saddled with financial, political, and temporal constrictions, have clamored for academic understanding of their needs for relevant theories and feasible evaluation techniques. The preceding chapter by Clifford Scherer and Napoleon Juanillo represents one of several recent efforts at "paradigm dialogues" between the disparate camps (see also Atkin & Wallack, 1990; Rice & Paisley, 1981), and contains insights and applications that will be of use to scholars and practitioners alike.

It is the case, however, that the vast majority of attempts to link theory and practice have focused only on those theories that will enhance the ability of professional communicators to achieve specific campaign goals. For the most part, these efforts involve the application of social psychological models of learning and/or persuasion, including three discussed in the Scherer and Juanillo chapter: social learning theory, information-seeking theory, and the uses and dependency model. A recent review essay by psychologists Patricia Devine and Edward Hirt (1989) has offered a more

Correspondence and requests for reprints: Charles T. Salmon, School of Journalism and Mass Communication, University of Wisconsin, Madison, WI 53706.

Communication Yearbook 15, pp. 346-358

expansive set of cognitive and social psychological theories for use in campaign planning, including McGuire's (1981) information-processing model, Greenwald's (1968) cognitive response theory, Petty and Cacioppo's (1986) elaboration likelihood model of persuasion, self-perception theory (Bem, 1972), dissonance theory (Festinger, 1957), operant conditioning (Scott, 1957), and heuristic approaches to social influence (Cialdini, 1988). To this list, we can add several other relevant theories and research approaches, including the health belief model (Becker, 1974), social judgment theory (Sherif & Hovland, 1961), social comparison theory (Festinger, 1954), diffusion theory (Rogers & Shoemaker, 1971), and the knowledge gap hypothesis (Tichenor, Donohue, & Olien, 1971). And there are others as well.

The genre of theory mentioned above, which I have labeled theory "for" campaigns (Salmon, 1989), is, or at least ought to be, of vital importance to campaign planners. In this genre, campaigns are implicitly conceptualized as independent variables, that is, stimuli that can be manipulated to induce changes in cognitions, attitudes, behaviors, and social norms. Similarly, theories are deemed relevant only to the extent that they facilitate the attainment of specific campaign goals and objectives. This genre has its roots in Paul Lazarsfeld's (1941) institutionalization of the "administrative" paradigm of communication research.

At the same time, however, this conceptualization of a communication process reflects only a meager subset of theoretical approaches that potentially could be brought to bear on communication campaigns. If we recognize campaigns as social phenomena, as "issues" rather than "facts" of contemporary social life (Rakow, 1989), it becomes clear that our research on these inherently social phenomena must not be restricted to the narrow confines of evaluation research procedures guided by theory "for" campaigns. As the distinguished social theorist Alvin Gouldner (1969) has observed:

> It is not enough . . . to examine the intellectual tools of applied social science in terms of their manifest scientific functions as technical instruments. They must also be considered in the light of their latent social functions for the peculiar system of human relations in which they are implicated. (p. 85)

The logical consequence of this perspective is the need for a parallel theory "of" campaigns, theory that examines campaigns as dependent variables, that is, as outcomes of a configuration of social, political, and ideological forces peculiar to a social system at a given point in time. In other words, while bridging theory and praxis is important, bridging theory "of" and theory "for" to create a theory "about" campaigns is at least equally so.

The remainder of this commentary is devoted to a discussion of how a blending of the two genres of theory leads to an enhanced understanding of the origins, manifest and latent functions, and outcomes of communication campaigns. In short, this essay investigates how implicit ideological and political factors influence policy decisions involving the use of communication to solve social problems. In the space allotted, it is not possible to provide an exhaustive inventory of relevant issues and concerns; instead, I will identify areas that might prove particularly fruitful for future scholarship in the area of developing an integrated theory of campaigns.

WHY COMMUNICATION?

A possible point of departure for an integrated theory about campaigns is a question that rarely is asked, but that should be, particularly in the wake of a number of review essays and research reports describing "disappointing" findings of campaign effectiveness: Why should we *expect* communication to be a panacea, a stimulus potent enough to induce addicts to disengage from cigarette smoking or drug use, to inspire adolescents and adults to temper powerful sexual urges, or to convince persons that they should drastically alter life-styles cultivated over a quarter of a century or more—especially in the face of research findings that appear to indicate that communication is incapable of achieving far more modest outcomes?

The popular response among contemporary communication researchers is to argue that we should not—that is, we should not expect *mass* communication *alone* to be capable of such ambitious outcomes. Scherer and Juanillo, for example, note:

> Given these findings [of temporary or limited impact] and the successful experiences in the early 1900s of combining mass media with strategies involving local participation, it is therefore surprising to discover present-day health communication programs that continue to rely *solely on mass media* to encourage complex behavioral change. (p. 330; emphasis added)

This passage echoes sentiments expressed by Steven Chaffee (1982) and Everett Rogers and Kathleen Reardon (1988), who criticize the conceptualization of mass and interpersonal communication functions as "competitive" rather than "complementary." Similarly, Everett Rogers and J. Douglas Storey (1987) note that "*mass media* communication is not a campaign panacea" (p. 836; emphasis added); they add that "interpersonal communication through peer networks is very important in leading to and maintaining behavior change." This line of reasoning has served as the basis for programmatic research on the effectiveness of using mass communication in conjunction with interpersonal communication strategies in health communication programs (e.g., the Stanford Three-Community Study and Five-City Project and the Minnesota Heart Health Program).

The perspectives articulated above imply the endorsement of a type of "vertical integration" in addressing a social problem. The argument is that because mass communication alone probably is unable to achieve imposing social objectives, we need to incorporate other modes or levels *of communication* in our persuasive efforts. Endorsement of this type of integration can be traced directly to the writings of Paul Lazarsfeld and Robert Merton (1948), who, in their seminal work on the functions of mass communication, write that "supplementation," the merger of mass and interpersonal communication strategies, is one of three conditions essential to the success of "prosocial" propaganda campaigns (the others being monopolization and canalization). This marriage is essential, they continue, for three reasons: (a) interpersonal communication reinforces mass media messages, (b) mass communication lessens the personal requirements of approaches relying heavily on interpersonal communication, and (c) mass communication legitimates interpersonal communication.

The adoption of the perspective of vertical integration is very likely a necessary, but not sufficient, condition for the success of social change efforts. It still implies that the use of communication per se is appropriate for tackling the most egregious of social problems, a conclusion that is, at the very least, questionable. By thinking vertically in terms of merging mass and interpersonal communication strategies, communication researchers have tended to neglect the alternative, what we might label "horizontal integration." Using this latter approach, public health specialists are not confined to a limited set of communication strategies, but instead are free to draw on mechanisms of change outside the realm of communication, such as power, facilitation, engineering/technology, or efforts to induce institutional change.

This latter prescription for change is the more practical and realistic of the two (and hence the more important in terms of public policy) because planners of social change rarely rely on vertical solutions exclusively; far more often, they integrate various elements of education, persuasion, facilitation or engineering, and power in efforts to induce change (Zaltman & Duncan, 1977).[1] For example, a coordinated effort to increase the wearing of helmets by motorcycle riders might include *communication* in the form of anxiety-producing mass-mediated public service announcements and in-person presentations to students in driver education programs, *power* in the form of passage of a helmet law, and *engineering* in the form of development of safer and more comfortable helmets. Such an effort would thus combine elements of vertical- and horizontal-integration change efforts.

If we look at the issue of cigarette smoking, the focus of many a public health campaign, we find evidence of tension between the endorsement of vertical and horizontal approaches to social change. Scherer and Juanillo, for example, quote communication researcher William Paisley (1981) as saying: "The decline in cigarette smoking in the population is not a consequence of engineering or enforcement. . . . The only strategy that can possibly counteract the advertisement [of tobacco] has been public communication in its many forms" (pp. 36-37). Such an interpretation of recent history does not do justice to the synergistic effect of the multitude of strategies that have been brought to bear on the smoker; instead, it attempts to extract artificially the influence of a single (vertical) strategy—communication— without considering the context in which the use of that strategy occurs. Because communication does not occur in a social vacuum, we must take into account the many forces operating in social, political, and economic environments that have, in combination with antismoking communication campaigns, resulted in lower rates of cigarette smoking. Some of these other forces include the use of medical research data, documenting the dangers of secondary smoke, to in part justify the passage and enforcement of "clean-air" acts and smoking bans in public and private buildings; increased taxation on cigarettes; a flurry of litigation by nonsmokers and individuals suffering from cancer; bans on the hiring of prospective employees who smoke; and successful inculcation of a social norm that makes smokers the new social "pariahs" (Goodin, 1989; Levin, 1987). Given the close proximity and even simultaneity of several of these occurrences, it is extremely difficult to argue convincingly that the influence of a single mechanism of change can be isolated.

Adopting the perspective of horizontal integration is a necessary step toward developing an integrated theory "about" communication campaigns because it compels us to specify the social conditions under which communication, rather than or in conjunction with some alternative, is selected as the mechanism of change. It forces us to consider the "whys" of policy options, not merely the "hows."

CAMPAIGNS, POLITICS, AND IDEOLOGY

Underlying a policy decision to deploy communication campaigns is a combination of two sets of influences: political and economic considerations, and the adoption of the ideology that the most expedient route to change is through individuals, not institutions. The use of the term *expedient* is critical, for policymakers do not necessarily believe that campaigns are the most efficient, fastest, or even most effective mechanisms of change. Indeed, communication is generally regarded as a relatively slow vehicle for change, at least relative to many types of power strategies (Zaltman & Duncan, 1977).

The use of communication campaigns has great political value. First, communication campaigns, by definition, are public in the sense of being highly visible and potentially noticeable to multitudes of persons in the public sphere. In this manner, they hold great symbolic value for policymakers, who can point to the dramatic efforts being made to solve a given social problem (Edelman, 1964; Paletz, Pearson, & Willia, 1977). This may have the effect of neutralizing criticism and, simultaneously, garnering public confidence and support even though a less visible, less "public" change strategy might ultimately be more capable of effecting meaningful change. This use of campaigns is most likely to occur for the most controversial of public health issues, those in which organized groups pose a viable threat to an incumbent's tenure.

Second, campaigns are attractive to policymakers because they can be relatively inexpensive to implement. Obvious examples of this include modest PSA campaigns in which states solicit donated agency expertise and free media space or time to implement a brief campaign about such issues as AIDS or drug abuse. Thus with minimal cost a government can achieve the visibility afforded by mass communication. On the other end of the cost continuum are the dozen or so massive programs described by Scherer and Juanillo, including Stanford's Three-Community Study and Five-City Project, the Pawtucket Heart Health Program, A Su Salud, and the Minnesota Heart Health Program. These programs tend to be highly visible in the academic community because their progenitors have published research findings extensively in academic journals. But we can expand this inventory to include such federal programs as the National AIDS Information and Education Program; the National High Blood Pressure Education Program; the National Cholesterol Education Program; the Depression/Awareness, Recognition, and Treatment Program; Healthy Mothers, Healthy Babies Public Information Program; and sundry programs sponsored by the National Institute for Drug Abuse.

Some of these programs have been in operation for a decade or so. They have provided employment for dozens of researchers, campaign planners, community organizers, and staff members; involved the dissemination of literally thousands of electronic, print, and interpersonal messages in a number of communities; and potentially changed the lives of hundreds—if not thousands—of citizens. Yet despite the ambitious nature of these programs, their costs still are modest in comparison with many other federal government expenditures. For example, the price tag for the seven-year Minnesota Heart Health Program—including the initial grant as well as its renewal several years later—was roughly the same as that of a *single* fighter plane deployed in the recent Operation Desert Storm, and far less than the cost of the military campaign itself.

Third, the use of campaigns is congruent with the underlying democratic principle of voluntarism (see Paisley, 1981, for an excellent discussion of the democratic origins of communication campaigns). That is, campaigns are seen as mechanisms that facilitate change by providing information, social support, and incentive rather than as mechanisms that compel individuals to change through the use of tangible punitive sanctions. At worst, campaigns create intangible sanctions by employing message appeals designed to make audience members feel afraid or guilty about the implications of performing a particular (undesirable) behavior. To the extent that this is deemed manipulative rather than merely educative, proponents of campaigns consider it manipulation of a benevolent sort because the ends of health and safety are seen as justifying the means of inducing anxiety or guilt.[2]

In contrast, power strategies, in which policymakers might pass laws prohibiting smoking or enforcing stiffer sentences for drug pushers, are deemed less desirable to a society that prides itself on self-determination and free will. In cases in which power strategies must be employed, however, communication campaigns still serve a vital role by laying the groundwork for and legitimating the use of coercive measures. For example, long before policymakers can use power strategies to violate civil rights and delimit individuals' freedoms, they must first use communication campaigns to convince society that a particular social problem is so egregious that it merits unusually harsh government responses. In recent years, there have been many such incidents in the form of mandatory drug testing, arrests of drug-addicted mothers for transporting drugs to a minor *in vitro,* and the use of demographic profiles to identify candidates for otherwise unwarranted drug searches. In each case, vigorous communication efforts elevated social conditions to the status of first "problems" and then "wars," thereby capitalizing on the public's general patriotic sentiments and concomitant acceptance of the need to make sacrifices during times of war. In such a practice, the effectiveness of a communication campaign should be conceptualized in terms of its ability to have the public accept the use of power strategies, not in its ability to elicit change per se. Thus it is entirely reasonable to assume that some communication campaigns have been labeled failures by evaluators using one set of criteria and simultaneously labeled successes by policymakers using a different set of criteria.

Fourth, campaigns are congruent with the democratic value of egalitarianism. Large-scale communication efforts through mass and interpersonal media usually are intended to promote equality of access to information. In a sense, campaigns represent conscious efforts to compensate for the inherent inadequacies of existing information systems in informing all segments of society equally about health hazards.

However, the ideal of egalitarianism is distinct from its achievement. That is, despite the best intentions of campaign planners, campaigns do not always equalize levels of knowledge about social problems; instead, there is a fairly substantial body of literature that suggests that some campaigns exacerbate knowledge differentials between the "haves" and "have-nots" of society (see Gaziano, 1983, for a review). Under any circumstances, knowledge inequities are antithetical to the democratic ideal of egalitarianism; in the realm of health information in particular, knowledge inequities are especially problematic because they literally can prove to be fatal.

In addition to political and economic factors, ideological factors are inextricably linked to campaign implementation and strategies. In her book

Hidden Arguments: Political Ideology and Disease Prevention Policy, Sylvia Tesh (1988) describes the paradox of individualism in the context of public health. First, she notes, the *ideals* of individualism provide the ethical foundations of most public health policies, which, if implemented, would protect the lives and welfare of individuals. However, the *doctrine* of individualism constitutes a barrier to the attainment of that protection by focusing on individual behaviors—rather than systemic or institutional conditions—as appropriate targets for change. Such a doctrine, she argues,

> supports a politically conservative predisposition to bracket off questions about the structure of society—about the distribution of wealth and power, for example—and to concentrate instead on questions about the behavior of individuals within that (apparently fixed) structure. One consequence is the assumption that health education is the best way to prevent disease. (p. 161)

In practice, communication campaigns are often treated as ideologically neutral solutions to social problems, despite their obvious bias, to which Tesh aptly alludes. Consider the concern about the sharing of needles among intravenous (IV) drug users and the spread of AIDS. One strategy of facilitation might endorse the distribution of clean needles to addicts, a proposal that would be—and has been—labeled controversial because, critics contend, it condones and promotes drug abuse. A second strategy of facilitation, eradicating poverty and other deleterious social conditions that foster drug use, also would be labeled controversial because it invokes the politically infeasible specter of redistribution of wealth. Similarly, a power strategy calling for the quarantine of IV drug users with AIDS would be labeled controversial because it would violate civil liberties. The use of an educative strategy, in sharp contrast, would be viewed as far less controversial. Its use would appeal to the great value Americans place on education in general. Whereas it would be easy for a politician to oppose "controversial" laws or "radical" proposals, it would be far more difficult for a politician to oppose the principle of education and enlightenment.

Yet the use of education in the form of communication campaigns clearly is a conservative, but not necessarily optimally effective, strategy; it is capable of engendering slow, manageable change. As one public health scholar has remarked:

> In relation to the social causation of disease it [the ideology of individualism] functions as a colossal masquerade. . . . What must be questioned is both the effectiveness and the political uses of a focus on life-styles and on changing individual behavior without changing social structure and processes. (Crawford, 1979, p. 256)

Perhaps therein lies one answer to the rhetorical question of why governments continue to invest large amounts of money in communication strategies when, as Scherer and Juanillo report, "evidence of possible gains and effects of public health communication programs on people's health lifestyles remains minimal" (p. 313). Rather than "benevolent" manipulation, some health education campaigns can be viewed in less altruistic terms, as efforts by the ruling elite to restrict the proffering of solutions to social problems to those that are the least threatening to the status quo. Because of their facilitation of individual rather than structural change, campaigns can be viewed as manifestations of the "blaming the victim" syndrome, in which individuals are censured for activities such as cigarette smoking at the same time the federal government subsidizes the growth of tobacco, condones the advertising of tobacco in print media, and permits the production and sale of tobacco domestically and internationally, and as corporations continue to manufacture and profit from products that are known to be dangerous to human life.

IMPLICATIONS

The above analysis provides a skeletal framework for an integrated theory "about" campaigns. First, we must understand the manifest and latent functions of such communication efforts, separating the symbolic benefits to sponsors from the tangible benefits to members of target audiences. Although Atkin (1981, p. 265) has differentiated "persuasion" campaigns from "information" campaigns by arguing that the latter are intended to benefit the receivers rather than the sponsors of campaign messages, all campaigns emanating from both the public and private sectors provide some tangible or intangible benefits to sponsors. In some cases—as in campaigns that are largely symbolic gestures—those benefits may actually exceed those accrued by the audience members themselves.

Second, we must neither blindly accept the use of communication to solve a particular social problem nor expect that it should be at all effective in a given situation. We must better define the conditions under which communication, rather than some alternative, is the most appropriate mechanism for change. For example, the technology now exists that would allow us to make foods healthier (i.e., to contain fewer carcinogens, pesticides, and other health hazards), but the use of this technology would disrupt current patterns of food production and sales. Under such circumstances, the decision to use communication to convince consumers to eat healthily rather than to direct power or engineering strategies at the food industry may be based more on a complex of political and ideological factors than on considerations of what actually would do the most good for individual consumers.

But if communication is deemed ineffective in this case, what are we to conclude? Far too often in the past, evaluators have blamed communication, concluding that campaigns are likely to be only minimally successful at social change. Alternatively, however, we could blame policymakers for selecting a solution that they know is not likely to be as successful as another, less politically attractive one. In comparison, the technology currently available to prevent the spread of AIDS is far less sophisticated than, for example, what is available to make foods safer to eat. Under such circumstances, the decision to use communication as a means of prevention is probably driven more by the lack of an appropriate technological solution (i.e., a vaccine to prevent the spread of the human immunodeficiency virus) than by political or ideological determinants.[3]

This approach has important implications for how we evaluate the effectiveness of communication campaigns. Currently, there is no objective benchmark against which communication can be measured as successful or unsuccessful. Claims of success have fluctuated wildly over the years and are defined in terms of idiosyncratic criteria established by specific evaluators. However, if we expand our frame of reference from the narrow confines of communication, the question of effectiveness become one of relativity; that is, How effective is our communication campaign relative to other options that we might have chosen? Rather than anchoring our expectations for success in terms of past communication campaigns (a vertical-integration approach), we should compare our success rate to that of the alternative options. For example, a statement that communication campaigns are ineffective against the use of illegal drugs should be questioned for its lack of context and specificity. First, it lacks context because we know that power strategies—laws—are not universally effective; the very existence of an "illegal" drug problem is evidence that other mechanisms of change are not always successful either. The real question that should be asked is, How much more—or less—effective are communication strategies than laws or technological solutions in curbing the use of illegal drugs? Second, the statement lacks specificity because it implicitly treats campaigns as homogeneous entities, generalizing from the findings of one specific communication activity to a class of communication activities. And yet we know with certainty that certain communication campaigns may be more effective than others and that evidence of lack of effectiveness may simply reflect poorly on the campaigner rather than on communication per se.

Focusing on issues of context and specificity forces us to abandon the conditioned pessimism that occurs in response to studies that seem to indicate that communication is capable of only modest change. The use of the term *modest* implies that stronger outcomes are either expected or at least possible, yet, without understanding the context of the situation in which communication has been deployed, we cannot validly make that value judgment. It may be that, given the formidable nature of a social problem and its particular sensitivity to power rather than communication strategies, what we have labeled modest results are actually more than should reasonably have been expected. Thus instead of pessimism upon encountering what appears to be limited evidence of communication effectiveness, our reaction should be one of curiosity;

that is, we should attempt to place our results in context and to specify further the conditions under which we can legitimately label those results as evidence of either success or failure. This, in turn, will ultimately enable us to strengthen the bridge between theory and praxis.

NOTES

1. Scherer and Juanillo draw on the work of McGuire (1984) initially to describe two broad classifications of health promotion programs—institutional strategies and communication strategies—and proceed to say that their chapter will focus on the latter rather than the former. Focusing on communication to the exclusion of other forms of social change is an example of vertical integration as described in this commentary. Yet the difficulty with such a classification of health promotion programs is made apparent when Scherer and Juanillo write, a few pages later, that the contemporary use of communication campaigns "is closely linked with other strategies that 'direct' changes through 'engineering' and institutionalize them through law enforcement" (p. 315). In other words, communication campaigns cannot truly be studied in isolation, divorced of consideration of their relationship to allied efforts or of the politics that gives rise to the specific configuration of forces brought to bear on a social problem. As such, we can expand Chaffee's (1982) distinction between "competitive" and "complementary" functions of mass and interpersonal communication to apply to the horizontal perspective as well. That is, communication, power, engineering, and other forms of change should be treated as complementary rather than competitive strategies for change.

2. The concept of "benevolent manipulation" is frequently discussed in philosophical treatises on "paternalism" (see Salmon, 1989, for a discussion). Dating back at least to the writings of John Stuart Mill in *On Liberty*, philosophers, change agents, and social critics have long questioned the conditions under which the attempted imposition of change is ethically and morally justifiable.

3. This is not to say that all campaigns involving, for example, diet are politically motivated and that all campaigns involving AIDS are not. As stated throughout this essay, the optimal approach is likely to involve an integration of multiple change strategies, one of which is communication. On the other hand, some health problems are more sensitive to engineering solutions than are others. It is important to recognize differences among issues and to realize that the prescription of communication may be more reasonable for one issue than for another.

REFERENCES

Atkin, C. K. (1981). Mass media information campaign effectiveness. In R. E. Rice & W. J. Paisley (Eds.), *Public communication campaigns* (pp. 265-280). Beverly Hills, CA: Sage.

Atkin, C. K., & Wallack, L. (1990). *Mass communication and public health: Complexities and conflicts.* Newbury Park, CA: Sage.

Becker, M. (Ed.). (1974). *The health belief model and personal health behavior.* Thorofaire, NJ: Charles B. Slack.

Bem, D. J. (1972). Self-perception theory. In L. Berkowitz (Ed.), *Advances in experimental social psychology* (Vol. 6, pp. 2-63). New York: Academic Press.

Chaffee, S. H. (1982). Mass media and interpersonal channels: Competitive, convergent, or complementary? In G. Gumpertz & R. Cathcart (Eds.), *Inter/media: Interpersonal communication in a media world.* New York: Oxford University Press.

Cialdini, R. B. (1988). *Influence: Science and practice.* Glenview, IL: Scott, Foresman.

Crawford, R. (1979). Individual responsibility and health politics in the 1970s. In S. Reverby & D. Rosner (Eds.), *Health care in America: Essays in social history.* Philadelphia: Temple University Press.

Devine, P. G., & Hirt, E. R. (1989). Message strategies for information campaigns: A social psychological analysis. In C. T. Salmon (Ed.), *Information campaigns: Balancing social values and social change* (pp. 229-258). Newbury Park, CA: Sage.

Edelman, M. (1964). *The symbolic uses of politics.* Urbana: University of Illinois Press.

Festinger, L. (1954). A theory of social comparison processes. *Human Relations, 7,* 117-140.

Festinger, L. (1957). *A theory of cognitive dissonance.* Stanford, CA: Stanford University Press.

Gaziano, C. (1983). The knowledge gap: An analytical review of media effects. *Communication Research, 4,* 447-486.

Goodin, R. E. (1989). *No smoking: The ethical issues.* Chicago: University of Chicago Press.

Gouldner, A. W. (1969). Theoretical requirements of the applied social sciences. In W. G. Bennis, K. D. Benne, & R. Chin (Eds.), *The planning of change* (2nd ed.)(pp. 85-98). New York: Holt, Rinehart & Winston.

Greenwald, A. G. (1968). Cognitive learning, cognitive response to persuasion and attitude change. In A. G. Greenwald, T. C. Brock, & T. M. Ostrom (Eds.), *Psychological foundations of attitudes* (pp. 361-388). New York: Academic Press.

Lazarsfeld, P. F. (1941). Remarks on administrative and critical communications research. *Studies in Philosophy and Social Science, 9,* 2-16.

Lazarsfeld, P. F., & Merton, R. K. (1948). Mass communication, popular taste and organized social action. In W. Schramm (Ed.), *Mass communications* (pp. 492-512). Urbana: University of Illinois Press.

Levin, L. S. (1987). Every silver lining has a cloud: The limits of health promotion. *Social Policy, 18*(1), 57-60.

McGuire, W. J. (1981). Theoretical foundations of campaigns. In R. E. Rice & W. J. Paisley (Eds.), *Public communication campaigns* (pp. 41-70). Beverly Hills, CA: Sage.

McGuire, W. J. (1984). Public communication as a strategy for inducing health-promoting behavioral change. *Preventive Medicine, 13,* 299-319.

Paisley, W. J. (1981). Public communication campaigns: The American experience. In R. E. Rice & W. J. Paisley (Eds.), *Public communication campaigns* (pp. 15-40). Beverly Hills, CA: Sage.

Paletz, D. L., Pearson, R. E., & Willia, D. L. (1977). *Politics in public service advertising on television.* New York: Praeger.

Petty, R. E., & Cacioppo, J. T. (1986). *Communication in persuasion: Central and peripheral routes to attitude change.* New York: Springer/Verlag.

Rakow, L. F. (1989). Information and power: Toward a critical theory of information campaigns. In C. T. Salmon (Ed.), *Information campaigns: Balancing social values and social change* (pp. 164-184). Newbury Park, CA: Sage.

Rice, R. E., & Paisley, W. J. (Eds.). (1981). *Public communication campaigns.* Beverly Hills, CA: Sage.

Rogers, E. M., & Reardon, K. K. (1988). Interpersonal versus mass media communication: A false dichotomy. *Human Communication Research, 15,* 284-303.

Rogers, E. M., & Shoemaker, F. (1971). *Communication of innovations: A cross-cultural approach.* New York: Free Press.

Rogers, E. M., & Storey, J. D. (1987). Communication campaigns. In C. R. Berger & S. H. Chaffee (Eds.), *Handbook of communication science* (pp. 817-846). Beverly Hills, CA: Sage.

Salmon, C. T. (1989). Campaigns for social "improvement": An overview of values, rationales, and impacts. In C. T. Salmon (Ed.), *Information campaigns: Balancing social values and social change* (pp. 19-53). Newbury Park, CA: Sage.

Scott, W. A. (1957). Attitude change through reward of verbal behavior. *Journal of Abnormal and Social Psychology, 55,* 72-75.

Sherif, M., & Hovland, C. I. (1961). *Social judgment: Assimilation and contrast effects in communication and attitude change.* New Haven, CT: Yale University Press.

Tesh, S. N. (1988). *Hidden arguments: Political ideology and disease prevention policy.* New Brunswick, NJ: Rutgers University Press.

Tichenor, P. J., Donohue, G. A., & Olien, C. N. (1971). Mass media flow and differential growth in knowledge. *Public Opinion Quarterly, 34,* 158-170.

Zaltman, G., & Duncan, R. (1977). *Strategies for planned change.* New York: John Wiley.

Risk Communication:
An Emerging Area of
Health Communication Research

VINCENT T. COVELLO
Columbia University

S CHERER and Juanillo provide an excellent review of the literature on public health communication. In their last section, they devote several paragraphs to a new and emerging area of public health communication research: risk communication (Covello, McCallum, & Pavlova, 1989; Covello, von Winterfeldt, & Slovic, 1986; Davies, Covello, & Allen, 1987; Fischhoff, 1987; Kasperson & Stallen, 1991; National Research Council, 1989; Sandman, 1985). Because this is one of the fastest-growing parts of the literature on public health communication—with hundreds of articles and books published over the last five years (Covello et al., 1989; Davies et al., 1987; Kasperson & Stallen, 1991; National Research Council, 1989)—the purpose of this commentary is to expand on the material presented in Scherer and Juanillo's review. By doing so, I also hope to provide the reader with a general outline of the risk communication literature and to relate this work to the larger literature on public health communication.

DEFINITIONS

Risk communication can be defined as the exchange of information among interested parties about the nature, magnitude, significance, or control of a risk (Covello, von Winterfeldt, & Slovic, 1987; National Research Council, 1989). Interested parties include government agencies, corporations or industry groups, unions, the communications media, scientists, professional organizations, public interest groups, communities, and individual citizens.

Correspondence and requests for reprints: Vincent T. Covello, School of Public Health, Center for Risk Communication, Columbia University, New York, NY 10027.

Communication Yearbook 15, pp. 359-373

Information about risks is communicated through a variety of channels, ranging from warning labels on consumer products to public meetings involving representatives from government, industry, the news media, and the general public. These communication efforts can be frustrating for both risk communicators and the intended recipients of the information (Covello et al., 1989; Hance, Chess, & Sandman, 1987; Johnson & Covello, 1987; Krimsky & Plough, 1988; National Research Council, 1989; President's Commission on the Accident at Three Mile Island, 1979; Press, 1987; Ruckelshaus, 1987; Thomas, 1987). Government officials, industry representatives, and scientists often complain that laypersons do not accurately perceive and evaluate risk information. Representatives of citizen groups and individual citizens are often equally frustrated, perceiving risk communicators and risk assessment experts to be uninterested in their concerns and unwilling to take action to solve seemingly straightforward health, safety, or environmental problems (Fessenden-Raden, Fitchen, & Heath, 1987; Krimsky & Plough, 1988). In this context, the media often serve as transmitters and translators of risk information (Sandman, Sachsman, Greenberg, & Gotchfeld, 1987). In this role, the media have at times been criticized for exaggerating risks and for emphasizing drama over scientific facts (Nelkin, 1984; Sandman, Sachsman, Greenberg, & Gotchfeld, 1987).

PROBLEMS AND DIFFICULTIES
IN EFFECTIVE RISK COMMUNICATION

A significant part of the risk communication literature focuses on problems and difficulties in communicating risk information effectively (Covello, 1988; Covello et al., 1986; Kasperson & Stallen, 1991; Krimsky & Plough, 1988; National Research Council, 1989; Nelkin, 1989). These problems and difficulties can be organized into four conceptually distinct, but related categories: characteristics and limitations of scientific data about risks; characteristics and limitations of government officials, industry officials, and other spokespersons in communicating information about risks; characteristics and limitations of the media in reporting information about risks; and characteristics and limitations of the public in evaluating and interpreting risk information. Each is discussed in turn below.

Characteristics and Limitations
of Scientific Data About Risks

One of the difficulties in communicating information about risks stems from the uncertainty and complexity of data on health, safety, and environmental risks. Risk assessments, despite their strengths, seldom provide exact answers (Cohrssen & Covello, 1989; Conservation Foundation, 1985;

National Research Council, 1983). Due to limitations in scientific understanding, data, models, and methods, the results of most risk assessments are at best approximations. Moreover, the resources needed to resolve these uncertainties are seldom adequate to the task (National Research Council, 1983).

These uncertainties invariably affect communications with the public in the adversarial climate that surrounds many risk issues. Scherer and Juanillo provide several examples in their discussion of communications about health promotion and disease prevention. In communications about environmental health risks, uncertainties often play an even larger role (Davies et al., 1987; Krimsky & Plough, 1988; National Research Council, 1989). For example, uncertainties in environmental risk assessment often lead to radically different estimates of risk. Important factors in many debates about risk are the different assessments of risk produced by government agencies, industry representatives, and public interest groups (Conservation Foundation, 1985; Johnson & Covello, 1987; Kasperson & Stallen, 1991; President's Commission on the Accident at Three Mile Island, 1979; Sandman, 1985, 1986; Sharlin, 1987).

Given these uncertainties, a critical flaw in many efforts to communicate risk information is the failure to provide information on the assumptions underlying the calculation of risks (Conservation Foundation, 1985; Covello, 1989). A related flaw is the failure to describe and characterize uncertainties. Risk reports that contain only single values ignore the true range of risk possibilities and often provide inaccurate pictures to the public.

Characteristics and Limitations of Industry Officials, Government Officials, and Other Spokespersons in Communicating Information About Risks

In their chapter, Scherer and Juanillo only briefly mention issues of trust and credibility. However, research on trust and credibility is a central thrust in the literature on risk communication. Given that the risk communication literature has focused largely on the environment or on environmental health issues, part of the explanation may lie in different perceptions of the credibility of health agencies compared with environmental agencies.

Two of the principal sources of environmental risk information—industry and government—often lack credibility (Kates, Hohenemser, & Kasperson, 1985; McCallum, Hammond, & Covello, 1990). In the United States, for example, overall public confidence and trust in government and industry as sources of information about environmental health risks have declined precipitously over the last two decades (Kates et al., 1985). The majority of people in the United States, for example, view industry and government as among the least trusted sources of information about the risks of environmental exposures to chemicals (McCallum et al., 1990). At the same time, the majority of people view industry and government as among the most knowledgeable sources of information about such risks (McCallum et al., 1990).

Public distrust of industry as a source of risk information is grounded in part in the belief that chemical companies have often been insensitive to facility neighbors, unwilling to acknowledge problems, opposed to regulation, closed to dialogue, unwilling to disclose risk-related information, and negligent in fulfilling their health, safety, and environmental responsibilities (Covello, Donovan, & Slavick, 1991; Covello, Sandman, & Slovic, 1988; Hance et al., 1987; McCallum et al., 1990). One of the costs of this heritage of mistrust is the public's willingness to believe that chemical risks represent some of the greatest risks posed by modern technology (McCallum et al., 1990).

The prospect of overcoming distrust of the chemical industry appears to be better locally than globally (Covello et al., 1988, 1991; Hance et al., 1987). Therefore, part of the solution to the global problem may be local. When chemical companies have built up track records of dealing openly, fairly, and safely with their employees, customers, and neighboring communities, the general distrust of the chemical industry may be reduced. In the meantime, many people view chemical plants as microcosms of an industry that they believe has been arrogant and careless and that has polluted the air, water, and land (Covello et al., 1991; Hance et al., 1987; McCallum et al., 1990). Building bridges locally, and explaining risk credibly, is difficult (Hance et al., 1987), but that work is essential because of the mistrust that faces most officials from the chemical industry.

Public distrust of government environmental agencies is grounded in a related set of factors (Covello et al., 1989; Hance et al., 1987; Krimsky & Plough, 1988; National Research Council, 1989; Ruckelshaus, 1983, 1984, 1987; Thomas, 1987). First, many government officials have engaged in highly visible debates and disagreements about the reliability, validity, and meaning of the results of environmental health risk assessments. In many cases, equally prominent government experts have taken diametrically opposed positions on the risks of nuclear power plants, hazardous waste sites, asbestos, electric and magnetic fields, lead, radon, PCBs, arsenic, dioxin, solid waste, the pesticide EDB, and ALAR (Bean, 1987; Johnson & Covello, 1987; Kasperson & Stallen, 1991; Morgan et al., 1985; President's Commission on the Accident at Three Mile Island, 1979; Sandman, 1985, 1986; Sharlin, 1987). While such debates may be constructive for the development of scientific knowledge, they often undermine public trust and confidence in industry and government.

Second, government resources for risk assessment and management are seldom adequate to meet demands by citizens and public interest groups for definitive findings and rapid action (Hance et al., 1987; Kasperson, 1986). Explanations by officials that the generation of valid and reliable toxicological or epidemiological data is expensive and time-consuming—or that risk assessment and management activities are constrained by resource, technical, statutory, legal, or other limitations—are seldom perceived to be satisfactory (Covello et al., 1989; Ruckelshaus, 1987; Thomas, 1987). Individuals facing what they believe is a new and significant risk are especially reluctant to accept such claims.

Third, coordination among responsible government authorities is seldom adequate. In many debates about risk, for example, lack of coordination among agencies has severely undermined public faith and confidence (Conservation Foundation, 1985; Davies et al., 1987; Johnson & Covello, 1987; Krimsky & Plough, 1988). Compounding such problems is the lack of consistency in approaches to risk assessment and management by government agencies and authorities at the local, state, regional, national, and international levels (Cohrssen & Covello, 1989; Conservation Foundation, 1985; National Research Council, 1983). Unfortunately, few requirements exist for regulatory agencies to develop coherent, coordinated, consistent, and interrelated plans, programs, and guidelines for managing risks. As a result, regulatory systems tend to be highly fragmented. This fragmentation often leads to jurisdictional conflicts about which agency and which level of government have the ultimate responsibility for assessing and managing a particular environmental activity or risk. Lack of coordination, different mandates, and confusion about responsibility and authority also lead, in many cases, to the production of multiple and competing estimates of risk. A commonly observed result of such confusion is the erosion of public trust, confidence, and acceptance.

Fourth, many government officials lack adequate training in community and media relations and in the specific requirements of risk communication (Covello & Allen, 1988; Hance et al., 1987; National Research Council, 1989). For example, many officials use complex and difficult language and jargon in communicating information about risks and benefits to the media and the public. Such language is not only difficult for the public to comprehend, it can also create a perception that the officials or experts are being unresponsive, dishonest, or evasive.

Finally, many government officials are insensitive to the information needs and concerns of the public (Fischhoff, 1985a; Fischhoff, Lichtenstein, Slovic, Derby, & Keeney, 1981; Ruckelshaus, 1987; Thomas, 1987). Officials often operate on the assumption that they and their audience share a common framework for evaluating and interpreting risk information. However, this is often not the case (Douglas & Wildavsky, 1982; Johnson & Covello, 1987; Krimsky & Plough, 1988). One of the most important findings to emerge from risk perception and communication studies is that people take into consideration a complex array of qualitative and quantitative factors in defining, evaluating, and acting on risk information (Covello, 1983; Fischhoff, 1985b; Fischhoff et al., 1981; Kasperson & Kasperson, 1983; Slovic, 1986, 1987).

To overcome public distrust and communicate more effectively, government agencies have initiated several programs. These include enhanced community relations and risk communication programs and extensive field testing of risk communication materials (Covello et al., 1989; Krimsky & Plough, 1988; Ruckelshaus, 1983, 1984; Sharlin, 1987; Smith, Desvousges, Fisher, & Johnson, 1987; Thomas, 1987). Furthermore, several federal and state agencies, including the Environmental Protection Agency (EPA) and the Minnesota Pollution Control Agency, have launched ambitious risk communication training programs for all employees. Finally, several agencies have published codes of management practice for effective risk communication. For example, in 1988 the EPA published a set of seven rules and guidelines for effective risk communication (Covello & Allen, 1988):

(1) Accept and involve the public as a legitimate partner.
(2) Plan carefully and evaluate performance.
(3) Listen to your audience.
(4) Be honest, frank, and open.
(5) Coordinate and collaborate with other credible sources.
(6) Meet the needs of the media.
(7) Speak clearly and with compassion.

In introducing the rules, the EPA noted that the goal of risk communication is not to diffuse public concern or avoid action, but rather to produce an informed public that is involved, interested, reasonable, thoughtful, solution oriented, and collaborative.

Characteristics and Limitations of the Media in Reporting Information About Risks

In their chapter, Scherer and Juanillo stress the importance of mass media in public health communication. The mass media also play a critical role in transmitting risk information (Friedman, 1981; Klaidman, 1985; Mazur, 1984; National Research Council, 1989; Nelkin, 1984, 1989; President's Commission on the Accident at Three Mile Island, 1979; Sandman, Sachsman, Greenberg, & Gotchfeld, 1987). However, mass media research in public health communication has had a different focus from that of mass media research in risk communication. Whereas the focus of public health communication research has been on the role and use of mass media for public health purposes, the focus in risk communication research has been on characteristics and limitations of the media that contribute to problems in risk communication (Friedman, 1981; Nelkin, 1989; Sandman, Sachsman, Greenberg, & Gotchfeld, 1987). For example, a major finding in the risk communication literature is that the media are biased toward stories that contain drama, conflict, expert disagreements, and uncertainties.

The media are especially biased toward stories that contain dramatic or sensational material, such as those concerning minor or major accidents at chemical manufacturing facilities or nuclear power plants (Slovic, 1987). Much less attention is paid to daily occurrences that kill or injure far more people each year but take only one life at a time. In reporting about risks, journalists often focus on the same concerns as the public: potentially catastrophic effects, lack of familiarity and understanding, involuntariness, scientific uncertainty, risks to future generations, unclear benefits, inequitable distribution of risks and benefits, and potentially irreversible effects (Slovic, 1986, 1987; Slovic & Fischhoff, 1982).

Media coverage of risks is frequently deficient in that many stories contain oversimplifications, distortions, and inaccuracies in reporting risk information (Friedman, 1981; Krimsky & Plough, 1988; Mazur, 1981, 1984; Nelkin, 1984, 1989; Sandman, Sachsman, Greenberg, & Gotchfeld, 1987). Media coverage is also deficient not only in what is contained in stories, but in what is left out (Davies et al., 1987; Kasperson & Stallen, 1991; Nelkin, 1984, 1989). For example, analyses of media reports on cancer risks show that these reports are often deficient in that they provide few statistics on general cancer rates for purposes of comparison and little information on common forms of cancer, do not address known sources of public ignorance about cancer, and provide little information about detection, treatments, and other protective measures (Combs & Slovic, 1979; Fischhoff et al., 1981).

Many of these problems stem from characteristics of the media and the constraints under which reporters work (Friedman, 1981; Nelkin, 1989; Sandman, Sachsman, & Greenberg, 1987; Sandman, Sachsman, Greenberg, & Gotchfeld, 1987). First, most reporters work under extremely tight deadlines that limit the amount of time for research and for the pursuit of valid and reliable information. Second, with few exceptions, reporters do not have adequate time or space to deal with the complexities and uncertainties surrounding many risk issues. Third, journalists achieve objectivity in a story by balancing opposing views. Truth in journalism is different from truth in science. In journalism, there are only different or conflicting views and claims, to be covered as fairly as possible. Fourth, journalists are source dependent. Under the pressure of deadlines and other constraints, reporters tend to rely heavily on sources who are easily accessible and willing to speak out. Sources who are difficult to contact, hard to draw out, or reluctant to provide interesting and nonqualified statements are often left out. Finally, few reporters have the scientific background or expertise needed to evaluate the complex scientific data and disagreements that surround many debates about risks. Given these limitations, effectiveness in communicating with the media about risks depends in part on understanding the constraints and needs of the media and adapting one's behavior and information to meet these needs (Fischhoff, 1985b; Sandman, Sachsman, & Greenberg, 1987).

Characteristics and Limitations of the Public
in Evaluating and Interpreting Risk Information

Risk communication research on public attitudes and beliefs parallels in many way the public health communication research described by Scherer and Juanillo. However, the risk communication literature has several distinctive elements not generally found in the public health communication literature. For example, much of the risk communication research focuses on characteristics and limitations of the public in evaluating and interpreting risk information. These include inaccurate perceptions of levels of risk; lack of interest in risk problems and technical complexities; individuals' overconfidence in their ability to avoid harm; strong beliefs and opinions that are resistant to change; exaggerated expectations about the effectiveness of regulatory actions; desires and demands for scientific certainty; reluctance to make trade-offs among different types of risks or among risks, costs, and benefits; and difficulties in understanding probabilistic information related to unfamiliar activities or technologies (Covello, 1983; Covello et al., 1987; Fischhoff, 1985b; Slovic, Fischhoff, & Lichtenstein, 1982).

An important implication of this literature for risk communication is the distinction between perceptions of risk and judgments of risk acceptability. Even though the level of risk is related to risk acceptability, it is not a perfect correlation. Two factors affect the way people assess risk and evaluate acceptability; these factors modify the correlation (Covello, 1983; Fischhoff et al., 1981; Slovic, 1986, 1987; Slovic & Fischhoff, 1982).

First, the level of risk is only one among several variables that determines acceptability (see Table 1). Among the other variables that matter to people in evaluating and interpreting risk information are fairness, benefits, alternatives, control, and voluntariness (Covello, 1983; Fischhoff et al., 1981; Lowrance, 1976; Slovic, 1986, 1987; Slovic et al., 1982). In general, a fairly distributed risk is more acceptable than an unfairly distributed one. A risk entailing significant benefits to the parties at risk is more acceptable than a risk with no such benefits. A risk for which there are no alternatives is more acceptable than a risk that could be eliminated by using an alternative technology. A risk that the parties at risk have some control over is more acceptable than a risk that is beyond their control. A risk that the parties at risk assess and decide to accept is more acceptable than a risk that is imposed on them. These statements are true in exactly the same sense in which it is true that a small risk is more acceptable than a large risk. Risk is multidimensional; size is only one of the relevant dimensions.

If one grants the validity of these points, then a whole range of risk-management approaches becomes possible (Covello et al., 1989, 1991; Hance et al., 1987). Because factors such as fairness, familiarity, and voluntariness are as relevant as size in judging the acceptability of a risk, efforts to

TABLE 1
Factors Important in Risk Perception and Evaluation

Factor	Conditions Associated with Increased Public Concern	Conditions Associated with Decreased Public Concern
Catastrophic potential	fatalities and injuries grouped in time and space	fatalities and injuries scattered and random
Familiarity	unfamiliar	familiar
Understanding	mechanisms or process not misunderstood	mechanisms or process understood
Uncertainty	risks scientifically unknown or uncertain	risks known to science
Controllability	uncontrollable	controllable
Voluntariness of exposure	involuntary	voluntary
Effects on children	children specifically at risk	children not specifically at risk
Effects manifestation	delayed effects	immediate effects
Effects on future generations	risk to future generations	no risk to future generations
Victim identity	identifiable victims	statistical victims
Dread	effects dreaded	effects not dreaded
Trust in institutions	lack of trust in responsible institutions	trust in responsible institutions
Media attention	much media attention	little media attention
Accident history	major and sometimes minor accidents	no major or minor accidents
Equity	inequitable distribution of risks and benefits	equitable distribution of risks and benefits
Benefits	unclear benefits	clear benefits
Reversibility	effects irreversible	effects reversible
Personal stake	individual personally at risk	individual not personally at risk
Origin	caused by human actions	caused by acts of nature or God

make a risk fairer, more familiar, and more voluntary are as appropriate as efforts to make the risk smaller. Similarly, because control is important in determining the acceptability of a risk, efforts to share power—such as establishing and assisting community advisory committees or supporting third-party research, audits, inspections, and monitoring—can be effective in making a risk more acceptable.

Second, deciding what level of risk ought to be acceptable involves not a technical question but a value question. People vary in how they assess risk acceptability (Douglas & Wildavsky, 1982; Fischhoff et al., 1981; Johnson & Covello, 1987; Kasperson, 1986; Kasperson & Kasperson, 1983; Krimsky & Plough, 1988). They weigh the various factors according to their own values, senses of risk, and stakes in the outcome. Because acceptability is a matter of values and opinions, and because values and opinions differ, debates about risk are often debates about values, accountability, and control (Johnson & Covello, 1987; Kasperson, 1986; Krimsky & Plough, 1988).

RISK COMPARISONS

A significant part of the risk communication literature deals with risk comparisons (Covello, 1989, 1991; Roth, Morgan, Fischhoff, Lave, & Bostrom, 1990; Slovic, Krauss, & Covello, 1990; Wilson & Crouch, 1987). Based on Scherer and Juanillo's review, there appears to be no parallel interest in this topic in the public health communication literature.

Interest in risk comparisons derives in part from the perceived difficulties in communicating complex, quantitative risk information to laypersons and the need to put risk information in perspective (Covello, 1991). Several authors have argued that risk comparisons provide this perspective (Cohen & Lee, 1982; Wilson, 1979, 1984; Wilson & Crouch, 1987).

In a typical risk comparison, the risk in question is compared with the risk associated with other substances or activities. Because comparisons are perceived to be more intuitively meaningful than absolute probabilities, it is widely believed that they can be used effectively for communicating risk information. A basic assumption of the approach is that risk comparisons provide a conceptual yardstick for measuring the relative size of a risk, especially when the risk is new and unfamiliar.

Risk comparisons have several strengths that address important facets of this problem (Fischhoff et al., 1981). They present issues in a mode that appears compatible with intuitive natural thought processes, such as the use of analogies to improve understanding; they avoid the difficult and controversial task of converting diverse risks into a common unit, such as dollars per life lost or per day of pain and suffering; and they avoid direct numerical reference to small probabilities, which can be difficult to comprehend and evaluate in the abstract.

Many risk comparisons are advanced not only for gaining perspective and understanding but also for setting priorities and determining which risks are acceptable (Wilson & Crouch, 1987). More specifically, risk comparisons have been advocated as a means for determining which risks to ignore, which risks to be concerned about, and how much risk reduction to seek (Cohen & Lee, 1982; Rothchild, 1979; Wilson, 1979, 1984; Wilson & Crouch, 1987). A common argument in many risk comparisons, for example, is that risks that are small or comparable to already accepted risks should themselves be accepted. Such claims cannot, however, be defended (Covello, 1991; Covello et al., 1988; Slovic, 1986, 1987). Although risk comparisons can provide insight and perspective, they provide only a small part of the information needed for setting priorities or for determining which risks are acceptable. For example, it is often tempting for industry or government officials to use the following argument when they meet with community groups or members of the public to discuss risks:

> The risk of *a* (emissions from the plant) is lower than the risk of *b* (driving to the meeting or smoking during breaks). Since you (the audience) find *b* acceptable, you are obliged to find *a* acceptable. (Covello et al., 1988)

This argument has a basic flaw in logic: its use can severely damage trust and credibility (Covello 1991; Covello et al., 1988). Some listeners will analyze the argument this way:

> I do not have to accept the (small) added risk of living near a chemical plant just because I accept the (perhaps larger, but voluntary and personally beneficial) risk of sunbathing, bicycling, smoking, or driving my car. In deciding about the acceptability of risks, I consider many factors, only one of them being the size of the risk—and I prefer to do my own evaluation. Your job is not to tell me what I should accept, but to tell me about the size of the risk and what you are doing about it.

Judgments of acceptability are related not only to annual mortality rates— the focus of most risk comparisons—but also to the broad and diverse set of factors that influence public perceptions of risk and acceptability (see Table 1). These factors explain, in part, public concerns about the risks of environmental exposures to toxic chemicals. Because of the importance of these factors, comparisons showing that the risks associated with environmental exposures to chemicals are lower than the risks of other activities or technologies may have no effect whatsoever on public perceptions and attitudes. For example, comparing the risk of living near a chemical manufacturing plant with the risk of driving X number of hours, eating X tablespoons of peanut butter, smoking X number of cigarettes a day, or sunbathing X number of hours may provide perspective but may also be highly inappropriate. Since such risks differ on a variety of qualitative dimensions—such as perceived benefits, extent of personal control, voluntariness, catastrophic potential, familiarity, fairness, origin, and scientific uncertainty—it is likely that people will perceive the comparison as irrelevant or meaningless.

The fundamental argument against such comparisons is that it is seldom relevant or appropriate to compare risks with different qualities for risk acceptability purposes, even if the comparison is technically accurate (Covello, 1991; Slovic, 1987). Several reasons underlie this argument. First, as noted above, there are important psychological and social differences among risks with different qualities. Risks that are involuntary and result from life-style choices, for example, are more likely to be accepted than risks that are perceived to be involuntary and imposed.

Second, people recognize that risks are cumulative and that each additional risk adds to their overall risk burden. The fact that a person is exposed to risks resulting from voluntary life-style choices does not lessen the impact of risks that are perceived to be involuntary and imposed.

Third, people perceive many types of risk in an absolute sense. An involuntary exposure that increases the risk of cancer or birth defects is perceived as a physical and moral insult regardless of whether the increase is small or whether the increase is smaller than risks from other exposures.

Finally, judgments about the acceptability of a risk can seldom be separated from judgments about the risk decision process (Kasperson, 1986). Public responses to risk are shaped both by the characteristics of the risky activity and by the perceived adequacy of the decision-making process. Risk comparisons play only a limited role in such determinations.

CONCLUSIONS

The literature on risk communication represents a growing and increasingly important part of the literature on public health communication. Many of the findings derived from research on risk communication parallel those reported by Scherer and Juanillo in their review of research on public health communication. For example, there are no easy prescriptions for effective communication. There are also limits on what people trying to communicate effectively can do, no matter how skilled, committed, and sincere they are. However, research has helped clarify the nature of the problem in public health communication and in risk communication. It has also helped identify solutions.

Given the passage of increasing numbers of right-to-know laws, and given increasing demands by the public for risk information, risk communication will be the focus of increasing attention in years to come. Industry, government, and public interest groups will continually be asked to provide information about health, safety, and environmental risks to interested and affected individuals and communities (Hadden, 1989; Ruckelshaus, 1983, 1984, 1987; Thomas, 1987). How they answer this challenge will have a profound affect on public perceptions of the risks of modern life.

REFERENCES

Bean, M. (1987). *Tools for environmental professionals involved in risk communication at hazardous waste facilities undergoing siting, permitting, or remediation* (Report No. 87-30.8). Reston, VA: Air Pollution Control Association.

Cohen, B., & Lee, I. (1982). A catalog of risks. *Health Physics, 36,* 707-722.

Cohrssen, J., & Covello, V. T. (1989). *Risk analysis.* Washington, DC: White House Council on Environmental Quality.

Combs, B., & Slovic, P. (1979). Newspaper coverage of causes of death. *Journalism Quarterly, 6,* 837-843.

Conservation Foundation. (1985). *Risk assessment and risk control.* Washington, DC: Author.

Covello, V. T. (1983). The perception of technological risks: A literature review. *Technological Forecasting and Social Change, 23,* 285-297.

Covello, V. T. (1988). Informing the public about health and environmental risks: Problems and opportunities for effective risk communication. In N. Lind (Ed.), *Risk communication: A symposium.* Waterloo: University of Waterloo.

Covello, V. T. (1989). Issues and problems in using risk comparisons for communicating right-to-know information on chemical risks. *Environmental Science and Technology, 23,* 1444-1449.

Covello, V. T. (1991). Risk comparisons and risk communication. In R. Kasperson & P. J. Stallen (Eds.), *Communicating risks to the public* (pp. 79-126). Boston: Kluwer.

Covello, V. T., & Allen, F. (1988). *Seven cardinal rules of risk communication.* Washington, DC: U.S. Environmental Protection Agency, Office of Policy Analysis.

Covello, V. T., Donovan, E., & Slavick, J. (1991). *Community outreach.* Washington, DC: Chemical Manufacturers Association.

Covello, V. T., McCallum, D., & Pavlova, M. (Eds.). (1989). *Effective risk communication: The role and responsibility of governmental and non-governmental organizations.* New York: Plenum.

Covello, V. T., Sandman, P., & Slovic, P. (1988). *Risk communication, risk statistics, and risk comparisons.* Washington, DC: Chemical Manufacturers Association.

Covello, V. T., von Winterfeldt, D., & Slovic, P. (1986). Communicating risk information to the public. *Risk Abstracts, 3,* 1-14.

Covello, V. T., von Winterfeldt, D., & Slovic, P. (1987). Communicating risk information to the public. In J. C. Davies, V. T. Covello, & F. W. Allen (Eds.), *Risk communication* (pp. 109-134). Washington, DC: Conservation Foundation.

Davies, J. C., Covello, V. T., & Allen, F. W. (Eds.). (1987). *Risk communication.* Washington, DC: Conservation Foundation.

Douglas, M., & Wildavsky, A. (1982). *Risk and culture.* Berkeley: University of California Press.

Fessenden-Raden, J., Fitchen, J., & Heath, J. (1987). Risk communication at the local level: A complex interactive progress. *Science, Technology and Human Values, 12*(3-4).

Fischhoff, B. (1985a). Managing risk perception. *Issues in Science and Technology, 2,* 83-96.

Fischhoff, B. (1985b, Winter). Protocols for environmental reporting: What to ask the experts. *Journalist,* pp. 11-15.

Fischhoff, B. (1987). Treating the public with risk communications: A public health perceptive. *Science, Technology, and Human Values, 12*(3-4), 13-19.

Fischhoff, B., Lichtenstein, S., Slovic, P., Derby, S. L., & Keeney, R. L. (1981). *Acceptable risk.* New York: Cambridge University Press.

Friedman, S. M. (1981). Blueprint for breakdown: Three Mile Island and the mass media before the accident. *Journal of Communications, 31,* 85-96, 116-128.

Hadden, S. (1989). *Citizen right to know: Communication and public policy.* Boulder, CO: Westview.

Hance, B., Chess, C., & Sandman, P. (1987). *Improving dialogue with communities: A risk communication manual for government.* Trenton: New Jersey Department of Environmental Protection, Office of Science and Research.

Johnson, B., & Covello, V. T. (Eds.). (1987). *The social and cultural construction of risk: Essays on risk selection and perception.* Boston: Reidel.

Kasperson, R. (1986). Six propositions on public participation and their relevance to risk communication. *Risk Analysis, 6,* 275-282.

Kasperson, R., & Kasperson, J. (1983). Determining the acceptability of risk: Ethical and policy issues. In J. Rogers & D. Bates (Eds.), *Risk: A symposium.* Ottawa: Royal Society of Canada.

Kasperson, R., & Stallen, P. J. (Eds.). (1991). *Communicating risks to the public.* Boston: Kluwer.

Kates, R., Hohenemser, C., & Kasperson, R. (1985). *Perilous progress: Managing the hazards of technology.* Boulder, CO: Westview.

Klaidman, S. (1985). *Health risk reporting.* Washington, DC: Institute for Health Policy Analysis.

Krimsky, S., & Plough, A. (1988). *Environmental hazards: Communicating risks as a social process*. Dover, MA: Auburn House.

Lowrance, W. W. (1976). *Of acceptable risk: Science and the determination of safety*. Los Altos, CA: Kaufman.

Mazur, A. (1981). Media coverage and public opinion on scientific controversies. *Journal of Communication*, pp. 106-115.

Mazur, A. (1984). The journalists and technology: Reporting about Love Canal and Three Mile Island. *Minerva, 22*, 45-66.

McCallum, D., Hammond, S., & Covello, V. T. (1990). *Public knowledge and perceptions of risks in six communities: Analysis of a baseline survey* (Report No. EPA 230-01-90-074). Washington, DC: Environmental Protection Agency.

Morgan, M. G., Slovic, P., Nair, I., Geisler, D., MacGregor, D., Fischhoff, B., Lincoln, D., & Florig, K. (1985). Powerline frequency and magnetic fields: A pilot study of risk perception. *Risk Analysis, 5*, 139-149.

National Research Council. (1983). *Risk assessment in the federal government: Managing the process*. Washington, DC: National Academy Press.

National Research Council. (1989). *Improving risk communication*. Washington, DC: National Academy Press.

Nelkin, D. (1984). *Science in the streets*. New York: Twentieth Century Fund.

Nelkin, D. (1989). Communicating technological risk: The social construction of risk perception. *American Review of Public Health, 10*, 95-113.

President's Commission on the Accident at Three Mile Island. (1979). *Report of the Public's Right to Information Task Force*. Washington, DC: Government Printing Office.

Press, F. (1987). Science and risk communication. In J. C. Davies, V. T. Covello, & F. W. Allen (Eds.), *Risk communication* (pp. 11-17). Washington, DC: Conservation Foundation.

Roth, E., Morgan, G., Fischhoff, B., Lave, L., & Bostrom, A. (1990). What do we know about making risk comparisons? *Risk Analysis, 10*, 375-387.

Rothchild, N. (1979, May 13). Coming to grips with risk. *Wall Street Journal*.

Ruckelshaus, W. D. (1983). Science, risk, and public policy. *Science, 221*, 1026-1028.

Ruckelshaus, W. D. (1984). Risk in a free society. *Risk Analysis, 4*, 157-163.

Ruckelshaus, W. D. (1987). Communicating about risk. In J. C. Davies, V. T. Covello, & F. W. Allen (Eds.), *Risk communication* (pp. 3-9). Washington, DC: Conservation Foundation.

Sandman, P. M. (1985). Getting to maybe: Some communications aspects of hazardous waste facility siting. *Seton Hall Legislative Journal, 9*, 442-465.

Sandman, P. M. (1986). *Explaining environmental risk*. Washington, DC: U.S. Environmental Protection Agency, Office of Toxic Substances.

Sandman, P. M., Sachsman, D., & Greenberg, M. (1987). *Risk communication for environmental news sources*. New Brunswick, NJ: Industry/University Cooperative Center for Research in Hazardous and Toxic Substances.

Sandman, P. M., Sachsman, D., Greenberg, M., & Gotchfeld, M. (1987). *Environmental risk and the press*. New Brunswick, NJ: Transaction.

Sharlin, H. (1987). EDB: A case study in the communication of health risk. In B. Johnson & V. T. Covello (Eds.), *The social and cultural construction of risk: Essays on risk selection and perception* (pp. 183-198). Boston: Reidel.

Slovic, P. (1986). Informing and educating the public about risk. *Risk Analysis, 4*, 403-415.

Slovic, P. (1987). Perception of risk. *Science, 236*, 280-285.

Slovic, P., & Fischhoff, B. (1982). How safe is safe enough? Determinants of perceived and acceptable risk. In L. Gould & C. Walker (Eds.), *Too hot to handle*. New Haven, CT: Yale University Press.

Slovic, P., Fischhoff, B., & Lichtenstein, S. (1982). Facts versus fears: Understanding perceived risk. In D. Kahneman, P. Slovic, & A. Tversky (Eds.), *Judgment under uncertainty: Heuristics and biases*. Cambridge: Cambridge University Press.

Slovic, P., Krauss, N., & Covello, V. T. (1990). What we should know about making risk comparisons. *Risk Analysis, 10,* 389-392.

Smith, V. K., Desvousges, W., Fisher, A., & Johnson, R. (1987). *Communicating radon risk effectively: A mid-course evaluation* (Report No. CR-811075). Washington, DC: Environmental Protection Agency.

Thomas, L. M. (1987). Why we must talk about risk. In J. C. Davies, V. T. Covello, & F. W. Allen (Eds.), *Risk communication* (pp. 19-25). Washington, DC: Conservation Foundation.

Wilson, R. (1979). Analyzing the daily risks of life. *Technology Review, 81,* 40-46.

Wilson, R. (1984). Commentary: Risks and their acceptability. *Science, Technology, and Human Values, 9*(2), 11-22.

Wilson, R., & Crouch, E. (1987). Risk assessment and comparisons: An introduction. *Science, 236,* 267-270.

8 Public Issues and Argumentation Structures: An Approach to the Study of the Contents of Media Agenda-Setting

HANS-JÜRGEN WEISS
Universität Göttingen

After a survey of conception, method, and selected results of an approach to the study of the contents of media agenda-setting, this chapter develops an approach termed *argumentation analysis*. This approach has been used in two studies on media contents concerning the tendencies with which the daily press covered and discussed the conflict of the coexistence of the public and commercial broadcasting systems in Germany. Argumentation analysis is a contribution to the further development of agenda-setting research because it measures important aspects of the stereotyping of issue-specific conflicts by journalists and the news media. With this approach, the hypothesis that the conflict structure of media issue coverage mediates the agenda-setting effect can be tested.

THE hypothesis of the agenda-setting function of the mass media is one of the most important concepts of recent media effects research. Since McCombs and Shaw's pioneering study on the 1968 presidential election campaign in the United States, studies working on the political effects of press, radio, and television, in election campaigns in particular, start from this approach (McCombs & Shaw, 1972; Patterson, 1980; Shaw, 1977; Weaver, Graber, McCombs, Maxwell, & Eyal, 1981).

AUTHOR'S NOTE: This chapter is based on a paper presented at the 39th Annual Conference of the International Communication Association, San Francisco, 1989. A revised version of this chapter was first published under the title "Öffentliche Streitfragen und massenmediale Argumentationsstrukturen," in M. Kaase & W. Schulz (Eds.), *Massenkommunikation. Theorien, Methoden, Befunde* (pp. 473-489). Opladen, 1989.

Correspondence and requests for reprints: Hans-Jürgen Weiss, Institut für Publizistik und Kommunikationswissenschaft, Universität Göttingen, Humboldtallee 38, D-3400 Göttingen, Germany.

The extensive attention paid to this research concept can be explained by the development of media effects research (Becker, 1982, p. 523). Under the impression that the mass media were omnipresent in modern industrial societies, the basic findings of the first phase of mass media research no longer did justice to the changed situation. Rather, theoretical alternatives had to diverge from the tenor of the early findings reduced by Klapper (1960) to the disillusioning formula that "mass communication does not serve as a necessary and sufficient cause of audience effects" (p. 8). In contrast to this negative conclusion, agenda-setting research has been successful in disproving the law of minimal consequences: "There can no longer be serious doubt over the ability of the mass media to influence the political agenda. The agenda-setting effect has proven to be quite robust, spanning a variety of issues, media channels, and target audiences" (Iyengar, 1988, p. 595). The explanation for this development can be based on the so-called paradigm change of recent research on media effects (Schulz, 1982). Klapper worked out the restrictions of the mass media to change attitudes. In the post-Klapper era of mass communication research it was necessary to direct the attention to what the media and journalists primarily do: "providing audience members with information" (Becker, McCombs, & McLeod, 1975, p. 22). From this perspective, agenda-setting can be seen as a latent consequence of the selection and transmittal of information by journalists in the mass media.

THEORETICAL FRAME:
THE CONCEPT OF MEDIA AGENDA-SETTING

Almost all reviews of agenda-setting research quote Cohen's (1963) famous statement: "[The press] may not be successful much of the time in telling people what to think, but it is stunningly successful in telling its readers what to think about" (p. 13). This quote provides agenda-setting research with a plausible metaphor. In analytic terms, Cohen's formulation means, first, that attitudes ("summary evaluations of objects by individuals") and cognitions ("stored information about those objects held by individuals") are to be distinguished from one another (Becker et al., 1975, pp. 25-26). Second, it assumes that cognitions are more easily influenced by the media than attitudes, because there is a hierarchy of media effects (see Figure 1).

If one discusses the validity of these theoretical prerequisites to the agenda-setting concept, one finds oneself in a paradoxical situation. On one hand, the empirical evidence of the agenda-setting function of the mass media seems to make this concept discussion superfluous (Iyengar, 1988; Rogers & Dearing, 1988; Weaver, 1982). On the other hand, reviews almost ritualistically label this approach as having "a high level of terminological imprecision" (Becker, 1982, p. 525) and "inconsistency of conceptualization, method and result" (Swanson, 1988, p. 604). The problem, simply stated, can be reduced to three questions (see Figure 2):

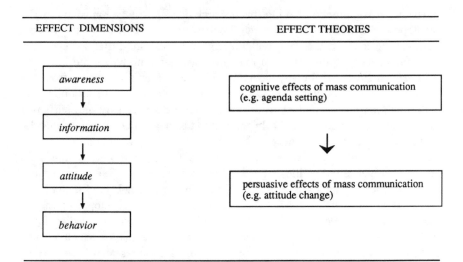

| EFFECT DIMENSIONS | EFFECT THEORIES |

Figure 1. A hierarchy of media effects?
SOURCE: "The Agenda-Setting Function of the Press," in D. L. Shaw & M. E. McCombs (Eds.), *The Emergence of American Political Issues* (p. 4). St. Paul, MN: West. Copyright 1977 by West Publishing Company. Reprinted by permission.

- What is defined and measured as *media information*?
- What are defined and measured as *audience cognitions*?
- What *type of influence* is to be seen as an agenda-setting effect of the mass media?

The discussion of these topics began immediately after the publication of McCombs and Shaw's influential study in 1972 (McLeod, Becker, & Byrnes, 1974). If one takes the most recent contributions as a criterion, however, the conceptual consistency of agenda-setting research has rarely been furthered. This chapter takes up a particular aspect of the conceptual debate on media agenda-setting underlying each of the three topics mentioned above. This issue is expressed well by Swanson (1988): "It seems obvious that if we wish to understand fully how the media influence the public's views, . . . then we must go beyond agendas and consider the *content* of persons' opinions and of news stories" (p. 613; emphasis added). The content aspect of agenda-setting is first of all related to the conceptualization and measurement of media information as the starting point for the analysis of mass media effects.

Defining the Contents of Media Agendas:
Issues and Conflict

McCombs and Shaw's (1972) particular translation of Cohen's formulation into a concrete research hypothesis was decisive for the entire develop-

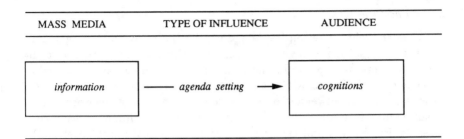

MASS MEDIA	TYPE OF INFLUENCE	AUDIENCE
information	—— *agenda setting* ——▶	*cognitions*

Figure 2. The basic model of media agenda-setting.

ment of agenda-setting research: "It is hypothesized that the mass media set the agenda for each political campaign, influencing the salience of attitudes toward the political issues" (p. 177). In this perspective the information of the media was conceptualized as an agenda of (political) issues. The term *issue* was never defined, because it had been used in election research for some time (Campbell, Gurin, & Miller, 1954). And *agenda* was nothing more than a metaphor referring to the schedule of public discussion. Indeed, the conceptual discussion did not pay much attention to the terms *agenda* and *issue*. They have been recently discussed by Rogers and Dearing (1988), but without clear results.

Rogers and Dearing (1988) define *agenda* rather narrowly as "a list of issues and events that are viewed at a point in time as ranked in a hierarchy of importance" (p. 565). Unlike Rogers and Dearing, McCombs and Shaw (1977) would like to include all possible "objects and their attributes . . . (topics, issues, persons, or whatever)" in their concept of agenda-setting (pp. 12-13). But Lang and Lang (1981) caution against a too "all-embracing and practically meaningless" (p. 450) concept if there is no clear definition of issue.

Issues and Events

At first sight, Shaw's (1977) differentiation between "(1) events, defined as discrete happenings that are limited by space and time, and (2) issues, defined as involving cumulative news coverage of a series of related events that fit together in a broad category," appears useful (Rogers & Dearing, 1988, p. 566). On closer examination, however, a general differentiation between events and issues proves to invite difficulties concerning the operationalization of these categories. Probable are ad hoc differentiations in the concrete research process that may be based on either the objects of media coverage themselves or the style of the media coverage of these objects. So it will in the end depend upon the individual research perspective as to whether a particular item will be conceptualized as an event or an issue.

Issues and Conflict

The relationship between issues and conflict is left open by Rogers and Dearing. In response to their question, "Is it necessary for an issue to involve contention?" (p. 566), they unfortunately quote only concurring statements from Eyestone (1974) and from Cobb and Elder (1971): "An issue is a conflict between two or more identifiable groups over procedural or substantive matters relating to the distribution of positions or resources" (p. 892). But Rogers and Dearing refuse to take a position themselves. In contrast, it is the main thesis of this chapter that *the agenda-setting concept, if limited to controversial issues, would gain significance.* This point of view is supported by the size of previous agenda-setting studies that have concerned themselves with this type of issue (normally in the field of political communication research; Schulz, 1984). Moreover, there are good reasons for the position that the public career of an issue is to a high degree regulated by the conflicts that it arouses. In the context of the agenda-setting concept, the question can be derived as to what role conflict dynamics play in the media effect to be analyzed. If one wishes to research this question empirically, one has to test the conflict content of issue coverage by the media as well as the perception of this conflict content by the audience.

Stereotypes: Reducing the Conflict Dimensions of an Issue

A primary step in the direction of content measurement in agenda-setting research is the approach of Benton and Frazier (1976), who differentiate among three different levels of media information about economic problems and correspond these to three levels of information holding:

- Level 1: the general issue (= issue name)
- Level 2: problems, causes, proposed solutions
- Level 3: persons and groups making proposals, rationales for proposals, pro/con positions taken on proposals

Benton and Frazier's concept is very helpful in two respects. On one hand, this system illustrates how unsystematically the term *issue* has been used in previous agenda-setting research. At least three issue categories are being mixed together: general issues (e.g., economy, foreign policy), problems (e.g., inflation, unemployment, crime), and solutions (e.g., disarmament, tax reduction). On the other hand, this concept draws attention to the fact that the issue content of the mass media (especially in the case of news coverage) normally is a package of observations, judgments, criticisms, and so on, thus permanently appealing not only to the cognitions but also to the attitudes of the audience.

It is therefore justified to suggest that the agenda-setting process is much more intensively connected with attitudes than previously assumed. Hyman

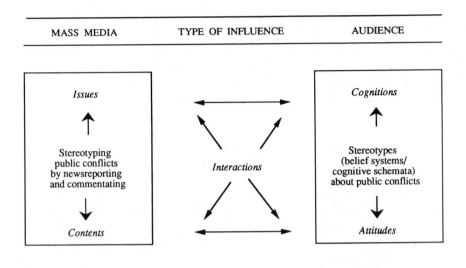

MASS MEDIA	TYPE OF INFLUENCE	AUDIENCE

Figure 3. An interaction model for the analysis of the contents of media agenda-setting.

and Sheatsley's (1947) early study of the possible effects of information campaigns and also the newest research on priming (Iyengar & Kinder, 1987) seem to favor an interaction perspective of cognitions and attitudes.

From this perspective the analysis of the transmittal of public conflicts and the contents dimension of the transmitting process can provide important conclusions. Agenda-setting is no longer understood to be an isolated, issue-specific media effect (issue by issue), but an effect that combines cognitions and attitudes (see Figure 3). This interaction can be outlined with the help of concepts such as those of "belief systems" (Converse, 1964; Fishbein & Ajzen, 1975) and "cognitive schemata" (Fiske, 1986; Fiske & Taylor 1984; Graber, 1984). Both concepts describe complex mechanisms with which the human being—for instance in his or her role as media user and voter—organizes perceptions and attitudes. On the basis of this, agenda-setting research would again be closer to Lippmann's (1922) often-cited conception of stereotypes. But prerequisite to this type of development of the agenda-setting research are methods by which the stereotyping of issues by the media (and the audience) can be measured and interrelated.

Gatekeeper research and especially news research have presented valuable suggestions on the newsworthiness of issues (Galtung & Ruge, 1965). The news factor "conflict" plays an important role in this context (Schulz, 1976). Journalists tend to simplify conflicts and stereotype them in the transmitting of information. As a result of professional norms, and in order to report news in an objective and neutral way (Weaver & Wilhoit, 1986), the stereotyping of conflicts ends up usually in reducing them to simple pro/con structures (Tuchman, 1978). Taking up this aspect, agenda-setting can be understood as a process that has two effects: (1) The media stereo-typing of a public debate draws the attention of the audience to the controversial problem as such (= issue dimension). (2) It leads to corresponding ideas about the contents of this conflict and its relevance for the individual, certain groups, the society, and so on (= contents dimension).

ARGUMENTATION ANALYSIS:
BACKGROUND AND CONCEPTION

The argumentation analysis described here starts with the media issue coverage tendency to polarize public controversies surrounding an issue. I developed this approach and tested it methodologically and empirically using two content analyses on the press coverage of broadcasting politics in Germany.[1]

The Studies

The first study analyzed newspaper coverage of the public discussion about the reorganization of the broadcasting system in Germany in 1984-1985. Actually, the debate served to produce a legal foundation (*Rundfunkstaatsvertrag*) for the coexistence of the public and commercial broadcasting systems. In this context the tendencies of the daily press in presenting this discussion and—as an interest group in favor of commercial broadcasting—in leading this discussion were examined.

The sample, consisting of two-thirds of the German newspapers ($n = 81$), was examined between October 1984 and January 1985. A total of 1,184 articles concerning this issue were discovered. A basic list was established that contained altogether 43 controversial arguments under discussion. The articles were examined with respect to whether and how they covered one or more of these arguments. The coding unit was the specific context in which the argument was transmitted to the public (= "argumentation"). A total of 4,012 argumentations were identified, coded, and analyzed (Weiss, 1985, 1986).

The second study examined the news reporting and commentating of the daily press on a conflict in 1987-1988 that also resulted from the competition of the commercial and public broadcasting systems in Germany. The politicians had to decide how much to increase broadcasting user fees. In this context, the sum that was recommended by a commission became the line of battle for public debate (it was criticized by the public broadcasting system as being too low). This study contained a sample of 633 articles referring to this issue that were published in the German daily press between October 1987 and January 1988. With a list of 68 basic arguments, 2,940 coding units (argumentations) were identified, coded, and analyzed (Weiss, 1988).

The Basic Concept: An Overview

The goal of argumentation analysis is to ascertain how public discussion of a particular issue is transmitted in news coverage and how it is discussed in media commentaries. Principally, two steps of analysis are to be differentiated: In a *prestudy*, the arguments used in the discussion of the critical issue are gathered. These arguments are ordered and placed in a list. The argument list is the starting point for the development of a coding scheme and the conduct of content analysis. In the *main study*, every contribution (articles and so on) to the critical issue in the sample is examined to determine whether or not it contains arguments from the argument list. If such an argument is found, the semantic context is identified (Is the argument quoted or mentioned as the author's opinion? Is it additionally evaluated? If so, by whom?). This context, defined as *argumentation*, is isolated as the coding unit and is subjected to a systematic content analysis. For both parts of the argumentation analysis, the conceptual assumptions and methodological procedures will be described and, as far as they are conceptually of interest, empirical data will be presented.

The Prestudy: From Arguments to Conflict Scales

The first step of the prestudy is to ascertain the full spectrum of the arguments actually applied to a controversial issue. In this context an *argument* is defined as an evaluative statement on the basic conflict that is connected with the controversial problem.

The prestudy can be done as a preliminary survey of the sample of articles and so on that will later be subjected to a quantitative content analysis. It would indeed be better, however, to expand the range of exploration to include such primary sources as party platforms, special publications, and press releases of interest groups. Ideally, this step should ascertain the entire spectrum of arguments that are used to "handle" a particular issue in the forefront of news reporting. There then would be a frame of reference from which the tendency of the argumentative selection of media coverage of a certain issue could be measured. After the arguments surrounding a controversial issue have been collected, they are ordered under two perspectives.

Methodologically, it is of great importance to *assign the arguments to a conflict scale* with which the argumentative polarization of the analyzed debate is measured. Thus, for example, in the study on the establishment of a legal foundation for the coexistence of public and commercial broadcasting systems, every argument had to be classified with respect to its favoring the position of the public or the point of view of the commercial system (and vice versa, criticizing one of the positions). The very simple two-dimensional structure of the public discussion of this controversial problem can be rather easily transferred to a one-dimensional conflict scale (see Figure 4).

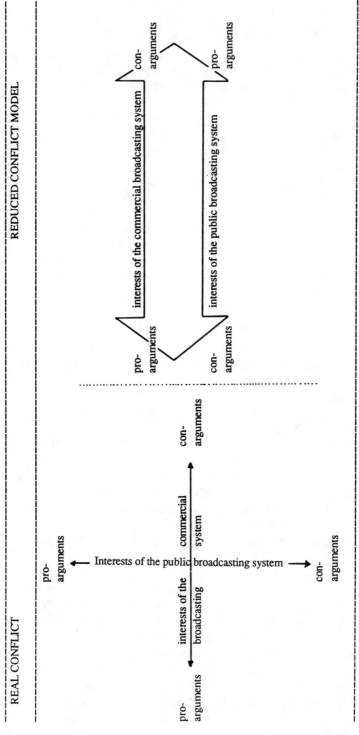

Figure 4. Constructing a one-dimensional conflict scale. The basic issue is the legal foundation for the coexistence of public and commercial broadcasting systems in Germany.
SOURCE: Weiss (1985, 1986). Reprinted by permission.

Generally speaking, this means that assumptions about the basic structure of the conflict—the transmittal of which by the media is to be analyzed—find their way into the design of the research instrument. On the basis of these assumptions, every argument of the instrument is assigned a *pro* or *con* value on the dichotomous conflict scale. This is done by an expert rating.

A further refinement of the research instrument can be achieved by *arranging the arguments on separate conflict dimensions* that can be distinguished with respect to their contents. For example, in the study on the increases in broadcasting user fees, two fields of argumentation referring to the conflict issue could be differentiated: First, there were several different variants of the increase rate suggested in the discussion (labeled "manifest arguments"). Second, different rationales were brought into the discussion that more or less directly favored one or the other of the suggested variants ("latent arguments"). What was common to all of these arguments was that they were either directly or indirectly for or against the interests of public broadcasting (see Figure 5).

First, the coding scheme differentiates between manifest and latent arguments. Second, the latent conflict dimension is subdivided into economic arguments, program arguments, technical arguments, and so on. After that, each of the altogether 68 basic arguments was assigned either to the manifest or to one of the latent conflict dimensions.

There is, of course, a systematic relationship between the "vertical" and the "horizontal" ordering of the arguments to the researched issue (i.e., the ratings of their evaluative pro/con tendencies and of the particular conflict dimensions they refer to; see Figure 6):

- Every conflict dimension is internally polarized in pro and con arguments.
- The pro/con arguments to the different conflict dimensions can be summed into a total conflict scale that measures the polarization of the discussion on a conflict issue at the most general level.

With this conception, the argumentation analysis can relatively flexibly explore and reconstruct the conflict structure of public debates. The range of arguments the analysis has at its starting point is very broad because the actual discussion of an issue is explored inductively. The ordering of arguments under content dimensions and the fixing of the number of content dimensions for a specific issue can be done stepwise. It would be optimal to begin the analysis with a broadly laid out content pattern of the researched conflict issue and then consolidate these clusters step by step in the course of data analysis.

A second advantage of this approach lies in the level of measurement in connection with statistical data analysis. The transformation of a long and very cumbersome nominal scale (= the nominal argument list) into one or more conflict scales that are more strongly consolidated at a higher measurement level is an important condition for more sophisticated procedures of data analysis that can be used in reconstructing public communication processes.

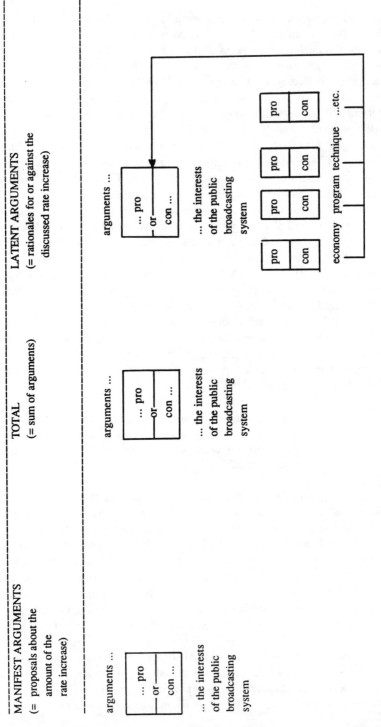

Figure 5. Constructing a multidimensional conflict scale. The basic issue is a rate increase in broadcasting user fees in Germany.

SOURCE: Weiss (1988). Reprinted by permission.

384

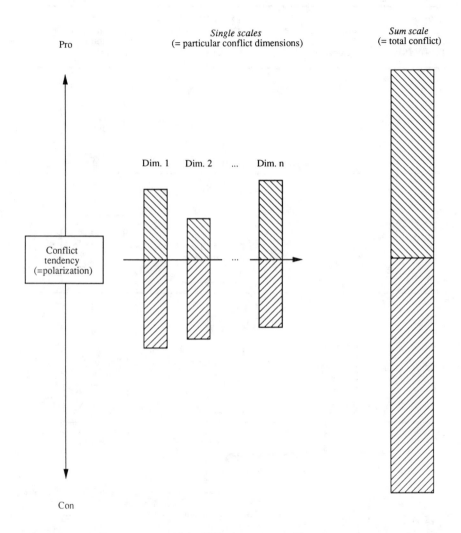

Figure 6. Relationships between the measurement of the polarization and the conflict dimensions of an issue debate.

The Main Study: From Argument to Argumentation Analysis

At the core of argumentation analysis are the above-described argument list and the conflict scales derived from it. However, this approach is not limited simply to describing the presence of these arguments in a sample of newspaper articles and the like. Moreover, the semantic contexts in which these arguments are passed on to the public at large by the mass media must be reconstructed (see Figure 7). There are three basic questions to be asked:

LEVELS OF ARGU-MENTATION	ONE-STEP ARGUMENTATION (= own argumentation)	TWO-STEP ARGUMENTATION (= simple quotation)	THREE-STEP ARGUMENTATION (= complex quotation)

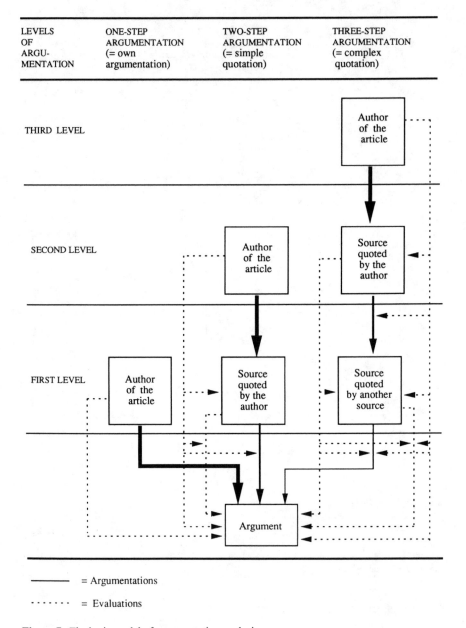

——————   = Argumentations

· · · · · ·   = Evaluations

Figure 7. The basic model of argumentation analysis.

- Which argument on the issue being researched is mentioned by whom?
- Who mentions whom, and with which arguments?
- Are the arguments (which themselves already express tendencies) and their sources additionally evaluated?

Especially in connection with the last question, it is clear that the mass media's argumentation and evaluation structures, with respect to news and commentary can overlap to such an extent that the original meaning of an argument—taken to the extreme—can be reversed. The validity of an empirical analysis is then dependent upon whether argumentation and evaluation structures and their potential interlacing can be respectively modeled. For this research problem, argumentation analysis is a conception that is relatively simple, but quite well adapted to the "language" of the media.

Argumentation Structures

In the study on the rate increase in broadcasting user fees, the complexity of mass argumentation structures was examined systematically (Weiss, 1988). It became evident that, at least with regard to press analysis, it is sufficient to differentiate among three patterns of argumentation.

The most common pattern is the two-step argumentation: The author of an article reports about a person, an institution, or the like that had taken a position on a particular issue. Of the just under 3,000 arguments that were taken from a sample of more than 600 articles about the increase in broadcasting user fees, 80% were presented in this form—that is, a simple quotation. Clearly, this type of argumentation is characteristic of the news reporting language in the daily press.

The second most common is the simple one-step argumentation pattern: The author him- or herself takes a position on a particular issue. Naturally, this form of argumentation is usually found in the commentating newspaper genres (in the case of the fee study, 15%). The reverse assumption—that commentaries consist mainly of this type of argumentation—is incorrect, however. Even in commentaries, the simple quotation form (= two-step argumentation) ranked clearly above the form in which the author took an explicit position.

The least often used form is the three-step argumentation, in which the author of an article reports about a public controversy in which person A comments on the statement of person B. This type of argumentation was found in only 5% of the data examined. But what is even more important than this rather low rate is the fact that argumentation structures more complex than the three-step form did not appear at all in the daily press.

Evaluation Structures

As shown in Figure 5, the network of evaluations with which an (per definitionem evaluative) argument may be related is very complex. The higher the level of argumentation, the more complex the structures of (potential) evaluations. But, parallel to the empirical argumentation structures, the media coverage of a controversial debate also shows typical patterns of evaluating arguments.

In the case of the press coverage of the controversy about broadcasting user fees, about three-fourths of the examined arguments were free of any additional evaluations. In only slightly more than one-fourth of the examined cases was a combination of an (evaluative) argument and an (additional) evaluation found. Within this group a clear priority of quoted evaluations became apparent (75% in the study concerning broadcasting user fees), and most of them were incorporated in the two-step argumentation (60%). This means that it is not the commentating genres that transmit most of the opinionated positions to arguments in a discussion, but the news reporting genres (in which, as mentioned, these evaluations are generally quoted positions).

Second in rank is the number of evaluations (16%) connected with the three-step form of argumentation in a very specific way. A "double quotation" appears in news coverage only when a reported argumentation is coupled with an evaluation: Person A quotes and reviews the argumentation of person B. Obviously, it is this evaluation that makes the news.

The evaluations that can be attributed to the authors of the articles themselves (nearly one-fourth) fall into two groups. Slightly more than half are evaluations that refer to the arguments of others, and less than half are part of the argumentations of the author. This evaluation style seems to be the typical "language" of a commentary.

Overall Tendency

The basis for the reconstruction of an overall pro/con tendency of the analyzed argumentation is the tendency of the coding unit argument. The positive or negative evaluation of the argument is coded at each level of argumentation. The last evaluation (that is, the evaluation at the highest argumentation level) is decisive for further analysis.

If one proceeds from the last evaluation, two variables are available for the calculation of the overall tendency of the analyzed argumentation: (a) the argument tendency as measured on the conflict scale and (b) the evaluation tendency as measured on the (last) evaluation scale.

When argumentation analysis was first applied, the study results were presented in a two-dimensional form (Weiss, 1986, p. 59). An alternative to this is to transform the tendency of the argument and the tendency of the evaluation into a new variable ("evaluated tendency") (Weiss, 1988). Especially for causal analyses—the tendency of the transmitting of a problem being either the dependent or the independent variable—this alternative is undoubtedly the better solution.

Validity and Reliability

With respect to *validity*, the main questions are whether the method of argumentation analysis can (a) *adequately register the public debate* with all of the important aspects of the issue and (b) *adequately reconstruct it.*

The quality of the registration of the basic arguments around an issue is first of all dependent on the strategy of the prestudy. The question is whether the prestudy should focus on extramedia sources or on the media themselves. Given a specialist's knowledge and thorough procedure, essential arguments of such a debate can be registered with both strategies. More crucial, however, can be the demand for completeness, the basis of which should be an objectifiable concept that delimits the potential debaters and sources of arguments. Independent of the chosen concept of registration (essential versus complete), the validity of argumentation analysis is always dependent on the argument list, which is the result of the prestudy. Argumentation analysis therefore does not measure *the* public discussion on a particular issue as such, but whether and how a selected number of arguments about an issue are conveyed by the media.

The quality with which argumentation analysis reconstructs the media transmittal of the public discussion of a conflict issue depends on the scaling of the arguments in the prestudy. And, as mentioned previously, this scaling is influenced by hypotheses on the structure of the conflict to be analyzed. But these hypotheses can be made explicit and—for instance, by expert ratings—objective. Second, the question is whether the instrument of the main study offers valid reconstruction of the semantic contexts in which arguments concerning the researched conflict are transmitted by the media. The methodological tests of this instrument undertaken up to now suggest that the coding scheme that has been developed for these purposes is an acceptable solution.

Concerning the *reliability* of the argumentation analysis, two problems must be discussed. The first is the reliability of the *identification and determination of the argumentation contexts* in the analyzed articles (and thus the *establishment of the coding units* of the argumentation analysis). Simply structured news generally poses no problems. According to my experience, however, the most difficult part of the argumentation analysis is the development of a reliable procedure with which to divide complex *argumentation chains* (e.g., in longer articles) into single argumentations to be coded separately. This is of central importance because through this procedure the coding units for the analysis are simultaneously set. Different reliability tests on this procedure have shown an agreement among the coders of about 70% on the average.

The second problem of reliability—the *coding of the established study units* (i.e., the actual argumentation analysis)—can be handled quite easily. It mainly consists of the following three steps: (a) identification of the argument, (b) determination of the number of argumentation levels, and (c) identification of the source of argumentation and evaluation at each level of argumentation. In this part of the coding process, coder reliability has been relatively high and stable, with agreement amounting to an average of 80-85%.

APPLICATIONS OF ARGUMENTATION ANALYSIS

A few examples are given below of research questions for which argumentation analysis can yield substantial results.

Focusing

The stereotyping of controversial problems by the media results not only in a polarization but also in an argumentative accentuation of the conflict. This process is called *focusing*. By comparing the range of the instrument's argument list with the empirical distribution of the arguments in the media, the degree of media focusing can be examined.

The two studies in which argumentation analysis has been used up to now showed similar results regarding focusing. In both cases, the press coverage of political problems concerning broadcasting was examined over a period of four months. The bases for the examinations in the two studies were argument lists with 43 and 68 arguments, respectively.

Starting from these argument lists, about 4,000 argumentations were analyzed in the first study and about 3,000 in the second. All had been identified in the relevant newspaper articles. The focusing effect was nearly identical in both studies (Weiss, 1985, p. 854; 1988, p. 483). About one-fourth of the analyzed articles concentrated on two or three different arguments. Half of all the news reporting and commenting concerning these two problems included only eight different arguments. These results suggest a strongly restricted complexity of media issue coverage.

Selection Tendencies

There can be no doubt about the de facto selection with which the transmitting of public discussion of an issue by the media is connected. It is, however, difficult to grasp empirically the tendency of this selection. Argumentation analysis offers an empirical approximation to this research question, if the argument list is first of all produced upon the basis of extramedia sources (i.e., on the basis of papers and so on from the conflicting interest groups), and, second, if one can say with any certainty that this list is complete (a prerequisite that would indeed prove to be difficult to validate).

Such an attempt was made in the study about news reporting on the reorganization of the broadcasting system in Germany (Weiss, 1985, p. 857; 1986, p. 65). The 43 arguments established in the prestudy were ordered on a polarization scale. Assuming that this scale was complete, at least during the time of the study, and that each argument had had the same chance to enter the public debate, an extramedia scale mean was calculated for the description of the initial situation of the conflict (Weiss, 1985, p. 857). This was defined as a theoretical balance measure and was compared to the respective empirical mean of the press coverage of this issue.

The results of this comparison are at least plausible. They show clearly that all genres and especially the commentaries in the daily newspapers were beyond the extramedia scale mean. That means that out of the total spectrum of arguments referring to this issue, a politically biased sample was extracted by the press—that is, arguments in favor of commercial and to the detriment of public broadcasting interests.

Construction Tendencies

The difficulty in comparing extramedia and media reality is well known (Rosengren, 1970; Schulz, 1976). The same difficulty arises as in the investigation of the argumentative tendency with which a social or political conflict is transmitted by the mass media to the public. But it is possible to reconstruct the tendencies of reality construction by the media as such and to compare the different tendencies of reality construction within the media system.

In developing and applying argumentation analysis, these comparisons have up to now been established primarily on issues that refer to broadcasting politics. My interest has so far concentrated on the question of whether the journalistic variety of the German press is also guaranteed when transmitting issues that touch the economic interests of the publishers. To go into depth on this issue, the argumentations on broadcasting issues were analyzed and compared at the level of different newspapers (e.g., conservative versus liberal), different press markets (e.g., local versus national), journalistic genres (e.g., news versus commentaries), and so on.

On the basis of a two-dimensional view of the tendencies and additional evaluations of arguments concerning the reorganization of the broadcasting system in Germany, for example, the diametrically opposed commentating by liberal and conservative national newspapers as well as the mainly conservative orientations of the local press could be demonstrated (Weiss, 1986, p. 59; see Figure 8 and Table 1).

If one sums up the arguments and evaluations concerning this issue within an overall argumentation scale and an evaluation scale, respectively, clear commentary clusters are to be seen:

- The liberal national papers favored in their commentaries arguments that supported public broadcasting, and evaluated these arguments more positively.
- The exact opposite viewpoints were presented in the commentaries of the conservative national papers.
- The majority of the local papers' commentaries were along the same lines as those of the conservative national dailies.

In the follow-up study concerning broadcasting user fees, the tendencies of the arguments and their evaluations were transformed into a single variable ("evaluated tendency"). It could then be shown that the local as well

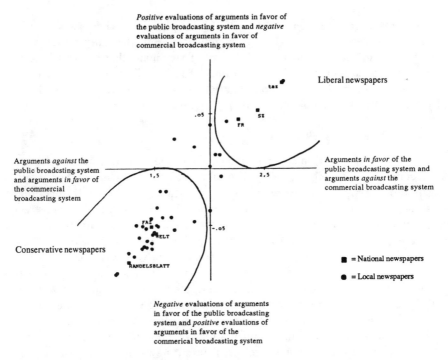

Figure 8. The tendencies of newspaper commentaries on the legal foundation of the coexistence of public and commercial broadcasting systems in Germany.

as the national press argued against the public broadcasting system. While the position of public broadcasting was indeed reflected in the news, the entire daily press commentated in disturbing consonance against this position.

CONCLUSION: RESEARCH PERSPECTIVES

What is the link between these results relevant for media policy and the application of argumentation analysis in research on media effects? On the one hand, a link can be found in the fact that the lack of variety that could be proved for a portion of the German press could also be called *consonance*—a phenomenon that has been given particular attention in the concept of the spiral of silence (Noelle-Neumann & Mathes, 1987). On the other hand, a link can be found in a consideration based on the agenda-setting hypothesis. The construction tendencies with which a controversial problem is shaped by the mass media and transmitted to the public may influence individuals' issue awareness as well as salience of an issue for individuals (Ükermann & Weiss, 1983). It seems useful here to take up the above-mentioned criticism that the

TABLE 1
The Tendencies of West German Local Newspapers: News Coverage
versus Commentaries on Rate Increases in Broadcasting User Fees

| | Evaluated Tendency | | |
Conflict Dimensions	*News*	*Commentaries*	*News Versus Commentaries*
Manifest tendency (= proposals about the amount of the rate increase)	$2,8^b$ $(n = 758)^c$	2,3 $(n = 166)$	$p \leq .001$
Latent tendency (= rationales for or against the discussed rate increase)	2,6 $(n = 1.100)$	2,3 $(n = 461)$	$p \leq .001$
Selected subdimensions			
Revenue and expenditures of the public broadcasting system	2,3 $(n = 167)$	2,1 $(n = 154)$	$p \leq .01$
Overall economic situation of the public broadcasting system	2,6 $(n = 365)$	2,4 $(n = 69)$	$p \leq .05$
Program of the public broadcasting system	2,7 $(n = 363)$	2,3 $(n = 119)$	$p \leq .001$
Overall tendency (= total of manifest and latent arguments)	2,6 $(n = 1.858)$	2,3 $(n = 627)$	$p \leq .001$

a. Results of one-way analysis of variance.
b. Mean (x); minimum = 1 (= clearly against the interests of the public broadcasting system), maximum = 4 (= clearly in favor of the interests of the public broadcasting system).
c. Number of argument in the pro dimension, drawn out of a total of n = 397 news and n = 126 commentaries.

content of the agenda-setting process until now has not been satisfactorily analyzed, either for the media or for the audience:

As we have seen, the public's agenda tells us comparatively little about the contents of citizens' views. Similarly, the media agenda is uninformative about the content of news coverage of topics or issues. It seems obvious that if we wish to understand fully how the media influence the public's views or the actions of policymakers, then we must go beyond agendas and consider the content of persons' opinions and of news stories. (Swanson, 1988, pp. 612-613)

In this context an interaction of media issues and media contents can be assumed (and, parallel to this for audience members, an interaction of cognition and attitudes in complex belief systems or cognitive schemata, respectively). The thesis derived from this states that agenda-setting depends largely upon the selection and construction of the contents of an issue by the media and upon the perception and evaluation of these contents of an issue by the audience. This approach makes it possible to get over the linear hierarchical model of media effects, substituting for it an interactional perspective (Huegel, Degenhardt, & Weiss, 1989; Swanson, 1988; Weaver, 1980).

In its thus far developed and tested form, argumentation analysis is an adequate method for reconstructing the issue-content interaction in media coverage of a public controversy. Two aspects of the stereotyping of the public debate by the media especially can be explored and measured: The first is the focusing of public discussion on a few arguments (independent of how broad the extramedia range of actual arguments concerning an issue is), and the second is the polarizing of the controversy surrounding an issue.

Argumentation analysis is well suited to reconstructing and indexing the "latent conflict management" done by media issue coverage. This is, however, not yet a direct contribution to the explanation of the effects of the contents dimension of such media transmitting processes. Necessary for this would be the analogous use of argumentation analysis in audience analyses. Only on this basis could one test Swanson's (1988) assumption that the transmittal of the conflict dynamics of an issue (i.e., its content) is decisive for the way a political controversy shapes the minds of the public.

NOTE

1. Apart from the method of argumentation analysis, two other advanced approaches to the analysis of media contents with which complex argumentations may be reconstructed have been developed in Germany. These are the module approach (Mathes, 1988) and the semantic structure and content analysis (Frueh, 1989).

REFERENCES

Becker, L. B. (1982). The mass media and citizen assessment of issue importance: A reflection on agenda-setting research. In D. C. Whitney, E. Wartella, & S. Windahl (Eds.), *Mass communication review yearbook* (Vol. 3, pp. 521-536). Beverly Hills, CA: Sage.

Becker, L. B., McCombs, M. E., & McLeod, J. M. (1975). The development of political cognitions. In S. H. Chaffee (Ed.), *Political communication: Issues and strategies for research* (pp. 21-63). Beverly Hills, CA: Sage.

Benton, M., & Frazier, P. J. (1976). The agenda-setting function of the mass media at three levels of "information holding." *Communication Research, 3*, 261-274.

Campbell, A., Gurin, G., & Miller, W. E. (1954). *The voter decides*. Evanston, IL: Row & Peterson.

Cobb, R. W., & Elder, C. D. (1971). The politics of agenda-building: An alternative perspective for modern democratic theory. *Journal of Politics, 33*, 892-915.

Cohen, B. C. (1963). *The press and foreign policy*. Princeton, NJ: Princeton University Press.

Converse, P. E. (1964). The nature of belief systems in mass publics. In D. E. Apter (Ed.), *Ideology and discontent* (pp. 206-261). Glencoe, IL: Free Press.

Eyestone, R. (1974). *From social issues to public policy*. New York: John Wiley.

Fishbein, M., & Ajzen, I. (1975). *Belief, attitude, intention and behavior.* Reading, MA: Addison-Wesley.

Fiske, S. T. (1986). Schema-based versus piecemeal politics: A patchwork quilt, but not a blanket, of evidence. In R. R. Lau & D. O. Sears (Eds.), *Political cognitions* (pp. 41-53). Hillsdale, NJ: Lawrence Erlbaum.

Fiske, S. T., & Taylor, S. E. (1984). *Social cognition.* Reading, MA: Addison-Wesley.

Frueh, W. (1989). Semantische Struktur- und Inhaltsanalyse (SSI). Eine Methode zur Analyze von Textinhalten und Textstrukturen und ihre Anwendung in der Rezeptions-analyse. In M. Kaase & W. Schulz (Eds.), *Massenkommunikation. Theorien, Methoden, Befunde* (pp. 490-507). Opladen.

Galtung, J., & Ruge, M. H. (1965). The structure of foreign news. *Journal of Peace Research, 2,* 64-91.

Graber, D. A. (1984). *Processing the news: How people tame the information tide.* New York: Longman.

Huegel, R., Degenhardt, W., & Weiss, H. J. (1989). Structural equation models for the analysis of the agenda setting process. *European Journal of Communication, 4,* 191-210.

Hyman, H. H., & Sheatsley, P. B. (1947). Some reasons why information campaigns fail. *Public Opinion Quarterly, 11,* 412-423.

Iyengar, S. (1988). New directions of agenda-setting research. In J. Anderson (Ed.), *Communication yearbook 11* (pp. 595-602). Newbury Park, CA: Sage.

Iyengar, S., & Kinder, D. R. (1987). *News that matters: Agenda-setting and priming in a television age.* Chicago: University of Chicago Press.

Klapper, J. T. (1960). *The effects of mass communication.* New York: Free Press.

Lang, G. E., & Lang, K. (1981). Watergate: An exploration of the agenda-building process. In G. C. Wilhoit & H. DeBock (Eds.), *Mass communication review yearbook* (Vol. 2, pp. 447-468). Beverly Hills, CA: Sage.

Lippmann, W. (1922). *Public opinion.* New York: Harcourt Brace.

Mathes, R. (1988). Quantitative Analyse qualitativ erhobener Daten? Die hermeneutisch-klassifikatorische Inhaltsanalyse von Leitfadengesprächen. *ZUMA Nachrichten, Heft, 23,* 60-78.

McCombs, M. E., & Shaw, D. L. (1972). The agenda-setting function of mass media. *Public Opinion Quarterly, 36,* 176-184.

McCombs, M. E., & Shaw, D. L. (1977). The agenda-setting function of the press. In D. L. Shaw & M. E. McCombs (Eds.), *The emergence of American political issues: The agenda-setting function of the press* (pp. 1-18). Saint Paul, MN: West.

McLeod, J. M., Becker, L. B., & Byrnes, J. E. (1974). Another look at the agenda-setting function of the press. *Communication Research, 1,* 131-166.

Noelle-Neumann, E., & Mathes, R. (1987). The 'event as event' and the 'event as news': The significance of 'consonance' for media effects research. *European Journal of Communication, 2,* 391-414.

Patterson, T. E. (1980). *The mass media election: How Americans choose their president.* New York: Praeger.

Rogers, E. M., & Dearing, J. W. (1988). Agenda-setting research: Where has it been, where is it going? In J. Anderson (Ed.), *Communication yearbook 11* (pp. 555-594). Newbury Park, CA: Sage.

Rosengren, K. E. (1970). International news: Intra and extra media data. *Acta Sociologica, 13,* 96-109.

Schulz, W. (1976). *Die Konstruktion von Realität in den Nachrichtenmedien.* Freiburg, Germany: Alber.

Schulz, W. (1982). Ausblick am Ende des Holzweges. Eine Übersicht über die neuen Ansätze der Medienwirkungsforschung. *Publizistik, 27,* 49-73.

Schulz, W. (1984). Agenda-setting und andere Erklärungen. Zur Theorie der Medienwirkung. *Rundfunk und Fernsehen, 32,* 206-213.

Shaw, D. L. (1977). The press agenda in a community setting. In D. L. Shaw & M. E. McCombs (Eds.), *The emergence of American public issues: The agenda-setting function of the press* (pp. 19-31). Saint Paul, MN: West.

Swanson, D. L. (1988). Feeling the elephant: Some observations on agenda-setting research. In J. Anderson (Ed.), *Communication yearbook 11* (pp. 603-619). Newbury Park, CA: Sage.

Tuchman, G. (1978). *Making news: A study in the construction of reality.* New York: Macmillan.

Ükermann, H. R., & Weiss, H.-J. (1983). Agenda setting: Zurück zu einem medienzentrierten Medienkonzept? In U. Saxer (Ed.), *Politik und Kommunikation* (pp. 69-79). Munich.

Weaver, D. H. (1980). Audience need for orientation and media effects. *Communication Research, 7,* 361-376.

Weaver, D. H. (1982). Media agenda-setting and media manipulation. In D. C. Whitney, E. Wartella, & S. Windahl (Eds.), *Mass communication review yearbook* (Vol. 3, pp. 537-554). Beverly Hills, CA: Sage.

Weaver, D. H., Graber, D. A., McCombs, M. E., Maxwell, E., & Eyal, C. H. (1981). *Media agenda-setting in a presidential election: Issues, images, and interest.* New York: Praeger.

Weaver, D. H., & Wilhoit, G. C. (1986). *The American journalist: A portrait of U.S. news people and their work.* Bloomington: Indiana University Press.

Weiss, H.-J. (1985). Die Tendenz der Berichterstattung und Kommentierung der Tagespresse zur Neuordnung des Rundfunkwesens in der Bundesrepublik Deutschland (Oktober 1984 bis Januar 1985). Ergebnisse einer quantitativen Inhaltsanalyse. *Media Perspektiven,* pp. 854-866.

Weiss, H.-J. (1986). Rundfunkinteressen und Pressejournalismus. Abschliessende Analysen und Anmerkungen zu zwei inhaltsanalytischen Zeitungsstudien. *Media Perspektiven,* pp. 53-73.

Weiss, H.-J. (1988). Meinungsgestaltung im Interesse der Zeitungen? Eine Analyse der Zeitungpublizistik zur Erhöhung der Rundfunkgebühr (Oktober 1987 bis Januar 1988). *Media Perspektiven,* pp. 469-489.

Public Issues,
Agenda-Setting, and Argument:
A Theoretical Perspective

RENÉE A. MEYERS
University of Wisconsin—Milwaukee

A T a time when scholars in political science, journalism, mass communication, and communication studies are all bemoaning a lack of theoretic and methodological progress in the agenda-setting research domain (Eyal, 1981; Iyengar, 1988; Iyengar & Kinder, 1987; Rogers, 1986; Rogers & Dearing, 1988; Swanson, 1988), Weiss's chapter offers a breath of fresh air. Drawing upon Swanson's (1988) recent conclusion that "if we wish to understand fully how the media influence the public's views or the actions of policymakers, then we must go beyond agendas and consider the *content* of persons' opinions and of news stories" (p. 613; emphasis added), Weiss has proposed an elaborate and detailed model for investigating the *content* of news stories in national and local newspapers. Weiss labels his approach *argumentation analysis*, and focuses upon the arguments (pro and con) that journalists utilize in constructing news stories for consumers. Utilizing this argumentation approach, Weiss's research has produced some interesting, if not disturbing, conclusions. In brief, his results reveal (a) that journalists focus the public discussion on a relatively limited number of arguments, and (b) that writers are decidedly polarized in the types of arguments they present.

Central to Weiss's argumentation analysis is a firm belief that "the agenda-setting concept, if limited to *controversial issues*, would gain significance" (p. 378; emphasis added). Unlike many past agenda-setting researchers who have skirted the question of what constitutes an issue, or whether issues are inherently controversial, Weiss attacks the problem head-on. He contends that issues are best viewed as controversial, that the

Correspondence and requests for reprints: Renée A. Meyers, Department of Communication, P.O. Box 413, Merrill Hall, University of Wisconsin, Milwaukee, WI 53201.

Communication Yearbook 15, pp. 397-409

public career of an issue is governed by the conflict it engenders. This notion of issues as controversial undergirds the construction of his argumentation model, and guides his analysis of newspaper argument.

Beyond Weiss's ability to offer a clear definition of issues, his essay is commendable on at least three additional counts: (a) He provides a complex and detailed method for analyzing the construction of issues in news media, (b) he teaches us much about *how* those issues are argumentatively designed and executed, and (c) he offers results that are both significant and provocative. These factors alone make his essay valuable reading for scholars in several research domains, including mass communication, political science communication, argumentation, agenda-setting, and public policy. In addition, because Weiss has creatively integrated an area of study—argumentation—into his work that is not "agenda research" per se, his results have the potential to stimulate new ways of thinking and theorizing about agenda-setting research. Recently, Swanson (1988) has encouraged the practice of attending to theories and research findings from outside the immediate agenda-setting research domain. He states that "attempting to find answers to the questions raised by agenda studies in programs of research based on local theories, including *research that is not "agenda research" per se*, may offer ways around some difficulties that seem to be inherent in agenda research" (p. 617; emphasis added).

One difficulty inherent in much previous agenda-setting research, and evident in Weiss's work as well, is a lack of comprehensive theoretical frameworks for guiding the research and for synthesizing existing findings. Past reviews and commentaries on agenda-setting research have both acknowledged and lamented this state of the art (Iyengar & Kinder, 1987; Rogers & Dearing, 1988; Swanson, 1988). These reviews, and Swanson's conclusion that scholars should begin attending to research outside the agenda-setting research domain, serve as points of departure for this commentary.

My purpose in the next few pages is to propose a theoretical framework, from outside the agenda-setting research arena, that seems particularly suited to understanding the relationships Weiss proposes in his essay among issues, media coverage, and argument. I am not suggesting that this theory (or metatheory, as it is more correctly labeled) is the only framework that can accomplish this objective, or even that it is the best framework. Instead, as one who comes to this review from outside the agenda-setting research domain, I offer it as food for thought. Those most familiar with the agenda-setting line of research are best qualified to judge its potential utility and value.

Three tasks are undertaken here. First, Giddens's (1984) theory of structuration is introduced as one possible framework for understanding the agenda-setting model Weiss proposes, linking issues, media coverage, and argument. Second, the structurational perspective is utilized (a) to conceptualize issues as inherently controversial (as Weiss defines them), (b) to account for the link between issues and media coverage, and (c) to explain the role of argument in producing focused and polarized media accounts (as Weiss's findings reveal). Finally, by way of conclusion, the advantages and implications of this theoretical perspective for framing Weiss's argumentation analysis are summarized and discussed.

OVERVIEW OF THE STRUCTURATIONAL PERSPECTIVE

The structurational position has been explicated in several books by Anthony Giddens (1971, 1972, 1974a, 1974b, 1976, 1977, 1979, 1984) and was recently introduced to the domain of communication studies by Poole, Seibold, and McPhee (1985, 1986). At the core of all structurationally grounded research must be a focus upon social actors' day-to-day activities as a basis for understanding the reproduction of institutionalized practices. As Giddens (1984) states, "The basic domain of study of the social sciences, according to the theory of structuration, is neither the experience of the individual actor, nor the existence of any form of societal totality, but social practices ordered across space and time" (p. 2). These routinized activities provide a rich context for wedding macro- and micro-level analyses into a single coherent framework.

Central to the study of social action as structurated practice are the concepts of *structure, system,* and *duality of structure.* From a structurational perspective, structure is conceived as recursively organized sets of rules and resources, and social systems are reproduced relations between actors in which structure is implicated. The duality of structure is in its production and reproduction as accomplished by active subjects in social interaction. Giddens (1984) states that "one of the main propositions of structuration theory is that the rules and resources drawn upon in the production and reproduction of social action are at the same time the means of system reproduction (the duality of structure)" (p. 19). In this sense, structure is both medium and outcome of the practices it recursively organizes (p. 25).

The structurational perspective is especially appealing to communication researchers because Giddens accords interaction a central role in the production and reproduction of social practices. Giddens (1984) contends that "the study of . . . the contextualities of interaction is inherent in the investigation of social reproduction" (p. 282). In short, understanding the reproduction of institutionalized practices demands investigation of communicative behavior.

Although this overview of the structurational perspective is necessarily brief, it lays the groundwork for the analysis I provide next, in which I apply this framework to Weiss's model of issues, media coverage, and argument. For purposes of this analysis, I will focus most heavily upon two facets of Giddens's structuration theory: (a) the notion of *structural contradictions* as a framework for conceptualizing issues, and (b) the notion of *duality of structure* as a format for explaining the relationships among issues, media coverage, and argument.

In the next section, I focus on the first of these two tasks—conceptualizing issues within the structurational perspective. As a foundational step, I briefly overview past attempts to define issues as an object of study both within and outside the agenda research domain. Second, I introduce Giddens's notion of structural contradictions as one way of viewing and identifying media issues, and argue that contradictions can be conceived as the interplay between opposing fundamental value structures. Moreover, I propose that it is exactly when these value differences are exposed as *public* conflict that issues are born. As detailed in the next sections, these issues are subsequently both revealed and constructed by the press via argumentative discourse. This process serves not only to produce issues for the public audience, but to reproduce them as well.

ISSUES AS STRUCTURAL CONTRADICTIONS

What Is an Issue?

Because the examination of issues is central to agenda-setting research, many past investigations in this domain have struggled with the question of what constitutes an issue. To date, little accord exists among scholars regarding an appropriate answer to this inquiry. As Rogers and Dearing (1988) note, "A rather wide range of issues have been studied in past agenda-setting research, and little care has been given to defining exactly what an issue is" (p. 566). Some scholars have attempted to distinguish between *issues* and *events*, but conceptual confusion still reigns in discussions of the distinctions between these two objects of study (McCombs, 1976; Shaw, 1977). Lang and Lang (1981) indicate that the consequence of this ambiguity is that, without a clear definition, the study of agenda-setting becomes so overly inclusive as to render it almost meaningless.

Yet ambiguity about what constitutes an issue is not unique to the agenda-setting research domain. Scholars in the issues management area (which includes researchers from organizational communication, management, public relations, and marketing, among other related disciplines) have encountered the same confusion in seeking to define and study issues. Among other definitions, researchers in this domain have variously conceptualized issues as follows:

- developments or trends that emerge from an organization's internal or external environment (Ansoff, 1980; Dutton & Ottensmeyer, 1987; King, 1982)
- conditions or pressures, either internal or external to an organization (Brown, 1979; Zentner, 1984)
- changes in the external environment (Arrington & Sawaya, 1984)

- social, regulatory, or legislative debates (Zentner, 1984)
- significant situations or perceived problems (Crable & Vibbert, 1985)

Issues management researchers Wartick and Rude (1986) indicate the ambiguity created by this state of the art:

> The most fundamental question in Issues Management is "What is an issue?" The answers to this question range from the "pornographic" approach ("We know it when we see it") to the passive approach ("An issue is what others tell us an issue is"). However, neither of these two extremes leads to effective Issues Management. (p. 139)

Some political scientists have argued that issues should be viewed as inherently controversial. For example, Cobb and Elder (1971) define an issue as "a conflict between two or more identifiable groups over procedural or substantive matters relating to the distribution of positions or resources" (p. 82). Similarly, Eyestone (1974) has suggested that "an issue arises when a public with a problem seeks order and governmental action, and there is public disagreement over the best solution to the problem" (p. 3). In his essay, Weiss strongly supports this view of issues, stating "it is the main thesis of this paper that the agenda-setting concept, if limited to controversial issues, would gain significance" and argues that "there are good reasons for the position that the public career of an issue is to a high degree regulated by the conflicts that it arouses" (p. 378).

Certainly, identifying issues as controversial, as Weiss does, is an important first step toward narrowing the field of possible definitions. Yet it does not fully answer the question of what issues are. Because this definition merely identifies a central characteristic of issues, it lacks an explanatory framework for explicating *why* issues are controversial, for determining *how* issues arise, and for identifying *what* are (and what are not) issues.

In the next section, I propose a structurational conception of issues grounded in Giddens's notion of structural contradictions. In this view, issues are conceived as inherently controversial, the public manifestation of clashes between opposing underlying value structures (or structural contradictions) in the system. These contradictions are an inherent part of the system, becoming significant *issues* when brought to public attention. Drawing heavily from past theoretical work in which organizational issues were similarly conceived (Meyers & Garrett, in press), the next section develops the relationships among structural contradictions, values, and issues in more detail.

Structural Contradictions, Values, and Issues

Giddens's notion of structural contradictions offers one avenue for conceptualizing issues. Giddens (1984) defines contradictions as "structural principles that operate in terms of one another but yet also contravene each other" (p. 193). Structural principles are "institutionalized sets of interconnections which govern system reproduction" (Giddens, 1979, p. 141). In simplest terms, contradictions represent "fault lines," fundamental characteristics of the structure that oppose or work against each other. For example, Giddens (1984) views the capitalist state as a primary contradiction, and contends that "the capitalist state, as a 'socializing' centre representing the power of the community at large, is dependent upon mechanisms of production and reproduction which it helps to bring into being but which are set off from and antagonistic to it" (p. 107).

Recently, Poole et al. (1985) have interpreted Giddens's concept of structural contradiction for communication research. They indicate that a contradiction represents a dysfunction, a pair of opposing forces that is a central property of the system, not an incidental or temporary problem that is readily solved. "Contradictions exist when fundamental characteristics of the structuring processes that reproduce a system oppose or work against each other" (p. 93). Moreover, they state that contradictions can be seen as the "generative principle of much of the system's activity, activities devoted to working through and responding to the contradiction as well as to the reproduction of the system" (p. 93).

In another paper, I have posited that contradictions can be viewed as sites of opposing and incompatible value structures (Meyers & Garrett, in press). Although the notion of value is itself vague, I have defined values as basic and treasured principles or tenets that are central to an individual, group, or larger collectivity. Values represent right and wrong, good and evil, morality and immorality. They are important motivating forces behind a person's or collectivity's actions, and are utilized to explain behavior and decisions (Wiener, 1988). Values are primarily revealed in the ongoing discourse of those individuals or collectivities (Cheney & Vibbert, 1987, p. 175).

Structural contradictions represent the clash between central and opposing values in a system. Giddens (1984) and Poole et al. (1985) contend that any complex system may have multiple contradictions implicit in its practices. In considering the capitalistic, democratic society within which the press resides (and perhaps sets agendas), a number of key contradictions seem readily apparent. One example of such a contradiction is the inherent and persistent tension that exists in our society between individual freedom and the welfare of society as a whole. While members of a democratic society want to maintain as much individual freedom as possible, some form of control and order is needed to guarantee the good of the society as a whole. For instance, while smokers typically want to be free to smoke cigarettes at their pleasure, laws have recently been enacted that limit those freedoms to private residences where other members of society will not be subjected to the potentially hazardous effects of passive smoke. The underlying foundation of the smoking controversy is a basic clash between individual rights and societal welfare. In recent times, the clash of these same values has undergirded such issues as flag burning, abortion, seat belt use, gun control, pollution control, and equal opportunity employment, among other issues. The basic question of when individual rights are foremost and when the good of society should take precedence is an inherent and stable contradiction embedded in the value structure of our society.

A second example of a key contradiction in our society arises from the clash between the values of profitability and corporate social responsiveness. Clearly, a business must be profitable if it is to survive in a capitalistic system. Yet many critics of this system argue that short-term corporate profits are being maximized at the expense of society's general welfare. Boycotts, for instance, are primary instigators of criticism against allegedly unethical business practices, and therefore play a particularly important role in exposing the clash of these two values to the public (Garrett, 1987; Garrett, Bradford, & Meyers, 1989; Garrett, Bradford, Meyers, & Becker, 1989). Perhaps one of the most widely publicized of these boycotts was the action taken by Infact against Nestle Corporation in the 1970s and 1980s, when Infact accused Nestle of selling powdered milk to Third World countries as a profitable and unethical practice (Jackson & Jackson, 1982; Miller, 1983; Murphy & Cancellier, 1982). Nestle countered by arguing that the company's actions represented efforts to ensure that babies in Third World countries received proper nutrition. The basis of this conflict, and many other conflicts in recent times, including controversies over chemical dumping, nuclear energy, pesticide spraying, food additives, and depletion of forests, is the clash between the underlying values of profitability and corporate social responsibility.

Although there are certainly other value conflicts that figure prominently in the formation of issues in our society, these two sets of opposing values seem to represent fundamental contradictions in the structuring process. As Giddens (1984) states, such contradictions "tend to involve divisions of interest between groupings or categories of people (including classes but not limited to them)" (p. 198). It follows then that contradictions are often the focal point of controversy. Yet Giddens (1984) indicates that not all structural contradictions breed controversy; only if actors are aware of their opposing interests and are willing to act on them does controversy erupt. Hence some structural contradictions remain a dormant part of a system. Other contradictions however, are brought to the surface, and are exposed for public scrutiny and judgment. It is at this point, at the point of public exhibition, that a contradiction becomes an issue. At the juncture when opposing values are publicly exposed, an issue is born.

While many vehicles exist in our society for bringing underlying opposing value structures to a public level of awareness, I submit here that the media—radio, television, newspapers—constitute one of the most prominent of these vehicles. These organizations are instrumental in identifying and constructing issues for public consumption. The forms through which this is accomplished are the news story, the editorial, and the commentary, all of which are produced via argumentative discourse. In the next sections, I more fully explicate the link between issues and media argument, and, focusing on Giddens's notion of duality of structure, indicate how this discourse serves not only to produce the issue, but to reproduce it as well.

Issues, Argument, and Duality of Structure

Giddens (1984) states that "one of the main propositions of structuration theory is that the rules and resources drawn upon in the production and reproduction of social action are at the same time the means of system reproduction (the duality of structure)" (p. 19). In applying Giddens's notion of duality of structure to agenda-setting research, and Weiss's analysis in particular, the importance of investigating argument use by the press is both clarified and validated. Arguments can be viewed as part of the set of rules and resources that enable the production and reproduction of issue coverage. In Giddens's terms, arguments serve as *structures* (the unobserved rules and resources) drawn upon by journalists to produce the *system* (the regularized, observable content) of newspaper discourse. These argumentative structures include socially derived arguments, culturally approved rules for utilizing those arguments, and appropriately sanctioned sets of arguments that can be used in creating a news story, among other possible resources (Meyers & Seibold, 1990). Journalists, for example, may draw upon rules that suggest that rational, logical arguments are more appropriate for newspaper prose than are emotional, value-laden arguments. Conversely, journalists may have learned through experience that only certain types of arguments (those that favor a liberal stance, for instance) are appropriate for stories in a given newspaper.

Since these structures are unobservable, one format for uncovering them is a detailed analysis of the observable system of discourse in which they are embedded. This seems to be the very task that Weiss has undertaken in his argumentation analysis. By framing his results within the structurational perspective, however, I hope to both enrich and clarify the explanation of his findings. From a structurational view, Weiss offers us an initial glimpse into some of the rules and resources that journalists use when constructing news stories about various controversial issues. He reports two rather disturbing findings. First, in his studies the press, across all newspapers, utilized a limited number of different arguments. As Weiss states, "About one-fourth of the analyzed articles concentrated on two or three different arguments. Half of all the news reporting and commenting concerning these two problems included only eight different arguments" (p. 390).

Second, Weiss found that the news reporting was decidedly polarized and biased, and that "the entire daily press commentated in disturbing consonance" (p. 392). For the most part, journalists presented only those arguments that were consonant with the value structures espoused by their newspapers. Journalists working for liberal national newspapers favored arguments that supported public broadcasting and evaluated those arguments more positively. Journalists writing in more conservative papers presented arguments that favored the opposite stance.

In short, the press's production of the issue in the respective newspapers revealed stereotypical, rather than objective, portrayals of the controversy. From a structurational view, identifying the underlying rules and resources that journalists used to construct such discourse and verifying their existence would provide important theoretical insights into the agenda-setting process and the link between institutionalized practices and journalists' day-to-day activities.

What is perhaps even more interesting about Weiss's analysis from a structurational perspective, however, is the apparent role the press also plays in *reproducing* the issues. In essence, the press's rhetoric defends and reinforces the current value structure, rather than advocating change or compromise. As Weiss's results so clearly reveal, journalists draw upon only a limited number of arguments, and select only those arguments that are consonant with the philosophy of the organization in which they are employed. These arguments are thereby validated and reproduced, serving to sustain the issue and the underlying conflict. In short, the process is a cyclical one. The press brings issues to public attention and, in the very act of performing this activity, serves to validate and sustain the issue. Journalists not only feed public opinion, they also shape the focus of public debate. The arguments act as both medium and outcome of the communicative process.

CONCLUSION

Although this overview of the structurational perspective and its application to Weiss's argumentation analysis is decidedly brief, it illustrates that such an approach promises several advantages. In this final section I briefly summarize three of the most important of these advantages, and discuss their implications.

Structurational theory offers a comprehensive view of the agenda-setting process. As indicated earlier in this review, many scholars in the agenda-setting research domain have recently called for the development of theoretical perspectives for guiding agenda research and synthesizing existing results. Additionally, Swanson (1988) has encouraged scholars to attend to theories outside the immediate research arena in an effort to answer difficulties that are inherent in agenda research. These calls for theory building and for fresh insights can both be addressed within the structurational perspective. This perspective offers a framework capable of accounting for the complexities of the agenda-setting process. It incorporates both macro- and

micro-level analyses within a single theory, so that the study of institutionalized practices is intimately bound up with the investigation of individuals'
activities. This perspective encourages scholars to study agenda-setting at
several different levels, and allows for multiple layers of meaning within a
single coherent framework. Hence this theory may be particularly suited to
integrating past research efforts in this domain that address agenda-setting
at different levels—media agendas, policy agendas, and public agendas
(Rogers & Dearing, 1988).

Second, because structurational theory is not endemic to the agenda research domain per se, it offers a fresh perspective for viewing past research
efforts and contemplating future endeavors. It has the potential to serve as
a stimulus for renewed theoretical development in the agenda-setting research area or to provide the foundation for programmatic investigation of
the links among institutionalized practices, individual activities, and public
awareness of issues. In sum, the structurational perspective offers a framework commensurate with the complexity of the agenda-setting process and
allows for the integration of multiple levels of meaning.

*Structurational theory addresses the role of issues in agenda-setting re-
search.* Central to the study of agenda-setting is the investigation of issues—
what they are, how they emerge, and the links among issues, media coverage,
and public awareness. To date, few researchers have satisfactorily answered
the question, What is an issue? Yet, addressing that problem seems a necessary first step toward establishing a research domain in which diverse findings
can be synthesized and results generalized across investigations. The
structurational theory provides a framework for conceptualizing issues that
serves simultaneously to narrow and enrich previous definitions of issues. In
this view, issues can be conceived as manifestations of structural contradictions in the system. At the simplest level, they are composed of at least three
facets: (a) incompatible value structures, (b) opposing factions or groups, and
(c) public controversy or conflict concerning those values.

A theoretically grounded conception of issues such as this provides a
more stable framework for generating research questions and guiding investigative efforts. For example, in Weiss's analysis, such a conceptualization might be helpful in determining arguments of the prestudy. Weiss
readily admits that generating a complete set of arguments from extramedia
and media sources is difficult. Moreover, since the validity of the argumentation analysis is dependent on the argument list from the prestudy, Weiss
concludes that his analysis "therefore does not measure *the* public discussion on a particular issue as such, but whether and how a selected number of
arguments about an issue are conveyed by the media" (p. 389). While this latter information is clearly important in determining how the media transmit issues to the public, it begs the question of whether the media are truly restricted
in their argument use. Given Weiss's findings, we cannot be sure whether

(a) only a few arguments really exist regarding this issue, or (b) the press chose to present only a limited number of all possible arguments.

If, however, a theoretical basis for deriving these prestudy arguments were available, such as the definition of issues that the structurational perspective offers, then perhaps prestudy arguments could be generated deductively and on a theoretical basis, rather than inductively from various media accounts. Or perhaps it might be more fruitful to begin with a study of the values espoused in the newspaper's stories and commentaries, and then consider how those values are variously presented in different argument forms. At any rate, a theoretical conception of issues seems to be an important first step in conducting agenda-setting research and synthesizing its findings.

Structurational theory accords communication a central role. Because the study of agenda-setting investigates communicative links among institutions, media, and the public, the structurational perspective, with its focus on interaction as a central feature, seems ideally suited to frame this research. The system-structure identification allows for the investigation of multiple layers of communicative behavior. Moreover, the structurational perspective provides a conception of communication that is inherently complex and rich—a view commensurate with the communicative processes inherent in agenda-setting research.

Certainly much work remains to be done before a complete structurational account of the agenda-setting process is accomplished. What I have outlined here is merely a thumbnail sketch of a very complex and integrated task. Yet, whether the future proves this perspective fruitful for research in this domain or not, it is clear that investigators of agenda-setting processes will continue to seek theories and answers to some very difficult and important questions. Researchers such as Weiss make that quest all the more commendable and promising.

REFERENCES

Ansoff, I. (1980). Strategic issue management. *Strategic Management Journal, 1*, 131-148.

Arrington, C. B., Jr., & Sawaya, R. N. (1984). Managing public affairs: Issues management in an uncertain environment. *California Management Review, 26*, 148-160.

Brown, J. K. (1979). *This business of issues: Coping with the company's environments.* New York: Conference Board.

Cheney, C., & Vibbert, S. L. (1987). Corporate discourse: Public relations and issue management. In F. M. Jablin, L. L. Putnam, K. H. Roberts, & L. W. Porter (Eds.), *Handbook of organizational communication* (pp. 165-194). Newbury Park, CA: Sage.

Cobb, W. E., & Elder, C. D. (1971). The politics of agenda-building: An alternative perspective for modern democratic theory. *Journal of Politics, 33*, 892-915.

Crable, R. E., & Vibbert, S. L. (1985). Managing issues and influencing public policy. *Public Relations Review, 11*, 3-16.

Dutton, J. E., & Ottensmeyer, E. (1987). Strategic issue management systems: Forms, functions, and contexts. *Academy of Management Review, 12*, 255-265.

Eyal, C. H. (1981). The roles of newspapers and television in agenda-setting. In G. C. Wilhoit & H. DeBock (Eds.), *Mass communication review yearbook* (Vol. 2, pp. 225-234). Beverly Hills, CA: Sage.

Eyestone, R. (1974). *From social issues to public policy.* New York: John Wiley.

Garrett, D. E. (1987). The effectiveness of marketing policy boycotts: Environmental opposition to marketing. *Journal of Marketing, 51*, 46-57.

Garrett, D. E., Bradford, J. L., & Meyers, R. A. (1989). A strategic model for issues management communication: How to respond to accusations of unethical behavior. *Journal of Business Strategies, 6*, 150-162.

Garrett, D. E., Bradford, J. L., Meyers, R. A., & Becker, J. (1989). Issues management and organizational accounts: An analysis of corporate responses to accusations of unethical business practices. *Journal of Business Ethics, 8*, 507-520.

Giddens, A. (1971). *Capitalism and modern social theory.* New York: Cambridge University Press.

Giddens, A. (1972). *Emile Durkheim.* New York: Cambridge University Press.

Giddens, A. (1974a). *The class structure of the advanced societies.* New York: Harper & Row.

Giddens, A. (Ed.). (1974b). *Positivism and sociology.* London: Heineman.

Giddens, A. (1977). *Studies in social and political theory.* New York: Basic Books.

Giddens, A. (1979). *Central problems in social theory.* Berkeley: University of California Press.

Giddens, A. (1984). *The constitution of society: Outline of the theory of structuration.* Berkeley: University of California Press.

Iyengar, S. (1988). New directions of agenda-setting research. In J. A. Anderson (Ed.), *Communication yearbook 11* (pp. 595-602). Newbury Park, CA: Sage.

Iyengar, S., & Kinder, D. R. (1987). *News that matters: Agenda-setting and priming in a television age.* Chicago: University of Chicago Press.

Jackson, T. M., & Jackson, T. Y. (1982). A response from Nestle. *Social Education, 46*, 531-533.

King, W. R. (1982). Using strategic issue analysis. *Long Range Planning, 15*(4), 45-49.

Lang, G. E., & Lang, K. (1981). Watergate: An exploration of the agenda-building process. In G. C. Wilhoit & J. DeBock (Eds.), *Mass communication review yearbook* (Vol. 2, pp. 447-468). Beverly Hills, CA: Sage.

McCombs, M. E. (1976). Agenda-setting research: A bibliographic essay. *Political Communication Review, 1*, 1-7.

Meyers, R. A., & Garrett, D. E. (in press). Contradictions, values, and organizational argument. In C. Conrad (Ed.), *The ethical nexus: Values, communication and organizational decisions.* Norwood, NJ: Ablex.

Meyers, R. A., & Seibold, D. R. (1990). Perspectives on group argument: A critical review of persuasive arguments theory and an alternative structurational view. In J. Anderson (Ed.), *Communication yearbook 13* (pp. 268-302). Newbury Park, CA: Sage.

Miller, R. D., Jr. (1983). Out of the mouths of babes. *Barron's, 63*, 11, 28.

Murphy, E. M., & Cancellier, P. M. (1982). The infant formula controversy: Is the boycott justified? *Social Education, 46*, 527-530.

Poole, M. S., Seibold, D. R., & McPhee, R. D. (1985). Group decision-making as a structurational process. *Quarterly Journal of Speech, 71*, 74-102.

Poole, M. S., Seibold, D. R., & McPhee, R. D. (1986). A structurational approach to theory-building in group decision-making research. In R. Y. Hirokawa & M. S. Poole (Eds.), *Communication and group decision-making* (pp. 237-264). Beverly Hills, CA: Sage.

Rogers, E. M. (1986). *Communication technology.* New York: Free Press.

Rogers, E. M., & Dearing, J. W. (1988). Agenda-setting research: Where has it been, where is it going? In J. Anderson (Ed.), *Communication yearbook 11* (pp. 555-594). Newbury Park, CA: Sage.

Shaw, D. L. (1977). The press agenda in a community setting. In D. L. Shaw & M. E. McCombs (Eds.), *The emergence of American public issues: The agenda-setting function of the press* (pp. 33-51). Saint Paul, MN: West.

Swanson, D. L. (1988). Feeling the elephant: Some observations on agenda-setting research. In J. Anderson (Ed.), *Communication yearbook 11* (pp. 603-619). Newbury Park, CA: Sage.

Wartick, S. L., & Rude, R. E. (1986). Issues management: Corporate fad or corporate function? *California Management Review, 29,* 124-140.

Wiener, Y. (1988). Forms of value systems: A focus on organizational effectiveness and cultural change and maintenance. *Academy of Management Review, 13,* 534-545.

Zentner, R. (1984). Issues and strategic management. In R. B. Lamb (Ed.), *Competitive strategic management* (pp. 634-648). Englewood Cliffs, NJ: Prentice-Hall.

The Mediacentric Agenda
of Agenda-Setting Research:
Eclipse of the Public Sphere

ED McLUSKIE
Boise State University

Freedom of expression is confined by the economic conditions of the media, the limited access to a forum of public discussion, and, perhaps most importantly, the inability to overcome the effects of an educational system that helps create and expand markets. . . . A contemporary theory of mass communication must identify, describe, and analyze the effects of these economic-political determinants of social communication in an effort to develop an alternative perspective. (Hardt, 1979, p. 229)

WEISS offers a model of "argumentation analysis" that considers mass media content as the intersection of constructions by media authors, by sources quoted through media authors, and by sources' quotations of still other sources used by media authors. The artifact produced is an "argument," understood as polarized issues that can be ranked on a scale of conflict. Weiss's intention is to operationalize a concept central for agenda-setting research, the concept of "issue." Once this is achieved, researchers presumably can plot the content of "public issues" while explaining their development via media sources for that content. Because the focus is on media content and not the public, nothing in Weiss's essay speaks to whether or how a bona fide public is poised for the reception of "public issues." Such silence is characteristic of agenda-setting research.

Weiss speaks the language of an empiricist research agenda developed in the United States. His embrace of agenda-setting research to analyze German media content is one consequence of intellectual migration in our field. My rejoinder results from other influences of intellectual migration, reflecting foci and issues developed in German critical theory as well as

Correspondence and requests for reprints: Ed McLuskie, Department of Communication, Boise State University, 1910 University Drive, Boise, ID 83725.

Communication Yearbook 15, pp. 410-424

American pragmatism. My position is that the public is best understood as a societal institution subject to the historical, evolutionary developments of the society in which it and other institutions, including mass media, are situated. Thus, where Weiss puts media content at the center of his analysis, I put the public as a historically produced social institution at the center, particularly the question of the shaping of its infrastructure. Weiss and I therefore probably differ over the reasons and the degree to which mass media play a leading role in the public arena.

Without discounting Weiss's contributions to content analysis, I prefer instead to address key issues he poses with a research decision to analyze only media-generated issues. I also wish to suggest a redirection of the notion of "audience agendas," a notion Weiss explicitly shelves but which presents itself as a still-open question for the wider community of agenda-setting researchers. This redirection entails abandoning the concept of "audience" for a concept of political communication understood in the context of an evolved formation of the public. Differences of approach and idiom emerge from my decision to address these matters. Accordingly, I shall not presume what Weiss presumes, specifically, the idea that a sociopolitical space already is built into society and maintained so that a "public" is available for agenda-setting effects to operate. On the surface of an unexamined public realm Weiss sees a populace adrift for events and issues to consider. While this public may well be adrift, Weiss's version of agenda-setting research cannot and will not demonstrate that condition. Instead, the image of a fundamentally media-bound, helpless public is taken for granted as a settled media effects issue. This image arguably vindicates Weiss's explorations of media content.

Agenda-setting research is a recurring example of mediacentric communication research. Even when envisioning ideas circulating through a public realm, even when construing media-defined issues as automatic definers of public issues, this variety of research manages to screen out the social, political, economic, cultural, and institutional conditions required to produce a stable public sphere. While this achievement no doubt sustains a general vision of the public's powerlessness, it does not address what could produce that condition in the public realm. What agenda-setting researchers see as powerful media effects more likely are symptoms of alterations in institutional configurations that have consigned mass media to their own powerlessness to invigorate the public. On that score I question that a single institutional set, the mass media, removes, supplies, or even maintains the conditions of another, especially the institution of the public sphere. While Weiss does not explicitly extend his work into such matters, these are precisely the kinds of issues opened up by mediacentric research fixed on media content, media sources, or media audiences. Those issues cannot be addressed through Weiss's explorations of media content or through his methodological innovations designed to clarify the nature of an "issue" in content. I therefore move away from the central content-analytic concerns of Weiss's essay to consider the question of the public sphere itself.

"THE PUBLIC SPHERE" AS A STARTING POINT

In a world where meaning, though not information, "is a scarce resource . . . becoming even scarcer" (Habermas, 1975), the concept of "agenda-setting" does appear to make sense. It appeals to the need to provide interpretations for public consumption as well as to supply information. Thus the concept is defined as the power of the mass media "to focus public attention on a defined and limited set of selected issues" where "some topics are widely debated, beyond the media in the public sphere, while others are ignored" (O'Sullivan, Hartley, Saunders, & Fiske, 1983, p. 6). Yet the inspiration for agenda-setting research incorporates a counterfactual ideal of democracy articulated in American pragmatism since the 1920s (see Hardt, 1989, pp. 569-570), then in Frankfurt critical theory since the 1960s. Critical theory captured this ideal when Habermas (1971) invoked the American pragmatist and sociologist, George Herbert Mead:

> Universal discourse is the formal ideal of communication. If communication can be carried through and made perfect, then there would exist the kind of democracy . . . in which each individual would carry just the response in himself that he calls out in the community. That is what makes communication in the significant sense the organizing process in the community. (p. 155; citing Mead, 1934, p. 327)

John Dewey (1916) optimistically foresaw the conditions for such a politics in local communities linked to the wider society through emerging systems of mass communication. In this way, he envisioned the institutionalization of democratic practices founded on "more than a verbal tie" among the concepts "common, community, and communication" (Dewey, 1922, p. 5). But when this theme of the formation of the communication-community (*Kommunikationsgemeinschaft*) is reiterated after 40 years of societal development, optimistic notes recede. Where Dewey pictured the realized hope for a politics animated by and through public discourse, Habermas (1962) emphasized its rise and decline both in theory and in practice. Transformations in modern institutional arrangements began with the unprecedented institutionalization of a sphere between state and society where otherwise private individuals freely conferred over "matters of general interest," fully expecting the state to act only as their executor; participants in this liberal public sphere did not behave, then, merely as "business or professional people transacting private affairs, nor like members of a constitutional order subject to the legal constraints of a state bureaucracy" (Habermas, 1974, p. 49). Instead, they performed the twin tasks of reasoned control and criticism, formally secured with regulations demanding that state proceedings be public (*Publizitätsvorschriften*). These tasks gave material form to the concept "public opinion," signifying that "publicity" had become a principle by which modern society was to be organized. But that was the 1700s.

Today, the "principle of publicity" survives as a remnant of sociocultural practice where only the *form* of public opinion making gives faint echo to critical functions long since undermined through societal evolution (Habermas, 1979). Agenda-setting research investigates only the *remnants* of a public that could fashion its own issues, a capacity now systematically and historically contained (Habermas, 1962, 1974, 1975, 1979, 1984, 1987; Hohendahl, 1974, 1979; McLuskie, 1978, 1981; Skogerbø, 1990). Habermas (1974) writes that today

> the process of making public simply serves the arcane policies of special interests; in the form of "publicity" it wins public prestige for people or affairs . . . in a climate of non-public opinion. The very words "public relations work" (*Öffentlichkeitsarbeit*) betray the fact that a public sphere must first be arduously constructed case by case, a public sphere which earlier grew out of the social structure. (p. 55)

The public as a public, not mere media audience, has not emerged from the social structure at least since Walter Lippmann (1922) wrote the book frequently cited within the agenda-setting research tradition, *Public Opinion.* Whatever agenda-setting researchers are "tracing" in media content or in audience issues, they are missing the real story even as their research capitalizes on that story: The theory of a form of politics animated by and through extensive public discourse is precariously counterfactual, no matter who or what "supplies" the issues.

Because agenda-setting research capitalizes on this sociostructural legacy, its role is ambiguous. It offers no theory of political communication to capture the dynamics of public issue formation in particular and practical discourse in general for otherwise presumed inhabitants of the public sphere. Yet agenda-setting research recognizes the need for such a theory.

In their review of agenda-setting literature, Rogers and Dearing (1988) recognize that need when they conclude that researchers of the "agenda-setting process, *especially those studying public agenda-setting*, need to become more fully aware of each others' research and theory, so that agenda-setting research can become more of an integrated whole" (p. 580; emphasis added). They make the point for theory more generally when they quote (p. 582) without argument Iyengar and Kinder's (1987) point, "Agenda-setting may be an apt metaphor, but it is no theory." Skogerbø (1990) argues that a theory of political communication is pertinent for mass communication research interested in any aspect of the relation between media and politics. Inheriting the Aristotelian objective of consensus, the concept of the public sphere challenges researchers to focus on public issues that in fact issue from a space in society protected not only from the state, but also from the economic market through which media-produced issues breed (Skogerbø, 1990; see also Garnham, 1990; Golding, 1990; Peters, 1989).

In its fully idealized vision, the public sphere reflects and enacts a politics fully empowered to make differences in the conduct of society's business. The concept "public sphere" emphasizes the "image of the citizen instead of the consumer" (Skogerbø, 1990, p. 45), challenging political mass communication theory and research to consider its normative roots. Weiss invokes those roots when he cites Lippmann's *Public Opinion* (1922). Agenda-setting research assumes, as did Lippmann, that a public exists in some ongoing way, however weakened it might be. Weiss in fact aligns his work with Lippmann's analysis of stereotypes. There, the opportunity to express even Lippmann's interest in a vigorous public passes into a quite different decision about where to launch theoretical and empirical energy.

SURRENDERING THE PUBLIC TO THE "MINIMAL VERSUS POWERFUL EFFECTS" DEBATE

Were agenda-setting research something more than empirical inquiry restricted to media content for Weiss, to media audiences for others (e.g., McLeod, Becker, & Byrnes, 1974), that intention would find expression through emphasizing the disparity between the theory and practice of political communication in the public sphere. The door to this disparity at best has been opened into silence, as when Becker (1982) concludes that public issues "can be understood only in the context of the effects of interpersonal discussion and of prior sensitization to the issues" (p. 532; see also Erbring, Goldenberg, & Miller, 1980). In the empirical research community, that matter is taken up on the "minimalist" side of the so-called minimal versus powerful media effects debate, primarily via inheritors of the Lazarsfeld tradition of media effects, proponents of the "uses and gratifications" approach (e.g., Katz, 1987; Swanson, 1988). Weiss categorically disenfranchises his research from minimalist research, and therefore from mass communication researchers who are closer to the site of activities related to political communication in the public realm.

There is academic folklore that seems to justify Weiss's decision. Most striking is Noelle-Neumann's (1983, 1990) strong implication that we would not have the minimal effects tradition had Paul Lazarsfeld not been pressured by the media to skew *The People's Choice* (Lazarsfeld, Berelson, & Gaudet, 1944/1968) toward the minimalist position. This historiographical episode is meant to write off analysis of active media audiences. It deflects the important question of what it takes to empower the public to set its *own* agendas. That question is avoided by the minimal effects tradition, too, as it reduces publics to audiences. Both sides of the debate are equally effective in ignoring the public sphere. From the vantage point of the public sphere, the entire minimalist/powerful effects debate is a sideshow. Both eclipse the public. Proponents of the powerful effects thesis, including Weiss, are simply further removed from the site of public (in)activity.

Weiss (p. 375) continues this sideshow when he endorses Iyengar's (1988) claim that agenda-setting research has obviously "been successful in disproving the law of minimal consequences" in media effects research (p. 595). This endorsement aims to legitimate agenda-setting as a valuable research enterprise. Weiss maintains his primary effort "is to ascertain how public discussion of a particular issue is transmitted in news coverage and how it is discussed in media commentaries" (p. 381). His chief focus is to show the workings of "argumentation analysis" as a method that permits identification of controversial issues as polarized issues in newspaper articles. In fact, the essay reports his recent study of 633 West German daily newspaper articles in which he identifies 2,940 "argumentations" (Weiss, 1988). Thus Weiss's essay stands as mediacentric in spite of a faintly backgrounded concern for what might be happening with the public itself. That concern is left for research at another time or for other researchers to move into the public realm and away from media content.

Why wait? Answers reach beyond agenda-setting research itself to general issues of inquiry, to the legitimation of research traditions, and to still other mediacentric metadebates.

GENERAL ISSUES IN INQUIRY

We can read those answers in the scope of our research foci, the addressees we assume for our theories, analyses, or other readings of human experience, and in the metascientific positions we hold. They proceed from research to action or recommendations beyond the academy. They also operate "behind the backs" of our research as metapositions on knowledge. As systematic linkages between our research and the wider society, they can be considered in the following way: Any research focus implies a range of possible addressees of research assigned status by virtue of our (usually implied) social theories of knowledge.

The topics we choose to investigate announce how far through the range of human experience and the history of its development we shall travel in our efforts to know and understand human communication in modern life. Whether these excursions include citizens' experience in society is an open question before research communities interested in media-related processes. The question implies an interest in historically informed theory, but the development of any theory remains distant. While there are calls in the literature of agenda-setting research for it, no actual plan has emerged to build theory. Occasional calls in the literature (Becker, 1982; Rogers & Dearing, 1988; Swanson, 1988) for connecting varied lines of research are the nearest to theory building one gets. It is fair to question, then, whether and to what extent agenda-setting research intends to develop theory, to say nothing about what kind of theory. Thus the status of any given research focus in a specific research project is, at best, ambivalent, at worst, unknowable. While it is clear that Weiss's work is located in content-analytic territory, the project of agenda-setting research itself stands at issue in spite of claims of settled scores regarding powerful effects (Weiss included; especially Noelle-Neumann, 1983, 1990). We are left not knowing whether research is paradigm generated, a mere occasion for the arbitrary application of concepts, or a simple projection of research tradition. We therefore lose criteria by which to characterize the communicational significance of research for communication and mass communication theory. Will accounts produced by agenda-setting researchers ever connect? Can they? Should they? Whether they do, can, or should, for whom are these narratives supposed to make any difference? Are addressees for research explicit and, if so, are they appropriate? The persistence of these questions is an overarching propensity in agenda-setting research. These questions open the idea of empowerment in society and within the specific institution of the public.

While these questions go to the heart of the malaise in agenda-setting studies, agenda-setting scholars appear disinterested in a program of research constantly evaluated by the interest in empowerment at this level. Such questions, however, are explored not in agenda-setting research, but in alternative perspectives, such as cultural studies of mass media (see Hardt, 1989) and historical-evolutionary studies of media (e.g., Carey & Quirk, 1970; Innis, 1950). Communication as part of the evolution of human societies, including modern "mass" societies, is appearing less and less likely to be of interest to agenda-setting researchers. The path of agenda-setting research discards the interest in "the people." It adopts, instead, an interest in media professionals consistent with the professionalizing of the academy (see the arguments by Jacoby, 1987).

Whether agenda-setting researchers are aware of it or not, the wider research community has before it a long-standing proposal to investigate the crisis in the health of political communication and of communication at all levels of human experience. This essentially Habermasian thesis does not trace the cause to mass media. Instead, it considers mass media as an institutional matrix among many in the social system, reflecting generic societal and cultural patterns that have been historically reproduced throughout society. Institutions other than mass media can reflect sociopolitical conditions suggested under the heading of "media effects." But the analysis of one or even a few institutions would not help us decide which, if any, are "steering" the course of human experience during the evolution of modern society. Our literacies and our opportunities for communication at all levels of society spell out the sociopolitical conditions for human communication—not just for journalists, not just for those connected with the information industries, not just for academics who are trying to make sense of such things, but for all. What have we done with such a proposal in mass communication research?

Our research foci indicate that we reject it, haven't heard about it, give it a rare hearing, or benignly coexist with it. Research then fails to coalesce at the pragmatically crucial point of connecting intellectual work within the academic community in ways that in turn connect with social experience. The problems of the destiny of the public and the role of research in that destiny are lost on the research community. Instead of considering that the scale of the proposal merits attention in itself, we fail to grasp the larger picture.

A research view that makes media and media-related institutions the center of both societal and social development can thrive without defense in the midst of this failure. That is one way to read the story of empiricism. To continue the tradition-made path of U.S. empirical research results in continuing decisions to confine our paradigms and research traditions to media-related matters.

This trend means that researchers' noses get closer to grindstones while theory shrinks in ambition as well as coverage. If concrete cases point beyond themselves, but theoretical ladders are not climbed, inquiry proceeds by caution while theory remains in cold storage. If we need to "ground" theory, we also need to take the concrete to theory—including actual content.

LEGITIMATING RESEARCH PRACTICES

Again, why delay these concerns? Another part of the answer rests with attempts to legitimate a research tradition. That effort is charted in agenda-setting research with the thesis that media are powerful. Media effects research in general and agenda-setting research in particular still refer to the issue of whether media effects are "minimal" or "powerful." Becker (1982) considers agenda-setting research "most appropriately classified" with the latter, given its consistent claim that minimal effects research overlooks "potential media effects of consequence" (p. 523). Noelle-Neumann (1983) flatly declares, "The long reign of the hypothesis of media reinforcers of public opinion is over at last" (p. 157). When Weiss (p. 375) aligns himself with arguments for the powerful effects thesis (Cohen, 1963; Iyengar, 1988; McCombs & Shaw, 1972), he selects a range of research foci on media content that justify taking the spotlight off the public. We can expect, then, that agenda-setting research will continue to be marked by treatments of media as though media were definers of public activity as well as of public thought. That amounts to shooting in the dark with received and unexamined wisdoms cultivated in graduate programs under the influence of both institutional and intellectual histories.

MEDIACENTRIC METADEBATES

Even other empirical researchers ask, Why wait to explore media audiences? They doubt both the endorsement and the worthiness of "agenda-setting" as a research-guiding concept. Perhaps the strongest statement is Swanson's (1988) summary assessment: "More penetrating and comprehensive understandings of the process of mass communication" probably require that we abandon "agendas as a construct for organizing research" (p. 617). Weiss ignores Swanson's point entirely here, preferring instead to take up one of Swanson's more specific suggestions: to "go beyond agendas and consider the content of persons' opinions and of news stories" (p. 613). Weiss then divides Swanson's point to leave behind "persons' opinions" and propose measuring "media information as the starting point for the analysis of mass media effects" (p. 376). Thus Weiss offers his proposal of argumentation analysis for examining media content, to focus on how the mass media portray controversy. Only at the end of his essay does Weiss recommend that his analytical method be applied to audiences, an "analogous use of argumentation analysis in audience analyses" (p. 394). There, too, the focus would be on controversial issues, as it was for media content.

Weiss's main thesis—"that the agenda-setting concept, if limited to controversial issues, would gain significance" (p. 378)—falls directly into a significant criticism by Rogers and Dearing (1988). "One of the strongest pieces of evidence of the media's agenda-setting influence may consist in [issues] completely ignored by the mass media on the public agenda," they write; but since most issues studied in agenda-setting research "are of very high salience," any claims about public processes that are derived from research on "high salience issues" are "certainly dangerous" if extrapolated "to those of much less salience" (p. 576). Thus whatever processes may be occurring at the level of political communication in the public sphere may be unknown to empirical researchers. Yet those processes hold the key to support needed for Weiss's assumptions that media influence those processes. Such evidence inevitably is inaccessible to Weiss due to his focus on issues tending toward high salience—that is, controversial issues.

A more damaging criticism applies to agenda-setting research as a whole, one that Rogers and Dearing (1988, p. 576) identify without apparently realizing what they have said. Suggesting that the most convincing evidence of the agenda-setting effect would show that issues "completely ignored by the mass media do not register on the public agenda," they cite McCombs's (1976) point: "This basic, primitive notion of agenda-setting" is the unproved assertion that, if media say "nothing about a topic," then the topic "simply will not exist on our personal agenda or in our life space" (p. 3). Rogers and Dearing equivocate: "It is extremely difficult or impossible for scholars to investigate such a 'non-agenda-setting' process" due to "the problem of identifying . . . issues that are not reported by the mass media, which by definition cannot be measured by a content analysis of the media." Just when agenda-setting researchers reach the edge of political processes in the public sphere, Rogers and Dearing put on the brakes in the face of a recurring methodological dilemma in agenda-setting research. They inform us that agenda-setting research is powerless to provide the strongest evidence for effects or influence in that very realm of society agenda-setting scholars claim to explain. Rather than face that dilemma as an occasion to consider an entirely different approach to political communication in society, agenda-setting researchers seem to prefer this reasoning: If political communication in society is not reported by the media, only political communication reported by the media exists. That is the conclusion that describes the boundaries of this tradition of scholarship. The trouble with it is more than logical: Agenda-setting research cannot reach beyond its presumptions about the public, whether conceived as media audiences or not. Given especially the persisting lament for linkages between media content and audiences/publics (Becker, 1982; Rogers & Dearing, 1988), this criticism cannot be ignored if "agenda-setting" is to have any connection to actual social and political processes outside media practices.

If the public sphere, however weakened, has any nonmediated activity going for it, then Weiss's focus on content analysis cannot explain political communication within it. Of course, agenda-setting research would have to move beyond its unduly mediacentric analyses to account for the formation of truly public issues. Perhaps that is why Rogers and Dearing (1988, p. 580) call for crossing the boundaries between agenda-setting research and those empirical traditions that have attempted to account for activity in media audiences: the uses and gratifications approach, Noelle-Neumann's (1980) "spiral of silence" research, and diffusion research. Such extensions also are subject to the dilemma just noted: How does one investigate an audience beyond its role as audience? The important distinction between "audience" and "public" is required to break through this mediacentric dilemma. Weiss's brand of mediacentrism is narrower, however. It aims to settle a conceptual problem while ignoring the challenge of that dilemma in agenda-setting research.

Rather than focus on the *formation* of public issues within the public sphere, Weiss intends to remove ambiguities over the concept "issue." Lang and Lang (1981) criticize the concept as "so all-embracing" as to make the idea of agenda-setting "practically meaningless" (p. 450). Weiss's essay is largely a response to the problem. It is not a response to the problem as it is characterized by Becker (1982) in his review of agenda-setting research, which concludes that any attempt to conceptually define . . . "issue" . . . must be sensitive to the implications of that definition for the audience variable as well. The work of Edelstein (1974) suggests that the term "issue" might well mean something quite different to a researcher from what it means to an audience member. How the mass media define issues might be something altogether different again. The assumption must be made, then, that audience members do not treat all issues equally. (p. 525)

While Lang and Lang's criticism locates Weiss's methodological response within agenda-setting research, Becker's calls for both a methodological and a substantive response that includes at least one outcome of political communication in the public realm, audience definitions of "issue." Weiss clearly endorses, then, key concepts that reduce our understanding of prospects for public participation to a mediacentric set of concepts from which we can only presume media effects—through the lens of the powerful versus minimal effects debate—for media audiences. Weiss's position on the powerful versus minimal effects debate and his predisposition to regard, though not actually investigate, audience issues as reflections of media-produced issues point at best to the symptoms of a public led, if it is, by mass media portrayals of issues. Unfortunately, Becker's version of "issue" would reduce "public" to "audience," at best scratching the surface of public processes.

Agenda-setting research and its surrounding empiricist metadebates fail to shed light on the fundamental question of the requirements for a truly public opinion to arise from within the social structure. Weiss's efforts to restrict attention to one narrow aspect of media practices, media content and its sources, reduces the focus even further. It blocks consideration of the public sphere with the presumption that to understand media content is to understand public opinion. The effect of Weiss's proposal is to exacerbate the gap between mass media and political communication.

CONCLUSION: ECLIPSE OF THE PUBLIC SPHERE

Any interest in an intact public is sequestered behind the focus on "public" issues reduced to media content. In the empirical critique of agenda-setting research, that interest is further relinquished through reducing the public sphere to media audiences. Perhaps consideration of what ails the public awaits future research on "the way a political controversy shapes the minds of the public" (Weiss, p. 394). But even this promised attention would leave silent the more essential matter of prerequisites for a robust, healthy public. So considered, the limiting of the agenda-setting concept to controversial issues supplied by media actually reduces the significance of the agenda-setting concept.

As with any decision, where one stands determines significance. If one stands with the public, then the only significant knowledge is what we already knew: that the predicament of the public is not one to be solved by mass media alone. If Weiss's essay has an intent beyond operationalizing the concept of "issue" in a content-analytic display of media-produced issues, it should lead toward understanding the public's relative vitality or frailty. A search of his essay for theoretical or methodological clues along such lines meets the obstacles and dilemmas outlined above.

The trajectory of Weiss's essay employs one mediacentric focus, content, in opposition to another, audience. When faced with proposals to bridge these empiricist camps, or with work that preserves their differing foci, communication scholars are asked to sustain reductions of media institutions to "media content" and the public sphere to "media audiences." For communication inquiry, these reductions encourage a mediacentric eclipse of the most basic story, the public's eroding infrastructure.

When the effects debate settles down, if ever it will, promised linkages between media content and media audiences will likely come up empty for explaining what happened to the public sphere. We have at our disposal a rich conceptual and empirical tradition in both the United States and Germany better equipped than empirical effects research to address directly the animating theory and practice of democracy behind agenda-setting research. Either we look at such proposals or we continue to let the tired effects pendulum swing between "minimal" and "powerful" media effects. When transfixed by that pendulum, the experience of movement is euphoria for scholars eager to celebrate the advent of the powerful effects thesis. While even a clock's pendulum does not tell time, the "effects" pendulum is attached to no clock at all. The historical birth and decline of the public sphere do not register on that pendulum.

From the vantage point of the public sphere as a social institution distinct from media institutions, the question of powerful versus minimal media effects flips in its meaning. If the present condition of the public sphere is weak, then mediated agendas are powerful only in that they help to reinforce and maintain the institutional arrangements that historically have set up that condition. If it is of central importance to revitalize the public sphere, then the media are themselves impotent no matter how much they may or may not tell the "public" what issues to ponder. A more basic question is whether media are powerful enough to help redirect the historical course of the public sphere. Investigation of that question by mass media effects researchers would require setting aside not only the idea of "agendas," but also the concepts "effects" and "audience." All three are too narrow in even their broadest formulations to grasp the societal and historical processes that form and contain that space for democratic participation known as "the public sphere."

Crowley (1982) recalls Lindblom's warning to social scientists

about a blind spot in their thinking if they went on focusing their analyses, designs, and judgments regarding the social world exclusively upon those centrally coordinated mechanisms and institutions (such as communication networks, information flows, and audience effects) through which modern societies attempted to manage aspects of their interaction. . . . this bias . . . could blind us to the many natural tendencies in society toward coordination, consensus, and commitment. "People," he said, "can coordinate with each other without anyone's coordinating them." (pp. 187-188; citing Lindblom, 1965)

That warning applies to advocates of *both* the powerful and minimal effects theses, to *both* agenda-setting researchers and their empirical "antagonists" who would have us investigate people as media audiences. It certainly applies to a fixation on content analysis and associated practices generating media content. The public that creates or is strained to create its opinions goes unheard and unstudied, from Weiss's analysis to the maze constructed of research agendas called for from Becker (1982) to Rogers and Dearing (1988). While the maze gets better mapped, the public sphere gets further eclipsed.

Redirecting the agenda of agenda-setting research requires abandoning its concepts to explore the nature of the public's ability to form itself—a question broader and deeper than media treatment of issues or the nature of media audiences. Attachment to mediacentric values, not methodological innovation and interempiricist bridge building, is a central problem facing the academic interest in political communication in society—unless we wish to argue that the media are powerful enough to revitalize the institution we call "the public." No agenda-setting researcher has suggested that degree of power.

At most, agenda-setting as a research tradition has suggested that media have the power to encourage public powerlessness in society. Problematic as this is, depending on which research one reads, its demonstration should not be confused with articulating an interest in explaining (a) how the public came to that powerless condition, (b) what institutional arrangements could alter that condition, and (c) how the mass media would fit into the institutional mix as part of the solution. On these questions, Weiss's essay must be read in the light of crosscurrents of intellectual migration between Germany and the United States and in the historical-institutional legacies for political communication in both societies.

REFERENCES

Becker, L. B. (1982). The mass media and citizen assessment of issue importance: A reflection on agenda-setting research. In D. C. Whitney, E. Wartella, & S. Windahl (Eds.), *Mass communication review yearbook* (Vol. 3, pp. 521-536). Beverly Hills, CA: Sage.

Carey, J. W., & Quirk, J. J. (1970). The mythos of the electronic revolution. *American Scholar, 39,* 219-241, 395-424.

Cohen, B. C. (1963). *The press and foreign policy.* Princeton, NJ: Princeton University Press.

Crowley, D. J. (1982). *Understanding communication: The signifying web.* New York: Gordon & Breach.

Dewey, J. (1916). *The public and its problems.* Denver: Swallow.

Dewey, J. (1922). *Democracy and education.* New York: Free Press.

Erbring, L., Goldenberg, E. N., & Miller, A. H. (1980). Front-page news and real-world cues: A new look at agenda-setting by the media. *American Journal of Political Science, 24,* 16-49.

Garnham, N. (1990). The media and the public sphere. In N. Garnham, *Capitalism and communication: Global culture and the economies of information* (pp. 104-114). London: Sage.

Golding, P. (1990). Political communication and citizenship: The media and democracy in an inegalitarian social order. In M. Ferguson (Ed.), *Public communication: The new imperatives* (pp. 84-100). Newbury Park, CA: Sage.

Habermas, J. (1962). *Strukturwandel der Öffentlichkeit. Untersuchungen zu einer Kategorie der bürgerlichen Gesellschaft.* Neuwied: Luchterhand.

Habermas, J. (1971). Der Universalitätsanspruch der Hermeneutik. In J. Habermas, *Hermeneutik und Ideologiekritik* (pp. 120-159). Frankfurt: Suhrkamp.

Habermas, J. (1974). The public sphere: An encyclopedia article (1964). *New German Critique, 3,* 49-55.

Habermas, J. (1975). *Legitimation crisis.* Boston: Beacon.

Habermas, J. (1979). *Communication and the evolution of society.* Boston: Beacon.

Habermas, J. (1984). *The theory of communicative action: Vol. 1. Reason and the rationalization of society.* Boston: Beacon.

Habermas, J. (1987). *The theory of communicative action: Vol. 2. Lifeworld and system: A critique of functionalist reason.* Boston: Beacon.

Hardt, H. (1979). *Social theories of the press: Early German and American perspectives.* Beverly Hills, CA: Sage.

Hardt, H. (1989). The return of the "critical" and the challenge of radical dissent: Critical theory, cultural studies, and American mass communication research. In J. A. Anderson (Ed.), *Communication yearbook 12* (pp. 558-600). Newbury Park, CA: Sage.

Hohendahl, P. (1974). Jürgen Habermas: The public sphere (1964). *New German Critique, 3,* 45-48.

Hohendahl, P. (1979). Critical theory, public sphere and culture: Jürgen Habermas and his critics. *New German Critique, 16,* 89-118.

Innis, H. A. (1950). *The bias of communication.* Toronto: University of Toronto Press.

Iyengar, S. (1988). New directions of agenda-setting research. In J. A. Anderson (Ed.), *Communication yearbook 11* (pp. 595-602). Newbury Park, CA: Sage.

Iyengar, S., & Kinder, D. R. (1987). *News that matters: Agenda-setting and printing in a television age.* Chicago: University of Chicago Press.

Jacoby, R. (1987). *The last intellectuals: American culture in the age of academe.* New York: Basic Books.

Katz, E. (1987). Communications research since Lazarsfeld. *Public Opinion Quarterly, 51*(4) (Part 2), S25-S45.

Lang, G. E., & Lang, K. (1981). Watergate: An exploration of the agenda-setting process. In G. C. Wilhoit & DeBock (Eds.), *Mass communication review yearbook 2* (pp. 447-468). Beverly Hills, CA: Sage.

Lazarsfeld, P. F., Berelson, B., & Gaudet, B. (1968). *The people's choice* (3rd ed.). New York: Columbia University Press. (Original work published 1944)

Lindblom, C. (1965). *The intelligence of democracy.* New York: Free Press.

Lippmann, W. (1922). *Public opinion.* New York: Macmillan.

McCombs, M. E. (1976). Agenda-setting research: A bibliographic essay. *Political Communication Review, 1,* 1-7.

McCombs, M. E., & Shaw, D. L. (1972). The agenda-setting function of mass media. *Public Opinion Quarterly, 36,* 176-184.

McLeod, J. M., Becker, L. B., & Byrnes, J. E. (1974). Another look at the agenda-setting function of the press. *Communication Research, 1,* 131-166.

McLuskie, E. (1978). Technical rationality and the public realm: A critical theory of responsibility as mass communication theory and practice. *Journal of Communication Inquiry, 3*, 13-29.

McLuskie, E. (1981). The embeddedness of communication in the slime of history: Themes leading to the thesis of a communication crisis. *Journal of Communication Inquiry, 7*, 3-31.

Mead, G. H. (1934). *Mind, self and society.* Chicago: University of Chicago Press.

Noelle-Neumann, E. (1980). *Die Schweigespirale.* Munich: R. Piper.

Noelle-Neumann, E. (1983). The effect of media on media research. *Journal of Communication, 33*, 157-165.

Noelle-Neumann, E. (1990). The people's choice—revisited. In W. R. Langenbucher (Ed.), *Paul F. Lazarsfeld: Die Wiener Forschungstradition der empirischen Sozial- und Kommunikationsforschung, Schriftenreihe der deutschen Gesellschaft für Publizistik- und Kommunikationswissenschaft 16* (pp. 147-155). Munich: Ölschläger.

O'Sullivan, T., Hartley, J., Saunders, D., & Fiske, J. (1983). *Key concepts in communication.* London: Methuen.

Peters, J. D. (1989). Democracy and American mass communication theory: Dewey, Lippmann, Lazarsfeld. *Communication, 11*(3), 199-220.

Rogers, E. M., & Dearing, J. W. (1988). Agenda-setting research: Where has it been, where is it going? In J. A. Anderson (Ed.), *Communication yearbook 11* (pp. 595-602). Newbury Park, CA: Sage.

Skogerbø, E. (1990). The concept of the public sphere in a historical perspective: An anachronism or a relevant political concept? *Nordicom Review of Nordic Mass Communication Research, 2*, 41-46.

Swanson, D. L. (1988). Feeling the elephant: Some observations on agenda-setting research. In J. A. Anderson (Ed.), *Communication yearbook 11* (pp. 603-619). Newbury Park, CA: Sage.

Weiss, H.-J. (1988). Meinungsgestaltung im Interesse der Zeitungen? Eine Analyse der Zeitungpublizistik zur Erhöhung der Rundfunkgebühr (Oktober 1987 bis Januar 1988). *Media Perspektiven*, pp. 469-489.

SECTION 3

INTERACTION IN THE SOCIAL CONTEXT

9 Dominance-Seeking Language Strategies: Please Eat the Floor, Dogbreath, or I'll Rip Your Lungs Out, Okay?

JO LISKA
University of Colorado at Denver

The last two decades have been witness to an explosion of research on linguistic features characteristic of dominance and power or the lack thereof. This explosion has been fueled by scholars especially interested in sex- and/or gender-linked differences in interaction behaviors reflective of dominance, leadership, influence, and power. Although sex and gender have received the most attention, variables such as status, context, personality, relational distance, and ontogeny have been examined relative to the acquisition, maintenance, and perception of dominance, influence, and power. Specifically, this chapter examines research directed at illuminating the characteristics and effects of language typically associated with or perceived as dominant and powerful, offers a methodological and theoretical/conceptual analysis and critique of that body of literature, and provides some rather specific directions for future research and suggestions for theoretical grounding.

DOMINANCE has long been a construct of prominence among scholars interested in social structure and interaction among humans and other social species. Indeed, dominance is considered a universal principle of social organization (see Bernstein, 1981; Sebeok, 1972). It is typically defined and measured using criteria based on outcome, such as rank order of individuals within a group, win/loss records, or preferential access to limited and/or desirable resources. Further, dominance is thought to be highly correlated with, or to result in, social power and influence. Capitanio (1982) suggests that the key mechanisms of dominance appear to be the ability to manipulate the behavior of others and the ability to affiliate and engage friendships and alliances. Mitchell and Maple (1985) "hypothesize that dominance is a summary statement about

Correspondence and requests for reprints: Jo Liska, Department of Anthropology, University of Colorado, Denver, CO 80204.

Communication Yearbook 15, pp. 427-456

an array of attributes that may be thought of as 'social skills' " (p. 50). For them, dominance is best conceived as dependent upon situational characteristics and individual social acuity. Thus, as is the case with many attributes (e.g., competence, credibility), dominance is negotiated within and constrained by particular social relationships.

In earlier work, I have argued:

> Dominance, and related constructs such as power, influence, and control, are outcomes that are attained using various strategies/tactics. One may be dominant or have power and influence in some areas but not in others. Power or dominance may be vested or earned. Vested dominance may result from birth order, kinship, or be institutionalized and granted as the rights and privileges of a particular role, e.g., college professor, judge, or corporate president. Vested dominance may also result in physical power dependent upon the physical characteristics of the individual. (Liska, 1990, p. 76)[1]

On the other hand, social dominance, power, and influence are earned and dependent upon social strategy selection and enactment abilities, empathic abilities, and the potential for affiliation. Finally, expert power is the result of some special knowledge or ability.

> Clearly, then, dominance is not unidimensional. Dominance may be assessed on a number of dimensions such as aggressiveness, politeness or deference, effectiveness, acceptability/desirability, and so on. Moreover, dominance is not dichotomous but continuous. One possesses degrees of dominance and the extent of dominance may vary from situation to situation. Further, dominance is not a trait but is bound by relationships, contexts, and time. (Liska, 1990, p. 77)

Dominance seeking takes many forms, and there are numerous cues or indicators of dominance-seeking attempts. Nonverbal indicators of dominance/ submissiveness have received considerable attention (see Ellyson & Dovidio, 1985; Omark, Strayer, & Freedman, 1980). Also numerous are investigations of verbal/linguistic strategies related to dominance. Linguistic markers generally associated with dominance include amount of interaction initiated by interactants, interruption, length of speaking turn, and overlaps in speaking among interactants. Lakoff (1975), writing about woman's language, and Goody (1978), reporting results of ethnographic research on politeness, have suggested several linguistic characteristics that constitute a style variously termed *woman's language, the female register, deferent, polite, powerless, conciliatory,* and *ingratiating.* These characteristics include "wh" imperatives, tag questions, qualifiers, apologies, polite or indirect commands, modal constructions, absence of coarse language and expletives, specific kinds of adjectives (e.g., charming, lovely, sweet, cute), hedges, indirect requests, rising inflection indicating tentativeness, and intensifiers such as *so* and *very.* These characteristics may be arranged along a dominance-seeking continuum with the absence of these characteristics, as well as the addition of words such as expletives that are generally not found in "polite" speech, indicating a highly assertive, direct, or dominant style, while the inclusion of all characteristics indicates a highly tentative, submissive, or deferential style.

Specifically, the thesis of this chapter is that perceptions of dominance/submissiveness based on language style are dependent upon culture, the constraints and affordances contained within specific situations, the goals (tacit and explicit) salient to the interactants, and the specific characteristics of the interactants. Further, the style one adopts is also dependent upon one's own goals, the characteristics and perceived goals of the other interactant, and situational affordances and constraints.

LINGUISTIC FEATURES
OF DOMINANCE/SUBMISSIVENESS

Robin Lakoff (1975, 1977), in writing about the typical character of women's speech, suggests several linguistic features that, when taken together, typify a style she describes as indicative of tentativeness, submissiveness, and triviality. Those linguistic features include the following:

(1) "wh" imperatives (e.g., "Why don't you open the door?")

(2) speaking less frequently

(3) tag questions (e.g., "It is cold in here, isn't it?")

(4) overuse of qualifiers (e.g., "I think that . . .")

(5) using more apologies (e.g., "I'm sorry, but I think that . . .")

(6) use of polite commands (e.g., "I would appreciate it if you would . . .")

(7) modal constructions (e.g., "can," "would," "should," and "ought")

(8) absence of coarse language and expletives

(9) use of more precise color terms (e.g., mauve, ecru, taupe)

(10) use of hedges (e.g., "Well, I am not really sure about this, but . . .")

(11) indirect commands and requests (e.g., "My, isn't it cold in here?")

(12) use of more intensifiers, especially *so* and *very*

Lakoff's characterization of this language style, and her suggestion that this style is best described as woman's language, are both based on introspection, intuition, and casual observation. In fact, well into the early 1970s, evidence for gender differences in communication was largely based on anecdotal data, conjecture, and untested hypotheses (Kramer, 1974; Thorne & Henley, 1975). Since that time, researchers in a number of disciplines have set about testing those speculations.

Liska, Mechling, and Stathas (1981) found that the absence of linguistic features such as tag questions, modal constructions, "wh" imperatives, and so on render judgments of speakers as believable, assertive, dominant, willing to take a stand, and less friendly and warm. Berryman-Fink and Wilcox (1983) found that, regardless of gender, speakers who use "male" language are perceived as more extroverted. Speakers who use language containing the features detailed by Lakoff are typically rated as more submissive, less assertive, less willing to take a stand, and less believable; they are also characterized as more polite and more friendly (Quina, Wingard, & Bates, 1987). In other studies, subjects rated language containing one or more of these features as less intelligent (O'Barr & Atkins, 1980), less assertive (Newcombe & Arnkoff, 1979), less commanding (Berryman & Wilcox, 1980), and both more credible (Berryman, 1980; Berryman-Fink & Wilcox, 1983) and less credible (Erickson, Lind, Johnson, & O'Barr, 1978). Rasmussen and Moely (1986) report that a language style lacking these features was rated by their subjects as more masculine, less feminine, more instrumental, and less socially positive than the opposite style. Their findings are based on responses on 23 scales (e.g., polite, gentle, powerful, competent, masculine, feminine, homosexual, uppity, good) applied to 14 short stories varying the sex of the speaker and the style of language. Chesler (1972) and Franks and Burtle (1974) report that an assertive style is seen as less appropriate for women than for men; Wiley and Eskilson (1985) report similar findings. Other studies have demonstrated that the use of language characterized as "powerless" tends to lower evaluations of speaker credibility and attractiveness (e.g., Bradac, Hemphill, & Tardy, 1981; Bradac & Mulac, 1984a).

There are exceptions to these general findings. Note, for instance, that Bradac and Mulac (1984b) report that a powerful style resulted in higher ratings of attractiveness and slightly higher ratings of empathy. Moreover, a powerful style is not necessarily associated with masculinity (Bradac et al., 1981). Also, polite forms are sometimes rated as relatively powerful (Bradac & Mulac, 1984a).

The extent of relationship between the gender-linked language effect and sex role stereotypes was tested by Mulac, Incontro, and James (1985), who found that their two measures were so congruent as to share 86% common variance. They speculate that "the two phenomena may well operate in a mutually reinforcing manner" (p. 1108). That is, people may tend to speak in ways consistent with sex role stereotypes and/or "examples of the language of men and women encountered daily might serve to reinforce the stereotypes" (p. 1108).

Zahn (1989) sought to determine the extent to which differences in subjects' evaluations of naturally occurring conversation were the result of speech differences between males and females, differences in sex role stereotypes maintained by subjects, and/or within-sex speech differences. Zahn concludes that, rather than supporting Lakoff's hypothesis, his data suggest that within-sex speech differences significantly affect subjects' ratings. Moreover, unlike Mulac et al. (1985), who found a pronounced effect for stereotypes, Zahn reports no effects for stereotyping on subjects' ratings of speaker superiority, attractiveness, or dynamism; that is, "unlike raters in some previous studies who gave the same message more negative ratings when attributed to a women than a man, the raters in this study did not make such stereotypic evaluations" (p. 70). Zahn concludes that "while some form of gender-linked variation has some influence on speech evaluation, the effects are unlikely to reflect an influence of sex-role stereotypes and are secondary to how individuals, male or female, communicate through other aspects of their encoding choices" (p. 72).

O'Barr and Atkins (1980) examined the characteristics suggested by Lakoff (excluding tag questions) by analyzing the testimony provided by male and female trial witnesses of differing ascribed status. They report great variation for both male and female witnesses in the use of polite forms, hedges, intensifiers, and so forth. They suggest that while among the witnesses they studied the women generally used more polite and uncertain forms than did the men, the speaker's status appeared to be influential. High-status women and low-status men used more of the characteristics of "woman's language." They further determined that ratings of the credibility of witness testimony were higher for those witnesses who used a powerful style.

Crosby and Nyquist (1977) examined the speech of males and females in three situations in order to assess the extent to which males and females engage in stereotypical styles of talk. The three situations involved Boston University undergraduates engaged in conversations with persons of the same sex, the speech of people making inquiries at an information booth in Boston, and police personnel and male and female clients engaged in conversation at a police station in Connecticut. They found significant differences between male and female subjects' use of "woman's language" in the first and third situations, but not in the second. They explain their findings by arguing that the second situation called for highly "ritualized" and routine interaction, and this may account for finding few sex differences in language use. Further, they argue that the use of different language styles will be highly influenced, and possibly exaggerated or attenuated, by situational demands.

Bradley (1981) manipulated tag questions, disclaimers, and supporting evidence and found that qualifying phrases had an adverse effect only when used by women. Females who used tag questions and disclaimers were perceived as having little knowledge, and, in general, women were not as well liked as men. Holmes (1984) found that tag questions were used more by nonleaders then by leaders. Fishman (1978, 1980, 1983) found that women used more verbal strategies characteristic of initiating and maintaining conversation than did men. Women more frequently used fillers such as "you know," questions that required responses, and attention-getting devices such as "Do you know what?" Fishman also found that while women initiated more topics than did men, topics initiated by men were more likely to evolve into conversations. Data were based on the tape-recorded conversations of three couples over a period of 4 to 14 days.

A study of the effects of hedges, intensifiers, and hesitations on subjects' perceptions of authoritativeness, sociability, character, and similarity conducted by Hosman (1989) revealed that "hedges lower evaluations of authoritativeness, while hesitations lower evaluations of authoritativeness and sociability" (p. 400). Based on the results of two studies, Hosman concludes that generally speakers wishing to appear "powerful" should avoid the use of hedges and hesitations. Intensifiers, on the other hand, do not necessarily contribute to perceptions of powerlessness or powerfulness. Nor is any effect for similarity found. Hosman concludes that not all of the features or characteristics typically associated with powerful/powerless actually or equally contribute to subjects' perceptions.

Brouwer, Gerritsen, and De Haan (1979) examined differences in the conversation of men and women engaged in the act of buying a train ticket in Amsterdam. Their analysis focused on number of words, diminutives, civilities, and forms of language indicative of insecurity (e.g., repetitions, hesitations). They found few significant differences between the language used by males and that used by females, but they did determine that the women in their study used more hesitations and requests for information than did the men. More interesting is their finding that the sex of the addressee affected almost all of the variables included in their study. That is, both men and women used more language characterized by markers of insecurity and politeness when talking with a male ticket agent than they used when talking with a female ticket agent. Since they were interested in gender differences between ticket buyers, the researchers did not explicitly control for sex of addressee beyond including one male and one female ticket agent. Thus their finding is suggestive of an important avenue for future research.

The use of coarse, profane, and/or obscene language has not received a great deal of attention. Some studies designed to test Lakoff's hypothesis have included such language in the conversations read by subjects (e.g., Liska et al., 1981). However, to my knowledge, no one has specifically examined the effects of coarse language independent of the other linguistic features. Mulac (1976) and Bostrom, Basehart, and Rossiter (1973), who tested the effects of obscenity generally, found that it produced negative evaluations of the speaker and inhibited the speaker's potential to effect opinion change.

Although it may appear that I am using the adjectives *coarse, profane,* and *obscene* interchangeably here, I am not. I think there are important differences among these terms. Coarse language is any language lacking in refinement or delicacy. "Hey, shut up!" is reasonably described as coarse when compared with "Be quiet" or "Please be quiet." *Profane* is typically reserved for language that denigrates religions or religious beliefs, artifacts, and so forth. The *American Heritage Dictionary* (1975) defines *profane* as "(1) Blasphemous, (2) nonreligious; secular, and (3) impure." Obscene language is offensive to accepted standards of decency, those standards determined by personal preference as well as group or cultural norms and expectations. Language littered with expletives is likely to be considered obscene. Of course, the effects of such linguistic forms are likely to depend upon individual idiosyncrasies, group and cultural standards, and contextual or situational expectations. Some comedians frequently use these forms, to the delight of their audiences. Lenny Bruce spent time in jail for using an obscene term in his act, and George Carlin is famous for his bit on the seven words one cannot say on television. These same routines would undoubtedly be deemed inappropriate and even vulgar in different circumstances, however. Where along a dominance-seeking continuum these linguistic forms would fall would depend upon who did the placement. In my opinion, the differences among them are a matter of degree, not of kind. And combining features of all three is likely to produce extreme forms of aggressive language, especially if such language is designed to undermine the target's self-esteem or self-worth. This aspect of the message, a personal orientation or tone, may be an important discriminator among perceptions of the degree or intensity of various types or levels of verbal aggressiveness. A study conducted by Greenburg (1976) provides some support for this idea.

Greenburg (1976) used a typology of verbal aggressiveness developed by Mosher (1956) and Mosher and Proenza (1968). This typology is composed of 10 levels of verbal aggressiveness, 3 of which are nonlinguistic (silence, intermittent distraction, and continuous distraction) and 7 of which are linguistic strategies (e.g., criticism, stereotypic derogation, severe derogation with cursing, stream of profanity, threat of physical attack). Profanity, as used by these researchers, included expletives other than those that denigrate religious beliefs. Greenburg used the 7 linguistic levels of verbal aggressiveness in his study and found that criticism was perceived as the least verbally aggressive, followed by various forms of stereotypic derogation and severe derogation, then stream of profanity, and finally threat of physical attack was perceived as the most aggressive. Examination of the statements included in this study led me to conclude that aggressive language strategies aimed at undermining the self-worth or safety of the target were also perceived as highly aggressive.

As mentioned earlier, while noted exceptions exist, the results of these studies tend to indicate that the language characteristics posited by Lakoff yield impressions of politeness, friendliness, and submissiveness. Moreover, speakers who use tag questions, hedges, hesitations, and so on are frequently rated as more feminine. However, while Mulac et al. (1985) report finding a rather consistent effect for gender-linked language, others do not. Such mixed results lead me to conclude that additional influences are operating on choices of and responses to language style. One theme in the research reviewed here, and in the communication literature generally, is the idea that communication behavior is frequently specific to situation or context. Thus, in this case, perceptions of language style are likely to be influenced by variables such as speaker status and sex of addressee. The results of research on interaction patterns lend support for the importance of these variables.

Interaction Patterns

Early studies of verbal interaction patterns in dyads and groups using Bales's (1950) interaction process analysis generally found that men focused their interaction on the task as indicated by offering suggestions, information, and opinions, while women focused on socioemotional aspects of the interaction by showing solidarity and agreement (see Aries, 1982; Lockheed & Hall, 1976; Piliavin & Martin, 1978; Strodtbeck & Mann, 1956). These findings are generally consistent with the stereotypical behaviors and concerns attributed to males and females; that is, women are thought to be more interested in social relationships, and thus provide social and emotional support and work to create an environment based on cooperation, and men are more interested in task accomplishment, and thus engage in instrumental behaviors that facilitate goal attainment. More recent studies indicate that even when women are more informed than the male members of a group, women still rely on socioemotional strategies (Leet-Pellegrini, 1980).

Bales (1970) suggests that the initiation of interaction and amount of time one talks are indications of power. Kenkel (1963), for example, found that the amount of talk generated by individuals in decision-making groups was related to their potential to influence. That is, those who talked the most were also perceived as highly influential. Additionally, when considering the length of utterances and overlaps in speaking turns, men are sometimes found to engage in longer utterances and to initiate more overlaps than are women (Duncan & Fiske, 1977; Frances, 1979; Zimmerman & West, 1975). However, Markel, Long, and Saine (1976) found that women used longer utterances than did men, and Esposito (1979) failed to detect gender differences in overlaps.

Interruptions have been viewed as important indicators of dominance relationships. Zimmerman and West (1975) suggest that interruptions are a means of topic control; they found that in mixed-sex conversations, men accounted for 96% of the total number of interruptions. In same-sex conversations, however, interruptions were equally divided between speakers. Bohn and Stutman (1983) found that interruptions were more characteristic of male-male dyads than of female-female dyads. LaFrance and Carmen (1980) report that when interruptive statements and interruptive questions are compared, women use significantly more interruptive questions than do men. They interpret these findings as suggestive of female responsiveness rather than assertiveness. Interruptions in the form of questions might also be used to indicate interest in the topic or might reflect a desire for the conversation to continue. Interest in the relationship might also be suggested by the use of interruptive questions. Finally, interruptive questions may be used simply to elicit clarification.

Aries (1987) has concluded that instead of assuming women's speech to be characteristic of low status, insecurity, and/or deference, the research may be suggesting that women use questions, tags, and back-channeling "to indicate involvement and connection in conversations and to facilitate conversations by soliciting responses from listeners" (p. 157). Thus these verbal strategies are used to encourage conversations. She goes on to suggest adopting a more functional approach for analyzing conversational characteristics.

Clearly, linguistic and interaction features influence perceptions of power, dominance/submissiveness, and control, with at least some of Lakoff's characteristics typically producing perceptions of tentativeness, uncertainty, socioemotional orientation, and submissiveness. Speakers who shun tag questions, hedges, hesitations, and so on, and who control conversations through interruptions, overlaps, and talking more, are perceived as more dominant, are rated as having greater potential to influence, and are seen as more task oriented and more instrumental. Studies examining the extent to which these speaking styles are typical of males and females have produced conflicting and complex results. Such results are in part due to differing methodologies and to variations in sample sizes, tasks, length of participation, and relationships between participants, as well as the operational definitions employed by various researchers.

Whether intended or not, these studies and others like them have demonstrated the need to expand research concerns beyond explicit hypotheses about pervasive sex differences and instead focus on how participant goals and situational characteristics (e.g., roles, interaction norms, and nature of interactant relationships) influence choice of language style, and the effects of those choices on subsequent perceptions, evaluations, and ongoing interaction. Haas (1979) writes:

> Sex is not the only variable to influence speech style. There is a complex interaction of personal characteristics such as sex, age, education, occupation, geographical region, ethnic background, and socioeconomic status and contextual factors such as communication, situation, environment, and participants. (p. 624)

A number of studies have attempted to assess the extent to which status, role, and other contextual and relational variables influence perceptions of language style. Those studies are the focus of the next section.[2]

SITUATIONAL CHARACTERISTICS: STATUS, ROLES, RELATIONAL INTIMACY, AND GROUP COMPOSITION

Kramarae (1981) claims that individuals of lower status, when compared with high-status speakers within a specific situation, will generally use verbal strategies employing the "female register." Research by Crosby and Nyquist (1977), McMillan, Clifton, McGrath, and Gale (1977), O'Barr and Atkins (1980), and Geis, Brown, Jennings, and Corrado-Taylor (1984) supports

Kramarae's claim. Bohra and Pandey (1984) had subjects rate the appropriateness of a number of interaction strategies with bosses, strangers, and friends. They report that ingratiation tactics were used more frequently with bosses than with friends or strangers. Because the subjects in this study were male students at an engineering institute in India, comparison of their findings with those from research based upon other cultures should provide some interesting insights into cultural variations found among the uses and effects of ingratiation tactics.

Holtgraves (1986) conducted two experiments to examine perceptions of direct and indirect speech acts and the speakers who use them. In the first experiment, subject read scenarios in which status and face threat were manipulated. Subjects then rated the direct and indirect questions and replies that followed the scenario on two 11-point scales designed to measure the extent to which each question/reply would be likely to be used in this situation, and the extent to which each question/reply would be considered polite in this situation. Results indicate that indirect replies were expected in face-threatening situations and evasive replies were deemed as more likely and polite than direct replies in face-threatening situations. Face threat had no effect on perceptions of questions. Subjects in the second experiment read the same scenario and replies and then rated the interactants' liking for one another, relative status, and degree of closeness of the relationship between interactants. Holtgraves (1986) reports that directness resulted in attributions of higher status in face-threatening situations, and direct replies were considered markers of liking and relational closeness.

Linehan and Seifert (1983) conclude that while the appropriateness of aggressive/assertive speech is dependent upon situational characteristics (in this case operationalized as relational intimacy), aggression is always rated as less appropriate than an assertive language style. Further, their results indicate that nonassertive speech is rated as being less likely to produce desirable goal attainment. Their subjects indicated that assertiveness is appropriate in the following relational types (moving from most to least): opposite-sex strangers, same-sex strangers, opposite-sex friends, spouses, and same-sex friends.

Rubin and Nelson (1983) tape-recorded simulated job interviews for a position at a fictitious fast-food restaurant. Subjects who participated in the interviews were tenth-grade students enrolled in a public school near Atlanta, Georgia. Transcripts of the interviews were coded using 16 categories typically associated with gender-linked speech style (e.g., intensifiers, polite forms, sentence trail-offs, allness terms, and rhetorical interrogatives). The effects of speaker sex, socioeconomic status, ability, rigidity, question type (open/closed), and communication apprehension on the 16 style markers were examined. Rubin and Nelson conclude that their findings are consistent with the results of other research in which no clear gender-linked differences in language style are apparent. Moreover, with the exceptions of "high ability," which was found to be associated with tentativeness, and "high rapidity," which was negatively associated with vague expressions such as "and stuff," no other effects for individual differences were obtained. They write that the "results of the present study concur with previous work in indicating that these stigmatized stylistic features occur in the speech of all members of the community in some contexts" (p. 287).

Cowen, Drinkard, and MacGavin (1984) asked sixth, ninth, and twelfth graders to write essays describing how they get their way with their fathers, mothers, and same-sex best friends. Essays were coded using 9 of Falbo and Peplau's (1980) 13 power strategies: asking, bargaining, persistence, negative affect, positive affect, laissez-faire, reasoning, stating importance, and telling. Demanding, evasion, and verbal manipulation (Falbo, 1977) were also included. Cowen et al. (1984) report that there is strong support for the pervasive effect of target on the use of power strategies, minimal support for age or grade effect, and no support for the effects of gender or gender by age. Thus they conclude that target power and status effects have a profound influence on the types of strategies adopted by children regardless of gender, age, or grade.

Siderits, Johannsen, and Fadden (1985) examined the effects of gender and role on "hostile" and "anxious" communications. College student volunteers participated in a role-play/role-reversal exercise based on the Melian Dialogues, stories in which the characters' power and status are manipulated. Each of the 14 groups had two negotiating teams of four men and four women. Participants read the Melian Dialogues and then spent 15 minutes negotiating the best deal they could for their side. All sessions were tape-recorded and later transcribed and content analyzed using the Gottschalk-Gleser system, which provides for analysis of content themes and intensity of expression. The dependent variables were content (hostile and anxious) and quantity of utterances. Siderits et al. (1985) found that assigned role had a highly significant effect on the content of communication, while gender and order in which roles were assumed had no effect. Typical of other findings, males tended to talk more than did females, especially when they were in clearly less powerful positions.

Sex composition of the group appears to have considerable influence on the style of interaction. Departures from stereotypical patterns of talk and interaction on the part of males in mixed-sex groups have been documented by Piliavin and Martin (1978), Bohn and Stutman (1983), and Marlatt (1970). They found men to disagree less, to use more supportive statements, and to talk longer about personal matters. Results indicate more stereotypical interaction behaviors among all male groups. A study by Hogg (1985) indicates that "particularly for female speakers speech produced in mixed-sex group discussion is less feminine and more masculine then in single-sex dyadic discussion" (p. 107). Hogg explains this finding by means of "speech accommodation theory," which predicts that high need for social approval will be marked by convergence in speech or language style. Hogg reasons that women are more likely to demonstrate convergence in a gender-salient situation (mixed-sex group) because they are more likely to desire approval, while men will maintain their already superior position by using a more stereotypically masculine speech/language style and thus maintain distinctiveness from female interactants. Hogg's predictions were confirmed.

The gender-linked language effect has been demonstrated in situations in which subjects act as third-party evaluators of, typically, scripted conversations. Mulac, Wiemann, Widenmann, and Gibson (1988) broke with that tradition to examine the gender-linked language effect in same-sex and mixed-sex dyads. In the first study subjects were randomly assigned to dyads, given a list of three problems relevant to college student concerns, and asked to choose one of them for discussion. Discussions were audiotaped and transcribed. Transcripts were analyzed by trained coders on the basis of 12 linguistic features, such as fillers, interruptions, questions, hedges, and personal pronouns. These results were submitted to discriminant analysis in an attempt to predict gender of the interactants. Then the discriminant scores for each interactant were used in an analysis of variance to determine the extent to which male/female language differences diminished in mixed-sex, compared with same-sex, dyads. Results indicate that interruptions, directives, and fillers beginning a sentence were typical of male interactants. Questions, justifiers, intensive adverbs, personal pronouns, and adverbials were typical of female speech. The outcome of the ANOVA showed greater gender-linked language behavior in same-sex than in mixed-sex dyads. It appears, then, that interactants influence and are influenced by their conversational partners.

In the second study naive coders judged the transcripts on three sets of measures associated with the gender-linked language effect: sociointellectual status, aesthetic quality, and dynamism. Results revealed that females in same-sex dyads were rated higher on measures of sociointellectual status and aesthetic quality, with no differences detected on measures of dynamism. On the other hand, in mixed-sex dyads, women interactants were rated higher on dynamism, while male interactants were rated higher on measures of aesthetic quality. Mulac et al. (1988) conclude: "Taken together, the analyses of the objective language data and the subjective attributional data provide partial support for the Gender-Linked Language Effect in same-sex dyads and for the attenuation of that effect in mixed-sex dyads" (p. 315).

POLITENESS AND DEFERENCE

Lakoff (1974) suggests that clarity and politeness are the two fundamental properties of interaction. Politeness, writes Lakoff, is "designed to get people through cooperative transactions with a minimal amount of waste, effort, or friction" (p. 19). Politeness serves to save face and reduces threats to the status, self-esteem, and "face" of others. Since some actions, such as criticism, requests, threats, orders, and eliciting promises, typically threaten others, polite forms are used to reduce or redress the face-threatening aspects inherent in these speech acts. Thus politeness facilitates cooperative behavior, maintains status distinctions, and saves face.

Ethnographic studies across a variety of cultures clearly indicate that politeness or deference is universal. Goody (1978) writes:

> The basic constraints on effective interaction appear to be essentially the same across cultures and languages; everywhere a person must secure the cooperation of his interlocutor if he is to accomplish his goals. To secure cooperation he must avoid antagonizing his hearer, and the same sorts of acts are perceived as threatening in Mexico, Wales and south India. If at this level the problem posed by interaction is everywhere the same, it is hardly surprising that the same devices have been developed to resolve it, that is to avoid giving the impression that the speaker intends to do these threatening acts. Hence the concept of 'face wants' is a formulation of the problem to which politeness forms provide the effective strategic response. To adopt the usage of Keenan, Schieffelin and Platt (1976), the communicative distress to which politeness forms are a response is the danger of threatening an interlocutor and thus jeopardizing the successful outcome of the speech act. (p. 6)

While linguistic forms of politeness have received considerable attention, theoretical development in the area is still lacking (Lim, 1988). Brown and Levinson (1978) provided the first systematic attempt at developing a theory of politeness based on their cross-cultural studies of the phenomenon. Lim (1988) has identified a number of limitations to their theory and provided several modifications. One specific area of concern was the fact that the Brown and Levinson model did not adequately explain "face-work." Subsequently, Lim and Bowers (1991) have tested the revised model's ability to explain face-work. Preliminary results reflect positively on the revised model.

Axia and Baroni (1985) argue for a definitional distinction between politeness and deference. They write, "Politeness is a complex linguistic means used to maintain good interactions with other people" (p. 918). Their interest is in the development of politeness, and they hypothesize that "children fully master the use of politeness when they are able to recognize the 'cost' of a request with reference not only to the status of both speaker and addressee but also to the interlocutor's reactions to the request" (p. 919). Politeness, then, is a complex ability requiring an understanding of listener cues, recognition of reciprocal status, and a need to produce common ground, establish mutual goals, and so forth. Deference, on the other hand, conveys respect for the other by either humbling oneself or raising the status of the other (Goody, 1978), and may be best conceived as one strategy of politeness.

Fraser and Nolen (1981) suggest that interactants enter into a conversational contract in which relational status is negotiated and acted out according to a set of social and cultural norms, expectations, and standards. Thus, for example, criticism and orders are not considered impolite if the source of the criticism or the command is of higher relational status than the recipient, as in a parent-child or teacher-student relationship. Moreover, the style in which criticism and orders are given is likely to exaggerate or attenuate their effect. Some are so skilled as to make criticism sound like praise; others are so inept that a request is delivered as an order. Judgments of politeness are dependent upon a number of characteristics. "First, politeness is a property associated with a voluntary action" (p. 96). Crass interruption of a conversation is not likely to be considered impolite if done by a small child. Second, politeness, or the lack thereof, is dependent upon the perceptions of the hearer, the nature of the relationship, and the specific context in which the utterance occurs. Finally, like dominance, politeness is not dichotomous but continuous. Utterances vary in the degree to which they are deemed polite/impolite.

Fraser and Nolen (1981) conducted a study in two phases in which subjects were asked to judge the relative deference associated with various forms of requests. Additionally, linguistic features of the sentences were analyzed to assess the relative deference of each request form. Results suggest that deference is signaled by interrogative rather than declarative forms (e.g., "Can you do that?" rather than "I must request that you do that"). The former construction apparently allows the target of the request more options than does the latter construction. Next, the conditional form of a request was judged as being more deferent than the indicative. Again, asking "Can you do that?" is less tentative and restricts the requestee's options more than the construction "Could you do that?" Finally, positive modal constructions ("can") were determined to be more deferent than negative ones ("can't").

Fraser and Nolen (1981) included in their study a comparison of the forms of deference in both English and Spanish. They conclude that the "rankings across the two languages were very similar, thus supporting the view that certain semantic phenomena (e.g., negation, subjective) function similarly across languages" (p. 107).

The results of this study indicate that, at least in some respects, deference as conceived by Goody (1978) and others is related to the features of woman's language suggested by Lakoff (1975). The language style she describes appears to be one that suggests tentativeness and thus affords the listener a number of options for response. One effect of that style is clearly one in which the speaker's status is lowered while the hearer's status is elevated; that is, one signals recognition of the higher status of the other by adopting a language style based on indirect requests, positive modal constructions, and other devices that reflect tentativeness and uncertainty. At the very least, the studies that manipulate language style and status appear to support this stance.

Deference may be viewed quite differently when used in other contexts. Exaggerated features of deference may indicate insincerity, satire, attempts at manipulation, or hypersensitivity to rank and context. Shimanoff (1976) presents a well-argued case for the use of politeness for purposes of manipulation. She defines manipulation as "the act of getting someone to do something they would not ordinarily do, at a minimum cost to the speaker" (p. 1). Shimanoff goes on to expand Brown and Levinson's (1974, 1978) model of conventional politeness to incorporate politeness used for purposes of manipulation. She suggests several tactics that may be indicative of manipulative politeness (e.g., "Make the hearer believe she/he is a free agent," exemplified by constructions such as "You can say no, but . . . ," and "I have no right to ask, but . . . "). Additionally, she suggests using hedges and tag formations as well as indirectness as means of manipulating others.

Shimanoff does not reflect on the conditions under which such tactics will raise the suspicions of the target as to the sincerity or state of mind of the source. My speculation is that nonverbal demeanor would provide some clues to instances of manipulative politeness. Those nonverbal cues that normally accompany politeness or deference may be exaggerated or may contradict the thrust of the verbal message. The individual's past behaviors, personality, and situational demands may provide important clues to attempts at manipulation. Extreme differences in status between interactants may also be cause for caution. If, for example, the requester is of substantially higher status than the requestee and the request is couched in hyperpolite terms, the requestee may legitimately be suspicious of the motives of the other. Even so, if the self-esteem of the target of the request is especially low, the hyperpolite request might be perceived as extremely flattering.

Flattery and ingratiation are forms of deference used to elevate the relative status of one while humbling the other. Many of the characteristics associated with "woman's language" are likely to be found in ingratiating attempts. Again, indirect commands and requests, hedges, and the use of intensifiers may be characteristic of attempts to flatter others into doing one's bidding. At the very least, the effect will be to build the esteem of the target and raise the target's evaluation of the source of the flattery. Bradac, Schneider, Hemphill, and Tardy (1979) report that an ingratiating strategy based on flattery was judged as relatively likely to produce compliance and was directly associated with perceptions of communicator friendliness.

If taken to the extreme, however, ingratiation may be perceived as manipulative and thus may produce negative evaluations of the source of the strategy. Pandey and Singh (1986) found that subjects were less attracted to ingratiating actors than to nonmanipulative actors. They also report that ingratiating actors were seen as more interested in the conversational task then were nonmanipulators. Finally, successful actors were more positively evaluated than were unsuccessful actors. The message seems to be that if one is going to adopt a strategy of manipulative politeness, one best be good at it.

Liska and Hazleton (1990) found that while a deferential language style was generally deemed more positive than a nondeferential style, this effect was particularly pronounced when a speaker was confronting a "hostile" audience—that is, when advocating opinions with which his or her listeners disagreed. Under these conditions, deferential speakers were rated as more likable, more influential, and less dominant. While no effect (opinion change) measure was included, insofar as liking and perceptions of influence are related to an actual ability to influence, it seems reasonable to hypothesize that deferential communicators may be more effective at persuasion than are nondeferential communicators, at least when the audience is "hostile."

Wallace (1988) conducted a critical study in which he posed the question: What stylistic devices do speakers use when they are faced with the task of addressing a hostile audience? He analyzed eight political speeches, two speeches for each of four speakers, with one speech per speaker delivered to a hostile audience and the other delivered to a friendly audience. The stylistic devices included in the analysis were empathy, identification, similarity, deference, language intensity, equivocation, euphemism, and humor. He found that when addressing a hostile audience, all the speakers attempted to enact an environment of conciliation by using strategies of identification and empathy. Opinionated and intense language was minimal in speeches addressed to hostile audiences. In all cases, the speakers chose a language style midrange on a continuum of deference/nondeference. Given that the speakers were all of political prominence and speaking in formal situations, adopting a deferential style could have undermined their positions of power. However, adopting a nondeferential style put them at risk of threatening and alienating their audiences. Consequently, adopting either a highly deferential or highly nondeferential approach could have jeopardized their credibility and potential to influence.

ASSERTIVENESS AND AGGRESSIVENESS

Norton and Warnick (1976) have identified four subdimensions of assertiveness: contentiousness, dominance, refusal to be intimidated, and low anxiety. Moreover, they found that assertiveness correlated highly with measures of talkativeness and verbal intensity, and indicated a "good" communicator style. However, adopting an assertive or nondeferential style may generate different responses depending upon perceived sex or gender role congruence, familiarity, situational constraints, nature of the audience or subject sample, goals of the interactants, and cultural norms and standards. That is, in many studies, males who use an assertive or nondeferential style have tended to be evaluated more positively than females who adopt the same style (Wiley & Eskilson, 1985). Furthermore, assertive language is rated more negatively when the speaker's opinions are in opposition to those held by the audience. Assertive language may generally improve an individual's ability to be commanding, credible, and powerful, but may inhibit impressions of friendliness and warmth. Thus assertive language may be a good choice when one is interested more in task accomplishment than in developing or maintaining friendships. Assertiveness may be expected and acceptable from those who command higher rank and status, and, in fact, "interactants often accept a wider range of communicative behaviors from interlocutors perceived as having high status or power than from their lower status counterparts" (Street & Cappella, 1986). The use of and response to assertive language is likely to vary depending upon individual differences, although it appears that individual differences have received little attention from researchers interested in the language styles associated with dominance/submissiveness.

Greenburg (1976) examined the relationship between verbal aggressiveness and intensity modification. Base sentences such as "You do that too slow" were modified using two levels of frequency adverbs: "sometimes" and "always." Base sentences were selected to reflect several verbal aggressiveness categories developed by Mosher (1956). Greenburg found that sentences modified with "always" were seen as more aggressive than sentences modified with "sometimes" or the base sentences, and reports that the "main finding from this study is that the language qualifiers work better to subtract from feelings of verbal aggressiveness than they do to add to them" (p. 137). That is, subjects were more sensitive to the use of modifiers to reduce aggressiveness than to modifiers added to already aggressive statements.

An exaggeratedly aggressive language style such as that used by staff sergeants in movies such as *Full Metal Jacket* and by the characters typically portrayed by Clint ("Make my day") Eastwood, while potentially effective in some circumstances and with some people, is unlikely to be viewed positively by most people in most situations. If one's goals are affiliation and the development of alliances and friendships, verbal aggressiveness is likely to frustrate goal attainment. But verbal aggression may be useful as a cathartic release, may be used for satiric or comic effect as in the case of Sam Kinison's approach to humor, may rouse an audience to action, or may give one the last word in an argument. Moreover, an aggressive style may be the last resort for dealing with phone solicitors or for demanding restitution for an injustice. However, regular and long-term reliance on verbal aggressiveness is likely to be counterproductive, especially when directed at one's friends, family, neighbors, and/or coworkers. Of course, this is largely conjecture because empirical studies specifically testing the uses and effects of verbal aggressiveness are rare. However, reports of research on nonverbal signs of aggression do suggest that this conjecture is plausible. Additionally, research on compliance strategies indicates that aggressive tactics are generally regarded as socially unacceptable.

COMMUNICATOR GOALS

It should be evident by now that the effects of language features associated with dominance/submissiveness, power, and influence vary, at least to some extent, in accordance with cultural, social, and group norms and standards, individual characteristics of the interactants (e.g., status, age, gender), constraints of the situation, and the goals salient and important to the communicators. While few researchers in this area have specifically examined or manipulated goals (exceptions will be noted shortly), several of the studies reviewed thus far carry implicit suggestions about the goals likely to be important and/or relevant. For example, studies exploring the uses and effects of assertive or nonassertive language in dealing with a hostile audience imply a goal of attaining influence without threatening audience beliefs and values. In such situations, the best strategy appears to be one based on conciliation, moderate deference, and low intensity. If one's goal is to develop friendship or to be perceived as warm, friendly, and likable, deference is again the choice. However, perceptions of success, power, and credibility appear to be facilitated by an assertive (but probably not aggressive) style. Therefore, if one wants to be perceived as a leader, especially in task groups, one should use the features of language associated with dominance. Finally, for those who wish to appear to be of high status and upwardly mobile, an assertive style may well facilitate such impressions. These are offered as tentative conclusions, because studies in which goals are specified or elicited are rare, and implicit goals are frequently confounded with other variables (such as status and relational context).

Bradac and Mulac (1984a) hypothesized that

> the various indicators of powerful and powerless speech—the presence or absence of tags, hesitations, etc.—do not necessarily affect ratings of power, competence, or attractiveness uniformly; i.e., in a given context the use of polite forms or intensifiers may be judged as an appropriate tactic for a powerful and competent communicator, whereas the use of hedges or hesitations may be judged as an inappropriate tactic for such a person. (p. 308)

They varied seven linguistic markers (e.g., tags, hesitations, polite forms) and manipulated goals ("social intentions") by telling subjects either that the interviewee desired to appear sociable or that the interviewee desired to appear authoritative. Subjects read an interview scenario followed by a set of messages in which the seven linguistic characteristics appeared. Subjects were asked to rate each message on measure of power and effectiveness (study 1) and on a "will-will not create the desired impression" scale (study 2). The researchers found a five- to six-level power hierarchy that was to some extent influenced by communicator goals, but consistent across studies, sexes, messages, and measures. Subjects indicated a greater tolerance or acceptance of powerless forms when the interviewee was attempting to establish a sociable impression.

CONCEPTUAL AND METHODOLOGICAL LIMITATIONS

The shortcomings and limitations evident in the research on the language and interaction devices considered here appear to revolve around three major areas of concern: First, the operational definitions, subject samples, stimulus messages, and dependent measures used differ substantially across studies, and thus comparability of findings is severely limited. Second, the ecological validity of the research has been constrained by overreliance on contrived rather than natural stimulus conversations, overreliance on stimulus conversations in which only the extremes of language style are represented, limited information about message sources and situations provided for the subjects, and overreliance on approaches that elicit only subjects' first impressions. Third, extensive descriptions or ethnographies of natural ongoing interactions in everyday situations are sorely lacking. Consequently, we have only a limited understanding of how language style functions in everyday encounters, although there are several excellent critiques of message variable research in general, and language style research in particular (Aries, 1987; Bradac, 1988, 1989; Jackson & Jacobs, 1983; Kramer, Thorne, & Henley, 1978; Street & Cappella, 1986).

Measurement

Aries (1987) points up two problems that arise in the research done on interruptions; these appear to be problems typical of the research on language style specifically, and message research generally:

> First, there has too often been a tendency to interpret a behavior in a particular way without direct evidence to validate that inference. (Interruptions, for example, are equated with dominance.) Second, operational definitions of specific behaviors vary across studies, resulting in inconsistent research findings and call into question the assumption that different measures can be interpreted similarly. (p. 153)

Not only do different researchers use different measures to assess language style, but variations in conceptualizations also abound (e.g., powerful/powerless, ingratiation, deferential/nondeferential, dominant/submissive, assertive/nonassertive, and woman's language or the female register). I have tried, in my discussion of these various conceptualizations, to point out differences and distill similarities from among them.

Differences in conceptualization are likely to have a profound effect on the measures and the types of stimuli employed by the researcher. More problematic is the fact that most of the conceptualizations suggest particular outcomes. It seems clear that to use terms such as *powerful/powerless language* or the *female register* gives the impression that specific features of language always denote power or the lack thereof, or are the province of females or feminine people. Politeness, for example, is frequently equated with lower status, less dominance, and less power. However, as Shimanoff's (1976) analysis implies, politeness can be used to manipulate others, and manipulation clearly suggests that wielding of power and influence. Thus politeness strategies may be powerful in some situations but not in others. Further, Bradac and Mulac (1984a) suggest that some situations may create a preference for one style over another. Moreover, the use of politeness strategies may not create an impression of power, but the effect on the behavior of others may indicate power, influence, and interpersonal control. Consequently, it seems readily apparent that research that focuses on or includes behavioral measures along with perceptual measures is necessary for understanding the relationship between how people perceive various strategies and the people who use them, encompassing the actual effects those strategies may have on subsequent behavior. Measures of opinion change or memory for various aspects of conversations could be used. Studies of compliance such as those referred to as "foot-in-the-door" and "door-in-the-face" provide useful models for constructing situations in which behavior beyond that of paper-and-pencil responses is elicited.

The extent to which choices of and responses to language style are context specific remains unanswered. According to Giles and Wiemann (1987), research on language in communication progressed from a virtual absence of research in which context variables were included (pre-1970s), through the idea that language reflected context (language choices and effects prescribed by situational influences), to the view that language built upon context, and currently to conceiving of language as a determinant of context. Whatever view one adopts regarding the relationship between language variables and contextual variables, the fact remains that a systematic understanding of the relationship is lacking. Bradac, Hopper, and Wiemann (1989) write, "At this point the issue is not so much whether context should be included or not in message-variable research but which contextual variable should be scrutinized given the message variable of interest?" (p. 309).

Stimulus Messages

Stimulus messages vary considerably across studies. Some messages are created by the researcher; others are based on transcripts of conversations that are rewritten into various styles. Some studies analyze spontaneous or experimentally contrived conversations (e.g., Cowen et al., 1984; Glauser, 1984; Schultz, Briere, & Sandler, 1984; Zahn, 1989), but those are clearly in the minority. Ethnographic studies such as those reported in Goody's (1978) edited volume on politeness and in *Language, Gender and Sex in Comparative Perspective* (Philips, Steele, & Tanz, 1987) provide detailed accounts of when, how, by whom, and in what contexts different language styles are used. These ethnographies provide interesting directions for theoretical development and for future research.

Messages constructed by researchers may appear contrived and artificial, in part because they are typically written to reflect extremes of language style. Bell, Zahn, and Hopper (1984) refer to this as the "hammer effect" because subjects are hammered with a large number of extremes in speech forms contained within brief transcripts of conversations. While people are likely to use extreme styles under some conditions, and some people may characteristically adopt extremes in language style, I suspect those conditions and people are in the minority. Consequently, ratings by subjects based on extreme forms of style cannot be applied generally. Research in which language style is varied along a theoretical continuum is necessary for developing our understanding of how subtle variations in style affect listener/reader perceptions.

Replications across messages are far too infrequent, both within and across studies. Bradac et al. (1989) suggest that comparability of messages across studies is made difficult by the fact that few researchers specify the strength of the message. Thus, while different researchers may term particular messages "high intensity," one cannot assume that the messages are equivalent. Bradac et al.'s suggestions for overcoming this particular problem include subjective scaling, in which subjects rate the power of various forms of language, and specifying the precise levels of a variable, for example, ratio of high-intensity words to all words in a conversation.

Additionally, the stimulus messages used may be so specific or so general as to be unrepresentative of actual messages. Consequently, the results obtained in these studies may be a function of the content or structure of the particular messages used. Certainly, using a broad range of types of messages and message content combined with stimulus conversations that are selected from sets of conversations collected under "natural" circumstances would greatly improve the ecological validity of the research.

Most research uses written rather than oral or videotaped messages, largely to avoid confounding the linguistic features of style with other characteristics (e.g., gender, vocal qualities, and physical characteristics such as appearance, body type, and gestures). While these characteristics are likely to have considerable influence on the way language style is perceived, these qualities are difficult to manipulate and control and thus have been excluded. The advantages of experimental control aside for the moment, there are several shortcomings inherent in this approach. First, people typically do not read the conversations of others. Second, it is difficult to rewrite and transcribe conversations in such a fashion that they appear natural and spontaneous. Creating conversations is even more problematic, as writing realistic dialogue seems to require special talents and training, to which I am certain most editors, publishers, and TV producers would attest. Third, there appear to be important differences in the production and reception of written versus oral messages that may have implications for the evaluation of those messages and their sources. For example, one may expect written messages to be more grammatically correct than oral messages. Or one may expect written messages to be more carefully worded than oral messages. Further, different forms of language style may be processed in different ways. "Some may be more salient in writing, others more salient in speech" (Vinson & Johnson, 1989, p. 20). Vinson and Johnson found, for example, that "subjects noted more hesitations in writing and hesitation forms, in turn, had the greatest negative impact on evaluations of the powerless witness" (p. 20).

Finally, perceptions of both written and oral messages may differ depending upon whether one is actively participating in the interaction or merely observing it. Observers are likely to have goals quite different from those of participants. Moreover, the importance of those goals is likely to be different. That is, a participant may be ego-involved in the topic or especially desirous of the other interactant's approval. Observers of the conversation, because they are not involved, are unlikely to be concerned about the extent of approval offered by one participant to the other in the interaction. They may be curious about the relationship, but the consequences of the interaction may have little direct effect on the observers. Unlike participants, observers may not be especially motivated to attend closely to the interaction. Furthermore, those aspects of the interaction that are salient to the participant may be quite different from those salient to the observer. Subtle indications of disapproval might be completely missed or ignored by the observer. Street (1985) provides evidence that observer and actor situations produce dissimilar responses. Bradac et al. (1989) offer an interesting discussion of what they term "evaluator role." They conclude by saying, "Thus some of our generalizations about message effects may be limited to third party respondents" (p. 306).

Social Context

Frequently, a researcher's only interest is in the perception and evaluation of language style, independent of other speakers and contextual variables. This approach maximizes experimental control and is useful for conducting manipulation checks. However, the artificiality of the experimental situation is greatly enhanced and, therefore, ecological validity is sacrificed. Some studies should include relevant source and contextual cues in specified combinations, in order to begin a program of research designed to assess the relationship among a variety of variables in a fashion that more closely resembles the processing of social stimuli in "real" life. In an interesting theoretical piece called "Toward an Ecological Theory of Social Perception," McArthur and Baron (1983) suggest that

the ecological approach calls for an examination of the information in dynamic human behavior as apprehended by an active perceiver. It also suggests that configural stimulus information may be more important than individual elements, a point that is consistent with evidence that the impact of particular facial features upon personality ratings may depend upon the other features with which they appear. (p. 227)

When descriptions of stimulus people and/or situations are included, they are typically presented in written form. Again, there are a number of problems with this approach, not the least of which is the fact that we infrequently engage in assessing people and situations on the basis of written descriptions. These descriptions are not likely to conform to "real" life, where we have access to a broad array of observable information. Since these descriptions are generally quite brief, subjects are free to "construct" additional data as they deem necessary. Cronkhite (1984) discusses this perceptual array and critiques the constructivist position in detail in a chapter titled "The Perception of Meaning." He argues that under normal circumstances, construction is unnecessary because the observable data array is so vast. However, as observable data are restricted, perceivers are forced to fill in the missing information. Since most brief stimulus descriptions do not include a great deal of information, subjects are forced to provide their own. Unfortunately, the information they provide may vary from subject to subject in ways that cannot be ascertained. One result is that their judgments may not be based on the stimulus presented, but on information they have "personally" provided. And "restricting social information is likely to produce stock cultural explanations without accessing the receivers' real coding processes" (Liska, 1986, p. 11).

SUGGESTIONS FOR FUTURE RESEARCH

It is my opinion that future research should entail considerably more observation and description of spontaneous communication behaviors as they occur in natural settings. Unlike those of many disciplines, our data are readily available and discernible and should be the object of analysis. While I am not in favor of borrowing methodologies and techniques with rampant abandon, field methodology, which is underrepresented in communication research, has several advantages of note. Approaches based on systematic observation, participant observation, and the use of unobtrusive measures would enhance ecological validity as well as provide greatly improved stimulus material for experimental studies. The naturalistic approach of studies such as those conducted by Schultz et al. (1984), O'Barr and Atkins (1980), Brouwer et al. (1979), and Crosby and Nyquist (1977) serve as excellent illustrations of the use of field methodology.

The relationship between nonverbal demeanor and language style seems an especially useful direction for future research. One might attempt to determine if there are nonverbal features characteristic of politeness, in much the same way that the nonverbal behaviors that indicate aggression have been cataloged. The research on status differences in nonverbal behavior would be relevant to this task.

Moreover, the effect of different language styles may be mediated by nonverbal behaviors in important and interesting ways. Note, for instance, that the polite form "Can you do that?" may be considered quite impolite if accompanied by a sarcastic tone of voice and a smirk. Messages that take the form of politeness may be accompanied by nonverbal cues that clearly distinguish those that are attempts at manipulation from those that are sincere. These cues are likely to be very subtle and thus processed at a low level of awareness, making them difficult for subjects to report. Therefore, careful observation and description of various types of messages in various situations seem essential to identifying those cues.

Individuals' nonverbal behavior is an important influence on the perceptions, judgments, and behaviors of others. Physical features such as height and physique are regularly associated with impressions of power and dominance. All other things held constant, the taller of two job candidates is more likely to get the job. A speaker's style of dress, the car he or she drives, and his or her home address may influence listeners' perceptions. Those characteristics are likely to be especially important and relevant to first impressions. Moreover, these physical features undoubtedly interact with linguistic markers of style in interesting and important ways. For example, a mildly assertive language style combined with greater height and size and the use of expansive gestures may exaggerate impressions of assertiveness. On the other hand, a moderately polite style coupled with petiteness and the use of smaller, more refined gestures may exaggerate impressions of deference, uncertainty, tentativeness, and so on.

Some people inherit physical traits that inhibit their ability to project an impression of dominance, assertiveness, submissiveness, and so forth. Further, the nonverbal images they project in one situation may carry over to other situations. Consider, for example, that Clint Eastwood probably has a difficult time acting deferent. His facial features and build simply do not lend themselves well to the image of one who is deferent or submissive. Moreover, the style and demeanor typical of the characters he has played in the past have resulted in an overall impression of someone who always enacts social strategies assertively/aggressively. Thus the character, style, and demeanor typical of an individual's interaction may influence later impressions and evaluations. Bradac and Street (1986) write:

> Generally, it might be suggested that the initial effect of any particular message feature, whether positive or negative, will tend to attenuate with repeated exposure because the audience has an increasingly large base of knowledge and beliefs which can be used to assess the communicator and the message. (p. 8)

Clearly, examining how past interactions affect present and future interactions is an area in need of attention.

Analyzing the style of various compliance strategies/tactics appears to be another interesting direction. The style used for articulating a compliance-gaining or -resisting attempt may interact with the nature of the strategy. For example, using polite forms may make a moderately unacceptable social strategy more acceptable, whereas a socially acceptable social strategy may become less acceptable if delivered in a style characteristic of aggression. And some strategies may be perceived as inherently more polite/impolite than others. Hinting, for example, may be considered generally more polite than making a direct request. Again, the nonverbal behaviors that accompany these strategies may influence how they are perceived as well as the extent to which they are likely to be effective.

Aside from sex and/or gender, the influence of individual characteristics and differences on the uses, perceptions, and effects of language style has received little attention. This situation persists in spite of the fact that results of research on communication processes generally underscore the importance of individual characteristics on the production and reception of messages. For example, receiver self-esteem (Glauser, 1984) and need for approval (Giles & Powesland, 1975) have been found to play an important role in responses to messages.

Finally, rigorous and systematic analyses of how needs/goals influence communication processes are severely lacking. As is the case with other variables frequently associated with individual differences, the research considered here largely ignores the role of goals in influencing perceptions, evaluations, and/or effects of language style. McArthur and Baron (1983) emphasize the importance of goals in perception:

> Different information is essential to the behavioral goals of different people. What low-status people need to perceive in order to interact effectively with their environment may often be different from what high-status people need to perceive; . . . what people in one occupation need to perceive may differ from what people in another occupation need to perceive; and so forth. Thus, the ecological approach suggests that we may discover much of the interest in the domain of individual differences in social perception if we begin our investigations with a careful analysis of what it is that various individuals most need to perceive in order to interact effectively with their social environment. (p. 220)

CONCLUSION

I have attempted to illustrate the thesis that the perceptions, evaluations, and effects of language style are dependent upon the constraints and affordances contained within specific situations, the goals that are relevant and salient to the interactants, and the specific observable characteristics of the interactants. I have further suggested that this research would benefit from greater attention to concerns of ecological validity (e.g., more realistic stimulus conversations, assessments of behaviors beyond those elicited in paper-and-pencil tests, greater attention to combinations of variables hypothesized to interact with language style, and increased use of detailed information about message sources and interaction situations). Finally, I have argued that the study of language style would be enhanced by the production of detailed descriptions of spontaneous conversation as it occurs in natural settings.

NOTES

1. I am not using these terms interchangeably. I have elected to use the term *dominance-seeking* for two reasons. As I have written elsewhere:

> First, problems of definition and measurement notwithstanding, the term "dominance" is common to a variety of disciplines and applied to a wide array of species. Second, at least from the standpoint of earned dominance based on relational or social skill, it appears to be the most parsimonious. That is, attaining some degree of dominance appears to be fundamental to achieving other outcomes such as control, influence, power, and compliance. (Liska, 1990, p. 6).

2. The influence of status and role upon perceptions of various language characteristics such as accent, dialect, and lexical diversity have received considerable attention. Since I am dealing with a rather limited set of language characteristics in the present discussion, I will not review that aforementioned literature. For those readers interested in a broader view of the research on language style, Bradac (1988, 1989) and Street and Cappella (1986) provide excellent discussions.

REFERENCES

Aries, E. (1982). Verbal and nonverbal behavior in single-sex and mixed-sex groups: Are traditional sex roles changing? *Psychological Reports, 51*, 127-134.

Aries, E. (1987). Gender and communication. In P. Shaver & C. Hendrick (Eds.), *Sex and gender* (pp. 149-176). Newbury Park, CA: Sage.

Axia, G., & Baroni, M. R. (1985). Linguistic politeness at different age levels. *Child Development, 56*, 918-927.

Bales, R. F. (1950). *Interaction process analysis.* Chicago: University of Chicago Press.

Bales, R. F. (1970). *Personality and interpersonal behavior.* New York: Holt, Rinehart & Winston.

Bell, R., Zahn, C., & Hopper, R. (1984). Disclaiming: A test of two competing views. *Communication Quarterly, 32*, 28-36.

Bernstein, I. S. (1981). Dominance: The baby and the bathwater. *Behavioral and Brain Sciences, 4*, 419-457.

Berryman, C. L. (1980). Attitudes toward male and female sex-appropriate and sex-inappropriate language. In C. Berryman & V. Eman (Eds.), *Communication, language and sex* (pp. 195-216). Rowley, MA: Newbury House.

Berryman, C. L., & Wilcox, J. R. (1980). Attitudes toward male and female speech: Experiments on the effects of sex-typed language. *Western Journal of Speech Communication, 44*, 50-59.

Berryman-Fink, C. L., & Wilcox, J. R. (1983). A multivariate investigation of perceptual attributions concerning gender appropriateness in language. *Sex Roles, 9*, 663-681.

Bohn, E., & Stutman, R. (1983). Sex-role differences in the relational control dimension of dyadic interaction. *Women's Studies in Communication, 6*, 96-104.

Bohra, K. A., & Pandey, J. (1984). Ingratiation toward strangers, friends, and bosses. *Journal of Social Psychology, 122*, 217-222.

Bostrom, R. N., Basehart, J. R., & Rossiter, C. M., Jr. (1973). The effects of three types of profane language in persuasive messages. *Journal of Communication, 23*, 461-475.

Bradac, J. J. (1988). Language variables: Conceptual and methodological problems of instantiation. In C. H. Tardy (Ed.), *A handbook for the study of human communication* (pp. 301-322). Norwood, NJ: Ablex.

Bradac, J. J. (Ed.). (1989). *Message effects in communication science.* Newbury Park, CA: Sage.

Bradac, J. J., Hemphill, M., & Tardy, C. (1981). Language style on trial: Effects of "powerful" and "powerless" speech upon judgments of victims and villains. *Western Journal of Speech Communication, 45*, 327-341.

Bradac, J. J., Hopper, R., & Wiemann, J. M. (1989). Message effects: Retrospect and prospect. In J. J. Bradac (Ed.), *Message effects in communication science* (pp. 294-317). Newbury Park, CA: Sage.

Bradac, J. J., & Mulac, A. (1984a). A molecular view of powerful and powerless speech styles: Attributional consequences of specific language features and communicator intentions. *Communication Monographs, 51*, 307-319.

Bradac, J. J., & Mulac, A. (1984b). Attributional consequences of powerful and powerless speech styles in a crisis-intervention context. *Journal of Language and Social Psychology, 3*, 1-19.

Bradac, J. J., Schneider, M. J., Hemphill, M. R., & Tardy, C. H. (1979). Consequences of language intensity and compliance-gaining strategies in an initial heterosexual encounter. In H. Giles, W. P. Robinson, & P. M. Smith (Eds.), *Language: Social psychological perspectives* (pp. 71-75). Oxford: Pergamon.

Bradac, J. J., & Street, R. L., Jr. (1986, November). *Powerful and powerless styles re-visited: A theoretical analysis of language and impression formation.* Paper presented at the annual meeting of the Speech Communication Association, Chicago.

Bradley, P. (1981). The folk-linguistics of women's speech: An empirical examination. *Communication Monographs, 48*, 73-90.

Brouwer, D., Gerritsen, M., & De Haan, D. (1979). Speech differences between women and men: On the wrong track? *Language in Society, 8*, 33-50.

Brown, R., & Levinson, S. (1974). *Universals in linguistic usage: Politeness phenomena.* Unpublished manuscript, Cambridge University, Department of Linguistics.

Brown, R., & Levinson, S. (1978). Universals in language usage: Politeness phenomena. In E. Goody (Ed.), *Questions and politeness* (pp. 56-289). Cambridge: Cambridge University Press.

Capitanio, J. P. (1982). *Early experience, behavior and organization in rhesus monkey social groups.* Unpublished doctoral dissertation, University of California, Davis.

Chesler, P. (1972). *Women and madness.* Garden City, NY: Doubleday.

Cowen, G., Drinkard, J., & MacGavin, L. (1984). The effects of target, age, and gender on use of power strategies. *Journal of Personality and Social Psychology, 47*, 1391-1398.

Cronkhite, G. (1984). The perception of meaning. In C. C. Arnold & J. W. Bowers (Eds.), *Handbook of rhetorical and communication theory* (pp. 51-229). Boston: Allyn & Bacon.

Crosby, F., & Nyquist, L. (1977).The Female Register: An emprical study of Lakoff's hypothesis. *Language in Society, 6*, 313-322.

Duncan, S., & Fiske, D. (1977). Face-to-face interaction. Hillsdale, NJ: Lawrence Erlbaum.

Ellyson, S. L., & Dovidio, J. F. (Eds.). (1985). *Power, dominance, and nonverbal behavior.* New York: Springer-Verlag.

Erickson, B., Lind, E., Johnson, B., & O'Barr, W. (1978). Speech style and impression formation in a court setting: The effects of "powerful" and "powerless" speech. *Journal of Experimental Social Psychology, 14*, 266-279.

Esposito, A. (1979). Sex differences in children's conversation. *Language and Speech, 22*, 213-220.

Falbo, T. (1977). Multidimensional scaling of power strategies. *Journal of Personality and Social Psychology, 35*, 537-547.

Falbo, T., & Peplau, L. A. (1980). Power strategies in intimate relationships. *Journal of Personality and Social Psychology, 38*, 618-628.

Fishman, P. (1978). What do couples talk about when they're alone? In D. Butturff & E. Epstein (Eds.), *Women's language and style* (pp. 11-22). Akron, OH: L&S.

Fishman, P. M. (1980). Conversational insecurity. In H. Giles, W. P. Robinson, & P. M. Smith (Eds.), *Language: Social psychological perspectives* (pp. 127-132). Oxford: Pergamon.

Fishman, P. M. (1983). Interaction: The work women do. In B. Thorne, C. Kramarae, & N. Henley (Eds.), *Language, gender, and society* (pp. 89-101). Rowley, MA: Newbury House.

Frances, S. (1979). Sex differences in nonverbal behavior. *Sex Roles, 5*, 519-535.

Franks, V., & Burtle, B. (Eds.). (1974). *Women in therapy: New psychotherapies for a changing society.* New York: Brunner/Mazel.

Fraser, B., & Nolen, W. (1981). The association of deference with linguistic form. *International Journal of Social Language, 27*, 93-109.

Geis, F. L., Brown, V., Jennings, J., & Corrado-Taylor, D. (1984). Sex vs. status in sex-associated stereotypes. *Sex Roles, 11*, 771-785.

Giles, H., & Powesland, P. F. (1975). *Speech style and social evaluation.* London: Academic Press.

Giles, H., & Wiemann, J. M. (1987). Language, social comparison, and power. In C. R. Berger & S. H. Chaffee (Eds.), *Handbook of communication science* (pp. 350-384). Newbury Park, CA: Sage.

Glauser, M. J. (1984). Self-esteem and communication tendencies: An analysis of four self-esteem/verbal dominance personality types. *Psychological Record, 34*, 115-131.

Goody, E. N. (Ed.). (1978). *Questions and politeness.* Cambridge: Cambridge University Press.

Greenburg, B. S. (1976). The effects of language intensity modification on perceived verbal aggressiveness. *Communication Monographs, 43*, 130-139.

Haas, A. (1979). Male and female spoken language differences: Stereotypes and evidence. *Psychological Bulletin, 86*, 616-626.

Hogg, M. A. (1985). Masculine and feminine speech in dyads and groups: A study of speech style and gender salience. *Journal of Language and Social Psychology, 4*, 99-112.

Holmes, J. (1984). Women's language: A functional approach. *General Linguistics, 24*, 149-178.

Holtgraves, T. (1986). Language structure in social interaction: Perceptions of direct and indirect speech acts and interactants who use them. *Journal of Personality and Social Psychology, 51*, 305-314.

Hosman, L. A. (1989). The evaluative consequences of hedges, hesitations, and intensifiers: Powerful and powerless speech styles. *Human Communication Research, 15*, 389-406.

Jackson, S., & Jacobs, S. (1983). Generalizing about messages: Suggestions for design and analysis of experiments. *Human Communication Research, 9*, 169-191.

Keenan, Schieffelin, , Platt, (1976). *Proposition across utterances and speakers.* Paper presented at the Stanford Child Language Research Forum, Stanford University, Palo Alto, CA.

Kenkel, W. F. (1963). Observational studies of husband-wife interaction in family decision-making. In M. Sussman (Ed.), *Source book in marriage and the family* (pp. 144-156). Boston: Houghton Mifflin.

Kramarae, C. (1981). *Women and men speaking.* Rowley, MA: Newbury House.

Kramer, C. (1974). Women's speech: Separate but unequal? *Quarterly Journal of Speech, 60*, 14-24.

Kramer, C., Thorne, B., & Henley, N. (1978). Perspectives on language and communication. *Signs, 3,* 638-651.

LaFrance, M., & Carmen, B. (1980). The nonverbal display of psychological androgyny. *Journal of Personality and Social Psychology, 38,* 36-49.

Lakoff, R. (1974). What you can do with words: Politeness, pragmatics and performatives. *Berkeley Studies in Syntax and Semantics, 16,* 1-55.

Lakoff, R. (1975). *Language and women's place.* New York: Harper & Row.

Lakoff, R. (1977). Language and sexual identity. *Semiotica, 19,* 119-130.

Leet-Pellegrini, H. M. (1980). Conversational dominance as a function of gender and expertise. In H. Giles, W. P. Robinson, & P. M. Smith (Eds.), *Language: Social psychological perspectives* (pp. 97-104). Oxford: Pergamon.

Lim, T. S. (1988, November). *A new model of politeness in discourse.* Paper presented at the annual meeting of the Speech Communication Association, New Orleans.

Lim, T. S., & Bowers, J. W. (1991). Face-work: Solidarity, approbation, and tact. *Human Communication Research, 17,* 415-450.

Linehan, M. M., & Seifert, R. F. (1983). Sex and contextual differences in the appropriateness of assertive behavior. *Psychology of Women Quarterly, 8,* 79-88.

Liska, J. (1986, November). *The problem of perceiving paper and pencil people.* Response presented at the annual meeting of the Speech Communication Association, Chicago.

Liska, J. (1990). Dominance-seeking strategies in primates: An evolutionary perspective. *Human Evolution, 5,* 75-90.

Liska, J., & Hazleton, V. (1990). Deferential language as a rhetorical strategy: The case for polite disagreement. *Journal of Social Behavior and Personality, 5,* 187-198.

Liska, J., Mechling, E. W., & Stathas, S. (1981). Differences in subjects' perceptions of gender and believability between users of deferential and nondeferential language. *Communication Quarterly, 29,* 40-48.

Lockheed, M. E., & Hall, K. P. (1976). Conceptualizing sex as a status characteristic: Applications to leadership training strategies. *Journal of Social Issues, 32,* 111-124.

Markel, N. H., Long, J. J., & Saine, T. J. (1976). Sex effects in conversation interaction: Another look at male dominance. *Human Communication Research, 2,* 356-364.

Marlatt, G. A. (1970). A comparison of vicarious and direct reinforcement control of verbal behavior in an interview setting. *Journal of Personality and Social Psychology, 16,* 695-703.

McArthur, L. Z., & Baron, R. M. (1983). Toward an ecological theory of social perception. *Psychological Review, 90,* 215-238.

McMillan, J. R., Clifton, A. K., McGrath, D., & Gale, W. S. (1977). Language: Uncertainty or interpersonal sensitivity and emotionality? *Sex Roles, 3,* 545-559.

Mitchell, G., & Maple, T. L. (1985). Dominance in nonhuman primates. In S. L. Ellyson & J. F. Dovidio (Eds.), *Power, dominance, and nonverbal behavior* (pp. 49-66). New York: Springer-Verlag.

Morris, W. (Ed.). (1975). *American heritage dictionary.* Boston: American Heritage Publishing Co. and Houghton Mifflin.

Mosher, D. L. (1956). *A pilot study to develop a laboratory measure of verbal aggressiveness* (Final Report No. 044). Columbus: Ohio State University.

Mosher, D. L., & Proenza, L. M. (1968). Intensity of attack, displacement and verbal aggression. *Psychonomic Science, 12,* 359-360.

Mulac, A. (1976). Effects of obscene language upon three dimensions of listener attitude. *Communication Monographs, 43,* 300-307.

Mulac, A., Incontro, C. R., & James, M. R. (1985). Comparison of the gender-linked language effect and sex role stereotypes. *Journal of Personality and Social Psychology, 49,* 1098-1109.

Mulac, A., Wiemann, J. M., Widenmann, S. J., & Gibson, T. W. (1988). Male/female language differences and effects in same-sex and mixed-sex dyads: The gender-linked language effect. *Communication Monographs, 55,* 315-335.

Newcombe, N., & Arnkoff, D. B. (1979). Effects of speech style and sex of speaker on person perception. *Journal of Personality and Social Psychology, 37*, 1293-1303.

Norton, R., & Warnick, B. (1976). Assertiveness as a communication construct. *Human Communication Research, 3*, 62-68.

O'Barr, W. M., & Atkins, B. K. (1980). "Women's language" or "powerless language"? In S. McConnell-Ginet, R. Borker, & N. Furman (Eds.), *Women and language in literature and society* (pp. 93-110). New York: Praeger.

Omark, D. R., Strayer, F. F., & Freedman, D. G. (Eds.). (1980). *Dominance relations.* New York: Garland STPM.

Pandey, J., & Singh, A. K. (1986). Attribution and evaluation of manipulative social behavior. *Journal of Social Psychology, 126*, 735-744.

Philips, S. U., Steele, S., & Tanz, C. (Eds.). (1987). *Language, gender and sex in comparative perspective.* Cambridge: Cambridge University Press.

Piliavin, J. A., & Martin, R. R. (1978). The effects of the sex composition of groups on style of social interaction. *Sex Roles, 4*, 281-296.

Quina, K., Wingard, J. A., & Bates, H. G. (1987). Language style and gender stereotypes in person perception. *Psychology of Women Quarterly, 11*, 111-122.

Rasmussen, J. L., & Moely, B. E. (1986). Impression formation as a function of the sex role appropriateness of linguistic behavior. *Sex Roles, 14*, 149-161.

Rubin, D. L., & Nelson, M. W. (1983). Multiple determinants of a stigmatized speech style: Women's language, powerless language, or everyone's language? *Language and Speech, 26*, 273-290.

Schultz, K., Briere, J., & Sandler, L. (1984). The use and development of sex-typed language. *Psychology of Women Quarterly, 8*, 327-336.

Sebeok, T. A. (1972). *Perspectives in zoosemiotics.* The Hague: Mouton.

Shimanoff, S. B. (1976). *The tyranny of politeness or how to get the fence white-washed.* Paper presented at the annual meeting of the Western Speech Communication Association, San Francisco.

Siderits, M. A., Johannsen, W. J., & Fadden, T. F. (1985). Gender, role, and power: A content analysis of speech. *Psychology of Women Quarterly, 9*, 439-450.

Street, R. L., Jr. (1985). Participant-observer differences in speech evaluation. *Journal of Language and Social Psychology, 4*, 125-130.

Street, R. L., Jr., & Cappella, J. N. (1986). *Message variables: A theoretical analysis.* Paper presented at the annual meeting of the Speech Communication Association, Chicago.

Strodtbeck, F. L., & Mann, R. D. (1956). Sex role differentiation in jury deliberations. *Sociometry, 19*, 3-11.

Thorne, B., & Henley, N. (Eds.). (1975). *Language and sex: Difference and dominance.* Rowley, MA: Newbury House.

Vinson, L., & Johnson, C. (1989). The use of written transcripts in powerful and powerless language research. *Communication Reports, 2*, 16-21.

Wallace, M. (1988). *A critical analysis of stylistic devices speakers use when confronting hostile audiences.* Unpublished master's thesis, Indiana University, Bloomington.

Wiley, M. G., & Eskilson, A. (1985). Speech style, gender stereotypes, and corporate success: What if women talk more like men? *Sex Roles, 12*, 993-1007.

Zahn, C. J. (1989). The bases for differing evaluations of male and female speech: Evidence from ratings of transcribed conversation. *Communication Monographs, 56*, 59-74.

Zimmerman, D. H., & West, C. (1975). Sex roles, interruptions and silences in conversation. In B. Thorne & N. Henley (Eds.), *Language and sex: Difference and dominance* (pp. 105-129). Rowley, MA: Newbury House.

Thoughts About Floors Not Eaten, Lungs Ripped, and Breathless Dogs: Issues in Language and Dominance

JAMES J. BRADAC
University of California—Santa Barbara

T HE language of power or dominance produces effects that vary as a function of contextual differences. This is the important claim offered in Liska's chapter and developed at some length therein. This claim is compatible with the most recent research on message effects that has examined with some fervor contextual influences upon message recipients' reactions to stylistic variation. In this commentary I, too, will discuss the role of context, offering some supplementary observations. Additionally, I will address some other issues that have emerged from my reading of both Liska's chapter and the research literature on language and power, such as types of evaluative reactions to power of style, style as a trait versus style as a state, and explanations for consistently obtained effects in experiments. The several issues will be presented serially, moving from rather particular or localized issues to others that are quite general.

EVALUATIVE DIMENSIONS

Power of style, verbal assertiveness, or dominance of style affects message recipients' evaluative reactions, and such reactions can be modeled as a three-dimensional or cubic space: status (high versus low), intelligence (high versus low), and dynamism (high versus low). These are the primary dimensions of message recipients' impressions of communicator power

Correspondence and requests for reprints: James J. Bradac, Department of Communication, University of California, Santa Barbara, CA 93106.

Communication Yearbook 15, pp. 457-468

(Bradac & Street, 1989-1990). Thus a communicator may be judged as high in status and intelligence but low in dynamism, or high in intelligence but low in status and dynamism, and so on. This suggest that evaluations along the three dimensions can fall into one of eight cells. Status is a group characteristic, for one acquires status by virtue of membership in a valued group, whereas dynamism and intelligence are characteristics of individual communicators (Giles & Ryan, 1982).

Another type of evaluative space, solidarity × attractiveness, is probably less pertinent for power of style than for other aspects of language, such as ethnicity markers. Solidarity is a group characteristic reflecting a message recipient's judgment of similarity to the communicator in terms of group affiliations, while attractiveness is an individual characteristic, involving, for instance, judgments of communicator warmth and friendliness. Still, as Professor Liska points out, some power-related linguistic features may cross both "evaluative spaces," as in the case of an aggressive style that may seem both dynamic and unfriendly.

An important point here is that some linguistic features may produce high ratings on one of the impressions-of-power dimensions and low ratings on the others. For example, commission of grammatical errors and use of action verbs may reduce communicators' ratings of status but increase their ratings of dynamism; conversely, use of adverbials at the beginnings of sentences may increase status ratings but reduce ratings of dynamism (Mulac, Incontro, & James, 1985; Mulac, Lundell, & Bradac, 1986). So are grammatical errors, action verbs, and initial adverbials indicators of high or low communicator power?

This suggests that the global power-of-style or dominance-of-style construct may have to be conceptualized more molecularly in some cases. A communicator may gain the impression of power at one level and lose it at another. From the standpoint of the communicator making language choices, it may be desirable, even necessary, to decide whether status is the most important dimension along which to be evaluated or whether dynamism should be weighted most heavily. In other cases the decision may entail a choice between status and intelligence or between intelligence and dynamism (Bradac & Wisegarver, 1984).

On the other hand, some linguistic or paralinguistic features appear to produce consistent effects across the three impressions-of-power dimensions and even across solidarity or attractiveness. Hedges ("I sort of like it") and hesitations ("I . . . uh . . . like it") seem to be quite generally stigmatized (Bradac & Mulac, 1984; Hosman, 1989). Communicators desiring to appear authoritative or attractive would probably be well advised to eliminate these features from their messages. (However, there are no doubt circumstances in which one strongly desires to appear to be an unattractive know-nothing, and in such circumstances heavy use of these features would be highly recommended.)

IS THERE A POWERFUL STYLE?

Some features of language are noticed by message recipients, and many others are not. This is the way it has to be for language to do what it does best: convey the intentions and thoughts of speakers efficiently and effectively. If we were constantly scrutinizing the details of communicators' messages, constantly aware of language choices made, and constantly asking, "Why did she say it in that way?" we would often miss the point of utterances. Language must be transparent for us most of the time. Frequently we notice particular linguistic features and use these to make attributions about a speaker's ethnic identity or personality traits. These features are marked, and those that are not noticed are unmarked.

The question now is: Is there a powerful style that is marked and used to make the inference "The communicator is powerful"? Or is there instead a powerless style that is marked? Or might it be the case that both powerful and powerless styles are marked, deviating in opposite directions from some neutral point of unnoticed linguistic form? Since to my knowledge this question has not been asked explicitly by researchers, there is much room to speculate. But there are some data that can inform this speculation.

At the outset, it may be useful to point to an apparent conflict in the research literature. Bradac and Mulac (1984) found that ostensibly powerful messages (in the sense of O'Barr, 1981; that is, messages that were terse and direct), messages containing polite forms, and messages containing intensifiers ("I really like it") were rated to the powerful or positive side of the midpoint of a powerful-powerless continuum, while tag questions, hedges, and hesitations were rated to the powerful or negative side of the midpoint. This suggests that both powerful and powerless forms may be marked.

A later study exposed respondents to powerful or powerless messages on a belief-discrepant topic and then had them engage in a thought-listing task (Gibbons, Busch, & Bradac, in press). Respondents generated thoughts about both message substance and style, but virtually all of the thoughts about style occurred in the powerless condition, and these thoughts were negatively valenced. Very few positive thoughts about style were produced for the powerful message. It appears that respondents did not think about this message's style, perhaps because its language, characterized by the absence of tag questions, hedges, and hesitations, was not noticed. This suggests that powerless forms alone are marked.

There is an important difference between the two studies, namely, that Bradac and Mulac used a within-subjects experimental design, whereas Gibbons et al. used a between-subjects design. This means that respondents in the former case were probably able to develop a clear sense of an anchoring midpoint and both positive and negative departures from this point through immediate comparison and contrast (indeed, all respondents rated all powerful and powerless messages, one after another), whereas in the latter case respondents had no immediate basis of comparison (responding to only one message, either powerful or powerless) and thus were unable to establish a midpoint anchor from which to view departures. Yet it appears that for these latter respondents negative "departures" were noticed. This suggests that for these respondents an enduring anchoring point, established not during the experiment but rather in prior everyday experience, resided somewhere in the positive range and from this point low-power language became "visible." Another way of saying this is that these persons may have expected high-power language, they may have found it normal and unremarkable, at least in a formal persuasion context of the sort used in the Gibbons et al. study; by contrast, low-power language may have seemed relatively abnormal and remarkable.

The conflicting results of these two studies are compatible at the level of a general principle: Persons have expectations for language behavior, established locally in a specific situation (as in the within-subjects experiment) or globally across situations (as in the between-subjects case), which are used to process discourse; violations of expectations are noticed, whereas fulfillments are not (Burgoon, 1990; Burgoon & Miller, 1985). Thus powerful forms of language that violate expectations will be noticed, as will expectancy-violating powerless forms. On the other hand, neither powerless nor powerful language will be noticed if message recipients expect this type of language behavior from communicators.

To the extent that this argument regarding expectancy violations and fulfillments is viable, it is reasonable to suggest that neither the powerful nor the powerless style is marked necessarily. Rather, markedness emerges from a violation of stylistic expectations, from the interaction of the language form of communicators and an aspect of the cognitive structure of message recipients. It may be that the low-power style (i.e., a heavy use of hedges, hesitations, and tags) is noticed more often than not because it is unexpected by many people in a wide range of communication situations. Of course, some of the powerful or dominant forms discussed by Liska, such as expletives or insults, seem likely to be widely noticed also, again because they are unexpected.

POWER OF STYLE: A TRAIT OR A STATE?

Some linguistic features do not vary much across situations. For example, a given speaker's dialect or accent may be constant as he or she moves from a bar to a doctor's office to a family dinner. But even here one can see examples of style shifting: Some persons are bidialectal and will shift from one dialect to another in accordance with situational demands (Genessee & Bourhis, 1982), and some persons will broaden their accents to emphasize their identification with valued ethnolinguistic groups if such identification seems desirable (Giles, 1973). Other linguistic or paralinguistic features are highly variable: Baby talk is used in the presence of babies, not when adults only are present; a loud volume of voice is used at a rally, and not when whispering sweet nothings.

What about power of style? Do some people carry a low-power style around with them from situation to situation? Or is use of a low-power style largely context-bound, perhaps reflecting a transitory state of mind? The answers to these questions do not emerge unambiguously from empirical research, but there are data that can inform the discussion. I think it is accurate to say that the early work of O'Barr (1981) and Lakoff (1975) assumed that forms such as hedges, tag questions, and so forth were frequently used by members of particular groups across situations and less frequently used by members of other groups. Specifically, Lakoff's "feminine register" was presumably used more commonly by women than by men; the same linguistic features constituting this register but labeled the "low-power" or "powerless" style by O'Barr were presumably used more commonly by persons low in social power, such as uneducated defendants.

But O'Barr's data were collected in one type of setting (a courtroom) and thus could not be inspected for cross-situational variability, and Lakoff's data were essentially introspective, formed on the basis of her own linguistic intuitions and informal observations. However, a few other studies do offer some clues about the variability/stability issue. For example, analysis of transcripts of a patient in psychotherapy showed that her use of tag questions increased across therapy sessions, presumably because she felt increasingly self-confident (a surprising interpretation; Winefield, Chandler, & Bassett, 1989). On the other hand, filled pauses and various disfluencies may increase as a communicator's uncertainty level or anxiety increases (Berger & Calabrese, 1975). Use of polite forms (which Lakoff and O'Barr see as potential indicators of low power) may increase as a situation becomes increasingly face-threatening to the target of a request or a criticism (Lim & Bowers, 1991).

Thus it seems reasonable to suggest that at least some of the linguistic indicators of low power are situationally variable. Some language forms associated with judgments of high communicator status and dynamism—that is, high-power forms—have also been shown to vary across situations. For example, high lexical diversity has been shown to stimulate judgments of high communicator status (Bradac, Bowers, & Courtright, 1979), and high diversity is more likely to occur in low-anxiety situations than in situations high in anxiety potential (Höweler, 1972). A rapid rate of speech has been shown to produce ratings of high communicator intelligence and dynamism (Brown, 1980), and there is some evidence that speech rate increases as communicator arousal increases (Siegman & Pope, 1972).

To suggest that use of high- and low-power language is situationally variable is not to deny the competing reality of linguistic stability—some persons tend to speak rapidly, others habitually deploy rich vocabularies, others are often hesitant, and so on. There is almost certainly a degree of idiolectal or person-specific variation in the realm of high- and low-power language. There is also evidence for stability at the level of groups of speakers; for example, American men tend to use language forms that produce judgments of high dynamism, while the language of American women tends to elicit judgments of high aesthetic quality (Mulac & Lundell, 1980); some accents exhibited by groups of speakers produce judgments of low status, while other accents produce judgments of high status (Giles & Sassoon, 1983).

But, for some of the powerful and powerless forms, particularly those entailing lexical and syntactic variation as opposed to phonological and paralinguistic variation, there is reason to believe that situational differences may account for more of the variability in language behavior than do between-speaker differences (Zahn, 1989). This is probably worth keeping in mind in light of many published discussions of power of style that emphasize stylistic stability and downplay situational variability.

CONTEXT AND LINGUISTIC POWER

It is difficult to overestimate the importance of context in examining connections between language and power, a point with which Liska would probably concur. The concept of context has already been invoked several times in this essay; for example, stylistic expectations are often context-bound, and situational context is a source of stylistic variation. What else can be said about this important notion?

Perhaps most basically, the very existence of power or dominance depends upon social context—one achieves dominance over others at specific times and places. One cannot dominate all by oneself. Dominance is essentially relational, rather different from, say, intelligence in this regard (which is not to deny the importance of social factors for the latter concept). Moreover, dominance or power is pervasive, crossing all social contexts always; communicators necessarily issue commands regarding how the points of their messages are to be taken by message recipients (Watzlawick, Beavin, & Jackson, 1967).

It seems to me that the essence of power is fulfilling one's intentions socially—in other words, getting what one wants from others. This invites the possibility that in some contexts power may be achieved by using the language of deference and by avoiding use of the language of dominance. Indeed, this should be the case if I want others to see me as a deferential person (of course, others may not accept my use of deferential language as a valid indicator of true deference—Uriah Heep in *David Copperfield* is an instructive case in point). This suggests that the term *powerful style* or *dominant style* should be construed as referring to language forms that tend to produce the appearance of possessing high power or dominance as opposed to forms that have a high probability of leading to the actual fulfillment of any intention whatsoever.

Limiting discussion now to language and the appearance of power or powerlessness, I can suggest that once again context plays an important role. For example, message recipients' generally negative evaluations of the low-power style may be attenuated by contextual factors. Brown, Giles, and Thackerar (1985) found that a communicator's competence rating was not reduced by use of a slow speech rate when the context was described as one where the speaker was lecturing on a technical topic to a naive audience. Presumably in this case persons evaluating the speaker inferred that he intentionally reduced his speech rate in order to meet the needs of his audience. Bradac, Mulac, and House (1988) found that a speaker who lowered his level of lexical diversity, thereby converging to the diversity level of the person to whom he was talking, received especially high competence ratings. In this case lower diversity may have signaled an attempt to accommodate to the other person's style (Giles & Powesland, 1975).

Several studies have found that initial perceptions of speaker status—that is, perceptions existing prior to production of a message—can affect reactions to a speaker's high- or low-power language style. For example, Bradac and Wisegarver (1984) found that a high-status person exhibiting high lexical diversity received maximally high competence ratings and that a low-status person exhibiting low lexical diversity received maximally low competence ratings, with the combinations high status/low diversity and low status/high diversity falling between these extremes. Similarly, Ryan and Bulik (1982) obtained the following ordering of conditions for speaker status ratings, from highest to lowest: Standard American English/high initial status, German-accented English/high initial status, Standard American English/low initial status, and German-accented English/low initial status.

Thus there appears to be an additive relationship between the contextual variable "initial perceptions of speaker status" and status- or competence-related language variables. That is, readers or hearers weigh orthogonally both contextual information about a speaker and speaker-generated linguistic information in forming a unified impression of status or competence level. Perhaps other types of extra-message information about speakers (e.g., gender) are processed along with other types of linguistic information (e.g., gender-linked language) according to this same additive logic (Mulac et al., 1985).

More generally, recent research examining the effects of language variation in context has demonstrated in a large majority of cases that contextual factors qualify the effects of language style. The earliest research on language effects (e.g., early studies of "language attitudes") largely ignored context as a variable, and this now seems to have been a misguided or at least severely limited approach (Bradac, 1990). The systematic examination of context-language style relationships can advance theory construction in the area of language and power, which points to the next and last issue to be discussed here.

EXPLAINING LANGUAGE AND IMPRESSIONS OF POWER

The early work on language and power by O'Barr and Lakoff was largely atheoretical in that forms of language variation were described and linked to social power or gender (respectively), but not explained. The subsequent research on language and impressions of power was also essentially atheoretical, concerned more with demonstrating effects than with explaining them. Research in this area continues to have a largely atheoretical quality. The question, then, is: Why are some forms of language perceived as powerful or powerless and used as a basis for inferring speaker status, competence, or dynamism? Obviously, I will not attempt to answer this question definitively here, but will instead sketch some possible explanations.

One promising avenue is to examine cognitions that mediate perceptions of certain forms of language and subsequent evaluations of communicators: What are people thinking about when they are listening to or reading messages exhibiting high- or low-power styles? This sort of examination could yield a cognitive explanation of consistently obtained effects (Berger, 1989). The Gibbons et al. (in press) study discussed above suggests that people may not think much about the high-power style, at least in a formal situation, but may think quite a bit about the low-power style. Further, the types of thoughts generated by low power included negative thoughts about the speaker's language (not surprisingly) but also negative thoughts about the speaker's ability to formulate arguments. There was also evidence that the low-power style elicited negative thoughts about speaker control, both self-control and control of others.

So one possibility is that use of the low-power style triggers in message recipients thoughts that the communicator has a low level of some specific ability, such as ability to argue, and that this generalizes to a global evaluation of low intellectual competence. Further, thoughts about low self-control and low control of others may lead to the inference that the speaker has low social status. The simple (no doubt overly simple) explanatory model would be as follows: power of style → thought—ability to argue → evaluation—intellectual competence; power of style → thought—control → evaluation—status.

There are other cases where particular language forms are likely to lead hearers to access cognitive categories pertaining to speaker group membership, and these categories may be linked to evaluative reactions. For example, a speaker's use of Black English vernacular may lead to the inference "urban black," which may yield the evaluation "dynamic/low status" (needless to say, not all hearers will share this stereotypical evaluation). Regional accents and ethnic dialects are especially likely to generate in hearers inferences about speakers' group affiliations (Gudykunst & Ting-Toomey, 1990).

The general model in this case is as follows: language → belief about speaker group membership → evaluation of status, and so on. This might be described as an associational model, because it suggests that persons learn to associate language forms with group membership on the one hand

and group membership with specific qualities (status, intelligence) on the other. These associations or pairings constitute ideas formed as part of the process of socialization, and their validity will vary from case to case. Some language forms are strongly attached to specific groups and are accordingly reliable indicators of membership—for example, use of the Welsh language is strongly linked to residence in Wales (of course, this is not an inevitable connection). Contrarily, connections between group membership and particular speaker attributes, such as intelligence, are likely to be objectively unreliable in the individual case.

The associational model described above is also a conventional model to the extent that it entails the learning of stereotypes; that is, connections among particular language forms, beliefs, and evaluative reactions are transitory social constructions that are not biologically inevitable. The major alternative to this view is the "inherent value" hypothesis, which argues that some language forms are inherently and naturally better or stronger than others. There is little support for this view (Giles & Powesland, 1975), although some paralinguistic features tend to be connected naturally to particular evaluative reactions; for instance, speaker loudness may tend to trigger judgments of dynamism as a result of its arousal potential—loud voices are relatively prominent and therefore arousing. However, "natural" connections may be easily overturned by learned conventions, as in the case of movie tough guys, who typically whisper rather than shout (Bradac & Street, 1989-1990).

Apart from explaining the effects of verbal dominance or power via general cognitive models and specific hearer thoughts about language, the potential explanatory value of particular communication theories should be noted (or reiterated) here. Uncertainty reduction theory might suggest that in initial-impression contexts, message recipients will use a communicator's powerful or powerless style to reduce their uncertainty about the kind of person he or she is (Berger & Calabrese, 1975). Perhaps power-related cues are especially important for uncertainty reduction. Such cues may also be important for predicting how rewarding or punishing future interaction will be; perhaps a communicator's use of a low-power style will lead to low "predicted value outcomes" for many message recipients (Sunnafrank, 1986). Thus subjective uncertainty and predicted outcome values may mediate reactions to high- and low-power language.

As suggested above, message recipients' expectations about language may render the low-power style highly noticeable in many contexts via expectancy violations. The suggestion here is that linguistic expectations mediate reactions to power of style. It can be suggested further that violated linguistic expectations increase message recipients' uncertainty about communicators. Thus the prediction would be that in many contexts power of style will be inversely related to message recipients' subjective uncertainty (and, further, directly related to their liking for communicators; Kellermann & Reynolds, 1990).

Finally, communication accommodation theory suggests that a person shifting from a low-power to a high-power style in order to match another person's use of high-power language will be evaluated favorably if the style shifter has a right to claim a high-status role in the situation (Giles, Mulac, Bradac, & Johnson, 1987). The high-power form may indicate the style shifter's effort to present him- or herself in a positive and appropriate manner. Conversely, diverging from another person's use of high power by shifting to a low-power style should be evaluated very unfavorably if, once again, the style shifter can appropriately claim a high-status position. In this case, the low-power form may indicate an intention to communicate inappropriately, to engage willfully in counternormative behavior.

CONCLUSION

Perhaps the major general points to extract from the preceding discussion are these:

(1) What counts as powerful or powerless, dominant or deferential language depends upon the relationship between language style and message recipients' knowledge structures (e.g., expectancies). An implication of this point is that no lexical, syntactic, or phonological forms are always and inevitably powerful or powerless, dominant or deferential.

(2) Power of style varies with speakers (idiolectally) and with situations (normatively).

(3) Effects of power of style, particularly evaluative reactions, can be explained by existing models and theories, but nevertheless there is a strong need for theory construction focused uniquely upon power and for theoretically motivated empirical research on the language-power relationship.

REFERENCES

Berger, C. R. (1989). Goals, plans, and discourse comprehension. In J. J. Bradac (Ed.), *Message effects in communication science* (pp. 52-74). Newbury Park, CA: Sage.

Berger, C. R., & Calabrese, R. J. (1975). Some explorations in initial interaction and beyond: Toward a developmental theory of interpersonal communication. *Human Communication Research, 1*, 99-112.

Bradac, J. J. (1990). Language attitudes and impression formation. In H. Giles & W. P. Robinson (Eds.), *Handbook of language and social psychology* (pp. 387-412). New York: John Wiley.

Bradac, J. J., Bowers, J. W., & Courtright, J. A. (1979). Three language variables in communication research: Intensity, immediacy, and diversity. *Human Communication Research, 5*, 257-269.

Bradac, J. J., & Mulac, A. (1984). A molecular view of powerful and powerless speech styles: Attributional consequences of specific language features and communicator intentions. *Communication Monographs, 51*, 307-319.

Bradac, J. J., Mulac, A., & House, A. (1988). Lexical diversity level and magnitude of convergent versus divergent style shifting: Perceptual and evaluative consequences. *Language & Communication, 8,* 213-228.

Bradac, J. J., & Street, R. L., Jr. (1989-1990). Powerful and powerless styles of talk: A theoretical analysis of language and impression formation. *Research on Language and Social Interaction, 23,* 195-242.

Bradac, J. J., & Wisegarver, R. (1984). Ascribed status, lexical diversity, and accent: Determinants of perceived status, solidarity, and control of speech style. *Journal of Language and Social Psychology, 3,* 239-255.

Brown, B. L. (1980). Effects of speech rate on personality attributions and competency evaluations. In H. Giles, W. P. Robinson, & P. Smith (Eds.), *Language: Social psychological perspectives* (pp. 294-300). Oxford: Pergamon.

Brown, B. L., Giles, H., & Thackerar, J. N. (1985). Speaker evaluations as a function of speech rate, accent, and context. *Language & Communication, 5,* 207-220.

Burgoon, M. (1990). Language and social influence. In H. Giles & W. P. Robinson (Eds.), *Handbook of language and social psychology* (pp. 51-72). New York: John Wiley.

Burgoon, M., & Miller, G. R. (1985). An expectancy interpretation of language and persuasion. In H. Giles & R. N. St. Clair (Eds.), *Recent advances in language, communication, and social psychology* (pp. 199-229). London: Lawrence Erlbaum.

Genessee, F., & Bourhis, R. Y. (1982). The social psychological significance of code switching in cross-cultural communication. *Journal of Language and Social Psychology, 1,* 1-27.

Gibbons, P., Busch, J., & Bradac, J. J. (in press). Powerful and powerless language styles: Consequences for persuasion, impression formation, and cognitive response. *Journal of Language and Social Psychology.*

Giles, H. (1973). Accent mobility: A model and some data. *Anthropological Linguistics, 15,* 87-105.

Giles, H., Mulac, A., Bradac, J. J., & Johnson, P. (1987). Speech accommodation theory: The first decade and beyond. In M. McLaughlin (Ed.), *Communication yearbook 10* (pp. 13-48). Newbury Park, CA: Sage.

Giles, H., & Powesland, P. (1975). *Speech style and social evaluation.* London: Academic Press.

Giles, H., & Ryan, E. B. (1982). Prolegomena for developing a social psychological theory of language attitudes. In E. B. Ryan & H. Giles (Eds.), *Attitudes toward language variation: Social and applied contexts* (pp. 208-223). London: Edward Arnold.

Giles, H., & Sassoon, C. (1983). The effect of speaker's accent, social class background and message style on British listeners' social judgments. *Language & Communication, 3,* 305-313.

Gudykunst, W. B., & Ting-Toomey, S. (1990). Ethnic identity, language and communication breakdowns. In H. Giles & W. P. Robinson (Eds.), *Handbook of language and social psychology* (pp. 293-308). New York: John Wiley.

Hosman, L. A. (1989). The evaluative consequences of hedges, hesitations, and intensifiers: Powerful and powerless speech styles. *Human Communication Research, 15,* 383-406.

Höweler, M. (1972). Diversity of word usage as a stress indicator in an interview situation. *Journal of Psycholinguistic Research, 1,* 243-248.

Kellermann, K., & Reynolds, R. (1990). The role of motivation to reduce uncertainty in uncertainty reduction theory. *Human Communication Research, 17,* 5-77.

Lakoff, R. (1975). *Language and woman's place.* New York: Harper & Row.

Lim, T. S., & Bowers, J. W. (1991). Politeness: Solidarity, approbation, and tact. *Human Communication Research, 17,* 415-450.

Mulac, A., Incontro, C. R., & James, M. R. (1985). A comparison of the gender-linked language effect and sex-role stereotypes. *Journal of Personality and Social Psychology, 49,* 1099-1110.

Mulac, A., & Lundell, T. L. (1980). Differences in perceptions created by semantic-syntactic productions of male and female speakers. *Communication Monographs, 47,* 111-118.

Mulac, A., Lundell, T. L., & Bradac, J. J. (1986). Male/female language differences and attri-
    butional consequences in a public speaking situation: Toward an explanation of the gender-
    linked language effect. *Communication Monographs, 53*, 115-129.
O'Barr, W. M. (1981). *Linguistic evidence: Language, power, and strategy in the courtroom.*
    New York: Academic Press.
Ryan, E. B., & Bulik, C. M. (1982). Evaluations of middle class speakers of Standard Ameri-
    can and German-accented English. *Journal of Language and Social Psychology, 1*, 51-62.
Siegman, A. W., & Pope, B. (1972). The effects of ambiguity and anxiety on interviewee ver-
    bal behavior. In A. W. Siegman & B. Pope (Eds.), *Studies in dyadic communication* (pp.
    29-68). Elmsford, NY: Pergamon.
Sunnafrank, M. (1986). Predicted outcome value during initial interactions: A reformulation
    of uncertainty reduction theory. *Human Communication Research, 13*, 3-33.
Watzlawick, P., Beavin, J., & Jackson, D. D. (1967). *Pragmatics of human communication.*
    New York: W. W. Norton.
Winefield, H. R., Chandler, M. A., & Bassett, D. L. (1989). Tag questions and powerfulness:
    Quantitative and qualitative analyses of a course of psychotherapy. *Language in Society,
    18*, 77-86.
Zahn, C. J. (1989). The basis for differing evaluations of male and female speech: Evidence
    from ratings of transcribed conversation. *Communication Monographs, 56*, 59-74.

Gender and Dominance

CHERIS KRAMARAE

University of Illinois at Urbana-Champaign

JO Liska has provided an extensive review of academic literature that will be welcomed by academics doing language and power work (and thus *should* interest anyone doing communication work). She has obviously done a careful review of studies that consider many of the favored variables, including interruptions, qualifying phrases, hedges, and amount of talk. The review focuses on what these studies say about gender and dominance (even when the studies do not explicitly address dominance behavior). The review also focuses on empirical academic literature to the near exclusion of feminist literature from other genres.

Because of the thoroughness of this specialized review, readers are in an excellent position to address many questions to this body of work. One that will probably come quickly to many is the following: Why is there so little academic research done with dominance and the interaction of gender, race, class, and age? That is, where is discussion of the other social groups that experience frequent areas of comparison and conflict? Liska's review can help us see how as researchers we have treated gender, race, class, and age as isolated variables when in life they are often closely related constructs.

The essay raises another immediate question. Why has there been this "explosion of research" about gender and dominance and power? Who have been the interested sources of this research and what have their questions been? Certainly the answer is not that the most respected leaders of the academy determined this to be a vital area of research. Rather, it is certainly that the women (and men) in the feminist movement have been asking questions and offering answers that form the background stories that are hardly mentioned in this review or in the research studies. So we can ask what impact the social agenda of the movement has had on the questions, experiments, and interpretations reported. The researchers are intelligent and well trained, and have tried to design careful and thoughtful

Correspondence and requests for reprints: Cheris Kramarae, Speech Communication, University of Illinois, Urbana, IL 61801.

Communication Yearbook 15, pp. 469-474

studies. But many of us find that the governing assumptions, the starting questions, and the social agendas of the movement are quite different from those of the academy. In what ways have we tried to resolve these conflicts?

Another immediate question comes to me from reading this review. Why in all this literature does a reader get almost no sense of men talking about the location and practice of their dominance, and the various harms that result from that dominance? The idea that gender—like class and race—is a division of inequality has been widely accepted at least in theory and discussed in this country for almost 150 years. How such divisions and hierarchies are supported or condemned by institutions, including universities where this research is done, is hardly addressed in this literature. These are complex topics that are common in the now vast feminist literature published in other genres inside academe and in feminist literature published outside academe. This review reveals, in a way no single study can, the constriction and distortion of much of our research on language and gender.

Here, however, I am going to ask an even more basic question of this work, and of several new books on language and power (such as Lakoff, 1990; Tannen, 1990). Are we listing as *givens* gender categories that are actually formed by the interaction we try to ascribe to the categories? What if, as much feminist theorizing argues, the categories "women" and "men" are *ideas* that must be learned and reinforced, and what if our gender identities are the result, not the cause, of the behaviors most of the literature reviewed describes as gender related? (A few of the articles or books reviewed do deal, at least in part, with this possibility. Philips, Steele, & Tanz, 1987, and Zimmerman & West, 1975, for example, do consider the ways gender is constructed.) What then would our research questions look like if we treat gender as an idea rather than a real-in-nature dichotomous category? What would our research questions look like if we, working from the writings of such scholars as Anne Fausto-Sterling (1985) and John Stoltenberg (1989) (who themselves have paid attention to dozens of other feminist scholars), were to focus our investigations on how gender gets constructed through talk and other actions, rather than on how girls and boys, and women and men, talk?

Let us posit the following. People are born with various physical characteristics that we can note, including a wide range of genital and gonadal variations. In general, women and men have different reproductive systems, and hormones that may differ in amount. Hormones make some differences in muscle size and fat distribution. These differences may be large or small, depending on life-cycle rhythms and experience. Many men are a bit taller and stronger than many women. The research cited in Jo Liska's review, as well as the research and folklore of most of the Euro-American culture at the present, makes clear that rather than a continuum of variation, we are trained to see two sexes. And then we do a lot of work to continue to see only these two sexes, which we call male and female, boys and girls, men and women. What being a male means differs somewhat depending

upon the decade and geographical location, but in this culture identifying
and being identified as a male generally includes being seen and heard as
being able to control and to own other people and earthly resources, and as
being able to use, or talk about using, the penis as a driving force of life.

John Stoltenberg (1989) writes that the idea of the male sex is like the idea
of the Aryan race. The Nazis believed that the Aryan race really existed, physically in nature, and put a great deal of effort, of life, into making it real. They
constructed a race. He writes, "This happened through hate and force, through
violence and victimization, through treating millions of people as things, then
exterminating them" (p. 30). The belief system shared by people who believed
they were all Aryan could not exist apart from that force and violence as they
defined as inferior and exterminated those they named non-Aryan. Considering the construction of gender, we can say that penises exist, but the notion
that they make for a distinct sex comes from a notion that is enforced by
deeds, actions, and adherence to particular value systems.

Now, instead of using gender in our research as two human nature categories
that exist prestudy, we could ask how gender is experienced and expressed,
about how much or little of our lives is concerned with gender actualizing, with
making ourselves or others sexualized. We can ask what conventional masculinity sounds like in various settings, how it is learned and displayed in speech,
what labels are used for those who do challenge a worldview that divides all humans into two sexes based on a visual inspection of groins at birth.

These questions are already being asked by many (although not in most academic communication studies). For example, women often discuss the degree
of genderness of their lives by talking about the times when they thought they
were talking to another person about work, and all of a sudden the other said
something that made them realize that he was thinking about them as a gender.
They had not been thinking about a sex-class system or their place in that system before being reminded of it. They also talk about times when they are
walking alone at night and are very, very conscious of how any man on the
street might try to sexually objectify and terrorize them, and mark public
streets as his and other men's turf. Some have labeled these experiences "gender shock," as women realize that their sense of self and concerns are rejected
by others near them, by men (usually) who once again have defined women
much more narrowly than they (the men) would define themselves.

This is not to say that there are no such things as girls and boys, women
and men. The categories may be man-made and enforced, but they now
exist. There may be no such thing as a "real" man in any "natural" sense,
but the cultural notion of the real man has central implications for us humans (and for the other species humans have designated). Races are also
created by humans, but their creation has very real consequences.

This is not to say that women have not learned to look and sound the part
of a real woman. From a young age they are taught in this culture that if
they are to be successful women they should use their bodies and actions to

trigger sexual objectification in others. But it is men who are taught that their attention, buying habits, speech, and other actions are to be so closely linked to sexual objectifying that the presence of a real woman is to make them feel very male (and even to think that the woman should consider their expressions of maleness flattering). This is a minisketch of some aspects of the examination of male sexual identity in many feminist sources. They are explanations and constructs that need further discussion. My point here is that they have received very little attention from communication scholars. There has been plenty of time for their inspection, as these are issues that have been raised many times for more than 100 years in the United States.

For example, men's fear that women might lose their "femininity" and become "like males" seems to have been one of the enduring characteristics of Euro-American culture in the last several centuries, although this characteristic has been little inspected in our research. As Elizabeth Cady Stanton wrote in 1868:

> People object to the demands of those they choose to call the "strong-minded" [the term used to describe women in the nineteenth-century women's movement], because, they say, it will make women "masculine." . . . Men profess to have great fear lest women should become men, yet they are always ridiculing the womanly wherever they find it. With what contempt they speak of "woman's way." In fact what they seem to desire in the sex is, a lower order of subservient, obedient men [who will reflect men's opinions and will be charitable toward their vices]. (*The Revolution*, December 31, 1868; see excerpts in Rakow & Kramarae, 1990)

Other "strong-minded" women wrote about the vacillation of "masculine writers" on the question of natural characteristics of women, and about the difficulty of figuring out where one can find "a really good woman" that men talk about so often. Francis Power Cobb wrote that men write of woman as if she is a plastic material "which can be manipulated to fit" men's theories about her nature and status, while male theorists present men as just growing like trees, naturally (*The Revolution*, October 21, 1869). Feminist writer Parker Pilsbury wrote articles about the construction of man and woman, beginning one article, "Mandom, in all generations, exhausts wit and wisdom to find and fix the sphere of woman" (*The Revolution*, July 8, 1869). These nineteenth-century analyses (some of which also considered designations of races as social, not biological, constructs) were not considered important by contemporary academic men and statesmen, and thus are difficult to find today, although by all evidence they were abundant. (There were at least a half dozen "strong-minded" newspapers in the 1850s alone; Russo & Kramarae, 1990.) Similar analyses are not considered important today by most communication researchers published in our journals, and so alternative frameworks for studying gender and language are still not widely used, critiqued, and developed in our academic literature.

What might our research questions and methodology look like if we began from the general explanation of gender above? First, researchers would not treat gender as first cause. While many researchers give lip service to the idea that gender is in some ways a social construct, we still usually begin our studies by sorting everyone out into the two categories of male and female, without discussion of the nature of those distinct categories. Gender categories are generally uninspected even in dominance studies. We *could* consider the lifelong assignment of people to one of these categories of gender hierarchy as *the* most central of dominance behaviors.

The androgyny research in communication in the late 1970s was an attempt to recognize variation in the interests and behaviors of people. But that work, by suggesting that masculinity and femininity were equally valuable and valued, ignored the gender *hierarchy* and, by suggesting that individuals could freely choose the degree of masculinity and femininity they wished to portray, ignored the insistence, present in almost all institutions, of two distinct categories. That work also accepted, in general, present-day constructs of masculinity and femininity as the two poles of the continuum of gender, although we know that these constructs change somewhat from decade to decade.

If we considered the relativity of gender, our interpretations of study results would reflect an interest in the varying significance of gender in different situations. We would have more concern with the sites of gender maintenance. For example, on public streets women have greater exposure to blatant genderizing statements from males than in some other sites. Little academic work has been done on what is said at such times.

Instead of just listing differing numbers of hedges, interruptions, and so on from women and men, we would look at the ways gender is *negotiated* in various situations, and look at strategies women use to cope with the process, including acceptance, withdrawal from the situation or conversation, and confrontation. (Some of this work is now being done in studies of sexual harassment.) Participants' perceived places in class, age, occupation, and race hierarchies would become more important than they are in contemporary research, since the ways we respond to others depend a lot on what safe and effective options we feel we have. We would pay more attention to what benefits come from various verbal initiations and responses in various situations.

Finally, we might recognize some very possible biases in the way academic researchers consider gender questions. We are becoming somewhat sensitive to cultural differences (including those involving cultures based on race groups) in what power and dominance mean and how they are represented in conversations (although this is not evidenced in the books by Tannen and Lakoff). We know that dominance means different things and is expressed differently in a society such as the United States, which has a strong focus on individual rights, and in a society such as Japan, which has a stronger interest in harmony and community. We are learning not to assume that what sounds "feminine" in the United States may sound "human" in another culture. But we still need to recognize that our questions might not represent very well the questions and concerns of many. Gender has particular histories. Women are more likely to perceive gender hierarchies than are men. Women and men with a lot of formal education tend to be less favorable toward efforts to reduce gender inequalities than are people who are less "well educated" (Davis & Robinson, 1991). We are not just researchers, we are also women and men who have our own daily gendered experiences. Our fears, wishes, guilt, defensiveness, and denials are present in our past research and will be in our future.

REFERENCES

Davis, N. J., & Robinson, R. (1991). Men's and women's consciousness of gender inequality: Austria, West Germany, Great Britain, and the United States. *American Sociological Review, 56,* 72-84.

Fausto-Sterling, A. (1985). *Myths of gender.* New York: Basic Books.

Lakoff, R. T. (1990). *Talking power.* New York: HarperCollins.

Philips, S. U., Steele, S., & Tanz, C. (Eds.). (1987). *Language, gender and sex in comparative perspective.* Cambridge: Cambridge University Press.

Rakow, L., & Kramarae, C. (Eds.). (1990). *The revolution in words: Righting women, 1868-1871.* New York: Routledge.

Russo, A., & Kramarae, C. (Eds.). (1990). *The radical women's press of the 1850s.* New York: Routledge.

Stoltenberg, J. (1989). *Refusing to be a man: Essays on sex and justice.* New York: Penguin.

Tannen, D. (1990). *You just don't understand: Women and men in conversation.* New York: William Morrow.

Zimmerman, D. H., & West, C. (1975). Sex roles, interruptions and silences in conversation. In B. Thorne & N. Henley (Eds.), *Language and sex: Difference and dominance* (pp. 105-129). Rowley, MA: Newbury House.

10 Communication as the Interface Between Couples and Culture

BARBARA M. MONTGOMERY
University of New Hampshire

Communication occurs at the intersection of multiple dimensions of social existence, where individuals, dyads, groups, and societies meet. This chapter examines the specific link between couples and culture as they engage in an ongoing negotiation to develop their identities vis-à-vis each other. The chapter describes communication messages by which couples and cultures assert their positions, specifically in relation to autonomy and connection; patterns that have emerged over the last few decades in those messages; and potential patterns accessible to couples and cultures as they negotiate their association.

IF personal relationships came with an instruction booklet, it would be filled with tips for new partners about how to manage the seemingly contradictory states of independence—being separate identifiable selves—and dependence—being an integrated social unit, a couple. The work of both theorists and researchers tells us that this is the fundamental challenge facing members of close relationships (Altman, Vinsel, & Brown, 1981; Baxter, 1988; Rawlins, 1989b). But relationships do not come with "how to" manuals. No set of "dos and don'ts" is distributed to neophyte friends, lovers, or spouses. Relationship development models emphasize that couples must work these things out for themselves, learning and developing ways of relating that are effective for them (Altman & Taylor, 1973; Knapp, 1984; McCall, 1970).

Or must they? After all, relationships exist in the context of a larger social order. Researchers have described a variety of laws, rules, customs, stories, suggestions, and directions that guide couples in the conduct of their relationships (Argyle, Furnham, & Graham, 1981; Ginsburg, 1988).

AUTHOR'S NOTE: I wish to thank Irwin Altman, Barbara Brown, Steve Duck, Aileen Estrada-Fernandez, Jack Lannamann, William Rawlins, Brenda Staples, and Carol Werner for their comments and suggestions on earlier drafts of this chapter.

Correspondence and requests for reprints: Barbara M. Montgomery, Office of the Vice President for Academic Affairs, Thompson Hall, University of New Hampshire, Durham, NH 03824-3538.

Communication Yearbook 15, pp. 475-507

Thus exists a fundamental tension in interpersonal scholarship between seeing dyadic relationships as orderly, predictable interactions that are anchored in the institutions and practices of society and seeing them as opportunities for spontaneous, interpersonal expressions that lead to unique relational experiences. This tension in the scholarly literature reflects a corresponding tension in the actual conduct of personal relationships, namely, how does a couple develop and maintain an identity as a distinct social unit while remaining a part of the larger social order? Or, looking at the issue from society's vantage point, how does society gain the couple's conformity to social norms, a necessity for the society's continued existence, while encouraging the level of independence that allows individuals to develop close associations between themselves?

This dilemma about couple identity is akin to the dilemma about self-identity that is currently commanding much scholarly attention (see, e.g., Berger & Luckmann, 1966; Gergen, 1982; Shotter, 1984). Harre (1983), for instance, describes the need for individuals to develop a "social identity"—one that is consistent with the prevailing social order—and a "personal identity"—one that is individually distinctive. The focal point of this chapter moves from the individual to the couple. At issue is how does a couple develop an identity that fits with society's relationship ideology while still being distinctive enough to sustain interpersonal intimacy.

A key assumption is that this dilemma is dealt with interactively, between society and the couple. That is, the couple and society use communication to manage the tension between being autonomous from one another and being connected to one another. Blumstein (in press) has recently referred to this process as "couple identity work." This chapter develops the idea of such couple-culture interaction by placing it within a theoretical frame and by reviewing relevant research findings that suggest the lines and contours of the interaction.

Making the assumption that couple identity work is an interactive process necessitates the view that societies as well as couples act as communicative agencies. Put most simply, it is assumed that society and a couple can and do mutually act on the basis of messages attributed to each other. Such a view is less familiar in interpersonal studies, than it is in sociological, media, and cultural studies (see, e.g., Billig et al., 1988; Fiske, 1987; Hall, 1979; Shotter, 1984). These fields have more fully integrated the notion that the social order is continuously emerging in a multifaceted process of socialization, interaction, and modification. Thus the social group is viewed as a dynamic agency that pressures members to conform and, at the same time, fosters interaction among members that both reaffirms the existing order and leads to change in that order.

The interpersonal communication field has tended to overlook this process and the significance it has for understanding interpersonal interaction. Lannamann (1991) has suggested that this oversight is explained by at least five ideological biases that characterize most interpersonal scholarship:

(a) a theoretical preoccupation with the individual as opposed to the culture as the focus of selfhood; (b) an assumption that reality is constructed by perceptions as opposed to practices; (c) an overestimation of the role of formal, operational thought in social processes; (d) an emphasis on individual intentionality at the expense of considering collective action, social and material construction of goals, and unintended consequences; and (e) a pervasively ahistorical approach. While this chapter is not entirely free of these biases, it represents an earnest attempt to bridge them in order to explore the establishment and functional management of the couple-society interface within a dynamic communicative system.

Many of the ideas here, particularly about how society acts as a communicative agency with regard to personal relationships, are in the early stages of development and should be viewed as tentative and evolving. Other notions, especially about how a couple's interaction establishes them as a communicative agency, have developed over a decade of work and writing and, therefore, are asserted more tenaciously.

THE THEORETICAL UNDERPINNINGS

The conceptual foundation for an exploration of couple-society interaction must be able to address both interpersonal and cultural contexts of communication. It must capture the interactive and reflexive quality of communication, and it must suggest the kinds of messages by which couples and society manage the dilemma created by opposing needs for autonomy and connection. No single existing theoretical frame meets these criteria. However, relational theory and dialectics, together, suggest potentially useful avenues of scholarly pursuit.

Communication and Relationship Negotiation

Relational theory was introduced by Bateson (1972) and subsequently developed by a diverse, interdisciplinary group of scholars, many associated with the Mental Research Institute in Palo Alto, California (see Haley, 1973; Ruesch & Bateson, 1951; Wilder-Mott & Weakland, 1981). Perhaps the most cogent explication of the perspective is contained in *Pragmatics of Human Communication*, by Watzlawick, Beavin, and Jackson (1967). To date, relational theory has been applied most often in dyadic and small group contexts. However, its basic propositions, which stem from systems and cybernetic models, are relevant for other communication contexts as well. In this chapter they are used to understand the intergroup communication system formed when couples and groups of couples (i.e., social collectives) interact (Montgomery, 1984a). This kind of application is much in keeping with Bateson's (1972) early articulations of a relational perspective.

Before exploring the relevance of relational theory to this broader context, however, it is important to understand its basic theoretical tenets.

Relational theory maintains, first, that relationships and communication are inextricably intertwined. Neither can exist without the other. To relate is to interact, and to interact is to relate. Admittedly, an isolated individual can think about relationships, imagining, planning, or evaluating them. But a relationship does not happen unless or until communication is established between two social entities.

Second, the nature of a relationship emerges from the communication between its members. Relational theory assumes that every message has both a content aspect and a relational aspect. The former conveys referential information about the topic at hand; the latter conveys information about how interactants relate to each other. While the potential themes of relational information are many (see Burgoon & Hale, 1984; Rogers & Millar, 1988), the three that are the most prominent are *control*, or who is to be dominant and who submissive; *affection*, or how positively partners feel and act toward each other; and *affiliation*, or how interdependent partners are (see also Schutz, 1958). Assuming the existence of such relational themes implies that in day-to-day exchanges, interactants are continuously making claims and counterclaims about the nature of their relationship.

Third, these claims and counterclaims are more often communicated *implicitly* rather than explicitly. For instance, in dyadic systems saying "Come here" typically indicates at the content level a desire for a person to move closer. Yet the way "Come here" is said (e.g., loud or soft voice, tense or relaxed posture), its grammatical structure (command versus request), the relational context of the statement (e.g., boss to employee or lover to lover), and the situational circumstances (e.g., boardroom or bedroom) suggests whether the statement is an expression of anger or sexual arousal, an assertion of dominance or an invitation for togetherness.

The existence of implicit, overlaid relational meanings allows dyadic interactants to negotiate relationships with a minimum of social trauma. A person need not risk rejection by explicitly stating to another, "I think we are friends rather than acquaintances; what do you think?" Instead, the two can surreptitiously and safely work out their relationship by repeatedly treating each other like friends or like acquaintances and noting the responses. This explanation is borne out by a number of studies, particularly from Leslie Baxter's program of research, reporting that partners are reluctant to discuss the state of their relationship explicitly (Baxter & Wilmot, 1985), that they readily employ secret relationship tests (Baxter & Wilmot, 1984), and that even at major turning points in the relationship, direct talk is avoided about half the time (Baxter & Bullis, 1986).

A fourth assumption of relational theory is that the negotiation process continues throughout the interactive life of the relationship. Some relationship eras are characterized by rapid change in which claims and counterclaims lead partners to explore new relationship forms. Other eras are characterized by exchanges in which claims tend to confirm existing patterns of interaction. The impact is to stabilize or merely "fine-tune" the relationship definition. Relationship lifelines typically show a number of fluctuations between eras predominated by change and eras predominated by stability (Altman et al., 1981; Gergen & Gergen, 1987; Huston, Surra, Fitzgerald, & Cate, 1981).

This same set of assumptions can be used to understand larger communication systems. A person's social existence occurs simultaneously in a number of dimensions. For instance, Cathy Stone, as a wife, is one half of "the Stones," who join with other couples in neighborhood gatherings, family get-togethers, PTA meetings, and other events in which the interaction defines the larger social unit of a community. Some of this interaction involves Cathy as an individual, but some of it involves Cathy primarily insofar as she is part of the couple called "the Stones." Thus Cathy, as a social communicator, takes part in defining her relationship with her husband, and both of them, *as a couple,* interact with others to define relationships that might be labeled families, communities, and cultures.

In this way, relational theory encourages us to view society and couples as constantly engaged in a process of defining themselves in relation to one another. Communication is at the heart of this process. And while the communication agencies do not possess the physical presence of interpersonal interactants, they nevertheless are recognizable in the force of their collective actions. The means, medians, and modes—realized or idealized—of couples' actions serve to create and maintain a pattern recognizable as a social order. But such an order does not exist in the mere description of a pattern. Rather, a kind of relational ideology emerges in this order that carries with it the power to influence the way couples continue to act, thereby creating a reflexive communication system. Thus "The average couple in the United States has 2.4 children" is not just a descriptive statement; it also carries the persuasive force of the mass of American couples, encouraging any one couple to follow suit. To have many more children or none at all is to be at odds with one's culture; to have two or three children is to affirm the pattern and to strengthen it. Taking this relational view that the social order is simultaneously an antecedent, consequent, and manifestation of intergroup interaction is quite compatible with a number of current scholarly positions about culture and communication (see Corcoran, 1989).

Despite these conceptual advantages, the relational perspective alone does not provide sufficient guidance in addressing the key questions of this chapter. This is because relational theory does not attend closely to the underlying structure of relationship negotiation. Dialectics offers some theoretical support in this area.

Dialectics and Relational Negotiation

The term *dialectic* can refer to a style of reasoning or to a metatheoretical conception of the nature of phenomena. This second sense is relevant here, because it provides a substantive orientation for understanding social processes. Since this orientation has been described in considerable detail elsewhere (see, e.g., Altman et al., 1981; Billig et al., 1988; Rawlins, 1989b), it is only summarized here.

The foundation for this orientation rests on three key notions, two of which closely resemble central assumptions of relational theory. The first is that social phenomena are defined by the relations among their character-istics—be they people, places, goals, or behaviors—not by the characteris-tics themselves. The second is that change is inherent in social phenomena. The third tenet is unique to the dialectical model, and it specifies that con-tradictions are the basis of social processes. That is, social identities emerge from conflicting and interconnected opposites.

The advancement of this latter assumption to a place of prominence by those who study personal relationships has produced insightful analyses of re-lational negotiations among intimates and friends. For instance, Altman et al. (1981) have explored the implications of the openness/closedness and stabil-ity/change contradictions in behavioral patterns for the development of close relationships. Baxter (1988) has identified three contradictions that permeate romantic relationships—autonomy/connection, openness/closedness, and pre-dictability/novelty—along with partners' strategies for managing them during the developmental process. Rawlins (1983a, 1983b, 1989b) has concentrated his application of dialectical analysis on friendships, identifying such inherent contradictions as independence/dependence, affection/instrumentality, judg-ment/acceptance, and expressiveness/protectiveness. Finally, Billig and his colleagues (1988) argue that dialectical contradictions are at the center of so-cial ideologies in the form of opposing beliefs, values, and actions that perme-ate the historical context that people bring to bear on their everyday lives. From a dialectical perspective, then, relationships are forged in contradictions.

THE AUTONOMY/CONNECTION DIALECTIC

One particular contradiction predominates among all others in social con-texts. It is the one formed by the opposites of autonomy and connection. Indi-viduals pursue both contact with and separation from one another. They regulate their personal boundaries, being dependent, sociable, accessible, and affected by each other under some circumstances, and being independent, soli-tary, inaccessible, and unaffected by each other under other circumstances (Alt-man et al., 1981). Rawlins (1989b) argues that one without the other would undermine the very nature of friendship: "Complete independence means no relationship at all, and total dependence constrains both persons by subverting their individual integrity" (p. 171). Baxter (1988) states that this contradiction is "so central to the essence of relationships on definitional grounds alone that it can be regarded as the principal contradiction" (p. 259). Such arguments provide strong support for the centrality of the autonomy/connection dialectic to the development of a relationship between two partners.

The domain of the autonomy/connection dialectic is broader than the interpersonal context, however. Couples are challenged by the need to be apart from and, at the same time, a part of the larger social community. And the social community is equally challenged to both integrate couples with and segregate couples from the larger social order. More detailed examination of these assertions is warranted.

Connection is the lifeblood of society. A society does not just encourage connection, it demands it. A society is, by definition, a product of the interdependent ties among its members. These form the "habits of the heart that are a matrix of the moral ecology, the connecting tissue of a body politic" (Bellah, Maddsen, Sullivan, Swidler, & Tipton, 1985, p. 251). These ties are not merely descriptive of associations, they are the ties of mutual reinforcement. The society ceases to exist if its identifying patterns are not confirmed in the values, beliefs, and behaviors of its members.

In addition to defining social existence, connection also facilitates it. Connection, in the form of a shared sense of how relationships work, reduces uncertainty about how couples will act. Thus outsiders' expectations about what a particular couple is likely to do and say are typically confirmed. The resulting reduction in social stress benefits society as a whole.

Connection is equally as important for the couple. Connection brings with it an understanding of how to act well in society because one is a part of that society. Shotter (1984) explains:

> Part of what it is to be recognized as a competent member of a society by others who are already competent members of it is to be able to sense or know directly—without the need to stop and reflect, nor to have to gather any evidence relevant to the matter—what should appropriately be said or done in most of the mundane circumstances one confronts in that society. (p. 129)

This kind of "insider's" knowledge brings with it a host of social rewards, including acceptance, protection, and security. It also provides a couple with a touchstone for developing their own relationship, a kind of broad-stroked guideline for deciding what is proper and not proper, what is likely to work and not to work for the couple.

In the dialectical tradition, however, it is recognized that autonomy of the couple is also necessary, because it allows them to develop a recognizable identity, separate from society. This identity sets the couple apart, contributes to their sense of worth and specialness, and thereby provides a motivation for continuing the relationship. McCall (1970) argues that this sense of uniqueness, the feeling "that there has never been a relationship (a love or a friendship, for example) quite like theirs," is part of the intrinsic sentimentalism of close relationships.

Establishing autonomy is in the interests of society as well. Autonomy facilitates deviance in the ways couples conduct their relationships, some of which is likely to be innovative and productive. Thus, autonomy is the avenue for continued societal growth and advancement.

Given that both society and the couple have simultaneous and contradictory needs for both autonomy and connection, the two are as likely to work with each other as against to manage the resulting dialectical tension. At issue is to what extent their relationship should be autonomous or connected in nature.

COMMUNICATING AUTONOMY AND CONNECTION

The couple's resources for communicating their autonomy and their connection with society are associated with two major aspects of relating within a social context. The first involves developing a sense of the relationship, what it is and what it is not, the essential qualities that produce the partners' "coupleness." The second involves signaling these qualities of the relationship to others.

Developing a Sense of the Relationship

Two individuals must achieve a significant level of dyadic coordination in order to act together as a couple (Pearce & Cronen, 1980). While it may not be necessary for partners to think about or describe their relationship in exactly the same way, it is important that their actions fit together in a way that both find meaningful. Although couples can achieve this level of coordination in a variety of ways, two general trends predominate, each stressing a different pole of the autonomy/connection dialectic.

Adopting the Social Norm: A Vehicle for Connection

One way to achieve coordination as a couple is for partners to act as others act in similar relationships. In acting normatively, partners achieve a kind of coordination that emanates from the social order. Partners use the knowledge they have of various relationship types within their culture to inform them about their own relationship.

Assuming the existence of relationship prototypes suggests one way for understanding this process. Prototypes are conceptualizations people have of the typical features of different relationship types. A prototype represents the clearest example of a relationship category. For instance, recent research has drawn the basic outlines of people's conceptualizations of friendship and love relationships (Davis & Todd, 1985; Fehr, 1986). These two relationship types share such qualities as affection, trust, and companionship, but differ in terms of passion (fascination, exclusiveness, and sexual desire) and depth of caring (willingness to make sacrifices, being the champion of the partner's interests).

Davis and Roberts (1985) argue that people adopt such prototypical conceptualizations to different degrees, but they describe one type of couple, composed of "rote status assigners," who exist in a "prefab" world created entirely in the social order. The authors compare this kind of couple to chess players who play "only games that have already been written in the chess book— never inventing a new opening or a new pattern of moves" (p. 149). The relational negotiation for this kind of couple is uncomplicated, effortless, and smooth. Passionate conflict is minimal because both partners are following the same guidebook for how to relate. That guidebook contains the conventional rules, roles, and scripts of the existing social order. Considerable research effort has been directed to describing such social conventions in personal relationships (see review by Argyle, 1986; Fitzpatrick, 1988; Ginsburg, 1988).

Establishing a Relational Culture: A Vehicle for Autonomy

Couples also can define their coupleness in such a way as to assert their autonomy from society. Specifically, they can separate themselves from the larger social culture by establishing a culture of their own. Styles of relating can be worked out over time, with partners adapting to each other and their circumstances, negotiating their expectations about appropriate ways to act, to divide responsibilities, and to contribute time and material resources in support of the relationship (McCall, 1970). Partners also can develop unique interpretations of communicative events. Private message systems can emerge that often bear little resemblance to public language rules. These unique understandings and ways of relating make up what has been called a "private culture" (McCall, 1970) or a "relational culture" (Wood, 1982).

The more a couple establishes a unique relational culture, the more they assert their autonomy from society. A unique culture sets them apart from other couples and groups. It emphasizes the differences between what other people do, say, and think and what the couple does, says, and thinks.

Of interest here is what communication characteristics lead to the establishment of a relational culture. The simplest answer is the sheer amount of interaction between partners. That is, the more two people talk with each other, the more likely they are to develop a shared unique approach to the world and to each other. Such an explanation is suggested in a number of theories that link communication and relationship development (e.g., Berger & Bradac, 1982; Knapp, 1984; Miller & Steinberg, 1975).

There is no doubt merit to this conclusion in that it is definitionally impossible for couples to develop a relational culture without any communication. But the frequency of interaction alone is not sufficient to explain a uniquely shared worldview. This conclusion is supported by Stephen's (1986) investigation of geographically separated and nonseparated couples, which indicates that while all communication between partners contributes to defining the relationship, separated couples evidently concentrate and compress culture-building qualities into their more limited interactions.

Denzin (1970) suggests some qualities that count in building a relational culture:

> Each social relationship may be viewed as a peculiar moral order, or social world. . . . Contained within it are special views of self, unique vocabularies of meaning and motive, and, most important, symbol systems that have consensual meaning only to the participants involved. In relationships of long duration . . . rules of conduct are built . . . giving order, rationality, and predictability to the relationship. (p. 71)

More recent work elaborates on Denzin's ideas. In fact, the notion that relationship partners develop unique meanings for behaviors has received wide endorsement and support (Gottman, 1979; Montgomery, 1988; Watzlawick et al., 1967). An almost universal axiom in the study of interpersonal communication is that meanings are not brute facts; they are not indisputable assertions of what is and what is not represented by a particular symbolic behavior. Rather, meanings are a product of social negotiation. To be sure, this negotiation is usually subtle, implicit, and sometimes even unconscious. For the sake of communicative efficiency, we typically build current negotiations upon past ones, making use of established meaning systems, but relying on standardized meanings is not necessary or even desirable at times.

This is particularly so within the context of intimate relationships. Harris and Sadeghi (1987, p. 484) illustrate the potential of created meanings with the example of Sue and Fred, for whom such statements as "Your cooking smells" and "So does your breath" count as acts of affection. Baxter (1987) provides additional examples as she explicates the concept of relationship symbols, which typically take the form of interaction routines and games, special nicknames and idioms, and events, places, or objects that are imbued with relational significance.

Jointly enacted relationship symbols carry an overlaid message that the relationship is special, unique, and differentiated from other relationships. As Hopper, Knapp, and Scott (1981) suggest, symbols such as idioms

> promote relationship cohesiveness and identify relationship norms. Romantic pairs may use personal idioms as expressions of mutual commitment in the task of working out the integration of their behavioral styles.

Interviews with partners in intimate relationships substantiate these conclusions. Among other functions, couples report that relationship symbols represent the closeness, intimacy, and affection between partners, promote togetherness and sharing, and provide a sense of privacy or exclusivity from others (Baxter, 1987).

The notion of *relational schemata* may help to explain how partners develop and maintain such private meaning systems. Planalp (1985) defines relational schemata as "coherent frameworks of relational knowledge that are used to derive relational implications of messages and are modified in accord with ongoing experience with relationships" (p. 9). Relational schemata are pertinent to this discussion to the extent that they are particularized to a specific relationship, providing a reference frame of expectations, salient concepts, stored experiences, explanations, and rules useful for dealing with the partner. Morgan (1986) calls such specific schemata "shared knowledge structures"—a similarity between partners in the way that information is gained, organized, and interpreted that evolves from the couple's interaction.

Creative relational standards for good communication (Montgomery, 1988) are an example of a shared knowledge structure. Creative standards are a unique set of mutually held beliefs that partners develop about what constitutes competent interaction between them. They are distinguished by being decidedly different from more global, societal standards and by being the product of negotiation and agreement between partners. Thus partners are free to agree to count arguing as caring, lying as saving face for the partner, or put-downs as attentiveness. No matter the exact meaning system negotiated, it appears beneficial to relationships to have developed some unique standards (Sabatelli, Buck, & Dryer, 1980; Stephen, 1984).

In summary, communication can function to particularize the association between intimate partners. As with cultures in general, a relational culture arises when a couple develops a meaning system and evaluative norms that set them apart from other couples. These unique ways of engaging in, interpreting, and evaluating communication behavior represent and reinforce the unique identity of the couple in comparison with others. In other words, private meaning systems help intimate partners realize autonomy from the rest of society in the uniqueness and specialness of their relationship.

Summary

To enhance conceptual clarity, I have isolated the discussions of conventional and unique ways of defining relationships. Realistically, however, it is hard to imagine many couples living entirely within the confines of society's conventions or entirely outside of them in their own relational culture. Most couples likely define their relationships by incorporating aspects of both society's norms and uniquely negotiated patterns of relating. At minimum, society's stereotypical conceptions and expectations must inform the couple about their own relationship, either as an ideal to be sought in their relationship or as an initial reference point for creating their own relational culture.

Signaling Coupleness to Outsiders

Asserting autonomy and connection involves not only developing a sense of coupleness, but also communicating that coupleness to others. Couples regularly signal how dependent or independent they are with regard to the rest of society. They do this in two different spheres of social existence— the physical and the psychological.

Couples regulate their *physical accessibility* by controlling the amount and the kinds of exchanges they have with outsiders. A couple signals physical autonomy by separating themselves from others (Baxter, 1987) and by discouraging intrusion when they are in the presence of others (Scheflen, 1965). Conversely, couples can emphasize their physical connection with society by being available and accessible to interact with others. They can spend relatively long periods of time in public places and in close proximity with others. They can encourage interaction with outsiders with various nonverbal immediacy behaviors (Mehrabian, 1981). In so doing, the couple signals a physical connection with society.

Couples also regulate their *psychological accessibility*, stressing either separation from or integration with the meanings, beliefs, and values of society. Separation is communicated with the use of private meaning systems—idioms, games, rituals—in public (Baxter, 1987). Bell, Buerkel-Rothfuss, and Gore (1987) explain how the public use of private message systems enables outsiders to make attributions of intimacy in two different ways. First, outsiders are likely to conclude that two people have a special relationship when they appear to interpret messages differently from others who are present. Second, even when outsiders are not aware of idiosyncratic interpretations, they may be aware of highly coordinated behavior between the intimates that stems from idiom use. Partners' use of secret codes to coordinate leave-takings, requests, or out-of-bounds conversational topics, for example, produce highly synchronized interactions that outsiders are likely to notice. From outsiders' points of view, the use of these kinds of relationship symbols emphasizes the privileged, particularized quality of the couple's relationship and sets it apart from other relationships.

Mandelbaum's (1987) research on partners' joint storytelling activity illustrates another way that couples can signal psychological separation from society—by engaging *together* in an activity that is typically engaged in by *one* person. The unusually high level of interpersonal coordination required in *interactively* initiating, developing, and emphasizing an unfolding story signals not only that the partners shared in a past experience that can be turned into a narrative, but that they also share in the present experience of the telling as well. For the observer, the unusualness of the latter, particularly, is likely to foster a sense of separateness from the couple. Other examples of joint behavior include two partners shopping for clothing for one of them, or two guests bringing the same bottle of wine for the dinner host.

Communication behaviors like these call the public's attention to the couple status of two people by setting them apart from others.

Psychological integration is asserted in opposite ways. Couples employ the traditional meaning system in the presence of others. Thus the sharing of meanings expands past the couple to include the community. Private stories and signals are avoided. Jokes are grounded in community knowledge, not intimate knowledge. The couple partakes in the cultural practices of the day, affirming in their actions the actions of the community.

Some writers have noted the particularly presentational quality that such psychological integration can take (Patterson, 1988; Rawlins, 1989a; Scheflen, 1974). That is, couples sometimes orchestrate their interaction so as to foster impressions about the kind of intimate relationship they would like others to think they have. For instance, Goffman (1959) discusses team presentations or performances that require the conspiratorial cooperation of team members to project and maintain a particular definition of the situation. In a similar vein, an intimate couple can manipulate communicative cues to encourage certain kinds of attributions about their relationship and discourage others. Patterson (1988) gives the example of a quarreling couple who, when they arrive at a party, conceal their argument by holding hands and smiling at each other.

Goffman (1971) has referred to such behavior as "tie-signs," behavioral evidence as to the type, relevant conditions, and stage of a relationship. He presents a detailed analysis of hand-holding as an illustration of how partners can signal the exclusiveness and sexual potential of their relationship to others. Goffman suggests that such tie-signs are often employed when mere proximity is not sufficient to signal the nature of a relationship and to ensure that the definition will be honored by others. Thus a couple arriving at a party where they will be mingling separately may, just before they part, smile warmly at each other or touch hands. Not only does such a display reinforce the intimacy they feel for each other, it also serves "to provide the gathering with initial evidence of the relationship and what it is that will have to be respected" (Goffman, 1971, p. 203).

Public celebrations and rituals are among the most visible of tie-signs that signal a couple's identity to others. A wedding ceremony, for instance, not only legally, socially, and emotionally binds partners together, it also broadcasts new limits on the relationships others may have with the spouses. These limits, set in the social order, are affirmed by the couple when they participate publicly in the marriage ceremony. In Western culture, for instance, a wedding marks the exclusivity of the partners, discouraging outsiders from engaging them in some kinds of interactions—romantic encounters, for instance—and encouraging other kinds of interactions—encounters with couples rather than individuals, for instance.

Thus communication functions to inform the public of the partners' bond and to contextualize that information with an assertion of connection with social norms or autonomy from them. This communication occurs more at the relational level than at the content level. The implicit message of autonomy overlays the joint telling of a story just as the message of connection overlays the couple's participation in social rituals.

Society as an Agency of Communication

Societies have a vested interest in the nature of their constituents' interpersonal associations. A society's ethical, political, and economic well-being is tied to its social well-being. In the cause of self-protection, then, society—the people in collective—attends to the ways its members relate to one another.

Understanding the nature of this attention is complicated by the need to take into account the collective nature of society. The members of any society form a great number of collectives, depending upon the criteria one chooses with which to divvy them up. A list of the collectives with immediate, vested interests in how personal relationships are conducted would have to include children, spouses, educators, lawyers, therapists, religious groups, social scientists—and the list goes on.

Further, sociologists tell us that each of these collectives is likely to have a *distinctive* interest with regard to how personal relationships are conducted (e.g., Bellah et al., 1985; McCall & Simmons, 1982). These interests, while distinctive, are not independent. Rather, they partially repeat, reformulate, and rebut one another. Complicating matters further, any collective usually has more than one set of interests, and these sets are often contradictory and sometimes mutually exclusive (Hall, 1988). This is the essence of the dialectical tension in social processes. Adolescents, for an example, want the protection and security that dependence on parents brings, but also want the feeling of self-determination that can come only with independence from parents. Their age-defining struggle, therefore, tends to be as much with their own conflicting interests as with members of other collectives (e.g., parents).

Given that society contains many collectives with varied and sometimes contradictory interests, the assertion that society is a communicative agency challenges one to specify what exactly constitutes the "agency" and the "communicative" message. Within the frame of relational theory, the agency and the message are metaphors for relational information contained in patterns of the collectives' behavior. These patterns emerge from the ways members of collectives represent the world to one another; how they talk about it, act within it, and present it in classrooms, at family get-togethers, in churches and theaters, on television, and in scholarly texts. Bateson (1979, p. 138) suggests that these generated and enduring patterns of interaction emerge through a process of "practice." Interestingly, a similar notion is advanced within the cultural perspective, which uses the label "practices" to describe the patterns of interaction that carry the communicative force of social ideology (Althusser, 1971).

Relational theory assumes that these messages, or practices, are open to multiple and different interpretations, depending upon the circumstances of the particular communication events. Members of different collectives, with different histories and interests, are likely to interpret patterns differently. What ensues, then, is a process of intergroup negotiation in which collectives work out appropriate meanings for these messages.

This process of negotiation underscores the active, dynamic involvement in a communicative system of both the "readers" of a relational pattern and the "enactors" of a relational pattern. Neither enactor nor reader resigns indifferently in the face of the other's assertions. As in any communication system, each element is constantly informing, interpreting, and influencing the other. In this way a recursive system emerges in which members of society, in this case couples, both read and enact relationship practices. That is, couples actively participate in the reproduction and reconstitution of society's relational ideology.

The Logical Force of Society's Assertions

Assertions by a collective about the nature of things, including its relationship with particular couples, exist in a rhetorical context. That is, the assertions have a logical force. Different possibilities exist for understanding the nature of this force.

First, society's assertions may be *descriptive*. They may assert the way "things are," reflecting how couples actually relate in and to the larger social order. A few have argued that this is so, for instance, in the portrayal of relationships in novels (Alberts, 1986; Ragan & Hopper, 1984). Further, historical tracings regularly cite such literary sources as *The Iliad* or the Bible as evidence for how relationships were conducted in times gone by (see, e.g., Kirkpatrick, 1963). Strong voices, however, have argued that these kinds of social practices distort "reality." Ulrich (1986, pp. 146-148) cites an array of researchers who have found significant inconsistencies when comparing fictional novels, television series, and docudramas to real-life interpersonal experiences. Similar conclusions have been reached in studies of magazine ads (Brown, 1982) and informally communicated folk wisdom (e.g., "Love conquers all," "Women are romantics at heart"; see Walster & Walster, 1978). Parks (1982) examines another social practice in the form of scholarly portrayals of personal relationships in texts and journals and reports significant inconsistencies between the prevailing social scientific depictions and much "empirical" evidence.

A troubling aspect of this debate about whether or not practices reflect reality, however, is the assumption made by both camps that reality can be known apart from socially constructed practices. Only if the two are independent can either be used to validate the other. A growing number of scholars are arguing that this independence does not exist (Gergen, 1985; Harre, 1983; Livingstone, 1987; Shotter, 1984). For instance, Hall (1985) makes the point that "there is no experiencing *outside* of the categories of representation or ideology" (p. 105). Bateson (1979) contends that "all experience is subjective" (p. 31). If one accepts this tenet, then the question of descriptive representation becomes moot. There is no "reality" to be described by social assertions; there are only different forms and contents of social assertions.

An alternative to descriptive force is to view a collective's assertions as vested with *persuasive* force; that is, collectives promote particular ways of life. With this view, a rich and varied literature of social scientific theory has attempted to describe socialization strategies that are grounded in systems of rewards and punishments (see McCall & Simmons, 1982). Some notable examples include social control theory (Nye, 1958), social exchange theory (Thibaut & Kelley, 1959), and modeling-identification theory (Bandura & Walters, 1963).

With regard to personal relationships, rewards and punishments are often formally and explicitly offered as incentives to couples to act in certain ways. For instance, refusing to follow societal norms about incest results in execution in some cultures and imprisonment in others (Goody, 1968). In many societies marrying the appropriate mate, as defined by economic, social, or political criteria, brings riches in the form of dowries, legally sanctioned provisions for offspring, contractual economic alliances between family groups, and formally recognized (often via title) social position and status.

While such formal rewards and costs demand our attention because of their frequently dramatic and extreme nature, the system of informal reinforcements behind social assertions is much more ingrained in social organizations. These are the subtle social promises and threats that underlie personal beliefs, expectations, fantasies, and values. The folk belief that AIDS is a curse levied against those who defy social practices regarding who may properly mate is an example, as is the notion that those partners who "truly" love one another will live happily ever after.

In summarizing this discussion, the following observations are offered. Society is composed of multiple collectives representing special interests in social, political, and economic events. Collectives act as communication agencies with the enactment of various practices that carry implicit assertions about, among other things, the relative autonomy versus connection in the couple-society relationship. These assertions are rhetorically persuasive, in that they influence particular couples' actions. Society and couples actively exchange assertions, negotiating the nature of their relationship. This negotiation is ongoing and evolving. Positions, contexts, and negotiated outcomes continually change. With these stipulations in mind, we can consider some specific social practices relevant to the couple-culture interaction.

Assertions of Autonomy and Connection in Social Practices

Providing a comprehensive catalog of social practices that assert the relative autonomy or connection of couple and society is beyond the purposes of this chapter. Any such treatise, however, would necessarily include exposition of institutional influences, cultural artifacts, and social networks. In the following admittedly limited review, each of these will be briefly described in turn to provide a sense of how collectives, at least in Western cultures, act as communicative agencies concerned with the conduct of personal relationships.

Institutional Influences

Institutionalization occurs when a collective, small or large, habitualizes behavior. This behavior, happening over and over, develops a history that imparts some control over any one happening. As this history is passed on to new initiates in the collective, and as time intercedes between the early, more conscious repetitions and later ones, the behavior takes on a certain objectivity, seemingly existing apart from the group members. Explanations and justifications are constructed to legitimate the institution to those who were not present during its early development. Mechanisms of social control are incorporated into the institutional framework to ensure the compliance of newer generations in the collective (Berger & Luckmann, 1966). This process of institutionalization is represented in the laws, rules, roles, customs, rituals, ceremonies, and scripts of the social order. We typically organize these into areas of interest by recognizing religious, educational, or legal institutions, but the same habitualized practice can serve a variety of interests. An extended look at the custom of marriage illustrates how institutional practices make assertions about autonomy and connection.

The wedding ceremony, itself, has carried diverse messages about autonomy and connection throughout history. In ancient Rome, different ceremonies coexisted. The upper class typically participated in a highly structured ritual called *confarreatio*, which consisted of eating a sacred cake, making a procession to the husband's house, carrying the bride across the threshold, and the bride's then reciting a public and standardized declaration of her attachment to her husband. In contrast, marriage for the lower class was more often accomplished by the couple's cohabiting for a year without separation. The first form implicitly asserted a high degree of connection, in that specific and elaborate procedures formally and publicly tied the couple to the larger collective. By comparison, the second form asserted considerably more autonomy: the formal, public, moment-marking ceremony was replaced by more informal, private, and diffused behavior. Within a broad parameter of what constituted marriage for lower-class couples, they were free to enact any number of variations in their declarations and interactions that resulted in "getting married."

A similar contrast is evident in the historical tracings of the church's and the state's involvement in English marriage ceremonies. In the fourth century marriage was a family matter, with no direct church or state involvement. Over the centuries, however, both forces took on more central roles in legitimating marriage. By the mid-eighteenth century an elaborate set of procedures, stipulated by the Hardwicke Act, was in place. These procedures required that banns be published, that an Anglican clergyman—acting as an agent of the state as well—perform the ceremony in a church, that witnesses be present, and that marriage records be kept (Kirkpatrick, 1963). This progression of changes resulted in the marriage ceremony, as a social practice, asserting more connection between the couple and the collectives represented by the church and state.

By comparison, ceremonial options available to contemporary Americans carry very different implications for the autonomy/connection dialectic. Couples may choose to have a "traditional church wedding" or they may choose to construct their own, unique rites of passage into marriage, with numerous and imaginative possibilities lying between these two extremes. While the presence of a state official is typically required, the multitude of socially endorsed possibilities asserts a sense of autonomy between couple and society.

Bellah and his associates' (1985) broader analysis of marriage sensitizes us to a recent historical trend toward more emphasis on autonomy. They recount numerous changes in marriage practices since the mid-1800s that have increasingly emphasized the autonomy of the couple. These include a narrowing of the kinship network—an important source of social constraint—and the increased emphasis on expressive individualism in patterns of relating.

A similar historical analysis is supplied by Buunk and van Driel (1989), albeit the time frame is more curtailed. These authors identify the 1970s as a time when predominant social collectives became noticeably more accepting and tolerant of many relationship life-styles that had been considered deviant or immoral in earlier times. They give the examples of deliberately remaining single, engaging in premarital sexual intercourse, cohabiting, divorcing, forming friendships with homosexuals, husbands and wives taking separate vacations, choosing to have children when single, and choosing not to have children when married. Yankelovich (1982), in looking at the same era, notes that "virtually all recent normative changes in America have moved toward greater tolerance, openness, choice and a wider range of acceptable behavior" (pp. 85-86). Whether or not this trend will continue through the 1990s is open to speculation, but the pattern established over the last three decades has been one of increased emphasis on autonomy through accepted diversity and choice in marital arrangements.

This same pattern, to different degrees, is evident in other institutional practices related to personal relationships. Laws discouraging nonmarital cohabitation and homosexuality are enforced much less stringently today than in the past (Buunk & van Driel, 1989). Equal opportunity provisions have been instituted in many facets of social life to reduce the incidence of social punishment for variant life-styles. Some religious organizations, such as the American Catholic church, traditionally noted for their strict pronouncements about how personal relationships should be conducted, recently have allowed their members more personal choice in matters such as living together outside of marriage, birth control, divorce, and remarriage. Carried in all of these changes is an assertion of more relative autonomy for couples from the involved collectives.

Cultural Artifacts

In this category are books, films, magazines, music videos, drawings, sculpture, music, public addresses, billboards, newspapers, and the like. These media have a strong fascination with personal relationships, and regularly spin out texts structured around the basic themes of relating. For practical purposes, I have chosen to narrow considerably the window of this review to examine a few representative examples of relevant research in the areas of television, novels, and journalism.

Scholars have shown considerable interest in how the portrayal of relational themes in these media is relevant to how readers of these cultural messages conduct their relationships. Alberts (1986), for instance, argues that romance novels act as relationship guides for their readers, predominantly women and young female adolescents, providing "a model for how romantic talk should be performed and [creating] expectations for how others should and do talk in similar situations, or at least how they expect communicators to talk in real life" (p. 129). Others have similarly stipulated that, at minimum, such public media provide informative, analytic frameworks that viewers consider in evaluating their own and others' personal relationships (Alexander, 1985; Brownstein, 1982). Livingstone (1987) makes this point with regard to the significance of television's content:

> The point is not that television representations, say, indicate, correctly or not, that most women want to get married, or that they incorrectly reflect the proportion of parents to non-parents in our society, but that these representations "set the agenda" for viewers' thinking on these issues. Such representations thus suggest, for example, that there is no viable alternative to marriage and that having children is an uninteresting and unimportant activity. (p. 260)

Turning specifically to the agenda regarding autonomy versus connection between the couple and society, a historical trend similar to the one observed in social institutions is evident in the messages embedded in cultural artifacts. This trend represents a shift, over about a 40-year period, from assertions emphasizing connection to assertions emphasizing autonomy. Kidd's (1975) analysis of women's magazines illustrates the pattern. In the 1950s, magazine articles endorsed secure romantic relationships in which partners adopted traditional sex roles, valued unselfish togetherness, and followed closely society's prescriptions for conducting their relationships. Kidd labels this the "ten easy steps to a happy marriage" genre. By the late 1970s a new genre had emerged and gained strength: the "we can talk it out" genre. Within this frame partners were challenged to develop personal relationships creatively. Meanings were negotiated between partners, and no set standards need guide their behavior together.

A similar developmental theme emerges from Hubbard's (1987) analysis of romance novels published from 1950 into the 1980s. The 1950s stories elevate sexual conservatism and social norms for emotions and behavior. Heroes and heroines cope with their problems by fitting "themselves neatly into the societally ordained stereotypes of the decade" (p. 116). Over the years, however, more and more prominence has been given to interpersonal intimacy, individualism, negotiated meanings, and multiple valid value systems, earmarks of the autonomy theme. In the books published in the 1980s, for instance, heroines come in all manner of shapes, sizes, ages, and backgrounds. They live in complex social worlds, challenged by a range of acceptable goals regarding careers, friendships, and romances. They work out personal solutions to these challenges by negotiating with their social networks.

Livingstone (1987) emphasizes this new complexity of choices as it is offered to contemporary consumers of television soap operas. She presents, as an example, some of the mixed messages about adultery contained in a particular 1984 episode of a British soap. Assertions were made that "old values . . . are no longer respected," and a variety of alternatives, some contradictory, were stipulated and given contextual credibility. Livingstone notes that this multiplicity of positions offered opportunities for the viewer to discriminate among, select from, and contrast different viewpoints. This range of choice, as opposed to narrowly prescribed actions, implicitly asserts more autonomy between predominant social collectives and any particular couple making such choices. Livingstone notes as well, however, that these choices are presented within a wider frame of conventional rhetoric about relationships, so complete autonomy is never endorsed. Nevertheless, current media practices do seem to assert more relative autonomy than in previous times.

Bellah et al. (1985) also make this point about contemporary television, arguing that it does not present a clear ideology. Rather, it merely "casts doubt on everything" at the societal level, thereby justifying a high degree of autonomy between viewers and the social order. The authors cite examples in negative portrayals of big business, government, labor, and smaller task and social groups.

Social Networks

Any particular dyadic relationship exists within a matrix of other relationships. A friend, who is likely to be one of many, has other friends as well. Both friends may have parents, siblings, colleagues, acquaintances, bosses, pastors, spouses, children. The pattern of association among all of these individuals forms a social network. What the people in this network say and do, and what they value, influences any particular dyadic relationship within the network. Relationship beginnings and endings, as well as the quality of the time between, have been linked to influential characteristics of the overarching social network (Altman, Brown, Staples, & Werner, in press; Milardo, 1983; Parks & Adelman, 1983; Ridley & Avery, 1979; Surra, 1988).

These influential characteristics can be substantive, in the sense of direct or indirect messages being communicated by the network about how a particular couple should proceed in their relationship. So parents may directly and explicitly forbid a child to associate with another child. Parents also may influence their child's associations indirectly by choosing a family residence in a rural versus an urban location, by teaching their child particular interpersonal values, or by raising their child in a particular religion (Surra, 1988).

Influential characteristics can also be structural in that the pattern of interconnections among all network members influences the activities of any two members (Bott, 1971). So whether or not networks are tightly clustered or loosely clustered, as well as how these clusters involve the particular couple, makes a difference. Generally speaking, the more tightly clustered and involving the network is, the more influence it has over the couple (Surra & Milardo, in press).

Network influence is accomplished in at least three ways. First, networks facilitate the accumulation of knowledge about partners and their relationship. Partners ask each other's friends about one another and watch each other interact with family. Through this process they reduce their uncertainty about each other and their relationship (Berger & Bradac, 1982). Second, networks provide a baseline for social comparisons that partners use to evaluate their beliefs, values, and abilities associated with the particular relationship. Current loves, for instance, are evaluated on the basis of past loves and other known people's loves (Surra & Milardo, in press). Third, networks function to set and enforce norms (Kelley, 1952). Parents, relatives, teachers, and peers socialize children about the characteristics of a "good" relationship and the qualities a partner should have (Romberger, 1986). These teachings are reinforced by the network with a system of social sanctions that continue to be applied through adulthood (Surra & Milardo, in press).

In general, the nature of couples' social networks, at least in this country, is currently more indicative of implicit messages asserting autonomy over connection between couples and the culture (Bellah et al., 1985). Kinship, religious, civic, and friendship ties are less important, less central, and less strong today than they have been in times past. While the notion of "personal support networks" has gained prominence as a result of what Bellah and his colleagues call the "therapeutic" perspective in contemporary America, these tend to be less influential than more traditional network types. People are more inclined to trust their abilities to work out effective ways to conduct personal relationship matters than to listen to or learn from others. This state of affairs represents a shift from times in this country when social networks were more tightly knit and, therefore, more influential. To be fair to contexts, however, it should be noted that American social networks may never have been extremely close-knit. Tocqueville (1981), in a work originally published between 1835 and 1840, argues, for instance, that the nature of a democracy has always precluded the kind of very close social networks found in some other kinds of cultures. A recent study of the ways people from seven different countries conduct their personal relationships confirms Tocqueville's position (Buunk & Hupka, 1986).

Summary

This analysis identifies a pattern in social practices enacted over the last few decades. That pattern has been toward couples' asserting more and more relative autonomy. Two points temper this conclusion, however. The first is that considerable variability exists among the messages asserted by the various social collectives within any particular time frame. Thus, although we can generalize about a stronger assertion of autonomy in the 1980s, numerous exceptions to this general trend exist. These exceptions indicate that the dialectical tension between autonomy and connection plays out within the body of cultural discourse as well as between culture and the couple. Second, the historical trend is identified by its *relatively* increasing emphasis on autonomy. There can never be absolute autonomy from the culture for the couple, because this would make communication impossible, and society would cease to exist. Thus the trend toward autonomy is observed within a larger set of contextualizing and more diffuse assertions that stress connection between couple and culture.

NEGOTIATING AUTONOMY AND CONNECTION

Couples and collectives have available to them a set of strategies for dealing directly with the contradictory polarities of autonomy and connection represented in their communication. These strategies are incorporated into the negotiation process between a couple and a collective. They represent patterns in the way the couple and the collective work out their association. I have taken a cue from Baxter's (1988) analysis of interpersonal dialectical structures in labeling these strategies. The basic patterns she describes are relevant in intergroup circumstances as well.

Cyclic Alternation

With this strategy the couple and the collective cycle between periods of high autonomy and periods of high connection. This notion is consistent with Chapple's (1970) view that a social system is a "population of oscillators," with actors trying to coordinate their behavioral rhythms. In a similar vein, Altman et al. (1981) have suggested that cycles are evident in dyadic patterns of interpersonal relationships, and the same appears to be so for intergroup associations as well.

Consider the pattern observed over the last 40 years in social practices of moving away from assertions of connection and toward assertions of autonomy. This pattern suggests the possibility of a macrocycle of long duration, perhaps defined over decades, in the relationship between any particular couple and predominant collectives. Indeed, a situation compatible with this pattern, but beginning later in the cycle, is described by one of the couples interviewed by Bellah et al. (1985). Their marriage's beginning was steeped in cultural norms and roles, learned primarily from the family network. A few years later, the couple experienced relationship problems and entered a counseling program that stressed expressing self-interests, working things out, and not following traditions simply because they are traditions. After the therapeutic experience, the couple acted more in terms of a relational culture they worked to create than in terms of societal-level norms.

This change was a negotiated one in that both the couple and particular collectives reinforced each other in the movement toward autonomy. Social practices initially encouraged more connection by implicitly conveying the message, "Conduct your marriage as others in society conduct their marriages." Later, social practices encouraged more autonomy: "Be your unique selves and create your own relationship rules and norms." The couple participated in the negotiation in a confirmatory fashion by choosing, initially, to follow social norms and later to create their own, relational norms. These choices reinforced the position advocated by predominant collectives. Of course, for the cycle to be complete, the couple would have to experience another period of greater connection to social collectives as their relationship matures further.

While the above analysis represents a macro-level view of cyclic alternation, it is productive to think in terms of micro-level analyses as well. Cycles can be much more frequent in number when we consider relationship development issues, for instance. Momentous occasions in the life of a relationship appear to be times of stronger (i.e., higher amplitude in the cycle) connection between collectives and a couple than in the conduct of the mundane. Relationship beginnings and endings, as well as a few intervening critical events (e.g., having a baby, handling an affair, dealing with a death) appear to receive considerably more attention from social networks, institutions, and the media. And while much variation is portrayed in these cultural representations, a good many include an implicit commentary that generally favors following the social rules. It is easy to imagine a typical couple's part in the negotiation as well. Finding out that "they" are pregnant, for instance, leads them to trade the motorcycle for a station wagon, cohabitation for marriage, and the communal apartment for a house (in a good school district, of course). The result of such negotiated connection occurring primarily at key events over the course of the relationship would be to produce relatively frequent cyclic alternations between connection and autonomy.

A conceptual advantage to using the cycle metaphor to understand at least some cases of intergroup negotiation is that it includes the notion of analyzing cycles to examine constituent patterns. Some cycles are more complex than others because they are made up of subcycles. Associations between these subcycles is informative. In intergroup relationships, they could represent patterns within patterns; that is, multiple, overlying approaches for managing the dialectical tension in the relationship between a couple and a culture. One example could be a subcycle with short durations and high amplitudes, representing swings between stressing connection when the couple is in public and stressing autonomy when the couple is in private (more will be said about this kind of segmentation in the following section). Superimposed upon this might be another subcycle with much longer durations but lower amplitudes, representing more subtle shifts between connection and autonomy that occur as cultural values fluctuate over many years.

Segmentation

This strategy is employed when the couple and a collective isolate particular context domains as appropriate for stressing autonomy while other domains are isolated for connection. Both situation and topic define context domains in intergroup relationships. Situation-based definitions lead to distinctions such as formal/informal, with family/with friends, after work/during work, and in front of the children/not in front of the children. Topic-based definitions lead to distinctions being made among various content concerns, such as sex, finances, love, friendship, household responsibilities—any topic around which a couple's interaction takes place.

One of the more pervasive situational distinctions is the public/private one, mentioned earlier. A typical pattern in negotiations between a couple and a collective is that more autonomy is deemed appropriate for private situations and more connection is deemed appropriate for public ones. Rawlins (1989b) notes that this negotiated strategy is central in friendship, allowing friends "to develop and share private definitions and practices while orchestrating social perceptions of their relationship" (p. 166). It also serves the persuasive agenda of collectives well by reinforcing the social order when such reinforcement carries the most influence—that is, in the presence of others—while allowing some measure of intimacy to develop between partners in their private expressions of autonomy.

Thus a couple and a collective can work out an arrangement in which autonomy is stressed in private ("I don't care what they do behind closed doors") and connection is stressed in public. The couple complies by following social norms when in the presence of others, and the collective complies by offering more exact norms for public behavior and more explicit penalties for noncompliance. Blumstein's (in press) discussion of couple identity work, Goffman's (1971) discussion of tie-signs, Patterson's (1988) discussion of presentations, and Scheflen's (1974) discussion of witness cues stem from this distinction between public domains and private domains, and document the many ways couples and society work together to orchestrate public performances that assert their connection.

Segmentation can also occur across topical concerns. Case studies have found that couples vary widely in the topics they single out for stressing connection and autonomy. Concomitantly, the diversity among messages embedded in social practices related to any one topic is great, despite the frequent presence of a general trend. This allows for very different negotiated resolutions to the autonomy/connection dialectic across couples and collectives. The topic of sexual interaction illustrates the point. Blumstein and Schwartz's (1983) detailed study of American couples documents considerable variability in sexual attitudes and behaviors, ranging from extremely traditional to unique, depending on the couple. The corresponding variety in social representations about sexual interaction through books, films, and educational and religious institutions reinforces this variability, facilitating connection in some couples and autonomy in others.

Selection

Selection occurs when a couple and a collective repeatedly and consistently choose to stress only one of the dialectical polarities. Stressing connection, for instance, produces the broad-based traditionalism found in a significant number of couples (Blumstein & Schwartz, 1983; Davis & Roberts, 1985; Fitzpatrick, 1988). These couples live the major portion of their lives together following the predominant collectives' notions about relationships rather than creating their own. Historical analyses of cultural practices suggest that most collectives are not as positive in their positions relative to these couples as they has been in past eras (Bellah et al., 1985; Buunk & van Driel, 1989). Thus it is not surprising that traditional couples feel some measure of uneasiness associated with their extremely consistent pattern of life (Bellah et al., 1985).

The outcome of selection does not seem any more rosy for couples who live primarily autonomously, divorced from society's norms. Research indicates that these couples are more prone to loneliness, alienation, and health problems. They are in therapy at a higher rate than are more connected couples, and their relationships tend to be less satisfying (Buunk & van Driel, 1989). Many of these problems undoubtedly can be traced to the definitional truism that extreme levels of autonomy undermine the very existence of a social order. So, while selection is a strategy that has some proponents among couples, it does not appear to be as effective in managing the dialectical tension between autonomy and connection.

Integration

Integration is evident when a couple and a collective respond simultaneously to both contradictory poles. Two different trends in integrative strategies are evident. The first is *neutralization*, in which a balance between autonomy and connection, a "happy medium," is sought. The couple and the collective craft their relationship so that it is consistently neither highly connected nor highly autonomous. Partners work out solutions to problems, but those solutions do not stray far from social norms. A woman who participated in a study of intimate couples described this sense of balance this way:

> We're traditional in some things, but when I start talking to other people about their marriages that I know, we're not. I get upset if I have to do more than fifty percent of the work, and everybody else [of her women friends] thinks it's super if they have to do only ninety-five percent. . . . So I guess we're not traditional, but this doesn't make us renegades either. Why should helping each other mean we are social outcasts? (quoted in Blumstein & Schwartz, 1983, pp. 391-392)

A second type of integration, *reframing*, is perhaps the most sophisticated of the strategies because it requires a collective and the couple to transcend the apparent contradiction between autonomy and connection. Reframing results in a redefinition of the social situation such that autonomy and connection are no longer poles apart. For instance, the intimate couple who repeatedly stress that the uniqueness of their relationship is a manifestation of the truism that "all intimate relationships are unique" has reframed the tension between autonomy and connection. The couple has concluded that developing their own relational culture conforms to a value deeply ingrained within the larger culture. That is, to be autonomous is to be connected. This conclusion is supported by the equally paradoxical message implicit in many social practices that "all intimate relationships are alike in that each is unique and unparalleled."

Another theme that anchors a reframing strategy is the view that "to be an exemplar is very unusual." Within this logical frame, a couple who is totally connected with a collective has an exceedingly unique and extraordinary relationship. Such a view is expressed by one couple, "Keith" and "Jean," in the Blumstein and Schwartz (1983) study, who feel that they have a very special and unusually happy relationship compared with others in society, simply because they have followed social traditions so closely.

FUTURE RESEARCH DIRECTIONS

The purposes of this chapter have been (a) to situate the issue of couple-culture identity work in the communication process; (b) to ground the thought about this topic in a useful theoretical framework, namely, an integration of relational theory and dialectics; and (c) to relate research efforts to the tenets of this framework. This last exercise points to as many questions to be addressed by future research as answers provided by extant research. Some of the more encompassing of those questions are considered in this section.

How is the couple-culture negotiation of autonomy/connection related to dyadic relationship stages and cultural eras? Both relational theory and dialectics draw attention to the developmental, evolutionary nature of couple-culture interaction and, concomitantly, the emerging nature of their negotiated relationship. The review of existing research presented here hints at possibilities for both linear and cyclical patterns of change as a result of these negotiations over the lifetime of a couple's relationship and over extended historical time lines in Western culture. Obviously, it would be useful to document these trends more clearly, but it also is important to investigate the possibilities for other time-related patterns. For example, a transformational pattern of change (i.e., a sudden and dramatic alteration in the nature of the relationship between a couple and a culture) might be a more frequent response to radical events in the couple's life (e.g., finding out one partner is terminally ill) and in the culture (e.g., the deep-seated political changes currently taking place in Eastern Europe and the Soviet Union). Understanding factors that affect not only the products of negotiation but also the timing, intensity, and efficiency of negotiation is important.

How do collectives' ideologies about personal relationships interrelate within a culture, and what are the consequences of that interrelationship? I have referred in this chapter to couples reacting to the communicative force of the "predominant collectives" in a culture, but this conceptualization is not entirely satisfying. Hall (1985) contends that the notions of dominant and subordinate ideological systems inadequately depict "the complex interplay of different ideological discourses and formulations in any modern society" (p. 104). Better understanding is needed of the nature of that interplay with regard to collectives' interests in personal relationships: How do such interests contextualize one another? What interests are shared among which collectives? How are those interests confirmed and disconfirmed in dialogue among and between collectives? How do couples prioritize conflicting cultural messages about relationships? The answers to these kinds of questions are more likely to emerge as we see applications of cultural studies approaches in the interpersonal field (see Lannamann, 1990).

Under what circumstances are the various strategies for handling the dialectical tensions in the couple-culture relationship most likely to be used? This chapter has discussed four basic strategies: cyclic alternation, segmentation, selection, and integration. Others could emerge from continued investigation. Further, that investigation should attempt to document the conditions under which each strategy is most likely to be used. The conditions undoubtedly will be related to couple types (e.g., the "traditionals" described by Fitzpatrick, 1988), relationship development phases, and cultural types and eras marked by particular political, economic, and social contingencies. It also will be important to understand what roles quality-of-life and quality-of-relationship factors (e.g., satisfaction, happiness, commitment) play, not only as antecedents to choosing a particular strategy, but also as consequences of that choice.

What research models are most useful for investigating the autonomy/connection dialectic? As the interpersonal field becomes more open to methodological pluralism (see Montgomery & Duck, in press), it will be useful to study the couple-culture interface with a variety of approaches. The most valuable of these will provide the "double description" that is such an integral part of relational theory (see Bateson, 1979). That is, the methods of choice should capture the interactive input of both the culture and the couple. The need to attend simultaneously to two communicative agencies has challenged relational researchers studying dyadic interaction, and it is likely to challenge equally those who study couple-culture interaction.

Nevertheless, some promising research models currently exist. Applying Kenny's social relations model (see Kenny & LaVoie, 1984), for instance, would document the dialectical presence of both autonomy and connection in couples' interactions. It would allow researchers to describe the extent to which interaction regularities exist across large numbers of couples within a culture, suggesting a high level of connection between couples and the culture, and it would assess the extent to which interaction characteristics are unique to particular couples, indicating autonomy between those couples and the culture. Similar methods could be used to investigate the complex interrelationships among collectives discussed above.

Altman et al. (in press) emphasize the value of ethnographic methods in the study of cultural practices, especially when contextual and temporal factors figure predominantly in the research issues. They also note that historical approaches are useful for understanding cultural changes over long periods of time. Both of these approaches hold promise for effectively addressing many of the issues raised in this chapter.

Of course, more traditional approaches are possible as well. In applying them, however, researchers must be mindful of the epistemological imperatives of relational theory and dialectics about accommodating and capturing the interactive quality of dyadic and intergroup phenomena, the temporal quality of change, and the contradictory quality of relationship issues.

CONCLUSION

The study of interpersonal communication, an area most directly and consistently concerned with the conduct of personal relationships, has had an exciting but perplexing history. Much of the excitement has been in directing scholars' attention to the everyday, commonplace interactions that make up so much of human life and affect so strongly the quality of that life. The perplexity has come from what can only be seen as radical swings in specifying what, appropriately, should be the focus for study. In the early years, with the prominence of individual-focused paradigms, no couples could be found in studies of interpersonal communication, and today it is a challenge to find anything but couples. The fixation on the individual has been replaced by a fixation on the couple. I believe that both show equal shortsightedness.

As I have stated elsewhere, communication is defined at the intersection of the multiple dimensions of social existence (Montgomery, 1984b, 1988). It happens where individuals, groups, and societies meet. Further, these "meetings" are interdependently woven into the fabric of social experience. Each one is tied to the others through related structures and processes (Bateson, 1979). So any understanding of one intersection must incorporate information about other intersections. In this chapter I have attempted to show how the nature of the person-to-person interface is intimately tied to the nature of the couple-to-culture interface. Each informs the other, and to the extent that we take notice of both, our understanding of couples and culture will be enriched.

REFERENCES

Alberts, J. (1986). The role of couples' conversations in relational development: A content analysis of courtship talk in Harlequin romance novels. *Communication Quarterly, 34*, 127-142.

Alexander, A. (1985). Adolescents' soap opera viewing and relational perceptions. *Journal of Broadcasting and Electronic Media, 29*, 295-308.

Althusser, L. (1971). *Lenin and philosophy and other essays* (B. Brewster, Trans.). London: New Left Books.

Altman, I., Brown, B. B., Staples, B., & Werner, C. M. (in press). A transactional approach to close relationships: Courtship, weddings, and placemaking. In B. Walsh, K. Craik, & R. Price (Eds.), *Person-environment psychology*. Hillsdale, NJ: Lawrence Erlbaum.

Altman, I., & Taylor, D. (1973). *Social penetration: The development of interpersonal relationships*. New York: Holt, Rinehart & Winston.

Altman, I., Vinsel, A., & Brown, B. (1981). Dialectic conceptions in social psychology: An application to social penetration and privacy regulation. In L. Berkowitz (Ed.), *Advances in experimental social psychology* (Vol. 14, pp. 107-158). New York: Academic Press.

Argyle, M. (1986). The skills, rules, and goals of relationships. In R. Gilmour & S. Duck (Eds.), *The emerging field of personal relationships* (pp. 23-39). Hillsdale, NJ: Lawrence Erlbaum.

Argyle, M., Furnham, A., & Graham, A. (1981). *Social situations*. Cambridge: Cambridge University Press.

Bandura, A., & Walters, R. H. (1963). *Social learning and personality development*. New York: Holt, Rinehart & Winston.

Bateson, G. (1972). *Steps to an ecology of mind.* New York: Ballantine.

Bateson, G. (1979). *Mind and nature: A necessary unity.* New York: Dutton.

Baxter, L. (1987). Symbols of relationship identity in relationship cultures. *Journal of Social and Personal Relationships, 4,* 261-280.

Baxter, L. (1988). A dialectical perspective on communication strategies in relationship development. In S. Duck, D. Hay, S. Hobfoll, W. Ickes, & B. Montgomery (Eds.), *Handbook of personal relationships: Theory, research and interventions* (pp. 257-274). Chichester: John Wiley.

Baxter, L., & Bullis, C. (1986). Turning points in developing romantic relationships. *Human Communication Research, 12,* 469-493.

Baxter, L., & Wilmot, W. (1984). "Secret tests": Social strategies for acquiring information about the state of the relationship. *Human Communication Research, 11,* 171-201.

Baxter, L., & Wilmot, W. (1985). Taboo topics in close relationships. *Journal of Social and Personal Relationships, 2,* 253-269.

Bell, R., Buerkel-Rothfuss, N., & Gore, K. (1987). "Did you bring the yarmulke for the Cabbage Patch Kid?" The idiomatic communication of young lovers. *Human Communication Research, 14,* 47-67.

Bellah, R., Maddsen, R., Sullivan, W., Swidler, A., & Tipton, S. (1985). *Habits of the heart: Individualism and commitment in American life.* New York: Harper & Row.

Berger, C., & Bradac, J. (1982). *Language and social knowledge.* London: Edward Arnold.

Berger, P., & Luckmann, T. (1966). *The social construction of reality.* Garden City, NY: Anchor.

Billig, M., Condor, S., Edwards, D., Gane, M., Middleton, D., & Radley, A. (1988). *Ideological dilemmas.* London: Sage.

Blumstein, P. (in press). The production of selves in personal relationships. In J. Howard & P. Callero (Eds.), *The self-society interface: Cognition, emotion and action.* New York: Cambridge University Press.

Blumstein, P., & Schwartz, P. (1983). *American couples.* New York: William Morrow.

Bott, E. (1971). *Family and social networks.* London: Tavistock.

Brown, B. (1982). Family intimacy in magazine advertising, 1920-1977. *Journal of Communication, 32,* 173-183.

Brownstein, R. (1982). *Becoming a heroine: Reading about women in novels.* New York: Viking.

Burgoon, J., & Hale, J. (1984). The fundamental topoi of relational communication. *Communication Monographs, 51,* 193-214.

Buunk, B., & Hupka, R. (1986). Autonomy in close relationships: A cross-cultural study. *Family Perspectives, 20,* 209-221.

Buunk, B., & van Driel, B. (1989). *Variant lifestyles and relationships.* Newbury Park, CA: Sage.

Chapple, E. (1970). *Culture and behavioral man.* New York: Holt, Rinehart & Winston.

Corcoran, F. (1989). Cultural studies: From old world to new world. In J. Anderson (Ed.), *Communication yearbook 12* (pp. 601-617). Newbury Park, CA: Sage.

Davis, K., & Roberts, M. (1985). Relationships in the real world: The descriptive psychology approach to personal relationships. In K. Gergen & K. Davis (Eds.), *The social construction of the person* (pp. 145-163). New York: Springer-Verlag.

Davis, K., & Todd, M. (1985). Assessing friendships: Prototypes, paradigm cases, and relationship description. In S. Duck & D. Pearlman (Eds.), *Understanding personal relationships* (pp. 17-37). Beverly Hills, CA: Sage.

Denzin, N. (1970). Rules of conduct and the study of deviant behavior: Some notes on the social relationship. In G. McCall, M. McCall, N. Denzin, G. Suttles, & S. Kurth (Eds.), *Social relationships* (pp. 62-94). Chicago: Aldine.

Fehr, B. (1986). *Prototype analysis of the concepts of love and commitment.* Unpublished doctoral dissertation, University of British Columbia, Department of Psychology.

Fiske, J. (1987). British cultural studies and television. In R. Allen (Ed.), *Channels of discourse* (pp. 254-288). Chapel Hill: University of North Carolina Press.

Fitzpatrick, M. A. (1988). *Between husbands and wives: Communication in marriage.* Newbury Park, CA: Sage.

Gergen, K. (1982). *Towards transformation in social knowledge.* New York: Springer-Verlag.

Gergen, K. (1985). The social constructionist movement in modern psychology. *American Psychologist, 40,* 266-275.

Gergen, K., & Gergen, M. (1987). Narratives of relationship. In R. Burnett (Ed.), *Accounting for relationships* (pp. 269-288). London: Methuen.

Ginsburg, G. (1988). Rules, scripts and prototypes in personal relationships. In S. Duck, D. Hay, S. Hobfoll, W. Ickes, & B. Montgomery (Eds.), *Handbook of personal relationships: Theory, research and interventions* (pp. 23-40). Chichester: John Wiley.

Goffman, E. (1959). *The presentation of self in everyday life.* Garden City, NY: Doubleday.

Goffman, E. (1971). *Relations in public.* New York: Basic Books.

Gottman, J. (1979). *Marital interaction: Experimental investigations.* New York: Academic Press.

Goody, J. (1968). A comparative approach to incest and adultery. In P. Bohannan & J. Middleton (Eds.), *Marriage, family and residence* (pp. 21-47). New York: Natural History Press.

Haley, J. (1973). *Uncommon therapy.* New York: W. W. Norton.

Hall, S. (1979). Culture, the media, and the "ideological effect." In J. Curran, M. Gurevitch, & J. Woollacott (Eds.), *Mass communication and society* (pp. 315-348). Beverly Hills, CA: Sage.

Hall, S. (1985). Signification, representation, ideology: Althusser and the post-structuralist debates. *Critical Studies in Mass Communication, 2,* 91-114.

Hall, S. (1988). The road in the garden: Thatcherism among the theorists. In C. Nelson & L. Grossberg (Eds.), *Marxism and the interpretation of culture* (pp. 35-73). Urbana: University of Illinois Press.

Harre, R. (1983). *Personal being.* Oxford: Basil Blackwell.

Harris, L., & Sadeghi, A. (1987). Realizing: How facts are created in human interaction. *Journal of Social and Personal Relationships, 4,* 481-496.

Hopper, R., Knapp, M., & Scott, L. (1981). Couples' personal idioms: Exploring intimate talk. *Journal of Communication, 31,* 23-33.

Hubbard, R. (1987). Relationship styles in popular romance novels, 1950 to 1983. *Communication Quarterly, 33,* 113-125.

Huston, T., Surra, C., Fitzgerald, N., & Cate, R. (1981). From courtship to marriage: Mate selection as an interpersonal process. In S. Duck & R. Gilmour (Eds.), *Personal relationships 2: Developing personal relationships* (pp. 53-88). London: Academic Press.

Kelley, H. (1952). Two functions of reference groups. In G. E. Swanson, T. Newcomb, & E. Hartley (Eds.), *Readings in social psychology* (pp. 410-414). New York: Henry Holt.

Kenny, D. A., & LaVoie, L. (1984). The social relations model. In L. Berkowitz (Ed.), *Advances in experimental social psychology* (Vol. 18, pp. 141-182). New York: Academic Press.

Kidd, V. (1975). Happily ever after and other relationship styles: Advice on interpersonal relations in popular magazines, 1951-1972. *Quarterly Journal of Speech, 61,* 31-39.

Kirkpatrick, C. (1963). *The family as process and institution.* New York: Ronald.

Knapp, M. (1984). *Interpersonal communication and human relationships.* Boston: Allyn & Bacon.

Lannamann, J. (1991). Interpersonal research as ideological practice. *Communication Theory, 1,* 179-203.

Lannamann, J. (1990). *Power, equality, and other unintended dialectical constructions.* Paper presented at the annual meeting of the International Communication Association, Dublin.

Livingstone, S. (1987). The representation of personal relationships in television drama: Realism, convention and morality. In R. Burnett (Ed.), *Accounting for relationships* (pp. 248-268). London: Methuen.

Mandelbaum, J. (1987). Couples sharing stories. *Communication Quarterly, 35,* 144-170.

McCall, G. (1970). The social organization of relationships. In G. McCall, M. McCall, N. Denzin, & S. Kurth (Eds.), *Social relationships* (pp. 3-34). Chicago: Aldine.

McCall, G., & Simmons, J. (1982). *Social psychology: A sociological approach.* New York: Free Press.

Mehrabian, A. (1981). *Silent messages: Implicit communication of emotions and attitudes.* Belmont, CA: Wadsworth.

Milardo, R. (1983). Social networks and pair relationships: A review of substantive and measurement issues. *Sociology and Social Research, 68,* 1-18.

Miller, G., & Steinberg, M. (1975). *Between people.* Chicago: Science Research Associates.

Montgomery, B. (1984a). Communication in intimate relationships: A research challenge. *Communication Quarterly, 32,* 318-325.

Montgomery, B. (1984b). Individual differences and relational interdependencies in social interaction. *Human Communication Research, 11,* 33-60.

Montgomery, B. (1988). Quality communication in personal relationships. In S. Duck, D. Hay, S. Hobfoll, W. Ickes, & B. Montgomery (Eds.), *Handbook of personal relationships: Theory, research and interventions* (pp. 343-362). Chichester: John Wiley.

Montgomery, B., & Duck, S. (Eds.). (in press). *Studying interpersonal interaction.* New York: Guilford.

Morgan, D. (1986). Personal relationships as an interface between social networks and social cognitions. *Journal of Social and Personal Relationship, 3,* 403-422.

Nye, F. I. (1958). *Family relationships and delinquent behavior.* New York: John Wiley.

Parks, M. (1982). Ideology in interpersonal communication: Off the couch and into the world. In M. Burgoon (Ed.), *Communication yearbook 5* (pp. 79-108). New Brunswick, NJ: Transaction.

Parks, M., & Adelman, M. (1983). Communication networks and the development of romantic relationship: An expansion of uncertainty reduction theory. *Human Communication Research, 10,* 55-79.

Patterson, M. (1988). Functions of nonverbal behavior in close relationships. In S. Duck, D. Hay, S. Hobfoll, W. Ickes, & B. Montgomery (Eds.), *Handbook of personal relationships: Theory, research and interventions* (pp. 41-56). Chichester: John Wiley.

Pearce, W. B., & Cronen, V. E. (1980). *Communication, action, and meaning: The creation of social realities.* New York: Praeger.

Planalp, S. (1985). Relational schemata: A test of alternative forms of relational knowledge as guides to communication. *Human Communication Research, 12,* 3-29.

Ragan, S., & Hopper, R. (1984). Ways to leave your lover: A conversational analysis of literature. *Communication Quarterly, 32,* 310-317.

Rawlins, W. (1983a). Negotiating close friendship: The dialectic of conjunctive freedoms. *Human Communication Research, 9,* 255-266.

Rawlins, W. (1983b). Openness as problematic in ongoing friendships: Two conversational dilemmas. *Communication Monographs, 50,* 1-13.

Rawlins, W. (1989a). Cultural double agency and the pursuit of friendship. *Cultural Dynamics, 2,* 28-40.

Rawlins, W. (1989b). A dialectical analysis of the tensions, functions, and strategic challenges of communication in young adult friendships. In J. Anderson (Ed.), *Communication yearbook 12* (pp. 157-189). Newbury Park, CA: Sage.

Ridley, C., & Avery, A. (1979). Social network influence in the dyadic relationship. In R. Burgess & T. Huston (Eds.), *Social exchange in developing relationships* (pp. 223-246). New York: Academic Press.

Rogers, E., & Millar, F. (1988). Relational communication. In S. Duck, D. Hay, S. Hobfoll, W. Ickes, & B. Montgomery (Eds.), *Handbook of personal relationships: Theory, research and interventions* (pp. 289-306). Chichester: John Wiley.

Romberger, B. (1986). "Aunt Sophie always said . . . ": Oral histories of the commonplaces women learned about relating to men. *American Behavioral Scientist, 29,* 342-367.

Ruesch, J., & Bateson, G. (1951). *Communication: The social matrix of psychiatry*. New York: W. W. Norton.

Sabatelli, R., Buck, R., & Dryer, A. (1980). Communication via facial cues in intimate dyads. *Personality and Social Psychology Bulletin, 6*, 242-247.

Scheflen, A. (1965). Quasi-courtship behavior in psychotherapy. *Psychiatry, 28*, 245-257.

Scheflen, A. (1974). *How behavior means*. Garden City, NY: Anchor.

Schutz, W. (1958). *FIRO: A three-dimensional theory of interpersonal behavior*. New York: Holt, Rinehart & Winston.

Shotter, J. (1984). *Social accountability and selfhood*. Oxford: Basil Blackwell

Stephen, T. (1984). A symbolic exchange framework for the development of intimate relationships. *Human Relations, 37*, 393-408.

Stephen, T. (1986). Communication and interdependence in geographically separated relationships. *Human Communication Research, 13*, 191-210.

Surra, C. (1988). The influence of the interactive network on developing relationships. In R. Milardo (Ed.), *Families and social networks* (pp. 48-82). Newbury Park, CA: Sage.

Surra, C., & Milardo, R. (in press). The social psychological context of developing relationships: Interactive and psychological networks. In W. Jones & D. Perlman (Eds.), *Advances in personal relationships* (Vol. 3). Greenwich, CT: JAI.

Thibaut, J. W., & Kelley, H. H. (1959). *The social psychology of groups*. New York: John Wiley.

Tocqueville, A. de. (1981). *Democracy in America*. New York: Modern Library.

Ulrich, W. (1986). The uses of fiction as a source of information about interpersonal communication: A critical view. *Communication Quarterly, 34*, 143-153.

Walster, E., & Walster, G. W. (1978). *A new look at love*. Reading, MA: Addison-Wesley.

Watzlawick, P., Beavin, J., & Jackson, D. (1967). *Pragmatics of human communication*. New York: W. W. Norton.

Wilder-Mott, C., & Weakland, J. (1981). *Rigor and imagination: Essays from the legacy of Gregory Bateson*. New York: Praeger.

Wood, J. (1982). Communication and relational culture: Bases for the study of human relationships. *Communication Quarterly, 30*, 75-83.

Yankelovich, D. (1982). *New rules: Searching for self-fulfillment in a world turned upside down*. New York: Bantam.

Close Relationships in the Physical and Social World: Dialectical and Transactional Analyses

BARBARA B. BROWN
IRWIN ALTMAN
CAROL M. WERNER
University of Utah

FOR a long time, social scientists have worked on familiar terrain, investigating the relationship between individuals and society. However, a small number of scholars have extended the scope of this investigation by considering how *couples* relate to society. Barbara Montgomery's chapter provides us with one of the few comprehensive maps for this new terrain. Because her explorations are somewhat parallel to our own, we will try to provide a coherent travelogue by drawing from both explorations. Both parties want to understand how couples in close relationships are both autonomous from and connected to the larger social context. For Montgomery, the question has been how couples relate to society in general. She demonstrates how "the couple and society use communication to manage the tension between being autonomous from one another and being connected to one another" (p. 477). For us, the question has been how couples relate to kin and others over the life course of their relationships, from the time of courtship, through weddings, to placemaking (i.e., the process of setting up a home). In this work, we illustrate how the relationships within the dyad and between the couple and their kin are both relatively autonomous and connected, as reflected in the physical and social contexts of couple relationships.

What is striking from a review of Montgomery's and our own journey is a reassuring convergence of ideas, especially ideas about *how* to explore

Correspondence and requests for reprints: Barbara B. Brown, Family and Consumer Studies, 228 Alfred C. Emery Building, University of Utah, Salt Lake City, UT 84112.

Communication Yearbook 15, pp. 508-521

the connections between couples and society. Drawing from Altman, Vinsel, and Brown's (1981) dialectical analysis of close relationships, our more recent work on transactional analysis (Altman, Brown, Staples, & Werner, in press; Altman & Rogoff, 1987), and Montgomery's chapter in this volume, we will offer what we have learned about useful ways to study couples in context. Although we focus our comments on the study of connections between couples and society, the general features of Montgomery's and our approach may be useful to researchers who wish to study other relationships or social phenomena in context.

The general features of our dialectical and/or transactional approach include the following: (a) an emphasis on the holistic quality of relationships; (b) an assumption that change and stability are both intrinsic to relationships; (c) a recognition that relationships exist in physical, social, and temporal contexts that are inseparable from the processes characterizing the relationships; and (d) an advocacy of the use of a wide range of techniques to investigate cross-cultural and historical variations in the patterns of relationships. To some extent, these features are present, more or less explicitly, in Montgomery's analysis as well. To convey a sense of our somewhat similar journeys, important elements of our respective works are summarized below.

PARALLEL EXPLORATIONS

Montgomery's essay addresses how couples and society negotiate the degrees of connection and autonomy that exist between them. Drawing from Bateson's (1972, 1979) relational theory, Montgomery argues that claims to particular forms or degrees of autonomy and connection are often offered implicitly, although the communication may be explicit as well. Through a continuous process of negotiation, couples and society define, redefine, and negotiate the terms of their relationship. Again drawing from Bateson, Montgomery suggests that these implicit negotiations place interactants along the dimensions of control, affection, and affiliation. Thus connection and autonomy for Montgomery stem from some combination of control, affection, and affiliation messages implicit in the communication between couples and society.

Montgomery then illustrates how current research on close relationships reveals multiple mechanisms for achieving autonomy and connection. For example, partners create a sense of couple unity by creating their own unique relational culture or by adhering to social norms regarding relationships. The couple sustains a unique relationship by selectively regulating their physical and psychological accessibility to outsiders. Conversely, societal groups try to define the relationship with the couple by exerting persuasive forces in the form of institutionalized influences, cultural artifacts, and social networks. Thus couples and society are both active forces in negotiating the degree of autonomy and connection characterizing the link between couples and society.

Although not addressing the links between couples and society, Altman et al. (1981) have proposed a similar dialectical analysis, which they applied to the level of individuals within a close relationship. Altman et al. argue that viable social relationships require both openness and closedness (as well as stability and change). A challenge for partners is to mesh or synchronize, to some extent, their degree of openness/closedness currently and in the future. The close relationships considered in Altman et al.'s analysis occurred between relatively equal partners, and openness generally involved sociability and intimacy. Thus viable relationships were those in which the fluctuating desires for sociability and intimacy by one partner were responsive to and compatible with the fluctuating desires of the other partner. The focus on change and fluctuation was conceived as a necessary antidote to the proliferation of social psychological approaches emphasizing stability, consistency, or homeostasis as a relational goal to the exclusion of needs for change, growth, and movement. Hence the emphases were on changing and oppositional dialectical processes examined from the perspectives of each individual within a close relationship.

Like Montgomery, we have extended the dialectical analysis in our more recent work to include couples, not just individuals (Altman et al., in press). We still address how individuals within a dyad are related to each other, but we add another dimension of analysis by examining how the dyad as a unit is related to family and kin outside of the dyad. Across a variety of cultures we examine how physical and social practices serve to define the degree of connection between members of a couple and between the couple and their kin. Cultures vary widely in the extent to which couples take the initiative in meeting, courting, arranging the wedding, and creating a place to live. By examining who participates in these events, where they take place, and what symbolic and material objects are involved, we can understand how strongly or loosely connected couples are with respect to wider kinship and family ties. By tracking these connections across the phases of courtship, wedding, and placemaking, we demonstrate the changes and stabilities inherent in the connections between couples and kin.

In sum, the particular aims of our work show striking similarities, and we can draw from both approaches to highlight possible new paths of exploration for future research. At times, our different approaches in combination provide broader coverage of this new terrain. For example, our analysis focuses on the behaviors and particular interactions involving couples and their kin, while Montgomery focuses more on mental constructions, such as relational ideologies, or social norms. We rely on ethnographic accounts as untapped sources of data on relationships, while Montgomery provides a scholarly review of studies conducted to reveal relationship processes.

Both our work and Montgomery's reveals several common understandings of the nature of close relationships, of how close relationships can be studied, and of promising directions for relationship research. We have distilled these understandings into succinct statements about relationships, which are discussed in turn below.

Couples are worthy of study, but neither couples nor individuals exist in isolation; all exist within a wider social context and can be profitably understood within that context. As Montgomery notes, social scientists often focus on individuals rather than on other social units, such as couples. Thus many social scientists, especially psychologists, often proceed as if the development of a close relationship depends exclusively upon physical attraction, complementary needs, or other individual-level psychological processes, as they add or combine together across two individuals. Such research fails to acknowledge that individuals and groups from wider social contexts actively participate in the development of any close dyadic relationship. This participation goes beyond the fact that the larger social context often influences the development of individual standards of attractiveness. More important, the wider social context also provides the substantive reality within which any new relationship must develop. By recognizing these multiple social commitments, we try to understand how sons, daughters, siblings, and other individuals with particular kinship ties can simultaneously initiate and nurture a close relationship such as a marriage. The broader kinship, friendship, and other relationship networks participate in individuals' identities and patterns of interaction, facilitating or hindering the development of particular dyadic relationships. Hence relationships do not occur in a vacuum, but within a rich and ongoing network of kin, friends, coworkers, and neighbors. Montgomery's essay and our more recent work (Altman et al., in press) both focus on these issues: How do couples achieve their unique identity as a couple while simultaneously participating in wider social groups?

Although the goal of Montgomery's chapter is to focus exclusively on the couple-society interface, it is useful for researchers to remember that dialectical processes apply to many social units at the same time. For example, dialectical processes characterize individuals as well as couples. An individual must possess a viable individual sense of identity in order to become a viable member of a couple. Just as couples sometimes want to be more autonomous from their families, so do partners sometimes want to be more autonomous from each other.

Because any one relationship exists in the context of others, researchers can add to our understanding by focusing their lens on both finer and larger units within the entirety of the social context. In Altman et al. (in press), we focus on both within-dyad dialectics and dyad-kin dialectics. Each member of the dyad must deal with his or her own individual autonomy/connection needs, protecting and maintaining a sense of individuality and uniqueness while also forging connections with the partner.

In addition, we think interesting research questions can be posed by juxtaposing one level of analysis with another. For example, at the dyadic level, private and unique communications can create openness (or connection) with that other person. At the level of couple-kin relationship, the openness within the dyad can imply closedness (or autonomy) with respect to others. For example, Montgomery describes Goffman's (1971) analysis of how couples hold hands as a reflection of and communication of their own intimacy. This intimate gesture communicates that the members of the couple are connected with each other and are relatively autonomous from others. Future researchers can benefit by explicitly varying their perspective, trying to understand how events in any one relationship have consequences for other relationships, especially with respect to autonomy and connection.

We should also note that these juxtaposed levels do not imply a hydraulic model of autonomy/connection, such that greater connection in one relationship entails lesser connection in others. In the above example of hand-holding, greater connection within the couple means lesser connection with others; however, other patterns can emerge as well. For example, in Altman et al. (in press) we describe how wedding showers are often events that serve to underscore gender identity, affirming links between a bride-to-be and her female peers. These celebrations underscore the fact that although a woman may be taking on the new identity of wife, an identity that connects her to her husband, she is still a woman, and this aspect of her identity contributes to her sense of individuality within her marriage as well as her sense of connection to groups of women beyond the marriage. Hence both individuality (within the marriage) and connection (beyond the marriage) are enhanced. Similarly, many young couples are expected to invite one or both sets of their parents to dinner early in the marriage. This dinner affirms connections between the generations while simultaneously providing an occasion to display the couple members' connections to each other. In sum, the degree of autonomy/connection in any one relationship may create patterns of autonomy/connection with respect to other relationships with other individuals or groups.

A dialectical analysis characterizes the relationship between couples and society: Couples are both autonomous from and connected to others, and these oppositional relationships operate in a unified and dynamic fashion. Montgomery's essay dovetails well with the dialectical analysis we presented in 1981. Specifically, we agree that dialectical analyses serve to highlight three fundamental aspects of relationship processes: opposition, unity, and change. Although researchers can use and have used a wide variety of themes to characterize the dialectical opposition (see Montgomery's essay and Baxter, 1988, for a review), both we and Montgomery have opted for themes that capture the classic dialectical opposition between the individual and society. Montgomery's choice of the autonomy/connection and our choice of openness/closedness describe the fundamental tension involved in developing and maintaining a unique social unit (e.g., person, couple, family) in relationship to larger groups (e.g., families, friends, society at large). Although we use different terms, we agree that couples are both autonomous from and a part of society at the same time.

We also agree that these oppositions exist within a unified system. Autonomy is understood in reference to connection and vice versa. So the opposing poles in a dialectical analysis help to define each other; both poles are necessary for the existence of either. Furthermore, change is inherent in any dialectical process, such that autonomy or connection may dominate only temporarily. When applied to couples in relationship to society, the couple must establish their autonomous existence within the context of their connections to society. The relative strength of autonomy and connection will change over time, creating different qualitative experiences of relationships.

Although both we and Montgomery adhere to the assumption of the unity of · dialectical opposites, this assumption plays out differently for each of us. Sometimes, in Montgomery's descriptions of temporal cycles of autonomy and connection or types of couples, it may be easy for the reader to miss the point that autonomy and connection do not completely alternate over time, one following the other. Instead, they always coexist (a point Montgomery makes but does not stress). A dialectical approach assumes that the coexistence of polar opposites is necessary at all times, as both poles give meaning to one another. Such cycles involve *relative* amounts of autonomy and connection; they are both present in varying degrees at all times.

Similarly, it would be impossible for one pole of the dialectic to determine the other pole completely. Thus connection gives meaning to but does not completely determine the nature of autonomy. At times, when describing couples whose actions are dominated by social conventions, the forces toward connection overshadow the existence of autonomy. Lest readers begin to think about couples as completely dominated by society, it is useful to reiterate that autonomy and connection are always intermeshed.

Indeed, the continued independent existence of forces toward autonomy is implicit in Montgomery's discussion of how privacy characterizes times when couples are most autonomous from society. She argues that social norms guide behavior when couples are in the presence of others, but society provides fewer and less exact norms for private behavior. Because societal advice on private moments and interactions may be inexact, sparse, or idealized (e.g., mass media portrayals of home life rarely ring true), the couple must themselves negotiate very private aspects of their relationship. Because there is less advice available from society, private aspects of relationships attain a certain degree of autonomy from society. Therefore, because community rules and guidelines are relatively absent, intimate communications should have more potential for creativity, variety, spontaneity, and uniqueness. Thus the seeds of autonomy are present in the very agreement between society and individuals to respect the private moments of relationships.

The emphasis on a dialectical unity of opposing forces also suggests a fruitful area for future exploration. Because forces toward autonomy and connection coexist at all times, research can be directed toward describing manifestations of this unity. Montgomery mentions examples of the concept of relationship symbols given by Baxter (1987), "which typically take the form of interaction routines and games, special nicknames and idioms, and events, places, or objects that are imbued with relational significance" (p. 484). Hence even individualistic overtures take into account the social standpoint, which Montgomery acknowledges elsewhere in the essay. Our point is that not only is there utility in identifying whether autonomy or connection dominate, there is also utility in noting how those themes intermingle and are simultaneously present and expressed at each phase of the relationship.

Autonomy and connection (a) are revealed through multiple levels of behavior, (b) are reflected in the physical environment, and (c) subsume multiple social processes.

Multiple levels of behavior. Relationships involve behaviors at many levels of functioning, and are impossible to understand when artificially divided into isolated systems (e.g., cognition, overt action, perception). Although it may be impossible to study all levels of behavior exhaustively, researchers can benefit by examining several. Montgomery, for example, attends to explicit and implicit aspects of communication, with the former emphasizing content and the latter emphasizing nonverbal or paraverbal behaviors. She also addresses a variety of cognitive aspects of relationships, including couples' understandings of norms, relational ideologies, and interpersonal expectations, and the way in which mass media and friends are often a source of these particular standards for interpersonal behavior. In our work, we argue that the physical environment is also an important aspect of social context that is inherent to close relationships. In combination, we and Montgomery propose a broad overview of the sources of information reflecting connections between couples and society.

A comparison of our two approaches also shows that both proximal and distal perspectives on relationships can be useful. Montgomery provides a distal perspective when she demonstrates how communications media, such as television or print publications, communicate standards that filter down to particular relationships. We address more immediate and proximal aspects of environments, demonstrating how symbolic and functional qualities of possessions, places, and ceremonial objects reflect different degrees of autonomy or connection in relationships. Similarly, Montgomery interprets the more general messages of events, such as suggesting that a traditional ceremony implies connection to society and a nontraditional one implies autonomy. We interpret the multitude of more specific messages within wedding ceremonies, which can reveal, for example, that even traditional Welsh marriages focus on how autonomous the couple will be from their kin. The message to future explorers is that couple-society connections involve environmental, social, and institutional levels of behavior as viewed from proximal and distal perspectives.

Reflection in the physical environment. The physical environment is one of the multiple levels of behavior that establish autonomy and connection.

Montgomery, for example, addresses how cultural artifacts and mass media are physical environmental entities that establish autonomy and connection between couples and society. Because the physical environment is so often overlooked in investigations of relationships, we will elaborate on its role. Our ethnographic analyses focus on places, ceremonial actions, and artifacts as keys to understanding relationships. Everyday and ceremonial artifacts and places are active contributors to meaning, especially to definitions of the relationships between couples and kin. To illustrate: In Taiwan the engagement process traditionally involved only the parents and the ancestors; the very physical absence of the couple reflected the fact that marital relationships were established in the interests of the family rather than of the couple. Furthermore, because Taiwanese couples live with and abide by the authority of the male's parents, many of the social and physical environmental aspects of marriage and placemaking practices illustrate how the bride must weaken connections with her own family and create connections with her husband's family. For example, as the bride leaves her house for the wedding, she literally turns her back on her family altar before leaving and a brother spits at her departing carriage, signifying that just as water cannot return to a vessel, she cannot return to her natal family. In her new home she must demonstrate ritual allegiance to the altar of her husband's ancestors and perform domestic service for his entire family. For a day or so after the wedding, because tradition holds that she does not yet begin her domestic service, she recognizes her new connections to her husband's family by leaving a packet of money to apologize for the fact that she is not yet doing her work. Thus the use of the physical environment in the transition to the married relationship conveys vividly the new interpersonal negotiations concerning connection and autonomy.

Another way in which researchers can recognize the importance of the physical context is to notice how essential the physical environment is to interpersonal processes that are usually discussed in a more abstract way, devoid of context. For example, Montgomery notes that opportunities for private talks enhance the development of a dyadic culture. An examination of how, where, and when these talks take place could show how couples' relationships must attain a certain maturity before couples are allowed by others and by themselves to have such private encounters. According to an ethnographic study of courtship in Wales (Leonard, 1980), initial courtship overtures take place in public places, with others present. In order for the relationship to progress, the couple seeks out more private encounters that, Montgomery would argue, create a public image of "coupleness." Ultimately, as the couple becomes formally engaged, the woman's parents allow them greater privacy in her home than was permitted at earlier phases of the relationship. To use Montgomery's terms, different places correspond to different norms and definitions of the relationship. Places provide for the qualities, such as privacy, that are needed to maintain the viability of the relationship. The couple cannot use places in an arbitrary fashion; they must cultivate their right to such autonomy by progressing through the proper temporal course of the relationship or by negotiating their legitimacy in the eyes of significant others such as the family. The couple's use of certain places both reflects and creates their identity as a couple. Because these places are so meaningful and intrinsic to relationships, we need to study how couples gain access to them, regulate their use, and use them to cultivate new stages of relationship, both in their own and others' eyes.

To underscore the importance of the physical environment, we have also noted that physical and social aspects of context are so intertwined that researchers focusing on one or the other aspect often reach the same conclusions. For example, both we and Montgomery describe how close relationships have changed historically toward more autonomy and individualism over time, but Montgomery traces this trend to changes in social institutions and values, while we trace it to changes in aspects of the physical environment. For example, Bailey's (1988) analysis of the change in courtship locales from "front porch" to "back seat" shows how changes in physical settings involve changes in social meanings. Courtship circa 1900, among upper and middle classes, was very much on the woman's territory. Courting was controlled by the woman at the outset, as she selectively acknowledged the cards left by visiting suitors. "Dates" took place in parlors or on front porches, where the woman chose the activities and had her family close by to supervise the progress of the relationship. When use of the automobile became more widespread, the initiation and control of courtship largely transferred to men, who took women out of the protective home environment into public settings as well as the private back seat, creating more autonomy from her kin in the process. Environmental changes, such as the availability of cars, were intrinsic to changes in the places of, meanings of, and control over courtship. Although one could trace the same evolution by referring only to changing norms and values, as Montgomery does, our point is that those norms and values do not change in a vacuum, but within particular physical, social, and temporal circumstances, all of which are important. To understand fully the overall context of relationships, we would argue, one must pay explicit attention to the social *and* physical aspects of contexts, including how they create and sustain meanings, opportunities, and constraints on relationships.

Finally, a focus on the physical environment suggests new topics of research that will enrich our understanding of couple relationships. In particular, placemaking, the process of creating a home, is an important aspect of close relationships that deserves greater investigation. Creating a home involves the creation of a particular spatial, temporal, and sociocultural order that contributes to one's sense of understanding self and world (Dovey, 1985). Placemaking connects one to the past, to the physical home, and with individuals both inside and outside the home. As an example, the creation of new homes by the Gabra, a nomadic desert culture, is central to marital relationships; in fact, their word for *marriage* means "to build a house." The wedding ceremony spans four days, during which a new couple's home is built, disassembled, and rebuilt in ways that involve both families and the couple. The house is built by blending parts of the bride's mother's home with new materials, and it incorporates items and has symbolic involvement of the groom's family. In addition, the couple plays an important role, with the husband specifying the location of the home and sanctifying it, and the bride furnishing it. Thus placemaking activities contribute to a sense of identity for members of the couple and provide links between the couple and their parents. In other cultures, placemaking involves a wide range of activities (e.g., saving money, giving bride prices or dowries), participants (e.g., the couple, their kin, peers, and community members), processes (e.g., privacy regulation, territoriality), and rituals or celebrations (e.g., engagement and housewarming parties, the custom of carrying the bride over the threshold, house blessings, and decorations of homes on religious or social occasions). In combination, these events often create places for use by individuals, couples, and larger groups; they define the places and times for appropriate contacts between the sexes, as well as between the couple and their kin. Thus placemaking mirrors, once again, cultural values regarding independence and autonomy within the dyad and between the dyad and their kin.

Multiple psychological processes. The degree of connection or autonomy in a relationship is a function of a variety of psychological processes that are often studied singly, rather than in the complicated mixtures that always characterize relationships. In our earlier work, we emphasized the processes of intimacy and liking that created openness between relatively equal partners (Altman et al., 1981). Montgomery acknowledges that connections often represent a blending of processes of control, affection, and affiliation. In our more recent work, we, like Montgomery, refer to a variety of social and psychological processes that serve to bind humans together in varying degrees.

The variety of forces that bind two people together are apparent in our description of the relationship between a Taiwanese bride and her new mother-in-law. During the wedding ceremony a Taiwanese bride resists her mother-in-law's attempt to slide the wedding ring all the way onto her finger because, tradition holds, this will establish the dominion of the mother-in-law in the relationship. This practice provides a vivid illustration of the fact that the Taiwanese bride is not linked to her mother-in-law because she likes her or has achieved intimacy with her through reciprocal self-disclosures. Instead, dynamics other than interpersonal affection serve to obligate her to the relationship. Specifically, the physical circumstances of the household, the absence of other opportunities for women, and the weight of cultural traditions and expectations regarding household labor and inheritance all establish the inevitable subservience of daughter-in-law to mother-in-law.

One advantage of a dialectical analysis is that it prompts us to think about how these various processes work in concert or contradiction. For example, in Wales women often experience love as their motivation for marriage, but other less romantic social processes, such as custom and economic necessity, participate as well. Young people are discouraged from moving away from home until they get married, and women can rarely get jobs that provide sufficient finances for independent living. Hence marriage bonds do not involve simply interpersonal love and affection; they are also cemented by economic and physical requirements for existence within a culture that regards marriage as the appropriate way to attain those necessities. Autonomy and connection do not arise from a specialized subset of social psychological dynamics concerning loving or liking; they also arise from complicated historical, economic, cultural, and practical circumstances and processes. Although researchers often tend to specialize in studying one or the other psychological process, a dialectical analysis provides a framework that can encompass the various processes involved in relationship bonds.

Relationships involve stability and change; full understanding of a relationship requires understanding of its temporal features. A final key to making sense of relationships is understanding that they involve essential temporal features of their own. Although many researchers call for an understanding of temporal features of relationships, this is difficult to accomplish. Even though Montgomery reiterates this call, we cannot help but notice that temporal features play more prominent roles in her conceptual introduction and in her call for future research than in the body of literature she reviews. Her review reflects the state of the art in our fields rather than our agreements about how to explore new terrain.

We both attend to large-scale temporal changes involving cultural and historical trends in the autonomy/connection dialectic; however, we also examine more micro-level temporal processes across phases or life histories of close relationships. In particular, Montgomery argues that researchers should examine the cycles of autonomy and connection across time, and our ethnographic case studies provide vivid examples of how this works in various cultures. In the Taiwanese example discussed above, it is clear that marriage, at least for the bride, entails a severing of connections with her natal family and creation of strong connections with her husband's family. Although females are somewhat close to their families before marriage, the bride's actions during her departure from home underscore the loosening of her ties with her natal family. Her services directed to her mother-in-law and her husband's ancestors at her new home reflect her new connections to the groom's family. The Welsh, on the other hand, have a more continuous theme of autonomy. The theme is clear, from early courtship, when parental involvement is construed as interference, through the wedding, where the father's "giving away" of the bride is mostly a formality, to placemaking, which is fairly independent.

At one point our mutual explorations of temporal aspects of relationships have led us to speculations somewhat different from Montgomery's. She observes that society has more interest at some points in the life cycle of relationships than others. So births, deaths, weddings, and other beginning and ending points of relationships receive more attention from society than do other phases. We did not make this observation, but it does make sense to us in retrospect. However, she argues that at these points society is *more* strongly connected to the couple than at other points. We agree that these "rites of passage" often call for explicit ceremony, but we question whether the substance of the ceremony would necessarily involve a strengthening of connections between the couple and society. To illustrate, Welsh wedding events, such as the honeymoon, often symbolize the launching of an independent couple rather than a strengthening of their connections to any particular part of society. Similarly, the ceremony may reveal how links to one part of society are weakened while ties to other parts of society are strengthened. In Taiwan, for example, the woman transfers allegiance from her natal family to her husband's family. While we agree that turning points in relationships often involve some ceremonial recognition of the change, we also believe that the changes may involve both the loosening and strengthening of a variety of bonds. In any case, it is clear that our explorations have pointed out that researchers might benefit by attending to both micro- and macro-level aspects of the temporal features of a relationship (for suggestions on how temporal features such as pace, rhythm, and scale are intrinsic to relationships, also see Werner & Haggard, 1985).

Multiple methods must be applied if we are to understand temporal, physical, and social aspects of relationships completely. We think it is useful to see how varied levels of behavior attain a certain force because of their unity and redundancy. A context is not divisible into separate strands of influence from institutions, cultural artifacts, and social networks; contexts always exist as a holistic unity with inseparable temporal, cultural, social, and physical aspects. This holistic perspective suggests that researchers consider being eclectic in methodology, drawing upon whatever tools can be used to describe holistic features of relationships.

We have especially found that historical and ethnographic methods are useful tools for understanding the longer-term phases wherein autonomy or connection is more or less dominant. For example, Taiwan provides a good example of a culture where connections dominate the kin-couple relationship, while in Wales autonomy is the more dominant pole of the dialectic. Similarly, earlier phases of Western history showed couples to be more strongly tied to family, state, and church interests than they are now.

At a more micro level, it may be useful to develop case studies of couples' progressions through phases of courtship, weddings, and placemaking. The intensive analyses we have drawn from have relied on qualitative and quantitative methods, including interviews and intensive systematic observation of contextual features of relationships. By noticing who is present for significant events, what gifts are given by whom, what is worn at wedding ceremonies, how individuals and couples spend their private and public moments, and so on, it becomes clear how contexts are aspects of relationships. Although the disciplines of communication and psychology have benefited from exploring abstract social processes, fruitful discoveries can also be made by looking at these processes as they unfold in actual social and physical contexts.

SUMMARY

We have suggested that a transactional analysis serves as a legend for the map of the new terrain, highlighting important aspects that are intrinsic to relationships and that deserve investigation. Researchers who emphasize the contexts of relationships, such as Montgomery, already include many of these aspects in their investigations; our transactional model simply provides explicit recognition for them (Altman et al., in press). Specifically, the model posits that relationships involve different levels of behavior, with the physical environment a prominent but overlooked level. Moreover, multiple relationships coexist (e.g., couple members relate to each other as well as to families, friends, and coworkers), and one relationship must be understood in the context of others. Furthermore, relationships are dynamic, and it is useful to trace relationships as they unfold over time. Finally, innovative methods, including qualitative and quantitative approaches, must be applied if we are to gain a rich understanding of relationships and their variations across history and across cultures.

We stated earlier that we felt great kinship with Montgomery's ways of exploring new terrain. We agree with her that a dialectical framework provides a useful map to the oppositional, unified, and changing nature of relationships. Montgomery's work emphasizes how societal and cultural processes contribute to the linkage between society and couples. Toward this end, she calls attention to the fact that any one relationship must be understood in the context of others, that multiple levels of behavior contribute to relationships, and that it is fruitful to look at historical variations in society-couple relationships. Finally, she advocates the adoption of innovative methods that can capture the complexity of the contexts of relationships. In sum, Montgomery's conceptualization provides a good map, as well as a fair amount of inspiration, for any researcher who would like to join us in exploring this mysterious and complex terrain.

REFERENCES

Altman, I., Brown, B. B., Staples, B., & Werner, C. M. (in press). A transactional approach to close relationships: Courtship, weddings, and placemaking. In B. Walsh, K. Craik, & R. Price (Eds.), *Person-environment psychology.* Hillsdale, NJ: Lawrence Erlbaum.

Altman, I., & Rogoff, B. (1987). World views in psychology: Trait, interactional, organismic, and transactional perspectives. In D. Stokols & I. Altman (Eds.), *Handbook of environmental psychology* (Vol. 1, pp. 1-40). New York: John Wiley.

Altman, I., Vinsel, A., & Brown, B. B. (1981). Dialectic conceptions in social psychology: An application to social penetration and privacy regulation. In L. Berkowitz (Ed.), *Advances in experimental social psychology* (Vol. 14, pp. 107-160). New York: Academic Press.

Bailey, B. L. (1988). *From front porch to back seat.* Baltimore: Johns Hopkins University Press.

Bateson, G. (1972). *Steps to an ecology of mind.* New York: Ballantine.

Bateson, G. (1979). *Mind and nature: A necessary unity.* New York: Dutton.

Baxter, L. (1987). Symbols of relationship identity in relationship cultures. *Journal of Social and Personal Relationships, 4,* 261-280.

Baxter, L. (1988). A dialectical perspective on communication strategies in relationship development. In S. Duck, D. Hay, S. Hobfoll, W. Ickes, & B. Montgomery (Eds.), *Handbook of personal relationships: Theory, research and interventions* (pp. 257-274). Chichester: John Wiley.

Dovey, K. (1985). Home and homelessness. In I. Altman & C. M. Werner (Eds.), *Home environments: Vol. 8. Human behavior and environment: Advances in theory and research* (pp. 33-64). New York: Plenum.

Goffman, E. (1971). *Relations in public.* New York: Basic Books.

Leonard, D. (1980). *Sex and generation.* London: Tavistock.

Werner, C. M., & Haggard, L. M. (1985). Temporal qualities of interpersonal relationships. In M. L. Knapp & G. R. Miller (Eds.), *Handbook of interpersonal communication* (pp. 59-99). Beverly Hills, CA: Sage.

Communication, Intimacy, and the Course of Time

TIMOTHY STEPHEN
Rensselaer Polytechnic Institute

MONTGOMERY reports the current consensus that intimate dyads—marriages or friendships—are, when successful, characterized by a high degree of mutual influence, resulting in the generation of private cultures and shared systems of meaning that impart to dyad members their senses of unique connection. As she indicates, this understanding is not new, but it would seem to have become consensual. Researchers can now begin to build upon, extend, and probe the implications of this foundation, rather than stabbing about adding to the discipline's already disparate literature (see Stephen, 1990). After devising reliable measures of a private culture's breadth and depth, this perspective should be pushed as far as possible. This can be done by identifying processes that facilitate or impede the development of a private culture, by mapping the rules that influence its construction (e.g., under what circumstances might a private culture be expected to be more the product of one partner than the other), and by examining relationships between it and other important social and individual variables. This agenda is clear, of considerable practical and theoretical relevance, and achievable. Thus the outlook for research on communication and intimacy is good, provided that it can stay on its theoretical track.

Where Montgomery's essay is freshest, however, is in its consideration of institutional influences on dyadic communication. Montgomery considers society and the dyad to be mutually influential, and, in an ultimate sense, they probably are. However, the magnitude of influence that any particular dyad is capable of exerting on larger institutional processes (e.g., the economy or government policy) is microscopic compared with in-

AUTHOR'S NOTE: I would like to thank Teresa M. Harrison for her valuable comments and advice during the preparation of this essay.

Correspondence and requests for reprints: Timothy Stephen, Department of Language, Literature, and Communication, Rensselaer Polytechnic Institute, Troy, NY 12180.

Communication Yearbook 15, pp. 522-534

fluence in the reverse direction. Thus, in prioritizing research, or in examining what has been accomplished within the discipline, it is how society's institutions act upon couples that deserves increased attention.

Such institutional influences *must* be taken seriously. So far, communication research has all but ignored them, and this lends a surrealistic aspect to the literature. One might ask, for example, how it is possible to draw conclusions about interaction dynamics in heterosexual couples without reference to the position of women in the United States. Although the world of intimacy is relatively private and, consequently, creative in structure, it stretches the imagination that marital dynamics could be disconnected from the influence of the continuing evolution of women's social power. Yet the communication literature has failed to address this connection. How can we understand links between communication and marital quality without reference to continuous change in patterns of work and productivity, to technological change, to industrialization and decentralization of work, and to other factors that are coupled to economic and political process? The literature fails to reflect these factors also.

What would communication look like if the discipline followed Montgomery's interest in links between interpersonal communication and societal processes? Is it possible to connect our knowledge about change in intimacy to knowledge about change in social institutions or to change in other macrosocial processes? What would our research look like if we took Montgomery's argument seriously, perhaps more seriously than she takes it herself?

Marriages and families have been visible historically and have been documented sufficiently well to substantiate that the face of intimacy—at least in the Western world—has changed in accordance with changes in a number of clearly relevant institutional factors. The importance of these factors may not come into focus, however, unless intimacy is viewed over a broad span of time. Time has been important in studies of intimacy and communication, but it has been time-in-micro—the passing of an interactional turn, the sequential structure of a marital conversation, the first moments of interaction. Observational studies typically record but a few minutes, longitudinal studies are rare, and life-span studies are unknown in the communication literature. There is no question that microanalytic studies have been responsible for a rich yield, but this level of focus deflects awareness from processes affecting interaction that are manifest only over broad expanses of time. I believe that there is something important to be gained in widening the conceptual perspective and seeing time on a larger scale: over the course of a life, over the course of generations of a family, over the course of civilization—indeed, over the course of the evolution of the human species.

In sympathy with Montgomery's desire to address links between society and the dyad, I will trace three societal-level factors that a historical analysis would suggest are relevant to communication in intimacy: the status of women in society, the development of capitalism and the centralization of work, and progressive improvements in health and longevity. Then, further broadening the span of analysis, I will discuss current thinking about connections between human evolution and intimate communication. Our challenge as a field will be to develop theory that is responsive to these macrotemporal processes.

WOMEN'S STATUS IN SOCIETY

Twentieth-century U.S. marriages represent the latest moment in a continuing redefinition of the nature of power relations between men and women. Today, perhaps less than yesterday, heterosexual relationships still appear to be patriarchal. Modern couples espouse an ideology of equality, but wives typically perform more than 50% of housework, even when they are employed outside of the home in full-time positions (Berardo, Shehan, & Leslie, 1987), and they continue to be the primary agents of child care and parenting. The roots of this inequality appear to extend at least to classical Greece, where women were disenfranchised and remained in a squarely inferior position, without political influence and consistently on the losing end in a system of double standards. The Greek word for *adultery*, for example, meant *only* intercourse between a married woman and someone other than her husband (Okin, 1982). Plato classified women as a particular kind of property, and Aristotle argued that women were unfit to partake of citizenship, thinking them to be, like children and slaves, unsuitable for participation in the polity.

Women's status in Western societies changed little through the ages until political philosophy evolved, under pressure, to admit equality in principle. In the seventeenth century, Locke's analysis of the social contract of marriage concluded that, though marriage was a matter of contractual consent, a mutually agreed-upon pact between man and woman, husbands should have ultimate authority in cases of a difference of will. Locke reasoned that since it is impossible to govern a dyad by majority rule, decision making could become deadlocked unless one member was vested with special authority. In his determination, authority should go to the male, since males, he thought, are inherently abler and stronger. Even by the nineteenth century, John Stuart Mill's liberal political philosophy could not shake free the classical patriarchal division of labor that assigned men to public life and women to private life. As his colleague and wife, Harriet Taylor, maintained, only with full employment of married women outside the home and women's full participation in political and economic life would it be possible to abolish patriarchy within the home (Krouse, 1982).

Within the colonial American patriarchal family, women's authority was minimal and marital relations were not always cemented with affection. In Puritanical New England, family roles were regarded "as a continuous chain of hierarchy and delegated authority descended from God" (Mintz & Kellogg, 1988, p. 8). Fathers were able to control their families because they controlled the family's property and wealth. Benjamin Franklin and his family provide a case in point (see Randall, 1984). Franklin had little regard or affection for either his wife or his children, and lived apart from his wife for more than a decade during his years in England. When he contacted her (typically at intervals of six months or longer), it was often to issue instructions for the management of his estates in America. He thought it his right to approve his children's selection in marriage partners and did not attend the wedding of either his son or his daughter when each married a partner he had not approved.

According to Mintz and Kellogg (1988), the American family's gradual transition from such rigid patriarchy to a more companionate form began in the late 1700s. At that time, husbands and wives started referring to each other by their first names or by pet names rather than as *Mister* and *Mistress*, and "a growing number of husbands openly sought out their spouses' advice" (p. 48). Expanding markets and improvements in transportation led to a decline in the number of families living on self-contained farms. Farms began to specialize in particular crops that could be sold for cash, and the cash was used to buy commodities that would formerly have been made within each family group. As the range of products produced within the home decreased, the role of women shifted from direct participation in the creation of the family's wealth to a supporting function within the domestic sphere. The creation of the housewife role further increased the affectionate quality of family life. It was during the mid-1800s that celebrations of family life such as birthday parties, Christmas festivities, and Thanksgiving became widely observed. Although the redefinition of women's roles enabled certain new domestic powers for wives, their absence from the public/economic world ensured that a fully democratic family form would remain an unfulfilled goal.

In their 50-year follow-up of the classic Middletown studies of the 1920s and 1930s, Caplow, Bahr, Chadwick, Hill, and Williamson (1982) found considerable continuity in the nature of family relations in Muncie, Indiana. However, they report evidence of a strikingly disproportionate rate of change in role for males and females. A male, they say, could step out of the pages of a 1930s issue of *Life* magazine into the present with hardly any notice, but a female could not. Not only have women's fashions changed, but women's role definitions have propelled increasing numbers to extend the focus of their lives beyond home and family. A woman of the 1930s would confront dizzying new role demands and life-styles, as well as significant new possibilities for self-definition.

The historical record thus suggests that the present context of intimacy is unique in that relatively recent gains in the social power of women have generated forces for change that are currently only beginning to be felt within relationships. The Middletown studies of the 1920s documented "the limited communication between husband and wives and the trivial nature of their conversation [that] left many of them isolated in their separate worlds" (Caplow et al., 1982, p. 118). The 50-year follow-up, however, reports considerable progress in the quality of marital communication, with more openness and disclosure and more mutual decision making. These gains are attributed in large part to the women's rights movement's efforts to garner a more equitable marital relationship. Since virtually no one would suggest that the sexes have yet achieved social equality, current norms with respect to power relations should be regarded as transitional. It would also seem prudent to keep an eye on the continuing impact on martial communication of changes in empowerment for males and females.

ECONOMICS, URBANIZATION, AND POLITICAL CHANGE

For most of pre-Renaissance civilization, the family was the principal means for ordering social and political life. It substituted for modern bureaucratic political systems and free market economies. The family was a principle of conduct, a way of ordering productivity and allocating loyalties and social/political obligations. Ancestral ties formed the basis of early political divisions, with groups often organized along lines of male genealogical descent, as in the Roman *Gens* and other clan-based political formations. By contrast, the Germanic cultures that predominated in Europe following the eclipse of the Roman empire organized into the *Sippe* or the *Sib*. These groups were organized afresh for each generation and consisted of brothers, cousins, uncles, and so on upon whom one could count for various kinds of support, including blood vengeance (Herlihy, 1985). Relatedness established potentials for mutual enterprise and social advancement, but also engendered distinct obligations toward kin. For example, in the absence of a bureaucratic system of jurisprudence, the members of a Sippe would be expected to contribute blood money to the kin of a victim of another member of the Sippe, or to swear oaths to his relative's innocence. Similarly, the head of the family was expected to perform judicial services for his own household, occasionally even to the point of pronouncing death sentences on members (Mitterauer & Sieder, 1982). Thus the view of the family as a social unit specializing in reproduction and socioemotional care, distinct from the world of extrafamilial instrumental relationships, as a private culture in which marital pairs support each other through mutual confirmation and dialogic exchange, is distinctly modern.

Embedded in clan and other manifestations of kinship networks were the seeds of political structure: feudalism, aristocracy, monarchy. However, with the accumulation of capital, it became possible to use wealth to create networks of nonrelated allies, and it became less important to base support on the comparatively unreliable allegiance of kinship. Thus there existed simultaneously a tradition of kin solidarity, acting as a force promoting endogenous support, and an increasingly sophisticated economic system that allowed the accumulation of wealth and promoted exogenous support. As Casey (1989) points out, this and the advance of opportunities for the development of wealth in the professions and the trades contributed to a collision between these two rival forms of social stratification, the one based on lineage and the other on capital accumulated through industry and merit. The beginnings of a market economy led to a shift from a system favoring ancestral ties to one favoring income and economic prowess. This, consequently, meant a shift in power from the noble class to the middle class of merchants. According to Casey, modern minds have difficulty appreciating the degree of interconnection between the private (affectional, reproductive) order and the public (political, economic) order in earlier periods of European civilization (a consideration extended by Gadlin, 1977, in his analysis of historical trends in American intimacy). Although some argue that the U.S. government is now increasingly assuming functions that previously fell within the purview of the family (e.g., education and health programs), historically, the trend has been toward increasing separation of the family from the political order.

By the late 1800s, this separation was greatly amplified by processes of industrialization and urbanization that propelled men and women from the home to earn wages in centralized workplaces. As economic activity moved out of the household and its surrounds, the prototypical family began to take on its more familiar modern form as a private microsociety in which the stock-in-trade is affectionate and relational and in which husbands and wives labor in highly differentiated environments. In the United States, urbanization brought men and women in contact in unprecedented numbers, fostering a marketplace ethic with respect to courtship—men and women could "walk out" with each other, testing their social currency and examining their prospects for intimacy. Inasmuch as urban courtship was less available to community surveillance, it became more of a private matter (D'Emilio & Freedman, 1988). Compared with modern times, white colonial America was a comparatively public but tolerant context for courtship and premarital sexuality (Flaherty, 1972); indeed, the rigors of travel in New England fostered the practice of "bundling," in which a courting couple slept together, though fully dressed and separated by a "bundling board" (Larkin, 1988). Perhaps because colonial courtship more often occurred within public purview and within small, often religiously oriented, communities, premarital sexuality was not seen to be dangerous, as it came to be seen in later periods. After all, in the small public communities of colonial New England, paternity was relatively easy to establish, marriage eventual, and social mechanisms available to reintegrate precocious parents within the community and church.

Marital relations in preindustrial times appear to have been colder and more distant than they are today. Consider, for example, Heinrich Rauscher's contemporary description of family relations in preindustrial Austria:

> Relationships between members of the family lack tenderness; people converse soberly and matter-of-factly with each other. They are loath to show their feelings,

as it is assumed to be a sign of weakness and affection. Only very young children are kissed and fondled. Relationships between spouses appear cold. (quoted in Mitterauer & Sieder, 1982, p. 127)

Numerous factors contributed to this state. In many times and places marriage was a matter of political or economic union, or it was a vehicle to supply children, who could be an important component of the labor force on a small farm. A great proportion of preindustrial European households contained live-in servants, perhaps between 7% and 15% (Mitterauer & Sieder, 1982), in addition to multiple marital pairs and some of their children. Dwelling spaces were cramped, and there was high turnover in household personnel as servants and children came and moved on (servants typically stayed until they were of marriageable age). High mortality, a factor discussed below, also contributed. Lack of stability in the household's composition may have discouraged the formation of attachment bonds and may have encouraged people to withhold emotional investment.

Even in the United States of the 1920s, marriage could be draining and distinctly instrumental by today's standards. In Caplow et al.'s (1982) description of 1920s Muncie, working-class husbands and wives were exhausted from providing for large families:

> For many wives, marriage meant poverty, cruelty, adultery, and abandonment. . . . the time couples did spend at home does not appear to have been filled with pleasant or stimulating conversation. Decisions about the children, the house payment, and the food budget were quickly dealt with in a bickering fashion, and, with those problems disposed of, couples often lapsed into "apathetic silence." (p. 117)

Things could be better in middle-class families, but both groups provide a bleak contrast to the higher levels of satisfaction found in marriages today. While other research attests to continuing differences in the quality of marital life for working- versus middle-class couples (Rubin, 1976), Caplow et al. comment that some characteristics that were once found only in working-class families have diffused recently to the middle class. These include wives' employment outside of the home, more hours on the job for males and females, and early rising on weekdays. The impacts of these changes on the quality of intimate life in middle-class couples would not be expected to be positive.

To summarize, the realm of intimacy—classically, the realm of socioemotional concerns—cannot be isolated from the instrumental (economic/political) sphere. One valid view of Western marriage is that it is itself an institution, defined in canon and secular law to provide for the continuity of ownership and fair distribution of property. It is not overstating the case to say that as goes the economy, so goes marriage—one might only reflect that divorce rates correlate negatively with periods of economic recession

(Nye & Berardo, 1973). Whether marital communication practices lead to the spinning out of a private culture; whether husbands and wives view their union as one in which psychological intimacy should play a significant part or rather, in the first instance, as a reproductive and economic partnership; whether courtship is private or public—all are influenced by the character of economic practices and by changes in the nature of work.

HEALTH AND LONGEVITY

Braudel's (1979) study of diet in Europe in the period 1400 to 1800 concludes that "eating consists of a lifetime of consuming bread, more bread, and gruel" (p. 130), and the bread was often months old, so tough it had to be cut with an axe. Coarse cereals such as rye, barley, oats, and buckwheat were the principal dietary staple, and often the primary source of calories. Consequently, dietary monotony was the rule and, for many, life was precariously dependent on the dynamics of the harvest. Braudel estimates that there were 89 devastating famines in France alone from the tenth to the eighteenth century, and this number does not include "hundreds and hundreds" of local famines. If the crop was abundant, there was fatigue from overwork and the flatness of existence, as well as cycles of disease. According to one source from 1775, at that time, smallpox affected 95% of the population and killed one in seven. Plague and epidemics of other fatal diseases ran rampant in cycles of devastation followed by lulls during which the agent had opportunity to mutate to a new form; it would then reappear. In one estimate, only 50% of children reached their twentieth year and as many as 33% died within 12 months of birth. According to Mitterauer and Sieder (1982), the average length of life in agrarian, preindustrial Europe was no greater than the early 30s.

The Industrial Revolution and scientific achievements of the 1800s in the fields of medicine, biology, and agriculture had a profound impact on longevity: In the last 100 years the average life expectancy in Western industrial countries has *doubled.* It is worth reflecting on the significance of this fact for the quality of marital and family relations. Mitterauer and Sieder report that the average age of marriage in the Middle Ages was often higher than it is today. Thus, at that time, marriage in the mid-20s for a mean duration of between 7 and 10 years would not have been uncommon. Similarly, according to Mintz and Kellogg (1988), low life expectancy meant that most marriages lasted fewer than 7 years in seventeenth-century Maryland, and in almost all cases it was the wife who survived. Remarriage for widows was routine, so the typical family represented a blending of nonrelated progeny and might often contain a number of half-siblings. Fertility was regulated haphazardly, if at all. Births occurred on average at two-year intervals in European peasant families—the duration of lactation (births were more frequent in upper-class families, which employed wet nurses). However, extremely high rates of infant and child mortality tended to limit family size. Due in part to the introduction of contraceptive devices and the dissemination of information on the topic within an increasingly literate population, in the United States the average number of children per family fell steadily, from slightly over 7 in 1800 to 4.24 in 1880 (D'Emilio & Freedman, 1988). Thus, though the patterns varied by nationality, race, ethnicity, and social class, by contrast with modern times, marriage tended to be a short-lived union in which women were almost constantly reproductive.

Mitterauer and Sieder (1982) argue that large family size, high turnover in household composition, and the continuous threat of death limited the development of intimacy and dampened the expression of affection within marriage and the family. Conversely, the increasing stability of the family, longer life expectancy, lower child mortality, and the gradual separation of work from home created conditions that encouraged sentimentality and the deepening of relationships. These factors helped to shape the family into a social system characterized by a high degree of intermember attachment, support, and mutual influence. Mintz and Kellogg (1988) report that these changes began to be evident in the United States at the close of the eighteenth century. The context of marriage and family is changing still, as marital pairs of the baby-boom generation begin to care for their parents, who will likely live for an unprecedented period. In light of the preceding discussion, recent increases in life expectancy and decreases in family size might be expected to contribute to the development of stronger bonds between marital couples and between adults and their aging parents. These bonds might be evidenced in greater overlap in worldview between marital partners and between the generations. Increased longevity, however, will create a new economic strain that will affect the work habits, home lives, and parental activities of marital couples.

BIOLOGY AND EVOLUTION

The preceding section discussed some of the ways in which biological functioning can influence patterns of intimate behavior. This link is most clearly illustrated by the fact that improvements in diet over the last 100 years have lowered the average age of menarche by two years, a fact of significance in understanding heightened rates of adolescent sexual contact (Caplow et al., 1982). Perhaps it has become trite to say that biology and social behavior are codeterminate—the principle seems to be ritually acknowledged and then routinely ignored—but one confronts such links head-on in the context of heterosexual intimacy, where failure to recognize them holds the potential to render a discipline's theoretical developments irrelevant. Unfortunately, the literature treating communication in heterosexual intimacy would lead one to conclude that intimacy is solely the creation of the mind, isolated from influences of the body. Yet, in addition to its role as purveyor of culture, and in addition to its role as a moderator of proximal stimuli (such as diet or disease) that moderate biological functioning and development, the family is the context in which the species is reproduced. It sits, therefore, at the intersection of evolution and social behavior.

Despite a period of resistance, social scientists are now beginning to accept the possibility that evolution, specifically genetic transmission, may play a role in shaping social life. A review of this controversy or the research literature that addresses biology, evolution, and human behavior will not be attempted here; however, it should be evident that the mere possibility of biological influence on human social behavior ought to be of paramount interest to those studying communication in the context of intimacy. At the center of this interest is the fact that family members share, on average, considerably more genetic material than nonrelated individuals (sibling and parent-child pairs share approximately 50% of their genes, but this amount decreases rapidly the more distantly related the pair). Thus any social characteristic that might be influenced by individual biology would be more likely to be copresent in family members than in nonrelated individuals. However, as Rossi (1984) points out, biological influences may also promote differentiation of male and female siblings, not only morphologically but also with respect to some areas of social behavior. Thus, while within-family similarity would be expected to be the rule, similarity should be heightened for same-sex family members. The significance of this effect, however, depends upon the existence of links between communication behaviors and biological processes that are themselves under genetic influence—no one would expect human behavior to be subject to direct genetic control.

With regard to this, Gottman and Levinson (1988) argue that differences in interpersonal conflict styles of males and females may be rooted in genetically calibrated biological processes. Negative affect, they argue, produces widespread physiological activation "consisting of such changes as increases in cardiac rate and cardiac contractility, sweating, deepened breathing, redirection of blood flow toward large skeletal muscles," and release of a number of chemicals into the blood. They believe that evidence suggests strongly that males may be more reactive physiologically than females to stressful emotional stimuli. This may provide a biological basis for understanding the differences in husbands' and wives' conflict styles that have been found consistently in the marital literature. These differences include (a) that wives function more effectively in a climate of negative affect; (b) that husbands are more likely to withdraw emotionally in conflictive, distressed marriages; (c) that wives are more likely to escalate conflict; and (d) that husbands are more likely to reduce conflict by conciliation.

It is also conceivable that some elements in an individual's characteristic style of interpersonal communication may be shaped by biological processes; communication behavior, after all, is overlaid on a biological structure. Attributes of interpersonal style, such as animation, pacing, and tension, would seem likely candidates for biological influence. The lymphatic or central nervous systems may influence an individual's interactional style by calibrating levels of activity and tension and thresholds for stress (see Gottman & Levinson, 1988). Although the functioning of such systems is surely influenced by cultural factors, their potentials are established biologically, creating the possibility of increased similarity in the communication styles of blood relations. Although only suggestive, an analysis of perceived communication styles among members of 44 families suggests that such correspondences exist (Stephen, 1989). Significantly heightened similarity in communication style has been found in the following family dyads: father-son, mother-daughter, sister-sister, brother-brother, and sister-brother. The three dyadic types that did not demonstrate greater similarity were the father-mother dyad, which compared two individuals from different bloodlines, and the mother-son and father-daughter dyads, which crossed categories of generation and sex.

CONCLUSION

I have attempted to illustrate the relevance of macrotemporal processes to the development and expression of intimacy in heterosexual dyads by drawing connections between historical and evolutionary processes and communication behaviors in marriage and the family. The effects of these processes may not be apparent in naive observation of everyday events, because historical and evolutionary forces operate generally at the level of ultimate rather than immediate causes. We also may not be sufficiently sensitive to these effects, viewing history, perhaps, as merely what has come before—a collection of discrete events, without direct impact on the present. Such a view is certainly always limiting, but of lesser consequence if the history one is tracking is the history of an abandoned technology (e.g., bloodletting), an isolated material artifact (e.g., the Hula Hoop), or perhaps a modern social practice (e.g., baseball). But the history of a central social institution, such as the family, is difficult to see in this way. The family's history is one of continuous adaption to changes in the values of a few central variables, variables that continue to change and to have impact upon the family today. As in a naturally occurring field study, viewing time in this way helps to illuminate factors that are difficult to bring to light in the normal course of social scientific analysis, reliant as it tends to be on cross-sectional designs.

It is also possible to take a shortsighted view of biological evolution. A reading of the communication literature would seem to suggest that, having created sexual dimorphism and *Homo sapiens*, the process of biological evolution has been rendered irrelevant by the innovation of linguistic culture. Such a view, if anyone actually holds it, might be excused as an understandable egocentrism in a discipline rooted in speech studies. More commonly, however, evolution is dimly understood as a process in which the successes and failures of a species to adapt to profound changes in the environment begin to favor mutation, a slow process that works its effects over millions of years. However, evolution is also apparent in the process of transmitting genetically coded information from generation to generation, a process that is immediately apparent in the family. Some of this information causes bodies to develop different potentials, among which may be potentials that affect communication behavior. It is worth reflecting on Rossi's (1984) warning that a discipline that ignores the biological substrate of behavior may be doomed eternally to miss the mark in its recommendations for social policy.

Montgomery notes that the interpersonal area has shifted emphasis from individuals to dyads, and observes that it is now concerned principally with personal relationships—marriages and friendships. If so, researchers must be careful not to lose sight of meaningful differences between these dyadic types. Friendship bonds are fundamentally different from bonds formed through family membership; after all, marital partners often think it remarkable that their spouses are *also* their friends. Friendship does not have a historical presence comparable to that of marriage and the family because forms of friendship have varied little over time. In addition, marital couples share social, material, and biological investments in their progeny, creating bonds of a nature altogether unknown in other forms of social relationships. It is important to understand common processes of intimacy that operate across categories of dyads (homosexual couples, friends, marriages, and so on), but there is a danger that in emphasizing similarities researchers may lose sight of critical differences.

Recognizing connections between political and economic processes and forms of family life helps to focus attention on the fact that it is not possible to speak of a modal family experience. Family life varies significantly by nationality, race, ethnicity, and social class (the history of the family varies in accordance with each of these factors as well), and our theories need to be responsive to these categorical divisions. For this reason, researchers must be cautious in using the label *traditional* in describing dyadic types, as the term loses sensibility without reference to whose traditions and which historical period. It is difficult to identify any feature of American intimacy more traditional than variability.

Modernity has burdened contemporary couples with the problems of an increasingly hurried, public, and diversified existence. Each layer of the social world—school, work, church, community, and so on—harbors its own demands and restrictions for self-expression. In consequence, Americans have turned increasingly to their intimate lives for sanctuary, for support for the unconventional aspects of self, or, as some might put it, for their "true" selves. Home and family provide a place to shed personae and the sediments of stress and alienation acquired in a day's navigation of the social milieu. As scholars have increasingly come to understand this, they have recognized that the microculture of the home has evolved in step with these changing conditions of modern existence. Prior to the last decades of the 1800s, the family was often described as a "little commonwealth"—a sort of private dominion for adult males. Such a model is out of step with modern times. What is required now is an environment that supports psychological nurturance, an environment in which people not only find relief from tension but in which they can tease apart the varied stimuli of the day and interpret them within the family's worldview. This is why the family context has come to be of increasing interest within the discipline. Will the economic, political, and biological conditions that have shaped family life remain as they are? Have they reached some final state, allowing communication theorists to disregard their influences safely? History's answer is clear.

REFERENCES

Berardo, D., Shehan, C., & Leslie, G. (1987). Jobs, careers, and spouses' time in housework. *Journal of Marriage and the Family, 49*, 381-390.

Braudel, F. (1979). *The structures of everyday life.* New York: Harper & Row.

Caplow, T., Bahr, H., Chadwick, B., Hill, R., & Williamson, M. (1982). *Middletown families: Fifty years of change and continuity.* Minneapolis: University of Minnesota Press.

Casey, J. (1989). *The history of the family.* Oxford: Basil Blackwell.

D'Emilio, J., & Freedman, E. (1988). *Intimate matters: A history of sexuality in America.* New York: Harper & Row.

Flaherty, D. (1972). *Privacy in colonial New England.* Charlottesville: University Press of Virginia.

Gadlin, H. (1977). Private lives and public order: A critical view of the history of intimate relations in the United States. In G. Levinger & H. L. Raush (Eds.), *Close relationships: Perspectives on the meaning of intimacy* (pp. 33-72). Amherst: University of Massachusetts Press.

Gottman, J., & Levinson, R. (1988). The social psychophysiology of marriage. In P. Noller & M. A. Fitzpatrick (Eds.), *Perspectives on marital interaction* (pp. 182-200). Philadelphia: Multilingual Matters.

Herlihy, D. (1985). *Medieval households.* Cambridge, MA: Harvard University Press.

Krouse, R. (1982). Patriarchal liberalism and beyond: From John Stuart Mill to Harriet Taylor. In J. B. Elshtain (Ed.), *The family in political thought* (pp. 145-172). Amherst: University of Massachusetts Press.

Larkin, J. (1988). *The reshaping of everyday life 1790-1840.* New York: Harper & Row.

Mintz, S. & Kellogg, S. (1988). *Domestic revolutions: A social history of American family life.* New York: Free Press.

Mitterauer, M., & Sieder, R. (1982). *The European family: Patriarchy to partnership from the Middle Ages to the present.* Chicago: University of Chicago Press.

Nye, F., & Berardo, F. (1973). *The family: Its structure and interaction.* New York: Macmillan.

Okin, S. (1982). Philosopher queens and private wives: Plato on women and the family. In J. B. Elshtain (Ed.), *The family in political thought* (pp. 31-50). Amherst: University of Massachusetts Press.

Randall, W. (1984). *A little revenge: Benjamin Franklin and his son.* Boston: Little, Brown.

Rossi, A. S. (1984). Gender and parenthood. *American Sociological Review, 49*, 1-19.

Rubin, L. (1976). *Worlds of pain: Life in the working class family.* New York: Basic Books.

Stephen, T. (1989). *Communication styles: Intergenerational links.* Paper presented at the annual meeting of the Speech Communication Association, San Francisco.

Stephen, T. (1990). *Research on the new frontier: A review of the communication literature on marriage and the family.* Paper presented at the annual meeting of the International Communication Association, Dublin.

11 The Politics of Common Sense: Articulation Theory and Critical Communication Studies

IAN ANGUS
University of Massachusetts, Amherst

This essay centers on the concept of articulation, beginning from the work of its major contemporary theorists—Ernesto Laclau, Chantal Mouffe, and Stuart Hall. Articulation theory conceptualizes the specific communication act as internally generative, but also situates it within an external context that is itself understood as communicatively constituted. It develops a conception of power that is not limited to the disjunction or consensus (convergence) between different constituted interests, but is directed toward the more fundamental level of the constitution of common sense. The interplay of poetic expression and rhetorical linkage in articulation provides the groundwork for a communication theory of society whose critical stance consists of its theoretical elaboration of the issues raised by the new social movements.

Our task is continually to struggle, lest mankind become completely disheartened by the frightful happenings of the present, lest man's belief in a worthy, peaceful and happy direction of society perish from the earth.

Max Horkheimer, 1939

Insofar as humans are not simply determined into a "natural" and unchanging social order, their participation requires that a particular social location be coordinated with the social order as a whole. This coordination relies on relationships based on understanding, affective interactions, and desire—in short, the establishment of meaning. To this extent, social order relies on the circulation of meaning for its legitimation and social change requires an intervention in this circulation. The rhetoric of order or change is thus not simply a coercive one, which would imply that all participation in social bonds has been broken and can be maintained only through the threat of violence, but above all a construction of meaning.

Correspondence and requests for reprints: Ian Angus, Department of Communication, University of Massachusetts, Amherst, MA 01003.

Communication Yearbook 15, pp. 535-570

Mainstream communication studies tend to isolate the communication process under investigation from the social order as a whole, thereby implicitly assuming that the specific process is not importantly affected by the wider social order and, more or less explicitly, resulting in an apologetic pluralism. Paradoxically, while communication is increasingly recognized across the human sciences as central to the social formation, communication studies rarely question the boundaries that seal its traditional domains of investigation off from wider social issues (Angus & Lannamann, 1988).

Critical studies of communication, on the other hand, emphasize the effect of the social totality on specific processes and analyze the dominating or liberating effect of a communication process in relation to it. The key, then, to the distinction between critical and administrative communication studies is the relation between a specific process and the social totality that is utilized in investigations. In both mainstream and critical studies (even when an explicit conceptualization is not attempted), epistemological, methodological, and ontological assumptions situate the investigation within this nexus of specificity and totality.

Critical studies have tended to conceptualize the social totality as a determinate structure—that is, as a positive phenomenon with identifiable characteristics that can be theoretically explained. This totality can then be expected to have regular and characteristic effects on a given communicative process. Thus, despite a circumscribed realm of specificity, the tendency is to subordinate communication processes to investigations of the social totality that are, in principle, of another type altogether—political economy, systems theory, historical evolution, and so forth. This approach tends to reduce the *generativity* of communication processes to being simply the effect of wider determinations.

As this essay will elaborate, articulation theory conceptualizes the specific communication act, or process, as internally generative, but also situates it within an external context that is itself understood as communicatively constituted. The interplay of poetic expression and rhetorical linkage in articulation provides the groundwork for a communication theory of society whose critical stance is theoretically justified but never statically presumed.

The concept of articulation that this essay investigates focuses on this relation between discursive intervention and the context, or field, of discourses. It incorporates, and attempts to develop, a conception of power that is not limited to the disjunction or consensus (convergence) between different interests, but is directed toward the more fundamental level of intersubjective meaning. "Convergence of belief or attitude or its absence presupposes a common language in which these beliefs can be formulated. . . . Much of this common language in any society is rooted in its institutions and practices; it is constitutive of these institutions and practices" (Taylor, 1977, p. 120; see also Lukes, 1974). The concept of articulation is concerned with the politics of common sense, in which discursive interventions modify the field of power. Thus legitimations of the social order succeed, not so much by repressing already formulated alternatives, but by preventing their formulation or, later, by recuperating formulated alternatives within the dominant articulation and thereby, of course, changing their meaning. The latter move is what we used to call *co-optation*. In the contemporary configuration of the field of common sense, the articulation of alternatives by new social movements must continually struggle with their de- and rearticulation, in which the mass media play a key role.

The concept of articulation has become central to recent critical studies of communication and cultural dynamics. The history of this concept links current empirical cultural studies to the development of Marxist theory and politics and refigures the relationship between theory and praxis.[1] The concept of hegemony emerged in Russian social democracy and became the center of the work of Antonio Gramsci. In this theoretical development, there was an increasing "expansion" of the realm of contingent specific circumstances to which the Marxist theory of historical development had to be adapted in order to attain practical relevance for political action. In articulation theory the significance of the realm of contingent hegemonic relations is radically reinterpreted so as to undermine the background of the logic of historical development against which it emerged. A figure/ground shift has taken place: Articulation theory is the form that hegemony takes when it has ceased to be the thematic concern against a presupposed background of historical logic and has itself become the background against which any historical figures emerge. This radicalization of the problematic of hegemony centers on the concept of articulation, which we could provisionally define as the "logic of contingent relations" extended to the entire social field. Put another way, the activist component of ideological intervention is conceived to be an inherent limit to any theoretical totalization, and therefore any historical logic, such that the unity of any social form is achieved through a political intention (rather than preceding it) and is therefore always a partial unity articulated against alternatives. As developed later, this figure/ground shift is not only a necessary condition of the emergence of the concept of articulation, but also needs to be understood as a key component of the concept itself.

Understood even in this provisional manner, it is clear why the concept of articulation is central for the practice of cultural criticism: Communication is understood not merely as a reflection of something underlying it, but as an active component (perhaps *the* active component) in the construction of social reality. From within Marxist theory, it offers a departure from the base-superstructure model that places cultural dynamics at the center of theoretical and political praxis. For cultural critics, it offers a connection to wider social and political criticism. For political activists, it offers a serious reflection on the everyday struggle for meaning in which they are engaged that surpasses such terms as *bourgeois ideology*, which are simply

dismissive and practically useless unless they can be compared with an existing revolutionary subaltern ideology. In all of these phrasings of this intellectual shift, communication becomes central to the process of meaning-making
in a culture and thereby to the possibilities of political intervention.

Moreover, these advantages converge in according due significance to
the new social movements that have been the main forces for social change
in advanced capitalist societies in the postwar period and that cannot be
properly understood if they are reduced to expressions of an underlying
class contradiction. Struggles over the definition of *common sense* have
been key in the ecology, antinuclear, antiracist, ethnic, feminist, sexual liberation, regionalist, nationalist, and other movements. These are, in large
part, struggles over the process of "normalization" by which the (de)legiti-
mation of movements for social change takes place and in which language
plays a key role. It is of primary importance to move forward with any concepts that can clarify these struggles in a manner that will help us to pass
beyond their mere enumeration. They need to be understood together
through some (as yet unclarified) notion of "totality," but not reduced to
expressions of an underlying (class) unity. In this sense, communication issues are central to the agenda of movements for social change.

This essay develops two main critical points with respect to the concept
of articulation as developed by Ernesto Laclau and Chantal Mouffe, and
utilized by Stuart Hall, and develops one corollary of each point. The four
central sections of the essay concentrate on each of these in turn. First, I
argue that the "elements" of an articulation are not satisfactorily theorized,
except to say that they are not the "moments" of a logical totality. With respect to the relation of elements and the discursive field, I suggest that this
relation should be understood as a theme/background relation as developed
in the phenomenological tradition. Articulatory practice not only forges a
linkage, but also focuses on, highlights, selected elements. This foregrounding
of selected elements allows them to become leading moments in the equivalences forged between moments of different articulations. A corollary of
this critique is that the notion of articulation is situated more effectively at
the point of political action—which is explicated through the notion of
"particularity."

Second, the rejection of the concept of totality by Laclau and Mouffe is
an arrested polemical reversal that remains within the logic of Hegelian rationalist totality. By contrast, I suggest that the phenomenological concept
of totality as a "horizon," which is built upon the theme/background relation, should become a central part of the theory of articulation. By denying
any concept of totality, Laclau and Mouffe reduce theoretical articulations
to those of common sense—thereby undermining one of the main purposes
of Laclau's introduction of the concept of articulation in his earlier work.

As a corollary of the lack of a reformulated concept of totality, Laclau
and Mouffe cannot account for the origin of modernity, even though this is

a crucial issue, because it is only at this historical moment that the problematic of articulation arises. In the present widening of the field of cultural criticism that can be called "postmodern," the origin and concept of modernity is essential to defining this contemporary open field.

While I do not wish to rediscover unblemished the French phenomenological Marxism of the 1950s, which was the global alternative to structuralism, this essay argues that the advances in Marxist theory that the concept of articulation achieves can, nevertheless, be secured and developed only within a theoretical perspective that retrieves a key experimental dimension.

TWO ASPECTS OF ARTICULATION: THEMATIZATION AND COMBINATION

The theory of articulation begins from Ernesto Laclau's *Politics and Ideology in Marxist Theory* (1977/1982). Laclau's critique of the Marxist reduction of all phenomena to class position and his alternative theory of articulation have been extended into cultural and communication studies by Stuart Hall[2] and, through the combined work of those associated with the Centre for Contemporary Cultural Studies in Birmingham, have become a significant influence on critical communication studies around the world. A discussion of the development of the problematic of articulation in British cultural studies will allow the introduction of this essay's first critical point: that the "elements" of an articulation must be understood as thematizations from a taken-for-granted background.

British cultural studies occurs at the intersection of the two traditions of structuralism and culturalism—associated in Britain with the work of Raymond Williams and Edward Thompson (Hall, 1986d). The latter emphasizes the experience of individuals and classes, whereas the former insists on the thorough mediation of any subjective experience of immediacy by the totality of the social formation. In the terms of international Marxism, these two traditions are most marked in the divergence between Gramsci's problematic of hegemony and Althusser's structuralism. Despite this divergence, the necessity of according due importance to both structure and subject is a key problematic of Marxism (Anderson, 1988, pp. 32-55). It is the considerable merit of British cultural studies to have attempted to mediate these two key poles of Marxist theory in a manner that enables concrete investigations.

In British Marxism, the monumental historical work of Edward Thompson, *The Making of the English Working Class* (1963), emphasized the notion of "experience," understood as the interaction of consciousness with the conditions of life (Hall, 1986a, p. 39). Despite the rejection of Thompson's formulation as an "expressive totality" (due to the structuralist influence), it formed the basis for the appropriation of Gramsci's concept of hegemony—which Hall (1982) has described as "the inventory of traditional ideas, the

forms of episodic thinking which provide us with the taken-for-granted elements of our practical knowledge, [which Gramsci] called . . . 'common
sense' " (p. 73; see also Hall, 1977, pp. 332-334; 1986b). It is through this
intellectual route that the experiential component entered the concept of articulation, though it has never been theoretically accounted for to the same degree as structuralism, even while this experiential component has usually
dominated both the choice of problems and the rhetoric of presentation. A
fuller theoretical treatment requires the inclusion of concepts adequate to theorizing the "immediacy" of experience that are best developed in the phenomenological tradition. In short, there is a hidden proximity between the emphasis
on subjectivity, experience, and decision in Thompson's historical writing and
the phenomenological tradition.

Hall's formulation of a cultural politics of common sense introduces the
component of the "taken-for-granted" into the concept of articulation.
When understood as constitutive of common sense, ideology is most effective precisely when it is invisible, when it has come to form the unquestioned basis *from which* people argue, rather than the explicit conclusions
that they *argue toward.* As Hall (1985) puts it:

> It is in and through the systems of representation of culture that we "experi-
> ence" the world: experience is the product of our codes of intelligibility, our
> schemas of interpretation. . . . Here we are most under the sway of the highly
> ideological structures of all—common sense, the regime of the "taken for
> granted." (p. 105)

In explaining his usage of the concept of articulation, Hall (1986b) has
pointed to two distinct meanings that are built into the concept:

> In England, the term has a nice double meaning because "articulate" means to
> utter, to speak forth, to be articulate. It carries that sense of language-ing, of ex-
> pressing, etc. But we also speak of an articulated lorry (truck): a lorry where the
> front (cab) and back (trailer) can, but need not necessarily, be connected to one
> other. The two parts are connected to each other, but through a specific linkage,
> that can be broken. An articulation is thus the form of the connection that *can* make
> a unity of two different elements, under certain conditions. It is a linkage that is not
> necessary, determined, absolute and essential for all time. (p. 53)

While the first sense of expressing has a clear affinity with the notion of
thematization, it is the poststructuralist notion of "linkage" developed by
Laclau that has come to dominate the definition and use of the concept of
articulation (see Hall, 1985, pp. 113ff.; 1986a, p. 45; 1986c, pp. 53, 56;
1988, pp. 9ff.). The influential studies *Learning to Labor* by Paul Willis
(1977) and *Subculture: The Meaning of Style* by Dick Hebdige (1979) focus
on this aspect when defining the term and its genealogy, but also utilize the

notion of the taken-for-granted in undertaking their empirical studies (see Hebdige, 1979, pp. 11, 13, 19, 91; Willis, 1977, pp. 60, 77, 120, 139). The dominant component in the definition emphasizes that an articulated cultural unity links components that do not necessarily belong together, but whose connection is forged in the activity of articulation itself. This component is very similar to Michael McGee's (1980) notion of the "ideograph," the meaning of which is established by the "cluster" of terms in which it operates. But, beginning from the above definition by Hall, one may say that articulation is also *enunciation*, the activity of "putting into words" that is captured by the notion of "thematization."

Before elements can be linked together, they must be focused upon, brought into the light, from a more global, undifferentiated, and presupposed background. The two aspects of the concept of articulation need to be distinguished and conceptually clarified: the *thematization* of elements from the undifferentiated background of interconnected presuppositions and the *combination* of these distinct elements. Thematization is a prior activity in which the anonymous interconnected field of assumptions preexisting the articulatory activity is selectively focused on to yield distinct elements. Subsequently, combination of these elements achieves a specific discursive formation that then enters into common sense. Common sense itself can be understood as the totality of these discursive formations, including their interrelationships, subsisting at any given spatiotemporal nexus and awaiting further articulation.

The activity of thematization that produces elements can thus be understood as a relationship between a taken-for-granted background and a focused-upon theme. This productive focusing captures the primary, and neglected, sense of articulation as an uttering, a bringing forth into language. Alfred Schutz's (1971) phenomenological sociology examined this process of selective focusing as a process of determining "relevances" for orientation in the commonsense world:[3]

> The selective function of our interest organizes the world in both respects—as to space and time—in strata of major or minor relevance. From the world within my actual or potential reach those objects are selected as primarily important which actually are or will become in the future possible ends or means for the realization of my projects, or which are or will become dangerous or enjoyable or otherwise relevant to me. (p. 227)

Thus we may say that the totality of discursive formations that constitute common sense are given their distinctive organization by a system of relevances interwoven with the conduct of practical life. Common sense is always *this* sense, here and now, and this particularity of its formation is constituted through thematization.

Despite the primacy of thematization, the later activity of combination can influence the productive process of thematization. The linkage of a prominent element with a less prominent one tends to transfer the prominence, or relevance, and with it, shall we say, the "strength" of thematization. But this transfer cannot itself produce a theme; even if a combination of a key ideological term such as *freedom* with a relatively minor element such as buying tennis shoes can serve to transfer and effect an association that makes buying tennis shoes, or even a specific brand of tennis shoes, more significant, it cannot accomplish the isolation and characterization of the element of "buying tennis shoes" in the first place. This element is pregiven to the activity of combination, the product of a thematization in the economic sphere that has separated out this kind of shoes from all others. Thus the linkage of elements derives a great deal of its efficacy from the prior process of thematization.

While thematization and combination function in an interrelated manner in the articulations that constitute common sense, an exclusive focus on the latter tends to obscure the manner in which a given articulatory practice not only recombines elements inherited from the previous formation, but focuses on and puts into circulation elements that had no existence in the previous formation. An articulation can function to silence certain experiences that still function within the assumptions of common sense. This is one of the main characteristics of ideology—it "anonymizes" certain elements of common sense that nevertheless do not entirely disappear. A rearticulation that combats such silences will indeed forge linkages with other competing but subaltern articulations. But it also does something else in the activity of thematization: It focuses on new elements; it slices up experience in new ways; it gives voice to the world. This giving voice is itself a fundamental aspect of articulation because it indicates where articulation cuts into the anonymous fabric of presuppositions.

The productive process of thematization can itself be analyzed into two components: There is the initial expression of a meaning in which the inchoate background is disclosed, and there is the preservation and extension of this known theme. The first of these is poetry, which, as Heidegger (1971a, 1971b) has elucidated, is at the origin of language, where the world is brought forth into human experience. In rhetoric, which is the second component, the given experience of the world is commemorated and made known to a wider cultural formation. The thematizing aspect of articulation is a speaking-forth-the-world that involves both disclosure and preservation and forms the cultural unity of a social identity. There is no identity, or experience, prior to this productive activity. Thematization is a determining of relevances for which we may use the term *expression* as long as it is understood as a *cultural* concept without the assumption of an initial mental internality that must be brought outside (Schrag, 1986, pp. 32-47).

The activity of thematization is assumed, and even occasionally described, by Hall and in cultural studies generally, but it is never theorized as such. Richard Johnson (1986-1987, p. 67) approximates the same concept and describes it as "public-ation," but this term carries too much baggage in implying separate social spheres and wrongly assumes the explicit preexistence of elements prior to their thematization. This crucial absence means that there can never be a satisfactory account of the origin of the elements and, consequently, a sufficiently *critical theory* of common sense. In order to account for this absence, we will have to recall the origin of the concept of articulation in the work of Ernesto Laclau that is the basis for its development in British cultural studies.

The introduction to Laclau's *Politics and Ideology in Marxist Theory* (1977/1982) gives a general formulation of the concept of articulation. The book consists of four essays that intervene in key disputes in the Marxist theory of ideology—dependency and underdevelopment in Latin America, the specificity of politics and the role of the state, fascism, and populism. The last three of these debates touch on an identical underlying issue: the extent to which features of political life have an independence from the economic and class forces toward which Marxist theory routes its explanations. With respect to populism, for example, Laclau points to "*the relative continuity* of popular traditions, in contrast to the historical discontinuities that characterize class structures." Marxist theory has failed to solve the issue of the class adherence of populism—which can take either a fascist or socialist direction—because it has failed to see that "popular traditions do not constitute consistent and organized discourses but merely *elements* which can only exist in articulation with class discourses" (pp. 166, 167). The problem requiring explanation shifts with this crucial reformulation. Rather than attempting to discover the *essential class ascription* of populist politics, the task becomes to explain the *specific conjuncture* of forces that articulate populism in either a right or left direction in a specific case.

The first essay in the book, which is a critique of Andre Gunder Frank's theory of dependency, centers on the concept of "mode of production" itself. Confronted with alternative analyses of Latin American societies, Laclau suggests a distinction between "economic system" and "mode of production" that, again, radically refigures the debate:[4]

> The concept of "world capitalist system" is therefore the nearest approximation to the concrete which a merely economic analysis permits, and . . . it cannot be *derived* from the concept of "capitalist mode of production" but must be *constructed* by starting from the theoretical study of possible articulations of the different modes of production. (Laclau, 1977/1982, p. 43)

Thus it is not possible to derive salient features of the current world system directly from the mode of production. Rather, it is the specific character of the *linkage*, or combination, of modes of production that characterizes the world system. This is a more fundamental critique of the Marxist base-superstructure model than contained in the other three essays. While they indicate limitations to the derivation of the political superstructure from the base and suggest a certain autonomy of elements and their combinations from economic determination, this argument suggests that the economic base itself is a unity only insofar as it is constructed by an articulation of more fundamental elements (modes of production).

In his introduction, Laclau generalizes these points by pointing out that the four essays demonstrate that there are two ways in which the theoretical debates he discusses have become confused: Either there is a failure to respect the proper level of theoretical abstraction, usually by substituting more concrete empirical determinations, or there is a denial of the specificity of the subject matter and its reduction to a another, supposedly more fundamental, one. His critique of Marxism thus focuses on the consequences of the failure to theorize adequately "abstraction" and "specificity." On this basis, Laclau develops a full-blown theory of articulation that focuses on the *elements* of a socioeconomic unity and the *linkage* whereby they are forged into such a unity.

The introduction begins with Plato's allegory of the cave and thereby links the theory of articulation to the social function of philosophy. Philosophy breaks up, or disarticulates, the connotative and evocative links of common sense, purifies theoretically their inherent meanings, and then rearticulates them as purely logical links. This dual movement has two related consequences. First, the purification of concepts dissolves the ideological identification of concepts with specific social forms. For example, "those concepts which defined for the bourgeoisie the abstract conditions of any possible society, lost their necessary articulation with the concrete forms in which those conditions were locally materialized" (Laclau, 1977/1982, p. 8). Philosophy functions as critical of the established order by measuring the given reality in relation to ideal determinations. Second, this critical practice is intertwined with a corresponding rationalist illusion that the whole of reality can be reconstructed in a logical and necessary manner. While common sense forms an interconnected whole absorbing every possible meaning through external links with all other meanings, philosophy claims to rearticulate a similar all-encompassing system but exclusively through inner logical links between meanings.

According to Laclau, the progress of Marxist theory has been hindered by both the connotations of common sense and essentialist rationalist paradigms due to its inadequate understanding of the relation between these two poles, or, we might say, a failure to resolve its relation to philosophy. On the one hand, connotative meanings from political practice have been inserted into theoretical discourse uncritically. For example, Marx's use of the term *capitalist* is purely as an abstract pole of analysis—a single and complete determination within the analysis of the capitalist mode of production. However, this is often confused with concrete social agents, also called capitalist, who, along with this determination in the mode of production, are also male and female, young or old, of a certain nationality, race, political party, and so forth. This confusion takes the theoretical determination to be the *name* of a social class and thereby reverses the theoretical determination of agency into a determination as one of several attributes of a concrete social subject. Any one attribute will then tend to evoke all the others connotatively. Theory is thus reduced to common sense.

On the other hand, when theory purifies common sense it often falls prey to the rationalist illusion of constructing a system of essential internal logical relations. The paradigmatic logical relation in Marxism is "class reductionism"—the idea that any element of social or political life is a necessary outgrowth of an underlying class contradiction.

> The paradoxical result is that theoretical practice has no need to correct the connotative articulations of political discourse, because if all political and ideological determinations have a necessary class ascription, they are also therefore expressive of the class essence of the subject. Since all of them, taken individually, express this subject equally, concretization of analysis can then only consist of the progressive unfolding of this essence. (Laclau, 1977/1982, p. 11)

Thus the twin errors in Marxist theory of reduction to common sense and rationalism reinforce each other in class reductionism, which is really another way of saying that the base-superstructure metaphor is characteristic of Marxism as such. If the essential logical relation in Marxist theory is the reduction to economic class position, then theoretical reflection will always determine attributes of class subjects. The givenness of these class subjects in common sense then reinforces theoretical reflection. This "bad infinity" of mutual reinforcement of essentialism and common sense will appear relatively stable if there is a relatively stable Marxist political culture. But with the breakdown of Marxist common sense a new radical situation is inaugurated for Marxist theory. "This enterprise [of abandoning class reductionism]," Laclau (1977/1982) concludes, "can in turn only be beneficial for socialist political practice, at a time when the proletariat must abandon any narrow class perspective and present itself as a hegemonic force to the vast masses seeking a radical political reorientation in the epoch of world decline of capitalism" (p. 12). Thus reduction of universal struggles to proletarian class interest is the youth, not the maturity, of Marxism. Maturity consists, rather, in the expansion from a single class to a universal hegemonic alliance.

If the various elements of political life have no necessary class ascription, then even less do the elements of cultural life generally. But this is emphatically not to say that these elements are independent of politics. Rather, the cultural and ideological sphere forms the commonsense assumptions that enter into explicit political views and positions. Thus the political sphere is expanded into a cultural politics of common sense. But this is no longer posed through the fixation of cultural elements to any necessary class belongingness, but rather through the mode of articulation of these elements into a cultural unity. It is the cohesion of elements and the overall hegemonic intent of this cultural unity that defines its political component.

Some of the implications of the first critical point that was introduced above through the discussion of British cultural studies—distinguishing poetic expression from rhetorical linkage—can be clarified on the basis of this full-blown account of articulation by Laclau. Let us pinpoint carefully the error that is involved in describing articulation solely in terms of linkage, or combination, of elements, thereby missing the activity of thematization. The error consists of taking the elements that are a *result* of the dearticulating activity of theoretical criticism to be simply there, that is, given prior to the thematization (see Angus, 1984, p. 53). This is a form of objectivism insofar as it anonymizes the (dearticulating) activity of theory and presents its results as simple givens. In short, failure to account for thematization leads to the error of empiricism, which wrongly takes the experienced everyday world to be a plurality of elements, rather than an articulated whole organized through relevances appearing as common sense. Since one of the main purposes of Laclau's first theory of articulation was to account for the role of theory in the (de)construction of common sense, this must be reckoned a key internal failure. The tendency to rediscover empiricism, which is the polemical complement of structuralism, indicates that the theory of articulation has not (yet) escaped the metaphysical oppositions it attempted to undercut. This problem is a motive for the later development of the theory of articulation by Laclau in collaboration with Chantal Mouffe.

Moreover, as will be shown later, this failure also implies that there can be neither a proper concept of totality nor a theory of the origin of modernity. While British cultural studies has concentrated successfully on an intermediate domain of culture in which elements were assumed as pregiven and the larger question of the historical epoch in which the problematic of articulation emerges was left aside, this larger context is central for the grander ambitions of the theory of articulation as conceived by Laclau. It is a task for specific cultural critiques to show that the activity of thematization, which I have also called "poetic expression," is an important component of cultural interventions.

A more comprehensive theory of cultural criticism must differentiate three levels of inquiry: the prior process of thematization, the intermediate level of linkages, and the historical level of transition between different epochs. But this critical revision can be developed further only through an analysis of the later theory of articulation developed by Laclau and Mouffe, in which the notion of element is clarified by distinguishing it from a "moment" of an articulated unity.

ANTAGONISMS IN THE DISCURSIVE FIELD

Hegemony and Socialist Strategy, coauthored by Ernesto Laclau and Chantal Mouffe (1985), develops the theory of articulation in a manner that follows out the consequences of Laclau's earlier work and transforms a theoretical development within Marxism into a post-Marxist political theory of "radical democracy" based on contemporary discourse theory. Laclau introduced the term "elements" of political ideologies in *Politics and Ideology in Marxist Theory* in order to supplant reductionism back to class origin and instead to orient toward the effectivity of a combination of these elements in an articulation. In the later work, this aspect is developed further through the distinction between "elements" and "moments" of a cultural unity, which allows them to understand the social field as constructed through *antagonism*. This notion of antagonism allows them to specify under what conditions a given social difference becomes experienced as oppressive or exploitative and, moreover, to extend such analysis beyond the terrain of class to the other antagonisms specified by the new social movements—struggles over the meaning of nation, race, sex, nature, and so forth. In each case, a given social difference, such as superpower/country, nation/region, white/black, male/female, humanity/nature, is given the inflection of an antagonism due to an effect emerging from the outside, or limit, of the social difference in question. The crucial contribution of this work is thus its rethinking of the Marxist notion of class struggle by investigating the conditions under which a social identity experiences a block to its realization. The point of political action is understood as constitutive of the social field, rather than as a circumscribed domain within it. A formulation of this issue in general terms is central to contemporary critical communication theory because, without it, studies of the construction of social identities focus simply on their plurality and heterogeneity—thereby becoming an apologetic pluralism—whereas a critical theory is concerned with the *differential* effects of power and the consequent *prevention* of the realization of social identities.

The articulation of a given cultural meaning is achieved through discursive practice oriented to linking what, in a slight shift of terminology, Laclau and Mouffe (1985) now call the various "moments" of a discourse. The identity, or meaning, of these moments within the given articulation is modified, or defined by, the particular character of the linkage established in each case. An "element," on the other hand, is defined as a "difference which is not discursively articulated" (p. 105). Articulatory practice, therefore, can be defined as the transformation of elements into moments.

> We now have all the necessary analytical elements to specify the concept of articulation. Since all identity is relational—even if the system of relations does not reach the point of being fixed as a stable system of differences—since, too, all discourse is subverted by a field of discursivity which overflows it, the transition form "elements" to "moments" can never be complete. The status of the "elements" is that of floating signifier, incapable of being articulated to a discursive chain. And this floating character finally penetrates every discursive (i.e. social) identity. (p. 113)

Elements must be conceived as preexisting the discursive formations into which they are articulated, since articulation is not a creation from nothing but a practice of linking. Moreover, the transformation of elements into moments can never be complete, because this would misinterpret the articulated discursive identity as a rationalist totality accomplished exclusively through mediation by logical relations. In consequence, any social identity must be understood temporary and partial, sustained only through a continuous articulatory practice that succeeds in repulsing alternative articulations that would dearticulate the given identity.

The key implication of this distinction (and relation) between elements and moments is the dynamic reformulation it allows of the notion of "antagonism." Without this term, articulation theory would bear no important relation to the Marxist tradition. Consequently, Laclau and Mouffe (1985) distinguish "subordination" from "domination" (pp. 154, 124). The former refers to any unequal social relation, whereas the latter refers to the same unequal relation experienced as "unjust," "insufferable," "exploitative," or some equivalent. An articulated set of social relations interpellates social differences in relations of subordination, such as lord/serf, capitalist/worker, white/black, man/woman, humanity/nature, and so forth. The Marxist question is: Under what conditions do such relations of subordination become experienced as relations of domination, or oppression, and give rise to struggles directed at their transformation? In other words, what occurs when relations of difference become experienced as antagonistic?

Within an articulated cultural unity, relations of difference are "moments" and experienced as normal. But since the transition from elements to moments is never complete, there is always the possibility of dearticulating these moments from this cultural unity into elements—which can, of course, enter as moments into a new articulation. It is at this point of dearticulation of moments into elements that antagonism arises, that the social difference is experienced as "not necessary and capable of being transformed."

Laclau and Mouffe (1985) reject the possibility of theorizing antagonism as occurring between positive social identities because such identities are understood as constituted by their articulation within a discursive formation. They exist "positively" only as a relations of subordination within a given articulation. In their words: "But in the case of antagonism, we are confronted with a different situation: the presence of the 'Other' prevents me from being totally myself. The relation arises not from full totalities, but from the impossibility of their constitution" (p. 125). A relation of antagonism thus implies a relation to a negativity, to the "outside" of the given discursive formation. It is this relation outside that transforms the internal relation of subordination into a relation of domination. Since society is not understood to be a *given totality* (whether expressive, rationalist, or empiricist) but an articulated social unity, antagonisms can be said to point to a "limit of the social," its inability to be fully present to itself. Thus power must be understood not as a conflict between constituted social identities, but as operative in the formation of identities themselves—their prevention, their temporary unity, and their dissolution—in relations of antagonism with other identities.

The limit of the social attains a presence within the discursive formation by an operation that Laclau and Mouffe designate as "equivalence." They give the example of a colonized country in which differences of dress, language, skin color, and customs become equivalent, or substitutable, as evidence of the oppressiveness of the dominant power and remark that "since each of these contents is equivalent to the others in terms of their common differentiation from the colonized people, it loses the condition of differential *moment*, and acquires the floating character of an *element*" (p. 127). This common differentiation should not be understood as various expressions of an underlying essentially antagonistic relation, which would be to revert to the positivity of the social that they criticize, but as the *construction* of equivalences that, through the antagonism, articulate the relation colonizer/colonized as domination, rather than as just subordination.

We may notice that the example in this case does not do the full duty the theory requires. Actually, Laclau and Mouffe (1985) speak of the dominant power being "made evident" in these different contexts (p. 127). But this misleading phrase is indicative of a problem that will allow us to draw out a corollary of the first critical point: If it cannot mean essential underlying relations of power that express themselves in various forms, as the phrase seems to imply (but that would be incompatible with their entire approach), then the issue is exactly how is this cultural unity of "the dominant power" constructed, and their terminology avoids this posing of the question.

To clarify that this key issue of antagonism has not been well enough illuminated by Laclau and Mouffe, let us instead refer to a dominated, but not colonized, country such as Canada, in which, we may say, the dependent relations between Canada and the United States are "like" the relations of labor/capital, which, in turn, are "like" the relations between Quebec and the federal government, "like" relations between men and women, and "like" relations between humanity and nature. This collection of similitudes, or equivalences, is not pregiven but constructed in the practical politics in which one and/or more of them is at issue. In each case, it is by no means self-evident that the best way to push one of these causes is by alliance with the dominated part of another social difference. Why not ally oneself with a dominant power in another discourse? And, of course, in the practical politics of the last 30 years—both in Canada and elsewhere—such alliances have indeed occurred. Feminism, to pick just one example, has been most "successful" where it has allied itself with the business mentality and possessive individualist notions of equality. To assume from the outset that one subordinated social difference, when it is experienced through antagonism as a domination, is in any "natural," or predictable, sense drawn to alliance with other subordinate sectors, is a remnant of exactly the Marxist essentialism that Laclau and Mouffe criticize. Let us finally say it clearly: The standpoint of the subordinated is not an epistemologically privileged one, though it is crucial politically. This certainly does not mean, however, that the question of how to ally various social identities experiencing themselves as dominated is not a fundamental issue for contemporary radical politics. But, contrary to Laclau and Mouffe, the present analysis suggests that this project cannot be formulated solely through the notion of "equivalences." It requires some theorizing of the expression of the particular domination experienced in a given social difference. Moreover, this prior cultural expression must also be placed within a conception of the social formation as a "whole," as an "epoch" characterized by a pervasiveness of the experience of domination—though this is to anticipate my second critical point, which will be discussed in the next section.

An antagonism, in Laclau and Mouffe's analysis, is constructed through the articulation of likenesses among various social differences. The construction of such equivalences is the assembling of a chain of substitutions in which each term stands as a metaphor for the others. Politics in the new social movements involves such a practice of metaphoric linkage. For this reason hegemony is fundamentally metonymical (Laclau & Mouffe, 1985, p. 141); the metaphoric equivalences, once established, are triggered by any one of them. Any part is displaced to all equivalent parts, and confirms the whole. This is true both of articulations that one could broadly call "status quo" and "progressive." Equivalences thus transform the moments of different discursive formations into floating elements that are not confined to any given formation since they tend to substitute in other formations. Such floating elements are the condition for the emergence of the problematic of hegemony in modern society—"a field criss-crossed by antagonisms and therefore suppose[ing] phenomena of equivalence and frontier effects" (pp. 135-136). But if we are not simply to presuppose the form that such equivalences may/should take—even to the point of assuming that the dominated relations have something in common—we must also focus on the constitution of specific antagonisms in the phenomenon of expression.

The construction of the equivalences that constitute antagonism requires an articulating subject. Clearly, this subject cannot preexist the articulation, since its identity is formed through the equivalences (interior to it); likewise, it cannot be entirely formed within the articulation, since its construction is a discursive *practice* that therefore requires an initiating action (exterior to it).

> If the exteriority supposed by the articulatory practice is located in the general field of discursivity, it cannot be that corresponding to two systems of fully constituted differences. It must therefore be the exteriority existing between subject positions located within certain discursive formations and "elements" which have no precise discursive articulation. (Laclau & Mouffe, 1985, p. 135)

It is this exteriority that becomes the " 'experience' of the limit of all objectivity" within a discursive formation that achieves "a form of precise discursive presence" as an antagonism (p. 121). The floating elements upon which articulatory practices operate are constructed by a chain of equivalences within the general field of discursivity. The totality of a certain discursive formation within this field is constituted by a negativity: It *is not* what is beyond the limit of its equivalences. This is termed, by Laclau and Mouffe, a transformation of limits into frontiers (p. 143). The frontier is thus the limit of a discursive formation (what it includes) transformed into a negation (what it excludes) by the construction of floating signifiers through articulating equivalences between discourses. In order to characterize the "form of presence" that this negation assumes, the term *experience* is utilized relatively often (pp. 104, 122, 125, 126; see also p. 146, ftn. 16), but it is always put in quotation marks, which implies a distancing probably due to the structuralist origins of their work. Nevertheless, it is significant that in certain contexts, especially the transformation of social subordinations into antagonisms, it is unavoidable. One would think that the task should be to abandon this embarrassment with one's language and to further the concept of articulation through a conceptualization of the experiential component that necessarily arises at this point. In this context Laclau and Mouffe state that antagonism cannot be apprehended by language—which they understand, following Saussure, as a system of differences—since "language only exists as an attempt to fix that which antagonism subverts" (p. 125). But this only serves to indicate the insufficiency of their conception of language (a structuralist-Wittgensteinian amalgam).[5] Language is not only a system of differences, and a cultural practice, but more fundamentally language-ing—the making known of the world through poetry.

The relation of interiority and exteriority of the subject to the articulation is, as was indicated at the outset of this essay, the core of the power of any given articulation. However, Laclau and Mouffe attempt to *reduce* interiority to exteriority; they investigate linkage but not thematization. Consequently, properly theorizing the power of articulation requires the utilization of the notion of "expression" as making known that was introduced as the first critical point in the previous section in connection with the extension of Laclau's earlier concept of articulation into British cultural studies.

Thus, to restate this point: The relation of elements and the discursive field should be understood as a theme/background relation as developed in the phenomenological tradition. Articulatory practice not only forges a linkage, but also focuses on, foregrounds, selected elements. This making known of selected elements allows them to become leading moments in the equivalences forged between moments of different articulations. It provides the theoretical basis for the expressive *difference* between the subordination/domination articulated by one social movement and that of another.

While I have left aside the vexing question of the interpretation of Marxism in this essay, I may note marginally at this point that the conception of thematization brings forward a key, but neglected, aspect of the base-superstructure model as it is formulated in the classic preface to *A Contribution* to the *Critique of Political Economy* (Marx, 1978). After asserting that the "legal and political superstructures" arise on the basis of, and correspond to, "material productive forces," Marx continues by distinguishing further among the types of changes in each of these realms. Material changes are said to be determinable with the exactness of natural science, which is not the case with the ideological forms, "in which men *become conscious* of this conflict and fight it out" (pp. 4-5; emphasis added). While "Marxism" has emphasized only the initial determinism of this passage, we may also see in it a problematic of "becoming conscious" that is key to social conflict. This phenomenological component of Marx's thought suggests that even the classic texts of "Marxism" have been read insufficiently. In this case, the initial "determinism" is rather a quickly sketched static topology from which the passage as a whole moves toward a dynamic formulation (in our present terminology) of the thematization central to any articulation within a contested field. The classical determinist interpretation, by contrast, reduces what is specifically new in this formulation back into the prior terms of *The German Ideology* (Angus, 1989). This is certainly not to suggest that contemporary theoretical contributions can be reduced to variant interpretations of canonical texts, but only to indicate that the accounting with Marx is not over once the spell of orthodoxy has been broken.

As the fundamental component of hegemonic struggle, an "element" is in the process of transformation into moments of various articulations, but this process is incomplete due to the competition between articulations. Thus it has a floating character that consists of not appearing outside a discursive formation, but rather appearing inside many, but in a situation of partial transformation into moments. The identity of this element is thus of a peculiar character. If it appeared outside an articulation (which it does not), it would be a positivity. If it were totally inside a given articulation (which it is not), it would be simply a moment. In this case, it would be a pure absence signifying the impossibility of equivalences, that is, the total externality of articulations. In short, an element appears as itself only within a field of competing discourses, as an expressed theme in relation to a background field, on the one hand, and in polemical opposition to the rejected Hegelian mediation of moments into a purely logical totality, on the other.

There are thus two senses of the term *element*, or, better, two ways in which the term is used in Laclau and Mouffe's theory of articulation. First, an element exists prior to its articulation into a moment of a discursive formation. Second, an element is constructed from moments of various articulations through equivalences. But this temporal terminology may be misleading. It is rather that an element-moment exists in a field of tension; it is a nodal point in a "space" crisscrossed by competing meanings. Element-moment is the name for this meaning tension as it tends to fall this way or that, into or away from the temporary unity of an articulated totality. In theorizing in this manner, the theory of articulation seeks to put itself at the point of political action, but, as indicated above, it does so only with respect to forging equivalences between existing movements, not with respect to the expression of domination itself.

The aspect of articulation that I have called thematization situates the theory of articulation more precisely at the point of political action. Laclau and Mouffe's denial of sutured totality is a valid response to the diffusion of political effects, which is to destabilize every given whole and to demonstrate that it appears as a unity only under conditions of continuous rearticulation in the face of dearticulations. But in order to approach more closely the point of politics, I may begin by noting that the denial of "necessity" to articulatory linkages is of relatively little use to any social identity attempting to *forge a specific articulation* in a situation of antagonism. While it is no doubt the case that political articulations have often falsely presented themselves as "necessary" in order to achieve hegemony, it is nevertheless the case that it is not usually a purely logical "necessity" that is meant. Moreover, the assertion of contingency amounts to only a bare assertion of the possibility of an alternative articulation.[6] It is of no help in deciding which articulation to project and thereby which equivalences to forge, which depends upon the resources enabled by the expressive poetic component of articulation.

The point of political intervention requires a distinction between contingency and "particularity." These are not complementary metaphysical opposites, as are contingency and necessity. Rather, *particularity* refers to the elements of an articulation as they are actively embraced *in the process of expression*—that is to say, at the very point where a given articulation comes into being. Particularity refers to a nonuniversal element of social identity that is expressed in it (Grant, 1969, pp. 23ff., 73ff.).[7]

Thematization of elements raises them from the contingency of an anonymous background to particular elements conferring identity. The construction of particularity through articulation is an anticipation of homecoming, a construction of a world in which the nonuniversal elements to which identities are attached become hegemonic (Angus, 1988c, p. xvii). In a world of leaky totalities, political action is not aided, and perhaps is diffused, by the assertion that it is pervaded by contingency. This is not false, it is merely the assertion of a truth inherited from previous political action—it is an effect, an afterthought. Enacting is a positing, both an expression and a linkage, that proposes a way of viewing the world. One cannot assert the contingency of an articulation in the same moment that one enacts it. The point of politics itself involves in its practical embodiment the assertion that the proposed articulation is not merely contingent, though neither can it claim necessity.

Political action can, in contrast, claim particularity, which involves a new formation of the part/whole relationship based on the phenomenological notion of thematization. Particularity "involves a step back from the relation between contingency and universality to the *condition under which* a specific being might apprehend a universal good. This regressive step back is made necessary by the absence of authoritative origin" (Angus, 1990a, p. 42). To those situated within them, the struggles of the new social movements and the new identities forged within them are particular, neither necessary nor contingent. They bring into focus new expressions of identity that do not have a similar claim on other identities, but that must be defended nonetheless. We are in the realm here not of reason but of love and hate, suffering and joy, wherein attachment to particulars resides.

The construction of equivalences between these particulars cannot reduce this specificity of attachment and, in this sense, Laclau and Mouffe's term "equivalences" is marred by the term "contingency." Thus, while Mouffe (1988) calls for a rethinking of the inherited universalism/relativism dichotomy, they cannot make any real progress toward it. The elements within the new social movements can never become strictly equal, even in a temporary fashion, since this would reduce the specificity of the antagonisms. Laclau and Mouffe's political theory of radical democracy contains within itself the ghost of the Marxist claim to universalize all struggles in that of the proletariat, though now as an articulated unity aiming at hegemony. The real political point now is a "difference in unity," a new relation of part and whole, that is not well served by a simple polemical denial of the whole and an assertion of equivalence between parts.

The "likeness" we find in different struggles can never predominate over the expression of difference. If metaphor is the process of forging equivalence, and metonymy the ideological triggering of a whole hegemonic articulation by any part, then the new social movements require also antimetonymy as a counterpart to metaphor. While there may be no ultimate literality of expression, antimetonymy can undo the displacements toward hegemonic universality toward the specific concrete particularity without which metaphoric equivalents become substitutions. The expression of the part in the midst of the dissolution of the whole field permeated by equivalences is the constitution of particularity.

I have argued above that the politics of the new social movements is indeed characterized by the metaphoric construction of equivalences, as Laclau and Mouffe suggest, but that it is also characterized by a more fundamental thematizing component that, in an antimetonymical, "regressive" move, expresses the particularity of a cultural identity and its experience of domination. The theoretical basis for this argument is the interpretation of the notion of the "element," from which the theory of articulation was developed, as a thematization from a nonthematically presupposed background. The next section examines more closely the background field, which is the space of operation of competing articulations.

TOTALITY AS WORLD-HORIZON

As has been anticipated in the previous section, the construction of equivalences in the field of discursivity requires a new notion of totality, not its abandonment. The polemical denial of totality by Laclau and Mouffe is a reversal that remains within the logic of Hegelian rationalist totality. By denying any concept of totality, they reduce theoretical articulations to those of common sense—thereby undermining one of the main purposes of Laclau's introduction of the concept of articulation in his earlier work.

Thematization, on the other hand, offers a way out of this alternative of necessity versus contingency. The universalization of contingency, the expansion of hegemony to the limit of the social, requires a new conception of the relation of part and whole. Whereas the last section focused on reformulating contingency into the notion of "particularity," this section sketches a phenomenological concept of totality as "world" derived from the theme/background relation, which is distinct from the criticized alternatives of organic, logical, or dissolved totality, and which is theorized beyond the negative statements of temporariness and unfixity. It is concerned to argue that such a phenomenological concept of totality does not fall into the errors pinpointed by Laclau and Mouffe. This argument leads to the corollary discussed in the next section, that, while the poststructuralist polemical rejection of totality is not adequate to conceptualizing the origin of modernity, this is not the case with the phenomenological concept of world-horizon.

As Laclau and Mouffe (1985) narrate, the elements on which articulations operate were specified in the eighteenth century as "fragments of a lost unity" (pp. 93-96). (It is significant that they turn to narration at this point. This is a common ploy when one cannot give an adequate theoretical account.) The analysis of modern society as a division and fragmentation was elaborated by German philosophy in contrast to their conception of the natural, organic unity of Greek culture. This unity could not be recaptured, since its very specification implies a conscious analysis that could not annul its own conditions of emergence. With the displacement of totality from origin to telos the theoretical task became the *construction* of a conscious and rational totality. Thus emerged the modern concept of alienation. Laclau and Mouffe (1985) argue that this new form of totality into which elements are to be unified may take two forms: "Either that organization is contingent and, therefore, external to the fragments themselves; or else, both the fragments and the organization are necessary moments of a totality which transcends them" (p. 94). While this is a clear alternative, one the theory of articulation seeks to address, it is nevertheless the case that the history of modern philosophy has tended to fudge the alternative. The history of Marxism has been no less clear in this respect.

A clarification of this alternative emerged in Louis Althusser's (1970) critique of Hegel through the notion of "expressive totality" (pp. 101-104). An expressive totality is a unity in which all of the elements and relations unfold from and therefore express an underlying principle. This principle of unity encompasses all transitions such that they take on a necessary and logical character. Hegel's rationalist totality claimed to be such a system of mediation through exclusively logical relations. Thus his conception of philosophy was based on the principle of the identity of logic and content. Through dialectic, speculative philosophy established the identity of thought and being (Hegel, 1979, pp. 33-35). Subsequent dialectical thought, up to Adorno, has always been skeptical of any separation of logic, or "method," and content. However, this claim masked the fact that nonnecessary, contingent relations were the basis for many so-called logical transitions, as any careful twentieth-century reader of *The Phenomenology of Mind* will have noticed. In other words, the putative banishment of rhetoric from philosophy concealed its return, disguised as logic, to shore up the system.

In contrast, Althusser, through the concept of "overdetermination," attempted to theorize the multiplicity of meanings inherent in any symbolic, or cultural, order. Laclau and Mouffe (1985) state the implication of this concept in the following manner:

> The symbolic—i.e., overdetermined—character of social relations therefore implies that they lack an ultimate literality which would reduce them to necessary moments of an immanent law. There are not *two* planes, one of essences and the other of appearances, since there is no possibility of fixing an *ultimate* literal sense for which the symbolic would be a second and derived plane of signification. Society and social agents lack any essence and their regularities merely consist of the relative and precarious forms of fixation which accompany the establishment of a certain order. (p. 98)

Laclau and Mouffe point out that this implication of Althusser's concept of overdetermination coexists in his work with an incompatible notion of "determination in the last instance by the economy" that holds it within Marxism and, indeed, reduces it back to an essentialism very much like the Hegelian type it criticizes (Laclau & Mouffe, 1985, p. 98; see, for example, Althusser, 1970, p. 111). The later deconstruction of Althusserianism allowed the possibility of merely shifting from an essentialism of expressive totality to an essentialism of elements (Laclau & Mouffe, 1985, p. 103). This alternative of expressive totality or disaggregated elements is thus a complementary metaphysical opposition within a similar essentialism (of part or whole). Laclau and Mouffe comment that this debate evaded the fundamental question, "by failing to *specify the terrain* in which the unity or separation among objects takes place, we once more fall back into the 'rationalism or empiricism' alternative" (p. 104; emphasis added). Thus it is only through the component of the "terrain," or "field," that the theory of articulation can avoid both a rationalist and an empiricist conception of totality.

The only path that Laclau and Mouffe see open at this point is "the critique of every type of fixity, through an affirmation of the incomplete, open and politically negotiable character of every identity." In an articulated identity "the presence of some in the others hinders the suturing of the identity of any of them" (p. 104). In fact, the only "positive" characteristic of an identity that Laclau and Mouffe can formulate is its lack of fixity, its temporary character. Fair enough, but how many times can one say this? The negative character of this assertion indicates that it makes sense only as a polemical assertion of postmodern antitotality in relation to the conceptions of totality to which it is opposed—Greek organic unity, modern rationalist logical totality, and the empiricist decomposition of totality into elements.

The notion of politics as the construction and deconstruction of equivalences must incorporate some notion of the general discursive field as a whole, since it is across the plural discourses constituting this field that equivalences are constructed. In the course of Laclau and Mouffe's (1985) argument, the important concept of the general "field," or "terrain," of discursivity is often used but not sufficiently clarified (pp. 111, 134, 135, 138, 182).

If we examine the manner of appearance of the field, the space of competing articulations, there are specific conditions for its emergence. If there were an articulation so successful as to achieve an uncontested hegemonic organization of the entire field, it would be Hegelian rationalist totality of mediation, rather than the space of articulations. But, also, the field cannot be simply a plurality of articulations, since it also constitutes the possibility of translation between them, through the construction of equivalences. Laclau and Mouffe (1985) say that "the *general field of the emergence of hegemony* is that of articulatory practices, that is, a field where the 'elements' have not crystallized into 'moments' " (p. 134; emphasis added). The general discursive field thus cannot be subsumed under one or any determinate number of articulations, but neither is it outside the articulations taken as a whole. Rather, it is to be sought in the very competition of articulations to hegemonize its space—a competition that, in principle, can have no decisive resolution without eliminating the entire problematic of hegemony and articulation.

These features of the field are captured in the phenomenological notion of horizon, which is built upon the theme/background relation introduced earlier to interpret the notion of an element. The element is a theme focused upon that appears only against a surrounding background. The background shades off indefinitely in all directions. It is given as "there," but not with an explicit clarity. Of course, elements previously part of the undetermined background can become themes, but this occurs precisely through a shift of theme and, thereby, a shift of background. The background can be determined only when it ceases to be background. As an undetermined surrounding to the theme, the background is not *in* time and space, but is the place and duration implicit in the theme. The shading off of the background is indefinite, but not infinite, and terminates in a *horizon* that circumscribes the background as a whole.

However, this limit of the background cannot be given as if it were a theme. There is a horizon because the background to any theme is specific to the theme due to the relevances (to use Schutz's term) to which it gives form. Related themes are related precisely by reference to an overlapping, but not identical, background and can be determined in their applicability with reference to the circumscribing horizon. The background and its horizon are therefore experienced in an entirely different manner from themes. As Husserl (1969) phrases it:

> These horizons, then, are "presuppositions," which, as intentional implicates included in the constituting intentionality, continually determine the objective sense of the immediate experiential surroundings, and which therefore have a character totally different from that of any of the idealizing presuppositions of predicative judging. (p. 199)

My second critical point pertains to the extension of the theme/background relation through the notion of horizon into a new concept of totality that is known in phenomenological terminology as the "world."

On the basis of the theme/background relation, we can define the central problem of rationalist logical mediation succinctly: Rationalism is a totality of relations among thematized elements that presents the *relations among* elements as if they were themselves thematized *elements*. The impossibility of this total thematization of all elements and relations surfaces periodically as the empiricist disaggregation. This reciprocal opposition confirms the point made in the last section: The opposition between necessary and contingent relations is an inadequate basis for the theory of articulation. Contingency is simply the absence of logical necessity. While the problematic of hegemony arises in this manner from within the rationalist dissolution, if it remains satisfied simply with the assertion of contingency, the elements are entrapped within the empiricist dissolution.

The figure/ground relationship means that any thematic unity is given within the context of a totality that, in principle, never appears thematically.[8] The background of a theme shades off indefinitely, but not infinitely, and is circumscribed by a horizon. Since there is a plurality of themes, there is also a plurality of horizons. Husserl (1973) calls the presupposed, nonthematic, *horizon of horizons* the "world" and emphasizes the difference between the evidence of the world and that of objects within it:

> There exists a fundamental difference between the way we are conscious of the world and the way we are conscious of things or objects . . . though together the two make up a fundamental unity. . . . we are conscious of this horizon only as a horizon for existing objects; without particular objects of consciousness it cannot be actual. (p. 143)

The totality of the world can never become an object. The indistinctness of the world, its characteristic of infinite continuation in time and space, provides the presupposed unity from which objects and their various backgrounds appear as belonging within the same horizon of the world. This is not to say that there is any object that cannot be thematized. On the contrary, thematization is inherently without barriers; any element can be picked up from the horizon and transformed into an explicit object. Rather, since thematization is itself the constitution of object-ness, or element-ness (in Laclau and Mouffe's vocabulary), the world is always, "prior," presupposed by elements within it. As Husserl (1973) puts it, "All that is together in the world has a universal immediate or mediate way of belonging together; through this the world is not merely a totality but an all-encompassing unity, a whole (even though it is infinite)" (p. 31; emphases removed). With this notion of world unity as "belonging together," the unity of the general discursive field can be understood without slipping into the difficulties with the notion of "totality" pointed out by Laclau and Mouffe.

We might surmise that the notion of the discursive field is not explicitly theorized by Laclau and Mouffe, precisely because the field encompasses a plurality of articulations, and thereby has a certain kind of unity. Their polemical rejection of any kind of unity may seem to suggest that the discursive field should itself be understood as an articulation. But this cannot be true. The discursive field emerges with the early modern experience of fragmentation that is the presupposition for the existence of hegemonic struggles. It cannot be reduced to a single articulation. While Laclau (1988) has affirmed the distinction of "horizon" from "foundation" to be key to the concept of postmodernity, their formulations provide no basis for theorizing it (p. 81). Thus the theory of articulation needs some conception of unity that surpasses the temporary unity of articulations. Only if this unity can be satisfactorily distinguished from both logical totality and empirical contingency can the theory of articulation theoretically account for the conditions of its own operation. The new conception of totality in the phenomenological concept of the world-horizon fulfills this function.

The totality of the horizon of the world is not a "fixity" in any of its forms (organic, rationalist, empiricist), which imply the total thematization of objects and their relations. The horizon changes with respect to the theme, and the world has a different character, or style, in different sociohistorical periods. Nonetheless, the existence of the horizon as such does not change, as the presumption of a unitary world to which themes belong does not change. This relation between change and perdurability is characteristic of nonthematic totality. It is always there, yet its particular style changes; if one were to attempt to define this style, aspects of it would be transformed into themes and there would remain an unthematized background. Its style is contingent, but its existence necessary, and this horizonal necessity can never be transferred to any specific themes.

The "world" thus has two interrelated aspects (Husserl, 1973, pp. 139, 147): On the one hand, the world is the culturally relative horizontal unity populated by social identities and with a characteristic spatial and temporal extension whose specific style is constituted by ongoing cultural practices. The "style" of a given world is instituted by a poetic expression that is successful rhetorically by being made known, commemorated, and continually rediscovered (Grassi, n.d.; Schurmann, 1987). In this sense, the instituting expression enables a discourse whose centrality in defining the style of a world is due to its ability to "translate" the other culturally relevant discourses and thereby implicate the world-horizon (Angus, 1992). Thus the "greater fundamentality" of some discourses is not a function of their "materiality," but rather of their ability to define the limits of the specific cultural world through its horizon. Similarly, the "unconscious" of a cultural unity can be addressed as "that which cannot be translated into a theme within this cultural unity," that is, as a limit concept of the horizon rather than as a repressed within a discourse. It is the general possibility of translation that constructs the limits of a discursive formation.

On the other hand, the world is a universality within which all these culturally relative worlds can encounter each other, and from whose relation global history and geography is constructed. This universality is not apprehensible apart from the culturally relative, but only *through* specific sociohistorical worlds, and is not revealed all at once, but only in glimpses.[9] It is especially important to pursue these glimpses in the turning point between two sociohistorical worlds. It is this contemporary turning point that is now discussed, with widely varying degrees of adequacy, under the heading of "postmodernity." One aspect of this turning point is that we should be able to account for the previous historical turning into the epoch out of which we are now proceeding. The next section pursues the question of the origin of modernity in this spirit.

THE ORIGIN OF MODERNITY

As a corollary of understanding the notion of totality as world-horizon, we can now address the question of the origin of modernity. As noted, Laclau and Mouffe, following German philosophy, specify the elements presupposed by articulatory practice as "fragments of a lost unity." But at this key point the theoretical status of this historically correct observation must be held up to scrutiny.

Now, either there is such a thing as an organic totality—that is, a nonconstructed, immediately given totality that encompasses each of its moments—or there is not. If there is, or was, such an organic totality, how could it disintegrate into elements? Disintegration could not come from its parts, since they serve in every case to confirm the whole. The whole is, by definition, without contradiction and could not disintegrate itself. Thus disintegration would have to originate externally, to operate from outside on an organic whole. But then, of course, it would not be a whole, but a merely apparent whole whose real partiality was later discovered.

"Greek unity" was, it would seem, either a false unity sustained only by ethnic arrogance and destined to be revealed as merely partial and dissolved from outside or a real organic unity and has not dissolved—we have merely forgotten it, but it is there for us to recapture. The progressive and conservative alternative here stems from the idea of an organic whole with which the analysis began. It is insoluble on this basis.

Laclau and Mouffe's polemical denial of totality makes it impossible for them to say anything about this crucial issue of the origin of modernity. Consequently, their starting point on this issue is narrative, rather than theoretical. When one cannot formulate a theory, one tells a story. They simply appeal, in contradiction to their own denial, to the classical historical characterization of fragmentation. But this characterization takes its content from a field defined through two totalities: the memory of a prior (Greek) organic totality and the anticipation of modern rationalist totality. But one cannot theoretically reject the Hegelian rationalist concept of totality, as well as organic totality, and simultaneously utilize the classical diagnosis of the modern world as "fragmentation," when it is precisely these conceptions of totality that make the diagnosis possible. At this point Laclau and Mouffe's analysis, or rather story, is entirely insupportable.

However, on the basis of the phenomenological critique sketched above, this issue can be sorted out. Organic totality can be defined as ascribing to thematic elements a real independence, ignoring their common relation to the world as horizon, in combination with the metaphoric elevation of one of these independent elements to the rank of a principle capable of subsuming all the rest. This is what Max Scheler (1960) calls a "relative natural worldview" (pp. 60-63; see also Angus, 1984, pp. 49-50). One example of this is the paradigmatic character of craft production throughout Plato's, and indeed Greek, philosophy (Schurmann, 1987, pp. 95-105). Unity is thus achieved by a subsumption that remains concrete because it derives from an element within the unity. Organic unity is thus a "tyranny of the part," elevated to an organization of the whole. The paradigmatic part thus metaphorically defines the horizon of the world.

Such traditional worldviews, though relatively stable in their own terms, do indeed have problems when they encounter an outside. This outside reveals the partial character of the organizing principle by confronting it with other organizing principles. The experience of "fragmentation" is thus a perennial possibility for such traditional organic unities, but it needs another condition for its emergence. The plurality of organic wholes can also lead to a simple eclecticism, which was indeed widespread in late antiquity.

Only with the rise of a new idea of universality, one that encompasses not merely elements but entire worldviews, can there be an analysis of modernity as a decay into fragments. This is a universality based not on a substantive organizing principle (which I have called here a "metaphorically elevated element"), but on the "bare possibility of an organizing principle at all" (see Husserl, 1969)—that is, a merely formal and therefore cosmo-politan claim to unity.[10] This principle defines the modern epoch. Its para-digmatic expression is, of course, Descartes's arraying of the world before himself as representation and securing its knowability in the self-evidence of immediate subjectivity.[11]

This new idea of universality reaches its apogee in the rationalist notion of a purely logical totality that is emblematic of modernity. Only on the basis of this twofold development—the combination of memory of substan-tive unity with the initial idea of formal cosmopolitan totality—could the emergent modern era be described as a fragmentation. The centrality of the notion of formal rational totality to modernity ensures that the diagnosis of fragmentation and the project of a recovery/discovery of wholeness contin-ually reemerges, especially in times of crisis.

This leads to the subsequent, and most characteristic, modern attempt at log-ical totality in Hegel, where the formal array of knowledge is acknowledged as insufficient but there is also an attempt to retrieve the fundamental project of modern subjective representation. This was attempted through accounting for the rationalist project as a historical culmination and thereby claiming to in-clude all experience within its purview. Thus the key role played in both mod-ern philosophy and social criticism of the notion of alienation, which charts a temporal path of the loss and recovery of totality—organic social totality, frag-mented individualism, new rational social totality incorporating individualism. This should serve to indicate that we can no longer simply appropriate the di-agnosis of modernity as described through the alienation story by German ide-alism, but must account for this story itself as characteristic of modernity.

Indeed, part of what is going on in the debates surrounding postmodern-ism is that it is impossible to imagine putting the fragments together again. But, in this case, they really should not be called *fragments* anymore, and the starting point of social critique must be reformulated.

The modern rationalist option begins from the elements but (unlike organic totality) cannot raise one of them into a substantive principle. Thus it begins from the pure principle of organization itself ("the bare possibility of an organ-izing principle at all"), not any particular organizing principle, and attempts to turn this formal-logical system into a substantive one by sleight of hand—though we should recognize that this "sleight of hand" is a fundamental and defining component of modernity. It consists of maintaining the concept of logical totality alongside the critique of formalism. But the critique of formal-ism, though valid, cannot of itself generate concreteness. Thus we may say that the modern rationalist totality understood as the "unconditioned condition of conditions," or "undetermined totality of determinations," in Kant and Hegel misinterprets the horizon of the world as if it were the totality of condi-tions. It does not view the whole as itself conditioned, as in organic unity, but as the sum of conditions. The unthematic horizon is thus treated as if it were the sum of thematized elements.

Thus in both ancient organic unities and modern rationalist totalities there is an obscuring of the horizon of the world as an unthematized background. The project of hegemony can emerge, as Laclau and Mouffe rightly assert, only with the decay of these two inclusive wholes. But the simple denial of totality (characteristic of many discussions of "postmodernism") makes it impossible to account theoretically for the transition to modernity and the subsequent decay of rationalism that enables hegemony to emerge and, as a consequence, for the whole of the practice of articulation itself.

By way of contrast, the present phenomenological reformulation of the concept of articulation begins from the undeveloped, but key, concept in Laclau and Mouffe's work of the "field of discursivity" to develop a conception of the world as the unthematized horizon of horizons that can address the problematic of the epochal shifts between types of world-horizons.

CRITICISM WITHOUT FOUNDATIONS

The concept of articulation emerged through the development of the key idea of structuralism—that the only alternative form of explanation to "reduction to" a prior or underlying sufficient cause is "structural determinism," or explanation with references to the organizing scheme of a totality. Thus the idea of structural totality emerged in polemical opposition to reductionism, or explanation with reference to determinate empirical contents.

Within Marxism, there is a continual resurgence of these two forms of explanation referring either toward totality or back to class origin. While these two types of explanation are different from each other, and one or the other is usually stressed by a given thinker or school, they are in a deeper sense mutually reinforcing. As Heidegger (1969) has shown, and Derrida (1982, p. 329) has elaborated, metaphysics consists of the mutual implication of origin and goal. Thus to argue for one trajectory of thought against the other misses the complementarity of the two. These local polemics do not alter the scheme of oppositions within which such reversals operate. Moreover, the ascription of origin and telos can shift their roles within these mutually reinforcing alternatives—class unity can be redefined as a goal and totality as an origin.

Since the complementarity of the two alternatives of structural totality and empirical content is now apparent, it is currently more to the point to rethink the theoretical basis of Marxism from the standpoint of the emergent concept of articulation. While the concept of articulation emerged from structuralism, or rather the unraveling of structuralism, it is not necessarily confined within the metaphysical complementarity. This essay has argued that the formulation of the theory of articulation has been sufficient to allow a break from structuralism that is significant for the development, and critique, of Marxism, but this formulation is not yet sufficiently strong to stand outside this polemical context. Should the break from structuralism

allow a new encounter with developments in, and beyond, the phenomenological tradition, it is possible that the investigation of cultural praxis can
elude metaphysical closure in a new postmodern open field.

In these days when a quote from Althusser seems to begin every discussion of ideology, and in which everything prior seems to have faded from
memory, it is necessary to recall that structuralism arose not only in the
local polemic against causal reductionism to empirical contents, but also in
opposition to the global alternative of routing theory toward everyday experience and mundane existence that is characteristic of phenomenology.
As Foucault (1980, pp. 116-118) has pointed out, French philosophy in the
1950s was polarized between structuralism and existential phenomenology.
It is in opposition to all theory oriented to finding its origin in experience
that the idea of structural determinism was articulated. In this larger context, Althusser (1970) opposed all Hegelian and "humanist" interpretations
of Marx, which, he argued, were based on a concept of "expressive totality" (pp. 202-204). The fundamental idea of expressive totality is that of a
whole that develops throughout all its aspects through an internal unfolding
of its essence. Against this, structuralism proposed the notion of "multiple
planes of determination" whose "conjunction," or intersection, could not be
conceptualized on any model of inner development. Whereas expressive totality, through its notion of internal development, relied on the mutual implication of origin and goal characteristic of metaphysical thought,
structuralism remains caught in metaphysics externally, as it were, through
its polemical denial of the relevance of origins and empirical contents.

Existential phenomenology—represented at that time in France primarily by
Sartre, Merleau-Ponty, and de Beauvoir—incorporated Marx by attempting a
synthesis of Hegel and Husserl. Thus it is not surprising that the structuralist
characterization of existential phenomenology followed their own self-concep-
tion in collapsing phenomenological (Husserlian) and Hegelian concepts of totality, though it continued by rejecting them in one fell swoop as expressive.
(Parenthetically, I may note that this confusion is still alive and well in
Habermas's recent work; 1987, pp. 300, 345-347; see also Angus, 1990b, pp.
27-29.) While this is not the place to offer a detailed critique of this attempted
synthesis, it is worthwhile to point out two key areas in which existentialists
departed from phenomenology: First, they rejected Husserl's transcendental
reduction in favor of a "mundane," or worldly, phenomenology. Second, they
did not distinguish between Hegelian and phenomenological notions of immediacy. For a Hegelian, immediacy is always mediated; thus the phenomenological retrieval of immediacy could be understood, in "expressive" fashion, to
mediate itself toward totality. The upshot of this is that the structuralist characterization was not without justification in the French context, but does not
apply to phenomenology as a whole.

The opposition between structural determination and experiential immediacy, the two concepts between which Marxism has lurched back and forth

without resolution, must now be brought into the theory of articulation itself. Not only Marxism but cultural theory in general has been articulated in the tension between viewing humanity as from a distant star and capturing the presence of experience in its presencing. The concept of articulation emerges through the structuralist denial of immediacy/origin and, in the hands of Laclau and Mouffe, engages in a complementary denial of any closed, or "sutured," totality/goal. It attempts to deny both sides of the metaphysical opposition between totality and immediacy and, for this reason, proposes an exit from the metaphysical closure in which Marxism has become trapped. This pro-Marxist critique rediscovers the rhetoric of meaning that (de)legitimates the social order and, thereby, connects the fortunes of Marxist critique of ideology to cultural criticism. For this reason, an extended focus on the concept of articulation is essential to a contemporary critical theory of communication.

This essay has argued that the polemical denial of origin and totality in which Laclau and Mouffe are engaged is itself still circumscribed by the complementary metaphysical oppositions it rejects. A genuine exit requires that these key terms be fundamentally rethought, criticized, and reformulated, which this essay has attempted to do by introducing the phenomenological terms *experience* and *world* into the space of the metaphysical deconstruction of origin and totality.

The new intellectual formation that has been coming into being in this space of metaphysical deconstruction denies the "foundationalist" and "essentialist" pretensions of modern thought and society. In particular, such a denial involves a rejection of the notion that the social totality is determinable as such. As this essay has argued, it does not (necessarily) involve the rejection of any concept of totality whatever—which would tend to reduce critical studies back to isolated studies of the mainstream type. Such a tendency is indeed widespread nowadays; it involves the consequence that radical social criticism is either silenced or reduced to sentimental and unjustified pronouncements. But, if totality is rethought as world-horizon, the social totality is not determinable as such, but only *through* the specific investigations (themes) undertaken. From this starting point, social criticism can be reconnected to both renewed theoretical formulations and specific empirical studies.

With the demise of foundationalism, this relation between specificity and totality can be understood as an internal/external relation, without any necessity to claim "fundamentalness," or priority, for either side. Social differences exist in all social formations. Only in some cases do they become "antagonisms" pressing for social change and invoking their centrality to the social form as a whole. Such antagonisms have become visible in the new social movements of the last 30 years—ecology, antinuclear, antiracist, ethnic, feminist, sexual liberation, regionalist, nationalist, and other movements. In the new social movements there has been a "step back" with respect to more conventional political events: It is not only an issue of a power struggle within a determined social formation, but primarily a question of under what conditions a given social difference is *experienced as insuffer-able* and imagination directed toward alternatives, which, thereby, *unsettles the presupposed understanding* of the social formation and provides a *glimpse into the universal dimensions* of cultural life. At this juncture, the teleology of modern society toward the ideals of "autonomy and equality" is displaced by a concern with an "ethics of difference" (Angus, 1988a). These movements invoke boundary phenomena pertaining to the relation between the internal social difference and its external context. But, as this essay has argued, they are also creatively formed by poetic expressions constitutive of their internality. The politics of common sense resides in this internal/external dynamism.

As Weber (1976, p. 78) has pointed out, the modern state maintains itself through a monopoly of the means of violence. But the question remains as to when these means can be "legitimately" used, without escalating the disintegration of the social meaning-fabric—which would, in turn, escalate the use of violence. The more fundamental question was posed in the mid-sixteenth century by Etienne de la Boetie (1975) in his *Politics of Obedience*: "The powerful influence of custom is in no respect more compelling than in this, namely, habituation to subjection" (p. 60). Since the king is only one man, what ensures that even his lieutenants will obey him? The rhetoric of meaning that (dis)establishes social order cannot be simply opposed to violence, but underlies even the use of violence and determines when, to what extent, and to what effect the means of coercion can be employed. Clearly, then, this rhetoric is always imbued with power—not only externally, due to the social position of the one who speaks (which is established in the social field as a whole), but also internally, as the power of a given speaking to (de)legitimate elements of the meaning-fabric and contribute to the (re)arranging of social order. It is the interplay between these external and internal dimensions of a given discourse that constitutes its contribution to the (de)legitimation of the social order. Every intervention in the circulation of meaning derives its power from the specific intervention in relation to the context of already existing discourses.

This new postmodern formation of totality and common sense implies a certain mutual liberation of theory and praxis. Setting aside the modern claim that theory and praxis should, or could, be a "unity," their different priorities can be acknowledged: Theory demands rigor, critical vigilance in the face of all "self-evidence," and an intelligence directed *through* all specific phenomena toward the world-horizon. Praxis involves immersion in the presuppositions of common sense as they are formed in a particular here and now in order to press for concrete change. These may be understood as poles of attraction between which any specific communication act is stretched—one intervention more to one side, the next toward the other. Theory and praxis are, in a sense, both abstractions; they are never experienced as pure types. Those of us who wish to further critical communication studies cannot do so without the immersion in praxis that generates issues and questions for theory, nor without the attempt to make theory speak in the world of common sense. But neither activity can be captured within the terms of the other, and a certain loosening of claims to unity should allow us to take each seriously on its own terms.

NOTES

1. I do not mean to imply by omission that the work stemming from the Birmingham Center is the only important tradition of critical studies of communication. The first stemmed from the pioneering work of the Frankfurt school, which remains today an important source of insight and research. An important connection between these two main waves of critical theory is that they both emerged from reformulations of the problematic of "Marxism and philosophy" that characterizes Western Marxism. A systematic comparison of the two traditions based on this common point of departure would shed a great deal of light on the role of the cultural problematic in a philosophy of communication. Neither, in any attempt at comprehensiveness, should studies of the political economy of communication be underestimated.

2. Hall refers to Laclau's *Politics and Ideology in Marxist Theory* as the source of his concept of articulation in many places (for example, see Hall, 1986c, p. 53; 1986d, p. 39; 1988, p. 10).

3. In conversation, Hall has admitted the influence of Schutz in developing his conception of the taken-for-grantedness of common sense and also that his failure to acknowledge this influence was due to the high profile of structuralism in British debates throughout the 1970s. In addition, early in his career Hall taught a seminar on Sartre's *Search for a Method.*

4. This debate also took place in Canada in the 1970s, without satisfactory resolution. Laclau's intervention became very significant for subsequent Latin American politics. One important political task for Canadian socialist theory, one that would link it directly to recent Latin American struggles, is the development of the theory of articulation with respect to Canada-U.S. relations. Concretely, this would mean a rearticulation of the work of Harold Innis with current Marxist theory. The Marx-Innis debate in the 1970s, since it did not achieve the level of rethinking of Marxism represented by Laclau's work based in Latin America, largely degenerated into a useless polemic between a so-called nationalist synthesis without theoretical foundation and a Marxist orthodoxy of independent capitalist development that totally ignored the specific features of Canadian political economy masterfully explained by Innis.

5. I can only assert, and not defend at this point, an alternative position with respect to the philosophical question of the nature of language. This position centers on "world-disclosing expression," which I would develop through reliance on Husserl, Heidegger, and Walter Benjamin. Laclau and Mouffe (1985) share the common misconception about Husserl that he traced cultural practice back to a "meaning-giving subject" (p. 105; see also Laclau, 1988, p. 70). Such constitution of meaning, in Husserl, can be addressed only transcendentally; the concrete, or mundane, ego does not confer meaning in this manner. A justification of the transcendental reduction would clearly be too far afield here. In any case, it is clear that, for Husserl, concrete egos encounter a world already permeated by cultural meaning. I might remark here also that the question of whether the whole cultural world can be adequately understood through language depends primarily on the notion of language that one adopts.

6. The consequences of a polemical denial of necessity rebounding simply to its complementary metaphysical opposition "contingency" are abundantly clear in Richard Rorty's *Contingency, Irony, and Solidarity* (1989), though it would be too far afield to document them here. Such a rebound is as likely to lead to self-satisfied (or even violent) assertion of one's own contingencies as a skeptical social critique of contingent social domination. The point, here as elsewhere, is to struggle toward concepts that encourage a thinking that exits from this sort of rebounding— which, as fashions change, will rebound back to another assertion of "necessity" soon enough.

7. Actually, George Grant uses both "particularity" and, more often, "one's own," which his rendering of Heidegger's *eigentlich*. See also Angus (1988b, pp. 14-24).

8. I am assuming here the convergence of the phenomenological and Gestalt conceptions of theme/horizon and part/whole that was established by Aron Gurwitsch. It involves a certain critique of Husserl on intrathematic organization of wholes and parts that puts to rest the residual empiricism in Husserl's work. Gurwitsch's position exerted considerable influence on Maurice Merleau-Ponty's *Phenomenology of Perception* through his lectures in Paris, which Merleau-Ponty attended, and is the basis for Merleau-Ponty's "most radical attempt to break with the essentialism inherent in every form of dualism" (Laclau & Mouffe, 1985, p. 146, ftn. 16).

9. This is the point at which the possibility of the transcendental reduction emerges. The cognoscenti will recognize that the suggestion that the universality of the world is apprehended only in glimpses (*Abschattungen*) entails a revision of Husserl's notion of the transcendental reduction. But, I believe, it is a consistent extension of his late view that the reduction needs to be continually carried out anew. Part of this revision is the suggestion that the term *transcendental subjectivity* is, in a certain sense, misleading. On these grounds, I am bound to disagree with the second part of Husserl's (1973) claim that we may attend to the general structure of the life-world "in its generality and, with sufficient care, fix it once and for all in a way equally accessible to all" (p. 139).

10. This brief theoretical account does not provide a crucial historical linkage between the decline of organic unities and the emergence of modern universality. The universal religions played a key role in this respect, since such "the pure possibility of organization as such" could not, in the first place, be conceived as the object of positive knowledge, but had to be placed beyond the knowable world.

11. For the connection of formalism and subjectivism, see Max Horkheimer's *Eclipse of Reason* (Angus, 1984, pp. 59-98).

REFERENCES

Althusser, L. (1970). *For Marx* (B. Brewster, Trans.). New York: Vintage.

Anderson, P. (1988). *In the tracks of historical materialism.* London: Verso.

Angus, I. H. (1984). *Technique and enlightenment: Limits of instrumental reason.* Washington, DC: Center for Advanced Research in Phenomenology and University Press of America.

Angus, I. H. (1988a). Displacement and otherness: Toward a postmodern ethics. In I. H. Angus (Ed.), *Ethnicity in a technological age.* Edmonton: Canadian Institute of Ukrainian Studies.

Angus, I. H. (1988b). *George Grant's platonic rejoinder to Heidegger.* Lewiston: Edwin Mellen.

Angus, I. H. (1988c). Introduction. In I. H. Angus (Ed.), *Ethnicity in a technological age.* Edmonton: Canadian Institute of Ukrainian Studies.

Angus, I. H. (1989). *Ideology as praxis: The teleology of Marx's work.* Unpublished manuscript, University of Massachusetts, Amherst.

Angus, I. H. (1990a, Spring-Summer). Crossing the border. *Massachusetts Review.*

Angus, I. H. (1990b). Habermas confronts the deconstructionist challenge: On the philosophical discourse of modernity. *Canadian Journal of Political and Social Theory, 14*(1-2, 3).

Angus, I. H. (1992). Learning to stop: A critique of general rhetoric. In I. H. Angus & L. Langsdorf (Eds.), *The critical turn: Rhetoric and philosophy in contemporary discourse.* Carbondale: Southern Illinois University Press.

Angus, I. H., & Lannamann, J. W. (1988, Summer). Questioning the institutional boundaries of U.S. communication research: An epistemological inquiry. *Journal of Communication.*

Boetie, E. de la. (1975). *The politics of obedience: The discourse of voluntary servitude* (H. Kurz, Trans.). Montreal: Black Rose.

Derrida, J. (1982). Signature event context. In J. Derrida, *Margins of philosophy* (A. Bass, Trans.). Chicago: University of Chicago Press.

Foucault, M. (1980). Truth and power. In M. Foucault, *Power and knowledge: Selected interviews and other writings 1927-1977* (C. Gordon, Ed. and Trans.). New York: Pantheon.

Grant, G. (1969). *Technology and empire.* Toronto: Anansi.

Grassi, E. (n.d.). *Rhetoric as philosophy: The humanistic tradition.* University Park: Pennsylvania State University Press.

Habermas, J. (1987). *On the philosophical discourse of modernity* (F. Lawrence, Trans.). Cambridge: MIT Press.

Hall, S. (1977). Culture, the media, and the "ideological effect." In J. Curran et al. (Eds.), *Mass communication and society.* London: Edward Arnold.

Hall, S. (1982). The rediscovery of "ideology": Return of the repressed in media studies. In M. Gurevitch, T. Bennett, J. Curran, & J. Woollacott (Eds.), *Culture, society, and the media* (pp. 56-90). London: Methuen.

Hall, S. (1985). Signification, representation, ideology: Althusser and the poststructuralist debates. *Critical Studies in Mass Communication, 2,* 91-114.

Hall, S. (1986a). Cultural studies: Two paradigms. In R. Collins, J. Curran, N. Garnham, P. Scannell, P. Schlesinger, & C. Sparks (Eds.), *Media, culture, and society: A critical reader.* Newbury Park, CA: Sage.

Hall, S. (1986b). Gramsci's relevance for the study of race and ethnicity. *Journal of Communication Inquiry, 10*(2).

Hall, S. (1986c). On postmodernism and articulation: An interview with Stuart Hall (L. Grossberg, Ed.). *Journal of Communication Inquiry, 10*(2).

Hall, S. (1986d). The problem of ideology: Marxism without guarantees. *Journal of Communication Inquiry, 10*(2).

Hall, S. (1988). *The hard road to renewal.* London: Verso.

Hebdige, D. (1979). *Subculture: The meaning of style.* London: Methuen.

Hegel, G. W. F. (1979). *Phenomenology of mind* (A. V. Miller, Trans.). New York: Oxford University Press.

Heidegger, M. (1969). *Identity and difference.* (J. Stambaugh, Trans.). New York: Harper & Row.

Heidegger, M. (1971a). The origin of the work of art. In M. Heidegger, *Poetry, language, thought* (A. Hofstadter, Trans.). New York: Harper & Row.

Heidegger, M. (1971b). . . . Poetically man dwells . . . In M. Heidegger, *Poetry, language, thought* (A. Hofstadter, Trans.). New York: Harper & Row.

Husserl, E. (1969). *Formal and transcendental logic* (D. Cairns, Trans.). The Hague: Martinus Nijhoff.

Husserl, E. (1973). *The crisis of European sciences and transcendental phenomenology* (D. Carr, Trans.). Evanston, IL: Northwestern University Press.

Johnson, R. (1986-1987). What is cultural studies anyway? *Social Text, 16.*

Laclau, E. (1982). *Politics and ideology in Marxist theory.* London: Verso. (Original work published 1977)

Laclau, E. (1988). Politics and the limits of modernity. In A. Ross (Ed.), *Universal abandon? The politics of postmodernism.* Minneapolis: University of Minnesota Press.

Laclau, E., & Mouffe, C. (1985). *Hegemony and socialist strategy: Towards a radical democratic politics* (W. Moore & P. Cammack, Trans.). London: Verso.

Lukes, S. (1974). *Power: A radical view.* London: Macmillan.

Marx, K. (1978). Preface to *A contribution to the critique of political economy.* In R. C. Tucker (Ed.), *The Marx-Engels reader.* New York: W. W. Norton.

McGee, M. C. (1980). The "ideograph": A link between rhetoric and ideology. *Quarterly Journal of Speech, 66*(1).

Mouffe, C. (1988). Radical democracy: Modern or postmodern? In A. Ross (Ed.), *Universal abandon? The politics of postmodernism.* Minneapolis: University of Minnesota Press.

Rorty, R. (1989). *Contingency, irony, and solidarity.* New York: Cambridge University Press.

Scheler, M. (1960). *Die Wissenformen und die Gesellschaft.* Munich: Francke Verlag.

Schrag, C. O. (1986). *Communicative praxis and the space of subjectivity.* Bloomington: Indiana University Press.

Schurmann, R. (1987). *Heidegger on being and acting: From principles to anarchy.* Bloomington: Indiana University Press.

Schutz, A. (1971). On multiple realities. In A. Schutz, *Collected papers 1: The problem of social reality* (M. Natanson, Ed.). The Hague: Martinus Nijhoff.

Taylor, C. (1977). Interpretation and the sciences of man. In F. R. Dallmayr & T. A McCarthy (Eds.), *Understanding and social inquiry.* Notre Dame, IN: University of Notre Dame Press.

Thompson, E. P. (1963). *The making of the English working class.* London: Galancz.

Weber, M. (1976). Politics as a vocation. In H. H. Gerth & C. W. Mills (Eds. and Trans.), *From Max Weber.* New York: Oxford University Press.

Willis, P. (1977). *Learning to labor.* New York: Columbia University Press.

Communication, Postmodernism, and the Politics of Common Sense

DENNIS K. MUMBY
Purdue University

Is a philosophical movement properly so called when it is devoted to creating a specialized culture among restricted intellectual groups, or rather when, and only when, in the process of elaborating a form of thought superior to "common sense" and coherent on a scientific plane, it never forgets to remain in contact with the "simple" and indeed finds in this contact the source of the problems it sets out to study and to resolve? Only by this contact does a philosophy become "historical," purify itself of intellectualistic elements of an individual character and become "life." (Gramsci, 1971)

IAN Angus's chapter represents the kind of scholarship that elicits simultaneous feelings of annoyance and admiration. On the one hand, the reader is confronted with prose that is so tightly argued that it requires an exegetical act of major proportions; indeed, one cannot read the chapter without sometimes feeling frustrated at both the density of the argument and one's difficulty in making sense of it. To paraphrase Clifford Geertz (1983, p. 58), the trick with Angus is to figure out what the devil he thinks he is up to. On the other hand, it is very clear that, with this essay, Angus is making an important contribution to extant critical studies in communication. As this is the case, I would like to bracket any residual feelings of annoyance (at either the article's moments of obscurity or my own moments of obtuseness) and instead thematize and engage with what I see as the most significant aspects of Angus's work.

The structure of this commentary is therefore as follows: First, a brief reading of Angus's paper is provided in which I highlight what I see as the principal thrust of his argument. Second, the importance of this argument is addressed. Finally, and most important, I want to extend the scope of Angus's theoretical project by suggesting how it might be most fruitfully employed within a communication framework, for while it is certainly the

Correspondence and requests for reprints: Dennis K. Mumby, Department of Communication, Heavilon Hall, Purdue University, West Lafayette, IN 47907.

Communication Yearbook 15, pp. 571-581

case that Angus locates himself within that part of the critical tradition that
concerns itself directly with communication issues, he does little to address the
question of how his revitalized conception of articulation helps us to rethink
the parameters of the communication discipline's "orthodox consensus." To
this end, I will more directly take on the relationship between communication
(as both field of study and practice) and the concept of articulation, situating
this discussion explicitly within a postmodern feminist frame of analysis.

MAKING SENSE OF
"THE POLITICS OF COMMON SENSE"

There is no doubt that Angus's project is an ambitious one, requiring a
high level of commitment and perseverance on the part of the reader (in
this context, the chapter's epigraph seems particularly apposite!). In this
case, however, perseverance is well rewarded. Let me try to make sense of
what I see as the central tenets of Angus's chapter.

Angus's title, "The Politics of Common Sense," juxtaposes what are ostensibly two differing, if not contradictory, terms. How can one have a "politics"
of "common sense"? Why should common sense be construed as political in
nature? Certainly in the ordinary scheme of things the notion of common sense
suggests one's orientation to the world that becomes developed and refined as
one gains in experience; in other words, it implies a taken-for-granted ability
to cope with the exigencies that daily life entails. In this context, "common
sense" connotes "practical knowledge" of everyday affairs (phronesis) or, as
Gadamer (1989) states, "It is a kind of genius for practical life" (p. 26). But it
is just this notion of *sensus communis* that lends itself to a political interpretation; that is, to an interpretation that focuses on the processes through which
social and power relations are constructed and reproduced, and that thus shape
common sense itself. Gadamer's (1989) appropriation of common sense is intended to exemplify the roots of a form of knowledge that constitutes an
individual's grounding in a particular tradition or historical community. As
such, common sense as a form of practical knowledge is differentiated from
theoretical knowledge as produced in the empirical-analytic sciences. Part of
Gadamer's purpose in making this distinction is to articulate an ontological
grounding for the human sciences that is fundamentally located at the level of
community. Thus the notion of *Bildung* (culture, self-formation), as conceptualized by Gadamer (1989, pp. 9-19), embodies the process of "becoming," in
which each individual's self-formation (i.e., development of common sense,
taste, judgment) is inextricably tied to his or her enmeshment in a particular
set of historically grounded cultural practices:

> What gives the human will its direction is not the abstract universality of rea-
> son but the concrete universality represented by the community of a group, a

people, a nation, or the whole human race. Hence developing this communal sense is of decisive importance for living. (p. 21)

Now, although Gadamer's notion of common sense is fundamental to his ontological grounding of the human sciences, the question remains whether he is able to articulate an adequate *politics* of common sense. In other words, is Gadamer able to conceive of the hermeneutic act as involving more than the explication of meaning as bound up in *Sprachlichkeit* (linguisticality)? Habermas, of course, would argue that Gadamer has no room for a politics of common sense because of his absolutization of language and tradition. By arguing for the fundamental linguisticality of understanding, and placing such understanding within the "concrete universality" of tradition, Habermas (1977) suggests that Gadamer leaves no room for reflection and hence critique of structures of domination:

> Language is *also* a medium of domination and social power. It serves to legitimate relations of organized force. In so far as the legitimations do not articulate the relations of force that they make possible, in so far as these relations are merely expressed in the legitimations, language is also ideological. Here it is not a question of deceptions within a language, but of deception with language as such. Hermeneutic experience that encounters this dependency of the symbolic framework on actual conditions changes into the critique of ideology. (p. 360)

Angus's notion of the politics of common sense is intended to explicate exactly this relationship—that is, to demonstrate the process through which specific linguistic meaning systems become attached to certain relations of organized force. Thus an "articulated cultural unity [Gadamer's 'tradition'?] links components that do not necessarily belong together, but whose connection is forged in the activity of articulation itself" (Angus, p. 541).

A *politics* of common sense, then, is grounded in the principle that notions of community, tradition, sense-making, and so on are always subject to a struggle over meaning. This "struggle" takes place through the various discursive practices in which different actors and social groups engage. Thus the construction of common sense is political to the extent that it is shaped by the given order of relations of power that make up a particular social system. As Angus points out in the context of both Gramsci's (1971) and Hall's (1985) work, common sense is inextricably tied up with systems of ideological hegemony that frame what is to be taken for granted as the given order of things.

In this context, Gramsci (1971, pp. 323-343) articulates a relationship among philosophy, politics, and common sense. This relationship has far-reaching consequences for our understanding of "the struggle over meaning" that lies at the heart of articulation theory. For Gramsci, "all men are 'philosophers' " (p. 322), involved not in abstract cogitation but in the concrete development of specific conceptions of the world. However, for the most part such philosophical thought takes a commonsense form that largely takes for granted the extant, externally imposed order of daily life. But, at a second level, philosophy is characterized by awareness and criticism, the starting point of which is "the consciousness of what one really is, and is 'knowing thyself' as a product of the historical process to date which has deposited in you an infinity of traces, without leaving an inventory" (p. 324). In this sense, philosophy supersedes common sense and takes a form that Gramsci refers to as "good sense."

The importance of this move is that it grounds philosophy firmly in a political context, and is one of the main anchoring points for Gramsci's (1971) "philosophy of praxis":

> Critical understanding of self takes place therefore through a struggle of political "hegemonies." . . . Consciousness of being part of a particular hegemonic force (that is to say, political consciousness) is the first stage towards a further progressive consciousness in which theory and practice will finally be one. . . . This is why it must be stressed that the political development of the concept of hegemony represents a great philosophical advance as well as a politico-practical one. For it necessarily supposes an intellectual unity and an ethic in conformity with a conception of reality that has gone beyond common sense and has become, if only within narrow limits, a critical conception. (pp. 333-334)

Of course, Gramsci's position is somewhat anachronistic, at least in the sense that he sets up the Communist party (the "Modern Prince") as the vehicle through which an "organic" link is established between intellectuals and the masses, and as the context in which the unification of theory and practice occurs. Such a position does not bear close scrutiny today, but provides an important beginning point for an elaboration of a viable relationship among politics, philosophy, and common sense. As such, one can argue that the theory of articulation as laid out by Angus is an extension of the model of the philosophy of praxis as developed by Gramsci. In other words, Angus's elaboration of a theory of articulation within the context of critical communication studies provides a framework for examining the specific communicative practices through which hegemonic meaning systems are maintained, reproduced, and transformed. Articulation theory is thus both a theory of the domination of one group or groups by another, and a theory of the emancipatory and transformative potential implicitly present in all relations of domination.

Ultimately, then, the notion of a politics of common sense is not oxymoronic, but on the contrary embodies within it the nature of the social actor's own understanding of his or her being-in-the-world. The issue of the struggle over meaning can be adequately addressed only by analyzing the processes through which certain signification systems come to hold sway over others. The analysis of the ongoing process of disarticulation and rearticulation is a crucial step in understanding how meaning becomes "fixed" and hence represented to the social actor in a particular way. Thus the theory of articulation is also a theory of ideology—that is, a theory that explains the "work of fixing meaning through establishing, by selection and combination, a chain of equivalences" (Hall, 1985, p. 93).

Much of Angus's chapter is devoted to an explanation of the limitations associated with Laclau and Mouffe's (1985) conception of articulation. While I am not particularly interested in recapitulating and critiquing the subtle twists and turns of this argument (I think Angus provides a coherent and well-"articulated" thesis), I would like to pick up on a couple of issues that I think are particularly important for critical communication studies. The first involves Angus's critique of Laclau and Mouffe's limited Saussurian conception of language. As he correctly points out, language is more than a system of differences; it is also both a cultural practice and "more fundamentally language-ing—the making known of the world through poetry" (p. 551). The second and related issue involves Angus's comment that critical communication studies tends to "subordinate communication processes to investigations of the social totality that are, in principle, of another type altogether. . . . This approach tends to reduce the *generativity* of communication processes to being simply the effect of wider determinations" (p. 536). In other words, communication as viewed from a critical perspective frequently takes on a representational, epiphenomenal dimension (i.e., it is seen as representing other, more deeply rooted, social and political phenomena) rather than being conceived as *constitutive* of social forces.

These two issues are clearly connected insofar as they both address the question of the role of communication in the production and reproduction of differences within the social totality. If communication were conceived of primarily as a play of differences (as in Saussurian structuralism; see Giddens, 1979, for a critique of this position), then any real notion of agency as a generative or transformative factor disappears. Similarly, the conception of communication as primarily an effect of other socioeconomic factors again reduces the social actor-as-language-ing agent to an epiphenomenal status within the play of both linguistic and social differences.

The principal issue, then, becomes one of formulating an appropriate (critical) conception of communication that can both account for the constitutive role that communicative practices play in the construction of systems of power and domination and, at the same time, provide a context for agentic possibilities of transformation and emancipation. Angus phrases this issue thus:

> It is not only an issue of a power struggle within a determined social formation, but primarily a question of under what conditions a given social difference is *experienced as insufferable* and imagination directed toward alternatives, which, thereby, *unsettles the presupposed understanding* of the social formation and provides a *glimpse into the universal dimensions* of cultural life. At this juncture, the teleology of modern society toward the ideals of "autonomy and equality" is displaced by a concern with an "ethics of difference." (p. 565)

Within Angus's frame of reference this ethics of difference provides the context for what he terms a "new postmodern formation of totality and common sense" (p. 566). That is, a politics of common sense is framed within a mode of critique predicated upon the dynamic relationship between internal and external social factors. If I understand this conception correctly, Angus is suggesting that the notion of totality should be viewed not as a static, determinable structure within which social forces vie for preeminence, but as a contingent social form ("world-horizon") that contextualizes and frames communicative practices. If this is the case, then Angus is suggesting a rejuvenated framing of the relationship between communication and social structure—one that moves beyond some of the difficulties associated with perspectives that attempt to privilege one or the other.

In the next section, I suggest how a postmodern conception of communication can provide us with greater insight into issues relating to the aforementioned "struggle over meaning" and the role of articulation in this process. More specifically, I want to address, briefly, postmodern feminism and its potential for advancing current critical approaches to communication studies.

POSTMODERN FEMINISM AND
CRITICAL COMMUNICATION STUDIES

My choice of postmodern feminism as a mode of critical analysis is not an arbitrary one used simply for purposes of illustration. The coming together of postmodernism and feminism is a development that has potentially important ramifications for critical communication studies, yet it is one that has not been explored in any depth in our field. Part of the significance of this development lies in its bringing together of theoretical and political issues that have previously been treated largely in a separate fashion. As Fraser and Nicholson (1990) state:

> [Postmodernists] have begun by elaborating anti-foundational metaphilosophical perspectives and from there have drawn conclusions about the shape and character of social criticism. For feminists, on the other hand, the question of philosophy has always been subordinate to an interest in social criticism. . . . As a result of this difference in emphasis and direction, the two tendencies have ended up with complementary strengths and weaknesses. (p. 20)

The tendency has been for postmodernism to concern itself in the main with epistemological questions relating to issues of subjectivity, rationality, and truth; however, at the same time it has neglected to address the important political dimensions of such questions. Feminism, on the other hand, has often fallen into an essentialist, reductionistic position through its privileging of "women's experience" as a mode of political critique of the hegemony of patriarchy. As such, it has tended to eschew extant theorizing as masculinist and by definition ideologically biased.

Postmodern feminism can move beyond this problem by being critical of modernist principles while at the same time remaining true to the political agenda that defines feminism as a social movement. For example, the question of subjectivity takes on great importance in postmodernist thought. Writers such as Derrida (1976), Foucault (1973, 1979, 1980), and Lyotard (1984) argue for a "decentered" notion of subjectivity in which we move beyond a logocentric/phonocentric view of the individual as the source of knowledge, rationality, and so on, and instead examine subjectivity as what is constituted through various discursive and institutional forms. Thus for Foucault (1979), "the subject who knows" is the effect of certain "power-knowledge" regimes that constitute our very understanding of reason, rationality, and so forth (p. 28).

From this perspective, a postmodern feminism requires that we examine the various discursive practices through which gender identity is constructed. Rather than viewing certain experiences as essentially masculine or feminine, the primary concern becomes one of showing how it is that knowledge is constructed in such a way that masculine discourse is privileged while feminine discourse becomes the marginalized other voice (Flax, 1990; Fraser, 1989; Weedon, 1987). In other words, the object of study is the articulatory system that connects certain relations of domination with a particular set of signifying practices such that a patriarchal structure of common sense becomes institutionalized.

A postmodern feminist approach can be brought readily to bear on communication studies in ways that provide insight into the relationships among communicative practices, meaning systems, and structures of domination. Such insight operates on two principal levels. First, and perhaps most obviously, communication as a signifying practice can be critiqued in terms of its gendered nature. Specifically, how do certain communicative behaviors constitute individuals as subjects in ways that privilege the masculine over the feminine? Second, because of its concern with the question of knowledge formation, postmodern feminism can provide critiques of disciplinary (i.e., research) practices that legitimate certain epistemological frameworks at the expense of others.

Clearly these two levels of critique are related. For example, Spitzack and Carter (1987) demonstrate how, in the communication field, the preoccupation with specific epistemological and methodological questions has led to an extremely narrow conception of "women's issues" in which the question of gender is reduced to its manipulation as a research variable. Communication research into "gender issues" generally gets reduced to an examination of the differences between male and female communication in various social contexts. In organization studies, for example, much of the "gender-based" research centers on the question of compliance gaining and examines the various communication strategies that women managers must employ to exercise authority over male subordinates. While such research may be vaguely feminist in tenor (i.e., women managers need to "make it" in the workplace), in reality the very notion of gender is depoliticized and rendered unproblematic, except to the extent that its "effect" has to be established. Thus gender becomes defined as an epiphenomenal dimension of communication, rather than as a political and epistemological construct within which the subjectivity of women and men is constituted.

Postmodern feminist theory therefore posits a particular kind of framework within which to situate the politics of common sense and the theory of articulation. On the one hand, it is true to Gramsci's philosophy of good sense in that it problematizes the basic assumptions of social science research, including its blindness to its own androcentric biases; any "commonsense" assumptions about gender issues are thus subject to critique. By questioning the epistemological foundations upon which most communication research is grounded, it brings into sharp focus the political implications of particular kinds of theory and research development. On the other hand, postmodern feminism provides a powerful means by which various communicative practices can be examined, understood not as a system of message transmission, but rather as the process through which the subjectivity of women and men is constituted within various discursive fields.

Within the field of communication, then, the goal of a radical perspective such as postmodern feminism is to interrogate the politics of common sense as it emerges both in everyday communication practices and in the conduct of communication research. Such a goal is frequently absent from mainstream communication theory and research because of its a priori acceptance of an objectivist ontological and epistemological stance. From such a position the empirical world is revealed through the communicative representation of the world in a particular way. This "ideology of representation" privileges and idealizes the development of a seamless, noise-free relationship between communicants on the one hand and communication researchers and their objects of study on the other. In both cases, communication is legitimated in terms of its capacity to represent.

Postmodern feminism, it can be argued, provides one perspective from which to deconstruct this process of legitimation through representation, in which communication is commonsensically viewed as representing to social actors and researchers alike the "objective" conditions of their existence. Postmodern feminism can deconstruct this process by looking at the ways in which communication practices objectify and normalize women and men within contemporary power-knowledge regimes.

But what does it mean to deconstruct the "ideology of representation" in communication? Here we can draw upon Lyotard's (1984) definition of postmodernism as "incredulity toward metanarratives" (p. xxiv). Communication-as-representation is a metanarrative that legitimates certain forms of theory and research in the communication field. That is, it provides a paradigmatic framework against which communicative practices are judged according to their fidelity to an objective norm. Because of its status as the received view, however, the ideology of representation is largely viewed as a neutral conception of communication, rather than as a perspective that has particular epistemological and political consequences.

That such a perspective is *not* neutral is demonstrated through the articulation of a form of discourse that falls outside of the purview of the dominant representational paradigm, presenting what Lyotard (1984) refers to as a *"petit récit"* (little narrative). Postmodern feminist theory might be viewed as such a *petit récit* insofar as it deconstructs patriarchal discourse to show how women's perspectives of the world are systematically excluded from serious consideration in areas ranging from literary theory (Culler, 1982) to political theory (Cocks, 1989) to anthropology (Rabinow, 1986). As already indicated, the field of communication has largely excluded women from its domain of study, either treating communication as "womanless" or viewing women as "other." In either case a patriarchal view of the world frames research on women's communication. In Lyotard's terms, one might say that women's communication and feminist research have fallen victim to the conformist, or "terrorist," ideals of the ideology of representation in communication studies. The primary source of this representation process is "absolutely centered, unitary, masculine" (Owens, 1983, p. 58).

Postmodern feminism, however, upsets the preeminence of the centered subject-as-masculine, through its challenging of the received notion of the individual-as-subject (i.e., as the stable, coherent wellspring of knowledge). At the same time, feminist theory attempts to exploit this decentering of the masculine subject by articulating alternative modes of discourse that address the positioning of the female subject. At the risk of appearing self-serving, I provide a brief example from my own work to illustrate this point.

Mumby and Putnam (1990) present a deconstructive critique of Simon's (1976) concept of "bounded rationality." The purpose is to show that, while Simon provides an important critique of classical notions of "pure" organizational rationality, his assumptive base is still firmly rooted within patriarchal conceptions of reason, rationality, and knowledge formation. As such, bounded rationality still conceives of organizations in ways that privilege technical and instrumental knowledge forms, and that marginalize knowledge based on mutual understanding and self-reflection. Our analysis is founded in Derrida's deconstructive criticism, and focuses on the play of opposites that reside in the texts articulated around the conception of bounded rationality. Thus oppositional terms such as *public/private, rationality/emotionality, mind/body,* and *formal/informal* serve to articulate a system of meaning in which the first term in each oppositional pair is given primacy over (but at the same time is defined by) the second term. In other words, the system of meaning that is articulated through the concept of bounded rationality is dependent upon oppositional but mutually defining terms; meaning is "fixed" through the privileging of one term and the marginalizing of the other term in each pair.

However, the analysis is not premised simply on the deconstruction of these oppositional pairs within the epistemological system constituted by bounded rationality. Rather, an attempt is made to "rescue" the marginalized terms articulated in this system of meaning. Thus the concept of "bounded emotionality" is juxtaposed against bounded rationality not simply as an oppositional, secondary term, but as the grounding for an alternative heuristic for organizing. By recouping emotionality as an organizational construct, an alternative epistemological framework is presented that provides the possibility for new forms of organizing.

Analyses such as this provide one way of examining the relationship between subjectivity and meaning, and demonstrate how communicative and research practices establish the range of subject positions available to women and men in institutional settings. As Weedon (1987) states, communication "is the place where actual and possible forms of social organization and their likely social and political consequences are defined and contested. Yet it is also the place where our sense of ourselves, our subjectivity, is *constructed*" (p. 21).

CONCLUSION

I have tried to show how the politics of common sense and its framing within the theory of articulation might get played out within a postmodern feminist conception of communication. What is common to both my own position and that laid out by Angus is an attempt to move beyond the traditional conception of communication as articulated by an originary, sovereign subject. That is, we need to recast the relationship between the subject and the communicative practices in which they engage. The theory of articulation provides for such a recasting by showing how communicative practices function to situate the individual within a complex system of signification. Thus subjectivity becomes not the origin of discourse but its effect.

What implications does this position have for communication studies in general? Such a move elevates communication as a field from its parochial concerns with endless theorizing about the nature of communication and the concomitant isolation of different communication contexts to be analyzed. Instead, communication studies must take on a greater degree of reflexivity, and recognize the extent to which it is bound up with the constitution of power relations and ideological meaning formations. The "decentering of the [communication] subject" that I am proposing does not assign the field of communication to an academic backwater, but rather repositions it at the center of social theory; it allows us to develop a more liberating conception of the human subject.

By viewing communication as both the medium and the outcome of social and political practices we can gain a more adequate account of the relationship between the individual and the social. Communication as a field has to figure out what "fixes" the normal; what creates the conditions under which a certain form of "common sense" prevails and allows one group to oppress another? A privileging of the sovereign subject cannot accomplish this because knowledge as such becomes grounded in the constitutive, transcendent experience of the individual. It is only through situating subjectivity within the dynamic interplay of articulated discursive practices that we can come to grips with the relationships among communication, knowledge, and power. Angus provides us with an important step in that direction.

REFERENCES

Cocks, J. (1989). *The oppositional imagination.* New York: Routledge.

Culler, J. (1982). *On deconstruction.* Ithaca, NY: Cornell University Press.

Derrida, J. (1976). *Of grammatology* (G. C. Spivak, Trans.). Baltimore: Johns Hopkins University Press.

Flax, J. (1990). *Thinking fragments.* Berkeley: University of California Press.

Foucault, M. (1973). *The order of things.* New York: Vintage.

Foucault, M. (1979). *Discipline and punish* (A. Sheridan, Trans.). New York: Vintage.

Foucault, M. (1980). *Power and knowledge: Selected interviews and other writings 1927-1977* (C. Gordon, Ed. and Trans.). New York: Pantheon.

Fraser, N. (1989). *Unruly practices: Power, discourse, and gender in contemporary social theory.* Minneapolis: University of Minnesota Press.

Fraser, N., & Nicholson, L. (1990). Social criticism without philosophy: An encounter between feminism and postmodernism. In L. Nicholson (Ed.), *Feminism/postmodernism* (pp. 19-38). New York: Routledge.

Gadamer, H.-G. (1989). *Truth and method* (2nd ed.) (J. Weinsheimer & D. Marshall, Trans.). New York: Continuum.

Geertz, C. (1983). *Local knowledge.* New York: Basic Books.

Giddens, A. (1979). *Central problems in social theory.* Berkeley: University of California Press.

Gramsci, A. (1971). *Selections from the prison notebooks* (Q. Hoare & G. Nowell Smith, Trans.). New York: International.

Habermas, J. (1977). A review of Gadamer's *Truth and method.* In F. Dallmayr & T. McCarthy (Eds.), *Understanding and social inquiry* (pp. 335-363). Notre Dame, IN: University of Notre Dame Press.

Hall, S. (1985). Signification, representation, ideology: Althusser and the poststructuralist debates. *Critical Studies in Mass Communication, 2,* 91-114.

Laclau, E., & Mouffe, C. (1985). *Hegemony and socialist strategy: Towards a radical democratic politics* (W. Moore & P. Cammack, Trans.). London: Verso.

Lyotard, J. F. (1984). *The postmodern condition* (G. Bennington & B. Massumi, Trans.). Minneapolis: University of Minnesota Press.

Mumby, D., & Putnam, L. (1990, August). *Bounded rationality as an organizational construct: A feminist critique.* Paper presented at the annual meeting of the Academy of Management, San Francisco.

Owens, C. (1983). The discourse of others: Feminists and postmodernism. In H. Foster (Ed.), *The anti-aesthetic: Essays on postmodern culture* (pp. 57-82). Port Townsend, WA: Bay Area.

Rabinow, P. (1986). Representations are social facts: Modernity and post-modernity in anthropology. In J. Clifford & G. Marcus (Eds.), *Writing culture: The poetics and politics of ethnography* (pp. 234-261). Berkeley: University of California Press.

Simon, H. (1976). *Administrative behavior* (3rd ed.). Glencoe, IL: Free Press.

Spitzack, C., & Carter, K. (1987). Women in communication studies: A typology for revision. *Quarterly Journal of Speech, 73,* 401-423.

Weedon, C. (1987). *Feminist practice and poststructuralist theory.* Oxford: Basil Blackwell.

The Politics of Articulation and Critical Communication Theory

LEONARD C. HAWES
University of Utah

A NGUS tells us his post-Marxist critique "argues that the advances in Marxist theory that the concept of articulation achieves can . . . be secured and developed only within a theoretical perspective that retrieves a key experiential dimension" (p. 539). In his account, contemporary Marxism is trapped within a metaphysical opposition between a denial of experiential immediacy, as argued by existential phenomenologists (e.g., Sartre), on the one side, and a denial of a sutured totality, as argued by Marxist structuralists (e.g., Althusser), on the other. Laclau (1977/1982, 1988), Laclau and Mouffe (1985, 1987), and Hall (1982, 1985, 1986a, 1986b, 1986c, 1988) work at denying both sides of this metaphysical opposition, and they propose articulation theory as the exit from this metaphysical trap. Angus contends, nevertheless, that those attempts are partially unsuccessful insofar as they remain trapped within the oppositions they struggle to deny. To make good on the escape, Angus argues that phenomenological terms must be introduced into the discourse, specifically the terms *experience* and *world*, for the deconstruction of immediacy and totality to be realized.

Just as Angus wants to move beyond the restrictions and constraints of orthodox, base-superstructure Marxism toward a phenomenologically adequate post-Marxist discourse theory, I want to extend the theory of articulation beyond, on the one side, sociological and cultural structuralisms toward the limits of biogenetic structuralism and, on the other side, beyond existential and transcendental phenomenologies toward the limits of the neurophenomenological production and reproduction of cultural embodiments. The aim of this particular expansion of post-Marxist discourse theory is to think through *subjectivity, meaning, experience*, and *consciousness* as materially embodied and socioculturally organized subjects of and for cultural praxis.

Correspondence and requests for reprints: Leonard C. Hawes, Communications Department, 304 LCB, University of Utah, Salt Lake City, UT 84112.

Communication Yearbook 15, pp. 582-594

Rather than entering the debate that rotates around the advantages and disadvantages of abandoning the base-superstructure formulation of Marxism that is theorized as a historical logic of modes of production, Angus begins with Gramsci's concept of hegemony, which is an attempt to account for a growing accumulation of contingent relations that do not fit into this historical logic. Laclau and Mouffe (1985) radically redefine the domain of contingent hegemonic relations in ways that dearticulate the logic of historical development; articulation logic takes the place of the presupposed background of historical logic. Angus refers to this reconfiguring as a "figure/ground shift." Articulation itself becomes the background against which historical and economic phenomena emerge; it is theorized as the logic of contingent relations extended to the entire social field and, as such, is central for the practice of cultural criticism.

BIOGENETIC STRUCTURALISM

I want to trace out another line of flight that spins off Angus's argument. I want to argue that individuated bodies, as material vehicles for, and embodiments of, cultural praxis, are cultural all the way down, and that proceeding "all the way down" entails phylogenetic, ontogenetic, and sociogenic structuring and organizing. I want to argue that material bodies, the several billions of neurophysiological/anatomical/chemical bodies, taken both individually and collectively, are each indefinitely dense massifications of networks of living cells that constitute living social subjects and, simultaneously, sociocultural (em)body(ments). Such bodies are by definition both complete and incomplete, both stationary and in process.

This biogenetic structuralist insight begins with, takes seriously, and both theoretically and empirically articulates the material relationships between brain and culture. Jean-Pierre Changeux (1983, 1985) argues that the increment of genetic material in humans compared with chimpanzees is too minuscule to account for the phenomenal increase in neural organizational complexity of the former over the latter. His theoretical focus is on the ways synaptic innervations are articulated (a process structurally similar, if not homologous, to Angus's two articulatory movements of *thematization* and *combination*) against a background field of potential synaptic relations. During the early developmental phase of the human organism, the structural organizing processes are highly redundant and largely determined by genetic coding. They thereby produce generic cell types that are capable of developmentally accommodating any neuronal configuration as a member. What follows developmentally is a selection process during which a field of synapses is laid down; some are grooved and reinforced through activity whereas others atrophy and are eliminated by means of cell inactivity.

Changeux's (1983, p. 475) conclusion is that the indefinite complexity of human symbolic expression and behavior can be both theoretically and empirically accounted for in terms of a relatively parsimonious and finite neurocognitive system in interaction with a complex and perpetually changing material environment. Recall that for Edward Thompson (1963), in *The Making of the English Working Class*, experience is understood as the interaction of consciousness with the conditions of life. Changeux's work accounts for cognitive processes in material terms: in terms of living cells. Any neuron's environment consists of the networks in which it works as a component, and such networks of reciprocal relationships build up the hierarchy of organization through the complete nervous system to the organizational level of the organism, at which point *environment* comes to take on its sociocultural connotations and its more macroscopic material manifestations. My claim here is that the neurological structure and organization of the nervous system, manifested in its material functions and mediated up through its ever-increasing levels of hierarchical complexity, interacts with an external world and articulates the world of consciousness as the horizon of horizons within which experience is produced and from which meanings are thematized and combined.

As an indefinitely marked and inscribed material surface and container, a body is indeed cultural all the way down, and no less material for all that. In fact, it is all the more material for all that. From the structure and organization of cells into communities of cells, and networks of such communities into organs, and so on, a living body is itself a variously inscribed cultural articulation. Bodies, as living, malleable, multiply layered material articulations, are the seams that at one and the same time separate and reintegrate structural determinism on one side and experiential immediacy on the other. Structures of experience are mediated through the neurophenomenological, and thereby the neuroepistemological, configurations of a material body, and such bodies, articulated as sociocultural subjects and objects, are the articulations of sociocultural structures and neurophysiologically inscribed experience.

Laughlin, McManus, and d'Aquili (1990) argue for the rather extreme position that "our experience at any moment of consciousness is produced by our nervous system, with or without stimulation from events occurring in the external world" (p. 43). But there can be no living system completely isolated from external events. It seems to me more plausible, and equally advantageous both theoretically and critically, to argue that consciousness is produced by our nervous systems in interaction with an external material world, and that the structure of experience is that part of the nervous system that is mediating experience. And as Laughlin et al. contend, "the structure of experience, being living tissue, develops" (p. 43). The result is a materially embodied neurophenomenology of consciousness, a material, social, and spiritual world consciousness that experience at one and the same time discloses and that temporarily laces and latches cultural praxis, weaving webs of common sense and disclosing horizons of possibility.

Angus stresses the need for developing the phenomenological aspects of Marxist thought. I am tracing out this line of implications further than Angus would probably underwrite. Nevertheless, I believe those implications are cultural all the way down. That does not necessarily mean that they are "only" cultural all the way down. This opens the doors and windows of the forum to discourses that may sound odd to ears used to listening and mouths used to speaking only Marxist and the traditionally related discourses of history and political economics. Conversely, these implications very probably will sound out of place to neurophenomenologists and biogenetic structuralists who have not considered the political dimensions and implications of their work. I want to politicize and materialize the neurophenomenological project and call into radical question the most elemental presuppositions of science: its presumed positions of objectivity and neutrality.

THEORIZING MATERIAL BODIES

The tension between structural determinism and experiential immediacy articulates both subject positions and contextual conditions. However, none of these positions and conditions is ever determined in the last analysis, and thus none is ever completely and entirely finished. This interanimative tension between structural determinism and experiential immediacy is the medium of power, and it is in and through this medium of power that *political in-tension* is articulated. Political in-tension, articulated as subject positions and relational alliances, is always a partial unity or, as Kristeva (1984) would say, a subject in process and on trial; Bakhtin's (1984) formulation is the hero. It is in this fashion that sociocultural subjects can be theorized as the material embodiments of the partial unities of political in-tensions.

Enter here, once again, the microanalytic concerns of biogenetic structuralism and neurophenomenology. I want to continue with the gloss of biogenetic structuralism that I began in the previous section. The purpose of the gloss is to point the way toward a theorizing of material bodies experientially inscribed and informed as sociocultural embodiments at the structural level of biogenetics. It is a material in-scribing and in-forming that results in a phenomenology organized at and grounded on the neurological level of epistemology. Neurons appear to be goal-seeking, living entities that become involved in hierarchy upon hierarchy of organization. This linking and combining (i.e., articulation) of neurons into increasingly complex networks and models is called *entrainment*, a subtle and complex pivotal construct in biogenetic structuralist theory (Laughlin et al., 1990, pp. 52-53). Neural structures function in accord not with the dynamic properties of equilibrial, homeostatic systems, but rather in accord with the dynamic properties of evolutionary, homeorhetic systems.

In other words, neural structures function by equilibrating on the move; each new equilibrial point is a transformation of the former equilibrial point. Such evolutionary growth is a result of its own internal development and adaptation to the environment. Varela (1979) refers to this evolutionary adaptation as "in-forming." The pathways of these neural equilibrating transformations in-form canals or grooves that are called *creodes*. Laughlin et al. (1990) summarize this line of theoretical development as follows: "Neurognosis, then, canalizes the developmental entrainment of neural systems into functional creodes that, in a successful organism or species, moderate and integrate the bipolar demands of growth and adaptation" (p. 56). Consciousness is theorized as the complex of integrations of neural functions that are entrained and reentrained from moment to moment. Consciousness is the function of these networks, which are the structures of consciousness. Conscious networks are living societies of cells and networks of cells whose patterns of entrainment are continuously changing.

In short, a "conscious network is a system perpetually transforming its internal organization and its engagement with the world. . . . This continual change in the organization of our conscious network underlies the remarkable flux we experience as our 'stream of consciousness' " (Laughlin et al., 1990, pp. 95-96). In a very truncated form, this is a biogenetic structuralist account of how experience is materially inscribed at the very cellular level of the human organism, transforming that biogenetic body into a sociocultural embodiment. Bodies, as indefinitely dense massifications of communities of networks of living cells, are structurally entrained; these layers of networks are materially in-tended. In other words, those biogenetic structures given to common sense as bodies are complexes of multilayered surfaces of neuronal networks and neurological patterns of relationships. On this account, consciousness, and the subjectivity it subtends, is *always* a partial unity articulated against alternative articulations, and these articulations are biogenetically structured at the microorganismic level.

THE STRUGGLE OVER MEANING

For Angus, *articulation* is the struggle over meaning under conditions of plurality. The shift in Marxist thinking is away from a logic of modes of production per se and toward the description and analysis of the myriad modes of articulation. The articulation of subjectivity in the form of experience—experience here is thought through as the interaction of consciousness with the (material and spiritual) conditions of life—is a process of inscribing, of marking, tracing, scarring, and touching, all of the sensual modes of entrainment. Angus distinguishes two aspects of articulation: its enunciative aspect and its combinatorial aspect. To enunciate is to thematize, to call out into the (at least partial) openness and away from its unthematized background. To link or combine is to formulate a partial unity of component thematizations.

As a medium of transformation, conversation works both to thematize elements and to combine those thematized elements in the microphysical production of common sense. Conversation both enunciates and combines; it cuts into the common sense of its contextualized and undifferentiated background and it cuts out previously unarticulated elements, thereby thematizing and positioning those elements as subjects. In the double movement of this articulatory process, it circulates those thematized subjects through a variety of discursive formations and passes them back into the common sense of hegemony, into the region of the unsaid, insofar as now it "goes without saying."

The political intentionality of partially unified subjects can be thought of as the struggle over meaning, under conditions of plurality, between the said and the unsaid, the speakable and the unspeakable, the acknowledged and the unacknowledged. Political intentionality is born in the silencing (Angus's term is "anonymizing"), in the elementalizing of what is potentially sayable. My interests and experiences may be silenced, and to call my interests and experiences out into the openness of discursive circulation risks calling other enunciated interests and experiences into question. Such enunciative and combinatorial work carries with it always the potential of silencing what is now said and what can be said. It is in this way that the study of articulation situates itself in the moment of the political; its critical investigation becomes a critique of ideology. In being cultural all the way down, and nonetheless material for all that, the focus on the logic of the modes of articulation is political all the way down, and nonetheless material and cultural for all that.

DIFFERENCE AND STRUCTURE

The issue of differences, of the macro and the micro, is indeed a matter of scale, much in the same sense that Ilya Prigogine (1980; Prigogine & Stengers, 1984) and Benoit Mandelbrot (1977), in their respective studies of chaos phenomena, have discovered that similar, if not identical, structures are iterated indefinitely, if not infinitely, across and throughout different scales. It is the same structure all the way down (or all the way across, to avoid a hierarchical analogue), divided by boundaries of chaos out of which emerge similar structures whether one moves "up" or "down," "in" or "out," "across" or "through" in relation to any given scale dimension. And so it may be, at least that is my argument at this point, that whether studying political subjectivity and intentionality at the level of the nation-state or at the level of the two-person conversation, the relations between structural determinism and experiential immediacy are homologous. Political intentionality exercises itself in and through the medium of power at whatever level of structure one chooses to focus. And conversation is a particularly rich location for the critical study of communication precisely insofar as conversational practices appear innocuous and innocent, minimal and inconsequential, the small change of the more macro-level concerns of nation-states and transnational conglomerates. The theory of articulation puts itself at the point of political action irrespective of the scale of the articulatory processes being investigated.

THE DISCURSIVE FIELD

One of several ingenious moves Angus makes in his essay is to point out the correspondence of the communicational concept of "discursive field" and the phenomenological concept of "the world." The discursive field can never be reduced to a single articulation, which means that the discursive is not a single element that remains unthematized, nor is it the sum of all the unthematized elements. It cannot be thematized. It can never "all" be said, and no saying says it "all." There is always what remains "outside" and "other." The fact that there is an "outside" of any particular discursive field, that there is an "other" to any given identity, reflects the partiality of that field and identity back onto itself. "Other" organizing principles always represent the partiality of any particular organizing principle to itself, and this experience of representational partiality, of fragmentation, is emblematic of modernity and the modern epoch.

When the claim to universality—a universality that encompasses entire worldviews—comes into contact with an "outside" and an "other," faith in that claim to universality is shattered. Such claims to universality undermine themselves by giving away their own negation and impossibility; universality is no longer the horizon of horizons, the phenomenological world. The plurality of worldviews is now always already the phenomenological background against which the universality claim is foregrounded. Once that claim is articulated, the preconditions for contact with an "outside," with an "other," are set in motion; the experience of fragmentation becomes inevitable. For Angus, modernity is the condition, or rather the predicament, of perpetually reclaiming and recalling a universality from the experience of dissolution into fragmentation. There is a rather heuristic correspondence here between the modernism/postmodernism debate in the social sciences and the humanities and the order/chaos debate in the natural sciences and life sciences, and I want to trace several of those lines of flight.

Rather than denying both totality and experience, as do Laclau and Mouffe (1985), and insisting on the equivalence of the parts, an alternative political stance is to presuppose differences in unity. What is called for is a foregrounded logic of different modes of articulation and a backgrounded logic of modes of production. In the staging of experience, political intentionality exercises itself as antagonism when difference moves from the experience of subordination to the experience of domination, when differences are rendered as equivalences, when a particular difference no longer makes a difference.

It is the politics of common sense, the particularity of *this* sense, here and now, that is itself being thematized in Eastern Europe. Chaos is overtaking and dearticulating the state-administered structures of Marxist-socialist regimes. Open fields of poststructures emerge from fixed bureaucratic structures: Chaos emerges from order. Common sense is being called into question as articulated elements are dearticulating and receding into the undifferentiated background and as unarticulated elements are being differentiated and articulated into discursive formations that have not as yet passed back into common sense. This is a theoretically and praxiologically fortuitous network of fault lines that have opened themselves up to disclose a history of the present. It is *a particular* opportunity to investigate the *mediation of theory and praxis* and to examine critically the transformation of the cultural practices of the politics of common sense.

One of the many destabilizing and seemingly disconcerting lessons of chaos theory is that the natural world is overwhelmingly nonlinear, and it is now undeniably evident that our sociocultural worlds are nonlinear as well. (This nonlinearity of the sociocultural domain has been, and is likely to continue to be, one of several paradoxes that animate the struggles for epistemological legitimacy on the part of the several social and behavioral sciences.) Sociocultural formations are aperiodic systems that are remarkably sensitive to seemingly small and inconsequential initial conditions. Aperiodic systems, unlike periodic systems, never find a steady state; rather than being homeostatic, with more or less fixed positions and ranges of equilibrium, aperiodic systems are homeorhetic. When perturbed, homeorhetic systems adjust to the state they *would have* evolved to had there been no perturbation. Erich Jantsch (1975, 1980) calls such systems *evolutionary.*

One of the foremost tasks for a critical theory of communication is to come to critical and theoretical terms with the politics and experience of chaos (see Deleuze & Guattari, 1986; Virilio, 1986). Chaos theory (see Hayles, 1990) teaches us that the structural shapes and configurations of sociocultural formations are not the material givens of a logic of historical necessity, but are rather formulae that generate and randomize the self-similar forms that compose the various levels of any particular sociocultural formation. Rather than theorizing objects and subjects as more or less homeostatic systems that define their unity by means of perpetual equilibration, the evolutionary fluidity of sociocultural formations is theorized as complexes of multiple self-similar layers working themselves out in quite different ways. Each layer advances in and through historical time at different rhythms and with varying intensities. Such sociocultural formations are theorized homeorhetically as the interactive evolution of internal structural principles that generate unfolding self-similar symmetries.

The fluidity of such evolutionary change is not the smooth progression over time mapped by conventional differential equations, but rather the discontinuous jumps from state to state that only difference equations can approximate. Such discontinuous jumps from state to state cannot simply be added together to predict the probabilities of various courses of evolution. This is the fundamental distinction between differential equations (the basis of calculus), which model continuous systems moving more or less smoothly through time as trajectories that can be broken down into arbitrarily small intervals, and difference equations (the basis of nonlinear dynamics), which model complex, discontinuous systems that jump from state to state in seemingly unpredictable ways.

Angus theorizes the sociocultural field as a complex of such discontinuous systems, incomplete articulatory unities, that configure themselves in relations of subordination and domination. For Angus, the concern that links articulation theory to a discourse theory of Marxism is the process whereby relations of subordination come to be experienced antagonistically, as relations of domination. This is true, as well, of my interest in chaos theory in this discussion. The Marxist question is:

> Under what conditions do such relations of subordination become experienced as relations of domination, or oppression, and give rise to struggles directed at their transformation? In other words, what occurs when relations of difference become experienced as antagonistic? (p. 548)

Angus's answer is that,

> within an articulated cultural unity, relations of difference are "moments" and experienced as normal. But since the transition from elements to moments is never complete, there is always the possibility of dearticulating these moments from this cultural unity into elements—which can, of course, enter as moments into a new articulation. It is at this point of dearticulation of moments into elements that antagonism arises, that the social difference is experienced as "not necessary and capable of being transformed. (p. 548)

In this fashion, articulated sociocultural unities, by definition, constitute partial objects, incomplete unities, or homeorhetic systems. Such incomplete and unfinalizable unities are evolutionary systems insofar as relations among moments remain articulated and also relations among moments, thereby, continue to be experienced as normal and natural. But, inasmuch as no element is ever completely and entirely articulated as a moment, it always already remains partially elemental. And it is when moments are dearticulated into elements that difference is experienced as antagonism, and that evolution opens itself to the possibilities of revolution. A difference that makes and marks a difference no longer does so; such a non-difference (an "equivalence") is now available for and capable of radical change or transformation to a moment in another sociocultural unity.

The partiality of sociocultural unities arises from the consciousness of the limits of the social as marked and represented by what is "outside" and "other." It is the realization of "other" competing articulatory processes as "outside" the boundaries of this particular unity here and now, as "other" than this identity, that limits the completion and finalizability of any sociocultural unity. And it is this "other" that prevents the total self-realization of this particular unity. Antagonism arises from the self-realization of the impossibility of the constitution of full totalities, insofar as "other" prevents complete "self"-realization. The presence of "other," to the "outside," transforms the internal relation of subordination into a relation of dominance, thereby producing the experience of antagonism.

Power, for Angus, is Foucauldian in the sense that it is not in the possession of social identities, but rather is exercised and is operative in the articulation of particular social identities. "The relation of interiority and exteriority of the subject to the articulation is . . . the core of the power of any given articulation" (p. 551). Here is Foucault (1980) on power:

> But in thinking of the mechanisms of power, I am thinking rather of its capillary form of existence, the point where power reaches into the very grain of individuals, touches their bodies and inserts itself into their actions and attitudes, their discourses, learning processes and everyday lives. (p. 39)

Power, in other words, is biogenetically coded and inscribed. At the sociocultural level it is in relations of domination, in consciousness of "other," of "outside," of exteriority as the limit of total self-presence, self-realization, interiority that the experiences of fragmentation and antagonism—the touchstones of modernism—originate. For Angus, "the expression of the part in the midst of the dissolution of the whole field permeated by equivalences is the constitution of particularity" (p. 554).

CONTEXTUAL SPACE

Rene Thom (1975) theorized *phase space* as the shaped and shaping multiply dimensioned context in and through which systems evolve and transform iteratively. A system and its phase space are articulated. They are integrally linked and combined in such a way that as a system evolves it reconfigures its topological features. In Angus's phenomenological terminology, a system articulates itself by selecting and combining elements against a background or horizon of the world (the horizon of horizons). The background is the topological surface on, over, and through which sociocultural systems articulate themselves. Such systems are the formulae by means of which they transform their internal structural principles. Topological surfaces, in this particular analogue, are the phase spaces—the contexts, the common senses, the background elements, the horizons—of and for the "outstanding," articulated, sociocultural systems.

Experience can now be theorized as the fluid, aperiodic, nonlinear, contextual evolution of what David Bohm (1980) calls the "implicate order." Meaning is that which is articulated—that is, foregrounded or thematized—over against this horizon of experience. Meaning is that which is made from the horizon of experience, from the phase space in and through which homeorhetic systems—and this most certainly includes the individuated embodiments (i.e., human subjects) of these sociocultural systems—struggle with and over the meanings (i.e., contents) of experiential contexts. It is the chaotic, and at times revolutionary, struggle and contestation over articulated meanings, the politics of common sense, that chaos theory leaves unarticulated, largely due to its origination in the world of the natural sciences. And it is chaos theory that can expand a post-Marxist phenomenology into the "natural scientific" worlds of biogenetic structuralism and into the "discursive" worlds of neurophenomenology.

For Stuart Hall (1985), experience manifests itself through the systems of sociocultural representation, which in turn are the codes of intelligibility for making meaning and sense. Insofar as experience is theorized as the interaction of consciousness with the conditions of life, and codes of intelligibility are such elementary conditions, I want to argue that consciousness constitutes the horizon of horizons, "the world," over against which codes of intelligibility articulate the partial meanings of experience. There are myriad codes of intelligibility and systems of representation that compete to make meaning of experience, and it is in and through this competition over meanings that political intentionality takes form and place.

What can be taken for granted and assumed to be in place, and what must be specified and made explicit against this implicit background of common sense? Herein lies the domain of the politics of common sense; herein lies the struggle over the articulation of meaning for experience; herein is determined which experience is given voice and which is silenced and "anonymized." Insofar as elements are unarticulated experiences, a rather broad assortment of experiences subsist in any particular system of articulated meanings. Experience, as consciousness interacting with the conditions of living, may never be given voice; experience may remain anonymized, or at best articulated as subaltern voices only sporadically spoken, and perhaps never heard, before being silenced once again.

IN CONCLUSION

My importation of seemingly foreign discourses into this critical theoretical conversation—the admittedly partial discourses of biogenetic structuralism, neurophenomenology, catastrophe theory, and chaos theory—has been designed to "question the boundaries that seal [communication studies'] traditional domains of investigation off from wider social issues" (Angus, p. 536, citing Angus & Lannamann, 1988). By taking structural determinism and experiential immediacy to the microscopically neurological level of analysis, and by extrapolating the social totality to the macroscopically "natural" level of analysis, my remarks have been intended to "emphasize the effect of the social totality on specific processes and [to] analyze the dominating or liberating effect of a communication process in relation to it" (p. 536). As a material element-moment, as an element-becoming-and-always-already-partial, a human body as a sociocultural embodiment is internally generative of consciousness of world, but that particular embodiment is at the same time situated "within an external context that is itself understood as communicatively constituted" (p. 536).

In several respects, some of which remain unwritten here, my critical commentary demonstrates its affirmation of Angus's work by proceeding in accord with an "ethics of difference" (Angus, 1988). I have been working with different, alternative, "other," and "outside" partial discourses in an effort to demonstrate that "the politics of common sense resides in this internal/external dynamism" (p. 566). Reading Angus's work has been at moments an immersion into common sense and at other moments an exercise in critical vigilance; it was necessary for me to work in the domains of both theory and praxis. It is not agreement that I found or expected, but the experience of engagement and contestation.

REFERENCES

Angus, I. H. (1988). Displacement and otherness: Toward a postmodern ethics. In I. H. Angus (Ed.), *Ethnicity in a technological age*. Edmonton: Canadian Institute of Ukrainian Studies.

Angus, I. H., & Lannamann, J. W. (1988, Summer). Questioning the institutional boundaries of U.S. communication research: An epistemological inquiry. *Journal of Communication, 38* (3), 62-74.

Bakhtin, M. (1984). *Problems of Dostoevsky's poetics*. Minneapolis: University of Minnesota Press.

Bohm, D. (1980). *Wholeness and the implicate order*. Boston: Routledge & Kegan Paul.

Changeaux, J. (1983). On the "singularity" of nerve cells and its ontogenesis. In J. Changeaux (Ed.), Molecular interactions underlying higher brain functions [Special issue]. *Progress in Brain Research, 58*, 465-478.

Changeaux, J. (1985). *Neuronal man: The biology of mind*. Oxford: Oxford University Press.

Deleuze, G., & Guattari, F. (1986). *Nomadology: The war machine*. New York: Semiotext(e).

Foucault, M. (1980). *Power and knowledge: Selected interviews and other writings 1927-1977* (C. Gordon, Ed. and Trans.). New York: Pantheon.

Hall, S. (1982). The rediscovery of "ideology": Return of the repressed in media studies. In M. Gurevitch, T. Bennett, J. Curran, & J. Woollacott (Eds.), *Culture, society, and the media* (pp. 56-90). London: Methuen.

Hall, S. (1985). Signification, representation, ideology: Althusser and the poststructuralist debates. *Critical Studies in Mass Communication, 2*, 91-114.

Hall, S. (1986a). Cultural studies: Two paradigms. In R. Collins, J. Curran, N. Garnham, P. Scannell, P. Schlesinger, & C. Sparks (Eds.), *Media, culture, and society: A critical reader* (pp. 33-48) Newbury Park, CA: Sage.

Hall, S. (1986b). Gramsci's relevance for the study of race and ethnicity. *Journal of Communication Inquiry, 10*(2), 5-27.

Hall, S. (1986c). On postmodernism and articulation: An interview with Stuart Hall. *Journal of Communication Inquiry, 10*(2), 45-60.

Hall, S. (1988). *The hard road to renewal.* London: Verso.

Hayles, N. (1990). *Chaos bound: Orderly disorder in contemporary literature and science.* Ithaca, NY: Cornell University Press.

Jantsch, E. (1975). *Design for evolution: Self-organization and planning in the life of human systems.* New York: Geroge.

Jantsch, E. (1980). *The self-organizing universe.* New York: Pergamon.

Kristeva, J. (1984). *Revolution in poetic language.* New York: Columbia University Press.

Laclau, E. (1982). *Politics and ideology in Marxist theory.* London: Verso. (Original work published 1977)

Laclau, E. (1988). Politics and the limits of modernity. In A. Ross (Ed.), *Universal abandon? The politics of postmodernism.* Minneapolis: University of Minnesota Press.

Laclau, E., & Mouffe, C. (1985). *Hegemony and socialist strategy: Towards a radical democratic politics* (W. Moore & P. Cammack, Trans.). London: Verso.

Laclau, E., & Mouffe, C. (1987). Post-Marxism without apologies. *New Left Review, 166,* 79-106.

Laughlin, C. D., McManus, J., & d'Aquili, E. G. (1990). *Brain, symbol and experience: Toward a neurophenomenology of human consciousness.* Boston: Shambala.

Mandelbrot, B. B. (1977). *The fractal geometry of nature.* New York: W. H. Freeman.

Prigogine, I. (1980). *From being to becoming: Time and complexity in the physical sciences.* New York: W. H. Freeman.

Prigogine, I., & Stengers, I. (1984). *Order out of chaos: Man's new dialogue with nature.* Boulder, CO: Shambala.

Thom, R. (1975). *Structural stability and morphogenesis* (D. H. Fowler, Trans.). Reading, MA: Benjamin.

Thompson, E. P. (1963). *The making of the English working class.* London: Galancz.

Varela, F. J. (1979). *Principles of biological autonomy.* New York: Elsevier North-Holland.

Virilio, P. (1986). *Speed and politics.* New York: Semiotext(e).

SECTION 4

THE PERSON
IN INTERACTION

12 Intrapersonal Communication: A Review and Critique

STANLEY B. CUNNINGHAM
University of Windsor

Intrapersonal communication (IaC) is regularly invoked as a distinctive form of communication. This chapter critically examines IaC to see whether or not it really has any distinctive value in the realm of communication theory. A first step is to identify representative descriptions of IaC and the settings in which they occur. This is followed by a sequence of criticisms that probe the soundness of the IaC construct. What emerges is that IaC appears to rest upon a mixture of linguistic improprieties and some highly dubious inferences. If IaC is to remain on the books, its theorists will have to answer some daunting questions.

IN the field of communication studies there is a widely held belief in *intrapersonal communication* as a unique process of message exchange and information transformation within the individual. Of all the commonly acknowledged forms of communication—interpersonal, small group, organizational, nonverbal, and mass communication—intrapersonal communication (IaC) is the youngest and least developed notion, and the one about which the least has been published. For all that, however, it is regularly mentioned and defended in the literature as an important component in the spectrum of communication types. Indeed, one of the strongest claims made repeatedly is that IaC is the basis and foundation of *all* other forms of communication. Quite simply, IaC has become an accepted model in communication theory, especially in the areas of speech and interpersonal communication.

Recently, questions have been raised about difficulties just in trying to define IaC (Cunningham, 1989). For the most part, however, it remains an uncontested model. Its theorists assume that IaC, either as a reality or as a powerful model, comprises a range of functions, and that it augments our understanding of both what communication is and what it means to be a human being. Many IaC theorists refer to the work of psychologists and neurophysiologists to reinforce their point that IaC comprises a number of

Correspondence and requests for reprints: Stanley B. Cunningham, Department of Communication Studies, University of Windsor, Windsor, Ontario, Canada N9B 3P4.

Communication Yearbook 15, pp. 597-620

intrapersonal processes. At first glance, that kind of referencing seems to lend scientific credence to IaC, but some weighty assumptions have been made. In most cases the scientific authorities alluded to are usually not talking about a form of communication, but, more conservatively, about inner processing in general: cognitive, perceptual, and motivational episodes. To call these psychophysiological processes *communication* is to exercise a transformation that exceeds the interests and insights of the allegedly supporting authorities. The fact that relatively few papers written on IaC have explicitly employed it as an investigative tool suggests that its empirical utility and scientific status are even more problematic. It is significant, perhaps, that the index of the *International Encyclopedia of Communications* (1989) contains no entry for IaC, nor does any listing for it appear in any of the dictionaries or encyclopedias of related scientific disciplines, such as the *International Encyclopedia of Social Sciences* or the *International Encyclopedia of Psychiatry, Psychology, Psychoanalysis, and Neurology.*

Now, an essential requirement in the life of any theory are those reflective moments in which its adherents adjudicate competing interpretations and respond unflinchingly to challenges directed against the model itself. Just as the phenomenon of mass communication has been exposed to a declension of competing interpretations in the course of efforts to understand what it is, how it works, and what kinds of effects it generates, there is a corresponding need for the same kind of interpretive exercises vis-à-vis IaC. The timing is propitious: The recent publication of *Intrapersonal Communication Processes* (Roberts & Watson, 1989), a compendium of 26 original studies, marks a point of critical mass at which the literature is now sufficiently ample and sophisticated to invite serious reflective analysis of the IaC construct. Unless and until IaC is prepared to withstand this sort of assessment, its theoretical probity remains untested and its utility uncertain at best.

This chapter examines what theorists say about IaC in order to see whether or not it really has any distinctive value in communication theory. The essay comprises both a review of IaC descriptions and an evaluation. Within the latter, an effort is made to unearth and assess the kinds of reasoning and motivation that have prompted communication theorists to posit IaC. Altogether, the procedure involves four steps:

(1) a brief description of the settings in which IaC is mentioned, used, and defended

(2) a representative inventory of the operations and properties commonly attributed to IaC

(3) a sequence of criticisms that probe the soundness of the IaC construct

(4) a number of inquiries that must be answered if the concept of IaC is to remain on the books

THE PUBLIC FACE
OF INTRAPERSONAL COMMUNICATION

IaC has emerged in three areas of communication literature: in lexicons, in introductory speech and mass communication textbooks, and in conference papers and theoretical writings of a more advanced nature. Blake and Haroldsen, in *A Taxonomy of Concepts in Communication* (1975), give a full-page entry in which we are told that IaC is a "distinct concept" (p. 25). It has also been itemized in *Key Concepts in Communication* by O'Sullivan, Hartley, Saunders, and Fiske (1983). Watson and Hill, in *A Dictionary of Communication and Media Studies* (1989), conclude that "it is what makes us unique" (p. 19).

The term appears with mounting frequency in other sectors of the literature. A number of mass communication textbooks state or assume that IaC is a genuine part of the communication spectrum, but in most cases treatment amounts to little more than a mention or a sentence. A few give longer treatment (e.g., Bittner, 1980, pp. 8-9). Introductory speech texts and a number of theory-level sources are much more ample. For example, Applbaum et al. (1973, pp. 12-31) devote an entire chapter to it. One of the earliest elaborations of the IaC construct was an influential journal article by Barker and Wiseman (1966). In 1980, Barker and Edwards published a 52-page instructional booklet titled *Intrapersonal Communication*. Their work was updated in 1987 with coauthor Charles Roberts under the title *Intrapersonal Communication Processes* (Roberts, Edwards, & Barker, 1987).

The widening recognition accorded to IaC has been enhanced by its recurrence in the conference forum. In the last decade or so, the Speech Communication Association has regularly scheduled multiple sessions and seminars dedicated to this model. In 1986, that recognition was formalized by the establishment of the Commission on Intrapersonal Communication Processes within the SCA. Each year a dozen or more presentations dealing with IaC and its applications are now listed in its conference program. To date, half or more of the material written about IaC is in the form of unpublished conference papers. For that very reason it is of limited value. Accordingly, the publication of a collection of 26 papers in *Intrapersonal Communication Processes* (Roberts & Watson, 1989) marks the first point at which the published literature is now sufficiently ample and complex to invite a review and assessment of this concept.

OPERATIONS AND PROPERTIES
OF INTRAPERSONAL COMMUNICATION

Collectively, the literature makes a surprising number of claims about IaC. Many of these claims identify functions, events, or operations, such as inner dialogue, reasoning, or the processing of information. Other claims have more to do with the characteristics or properties of IaC. For example, some believe that IaC is the foundation of all communication, and that it is an important source of self-knowledge. Accordingly, as a first step in understanding what IaC is supposed to be, it is important to provide a catalog of these operations and characteristics.

In the inventory that follows, both functions and properties commonly attributed to IaC have been identified and assembled into numbered classes.[1] These classifications do not pretend to be complete, but they are representative.

Operations

(1) *Talking to oneself*, the process of communicating with(in) oneself, of inner speech, or a self-contained communication system within the person is often mentioned (Applbaum et al., 1973, p. 12; Apple, 1989; Barker & Edwards, 1980; Blake & Haroldsen, 1975, p. 25; Brooks, 1978, pp. 12-13, 38; Hikins, 1989; Korba, 1989; Linkugel & Buehler, 1975, p. 16; Littlejohn, 1989, p. 8; O'Sullivan et al., 1983, p. 121; Pearson & Nelson, 1979, p. 6; Rogers, 1984, p. 7; Stacks & Sellers, 1989; Watson & Hill, 1989, pp. 90-91).

(2) *An internal dialogue* or interchange of meanings between parts of the person, such as consciousness and the unconscious (O'Sullivan et al., 1983, p. 22), or between the "I"—that "part of ourselves that is fundamentally idiosyncratic and personal"—and the "Me"—that "part of ourselves that is social product" (Davis & Baran, 1981, pp. 137-138) is also mentioned. A related operation is the transfer of messages between the brain and an individual's other parts (Bittner, 1980, pp. 8; Whetmore, 1985, p. 5).

(3) *A process whereby a person transacts with the environment* or adapts to the environment; a process of manipulating cues (stimuli) impinging upon us from without or even from within (Applbaum et al., 1973, pp. 13-19; Barker & Edwards, 1980; Barker & Wiseman, 1966; Blake & Haroldsen, 1975; Budd & Ruben, 1979, pp. 107-112; Linkugel & Buehler, 1975, pp. 16-17; Watson & Hill, 1989) is attributed to IaC.

(4) *Perception* is another operation, a process whereby the individual receives, stores, and retrieves information or symbolic abstractions (Applbaum et al., 1973, pp. 12-31; Barker & Edwards, 1980; Barker & Wiseman, 1966; Brooks, 1978, pp. 13, 24; Budd & Ruben, 1979, pp. 107-112; Harless, 1985, p. 8; Linkugel & Buehler, 1975, pp. 16-17; O'Sullivan et al., 1983, p. 121; Roberts et al., 1987).

(5) *An interactive process whereby the "raw data" of perception are endowed with meaning* or transformed into information of a more conceptual nature (Applbaum et al., 1973, pp. 12-31; Barker & Edwards, 1980; Barker & Wiseman, 1966; Brooks, 1978, p. 13; Linkugel & Buehler, 1975, pp. 16-17; Roberts et al., 1987) has been described. Budd and Ruben (1979) term this epistemic sublimation variously "the metabolism of information,"

"conversion," "extraction," and "inference" in order to underscore the more abstract level of the resultant information (p. 108). IaC, they write, supplies the individual with a "conceptual surrogate for environment data."

(6) *Data processing* functions are described as well. Given the functions recorded in 4 and 5 above, it is not surprising that some authors choose to think of IaC in metaphorical terms as a "data processing center" (Applbaum et al., 1973, pp. 27-31). Where that metaphor is not explicitly invoked, the recurrent use of the data and information-processing idioms encourages that and other sorts of biomechanical interpretations (e.g., Barker & Wiseman, 1966; Brooks, 1978, pp. 13, 24, 38; Roberts et al., 1987; Whetmore, 1985, p. 5).

(7) *Feedback* is sometimes identified (Applbaum et al., 1973, p. 14; Dance & Larson, 1972, pp. 124, 132; Roberts et al., 1987, pp. 122-130), but more often than not is implicit only in some of the operations identified in 3-6 above.

(8) Though individual accounts may stress this or that aspect, the literature attributes a *wide assortment of mentalistic operations* to IaC—that is, a range of epistemic functions that do not seem to be reducible to purely material changes or elements. These include the following:

(a) the assignment of meaning to, or interpretations of, perceptions, events, and experiences (Applbaum et al., 1973, pp. 12-13; Barker & Edwards, 1980; Barker & Wiseman, 1966; Blake & Haroldsen, 1975; Brooks, 1978, p. 13; LaFleur, 1985; Linkugel & Buehler, 1975, p. 17; O'Sullivan et al., 1983, p. 121; Roberts et al., 1987)

(b) thinking and understanding (Barker & Edwards, 1980; Barker & Wiseman, 1966; Harless, 1985, p. 8; Linkugel & Buehler, 1975, p. 17; O'Sullivan et al., 1983; Pearson & Nelson, 1979, p. 81; Roberts et al., 1987; Rogers, 1984, p. 7; Stacks & Sellers, 1989)

(c) problem solving, conflict resolution, applied thinking, evaluation, planning, decision making (Anderson, 1989; Applbaum et al., 1973, p. 13; Barker & Edwards, 1980; Brooks, 1978, p. 12; Pearson & Nelson, 1979, p. 6)

(d) memory (Barker & Edwards, 1980; Bruneau, 1989; Budd & Ruben, 1979, p. 110; Harless, 1985, p. 8; Jensen, 1989; O'Sullivan et al., 1983; Roberts et al., 1987, pp. 77-92)

(e) introspection; awareness, self-consciousness, and self-knowledge; reflection; metacognition (Anderson, 1989; Barker & Edwards, 1980; Barker & Wiseman, 1966; Blake & Haroldsen, 1975; Budd & Ruben, 1979, pp. 108-110; Davis & Baran, 1981, pp. 137-138; Hikins, 1989; Jensen, 1989; Pelose, 1989; Roberts et al., 1987; Watson & Hill, 1989)

(f) dreaming (Harless, 1985, p. 8; Lippard-Justice, 1989, p. 452)

(g) imaging (Honeycutt, Zagacki, & Edwards, 1989; Weaver, Bailey, & Cotrell, 1989)

(h) feeling (Barker & Edwards, 1980; Roberts et al., 1987; Rogers, 1984, p. 7)

(i) IaC comprises or is allied to a number of dispositions and emotional states that, in turn, affect overt behavior and speech. These inner states range from willingness to communicate to unconsciousness and mindlessness (Apple, 1989; Miller, Sleight, & deTurck, 1989; Richmond & McCroskey, 1989; Roloff, 1989; Vinson, 1989).

(9) In a move that is highly reminiscent of Immanuel Kant's intuition of time, Bruneau (1989) suggests that IaC is that *whereby we experience time in all its modalities.* IaC, he writes, is "basically and essentially temporalities concerning internal time dimensions, cycles, periods, rhythms and kinds of sequential phenomena" (p. 79).

(10) *IaC crops up as an easily recognizable synonym in the literature of persuasion.* More precisely, "self-persuasion" is taken to be an internal process involving the production and intransitive movement of messages within the individual. Thus Burks (1970) writes that there is "no intrinsic difference in the persuasion of another and the persuasion of self" (p. 112). The self-persuasion paradigm, we are told,

entails no external producer of messages. Rather people generate their own *original meanings*, containing reasons for changing beliefs or behaviors. . . . the process of actively thinking about an issue regarding the self or the environment usually results in a number of self-generated persuasive messages. (Smith, 1982, p. 18)

Self-persuasion, or the "active participation paradigm," as it is also called, has attracted the interest of communication scholars because it represents an area in which the individual is no longer interpreted as a passive recipient of externally induced messages or influences. Rather, the individual is now seen as playing a more active participatory role in the modification of his or her own attitudes, beliefs, and behaviors. Agency and initiation, not passivity, are the key notes. Much of this clearly coincides with, and recapitulates, the internalized message-production factor in IaC theory.

Properties and Characteristics

(11) *IaC is exclusively a neurophysiological activity,* and it can be "defined" through experimental procedures in purely neurophysiological terms (Brooks, 1978, p. 13; Roberts, 1985, 1986; Vinson, 1985). It is something that is "mainly a concern of the psychologist and neurologist" (Merrill & Lowenstein, 1979, p. 8). Roberts (1986) states that "*all* of the communication within the individual is physiological" (p. 6). Some argue, with less desire for precision, that IaC can be viewed as a mental process, a physical state, and a biological-psychological system (e.g., Stacks & Sellers, 1989).

(12) *IaC is virtually a continuous process in our waking state* (Bittner, 1980, p. 8; Pearson & Nelson, 1979, p. 6; Whetmore, 1985, p. 5).

(13) *From the earliest days of this theory, the relationship of IaC to language and symbols has been problematic* (Barker & Wiseman, 1966, p. 178). Though Budd and Ruben (1979) raise the possibility that "language may not be a requirement for Intrapersonal Communication" (p. 111), the consensus among most is that language (or some form of encoding/decoding) plays a "decisive role" and an "important part" (Applbaum et al., 1973, p. 27; Linkugel & Buehler, 1975, p. 17; O'Sullivan et al., 1983; Roberts et al., 1987; Rogers, 1984, p. 7; Stacks & Sellers, 1989, pp. 245, 255-263; Whetmore, 1985, p. 5).

(14) *IaC is essential to both the reality of and our understanding of all communication.* "All communication is to some extent intrapersonal communication" (Blake & Haroldsen, 1975). IaC is the *basis* or *foundation* of all communication (Applbaum et al., 1973, p. 13; Barker & Edwards, 1980; Barker & Wiseman, 1966, p. 173; Brooks, 1978, pp. 13, 38; Harless, 1985, pp. 8-9; Heun & Heun, 1989; Hikins, 1989, p. 32; Linkugel & Buehler, 1975, pp. 17; Pearson & Nelson, 1979, p. 6; Roberts et al., 1987, pp. 2-4; Stacks & Sellers, 1989). Barker and Edwards (1980, p. 20) are not alone when they say that interpersonal communication cannot occur without IaC going on simultaneously. Littlejohn (1989) says that it is "so pervasive that it cuts across all other contexts, making it a universal theme" (p. 8). Larson (1983) enthusiastically universalizes the significance and import of self-persuasion in a manner that parallels the claims made for IaC: "In one sense," he writes, "*all persuasion is self-persuasion*—we are rarely persuaded unless we *participate* in the process" (p. 6).

(15) *IaC, or knowledge of IaC, adds to our knowledge of ourselves and to our understanding of the process of communication with others* (Applbaum et al., 1973, p. 13; Apple, 1989; Emmert, 1989; Hikins, 1989, pp. 32). It is a source of personal development and self-discovery, of self-understanding, of our view of ourselves—both as a part of and apart from our environment (Barker & Edwards, 1980; Budd & Ruben, 1979, p. 109; Davis & Baran, 1981, pp. 137-138; Fletcher, 1989; Linkugel & Buehler, 1975, p. 17; Pearson & Nelson, 1979; Roberts et al., 1987; Watson & Hill, 1989).

(16) *IaC has therapeutic value.* By developing this level of communication, we can promote inner harmony, the union of body and soul; we can regain health and stability, and improve physical functioning (Apple, 1989; Hikins, 1989, pp. 48-49; Roberts et al., 1987).

(17) *IaC has a valid role in empirical research* (Brooks, 1978; Roberts, 1985, 1986; Surlin & Costaris, 1985; Vinson, 1985). It is something that can be studied through empirical methods (Apple, 1989; Behnke, 1989; Emmert, 1989; Fletcher, 1989; Korba, 1989; Richmond & McCroskey, 1989; Schedletsky, 1989).

CRITICAL EVALUATIONS OF
THE INTRAPERSONAL COMMUNICATION MODEL

The remainder of this chapter will identify a number of weaknesses in the IaC construct. At the outset, however, it is extremely important to make clear that the target of these evaluations and criticisms is not the reality of our inner operations, or indeed the causal and conditioning role they might play in the business of communicating with others. Rather, the focus of this critique is the uncritical extension of *communication* terminology and metaphors to the facts of our inner life space. It is one thing to say that communication behavior is rooted in intrapersonal events or processes, or that it has an important psychophysiological dimension. It is quite another to leap to the conclusion that these events or processes are themselves "communication."

The Ambiguity of IaC

There is a profound ambiguity at the core of the phrase *intrapersonal communication processes*. Depending upon how we bracket its phrase constituents, it is possible to come up with two different interpretations. [Intrapersonal] [communication processes] is the weaker reading, which may simply denote the inner behavioral aspects or foundations of communication in general without positing any distinctive communication type. This interpretation is not controversial, since no one would seriously question the reality of the inner physicopsychological basis of communicative behavior. Even though they appear in the general context of a unique communication type, a few articles seem to content themselves with this interpretation (e.g., Emmert, 1989; Schedletsky, 1989). On the other hand, [intrapersonal communication] [processes] is a much stronger reading; linguistically and semantically, it says that distinctive micromessages or communication units circulate within each of us. This latter interpretation is the majority view among IaC theorists and the object of this critique.

In any case, what we have here is more than just a piece of linguistic ambivalence. Because of this ambiguity it is difficult to know whether the referent of IaC theorizing is a unique mode of human exchange—Blake and Haroldsen (1975) call it a "distinct concept" (p. 25)—or whether "intrapersonal communication" is little more than a misleading label for the psychophysical dimension of all human communication. Without precision in its opening terms, we can scarcely expect clarity in the ensuing speculations. Indeed, what Frank Dance (1970) says about the starting point of communication inquiry in general should also serve as sobering instruction in the realm of IaC:

> The concept of communication with which one starts will substantively affect any additions to an already extant theory of communication or any efforts directed toward the development of a new theory. Concepts serve as a real, if unstated, rule for making observations and organizing experience. (pp. 201-202)

The specific difficulties enumerated below can be regarded as facets of this initial, core ambiguity.

A thicket of metadefinitional issues compounds this central ambiguity.[2] For example, it is uncertain whether the terms *intrapersonal communication* and *intrapersonal communication processes* signify one overarching theory, several theories, or, less ambitiously, one or more pretheoretical postulates. IaC theorists often seem to speak *as if* IaC has a solid theoretical status, but it may be closer to the intent of most (and fairer) to view IaC as a pretheoretical construct. None the less, it is difficult to know whether the manifold accounts of IaC operations and properties are posited as neutral descriptions, definitions, or explanations. As neutral descriptions they might simply stand as components of an abstract theory without any ontological commitment to the reality of IaC. Or are they nothing more than definitions, that is, linguistic stipulations that are intended not so much to augment our knowledge as to crystallize and stabilize meanings? Many accounts, however, especially those that invoke cross-disciplinary research and empirical grounding, present themselves as explanations that genuinely augment our understanding of human nature. This largely uncritical assumption is prevalent throughout the literature. Until these metadefinitional uncertainties are directly addressed by its theorists, the (pre)theoretical value of IaC remains indeterminate.

IaC as Countertheoretical

If only initially, the theory of IaC seems to be counterintuitive, and it violates customary usage. In both ordinary language and communication theory, the term *communication* typically denotes the exchange or sharing of messages between and among persons (including corporate entities), something situated within a community. That is, communication is typically regarded as a molar social phenomenon. In contrast to this normal acceptance, IaC posits a message transfer within the individual. This means that the IaC model is in sharp conflict with paradigm models of communication.

Now, the concept of communication is admittedly polymorphous, but in theoretical discussion (e.g., Dance, 1970; Dance & Larson, 1972; Fiske, 1982; Littlejohn, 1989) as well as in everyday discourse it characteristically entails a core of three features:

(1) a community of at least two persons
(2) a message, construed as something meaningful or informative
(3) a sharing, transfer, or exchange of that message

In many discussions, of course, one or more of these necessary conditions may be only implicit, yet each one is no less operative. For purposes of this critique, this threefold distillate of primary conditions may be viewed as a normative, if commonplace, model of communication.

To this invariant nucleus of defining features may be added several others that tolerate some degree of variety and intermittence:

(4) a system of symbols (e.g., natural language) whereby the message is structured
(5) a degree of consciousness or awareness
(6) an element of purpose or intent and/or an element of choice, either of which serves to distinguish communication as a human activity from mere mechanical impact or physical transfer (Dance, 1970, pp. 207-209)

For the sake of convenience and brevity, this enumeration does not include such standard features as noise, feedback, medium or channel, and effects—let alone the welter of more refined notions including rules, proxemics, redundancy, and so on. Notwithstanding these omissions, however, the six enumerated features, especially the first three, are theoretical requirements that spell out *minimal conditions* for communicative performance and theory building. They are necessary conditions mentioned, embedded, or implied in any theoretical discussion of communication, ranging from mass communication (e.g., DeFleur & Ball-Rokeach, 1975, p. 127; Dominick, 1990, p. 5) to nonverbal (e.g., Druckman, Rozelle, & Baxter, 1982, p. 24) and interpersonal communication (e.g., Littlejohn, 1989, p. 152). However, the various claims made about IaC are seriously compromised by the fact that these core features are not clearly instantiated, and when they are invoked, they figure only in a highly metaphorical and tenuous fashion. The tenuousness of these moves can be observed by attending more closely to IaC's reliance upon (a) the language of personhood, (b) its appeal to the concept of message, and (c) its inherent dependency upon the notion of private language.

By a Person or Persons Unknown

For one thing, the person within whom IaC is said to take place is not a community, but a single self. Some descriptions seem to respect partially that constraint by depicting IaC as something that goes on within the *single* person or individual or "within life space of one organism" (Barker & Wiseman, 1966, p. 175). In other accounts, it could be said that the indivisibility of the self is implied and protected by vesting plurality not in any parts or divisions of the person, but in reflexive verb forms and pronouns: "talking to oneself," "self-persuasion," "privately interpreting to oneself." In either case, the point is that any real community of persons is not apparent. The duality, so necessary for communication, seems to be nothing more than grammatical.

Some descriptions go further when they posit dyads within the individual. Thus Davis and Baran (1981) situate IaC between the "I" (that part of ourselves that is radically "idiosyncratic and personal") and the "Me" (that "part of ourselves that is social product") (p. 138). O'Sullivan et al. (1983) define it as an exchange between "different structures or levels," namely, the conscious and the unconscious (p. 121). Yet in cases such as these the alleged communication takes place not between wholly constituted persons, but between fractions thereof, between abstractions. Even though the language of personhood is used to identify these parts, the referents ("I," "Me," the unconscious) cannot be said to be different "persons" in any realistic sense of the term.

The strategy of analyzing IaC into inner dyads is also methodologically questionable. At least initially, IaC is not a clear and perspicuous notion. As noted above, it is highly ambiguous. To attempt to define it in terms or with principles that are equally or more abstract and speculative amounts to explaining the obscure through the equally obscure. Furthermore, the function or role of these hypothetical parts remains just as uncertain as their ontological status. IaC is commonly pictured as a "dialogue" or "exchange of meaning" between inner psychic structures, but just what are we to make of that subcutaneous exchange? It obviously lacks the normal conversational aspect of either spoken or written dialogue because wholly constituted persons converse, not parts of persons. (This sort of distinction is reflected in the etymology of the traditional language used to describe solitary utterance: *mono*logue, *soli*loquy.) Davis and Baran (1981) do even more to cloud the issue of inner communication when they equate that dialogue with "the only conscious awareness that we can have of this self-system" (p. 138). Few would disagree that consciousness is a normal condition of communication, but to equate awareness of the self with IaC seems unwarranted. And this same argument can also be directed to some of the other epistemic identities (e.g., thinking) made in the name of IaC.

The Message as Cipher

What is said and left unsaid about the message component compounds the uncertainty of IaC. The term *message* is frequently used in the literature, but just as often other synonyms are used, such as *dialogue, inner speech, meaning,* and *information.* In most cases the message element is described as a process in language that is intended to underscore its dynamism. Now, while most accounts ascribe a highly semantic and epistemic nature to the message process, its symbolic status remains indefinite. Descriptions such as "inner speech" and "talking to oneself" suggest that IaC is a fully language-mediated experience cast primarily in propositional form. Phrases such as "encoding-decoding process" and "symbolic abstractions" indicate that some form of symbolism is at work, though not necessarily a linguistic one. Budd and Ruben (1979) pose the possibility that language "may not be a requirement for intrapersonal communication" (p. 111). Indeed, more than 25 years ago, Barker and Wiseman (1966, pp. 178) viewed this whole question as a challenging research issue. Finally, in the more mechanistic descriptions that depict IaC as a process of interacting with one's environment or as a receptor and processor of stimuli, it is even less clear whether the message is to be construed as symbolically structured or as something mutely infrasymbolic. In sum, just what kind of message(s) do we have here?

There is a certain irony within this confusion. Language is not simply a conduit by which meanings are exported and imported between senders and receivers. On the contrary, language theory over the last few decades, and in a variety of disciplines (e.g., linguistics, speech theory, philosophy, sociolinguistics), has done much to show that language itself plays a central and constitutive role in the formation of meaning. IaC threatens to become unintelligible in direct proportion to the distance placed between it and the structure of symbols and language.

Until something is done to clarify or reduce the element of symbolic indeterminacy in IaC, it is virtually impossible to decide in what sense its "message" is to be interpreted as really being a message. That uncertainty is compounded when we try to relate the alleged message element to some of the purely affective processes attributed to IaC: feelings, emotional states, and dispositions such as unwillingness. These processes are clearly experiential, but many would hesitate to ascribe symbolized message structures to these affective states.

IaC as a Radically Private Language

This symbolic and linguistic indeterminacy should not be surprising, because of an unremovable barrier between IaC and its theorists: *By definition, the message is unavailable for public examination.* "Message," in its normal, nonmetaphorical sense, means a symbolically structured text that, in principle at least, is accessible to more than one person. But the message of IaC is so private and indeterminate that not only agreement but even *disagreement* about its symbolic or nonsymbolic status is ruled out of order. "Talking to oneself" might seem to escape that blanket constraint, but to the extent that it is verbalized or externalized, it thereby seems to disqualify itself as an inner, self-contained exchange. Besides, Barnlund (1968) seems to voice a consensus found in IaC discussions when he writes that "it is desirable to restrict 'intrapersonal communication' to the manipulation of cues *within* an individual that occurs *in the absence of other people*" (p. 8; emphasis added).

The situation here is not unlike the issue of private language that has exercised the attention of philosophers in the last few decades, and so it may be instructive to look at what Wittgenstein (1963) has to say. In the *Philosophical Investigations* (nos. 243-317), Wittgenstein raises the question of the possibility of a radically private language or notational system put together by an individual in order to record and describe inner experiences only, such as pain. (Adumbrations of the private-language problem can be found in John Locke and St. Augustine.) This purely hypothetical "language" would be completely self-generated, that is, totally unrelated to both external behavior and conventional language systems. It would be a *radically* private language. Inner recordings would be made without any reliance upon a derived system of rules grounded in such public benchmarks as overt speech behavior and the given conventions of natural language. Accordingly, the individual in his or her private selection of any sign, say "E," to register a sensation of pain would have nothing more to rely upon than memory or the personal belief that there is indeed a connection between E and past and present experience of the same kind. But that also means that there would be no "grammar" in the ordinary sense of that term since, *pace* Chomsky, grammar is a socially evolved rule system involving public agreement about the uses and arrangements of words and systems. Any encoding/decoding system involves that much. Moreover, since it is grammar that establishes regularity and linkages in the use of human signs, these hidden notations would lack fixity or meaning. Usage, grounded in behavior and socialization, determines that the language of, say, toothaches does not apply anywhere else but at the face level, and that it has nothing to do with color words, sewing, or the names of flowers. In a radically private language, however, without the constraints of grammatical usage, there would be nothing to guarantee consistency and regularity in predication. Put another way, without independent or outer criteria regulating the use of signs, the individual could never be sure that the memory of the connection between E and a sensation was really a rule governing that connection or merely the *impression of a rule* (no. 259). By analogy, if I am uncertain about train departure times, I acquire certainty not by flipping through the pages of my memory, but by consulting a *real* timetable (no. 265).

The notion of a *correct* linkage, then, between our hypothetical individual's private jottings and the experiences they allegedly signify would be elusive at best. Condemned to a solipsistic game of inventing and manipulating signs without the controls and safeguards of publicly anchored language rules, the boundary between illusion and reality disappears. The private-language undertaking, according to Wittgenstein, would be something meaningless, an empty ritual, and certainly not a "language" in any recognizable sense of the term.

Indeed, even the undertaking to invent a private sign system itself is not and cannot be all that private and independent. On the contrary, the very practice of privately recording our inner sensations is necessarily derivative because naming is itself a universal and integral part of all natural languages, something we learned to do as we learned our mother tongue. "When one says 'He gave a name to his sensation,' " writes Wittgenstein, "one forgets that a great deal of stage-setting in the language is presupposed if the mere act of naming is to make sense" (no. 257).

Wittgenstein's aphoristic reflections are relevant to the issue of IaC's message factor. Those accounts of IaC that posit or imply a privately generated symbolism, or that make IaC itself an originating condition or defining element for other levels of communication, veer into the same kind of tenuousness diagnosed by Wittgenstein. On the other hand, if IaC is taken to mean talking to oneself in words and phrases borrowed from another language already learned, then its so-called privacy or *intra*personal nature is seriously compromised. Such verbal behavior, it can be argued, is simply truncated conversation, a derivative practice that does not take place unless one already knows a publicly shared language (or elements thereof, in the case of children). About this kind of behavior one can say, without significant theoretical loss or penalty to communication theory in general, that there is indeed a type of nondirected, noncommunicative thinking and verbalizing—which we call *monologue* or *soliloquy*—that does nothing more than *imitate* some features of dialogue. To call it *intrapersonal communication*, however, is to make it into something much more than it has to be.

The Nonspecificity of IaC

The difficulties involved in trying to see how community, personhood, and message do or do not apply to IaC are facets of much more comprehensive defects in the model—namely, its nonspecificity and general aura of indeterminacy. Consider the proliferation of operations attributed to IaC. Pearson and Nelson, for instance, write that

> intrapersonal communication is not restricted to "talking to ourselves"; it also includes such activities as internal problem solving, resolution of internal conflict, planning for the future, emotional catharsis, evaluations of ourselves and others, and the relationship between ourselves and others. (quoted in Apple, 1989, p. 321)

Roberts et al. (1987) confidently pose an even greater totality in their *definition* of IaC as

> all of the physiological and psychological processing of messages that happens within individuals at conscious and nonconscious levels as they attempt to understand themselves and their environment. (p. 2)

Some might see the above definition as either harmonizing with or conveniently summarizing the catalog of functions commonly attributed to IaC. However, by virtue of its very comprehensiveness it becomes indistinguishable from a tautology. What psychological processing within the human agent is *not* IaC?

With an eye to such metatheoretical issues as the definability of IaC, more specific criticisms can be framed. For example, the identification of IaC or its message with an assortment of mentalistic and/or neurophysiological operations seems forced and hasty. No one would deny that any number of cognitive processes are somehow involved in communication behavior, but the descriptions of IaC for the most part unguardedly set up an identity between the *definiendum* and one or more of these operations. The move is premature because it rules out the possibility of other kinds of relationships. Might not these cognitive operations be related to IaC as conditions only, or as causes, or as components? If there really is such a phenomenon as IaC, maybe its nature is exhausted in only one or two specific functions. If IaC is to be defined as, say, thinking, or as interacting with our environment, or as the processing of information, does the reverse hold true? Is *all* thinking or interacting to be viewed as IaC? Are there instances of interpreting cues or the metabolizing of information that do not qualify as IaC? If so, what distinguishes some of these inner episodes as IaC from others that are not? Questions such as these are valid because many of the psychoneurophysiological operations mentioned in the descriptions are equally involved in areas of human behavior that one would not readily call or relate to communicative activity, for example, playing solitaire, humming a tune, jogging. To insist that these latter activities do involve IaC is to assume what is now being questioned.

Indeed, given its epistemic scope, there seems to be little difference between IaC and the philosophical concept of mind or, more comprehensively, the Greco-medieval concept of soul and its system of interactive sensory and intellectual powers. For receiving and interpreting cues from the environment one could just as easily substitute the powers of the sentient soul, including *sensus communis* and the *vis aestimativa* of, say, St. Thomas Aquinas. For IaC as metabolizer of information and the source of ideation, why not invoke the medieval theory of phantasm, impressed species, agent intellect, passive intellect, and expressed species? IaC as the inner dynamo of all information and message processing turns out to be neither less occult nor more explanatory than these older epistemologies or philosophical psychologies. By the same token, one is left to wonder what scientific or dialectical advance has been made by substituting the IaC construct for that of mind or soul.

It has already been shown that there is conflicting testimony as to whether or not IaC is linguistically or symbolically structured. Additional pairs of conflicting interpretations accentuate the overall indeterminacy of the IaC model. For one thing, it remains unclear from the literature whether IaC is a biomechanical agency explainable without residue in terms of neurophysiology or one that should be thought of (only? primarily?) in nonphysicalist or mentalistic terms. Some allow that IaC can be viewed as a mental process, a physical state, and a biological-psychological system (see, e.g., Stacks & Sellers, 1989). That sort of generous allowance, however, seems to do more to identify the confusion than to dispel it.

Second, it is equally unclear whether IaC should be thought of as atomic or particulate information, or as being a more discursive mode of cognition. Descriptions that underscore stimuli, raw data, storage, retrieval, and reacting with the environment seem to imply that it works at the level of discrete bits of information. Other accounts picture IaC as functioning at a more abstract level in which propositional and inferential forms of knowledge predominate: talking to oneself, inner dialogue, thinking; problem solving, planning, and evaluation. In either case, nonspecificity is compounded by the welter of qualitatively different functions attributed to IaC. To counterargue that IaC is a highly complex, highly diversified faculty is, once again, to beg the question.

Third, we have no way of knowing whether IaC should be construed as free or chosen behavior or whether, as merely physiological motion, it should be treated as something involuntary in which purpose and intention play no role. Descriptions that stress or incorporate the neurophysiological and the continuous data-processing aspects of IaC do much to minimize the element of personal agency in human communication. When it emphasizes biomechanical processes, IaC signalizes a retreat from the concept of human action by reducing communication or its genesis to series of physical episodes. That sort of reductionism, though not uncommon, does something to erode the specificity of human communication.

Merely to assume, as more than one account does, that IaC somehow incorporates one or more of these pairs of incommensurates serves only to exacerbate the problem of reconciling them. Such an assumption, in settling for proliferation and incompatibilities, is made at the expense of such theory values as economy and elegance.

The Circularity of IaC

The logical impropriety of IaC is evident in repeated claims that it is the basis and foundation of all other forms of communication. It is also said that *all* communication is to some extent IaC. Consistent with these claims are the added assertions that IaC contributes significantly to our understanding of all forms of communication as well as to our own self-knowledge.

There appears to be an embarrassing circularity here. Communication is a molar phenomenon that we first encounter and come to know through its public forms: interpersonal communication, group and mass communication, body language. IaC, on the other hand, is a later theoretical construct elaborated in the identical terms and metaphors already in use to explain these public forms: message, sender, receiver, dialogue, speech, talking, feedback, coding and decoding, and, of course, "communication" itself. Yet in the very same breath, theorists insist that IaC is the basis of these other forms of communication from which it has just borrowed it principal concepts and vocabulary. That sort of circular reasoning is evident in the following representative passage:

> The communication process involves the sending and receiving of a message through some channel—with a resulting response. However, the process does not always require two or more participants. Intrapersonal communication—

communication within oneself—involves all of the elements (e.g., "sender," "receiver," and "transmitter") of other levels of communication such as interpersonal, public speaking, or mass communication, but the process takes place within a single person. . . . The intrapersonal level of communication is the basis for all other communication levels. (Barker & Edwards, 1980, p. 1)

If we use a very simple method of translation or replacement to provide alternative readings for the propositional core of the basis/foundation claims, the redundant structure of these claims can be thrown into relief: "In order to communicate [with others], we must [first] [simultaneously] communicate with[in] ourselves." Since the propositional core simply iterates "communication," it is hard to see how this two-step communication flow is any more informative than a one-step mode.

An alternative and more economical line of reasoning is possible. Every communicator is an agent, the cause and initiator of his or her communicative action (after all, this is why we are held responsible for what we say and do). Why, then, should one assume that the communicator's agency must be further analyzed into yet another and somehow different level of cause (i.e., IaC) and effect (i.e., public communication behavior)? To insist that we do so is akin to insisting, quite fallaciously, that a chain of generative causes must terminate in that which is a cause of itself (*causa sui*). In the case of IaC's more mechanistic descriptions, it could even have the effect of reducing the distinctively human dimension of agency and responsibility.

Once again, the purpose of these criticisms is not to impugn the reality or even the complexity of our inner processes, but rather to diagnose the tenuousness of defining them as a unique form of communication.

Questions About IaC's Origins

The legitimacy of IaC's origins is suspect. IaC is very much a post-World War II construct, and it seems to have been prompted in large measure by what George H. Mead had to say about mind and consciousness (Davis & Baran, 1981, pp. 137). A generation ago, Lee Thayer (1987) urged upon us the importance of a multilevel approach to communication analysis, including the intrapersonal level. An adequate, humanistic theory of communication, he reasoned, should acknowledge the metabolizing function of the individual mind—that is, its taking-into-account abilities. Thus he writes:

It is conceptually useful, if not necessary, to conceive of the communication process as being compounded of all those subprocesses by which a living system acquires and converts ongoing event-*data* into *information* for processing or "consumption" to some end. . . . It is therefore consistent to define *communication* as all of those processes associated with the acquisition and conversion of raw event-data into consumable or processable information, culminating in an instance of taking-something-into-account. (p. 73)

It would be rash to conclude from Thayer's statements, however, that he subscribes to anything at all like an explicit faculty or process theory of IaC such as it has come to mean. On the contrary, his intent is primarily methodological: Theoretical analysis must include an appreciation of those epistemic realities that are part of the communication process. To urge that much, however, neither implies nor entails that those same epistemic realities are communication types.

Moreover, questions about the provenance of IaC are perhaps less germane to its evaluation than the chain of reasoning and assumptions behind it, because the theory seems to have been motivated less by empirical discovery and understanding than by a mixture of linguistic and logical improprieties. A likely genesis of the IaC construct can be reconstructed in the following declension of commonplace beliefs and inferences:

(1) Communication among people, groups, and institutions typically involves an exchange of messages, that is, a process in which movement, change, and cognition come into play.

(2) But that too involves a complex network of neurophysiological and/or mentalistic operations.

(3) The alliance between these inner operations and the more outward exchange of information in, say, conversation is close and marked by a high degree of integration and interdependency.

(4) At the same time, a good many of our inner workings are traditionally describable in process language: the association of images and ideas; thought processes; the discourse of reason; the processes of receiving, storing, and retrieving information; and so forth.

(5) Encouraged, then, by that tight contiguity between events taking place in our inner space and the more public business of exchanging messages, and encouraged, no doubt, by such commonplace expressions as "inner dialogue," "talking to oneself," "obeying one's conscience," and "convincing oneself," the inference is made that yet another form of communication process must be taking place—this time *within* the individual.

(6) As a sort of overlay, then, an extended and transposed concept of (overt) communication is now said to be or to comprise one or more of our inner psychophysical workings.

(7) At the same time, it is also assumed that these inner processes must surely recapitulate the dialogic form of public forms of communication.

First off, then, IaC theory makes its crucial move at the point where observable communication activities are seen to involve or entail a host of cognitive functions. But the IaC theorist appears to go one step further when he or she uncritically collapses that interaction and dependency into a strict identity.

Second, in all of this there appears to be a kind of legerdemain that consists of taking a set of metaphors and words that are very much at home in some regions of language—those of interpersonal and mass communication theory—and using those same expressions to interpret and describe operations in another and very different area—the intransitive activities of the inner human self. But it is already evident that in this new venue the original language of communication theory seems to work not nearly as well or not at all. The fact that IaC does not clearly instantiate the core defining features of communication suggests, that is, that the organism of the single self rejects the IaC transplant.

The reason for this is that the genesis of IaC lies in the same kind of mistake closely diagnosed by Gilbert Ryle in his celebrated work, *The Concept of Mind* (1964). According to Ryle, the traditional or Cartesian theory of an immaterial mind housed within a material body—what he calls the "official dogma of 'the Ghost in the Machine' "—arises from a special kind of blunder, the "category mistake." This mistake is one that "represents the facts of mental life as if they belonged to one logical type or category (or range of types or categories) when they actually belong to another" (p. 16). It is as if, he goes on to explain, a foreigner visiting Oxford or Cambridge for the first time were shown a number of colleges, libraries, museums, labs, and administration buildings, and were then to ask: "But where is the university?" The mistake, of course, lies in the questioner's assumption that *the* university is also a member of the same class and category of which these other units are members, whereas, in fact, it is a very different, more complex organizational form. Ryle argues that the Cartesian concept of mind commits this kind of mistake when it makes the inference that behind a person's thoughtful, feeling, and purposive behavior there must be a hidden immaterial substance within which a host of affective and epistemic functions take place. A person's characteristically human activities, such as thinking and choosing, then, are relegated to this inner sanctum, which then is called *mind* or *soul*. What we end up with is really a needless paramechanical agency that essentially duplicates the overt processes and operations of the whole person but that, its defenders insist, is different.

The IaC model commits the category mistake. It says that behind public communication activities there is another kind of communication that is their basis and source. Supposedly it is not the same as interpersonal, group, or mass communication, but the words and metaphors used to describe it are drawn from those types or categories of communication, in which they do indeed have their place. The result, then, is a double image or doppelgänger form of communication that, in the ensuing confusion, somehow is and is not like the other forms of communication.

Some very questionable reasoning lies behind this paradox, but that is not all. The incautious patterns of ordinary language itself have also contributed to the rise of IaC. IaC arises alongside interpersonal communication because, at first glance, it seems to parallel commonplace structures such as interuniversity and intrauniversity mail services, or intergovernmental and intragovernmental relations.[3] Not surprisingly, then, some thinkers assume that it is perfectly legitimate to have intracommunication accompany intercommunication. What they neglect to consider, however, is that *inter/intra* pairing is valid only when the prefix *intra* attaches to genuine communities, but that such twinning is forced and unconvincing when intracommunication is predicated of individuals.

Finally, there may be something about the language of the communication theory models themselves that has, if only inadvertently, encouraged the emergence of the concept of IaC. The sender-receiver or stimulus-response dyads on which communication theories are commonly based are usually (or too easily) interpreted mainly in biomechanical terms and metaphors. The basic unit of transfer or exchange between these dyads is some sort of physical impulse or signal. All too quickly, however, those same physical impulses and imprints are promoted to the status of *messages*— even before any provision has been made for the contributions of semantic and symbolic structuring, language, formation rules, and so forth. The result of that nearly imperceptible promotion is almost predictable when applied to the human organism. When, that is, the object of attention is the series of neurophysiological workings in individuals, and when these myriad events and reactions are said or assumed to be message-type relationships, it is not so surprising that the model of IaC should take root. Once again, however, that move has really been set up and facilitated by the unexamined belief that any impulse is already a message—different only in degree from the everyday kind of message that we leave for others beside the telephone or in the mailbox. If one drifts into those kinds of assumptions, then it is a short step to conclude further that there must be an inner world of communication, since all sorts of transferences—"messages"—are whizzing around inside our skulls.

SOME CONCLUDING QUESTIONS

The above critique throws into relief weaknesses in the concept of IaC conceived as a distinctive and elemental form of communication. Those weaknesses range from the inherent ambiguity of the phrase *intrapersonal communication processes* to questions about the very legitimacy of motives behind the IaC construct. Once again, the target of these criticisms is not our psychological and inner physical processes, but rather the practice among a growing number of theorists of identifying those inner events as constituting a distinctive communication type. Collectively, the arguments and reflections assembled above demonstrate that this translation is, if not unwarranted, at least highly questionable.

The following groups of questions will perhaps encourage IaC theorists to provide a clearer and more coherent account of their basic tenets.

(1) Can IaC theorists demonstrate that their model is a well motivated one? Can IaC theorizing defend itself against the argument that it arises from fallacious reasoning and linguistic seduction? Those who do not know their history of philosophy are condemned to repeat it. Do IaC theorists realize that they repeat virtually the same kinds of risky moves that have been diagnosed and criticized so compellingly by such frontline thinkers as Ryle and Wittgenstein?

(2) Can IaC theorists beat the circular-reasoning charge? Can they demonstrate to colleagues and critics that they are not assuming and invoking the selfsame principles of public communication that so many of them undertake to explain? If the model cannot avoid using concepts and terms borrowed from public communication, is it anything more than an oxymoron?

(3) There are related methodological concerns as well. Granted that interpersonal, group, and mass communication are molar phenomena, is there really a need to *ground* them in something so private, so imperfectly understood, and so controversial as the IaC construct? Is the IaC model or something like it even the right direction for communication theorists to move in?

(4) Is it not the case that IaC does more to obfuscate than to enlighten? In a field that undertakes to instruct us about the fundaments of community, culture, and society, does it not appear that IaC pulls us in the opposite direction by postulating a very private and opaque process that is said to be or to comprise parts of the psyche?

(5) Can IaC theorists formulate a more wieldy and consistent account? Must IaC comprise as many functions as it is alleged to? Can IaC theorists reduce or eliminate the apparent contradictions both within and among their definitions? Can they secure more agreement among themselves about what IaC is and what it is not?

(6) If IaC's epistemic scope is virtually indistinguishable from that of "mind" or "soul," what scientific or dialectical advance has been made by replacing these older conceptions with the newer construct? If IaC is neither less occult nor more explanatory than these older concepts, why retain it all? Is *intrapersonal communication* anything more than a neologism?

(7) Add to this the moot point of whether IaC can be accessed through research and empirical investigation. If IaC is a neurophysiological process, are its defenders poaching on other research domains and simply duplicating investigations done (better) in other disciplines? If IaC is primarily mentalistic or nonphysicalist in nature, how can it lend itself to empirical investigation? However they choose to respond, IaC theorists will have to make some sort of ontological commitment as to the metaphysical status of IaC. Can they?

NOTES

1. This is a revised and expanded version of the catalog that appears in Cunningham (1989, pp. 89-92).

2. For a more complete discussion of this point, see Cunningham (1989, pp. 87-88).
3. I am grateful to my colleague Stuart Selby for suggesting these analogies.

REFERENCES

Anderson, R. E. (1989). Kierkegaard on ethics in communication with self. In C. V. Roberts &
    K. W. Watson (Eds.), *Intrapersonal communication processes: Original essays* (pp. 411-
    440). New Orleans: Spectra.
Applbaum, R., Anatol, K., Hays, E. R., Jensen, O. O., Porter, R. E., & Mandel, J. E. (1973).
    Fundamental concepts in human communication. San Francisco: Canfield.
Apple, C. G. (1989). Freedom of choice: Intrapersonal communication and emotion. In C. V.
    Roberts & K. W. Watson (Eds.), *Intrapersonal communication processes: Original essays*
    (pp. 319-336). New Orleans: Spectra.
Barker, L. L., & Edwards, R. (1980). *Intrapersonal communication.* Dubuque, IA: Gorsuch
    Scarisbrick.
Barker, L. L., & Wiseman, G. (1966). A model of intrapersonal communication. *Journal of
    Communication, 16*, 172-179.
Barnlund, D. C. (1968). *Interpersonal communication: Survey and studies.* Boston: Houghton
    Mifflin.
Behnke, R. R. (1989). Issues of measurement, instrumentation, and analysis of physiological
    variables. In C. V. Roberts & K. W. Watson (Eds.), *Intrapersonal communication pro-
    cesses: Original essays* (pp. 203-216). New Orleans: Spectra.
Bittner, J. R. (1980). *Mass communication: An introduction* (2nd ed.). Englewood Cliffs, NJ:
    Prentice-Hall.
Blake, R. H., & Haroldsen, E. O. (1975). *A taxonomy of concepts in communication.* New
    York: Hastings House.
Brooks, W. D. (1978). *Speech communication* (3rd ed.). Dubuque, IA: William C. Brown.
Bruneau, T. J. (1989). The deep structure of intrapersonal communication processes. In C. V.
    Roberts & K. W. Watson (Eds.), *Intrapersonal communication processes: Original essays*
    (pp. 63-81). New Orleans: Spectra.
Budd, R. W., & Ruben, B. D. (1979). *New approaches to mass communication.* Rochelle Park,
    NJ: Hayden.
Burks, D. M. (1970). Persuasion, self-persuasion and rhetorical discourse. *Philosophy and
    Rhetoric, 3*, 109-119.
Cunningham, S. B. (1989). Defining intrapersonal communication. In C. V. Roberts & K. W.
    Watson (Eds.), *Intrapersonal communication processes: Original essays* (pp. 82-94). New
    Orleans: Spectra.
Dance, F. E. X. (1970). The "concept" of communication. *Journal of Communication, 20*, 201-210.
Dance, F. E. X., & Larson, C. E. (1972). *Speech communication: Concepts and behavior.* New
    York: Holt, Rinehart & Winston.
Davis, D. K., & Baran, S. J. (1981). *Mass communication in everyday life.* Belmont, CA:
    Wadsworth.
DeFleur, M. L., & Ball-Rokeach, S. (1975). *Theories of mass communication* (3rd ed.). New
    York: Longman.
Dominick, J. R.'(1990). *The dynamics of mass communication* (3rd ed.). New York: McGraw-
    Hill.
Druckman, D., Rozelle, R. M., & Baxter, J. C. (1982). *Nonverbal communication: Survey, the-
    ory, and research.* Beverly Hills, CA: Sage.
Emmert, P. (1989). The theory-research connection. In C. V. Roberts & K. W. Watson (Eds.), *In-
    trapersonal communication processes: Original essays* (pp. 98-110). New Orleans: Spectra.

Fiske, J. (1982). *Introduction to communication studies.* London: Methuen.

Fletcher, J. E. (1989). Physiological foundations of intrapersonal communication. In C. V. Roberts & K. W. Watson (Eds.), *Intrapersonal communication processes: Original essays* (pp. 188-202). New Orleans: Spectra.

Harless, L. (1985). *Mass communication: An introductory survey.* Dubuque, IA: William C. Brown.

Heun, R. E., & Heun, L. R. (1989). Intrapersonal communication processes in public speaking. In C. V. Roberts & K. W. Watson (Eds.), *Intrapersonal communication processes: Original essays* (pp. 493-503). New Orleans: Spectra.

Hikins, J. W. (1989). Intrapersonal discourse and its relationship to human communication: Rhetorical dimensions of self-talk. In C. V. Roberts & K. W. Watson (Eds.), *Intrapersonal communication processes: Original essays* (pp. 28-62). New Orleans: Spectra.

Honeycutt, J. M., Zagacki, S., & Edwards, R. (1989). Intrapersonal communication, social cognition, and imagined interactions. In C. V. Roberts & K. W. Watson (Eds.), *Intrapersonal communication processes: Original essays* (pp. 166-184). New Orleans: Spectra.

Jensen, M. D. (1989). Introspective writings as reflections of intrapersonal communication. In C. V. Roberts & K. W. Watson (Eds.), *Intrapersonal communication processes: Original essays* (pp. 111-134). New Orleans: Spectra.

Korba, R. J. (1989). The cognitive psychophysiology of inner speech. In C. V. Roberts & K. W. Watson (Eds.), *Intrapersonal communication processes: Original essays* (pp. 217-242). New Orleans: Spectra.

LaFleur, G. B. (1985, November). *Intrapersonal communication: Problems of context and meaning.* Paper presented at the annual meeting of the Speech Communication Association, Denver.

Larson, C. U. (1983). *Persuasion: Reception and responsibility* (3rd ed.). Belmont, CA: Wadsworth.

Linkugel, W. A., & Buehler, E. C. (1975). *Speech communication for the contemporary student.* New York: Harper & Row.

Lippard-Justice, P. (1989). The relationship between intrapersonal and interpersonal communication patterns. In C. V. Roberts & K. W. Watson (Eds.), *Intrapersonal communication processes: Original essays* (pp. 444-455). New Orleans: Spectra.

Littlejohn, S. W. (1989). *Theories of human communication* (3rd ed.). Belmont, CA: Wadsworth.

Merrill, J. C., & Lowenstein, R. L. (1979). *Media, messages and men* (2nd ed.). New York: Longman.

Miller, G. R., Sleight, C., & deTurck, M. A. (1989). Arousal and attribution: Are the behavioral cues nonspecific? In C. V. Roberts & K. W. Watson (Eds.), *Intrapersonal communication processes: Original essays* (pp. 273-291). New Orleans: Spectra.

O'Sullivan, T., Hartley, J., Saunders, D., & Fiske, J. (1983). *Key concepts in communication.* London: Methuen.

Pearson, J. D., & Nelson, P. E. (1979). *Understanding and sharing: An introduction to speech communication.* Dubuque, IA: William C. Brown.

Pelose, G. C. (1989). Metacognition as an intrapersonal communication process: The purpose of cognitive monitoring and methodology for its assessment. In C. V. Roberts & K. W. Watson (Eds.), *Intrapersonal communication processes: Original essays* (pp. 135-165). New Orleans: Spectra.

Richmond, V. P., & McCroskey, J. C. (1989). Willingness to communicate and dysfunctional communication processes. In C. V. Roberts & K. W. Watson (Eds.), *Intrapersonal communication processes: Original essays* (pp. 292-318). New Orleans: Spectra.

Roberts, C. V. (1985, November). *The definition and delimitation of intrapersonal communication: A physiological perspective.* Paper presented at the annual meeting of the Speech Communication Association, Denver.

Roberts, C. V. (1986, November). *A physiological approach to the teaching of intrapersonal communication.* Paper presented at the annual meeting of the Speech Communication Association, Chicago.

Roberts, C. V., Edwards, R., & Barker, L. L. (1987). *Intrapersonal communication processes.* Scottsdale, AZ: Gorsuch Scarisbrick.

Roberts, C. V., & Watson, K. W. (Eds.). (1989). *Intrapersonal communication processes: Original essays.* New Orleans: Spectra.

Rogers, W. (1984). *Communication in action: Building speech competencies.* New York: Holt, Rinehart & Winston.

Roloff, M. E. (1989). Issue schema and mindless processing of persuasive messages: Much ado about nothing? In C. V. Roberts & K. W. Watson (Eds.), *Intrapersonal communication processes: Original essays* (pp. 380-410). New Orleans: Spectra.

Ryle, G. (1964). *The concept of mind.* New York: Barnes & Noble.

Schedletsky, L. J. (1989). What evidence do we have for the psychological reality of nonconscious processing? In C. V. Roberts & K. W. Watson (Eds.), *Intrapersonal communication processes: Original essays* (pp. 345-379). New Orleans: Spectra.

Smith, M. J. (1982). *Persuasion and human action: A review and critique of social influence theories.* Belmont, CA: Wadsworth.

Stacks, D. W., & Sellers, D. E. (1989). Understanding intrapersonal communication: Neurological processing and implications. In C. V. Roberts & K. W. Watson (Eds.), *Intrapersonal communication processes: Original essays* (pp. 243-267). New Orleans: Spectra.

Surlin, S. H., & Costaris, G. (1985). Growth and preservation-oriented communication behavior. *Canadian Journal of Communication, 11*, 211-226.

Thayer, L. (1987). *On communication: Essays in understanding.* Norwood, NJ: Ablex.

Vinson, L. R. (1985, November). *A perspective of intrapersonal communication.* Paper presented at the annual meeting of the Speech Communication Association, Denver.

Vinson, L. R. (1989). The relative importance of three sources of emotion-eliciting stimuli: Toward an integrative model of naturally occurring emotion. In C. V. Roberts & K. W. Watson (Eds.), *Intrapersonal communication processes: Original essays* (pp. 337-349). New Orleans: Spectra.

Watson, J., & Hill, A. (1989). *A dictionary of communication and media studies* (2nd ed.). London: Edward Arnold.

Weaver, R. L., Bailey, M. L., & Cotrell, H. W. (1989). Imagio [*sic*]: Precursor to Inventio. In C. V. Roberts & K. W. Watson (Eds.), *Intrapersonal communication processes: Original essays* (pp. 4-27). New Orleans: Spectra.

Whetmore, E. J. (1985). *Mediamerica: Form, content and consequences of mass communication* (3rd ed.). Belmont, CA: Wadsworth.

Wittgenstein, L. (1963). *Philosophical investigations.* Oxford: Basil Blackwell.

Theoretical Choices
That Clarify the Present
and Define the Future

JAMES L. APPLEGATE
University of Kentucky

COMMENTARIES should note areas of agreement and disagreement with the essay in question and provide additional insights into the issue. Here, the issue is "intrapersonal" communication. Let me then offer (a) an assessment of Cunningham's rather bruising critique of the intrapersonal idea and the limited research explicitly studying it, (b) a different way to address the problems Cunningham correctly defines, and (c) my own argument for the best approach to this troubled notion of intrapersonal communication given my theoretical commitments and best sense of what is unique about the communication discipline.

THE FUTILITY OF
THEORY-FREE DEFINITIONS OF COMMUNICATION:
INTRAPERSONAL COMMUNICATION AS EXAMPLE

Cunningham's critiques of intrapersonal communication research are correct as far as they go (in addition to his chapter in this volume, see Cunningham, 1989). For those daunted by the many lists, references, and dense prose in his treatment, a brief elaboration of his key claims should be helpful. First, research explicitly employing the idea of intrapersonal communication is almost nonexistent, despite its initial "coming out" 25 years ago. Only when we count every area of research now interested in cognitive antecedents to communication, metacognition, and affect as intrapersonal communication research (an inclusion at which many doing that research

Correspondence and requests for reprints: James L. Applegate, Department of Communication, 227 Grehan Building, University of Kentucky, Lexington, KY 40506-0042.

Communication Yearbook 15, pp. 621-632

would balk) can enough references be included in an essay to suggest wide scholarly interest. However, the recent formation of an intrapersonal interest group in one of our national associations and publication of a collection of essays on the topic (Roberts & Watson, 1989) suggest the need for attention to the area.

Second, Cunningham details the conceptual confusion that informs efforts to define intrapersonal communication. I will not recount the various definitions. Most important, those using the term seem confused over whether they are studying (a) intrapersonal (read cognitive, affective, psychological, physiological) processes that serve as antecedents to and products of communication defined in behavioral contexts involving at least two people or (b) a distinct form of communication deserving a special adjective (intrapersonal) to distinguish it from more typical interactive applications of the term.

If the former is the case, then the idea seems at best superfluous and at worst distracting to those inside and outside the discipline attempting to sustain a sensible focus for research. My own review of the recent Roberts and Watson (1989) volume on the topic suggests the peripheral nature of the term for much of the work included there. For example, Pelose's (1989) contribution to the volume provides a discussion of metacognition well worth our attention, yet, despite her valiant attempts to distinguish intrapersonal communication from what is generally known as metacognition, the distinction she offers lacks substance. She writes:

> There is a sense in which intrapersonal communication and metacognition seem almost to describe the same process. However, metacognition . . . refers to one's awareness and control of one's cognitive endeavors . . . and one's social cognitive endeavors [only]. . . . intrapersonal communication can also refer to one's awareness of physiological processes or states.

So intrapersonal communication is metacognition about more than just cognitive processes? The usefulness of the distinction is not clear.

Throughout much of the Roberts and Watson volume, authors strain in similar ways to avoid marginalizing the intrapersonal term that anchors its title. Fletcher (1989) acknowledges that most researchers studying psychophysiological processes do not use the term *intrapersonal communication* (most probably have never encountered the term). However, he suggests they are studying it whether they know it or not. I am not sure what we or those researchers gain by adding another label to their work, especially when calling their work *communication research* clouds the meaning of that term for them and the rest of us. Several other essays in the Roberts and Watson volume ignore the intrapersonal idea entirely. Miller, Sleight, and deTurck (1989) offer a study of "*antecedent intraindividual processes* responsible for triggering particular displays of verbal and nonverbal behavior" related to deceptive exchanges between people (emphasis added). Richmond and McCroskey (1989) analyze "willingness to communicate" and Roloff (1989) explores mindless processing of persuasive messages with no substantial mention of the idea of intrapersonal communication. For these and other authors in this recent collection of intrapersonal communication research the contributors' focus is on variables conceived of as important antecedents to communication behavior, not communication itself.

What of the idea that intrapersonal communication is truly a distinct process involving message exchange inside the person, using, as Cunningham suggests from Wittgenstein, some "radically private language"? I will not spend much time on this point, since no recent research in the area seem to embrace this position. Cunningham details the reasons the position is untenable: most important, because the thinker and the researcher would be trapped in a "solipsistic game of inventing and manipulating signs" in which "the boundary between illusion and reality disappears" (p. 609).

So the picture Cunningham gives us of a somewhat ambiguous dialogue by intrapersonal communication scholars seems correct. We confront the general notion that *some* kind of process with *some* similarities (if not isomorphism) with both psychophysiological processes and *inter*personal exchanges occurs inside the head. This process serves as the foundation for all other behavior we might want to call communication. Intrapersonal communication encompasses metacognition, affect, perception, the reflective self, cognition generally, physiological responses to the environment, and so on, but treats them somehow as not just perception, metacognition, reflection, or affect but as an internal *communication* process.

Cunningham further argues that the ambiguous definition of communication that characterizes intrapersonal research is, as far as he can tell, counterintuitive. At least it is an idea of communication at odds with the commonsense definition shared across the discipline as evidenced in popular communication texts (e.g., Littlejohn, 1989). He wants intrapersonal researchers not only to clarify but to alter the conception of communication implied in the research.

However, in posing the challenge to intrapersonal communication researchers to clarify in this way, Cunningham creates an impossible task for them. He too, perhaps, falls into the very trap that I believe produced all this confusion in the first place. *The trap door shuts behind us when we assume we can decide whether to talk as if there is something called "intrapersonal communication" and define it independently of a commitment to some substantive theory of communication that embraces its own philosophy of human nature, language, and social life.*

The limited amount of writing explicitly about intrapersonal communication tries to define the process in terms of particular variables as objects of study (e.g., affect, neuron activity) or, worse yet, in terms of where "it" occurs (inside the individual). This approach leads to the unfortunate translation of theoretically based concepts into applications outside the theory that seem strange at best. For example, few are unfamiliar with Watzlawick, Beavin, and Jackson's (1967) analysis of the content and relational dimensions of communication. The ideas are grounded in a systems-oriented approach to *talk between people* that grounds the meaning of communication in the behavioral patterns that emerge in that talk. An interesting and coherent line of work in interaction analysis has grown from this approach.

Recently, Hikins (1989) introduced the content/relational theme in the intrapersonal domain, asserting that what counts as both content and relational dimensions is "determined wholly by what the self will certify while reflecting *with* itself" (p. 53). I am not sure where extracting the meaning of the content and relational dimensions of communication from interaction and planting it in metacognitive activity takes us ultimately, but it does take us to a theoretical place far from where these ideas live in Watzlawick et al.'s pragmatic theory of communication. My point is not to critique this particular translation, but to suggest that scholarly discourse attempting to define concepts and research domains independent of substantive theory invites piecemeal eclecticism and the type of ambiguity and confusion Cunningham documents.

The "theory-free" discourse now informing intrapersonal communication research and debates on the nature of intrapersonal communication produces a confusing use of concepts. It also encourages general definitional debates reminiscent of those arising in the younger days of the discipline, when we tried to define communication without reference to particular theories. These reflections produced definitions that excluded so little from consideration they did little to define. Take, for example, Fletcher's (1989) definition of communication taken from Thayer's (1968) work: Communication is the process from which reality evolves. That may be true, but it is not very helpful in guiding research. Hikins (1989), in an otherwise interesting article on the role of self-talk in producing communication behavior, provides an elaborate model of communication reminiscent of the complicated versions of the linear model of communication that emerged in the 1960s as we became less linear and more "systemic" in thinking about communication. Both those earlier models and Hikins's may be useful organizing frameworks for grouping variables. A mediational behaviorist *or* a symbolic interactionist could usefully employ such models. However, it is the theory they employ that defines variables and guides the interpretation of results. The model itself is useless for such purposes.

As noted, I believe Cunningham himself falls into this theory-free, definitional game when he critiques intrapersonal communication writers for a counterintuitive definition of communication and then offers his own synthetically derived set of minimal conditions for communication. While I am comfortable with the qualities Cunningham lists, I am uncomfortable with the atheoretical way he presents them. Later in this essay I offer an argument for a particular set of theoretical commitments that define communication using several of the qualities on Cunningham's list. Readers may accept or reject the perspective I embrace, but the theoretical nature of the argument is, I hope, clear. My criticism of intrapersonal research (and perhaps Cunningham's approach to critiquing it) is that I see *no* explicit theory of communication and little coherent philosophy explicitly informing either effort. Not until we identify the theoretical realm of our discourse can we hope to define clearly the idea of intrapersonal communication. The theory we embrace will not only define the idea but will establish its relative distinctiveness from other variables within the theory's range of convenience.

This point may be embarrassingly obvious to anyone who lived through the philosophy of science debates characterizing social science in the late 1960s and 1970s. In our own discipline, D. J. O'Keefe (1975) makes this point in his influential analysis of the theory/observation issue and the shift in our understanding of the role of theory in scientific reasoning. Suppe's (1977) encyclopedic description of the shift in our understanding of the role of theory and many other volumes on post-Kuhnian philosophy of science also show us we can neither define nor operationalize an idea (e.g., intrapersonal communication) independent of theory. Moreover, unless we explicitly subject our theories to rigorous scientific debate, our ideas will continue to be confused and ambiguous to ourselves and others (see especially Brown, 1989, for an illuminating account of the relation of metaphor, theory, science, and praxis).

Moreover, the need for clear theoretical constructs may be especially strong in research on communication-relevant intrapersonal processes. The indicators of these processes must be clearly defined. Many of the constructs may have no clear observable consequent or representation. Without straightforward theoretical definitions, intrapersonal variables are susceptible to multiple and contradictory operationalizations.

In the next section, I briefly review one well-explicated social scientific theory often referenced by communication researchers: symbolic interactionism. I describe how the theory defines the processes generally embraced by intrapersonal communication researchers within a general approach to human interaction. This application exercise is meant to evidence the clarifying effects of theoretical choice making. I chose this theory because intrapersonal communication researchers sometimes borrow its ideas in their efforts to study the role of the "self" in intrapersonal communication.

Symbolic interactionist theory developed from the pragmatic philosophy of George H. Mead, Robert Park, W. I. Thomas, and John Dewey and the work of the Chicago school of sociology (for more complete looks at Mead and the Chicago school, respectively, see Miller, 1973; Smith, 1988). Ironically, symbolic interactionism, while referenced in the intrapersonal literature, is one of several theories whose increased coinage among communication researchers over the last 20 years refocused communication research on ideas such as language, community, topoi, text, and interaction and to some extent away from the physiological/psychological processes of primary concern in intrapersonal research. (Other such theories include constructivism, ethnomethodology, critical theory, and a variety of linguistic theories of communication.) The resultant increase in analyses of message behavior *between* persons has produced what might be called a "turn to messages" in the discipline. Within this message-centered approach the variables of concern to intrapersonal researchers often are studied, if at all, as antecedents, consequents, or peripherals to core *communication* behaviors. Nevertheless, some of its concepts have been appropriated in the intrapersonal literature, and as a coherent theory it can serve as the basis for a discussion of intrapersonal communication.

INTRAPERSONAL COMMUNICATION IN
SYMBOLIC INTERACTIONIST TERMS:
THE CLARIFYING ROLE OF THEORY

Cunningham notes that many intrapersonal analyses focus on the idea of an internal dialogue between the "I" and "Me" components of the self as intrapersonal communication. In discussing "self-talk," "inner dialogue," "the reflexive self," and related ideas, these studies directly or indirectly reference work in the American pragmatic tradition, particularly the Chicago school and its research offspring in the social sciences. If this philosophical/theoretical position should be explicitly embraced by intrapersonal communication researchers, it would add the clarity Cunningham seeks in the intrapersonal discourse. Most of Cunningham's questions about intrapersonal research could be answered, if not in a way that pleased every researcher in the area.

Let me be brief and, I am afraid, necessarily indexical to those not already familiar with the pragmatic tradition, in demonstrating the point. This line of work grew out of initial concerns with the role of language and communication in maintaining social communities. Language as the basis for thought contains a shared set of "significant symbols" that derive their meaning from the similar "way of acting" toward the world they index. Use of these symbols enables social actors to establish common lines of action in pursuit of pragmatic social goals. Hence symbolic interactionism offers an action-centered theory of meaning. The internalization of such action blueprints empowers the individual to join the community. With the internalization of language we internalize a "generalized other"—a third-party "community" perspective on our actions. However, people are not social robots. The self contains a creative component (the "I") that drives action using symbols embodied in a generalized (cultural) perspective acquired through the internalization of language. The outcome of this language-based effort is the creation of specific social selves constructed in communication contexts (the "Me" component of the reflexive self). Internal dialogue is derivative from social language. The reflexive self encompasses these various components and processes that inform and also are informed by the interaction processes that produce socially shared definitions of situations.

Pragmatist/symbolic interactionist theory suggests that the internal dialogue referred to by intrapersonal researchers does not differ in any substantial way from interactive dialogue between persons. Its coinage is social language. Hence we have one example of the clarifying effect of a theoretical commitment. Questions Cunningham correctly raises about the exact nature of the internal activity referenced in intrapersonal research are answered (e.g., Does it employ a "private" language and if so how do we study it? No, language is not private but social). Moreover, the answer suggests how to study the process and its relation to interpersonal communication and social action. The research focus is the accomplishment of community in *inter*personal interaction. Communication is the social *use of language* populated with significant symbols that enable creation of shared ways of acting toward the world. The interpretive activities of the reflexive self are, in their substance, derivative of our shared language and this community-building process.

The adoption of a symbolic interactionist theory of communication enables us to define clearly the intrapersonal processes of interest. Our starting point is language and the social. Our entrance into the realm of inner dialogues and individual interpretation is guided by what we need to know about social interaction. Our theory suggests that those internal processes (a) use no "radically private language," (b) are more linguistically than physiologically driven, (c) gain meaning and visibility only in social interaction, and (d) are antecedent to core communication processes serving the primary purpose of identifying the individual with his or her language community. The self is reflexive, choice making, and symbolic, but its internal dialogues are defined by social interaction processes that produce the grist for intrapersonal reflections best thought of as analogic to communication in certain limited ways. It should be clear how these theoretical commitments address many of Cunningham's concerns about ambiguities in intrapersonal research. However, the questions are answered in a way likely to leave many intrapersonal communication researchers (e.g., those physiologically oriented) dissatisfied. At least clarifying answers are provided by the theory.

Adoption of other theories would provide different but equally clear answers to the important questions Cunningham raises. Constructivist communication theory, for example (Applegate, 1990; Burleson, 1989; Delia, O'Keefe, & O'Keefe, 1982), would grant a more independent and uniquely individual status to the cognitive and affective processes of interest to intrapersonal researchers. However, the idea of communication itself informing this theory would define intrapersonal processes as antecedents to communication behavior: sometimes necessary but seldom sufficient conditions to define the communication that occurs. Within constructivist theory communication is the process occurring where two or more people are mutually aware of the intention to make something private public: to create intersubjective meaning by using language organized around more specific communicative goals (e.g., persuasion). Cognition, metacognition, and their neurological or physiological counterparts may sometimes embody necessary conditions for certain types of communication. At other times they may reflect the consequences of communication. They do not however, constitute communication. Moreover, these antecedents are studied within a developmental framework tied to developments in strategic interactive communication ability that serve as the starting point for constructivist theory.

My belabored point is that *some* theoretical commitment is necessary if we are ever to argue sensibly about, much less resolve, the confusions and ambiguities Cunningham documents. Assuming I have made that point, let me acknowledge that a researcher committed to studying the very important processes now studied under the intrapersonal communication rubric (e.g., metacognition) could reasonably argue that, the need for some theory aside, I have been unfair in choosing theories that argue against thinking of intrapersonal processes as a form of communication. Certainly, one could embrace variants of very important cognitive theories in psychology that offer an almost exclusive focus on intrapersonal processes. A few of these even use the term *communication* isomorphically with these internal processes. To respond to this objection, I conclude with an argument not just for explicit theoretical commitment but for a commitment to theories that focus on communication as an independent process of message exchange between people not reducible to—or simply mirroring—cognition, culture, or physiology. This second argument reflects my own theoretical commitments and a sense of our discipline's status, strengths, and future.

AN INTERACTIVE STARTING POINT
FOR COMMUNICATION RESEARCH

The various internal cognitive, affective, and even physiological processes constituting the focus of current intrapersonal communication research relate in important ways to communication. Nothing written here should be taken as an argument that those processes should not be studied on their own and insofar as they affect communication. It is important, however, that these processes be studied within a clearly articulated theoretical framework that grants communicative interactions a status that is not confused with an operationalization of cognitive, affective, or, for that matter, cultural processes.

We do our discipline no service when we embrace theories that reduce communication to cognition or culture. Worse yet, we invite confusion among ourselves and our colleagues in other disciplines when we refer to what most of the world sees as cognition (thinking) or physiology as "communication." The focus of our discipline both past and present on the exchange of messages between people and the outcomes of that exchange for the individual and the group is lost in this terminological move.

The theoretical choices called for in this essay define what constitutes communication and in doing so define our focus, research problems, and method for addressing those problems. They define the starting point for all our work. At an earlier point in its development the communication discipline adopted theories focused on psychological processes as the starting point for research. Communication, from these perspectives, was studied as it operationalized those processes (see Delia, 1987, for a history of the discipline generally; see Duck, 1985, for an account of "when social psychology was king" in interpersonal communication research particularly). Since that time, the communication discipline has matured and increasingly has been populated by research programs taking symbolic message exchange between people as their starting place.[1] In this research the qualities of communicative messages and interactions are the focus. The idea of communication embraced then defines the dimensions of culture, cognition, and so on studied to illuminate what happens when communicative interaction occurs.

The increasing visibility of discourse-/conversation-/text-based approaches to communication exemplifies recent theoretical choices that "start" the research process with a focus on the construction and negotiation of realities by using symbolic resources. Specifically, Habermas's modern critical perspective on rational discourse (see Burleson & Kline, 1979), theories of pragmatics from linguistics (Levinson, 1983), conversation-analytic theories arising from ethnomethodology (McLaughlin, 1984), and hermeneutic (Gadamer, 1975) and modern critical (Habermas, 1984) approaches to communicative texts are but a few examples of interactive, message-focused theoretical approaches to communication research. In interpersonal, institutional, and media contexts, communication is studied as a rhetorical negotiation of reality more or less (depending on the theoretical position) informed and constrained by the resources of cognition or culture.

Research on compliance gaining (see Dillard, 1990) and uncertainty reduction in initial relational and cross-cultural interactions (e.g., Gudykunst, Chua, & Gray, 1987), continuing work on the emergence and effects of differing communication strategies and patterns in personal and family relationships (see reviews in Bochner & Eisenberg, 1987; Duck, 1985; Fitzpatrick, 1987), B. J. O'Keefe's (1988) recent work on message design logic, and constructivist research on person-centered communication (see reviews by Applegate, 1990; Burleson, 1989; Delia et al., 1982) are other examples of theoretical choices that provide an initial interactive message-centered focus for research. These perspectives allow the idea of communicative interaction informing the theory to guide the approach to the study of communication-relevant processes occurring at the individual or social level.

This is not the place to elaborate on the nature of the message-centered, interactive focus of these positions, or to explain fully why I see that focus as the best starting point for our discipline (see Applegate, Coyle, & Leichty, forthcoming). However, my claim is that the focus on message production, interactive organization, social goals, and outcomes for communication embraced by these positions is consistent with our disciplinary roots in rhetorical traditions. It also simultaneously differentiates and yet integrates us within the current research terrain populated by our colleagues in the critical and social sciences. It closely ties our research to our traditional disciplinary commitments to improve the practice of communication. This interactive focus is, in my view, the best starting point for our research.

Having said this, I conclude by restating a caveat. The many processes currently forming the diverse topical focus of intrapersonal communication research are important communication-relevant phenomena (e.g., the imaginary conversations people have with themselves, reflexive "self-talk," affective and physiological responses to situations), relevant at least from my constructivist theoretical perspective concerned with variables producing individual differences in communication behavior. However, to call physiological, cognitive, or most of the other processes described in Cunningham's review *communication* gives us the wrong starting point for our research. We are led to begin by trying to understand psychological processes and then to define communication in light of those. In doing so, we allow our attention to be drawn away from the common interactive-message focus of the many productive lines of research emerging in our discipline over the last 20 years. As Cunningham's essay suggests, this returns us to nonproductive debates about the definition of communication that blur our sense of the central problems serving as the starting point for communication research, debates and terminological twists that confuse us as well as our colleagues in related disciplines.

Of course we should continue to study intrapersonal processes, but only after making explicit theoretical choices that clarify the confusions Cunningham documents. Moreover, I believe we should choose theories that initially focus research on what is unique about communication as an interactive process in which human beings use symbolic resources to exchange messages in an effort to establish and sustain a sense of intersubjectivity. Useful accounts of communication-relevant intrapersonal processes no doubt will emerge from that starting point, but they will be framed in terms of communicative research problems. Shakespeare to the contrary, there is much to a name and the theoretical choice for a research focus it reflects.

NOTE

1. Of course, many research programs popular in communication still focus on psychological, physiological, or cultural variables as starting points for communication research. The intrapersonal communication research area topically reflects that starting point. Another example is the "elaboration likelihood model" of cognitive processing (see Petty & Cacioppo, 1986) popular in current persuasion research. This approach begins with a model of alternative "routes" for processing information and then studies the qualities of persuasive communication as they relate to model characteristics. The nature and effects of persuasion are defined in almost exclusively cognitive terms designed to confirm/refine the information-processing model. This is an example of a well-explicated psychological model that nevertheless seems a curious choice as a starting point for communication researchers interested in explaining the persuasive communication process as we typically think of it (for an excellent review of the use of this model in persuasive communication research, see D. J. O'Keefe, 1990).

REFERENCES

Applegate, J. L. (1990). Constructs and communication: A pragmatic integration. In G. Neimeyer & R. Neimeyer (Eds.), *Advances in personal construct psychology* (Vol. 1, pp. 203-230). Greenwich, CT: JAI.

Applegate, J. L., Coyle, K., & Leichty, G. (forthcoming). *The turn to messages: Discovering the core of communication research.* New York: Guilford.

Bochner, A. P., & Eisenberg, E. M. (1987). Family processes: Systems perspectives. In C. R. Berger & S. H. Chaffee (Eds.), *Handbook of communication science* (pp. 540-563). Newbury Park, CA: Sage.

Brown, R. H. (1989). *Social science as civic discourse.* Chicago: University of Chicago Press.

Burleson, B. R. (1989). The constructivist approach to person-centered communication. In B. Dervin, L. Grossberg, B. J. O'Keefe, & E. Wartella (Eds.), *Rethinking communication: Vol. 2. Paradigm exemplars* (pp. 29-46). Newbury Park, CA: Sage.

Burleson, B. R., & Kline, S. L. (1979). Habermas' theory of communication: A critical explication. *Quarterly Journal of Speech, 65*, pp. 412-428.

Cunningham, S. B. (1989). Defining intrapersonal communication. In C. V. Roberts & K. W. Watson (Eds.), *Intrapersonal communication processes: Original essays* (pp. 82-94). New Orleans: Spectra.

Delia, J. G. (1987). Communication research: A history. In C. R. Berger & S. H. Chaffee (Eds.), *Handbook of communication science* (pp. 20-98). Newbury Park, CA: Sage.

Delia, J. G., O'Keefe, B. J., & O'Keefe, D. J. (1982). The constructivist approach to communication. In F. E. X. Dance (Ed.), *Human communication theory* (pp. 147-191). New York: Harper & Row.

Dillard, J. P. (Ed.). (1990). *Seeking compliance: The production of interpersonal influence messages.* Scottsdale, AZ: Gorsuch Scarisbrick.

Duck, S. (1985). Social and personal relationships. In M. L. Knapp & G. R. Miller (Eds.), *Handbook of interpersonal communication* (pp. 655-686). Beverly Hills, CA: Sage.

Fitzpatrick, M. A. (1987). Marital interaction. In C. R. Berger & S. H. Chaffee (Eds.), *Handbook of communication science* (pp. 564-618). Newbury Park, CA: Sage.

Fletcher, J. E. (1989). Physiological foundations of intrapersonal communication. In C. V. Roberts & K. W. Watson (Eds.), *Intrapersonal communication processes: Original essays* (pp. 188-202). New Orleans: Spectra.

Gadamer, H. (1975). *Truth and method.* New York: Seabury.

Gudykunst, W., Chua, E., & Gray, A. (1987). Cultural dissimilarities and uncertainty reduction processes. In M. McLaughlin (Ed.), *Communication yearbook 10* (pp. 456-469). Newbury Park, CA: Sage.

Habermas, J. (1984). *The theory of communication action* (Vol. 1) (T. McCarthy, Trans.). Boston: Beacon.

Hikins, J. W. (1989). Intrapersonal discourse and its relation to human communication: Rhetorical dimensions of self-talk. In C. V. Roberts & K. W. Watson (Eds.), *Intrapersonal communication processes: Original essays* (pp. 28-62). New Orleans: Spectra.

Levinson, S. (1983). *Pragmatics.* Cambridge: Cambridge University Press.

Littlejohn, S. W. (1989). *Theories of human communication* (3rd ed.). Belmont, CA: Wadsworth.

McLaughlin, M. (1984). *Conversation: How talk is organized.* Beverly Hills, CA: Sage.

Miller, D. L. (1973). *George Herbert Mead: Self, language, and the world.* Austin: University of Texas Press.

Miller, G. R., Sleight, C., & deTurck, M. A. (1989). Arousal and attribution: Are the behavioral cues nonspecific? In C. V. Roberts & K. W. Watson (Eds.), *Intrapersonal communication processes: Original essays* (pp. 273-291). New Orleans: Spectra.

O'Keefe, B. J. (1988). The logic of message design. *Communication Monographs, 55,* 80-103.

O'Keefe, D. J. (1975). Logical empiricism and the study of human communication. *Speech Monographs, 42,* 169-183.

O'Keefe, D. J. (1990). *Persuasion: Theory and research.* Newbury Park, CA: Sage.

Pelose, G. C. (1989). Metacognition as an intrapersonal communication process: The purpose of cognitive monitoring and methodology for its assessment. In C. V. Roberts & K. W. Watson (Eds.), *Intrapersonal communication processes: Original essays* (pp. 135-165). New Orleans: Spectra.

Petty, R. E., & Cacioppo, J. T. (1986). *Communication and persuasion: Central and peripheral routes to attitude change.* New York: Springer-Verlag.

Richmond, V. P., & McCroskey, J. C. (1989). Willingness to communicate and dysfunctional communication processes. In C. V. Roberts & K. W. Watson (Eds.), *Intrapersonal communication processes: Original essays* (pp. 292-318). New Orleans: Spectra.

Roloff, M. E. (1989). Issue schema and mindless processing of persuasive messages: Much ado about nothing? In C. V. Roberts & K. W. Watson (Eds.), *Intrapersonal communication processes: Original essays* (pp. 380-410). New Orleans: Spectra.

Roberts, C. V., & Watson, K. W. (Eds.). (1989). *Intrapersonal communication processes: Original essays.* New Orleans: Spectra.

Smith, D. (1988). *The Chicago school: A liberal critique of capitalism.* New York: St. Martin's.

Suppe, F. (1977). *The structure of scientific theories.* Urbana: University of Illinois Press.

Thayer, L. (1968). *Communication and communication systems.* Homewood, IL: Richard D. Irwin.

Watzlawick, P., Beavin, J. H., & Jackson, D. D. (1967). *Pragmatics of human communication: A study of interaction patterns, pathologies and paradoxes.* New York: W. W. Norton.

Criteria for Evaluating
Models of Intrapersonal
Communication Processes

DEBORAH R. BARKER
LARRY L. BARKER
Auburn University

S CHOLARLY criticism is essential to the development and enhancement of scientific theories. Cunningham's essay deserves careful consideration by scholars who are studying intrapersonal processes, as do all thoughtful critical analyses of definitions, models, and theories. However, Cunningham appears to make several assumptions that may be invalid from the perspective of long-term, active researchers who are investigating intrapersonal processes.

The first assumption is that there is virtue in continuing to argue over whether intrapersonal processes should be labeled "communication." This issue has been addressed by critics and scholars on numerous occasions in the past and has been resolved in the minds of most active researchers. For example, when the Barker/Wiseman model was first published in the *Journal of Communication* in 1966, the words *intrapersonal communication* appeared in the title. Barker and Wiseman borrowed the phrase from Ruesch and Bateson's (1951) classic work, *Communication: The Social Matrix of Psychiatry.* In later publications, Barker and his colleagues modified the original definitions, model, and terminology associated with intrapersonal processes. Within the last five years, Barker and his colleagues (Barker, Barker, & Fitch-Hauser, 1988; Roberts, Edwards, & Barker, 1987; Watson & Barker, 1990)—as well as the majority of scholars who are interested in their study—have begun to construct models and research programs around "intrapersonal processes" as they affect human communication. This shift in focus from models of intrapersonal communication to intrapersonal

Correspondence and requests for reprints: Deborah R. Barker, Department of Communication, Auburn University, Auburn, AL 36849.

Communication Yearbook 15, pp. 633-643

processes is partially reflected in the addition of the word *processes* to the phrase *intrapersonal communication.* In short, those who are actively involved in research concerning intrapersonal processes seem to agree: Whether or not the concept should be labeled communication is a semantic issue—not a philosophical one. The number of fruitful research programs that have emerged that take an "intrapersonal processing" approach to the study of either intrapersonal processes, specifically, or human communication, in general, would seem to document this claim effectively (e.g., Andriate & Beatty, 1988; Beatty, 1989; Beatty & Behnke, 1980; Beatty & Payne, 1981, 1984; Craig, 1979; Delia & Clark, 1977; Hale & Delia, 1976; Krueger, 1982; Krueger & Harper, 1988; Miller, 1988; Miller, Sleight, & deTurck, 1989; Planalp & Hewes, 1982; Powers, Jordan, & Street, 1979; Roloff, 1980, 1989; Ruben, 1975; Stacks, 1983; Stacks & Sellers, 1986, 1989; Wheeless, 1975). Indeed, the inclusion of *communication* in the phrase *intrapersonal communication processes* has done little to hamper the work of these highly productive researchers.

The second assumption Cunningham makes is that, by providing a longitudinal literature review, he has adequately represented current thinking about intrapersonal processes. Most scholars who have ever written about "intrapersonal communication" or related processes are still living. They also are constantly modifying, expanding, relabeling, and enhancing previous thinking in both convention papers and refereed publications. By not citing the most recent thinking among intrapersonal researchers, Cunningham has kept them "time bound" by the most recent publication date he cites. If we date the study of "intrapersonal communication" (processes) back to Ruesch and Bateson, the field has been active for only four decades. If we set the date of its inception at 1966 and publication of the Barker/Wiseman article, the field is only a little over two and a half decades old. When criticizing the research and "concept development" in a discipline this young, one has to be aware of the dynamic and rapid evolution and change in thinking and terminology. One wonders how Cunningham would have criticized definitions, models, and theories in psychology after only two to four decades of scholarly activity.

The question then remains: How should scholars who are interested in intrapersonal processes proceed, given the contribution of critical evaluations such as Cunningham's and the role that clear conceptualizations indeed play in targeting phenomena for inquiry? The answer seems to lie in an awareness of three primary issues, each of which will be discussed in the pages that follow. First, the discipline of communication as a whole is still in the pre- or multiparadigmatic stage as a scientific discipline. Thus, if Thomas Kuhn (1970) was accurate in his assessment concerning the evolution of a scientific discipline, a number of research programs will (and should) continue to compete for attention and resources until a dominant paradigm concerning the study of human communication emerges. This statement should subsequently hold true for the study of "intrapersonal communication processes." Second, although critical evaluation serves several vital functions in theory building and research, critics and scholars alike must remember the goals, functions, and limitations of models before they can adequately assess the "goodness of fit" between a specific model and the phenomenon it serves to represent. Third, in order to maximize its utility, criticism must be followed by the presentation of viable alternatives. Indeed, until alternative definitions, models, and theories of "intrapersonal communication processes" are presented, we have little recourse but to work actively with those that have been developed.

THE COMMUNICATION DISCIPLINE
AS PRE- OR MULTIPARADIGMATIC

In reading Cunningham's blistering critique of current work in "intrapersonal communication," one is struck immediately by his apparent confusion regarding his own definitions, as indicated by his propensity to use scientific terms somewhat arbitrarily. For example, at different points within his review and analysis, Cunningham describes intrapersonal communication variously as a model, a theory, a construct, and a paradigm.

Although such confusion is problematic for a number of reasons, neither its existence nor its ramifications are the focus of this article. Rather, Cunningham's indiscriminate use of scientific terminology serves well as evidence for our first main point: Given the approximate age (75 years) of the communication discipline as a whole—adolescent when likened to psychology and infantile when compared with physics—the discipline is prone to the characteristics (and mistakes) of youth. For example, adolescents tend to believe they are more mature than they are. Thus when they attempt to model adult behavior (e.g., use an adult vocabulary)—they inevitably make mistakes; yet mistakes are the primary way they grow. More important, adolescents have yet to develop a strong sense of self and are often torn between a number of different identities. So it is with young disciplines, if we agree with Thomas Kuhn.[1] Because no single paradigm has emerged from which to approach the world (i.e., the phenomenon of interest), young disciplines often are characterized by a number and variety of identities. Indeed, one may liken the discovery of a discipline's dominant paradigm to the discovery of the human self, described by Gergen (1971) in *The Concept of Self.* Both involve the formation of an identity apart from other people (disciplines), an ability to conduct both timely and insightful self-evaluation, conflicts with other members of the society (scientific community) regarding what constitutes (scientific) integrity, and discovery of one's personal paradigmatic restrictions and limitations.

How does this analogy relate to the discussion at hand? Prematurely criticizing or labeling an approach, theory, or model as "ambiguous," "countertheoretic," or "nonspecific" can be counterproductive, especially when a body of ideas has not yet achieved theory status and/or if the discipline may be classified as multiparadigmatic. Prior to the formation of a dominant paradigm, all research programs should be viewed as viable, particularly if their proponents are adhering to established scientific principles. Indeed, until a dominant paradigm emerges,

> the assessment of which two [research] programs to prefer . . . is analogous to having Donald Trump and Harry Helmsley tossing pennies off the top of the World Trade Center, the title Grand Real Estate Baron of Manhattan being awarded the one whose penny lands first; it's a meaningless game without a criterion that they can employ to see who will reign as King of the Towers. (Casti, 1989, p. 36)

Evidence of a discipline being multiparadigmatic comes in three major forms:

(1) when brand new, speculative theories can still grow out of nothing and yet not be completely implausible (Collins, 1989, p. 205)

(2) when a number of different approaches to the study of a phenomenon are generating productive research programs

(3) when theories can be taken seriously because existing explanations do not exclude them by their own overwhelming greater plausibility (Collins, 1989, p. 205)

Certainly, upon examining the status of theory development in the communication discipline, one might conclude that we meet all three criteria for classification as multiparadigmatic. As an area of emphasis within the communication discipline, the study of intrapersonal communication processes likewise meets these criteria.

GOALS, CHARACTERISTICS, AND
LIMITATIONS OF MODEL BUILDING

As we stated earlier, several insights emerged as we perused the Cunningham article. The second of these focuses on the potential contributions of models to scientific inquiry—and the importance of remembering their goals, characteristics, and functions when developing and criticizing specific models.

Scholars construct models for a variety of reasons, ranging from scale models used to test aircraft in wind tunnels for aerodynamic properties, to instructional diagrams that depict gas molecules as billiard balls flying about inside a cylinder, to formal mathematical models such as $E = mc^2$. Of the wide array of models that are constructed by scholars, however, only two are used for scientific inquiry: models that allow theorists to generate intuitions about how a system will act under various circumstances (pretheoretic models) and models that are used to test theoretic statements (formal or mathematical models).

Another set of models that teachers and scholars commonly use are models designed for instructional or teaching purposes. These are designed for use in pedagogical settings to clarify or simplify complex phenomena. As such, their primary purpose is to optimize communication between teachers and students. (Note that these types of models are the primary models to which Cunningham refers in his chapter.)

Although our discussion of models to this point is certainly not new to communication scholars, confusion often surrounds (and arises from) the *evaluation* of models, especially when criteria that are used to evaluate scientific models are used to evaluate models designed for instructional purposes (and vice versa). For instance, the following constitutes a list of criteria that are commonly used to evaluate scientific models:

(1) *Accuracy:* Depiction of elements and their relationships in the model should accurately predict/reflect experimental outcomes.

(2) *Consistency:* The model should contain no internal contradictions, and should be consistent with currently accepted theories applicable to related aspects of the phenomenon.

(3) *Comprehensiveness:* The model should depict all known variables and relationships associated with the phenomenon in question.

(4) *Clarity:* The model should be clear, precise, and free of ambiguity.

Scientific models usually are presented in research articles or monographs; thus they frequently are characterized by the use of empirical language, operationalizations of variables and constructs, and mathematical equations depicting relationships.

Contrast these four criteria with those most often used to evaluate models developed for instructional purposes:

(1) *Simplicity:* The model should include basic elements and relationships; if necessary, some elements can be deleted so that basic concepts can be grasped with ease. Additional details can be added later, once the basic model is understood.

(2) *Clarity:* The model should be free of jargon, if possible, and should use terms and physical or pictorial representations that are easily comprehended by students and laypersons.

(3) *Dual-channel input:* The model should provide dual-channel (i.e., visual plus verbal) input to optimize understanding and memorization by students.

The primary purpose of models created for instructional purposes is to provide a connection point or bridge between previously known ideas and new concepts or relationships to be learned. Thus, most models of an instructional nature are characterized by the use of common language, simplified definitions of concepts and variables, and diagrammatic depictions of relationships. Additionally, they usually are found in the context of other instructional materials, such as undergraduate or graduate-level textbooks.

If one is attempting to evaluate a specific model, then, one must look at the intended audience and context for which the model was developed in order to determine which set of criteria to employ. Using criteria that are appropriate for scientific models to evaluate models designed for instructional purposes is an unfair and invalid use of those criteria. Likewise, scientists generally would not employ the latter criteria to evaluate the validity or usefulness of pretheoretic or formal models.

Unfortunately, the misapplication of these criteria is not uncommon among critiques of models in the discipline of communication. We would argue that this is precisely what has occurred in Cunningham's critique of current models of intrapersonal communication processes. He has mistakenly taken criteria that are commonly used for evaluating scientific models and applied them to models of intrapersonal processes designed for instructional purposes.

Discussed below are some other attributes and limitations scholars need to keep in mind when developing, using, or criticizing models.

Models are (or are derived from) analogues or extended metaphors. The geneticist's depiction of genes as beans arranged on a string is one example (Pronko, 1987); the brain depicted as a computer is another. Like metaphors, models both exclude and include properties of the objects or processes compared. As long as the scholar remembers that he or she is "presenting items of one sort in the idiom of another," he or she will have no problem; however, at the point where the thing being modeled becomes the thing itself, the scholar is no longer using the metaphor (model) but is being used by it (Pronko, 1987, pp. 122-123).

Models are cognitive maps of scientists' knowledge structures as well the categories they map. Their cognitive constructs structure and constrain how they perceive and categorize the world. Thus when using or criticizing a model, we must remember one important fact: That model has captured the essence of a scientist's perceptions at a given point in time. The world as the scientist experiences it in the future will influence both the directions in which his or her knowledge grows and the direction in which his or her concepts change (McCauley, 1987). The model—be it theoretical or designed for instructional purposes—indeed may be incomplete or inaccurate at the time we view it. However, to criticize or dismiss the scientist or the model prematurely would be akin to throwing the baby out with the bathwater.

Models function as road maps, not to well-defined answers, but to an understanding of the questions themselves. Models allow us to understand why an answer is possible at all and why it takes the form that it does (Casti, 1989). As Casti (1989) notes, "Research involves ideas, not answers. . . . What count[s] is developing a deep understanding of the question itself; whatever 'answers' there might be would then follow as corollaries of this insight into the real nature of the question" (p. 12).

Models can lead to discovery by showing scientists where to look. The delightful part of the journey, however, is what scholars can discover along the way simply by accident. Models are useful not only because they show scientists where to look, or how to plan an experiment and collect data; as a problem-solving tool, they can reveal that our initial descriptions or explanations are false and can lead us to alternative solutions. Herbert Simon (1989) offers the following analogy regarding the process of (scientific) discovery, which seems to be appropriate when applied to the building and testing of models as well:

> Searching for wildflowers, we are surprised to see something shining and golden in the rocks. To be surprised [and, hence, to perceive what appears to be gold], we must attend to the surprising phenomenon. Hence the dictum of Pasteur: "Accidents happen to the prepared mind." (p. 377)

How does the mind come to be prepared? One way is to construct and test alternative models.

THE ROLE OF CRITICISM AND
THE PRESENTATION OF VIABLE ALTERNATIVES

The third observation we made when perusing the Cunningham article is that critical evaluation involves more than basic criticism of scientists and their work. It involves synthesis and analysis of the highest order. Perhaps one stumbling block for critics is a misunderstanding about the fundamental building blocks of criticism, especially critical evaluation of a scientific body of knowledge.

According to the *Random House College Dictionary* (1982), *criticism* has a number of definitions, the first or most common of which is "the act of passing severe judgment, censuring, or finding fault." This type of criticism usually involves saying negative things about a person, place, idea, or event. In the scholarly arena, this definition of criticism is neither useful nor desirable. Critical evaluation needs to be of a constructive nature in order to encourage or contribute to advancement in a designated field of study.

A second definition of criticism that Random House offers is "the act of making judgments about the merits and faults of a literary or artistic work, musical performance, dramatic production, etc." When applied to work in a scientific community, this definition implies addressing both the merits and faults of a body of knowledge, particularly its definitions of concepts, variables, and empirical relationships. Although this type of criticism, if thorough, has merit in the scholarly arena, it falls one step short of the highest order of criticism. Generally, such evaluations fail to offer viable solutions to problems that are addressed, or to offer alternative or more plausible explanations than the theories they have critically assessed.

The third and highest order of criticism involves not only insightful synthesis and analysis, but also the contribution of a new or more plausible description or explanation, based on a thorough examination of a body of literature. To perform at this level in the scientific community, the critic must be armed with the tools that allow him or her to fully comprehend, understand, and make use of the information he or she is evaluating. Additionally, the critic must be able to make use of that information in an effort to contribute a more valid, plausible, and/or useful solution to a problem, or an explanation of the phenomenon in question.

In attempting to classify Cunningham's contribution to the study of "intrapersonal communication," we would argue that he has approached the second level of criticism, at best. We offer this assessment based on his critical evaluation of the literature in 1989 and his almost identical analysis offered in this volume, more than two years later. In both of these articles, Cunningham has done little more than offer a fairly brutal critique of the literature, without offering to discuss its merits or to present a superior theoretical alternative that is compelling enough for us to reject all that scholars who are interested in intrapersonal processes have done to this point. As McCauley (1987) argues:

> Our best accounts of reality are the ones that our best theories entail, and it is through scientific inquiry that we ascertain the relative value of our theories. The history of science is replete with examples of theoretical advances superseding what was, theretofore, the perceptually obvious. (p. 306)

However, it is theoretical accomplishments that supply reasons compelling enough to reject what has come before—not critical evaluation that falls short of the highest order.

SUMMARY AND CONCLUSIONS

In summary, we have attempted to accomplish three primary objectives: (a) to address Cunningham's critique of literature concerning the study of intrapersonal communication processes, (b) to advance a point of view that is based on the issues that Cunningham raises, and (c) to show how future analyses might be developed more thoroughly in order to advance the study of both intrapersonal and communication processes.

To accomplish these objectives, we have presented three major arguments. The first was that the discipline of communication may be classified as pre- or multiparadigmatic. Thus, criticizing research programs prematurely without offering viable alternatives could be construed as counterproductive to the growth of those programs and the field as a whole. We have also argued that, as long as the discipline can be classified as multiparadigmatic, any research program that employs rigorous scientific standards can and should continue to compete for attention and resources. We then pointed out that, as members of the discipline of communication, scholars who are addressing intrapersonal communication processes should be afforded the same academic privileges and rights.

Our second argument concerned the importance of remembering the goals, functions, and limitations of models when we, as scholars, develop, test, or criticize models. Specifically, we addressed the dangers of applying criteria designed for scientific models to models designed for instructional or pedagogical purposes. We then provided a list of additional attributes or limitations of models that scholars should remember when constructing and testing either scientific or instructional models.

Finally, we offered the argument that the presentation of viable alternatives is a necessary component of critical evaluations, if they are to contribute to a given body of knowledge. In doing so, we described three primary levels of criticism: the act of passing judgment, censuring, or finding fault; the act of making judgments regarding the merit or faults of a work; and the act of synthesizing and analyzing a body of knowledge— coupled with the presentation of viable alternatives that emerge from both the strengths and weaknesses of the theories or models evaluated. After pointing out that, of the three types of criticism, the third contributes most to the growth of a scientific community, we encouraged critics to go the distance when offering critiques of theories or models, and to offer viable solutions to problems they see in the research program being evaluated.

Perhaps all that remains to be emphasized is that Cunningham's critique provides an excellent point of departure for those scholars interested in intrapersonal processes to express their many divergent points of view. We have taken the opportunity to express our position concerning this complex but intriguing process and look forward to continuing dialogues between researchers and thoughtful critics in this area.

NOTE

1. Given the importance of clarity when defining terms (as Cunningham suggests), we will use the term *paradigm* in this section to mean "a [dominant] framework of presuppositions [or shared assumptions] about what constitutes a problem, a solution, and a method" within a given scientific discipline (Casti, 1989, p. 40). When operating within a field of study, such as physics or communication, a paradigm acts as a gestalt that affects the way scientists perceive the world they are studying.

REFERENCES

Andriate, G. S., & Beatty, M. J. (1988). Cognitive complexity and cognitive backlog in human information processing. In B. D. Ruben (Ed.), *Information and behavior* (Vol. 2, pp. 216-225). New Brunswick, NJ: Transaction.

Barker, D. R., Barker, L. L., & Fitch-Hauser, M. (1988). Origins, evolution, and development of a systems-based model of intrapersonal processes: A holistic view of man as information processor. In B. D. Ruben (Ed.), *Information and behavior* (Vol. 2, pp. 197-215). New Brunswick, NJ: Transaction.

Barker, L. L., & Wiseman, G. (1966). A model of intrapersonal communication. *Journal of Communication, 16*, 172-179.

Beatty, M. J. (1989). Decision-rule orientation as an intrapersonal communication construct. In C. V. Roberts & K. W. Watson (Eds.), *Intrapersonal communication processes: Original essays* (pp. 479-492). New Orleans: Spectra.

Beatty, M. J., & Behnke, R. R. (1980). An assimilation theory perspective of communication apprehension. *Human Communication Research, 6*, 319-325.

Beatty, M. J., & Payne, S. K. (1981). Receiver apprehension and cognitive complexity. *Western Journal of Speech Communication, 45*, 363-369.

Beatty, M. J., & Payne, S. K. (1984). Listening comprehension as a function of cognitive complexity: A research note. *Communication Monographs, 51*, 85-89.

Casti, J. L. (1989). *Paradigms lost: Images of man in the mirror of science.* New York: William Morrow.

Collins, H. M. (1989). Learning through enculturation. In A. Gellatly, D. Rogers, & J. A. Sloboda (Eds.), *Cognition and social worlds* (pp. 205-215). Oxford: Clarendon.

Craig, R. T. (1979). Information systems theory and research: An overview of individual information processing. In D. Nimmo (Ed.), *Communication yearbook 3* (pp. 99-121). New Brunswick, NJ: Transaction.

Cunningham, S. B. (1989). Defining intrapersonal communication. In C. V. Roberts & K. W. Watson (Eds.), *Intrapersonal communication processes: Original essays* (pp. 82-97). New Orleans: Spectra.

Delia, J. G., & Clark, R. A. (1977). Cognitive complexity, social perception and the development of listener-adapted communication in six-, eight-, ten-, and twelve-year-old boys. *Communication Monographs, 44*, 326-345.

Gergen, K. J. (1971). *The concept of self.* New York: Holt, Rinehart & Winston.

Hale, C., & Delia, J. G. (1976). Cognitive complexity and social perspective-taking. *Speech Monographs, 43*, 195-203.

Krueger, D. L. (1982). Marital decision making: A language-action analysis. *Quarterly Journal of Speech, 68*, 273-287.

Krueger, D. L., & Harper, N. L. (1988). Information, behavior, and meaning. In B. D. Ruben (Ed.), *Information and behavior* (Vol. 2, pp. 54-73). New Brunswick, NJ: Transaction.

Kuhn, T. (1970). *The structure of scientific revolutions* (2nd ed.). Chicago: University of Chicago Press.

McCauley, R. N. (1987). The role of theories in a theory of concepts. In U. Neisser (Ed.), *Concepts and conceptual development: Ecological and intellectual factors in categorization* (pp. 288-309). Cambridge: Cambridge University Press.

Miller, G. R. (1988). Media messages and information processing in interpersonal communication: "Generally speaking." In B. D. Ruben (Ed.), *Information and behavior* (Vol. 2, pp. 273-287). New Brunswick, NJ: Transaction.

Miller, G. R., Sleight, C., & deTurck, M. A. (1989). Arousal and attribution: Are the behavioral cues nonspecific? In C. V. Roberts & K. W. Watson (Eds.), *Intrapersonal communication processes: Original essays* (pp. 273-291). New Orleans: Spectra.

Planalp, S. K., & Hewes, D. E. (1982). A cognitive approach to communication theory: Cogito ergo dico? In M. Burgoon (Ed.), *Communication yearbook 6* (pp. 49-77). Beverly Hills, CA: Sage.

Powers, W. G., Jordan, W. J., & Street, R. L. (1979). Language indices in the measurement of cognitive complexity: Is complexity loquacity? *Human Communication Research, 6,* 69-73.

Pronko, N. H. (1987). Language with or without consciousness. In G. Greenberg & E. Tobach (Eds.), *Cognition, language and consciousness: Integrative levels* (Vol. 2, pp. 117-135). Hillsdale, NJ: Lawrence Erlbaum.

Roberts, C. V., Edwards, R., & Barker, L. L. (1987). *Intrapersonal communication processes.* Scottsdale, AZ: Gorsuch Scarisbrick.

Roloff, M. E. (1980). Self-awareness and the persuasion process: Do we really *know* what we're doing? In M. E. Roloff & G. R. Miller (Eds.), *Persuasion: New directions in theory and research* (pp. 29-66). Beverly Hills, CA: Sage.

Roloff, M. E. (1989). Issue schema and mindless processing of persuasive messages: Much ado about nothing? In C. V. Roberts & K. W. Watson (Eds.), *Intrapersonal communication processes: Original essays* (pp. 380-410). New Orleans: Spectra.

Ruben, B. D. (1975). Intrapersonal, interpersonal, and mass communication processes in individual and multi-person systems. In B. D. Ruben & J. Y. Kim (Eds.), *General systems theory and human communication* (pp. 164-190). Rochelle Park, NJ: Hayden.

Ruesch, J., & Bateson, G. (1951). *Communication: The social matrix of psychiatry.* New York: W. W. Norton.

Simon, H. A. (1989). The scientist as problem solver. In D. Klahr & K. Kotovsky (Eds.), *Complex information processing: The impact of Herbert A. Simon* (pp. 375-398). Hillsdale, NJ: Lawrence Erlbaum.

Stacks, D. W. (1983). Toward a preverbal stage of communication. *Journal of Communication Therapy, 3,* 39-60.

Stacks, D. W., & Sellers, D. E. (1986). Toward a holistic approach to communication: The effect of "pure" hemispheric reception on message acceptance. *Communication Quarterly, 34,* 266-285.

Stacks, D. W., & Sellers, D. E. (1989). Understanding intrapersonal communication: Neurological processing implications. In C. V. Roberts & K. W. Watson (Eds.), *Intrapersonal communication processes: Original essays* (pp. 243-267). New Orleans: Spectra.

Watson, K. W., & Barker, L. L. (1990). *Interpersonal and relational communication.* Scottsdale, AZ: Gorsuch Scarisbrick.

Wheeless, L. R. (1975). An investigation of receiver apprehension and social context dimensions of communication apprehension. *Speech Teacher, 14,* 261-268.

AUTHOR INDEX

SUBJECT INDEX

ABOUT THE EDITOR

STANLEY A. DEETZ (Ph.D., Ohio University) is an Associate Professor in the Department of Communication at Rutgers University, New Brunswick. He is the author of *Democracy in an Age of Corporate Colonization: Developments in Communication and the Politics of Everyday Life* and *Managing Interpersonal Communication*, and editor or author of four other books. He has published numerous essays in scholarly journals and books regarding communication theory, qualitative research methods, and communication in corporate organizations, and has lectured widely in the United States and Europe. He is Chair of the Organizational Communication Division and a member of the Legislative Council of the Speech Communication Association and a former Chair of the Philosophy of Communication Division and Board Member at Large of the International Communication Association. In addition to his work as editor of the prestigious *Communication Yearbook* series, he continues his research on workplace democracy.

ABOUT THE AUTHORS

IRWIN ALTMAN (Ph.D., University of Maryland, 1957) is Distinguished Professor of Psychology and Professor of Family and Consumer Studies at the University of Utah. His research interests focus on the role of physical environments in social relationships. He is coeditor, with Dan Stokols, of the *Handbook of Environmental Psychology* (Volumes 1-2) and is senior editor of the series Human Behavior and Environment (Volumes 1-12).

IAN ANGUS (Ph.D., York University, 1980) is Associate Professor in the Department of Communication at the University of Massachusetts at Amherst. He is the author of *Technique and Enlightenment: Limits of Instrumental Reason* and *George Grant's Platonic Rejoinder to Heidegger* and is editor or coeditor of *Ethnicity in a Technological Age, Cultural Politics in Contemporary America,* and *The Critical Turn: Rhetoric and Philosophy in Contemporary Discourse.* His main fields of interest are critical cultural theory, technology and ethics, comparative media theory, and philosophy of communication.

JAMES L. APPLEGATE (Ph.D., University of Illinois) is Professor and Chair of the Department of Communication at the University of Kentucky. He served as President of the Southern States Communication Association and as Chair of his research division in the Speech Communication Association. His research examines individual differences in the person-centered communication abilities of children and adults. His work has been published in *Human Communication Research, Communication Monographs, Communication Yearbook,* and elsewhere. His great joy is observing the communication development of an adolescent named Alexis. She finds having a communication professor in the family as a father a developmental challenge to be met with anything but silence.

ANNA BANKS (Ph.D., University of Southern California, 1989) is Assistant Professor of Visual Communication in the School of Communication at the University of Idaho. Her research interests include cultural and cross-cultural issues in film and photography.

DAVID BARKER (Ph.D., University of Texas, 1985), formerly Assistant Professor of Communication at the University of Missouri—Columbia, is a licensed professional counselor in private practice in Austin, Texas. In addition to research interests in encoding research and the impact of the mass media on the development of a sense of self, he is involved in consulting and public workshops and is currently at work on a history of individualism in the United States, *Being Yourself in America: Biography of an Idea.*

DEBORAH R. BARKER (Ph.D., Oklahoma University, 1985) is Assistant Professor of Communication at Auburn University and President of Windward Communications, a communication consulting and video production firm. Prior to taking her position at Auburn, she taught at the University of South Alabama. She is coauthor of *Nonverbal Communication* and has written numerous articles that have appeared in professional journals. Her current research interests include listening, nonverbal communication, and organizational behavior.

LARRY L. BARKER (Ph.D., Ohio University, 1965) is Professor of Communication at Auburn University. He has authored or coauthored more than 30 books and 80 journal articles. His current research interests include listening, organizational communication, and information processing. He has held offices in the International Communication Association and the Speech Communication Association, and is Past President of the International Listening Association.

THOMAS S. BIRK is a doctoral student in the Department of Communication at the University of Arizona and is employed by RESEARCH COMMUNICATIONS in Boston. He has done an extensive amount of media research.

JAMES J. BRADAC (Ph.D., Northwestern University, 1970) is Professor of Communication at the University of California, Santa Barbara. He is the author of numerous articles and chapters on language and impression formation. His book *Language and Social Knowledge*, coauthored with Charles Berger, received the Speech Communication Association's Golden Anniversary Award in 1983. He edited the volume *Message Effects in Communication Science* (Sage, 1989), and is currently editor of *Human Communication Research*.

BARBARA B. BROWN (Ph.D., University of Utah, 1983) is Associate Professor in the Environment and Behavior Area of the Family and Consumer Studies Department at the University of Utah. Her research areas focus on human territoriality and privacy regulation as they contribute to individual and group well-being.

MIKE BUDD (Ph.D., University of Iowa, 1975) is Professor of Communication at Florida Atlantic University in Boca Raton. He is the editor of *The Cabinet of Dr. Caligari: Texts, Contexts, Histories* (Rutgers University Press, 1990), and his research interests include critical and cultural studies of the media, especially film and television.

MICHAEL BURGOON is Professor and Head of Communication at the University of Arizona. He is a Fellow of the International Communication

Association and the author of numerous articles, chapters, and books. He is an active consultant for a number of media companies.

VINCENT T. COVELLO, Ph.D., is a Professor of Environmental Sciences in the School of Public Health at Columbia University. He is also Director of Columbia's Center for Risk Communication. He has authored or edited more than 25 books and has published numerous articles on risk assessment, management, and communication.

RICHARD E. CRABLE (Ph.D., Ohio State, 1973) is Professor in the Department of Communication Studies at California State University, Sacramento. He is former editor of *Communication Studies* and the author of five books and numerous papers and articles reflecting his interests in argumentation, rhetorical theory, public affairs/relations, and issue management.

STANLEY B. CUNNINGHAM (Ph.D., University of Toronto, 1965) is Professor in the Department of Communication Studies, University of Windsor. He has a background in philosophy and medieval studies, and his current interests include media ethics, propaganda, and the philosophy of communication.

DENNIS K. DAVIS is Professor and Director of the School of Communication at the University of North Dakota. He is coauthor of *The Effects of Mass Communication on Political Behavior* and *Mass Communication and Everyday Life: A Perspective on Theory and Effects.* He is currently working on textbooks dealing with political communication and mass communication theory.

CAREN J. DEMING (Ph.D., University of Michigan, 1976) is Professor and Head of the Department of Media Arts at the University of Arizona. Her primary research interests are television criticism and contemporary feminist theory. Publications representative of her work have appeared in *Critical Studies in Mass Communication, Journal of Broadcasting and Electronic Media,* and *Journal of Popular Culture.* She is the editor of *Media and Society: Readings in Mass Communication,* with Samuel L. Becker.

GINA M. GARRAMONE (Ph.D., University of Wisconsin, 1981) is Professor of Advertising at Michigan State University. Her research interests include information processing and political communication.

LEONARD C. HAWES (Ph.D., University of Minnesota, 1970) is Professor and Director of Graduate Studies in the Department of Communication at the University of Utah. His research interests include discourse analysis, cultural studies, and transformational contexts.

NAPOLEON K. JUANILLO, JR., is a Ph.D. candidate at Cornell University. He has conducted research on the communication patterns of families in relation to public health issues. His other research interests focus on risk and environmental communication, health and nutrition education, and international development.

CHERIS KRAMARAE (Ph.D., University of Illinois, 1975) is Professor of Speech Communication, and Sociology, at the University of Illinois at Urbana-Champaign. She has authored, edited, or coedited 10 books on women and communication, including *A Feminist Dictionary* (with Paula Treichler and Ann Russo) and *Technology and Women's Voices.* She is working on a book that deals with feminist theories of hierarchy, and with the categories used to describe race, ethnicity, crime, class, religion, sex, age, physical and mental abilities, nationality, and sexual orientation.

JO LISKA (Ph.D., University of Colorado, Boulder, 1976) is Research Professor of Anthropology at the University of Colorado, Denver. Her research interests include relationships among communication style, person perception, and social influence; evolutionary foundations of communication; and communication strategies used to facilitate interspecies empathy.

SONIA M. LIVINGSTONE (D.Phil., Oxford University, 1987) is Lecturer in Social Psychology at the London School of Economics and Political Science. Her research interests include the active television audience and reception theory, the domestic use of communication technologies, and the psychology of everyday understandings. She is author of *Making Sense of Television: The Psychology of Audience Interpretation* (Pergamon, 1990) and articles in communication and psychology journals.

ED McLUSKIE (Ph.D., University of Iowa, 1975) is Professor of Communication at Boise State University. His research interests include communication in the public sphere and, more generally, the social experience of communication, approached from critical-pragmatic philosophies of communication, metascience, and the theory and practice of communication versus control.

RENÉE A. MEYERS (Ph.D., University of Illinois, 1987) is an Associate Professor in the Department of Communication at the University of Wisconsin—Milwaukee. Her primary research interests include the study of argumentation in small groups and organizations. Her research has appeared in such publications as *Communication Monographs, Human Communication Research,* and *Communication Yearbook.* She is a past recipient of the SCA Distinguished Dissertation Award.

BARBARA M. MONTGOMERY (Ph.D., Purdue University, 1980), an Associate Professor of Communication, is currently Associate Vice President for Academic Affairs at the University of New Hampshire. In addition to her ongoing study of the communication process in close relationships, she recently has advanced a case for methodological openness and pluralism in her book *Studying Interpersonal Interaction*, coedited with Steve Duck (Guilford Press, 1991). She is Past President of the Eastern Communication Association and has served as an associate editor of both national and regional scholarly journals.

DENNIS K. MUMBY (Ph.D., Southern Illinois University, 1985) is Associate Professor of Communication at Purdue University. His research interests include the application of contemporary continental philosophy to the study of power and discourse in organizations. His most recent research examines the application of feminist theory to organizational settings. He is the author of *Communication and Power in Organizations* (Ablex, 1988), as well as many other articles and book chapters.

DEBORAH A. NEWTON (Ph.D., University of Arizona) was a faculty member at the University of Arizona at the time the chapter in this volume was written; she is now in private industry in San Francisco. She has published extensively in the areas of interpersonal communication and social influence.

SUZANNE PINGREE (Ph.D., Stanford University, 1975) is Professor of Family and Consumer Communication at the University of Wisconsin—Madison. Her research interests include developing approaches to understanding how people attend to and comprehend mass and electronic media content, and how they use media to inform themselves.

ANDREA L. PRESS (Ph.D., University of California, Berkeley, 1987) is Assistant Professor of Communication and Women's Studies at the University of Michigan, Ann Arbor. She is the author of *Women Watching Television: Gender, Class, and Generation in the American Television Experience* (1991) and of articles concerning feminist theory, feminist communication research, and ethnographic audience research. Currently she is studying the way mass media structure discourse about abortion in women of different social class and race groups.

THOMAS F. N. PUCKETT, (Ph.D., Southern Illinois University, Carbondale, 1991) is Assistant Professor of Communication Studies at Eastern Washington University. He is concerned with the relationship between personal speech and cultural discourse. His research in cultural studies focuses on entertainment television and film studies; he is the founder of the semiotics research group La Societe Des Vingt Dix.

LANA F. RAKOW (Ph.D., University of Illinois, Champaign-Urbana, 1987) is Associate Professor and Chair of the Communication Department at the University of Wisconsin—Parkside. She is coeditor, with Cheris Kramarae, of *The Revolution in Words: Righting Women, 1868-1871* (1990) and author of *Gender on the Line: Women, the Telephone, and Community Life* (1992).

MICHAEL REAL (Ph.D., University of Illinois) is Professor of Telecommunications and Film at San Diego State University. He is the author of *Super Media: A Cultural Studies Approach* and *Mass-Mediated Culture.* He has published studies of contemporary media and culture in *Critical Studies in Mass Communication, Journal of Communication, Journal of Popular Culture, Media Development, Journalism Quarterly, American Quarterly,* and elsewhere.

HERBERT J. ROTFELD (Ph.D., University of Illinois, Urbana, 1978) is Associate Professor of Marketing and Adjunct Associate Professor of Communication at Auburn University. His ongoing research analyzes issues of business self-regulation and advertising law, as well as pragmatic issues of advertising media and message management. His essays and commentaries published in a variety of newspapers and magazines have addressed the effects of advertising in modern society and the nature of U.S. higher education.

CHARLES T. SALMON (Ph.D., University of Minnesota, 1985) is Associate Professor of Mass Communication at the University of Wisconsin— Madison. He has worked in evaluation research for the Centers for Disease Control's National AIDS Information and Education Program and the Minnesota Heart Health Program. He is the editor of *Information Campaigns: Balancing Social Values and Social Change* (Sage, 1989) and, with Ted Glasser, *Public Opinion and the Communication of Consent* (Guilford, in press).

CLIFFORD W. SCHERER (Ph.D., University of Wisconsin—Madison, 1976) is Associate Professor of Communication at Cornell University. He is particularly interested in strategies and issues related to the communication of environmental and health risks to both the public and policymakers.

DMITRY SHLAPENTOKH (Ph.D., University of Chicago) is a Research Fellow at the Russian Center at Harvard University. His research interests include the role of the French Revolution in Russian and Soviet histories, the role of cosmological philosophy in Russian culture, ethnic relationships in the Soviet Union, and political developments in Gorbachev's time.

VLADIMIR SHLAPENTOKH (Ph.D., Academy of Science) is a Professor in the Departments of Community Health Science and Sociology at Michigan State University. His research interests include Soviet public opinion, Soviet politics, and Soviet ideology. Since emigrating to the United States, he has published 10 books and numerous articles.

CLAY STEINMAN (Ph.D., New York University, 1979) is Professor of Communications at California State University, Bakersfield. A former journalist, his recent research has focused on gender, race, and cultural theory. His work has appeared in anthologies and journals, including *Mediated Males: Men, Masculinity, and the Media* (Sage), the *Journal of Film and Video*, and *The Nation* and, with Mike Budd, in *Cultural Critique, Television Studies: Textual Analysis* (Praeger), *Critical Studies in Mass Communication* (also with Robert M. Entman), and the *Journal of Communication* (also with Steve Craig).

TIMOTHY STEPHEN (Ph.D., Bowling Green State University, 1980) is Associate Professor of Communication at Rensselaer Polytechnic Institute. His research has examined family interaction from several perspectives, including how it sustains a family's construction of reality, how it supports the transmission of member characteristics across generations, and how it relates to individuals' life outcomes. He is cofounder of the Communication Institute for Online Scholarship.

BERNARD M. TIMBERG (Ph.D., University of Texas, Austin, 1979) is Associate Professor of Communication at Radford University. He has written and produced programs for National Public Radio and PBS, as well as 16mm films that have been distributed nationally. His recent research and writing have been in film and television studies, applying critical thinking and cultural studies perspectives and pedagogic theory.

HANS-JÜRGEN WEISS, Ph.D., is Professor of Communication at the University of Göttingen and Research Director of the Göttingen Institute for Applied Communication Research. His major research interests focus on journalism, media use and media effects, public opinion, and media politics. His most recent coauthored book, *Programmbindung und Radionutzung*, deals with the process of program selection by radio listeners.

CAROL M. WERNER (Ph.D., Ohio State University, 1973) is a Professor of Psychology at the University of Utah. She is a social/environmental psychologist who studies how people use their environments to foster effective social interaction. She is also interested in the role of service in the university curriculum.

ROBERT H. WICKS (Ph.D., Michigan State University, 1987) is an Assistant Professor of Journalism at Indiana University. He has worked professionally as both a broadcast and print journalist. His research interests include audience behavior and cognitive processes associated with news usage.